THE POLITICAL DIARIES OF THE FOURTH EARL OF CARNARVON, 1857–1890

COLONIAL SECRETARY AND LORD LIEUTENANT OF IRELAND

THE POLITICAL DIARIES OF THE FOURTH EARL OF CARNARVON, 1857–1890

COLONIAL SECRETARY AND LORD LIEUTENANT OF IRELAND

edited by
PETER GORDON

CAMDEN FIFTH SERIES
Volume 35

CAMBRIDGE
UNIVERSITY PRESS

FOR THE ROYAL HISTORICAL SOCIETY
University College London, Gower Street, London WC1 6BT
2009

Published by the Press Syndicate of the University of Cambridge
The Edinburgh Building, Cambridge CB2 8RU, United Kingdom
32 Avenue of the Americas, New York, NY 10013-2473, USA
477 Williamstown Road, Port Melbourne, VIC 3207, Australia
Ruiz de Alarcón 13, 28014 Madrid, Spain
Dock House, The Waterfront, Cape Town 8001, South Africa

First published 2009

A catalogue record for this book is available from the British Library

ISBN 9780 521 194051 hardback

SUBSCRIPTIONS. The serial publications of the Royal Historical Society, *Royal Historical Society Transactions* (ISSN 0080–4401) and Camden Fifth Series (ISSN 0960–1163) volumes, may be purchased together on annual subscription. The 2009 subscription price, which includes print and electronic access (but not VAT), is £109 (US $183 in the USA, Canada, and Mexico) and includes Camden Fifth Series, volumes 34 and 35 (published in July and December) and Transactions Sixth Series, volume 19 (published in December). Japanese prices are available from Kinokuniya Company Ltd, P.O. Box 55, Chitose, Tokyo 156, Japan. EU subscribers (outside the UK) who are not registered for VAT should add VAT at their country's rate. VAT registered subscribers should provide their VAT registration number. Prices include delivery by air.

Subscription orders, which must be accompanied by payment, may be sent to a bookseller, subscription agent or direct to the publisher: Cambridge University Press, The Edinburgh Building, Shaftesbury Road, Cambridge CB2 8RU, UK; or in the USA, Canada, and Mexico: Cambridge University Press, Journals Fulfillment Department, 100 Brook Hill Drive, West Nyack, New York, 10994–2133, USA.

SINGLE VOLUMES AND BACK VOLUMES. A list of Royal Historical Society volumes available from Cambridge University Press may be obtained from the Humanities Marketing Department at the address above.

Printed and bound in the United Kingdom at the University Press, Cambridge

CONTENTS

LIST OF ILLUSTRATIONS   vii

ACKNOWLEDGEMENTS   ix

ABBREVIATIONS   xi

MANUSCRIPT COLLECTIONS CONSULTED   xiii

PREFACE   xv

INTRODUCTION   1

MINISTERIAL POSTS HELD   89

CARNARVON PEDIGREE   90

THE DIARIES

1857   93

1858   95

1859   103

1866   117

1867   143

1868   173

1869   177

1870   187

1871   197

1872 201

1873 203

1874 207

1875 247

1876 281

1877 283

1878 295

1879 311

1880 321

1881 323

1882 335

1883 343

1884 345

1885 377

1886 411

1887 443

1888 447

1889 451

1890 467

INDEX 473

LIST OF ILLUSTRATIONS

Frontispiece: Earl of Carnarvon, *Whitehall Review*, 16 February 1878.

1. Highclere Castle from the south-east.
2. 'The Fathers of the Confederation', London, December 1866.
3. Earl of Carnarvon, *Vanity Fair*, 11 September 1869, by Carlo Pellegrini (Ape).
4. 'The Awkward Squad', *Punch*, 24 February 1877. © British Library Board. All Rights Reserved.
5. Earl of Carnarvon at his desk in his study, Highclere Castle, *c*.1880.
6. Earl of Carnarvon with his son Aubrey Herbert, 1885.

Acknowledgements and thanks for permission to reproduce the illustrations are due to the Earl of Carnarvon for the cover image, frontispiece, and plates 2, 3, 5, and 6; to the British Library for plate 4; and to Tessa Gordon for plate 1.

ACKNOWLEDGEMENTS

My interest in the life and work of Henry Howard Molyneux Herbert, fourth Earl of Carnarvon, arose from a visit to Highclere Castle in Hampshire, the family home, in 1978, when I had the opportunity to discuss with Henry George Reginald Molyneux Herbert, the seventh Earl, aspects of his great-great-grandfather's political and literary career. It was largely due to his subsequent interest and encouragement that the present work was undertaken, and I wish to record my grateful thanks to him. Following his untimely death in 2001, I have much appreciated the generous access to the family papers at Highclere given by his son, Geordie, the eighth Earl.

During the course of the preparation of this volume, I have received valuable assistance from many individuals, libraries, and other institutions. I have particularly benefited from the advice and comments of Professor John Vincent during the last three decades. I am also most grateful to Dr Jon Lawrence, Literary Editor of the Royal Historical Society, Dr Hester Higton, copy-editor, and Pauline Gordon for their practical help during many stages of the production of this book. Jennifer Thorp, archivist at Highclere, was kind enough to share with me her detailed expertise on the fourth Earl's papers and was most helpful in answering many questions on the collection over the years. I would also wish to thank her husband, Neil, for making copies of most of the photographs that illustrate the work.

I should like to acknowledge the help given by the staffs of several of the institutions visited, particularly the British Library and the London Library, as well as the record offices, private individuals, and other bodies named in the list of manuscript collections consulted. All readily gave their permission to include relevant material in this book. John Rolton has been of outstanding help to me from the outset; he has done superb work in pursuing numerous and often obscure references and in providing background information on many topics.

My greatest debt, however, is to my wife, Tessa, for her very practical assistance at all stages of the project, taking much of the burden from me in many instances, and for her sustained interest in the subject of the book; this made the editing of the diaries a most enjoyable and worthwhile experience. To her, I dedicate this book.

ABBREVIATIONS

Bahlman	I 1880–1882 II 1883–1885 III 1886–1906	D.W.R. Bahlman (ed.), *The Diary of Sir Edward Walter Hamilton, 1880–1906*, 3 vols (vols 1–2, Oxford, 1972; vol. 3, Hull, 1993)
Buckle, *Disraeli*	IV 1855–1868 V 1868–1876 VI 1876–1881	G.E. Buckle and W. F. Monypenny, *The Life of Benjamin Disraeli, Earl of Beaconsfield*, 6 vols (London, 1910–1920)
Buckle, *Letters*	I 1862–1869 II 1870–1878 III 1879–1885	G.E. Buckle (ed.), *The Letters of Queen Victoria, 1862–85*, 2nd series, 3 vols (London, 1926–1928)
Cecil	I 1830–1868 II 1868–1880 III 1880–1886	Lady Gwendolen Cecil, *Life of Robert, Marquis of Salisbury*, 4 vols (London, 1921–1932)
CP, BL		Carnarvon Papers, British Library, Add MS
CP, TNA		Carnarvon Papers, The National Archives of the UK (Public Record Office)
Diary		Carnarvon Diaries, British Library
Hansard		*Hansard's Parliamentary Debates*, 3rd series
Hardinge	I 1831–1868 II 1868–1878 III 1878–1890	Sir A. Hardinge (ed. Elisabeth, Countess of Carnarvon), *The Life of Henry Howard Molyneux Herbert, Fourth Earl of Carnarvon, 1831–1890*, 3 vols (London, 1925)
Johnson		N.E. Johnson (ed.), *The Diary of Gathorne Hardy, later Lord Cranbrook, 1866–1892: political selections* (Oxford, 1981)

Ramm (1952)	I 1868–1871 II 1871–1876	A. Ramm, (ed.), *The Political Correspondence of Mr Gladstone and Lord Granville, 1868–1876*, 2 vols (London, 1952)
Ramm (1962)	I 1876–1882 II 1883–1886	A. Ramm, (ed.), *The Political Correspondence of Mr Gladstone and Lord Granville, 1876–1886*, 2 vols (Oxford, 1962)
Shannon, *Gladstone*, I		R.T. Shannon, *Gladstone, 1809–1865* (London, 1982)
Shannon, *Gladstone*, II		R.T. Shannon, *Gladstone: heroic minister, 1865–1898* (London, 1999)
Vincent, *Derby*, I		J.R. Vincent (ed.), *Disraeli, Derby and the Conservative Party: journals and memoirs of Edward Henry, Lord Stanley, 1849–1869* (Hassocks, Sussex, 1978)
Vincent, *Derby*, II		J.R. Vincent (ed.), *A Selection from the Diaries of Henry Stanley, 15th Earl of Derby (1826–93) between September 1869 and March 1878* (London, 1994)
Vincent, *Derby*, III		J.R. Vincent (ed.), *The Later Derby Diaries* (Bristol, 1981)
Vincent, *Derby*, IV		J.R. Vincent (ed.), *The Diaries of Edward Henry Stanley, 15th Earl of Derby (1826–93) between 1878 and 1893* (Oxford, 2003)
Zetland	I 1873–1875 II 1876–1881	L.J.L. Dundas, Marquess of Zetland (ed.), *The Letters of Disraeli to Lady Bradford and Lady Chesterfield*, 2 vols (London, 1929)

MANUSCRIPT COLLECTIONS CONSULTED

Aberdeen Papers	British Library
H.W. Acland Papers	Bodleian Library, Oxford
Ashbourne Papers	House of Lords Record Office
Bath Papers	Longleat House, Wiltshire
Benson Papers	Lambeth Palace Library
Brand Papers	House of Lords Record Office
British Archaeological Association Papers	Yale University, Manuscript Department
Cairns Papers	The National Archives of the UK (Public Record Office)
Duke of Cambridge Papers	Cambridge University Library, Department of Manuscripts
Carlingford Papers	British Library
Carnarvon Papers	British Library
	Highclere Castle Archives
	The National Archives of the UK (Public Record Office)
Charnwood Papers	British Library
Churchill Papers	Cambridge University Library, Department of Manuscripts
Clarendon Papers	Bodleian Library, Oxford
Cranbrook Papers	Suffolk Record Office, Ipswich Branch
Cross Papers	British Library
14th Lord Derby Papers	Liverpool Record Office
15th Lord Derby Papers	Liverpool Record Office
Dufferin Papers	PRO of Northern Ireland
Erskine May Papers	House of Lords Record Office
Gladstone Papers	British Library
Goodwood Papers	West Sussex Record Office
3rd Lord Grey Papers	Durham University Library, Archives and Special Collections
4th Lord Grey Papers	Durham University Library, Archives and Special Collections
5th Lord Grey Papers	Durham University Library, Archives and Special Collections
Hambleden Papers	W H Smith
Edward Hamilton Papers	British Library

Harrowby Papers	Sandon Hall, Staffordshire
Hatfield House Papers	Hatfield House, Hertfordshire
Herbert Papers	Hampshire Record Office
	Somerset Archives and Record Service
Hughenden Papers	Bodleian Library, Oxford
Iddesleigh Papers	British Library
Kimberley Papers	Bodleian Library, Oxford
London Library Papers	London Library
Lytton Papers	Hertfordshire Archives and Local Studies
	India Office, British Library
Masonic Papers	Library and Museum of Freemasonry, London
Minto Papers	National Library of Scotland
Molyneux of Teversal Papers	Nottingham University, Department of Manuscripts
Monck Papers	National Library of Ireland, Dublin
Phillimore Papers	Hampshire Record Office
Royal Archives	Windsor Castle
Society of Antiquaries Papers	Society of Antiquaries, London
Spencer Papers	British Library
Lady Spencer Papers	Althorp House, Northamptonshire
St Aldwyn Papers	Gloucestershire Record Office
Stanhope Papers	Centre for Kentish Studies
Lady Vincent Papers	Private Collection
Williams Papers	New Brunswick Museum, St John, Newfoundland
Wolseley Papers	Hove Central Library

PREFACE

It is generally recognized that Henry Howard Molyneux Herbert, fourth Earl of Carnarvon, figured prominently in Conservative politics during four decades of the second half of the nineteenth century. It is remarkable, therefore, that it is more than eighty years since the only biographical work on him, Sir Arthur Hardinge's *The Life of Lord Carnarvon*, was published. As one historian has recently remarked, '[This work] is all we have'.[1] The three-volume set well summarizes Carnarvon's achievements but suffers from a number of defects. After his death, his second wife, Elsie, commissioned the work, determined (as she wrote in the Preface) to 'endeavour faithfully to portray the character, thoughts, words and deeds of one who amidst the shifting sense of politics, held honour to be the soul of public and private life; it seeks whilst presenting the facts to hurt no feelings'.[2] As the self-appointed guardian of her husband's reputation, she was concerned to show him in the best possible light. Carnarvon's contemporaries, whose writings contained references to his political career, often received detailed letters from the Countess, pointing out factual errors and unwelcome criticism and demanding changes in the text. The correspondence with Sir Charles Gavan Duffy after the publication of R. Barry O'Brien's book on Parnell,[3] to which the former had contributed a chapter on Carnarvon's secret meeting with Parnell in August 1885, is a good example. Duffy's criticism of Carnarvon's attitude towards the Irish question was strongly challenged by Lady Carnarvon.[4] She was also 'less than helpful' in allowing Gwendolen Cecil access to her father's correspondence with Carnarvon when she was writing Salisbury's biography.[5]

Sir Arthur Hardinge, a career diplomat, had been Salisbury's personal secretary when the latter held the combined posts of Prime

---

[1] M. Bentley, *Lord Salisbury's World: conservative environments in late-Victorian Britain* (Cambridge, 2001), p. 326.

[2] Hardinge, I, p. viii.

[3] 'The Carnarvon controversy', in R. Barry O'Brien, *The Life of Charles Stewart Parnell* (London, 1899), II, pp. 58–95.

[4] Lady Carnarvon to Duffy, 5 Sept 1898 and Duffy to Lady Carnarvon, 12 Sept 1898: CP, BL MS 60828, fos 99–102, 125.

[5] H. Cecil, 'Lady Gwendolen Cecil: Salisbury's biographer', in Lord Blake and H. Cecil (eds), *Salisbury: the man and his policies* (Basingstoke, 1987), p. 70.

Minister and Foreign Secretary in 1885. Although he never knew Carnarvon closely, he would no doubt have met him on visits to Hatfield and at the Foreign Office.[6] Hardinge was chosen as the original author by Lady Carnarvon. Progress on the commission was slow because of his other commitments, so, in March 1922, she decided to become more closely involved with the project, though Hardinge had by this time produced a full and lengthy draft. Elsie was not happy with the result. She told him:

> The fact is, our past conversations and correspondence show that we are looking at the work from different angles. My mind is wholly set on biography – as perfect a picture of a man as can be achieved. The side which appeals to you is the historical and political one; and to compress into a two or three volume work the amount of matter which the two conceptions involve is not, I fear, a practical proposition.

She suggested, therefore, that Hardinge should deal with some special subjects, such as military and naval matters, defence, and freemasonry, and the rest would be left in her hands, according to the original agreement, 'to edit, alter and reduce in length and add the biographical portion, for which I propose to obtain the help of some members of my family'.[7] The book would be published with their joint names on the title page. Hardinge was happy to agree to this arrangement.

The book, published in 1925, was based on the extensive correspondence and papers, official and private, that Carnarvon meticulously preserved at Highclere. Part of the collection was presented by Lady Carnarvon to the Public Record Office (now The National Archives) in 1926 and by the sixth Earl of Carnarvon in 1959 (reference TNA PRO 30/6). Other Herbert family papers containing Carnarvon material were bought by the Hampshire Record Office in 1991 and further papers were deposited at the Somerset Archive and Record Service between 1981 and 1989. The vast bulk of the papers, however, was bought by the British Library in 1978, having been purchased at Sotheby's on 24 July of that year. This collection included the diaries: these, long regarded as lost, were found, along with other papers, in 1976 at Pixton, Somerset, the home of Aubrey Herbert, Carnarvon's elder son by Elsie. This discovery was made by Professor John Vincent of Bristol University, with the help of one of his students, the late Mrs John Montagu. The British Library deposit consists of 344 volumes, including the diaries. The latter amount to

---

[6] Sir A. Hardinge, *A Diplomatist in Europe* (London, 1927), pp. 78, 86.

[7] Lady Carnarvon to Hardinge, 14 March 1921: Herbert Papers, Hampshire Record Office, 75 M91/514/3.

sixty volumes, which follow in almost unbroken sequence from 20 June 1852 to 6 June 1890[8] and cover most of Carnarvon's adult life (Add MSS 60887–60934). They give a full picture of Carnarvon's political, social, and literary life and provide a valuable record of Cabinet meetings during his time in office. Although Hardinge quoted extensively from the diaries, he was necessarily selective and the quotations do not do justice to the richness of the entries themselves.

The Carnarvon diaries take their place alongside those of a few other Conservative Cabinet colleagues, particularly Derby, Cranbrook, and Northcote. Carnarvon was well aware of both the intended and unintended consequences of a Cabinet minister keeping a diary. During a holiday at his retreat at Portofino in North Italy, in 1888, he wrote:

> I have read through since we came here Lord Ellenborough's diary. It ought never to have been published whether as regards the Cabinet secrets which it freely gives, or as regards himself. He never can have intended to give to the world the reflections on himself, as to the office he held or which he desired to have – nor could he have intended that the remarks which he makes on other persons could all be given out without reserve. It shows the risk of leaving papers behind one – and yet this is what I have done: for I shall leave a great mass both public and private.[9]

It is likely that Carnarvon wished to place on record his version of events in order to justify his subsequent actions. During the 1880s, with an eye to the future, he began to trawl through his diaries. On 2 November 1882 he wrote, 'I spent a considerable part of the day in looking over and destroying old correspondence [. . .] as they went into the waste paper basket they reminded me of things passed away for ever'; and, near the end of his life, in October 1889, he started to sort through the letters of previous generations of his family. Intriguingly, there is a diary entry for 2 January 1884 that simply states, 'I have destroyed, having first read over, some parts of my Journal, a painful task', giving no indication of where or why the excisions were made. There is some obvious evidence of the large-scale physical removal of sections of the diary for a number of consecutive entries: for example, in late 1877 and early 1878, when Carnarvon was about to resign from the government over the Eastern Question. For the most part, however, his periods in office, which altogether totalled six years and eight months, are fairly well represented. The most complete years are those dealing with the struggle over the Reform Bill, 1866–1867,

---

[8] The years 1854 and 1855 are missing.

[9] Diary, 22 April 1888. Ellenborough's *A Political Diary, 1828–1830*, edited by Lord Colchester, was published in two volumes in 1881. Ellenborough was Lord Privy Seal and President of the Board of Control during these years.

his participation in the second Disraeli ministry (particularly 1874 and 1875), the manoeuvres over the Franchise Bill 1884, and Carnarvon's period as Lord Lieutenant of Ireland, 1885–1886. Little remains for the years 1872, 1873, 1876 (the only two entries of any significance for that year have survived only because they are written on the verso of family correspondence), 1880, and 1882. The many excisions from the diaries were probably made by Lady Carnarvon. For instance, in one of the pages of the diary for 1881 she had written, 'I have gone through this volume and extracted a few pages. The travels may at any rate remain'.[10] However, Carnarvon was an inveterate memorandum writer and these fill many of the gaps; he also described, on mature reflection, important events in which he participated.

The selection from the diaries that follows represents approximately one-third of the total entries. The editor has omitted the majority of entries that deal with domestic and day-to-day routine happenings. It was considered important to include details of Carnarvon's political activities, whether in or out of office, that throw light on his relations with colleagues, particularly in the years 1879 and 1884. The entries vary considerably in length, some consisting of a line or two, others covering several pages. Where the names of individuals appear only as initials in the original text, they are reproduced here in full wherever possible. It is hoped that this edition of the diaries will be of great interest both to the general reader and to researchers of nineteenth-century political and social history.

[10]Diary, 3 January 1881.

Frontispiece: Earl of Carnarvon, *Whitehall Review*, 16 February 1878, shortly after resigning from the Government.

INTRODUCTION

Henry Howard Molyneux Herbert, fourth Earl of Carnarvon (1831–1890), had the distinction of serving in all the Conservative ministries between 1858 and 1886, and was a member of Cabinets in three of them, under the fourteenth Earl of Derby, Disraeli, and Salisbury. What is equally remarkable is the fact that, although he resigned on two occasions, he was appointed a third time, in 1885. Throughout this time he kept a journal, in which he provided keen observations of his colleagues and comments on political happenings.

Carnarvon was the eldest son of Henry John George Herbert, third Earl (1800–1849) and his wife, Henrietta Anne (1804–1876), who was the eldest daughter of Henry Molyneux Howard, brother of the twelfth Duke of Norfolk. A sensitive man of a romantic and adventurous nature, the third Earl was the author of books based on his travels. His last important journey, which he undertook with his wife, his eldest daughter, Eveline, and the seven-year-old Carnarvon, then Viscount Porchester, was to Asia Minor. This plan was thrown into disarray by the boy's illness of Asiatic 'flu at Constantinople, which was so serious that the doctors ordered the family to return to England if he was to live. On the way there, his sister contracted fever, and both his nurse and his governess died in Italy. Thirty years later, in homage to his father, Carnarvon published the diaries of part of the journey, *Reminiscences of Athens and the Morea in 1839.*[1] In adult life, he too became a keen traveller. In 1860, together with his college friend Lord Sandon, he toured Asia Minor, visiting Babylon and Damascus. His love of antiquities was transmitted to his son, George, the fifth Earl, who, as patron of Howard Carter, was associated with the discovery of the tomb of Tutankhamun in November 1922.[2]

Porchester also followed his father in a liking for politics. The third Earl, before inheriting the title in 1833, had sat briefly in the Commons as MP for Wootton Bassett, Wiltshire, in March 1831, taking up his

---

[1] Carnarvon wrote, 'I have been engaged during the last few days in reading over my Father's Greek Journals. They are very interesting and written with all the care and grace and love of the imaginative and picturesque which he possessed in so full a measure' (Diary, 23 August 1867).

[2] H. Carter, *Tutankhamun: the politics of discovery* (London, 1998).

position three days before Lord John Russell introduced the first
Reform Bill. After making a speech on the second reading, ten days
after Porchester's birth, he was offered a post in the ministry but
refused.[3] As a Whig, he opposed the 'great and doubtful experiment',
as Carnarvon was also to do. Carnarvon always admired his father's
intellectual and literary powers and was saddened by the death of the
third Earl in 1849 at the age of forty-nine.

Porchester showed early signs of precociousness. At the age of six,
he delivered a speech to the Dulverton Troop of Yeomanry,[4] and at
nine and a half he appeared with his father in London at a public
meeting on behalf of the Royal Society for the Protection of Animals.[5]
He was reading Greek and Latin authors before he went to Eton,
where he took with him his private tutor, John Kent, who became a
lifelong friend. He had been at Christ Church, Oxford, for only three
months when he succeeded to the earldom at the age of eighteen, on
the death of his invalid father. He graduated in 1852, being awarded
a first class in Greats, though he admitted that laziness had almost
threatened a 'very premature termination' in his first year.[6]

Early years in politics

Since his Oxford days Carnarvon had been interested in politics.
His first opportunity on the wider stage came in January 1854,
when Lord Aberdeen, the Prime Minister of a coalition government,
requested him to move the Address in Answer to the Queen's Speech.
Although flattered by the proposal, Carnarvon anxiously replied
to the offer, an action which became typical of his later political
dealings. Admitting that he had not so far heard a single speech in
the House of Lords, Carnarvon asked for an interview with Aberdeen
on the Government's intention to enlarge the franchise 'for the upper
classes of the operatives'. He wrote to Aberdeen after the interview,
'having very distinctly impressed on my mind your Lordship's previous
emphatic avowal was distinctly Conservative I did not enter upon the
point so fully as I now wish I had done'.[7] Aberdeen testily replied that

---

[3] H.H.M. Herbert, 4th Earl of Carnarvon, *The Herberts of Highclere* (London, 1907), p. 67.

[4] A local paper reported on 30 December 1837, 'On the health of Lord Porchester being
given (a fine and noble boy of about six years of age, who had been brought into the room)
he was put on the table, and returned thanks in a maiden speech, such as it is hoped may
be the forerunner of many hereafter in the Senate': CP, BL 60994A, fo. 13.

[5] Hardinge, I, p. 25.

[6] Carnarvon to H.W. Acland, 12 December 1852: H.W. Acland Papers, MS Acland,
d. 77, fos 41–42.

[7] Carnarvon to Aberdeen, 13 January 1854: Aberdeen Papers, BL MS 43252, fos 56–57.

from my desire to afford you all the satisfaction in my power, I entered into an explanation of details which was not at all necessary to do for the purpose of the Address [...]. All therefore which is required from any person moving the Address is a general assent to the proposition that it is desirable to consider some measure of Parliamentary Reform.[8]

Carnarvon, now satisfied that he could undertake the task 'consistent with my own principles', moved the Address on 31 January. In his speech, which was well received, he spelled out his belief in a strong British Empire with the colonies living in harmony with their mother country. He wrote to John Kent the following day, 'Lord Aberdeen told me that it was one of the most successful first speeches.'[9]

Carnarvon's temperament was the subject of amusement for many of his Cabinet colleagues later in his career. Disraeli and others referred to him as 'Twitters' in their correspondence. His excitability at one stage of the Near East crisis in 1877 led Salisbury to send his colleague a quotation from Shakespeare's *Henry VIII*, 'Be advis'd; Heat not a furnace for your foes so that / it does not singe yourself.'[10] Sir Henry Ponsonby, Queen Victoria's private secretary, described him as a man 'with a nervous manner and a most distressing little cough which always attacks him when you ask him a question'.[11] Carnarvon himself believed that his personality was a family characteristic. He once confessed to an old family friend:

You are, I am afraid, right as to my restlessness, and also in a great measure as to its cause. At the same time you must remember that I have always had this 'restless' temper, from School days till now, and that it has been, to a great degree not least, a secret of whatever little success I have won. If it wearies me, it also prevents my rusting, which is a contingency I dread much more. Eveline [his sister] has a good deal of the same quality, but she makes excellent use of it. Auberon [his brother] has it largely and unfortunately in excess.[12]

Carnarvon's maiden speech, the Address in Answer to the Queen's Speech, took place while the Crimean War was in progress.[13] His brother-in-law described Carnarvon as 'not one of those who strike the popular imagination. He was not tall, nor capable of vigorous expression and his extreme refinement possibly gave to those who did not know him well an impression of weakness which was increased

---

[8] Aberdeen to Carnarvon, 16 January 1854: *ibid.*, fo. 64.

[9] Carnarvon to Kent, 1 February 1854: CP, BL 61063, fo. 1.

[10] Quoted in M. Bentley, *Lord Salisbury's World: conservative environments in late-Victorian Britain* (Cambridge, 2001), p. 128.

[11] Ponsonby to his wife, Mary Elizabeth, 15 September 1875: Royal Archives, Add A/36.

[12] Carnarvon to Sir William Heathcote, 18 September 1878: CP, BL 61074, fo. 153.

[13] *Hansard*, CXXX, 31 January 1854, cols 13–16.

by his short-sightedness and a thin voice in public speaking.'[14] With the ending of the war, Carnarvon toured the battlefields with an acquaintance, Admiral Lord Lyons. They sailed to Constantinople, where he visited the capital of Turkey for the third time. He was disillusioned with the state of the country. Giving an address the following year, Carnarvon stated:

> Without absolutely saying that the Turkish Government is wantonly cruel, it is not too much to assert that it has been singularly unfortunate in its internal administration [. . .]. In war, continual barbarities and massacres and the violation of all faiths: and in peace, systematic family murders, misrule, irresponsibility and extortion.[15]

Nor did he believe that civilization was the policy or property of Russia. A British presence in the East was probably the answer.

By 1857, Carnarvon noted that he had made 'considerable progress and certainly had greater confidence' since his maiden speech. He spent several days with Sir Edward Bulwer Lytton, whom he found very agreeable, and noted that Lord Stanley, later fifteenth Earl of Derby, 'sought me out – for his character is so peculiar that I have always feared to be the first to make advances – this summer in London to propose various plans of foreign travel together'.[16] The unexpected fall of Palmerston's ministry in February 1858 brought Derby into office. Within three days, Carnarvon received a call from the new Prime Minister, offering him the post of Under-Secretary at the Colonial Office. At their meeting, Carnarvon typically asked for reassurances, before accepting office, that Palmerston's Conspiracy Bill would not be proceeded with.

The Colonial Secretary was Lord Stanley, whom Carnarvon considered a conscientious and efficient head of office. When, after a short while, Stanley became Secretary of State for India, Bulwer Lytton succeeded him, and Carnarvon was pleased to be given more responsibility henceforth than was the case under Stanley. While being a good speaker on colonial matters, Lytton's powers of administration were poor and he had little capacity for business. He was frequently absent from the office, and Carnarvon was often left to make decisions and to sign Lytton's letters for him.[17] Lytton told Carnarvon, 'I would

[14] E.W. Howard, Baron Howard of Penrith, *Theatre of Life: life seen from the pit, 1863–1905* (London, 1935), p. 62.

[15] 'The present condition of the Turkish Empire in Asia: address to the Newbury Literary and Scientific Institution', in H.H.M. Herbert, 4th Earl of Carnarvon, ed. R.H. Herbert, *Essays, Addresses and Translations*, 2 vols (London, 1896), I, pp. 175–6.

[16] 'Memorandum of the Session 1857', 16 September 1857: CP, BL 60892, fo. 17.

[17] L. Mitchell, *Bulwer Lytton: the rise and fall of a Victorian man of letters* (London, 2003), p. 219.

much rather trust your signature than that of any other Secretaries of State [. . .]. As to Patronage I leave you *carte blanche*.'[18]

There was unrest at the time in the Ionian Islands, which was an independent state but under British protection, and a Special Commissioner was required to investigate the state of affairs there. It was Carnarvon who suggested that William Gladstone should be sent out for this purpose. At the same time, Carnarvon was also responsible for introducing two large measures in the Lords: the Medical Practitioners Bill to regulate the qualifications of doctors and surgeons, and a Local Government Bill. In addition, he was the instigator of a Jewish Oaths Bill, which would have admitted Jews to the House of Commons.[19]

The years out of office, 1859–1866

After eighteen months in office, the Derby government fell in 1859. For the next seven years Carnarvon was content to follow some of his non-political interests. He was delighted to be appointed High Steward of Oxford University in October 1859, and he travelled around Europe and the Middle East. In September 1861, he married Lady Evelyn Stanhope, the only daughter of the sixth Earl of Chesterfield. Algernon West described her as a person 'who had hardly emerged from girlhood to womanhood, fascinated with her almost mature beauty and charmed with her talents the men and women of an older generation'.[20] There were four children: one boy, George Edward, later fifth Earl; and three daughters, Winifred, Margaret, and Victoria. Meanwhile, Highclere Castle, Hampshire, near Newbury, became more than a domestic dwelling: Carnarvon made it a meeting place for politicians, from both Britain and overseas, throughout the rest of his life. Indeed, it was widely remarked that Carnarvon was the first Colonial Secretary to entertain ministers and other leading figures from the colonies in his home on such a scale.[21]

---

[18]Lytton to Carnarvon, 17 April 1859: CP, BL 60780, fo. 81. Lytton wrote to one of his officials at this time, naming Carnarvon as 'by far the first young man of his rank in public life': V.A.G.R.B. Lytton, Earl of Lytton, *The Life of Edward Bulwer, First Lord Lytton*, 2 vols (London: 1913), II, p. 281.

[19]Memorandum for 1858: CP, BL 60892, fos 42–45.

[20]A. West, *Recollections, 1832–1886*, 2 vols (London, 1899), I, p. 239.

[21]'In this period Colonial Secretaries were for the first time required to cultivate personal relations with prominent colonists. Canadian ministers from 1857 and Australians from 1866 onwards began to make the long journey across the oceans to deal direct with London. The earlier Canadian visits did not achieve much; the later ones successfully begot Confederation. Carnarvon, who was Under-Secretary or Secretary of State during most of them, put the visits to imaginative use. He would not allow the delegates to confine themselves to business

Fig. 1 Highclere Castle from the south-east, restored by Sir Charles Barry and completed in 1842.

The original Georgian house was set in a spectacular park landscaped by Capability Brown in 1770–1771. When the third Earl took up residence at Highclere, he called on the services of Charles Barry to transform the building into something more exotic. While retaining the inner core, the outside now resembles in many ways Barry's other best-known building, the Houses of Parliament, with its system of grid-like encrusted decoration with a Gothic feel.[22] The design was approved by the Earl and the foundation stone of the new great central tower was laid by the eleven-year-old Porchester. The latter completed the interiors in an Italian style, thus adding to the mixture of styles in the building. One of the many visitors, Disraeli, on seeing the front of the house for the first time exclaimed, 'How scenical! how scenical!'[23]

One of Carnarvon's lifelong interests was the relationship between penal policy and prison administration, he believing, like many of his contemporaries, that there was a need for a move from the penitential

but had them to stay with him at Highclere. The result was that they commonly returned home contented' (E.A. Benians, J. Butler, and C.E. Carrington (eds), *The Cambridge History of the British Empire, vol. 3: the Empire-Commonwealth, 1870–1919* (Cambridge, 1959), p. 735).

[22] M. Girouard, *The Victorian Country House* (New Haven, CT and London, 1979), p. 133.

[23] Lady D. Nevill, *Reminiscences* (London, 1906), p. 141.

and reformatory ideal towards one of punishment and deterrence. A Select Committee of the House of Lords that he chaired on the subject, reporting in 1863, recommended that 'during short sentences or the earlier stages of a long confinement, the prisoner should be made to dispense with the use of a mattress, and should sleep upon planks'.[24] He was appointed chairman of the Judicial Committee of Quarter Sessions in February 1860 at the age of just twenty-nine, and, at a local level, he took part in the deliberations at the Winchester Assizes. He also served on several Parliamentary Commissions on aspects of the penal system, and spoke as an authority on the subject in the Lords, introducing legislation such as the Reformatory Schools Bill in 1857.[25]

Derby's 1866 government and the second Reform Bill

When Lord Derby formed his new administration in July 1866, Carnarvon was once more appointed to the Colonial Office, though now as Secretary of State, with a seat in the Cabinet.[26] One outstanding issue that needed to be settled was the future constitution of Canada. The policy of confederation, announced in 1848 by Sir Edmund Head, Governor-General of British North America, involved the unification of Canada – including the United Provinces of Canada, Nova Scotia, and New Brunswick – and the creation of its own parliament. The seat of government was to be Ottawa. Not all Canadian politicians were in favour of this move: some from the Maritime Provinces preferred their own parliament and, more worryingly, the United States of America showed a lively interest in impeding the establishment of such a confederation.

Carnarvon was an advocate of a union of colonies, as he was later to attempt in South Africa and in Ireland. In a speech to the Canadian

[24]Quoted in P. Priestley, *Victorian Prison Lives: English prison biography, 1830–1914* (London, 1985), p. 31.

[25]S. McConville, *English Local Prisons, 1860–1900: next only to death* (London, 1995), p. 38.

[26]The senior Under-Secretary, Frederick Rogers, contrasted Carnarvon with his predecessor, Cardwell: 'He had more of generous desire to effect worthy objects, and also more, I think, of a wish to shine before the public and to distinguish himself in the ordinary sense of the word. His failing was rather too much self-consciousness, and a disposition to be caught by showy schemes.' Rogers also observed that his chief, 'though he was fully aware of his own abilities and desirous of receiving credit for them particularly in his measures and public appearances, he was given to take a second part in conversation, always wishing to draw others out than to speak himself': G.E. Marindin (ed.), *Letters of Frederick, Lord Blachford, Under-Secretary of State for the Colonies, 1860–1871* (London, 1896), p. 263.

delegates the following year he stated his philosophy:

> Once in the history of England it so happened that we parted from some of our great Colonies with a bad spirit and in a misunderstanding [. . .]. It taught us that conciliation is better than coercion; that if we give our confidence, it will be repaid us a hundredfold. It has taught us – and it taught the Colonies also – that their interests properly understood are not separate and distinct; but that the more prosperous the Colonies are, the greater the strength they confer on the Mother Country.[27]

At a formal meeting of delegates in London on 26 January 1867, Carnarvon and Lord Monck, the Governor-General of Canada, discussed the British North American Bill. By the time it received Royal Assent in July, Carnarvon, the architect of the measure, was out of office over a different issue. Looking back on this achievement a year later, he told Monck, 'This is after all the last chance for the great country which belongs to us in North America, but whatever the result I can see no ground for regretting the course taken in providing the Union of the Provinces.'[28]

Like his father, Carnarvon disliked the attempts by successive governments to bring about the reform of the franchise, though in this he was moving against the tide of general public feeling, and the Hyde Park Riots in July 1866 stimulated politicians to speed up the process. The Derby government came into office on 2 July, mainly owing to a group of Whigs known as the Adullamites – Liberal MPs led by such figures as Robert Lowe. By their actions, the Russell–Gladstone ministry fell. The minority government of Derby was not in a position to resist Reform but was reluctant to expedite legislation. Derby argued that the process could be slowed down by proceeding by resolutions in Parliament, which would be discussed in detail by a Royal Commission and might serve as the basis for future legislation. This approach was eventually agreed to by Disraeli, then Leader of the House, and after much discussion in Cabinet he introduced the resolutions in the Commons on 12 February 1867. However, without Cabinet approval, Disraeli pledged that a bill would be immediately introduced.

Carnarvon, together with his old friend Lord Cranborne, then Secretary of State for India, was dismayed at Disraeli's willingness to pacify Gladstone. They decided to take drastic action together. On 25 February, shortly before a Cabinet meeting to be held at midday, Cranborne wrote to Derby, pointing out that Disraeli's scheme was unacceptable, a view which was shared by Carnarvon. At the Cabinet meeting, the two men, along with General Jonathan Peel, Secretary

---

[27]Hardinge, I, p. 301.
[28]Carnarvon to Monck, 15 January 1868: Monck Papers, 27021 (3).

of State for War, were the only members to express their dissent.[29] In a desperate attempt to save the situation, Disraeli introduced a Ten Minute Bill in the Commons, which was unpopular with both Conservatives and Liberals. At the Cabinet meeting on 2 March, when it was agreed to proceed with household suffrage, the three men resigned. At this, as Carnarvon noted in his diary, 'Lord Derby closed a red box with a heavy sigh and said, "The Party is ruined," and Disraeli added rather cynically, "Poor Tory Party!"' The third reading of the Reform Bill was passed without division and became law in August. The 'leap in the dark' had been made.[30]

'I am convinced that we are in a very critical position', Carnarvon wrote to the Duke of Richmond a few days later. 'Household suffrage may be good or bad: but it is a revolution.'[31] And to his former guardian and friend Sir William Heathcote he added, 'I hardly see now how we can avoid a great break in the Party.'[32] Carnarvon had no doubt as to who was to blame for the 'painful scenes in which we have been engaged during the last two or three weeks [. . .]. The truth is that the Government is Disraeli and he is dragging them through their present discredit.'[33] In reply, Heathcote admitted that Disraeli 'probably looked forward with satisfaction to getting rid of you by the strong dose of democracy which I have no doubt he has determined from the beginning', but considered that this was not a deliberate Government plot.[34] When the three 'renegades', as the Queen called them, returned their seals of office, she was so furious that she refused to shake hands with them.

Out of office: Carnarvon's non-political pursuits

Carnarvon was gloomy about his own future. 'I am sadly out of heart', he confessed, 'and I am thinking of giving up all Politics as far as possible, and dividing my time between turnips and literature.'[35] He

[29] All three were members of the 'Bath clique', named after their leader, Lord Bath, who had attempted to remove Disraeli in 1860. See J. Ramsden, *An Appetite for Power: a history of the Conservative Party since 1830* (London, 1998), pp. 94–95. See also Carnarvon's correspondence with Bath in the Longleat Papers.

[30] Diary, 2 March 1867.

[31] Carnarvon to Richmond, 11 March 1867: Goodwood Papers, 822.97.

[32] Carnarvon to Heathcote, 28 March 1867: CP, BL 61070, fo. 209a. It had been on Heathcote's advice that Carnarvon had taken an interest in prison reform: see F. Awdry, *A Country Gentleman of the Nineteenth Century: being a short memoir of the Right Honourable Sir William Heathcote, Bart., of Hursley, 1801–1881* (Winchester, 1906), pp. 123–125.

[33] Carnarvon to Sandon, 7 March 1867: Harrowby Papers, 1st series, xxix, fos 28–29.

[34] Heathcote to Carnarvon, 13 May 1867: CP, BL 61070, fo. 222.

[35] Carnarvon to Heathcote, 6 April 1867: CP, BL 61078, fo. 212.

was anxious, however, not to appear disloyal to the Government. He wrote to Earl Grey towards the end of the year,

> I find that my presence in the House is a cause of dire irritation and I see no reason why I should not allow this feeling to cool down by a temporary absence. It will show at all events that I am not looking out for an opportunity to annoy them.[36]

Throughout his public life, Carnarvon often, in times of personal distress, turned to his great love, the classics. Thanking a fellow classicist, the fifteenth Earl of Derby, for his criticisms of a translation he had made of the *Agamemnon*, Carnarvon replied, 'It has been an amusement and an interest to me in the intervals of business: and there is, I think, a certain satisfaction in turning to some account the work on which so large a part of one's early life was spent.'[37] During a severe illness the following year he translated the fifth and eleventh books of the *Odyssey*, which he had privately published for his friends. A more ambitious project was a complete translation of the first twelve books of the same work, which he undertook shortly after resigning as Lord Lieutenant of Ireland in 1886. While at work on the book, he wrote to Sandon, 'I am personally well pleased to have shuffled off the coil of English politics and to get in exchange Dante and Aristotle and my best beloved Homer, which every day grow more wonderful to me.'[38]

Towards the end of his life, he turned once more to discovering more about his own ancestors. The result was a book, *The Herberts of Highclere*, written in 1887 but published twenty years later, a first-hand account of his father, grandfather, and great-grandfather, with some interesting comments on their activities. He then undertook a project which was to be his final work. The letters of Philip Dormer Stanhope, fourth Earl of Chesterfield (1694–1773), to his natural son, written daily from 1737 onwards concerning the education of a young man, and published by the Earl's wife in 1774, had long been considered a classic in the corpus of English literature. Carnarvon's first wife, Evelyn, was a Stanhope. Her father, the sixth Earl of Chesterfield, had given Carnarvon no fewer than 236 letters written subsequently by the fourth Earl to an illegitimate godson. Carnarvon had put them to one side and many years later he rediscovered them at the Chesterfields' home at Bretby. The letters, edited by Carnarvon, were published under the title *Lord Chesterfield's Letters to his Godson* in December 1889. In his introduction Carnarvon stated, 'I can honestly say that I began

---

[36] Carnarvon to 3rd Earl Grey, 27 November 1867: Grey Papers, 80/13.

[37] Carnarvon to 15th Earl of Derby, 18 April 1879: Derby Papers, 920 DER (15).

[38] Carnarvon to Harrowby, 22 February 1886: Harrowby Papers, 2nd series, lii, fo. 161.

my task with little interest, perhaps with prejudice, and ended with strong interest, sympathy and appreciation.' The 550 copies printed on large quarto by the Clarendon Press immediately sold out.[39] A second edition was published in 1890.

The Library at Highclere well reflected Carnarvon's tastes. Besides the books written by previous Herberts, many of whom were prolific authors, there are works of Italian, French, English, and classical literature, history, biography, travel, and theology. The oldest book is by the poet Ariosto, from 1538. The books, which were catalogued on behalf of Carnarvon in 1888, then consisted of over 5,600 volumes.[40] His favourite work was *Holy Living and Holy Dying*, published in 1650–1651 and written by Jeremy Taylor, who was chaplain to Archbishop Laud and Charles I. The book dealt with 'the duties and specimen of the devotions of a Christian'.[41] In 1880, he also prepared a catalogue of pictures at Highclere, based on an inventory drawn up by his mother, the third Countess, in the 1860s. Among the 142 listed are portraits of Anne Sophia, first Countess of Carnarvon, by Van Dyck; Henry, first Earl by Romney; and the second Earl by both Beechey and Reynolds.[42]

Highclere and his London home were meeting places for the entertainment of many eminent literary figures.[43] Robert Browning was often a welcome visitor at Highclere. As a member of a shooting party there in 1873, he was able to claim in a single day's sport 218 pheasants, 40 hares, 20 rabbits, and 1 partridge.[44] In 1883, Browning confided to Carnarvon that he was very much disturbed at the peerage recently bestowed on Tennyson, 'the very name of which has the sound of a bugle, apart from all other attractions'.[45] Henry James visited Lady Carnarvon at Highclere after her husband's death 'in memory of your kindness to me at Highclere and of Lord Carnarvon's in times that seem already far away'.[46] Carnarvon was also praised by others for his political ability and firm principles. On his setting out on one of his early Middle Eastern expeditions, he received a letter from Charles Kingsley urging, 'For God's sake take care of yourself. We have not so many young men of promise in England that we can afford to spare you

---

[39] See C. Franklin, *Lord Chesterfield: his character and characters* (Aldershot, 1993), p. 49.

[40] A.M. Deveson, *Highclere Library Catalogue* (Highclere, Hampshire, 1992), p. 1.

[41] Carnarvon to Salisbury, 3 June 1874: Hatfield House Papers, 3M/E.

[42] H.H.M. Herbert, 4th Earl of Carnarvon, *Catalogue of the Principal Pictures at Highclere Castle* (Newbury, 1880, rev. 1939).

[43] Carnarvon was a trustee of the London Library for many years and acted as chairman of its annual general meetings. See, for example, 31 May 1888, Minutes of Committee Meeting, London Library Papers.

[44] D. Thomas, *Robert Browning: a life within life* (London, 1982), p. 236.

[45] R. Lowell to Lady Carnarvon, 26 July 1887: CP, BL 60865, fo. 38.

[46] James to Lady Carnarvon, 6 May 1894: CP, BL 60865, fo. 129.

from public life.'[47] Walter Bagehot, another old friend, congratulated Carnarvon on becoming Colonial Secretary in 1874,[48] and Thomas Carlyle praised him for 'his fair and upright conduct befitting an English gentleman and statesman'.[49] Thomas Hughes, the author of *Tom Brown's School Days*, 'although only an acquaintance and on the other side in politics', congratulated Carnarvon on his resignation over the Eastern Question in 1878.[50]

Carnarvon's greatest pleasure, however, was discussing literary matters with distinguished authors. That he was well considered in this field can be seen in a letter from Matthew Arnold written shortly before the poet's death, when he stated that 'since the *Agamemnon* we have claims on you'.[51] Carnarvon had first been introduced to Alfred, Lord Tennyson in March 1877. He wrote in his diary afterwards, 'I naturally wish to know him and he was good enough to say that he wished to know me. On the whole I think we were mutually satisfied.'[52] They subsequently met on a number of occasions and the two men enjoyed each other's company. Two years later, Carnarvon described a further meeting where foreign affairs as well as other matters were discussed: 'He seemed to me to have recovered in some degree from his fit of jingoism of last summer. He deplored the Cape War, the Afghan War and the chance of a Burmah war, but he was curiously inconsistent on some points.'[53] Most memorably, in 1888 Carnarvon and his wife were invited to spend three nights with Tennyson at his house at Aldworth, near Haslemere in Surrey. Carnarvon was impressed with the intellectual powers of the eighty-year-old poet, and he described Tennyson's readings from his own works, particularly the recently composed *Locksley Hall Sixty Years After* (1886), and his criticism of Milton's *L'allegro et penseroso*.[54] Carnarvon was less impressed with George Eliot, whom he met at a dinner party: 'She is older than I expected,' he wrote, 'very different in appearance and less brilliant.'[55]

As a scholar, Carnarvon took a great interest in the promotion of education. Only three years after leaving Oxford, he became

[47] Kingsley to Carnarvon, 8 February 1860: CP, BL 60865, fo. 59.
[48] Bagehot, a frequent guest at Highclere, received a reply from Carnarvon, stating, 'How I pity any one who has to undertake the Colonial Office with no previous knowledge of it. Chaos would be a trifle compared to what he would pass through' (R. Barrington, *Life of Walter Bagehot* (London, 1914), p. 433).
[49] Carlyle to Carnarvon, 11 July 1875: CP, BL 60865, fo. 82.
[50] Hughes to Carnarvon, 25 January 1878: CP, BL 60865, fo. 74.
[51] Arnold to Carnarvon, 17 June 1887: CP, BL 60865, fo. 110.
[52] Diary, 8 March 1877.
[53] Diary, 28 March 1879.
[54] M. Thorn, *Tennyson*, (London, 1993), p. 502. See also Diary, 18 July 1888.
[55] Diary, 18 May 1876.

an examiner in Greek, Latin, and Divinity for the Newcastle Scholarship,[56] and was made Doctor of Civil Law on being appointed High Steward of the University. He was an active governor of King's College, London, Newbury Grammar School, and Repton School. When a new headmaster was to be appointed at Repton in 1874, Carnarvon was a member of the selection committee. One applicant on the short list, T.B. Rowe of Uppingham, was disqualified, as Carnarvon wrote approvingly in his Diary, 'on account of the Darwinianism of his opinion'.[57] The successful candidate, Henry Robert Huckin, a Doctor of Divinity, urged parents to keep their sons at school, where they could belong to 'a society with a moral and religious basis'.[58] On the whole, though, his views on the curriculum were forward-looking. While agreeing that the classics were valuable because of their humanizing qualities, he believed there was also a need for science to be taught in order to give a balanced education. He was in great sympathy with the enlightened headmaster of Uppingham, Edward Thring, who encouraged a wider curriculum than did most other public schools. There was a thriving modern side, with such subjects as music and handwork, and less emphasis on athletic prowess. After a visit to the school to present prizes in 1882, Carnarvon commented on Thring's energy, his clear-sightedness of purpose, and his good relationship with pupils. Remembering his own school days at Eton, where four previous generations of his family had attended, Carnarvon noted, 'The system I cannot doubt is for the educating of boys a far safer and more wholesome one than the great and overgrown accumulations of Eton, and, I suspect, Harrow. The former exists very much by and on her traditions.'[59]

Nevertheless, like many other Conservative politicians, he bitterly opposed the establishment of board schools created by the Elementary Education Act of 1870. The legislation allowed school boards to be elected by districts where there was a deficiency in the accommodation provided by voluntary effort. As a firm believer in religious education forming the basis of a sound education, Carnarvon was greatly disturbed by the conscience clause in the Act, which stated that no religious catechism distinctive of any religious denomination should be taught. He wrote to his Somerset agent in 1872, 'A denominational school means, in this Parish, a religious and a Church of England School; and a School-Board School, meaning the exact opposite of

[56]CP, BL 60842, fos 1–9.
[57]Diary, 22 January 1874.
[58]B. Thomas (ed.), *Repton 1557 to 1957* (London, 1957), p. 63.
[59]Diary, 30 January 1882; G.R. Parkin, *Edward Thring, Headmaster of Uppingham*, 2 vols (London, 1898), II, p. 120.

this, is one to which I will not contribute one shilling.'[60] He subsequently closely observed cases of possible injustice to Church schools and raised such instances in Parliament, as at Willesden in 1882, where a school board was to be imposed.[61] He was equally opposed to the Endowed School Commission, established in 1869 by a Liberal government, whose task it was to make sweeping reforms in matters of charitable endowments and to frame new schemes for schools. Together with Salisbury, he played a leading part after the return of a Conservative government in 1874 in dismantling and transferring most of the powers of the Commission to the Charity Commission.[62]

Carnarvon also took an interest in all aspects of adult education. He gave many addresses on the topic to such bodies as the Birkbeck Schools, literary institutes, and the National Association for the Promotion of Social Science, as well as writing articles on the subject. In 1871, Oxford University was approached by four bodies requesting the university to supply teachers to present a series of lectures in different towns for non-university audiences. (It later became known as extension education and achieved widespread popularity. Some of the areas that benefited from this movement were Nottingham, Derby, and Leicester, where three lecturers circulated between these towns.) At the inaugural meeting at Nottingham in October 1873, Carnarvon presided. As a result of this movement, a University College was established there four years later, and he was present at the foundation ceremony.[63] It was an association that continued for the rest of his life.[64] Carnarvon also urged the provision of higher education for women, especially in connection with the Church of England, as at King's College, London.[65]

Carnarvon had been appointed Constable of Carnarvon Castle, North Wales, in 1856, and was surprised at its dilapidated state.[66] In 1870, after spending some time surveying the castle, he embarked on a programme of restoration. He ordered the removal of trees growing in the walls and the removal of excessive ivy from the Ivy Tower. The moat was cleared and intrusive houses below the Eagle Tower removed. Iron rails were put in place and a number of passages roofed.[67]

[60] Hardinge, III, p. 372.

[61] See Willesden School Board, TNA, PRO Ed. 16/217; Diary, 13 June 1882.

[62] P. Gordon, *Selection for Secondary Education* (London, 1980), p. 73.

[63] A.C. Wood, *A History of the University College, Nottingham, 1881–1948* (Oxford, 1953), p. 18.

[64] See, e.g., Diary, 11 October 1889.

[65] Diary, 24 June 1881.

[66] Letters Patent appointing him as Constable: Highclere Castle Archives, A/A12.

[67] Correspondence concerning Carnarvon Castle, 1870–1873: Highclere Castle Archives, 3/20.

Two important political measures – an Irish Church Bill in 1868 and a Land Bill in 1870 – occupied much of Carnarvon's time. Although he was often regarded as a High Churchman, his early contact with his uncle's brother, Edward Bouverie Pusey, the Tractarian, made him an intermediary between the conflicting schools of Evangelical and High Church opinion on the Irish Church Bill. He believed that the disestablishment of the Irish Church was inevitable, and, when Gladstone introduced the bill in March 1869 after the return of a Liberal government, Carnarvon made his own position clear. At a meeting of Conservative peers on 5 June at Derby's house, 'Lord Derby made a very vigorous speech in his old manner, denouncing the bill in the strongest language and looking almost pointedly at me said there was anyhow no individual who did not dislike and protest against every part of the bill and regard it as revolutionary and abominable.'[68] Nevertheless, in a speech in the Lords nine days later, much to the annoyance of his colleagues, Carnarvon declared that he was unable to oppose the bill.[69] At a further meeting of Conservative peers at Derby's house to prepare further opposition to the bill, Carnarvon was the only one to speak 'in a semi-dissentient sense'.[70] During the later stages of the bill, Carnarvon called on Derby at St James's Square, to discuss the University Tests Bill. It was the first time he had visited the Prime Minister since his resignation. Carnarvon noticed that Derby was gravely ill, and at the end expressed the hope that they were still friends. Derby agreed. Carnarvon had written to him a few days before, 'Everyone of course must be free to hold his own opinion, but whatever happens, I shall not forget that I owed my first introduction to Office to you.'[71] This was the last time they met: Derby died on 23 October that year.

Gladstone's Irish Land Bill, which was introduced into the Commons on 15 February 1870, was supported by Carnarvon on the grounds that it would help pacify Ireland and benefit landlords.[72] At this time the question of the leadership of the House of Lords arose with the relinquishing of the position by Cairns. He preferred Salisbury as a successor, but the latter had vowed that he would not take the leadership while Disraeli remained leader in the Commons. Carnarvon acted as an intermediary, attempting unsuccessfully to persuade Stanley, Salisbury, and Richmond in turn to take the post.

---

[68] Diary, 5 June 1869.
[69] See R.B. McDowell, *The Church of Ireland 1869–1969* (London, 1975), p. 46.
[70] Diary, 29 June 1869.
[71] Carnarvon to Derby, 18 June 1869: Derby Papers, DER (14) 163/5A.
[72] The *Daily News* had earlier spoken out with what it described as 'a [. . .] contribution to the worst understanding of the Irish Land Question' (E.D. Steele, *Irish Land and British Politics: tenant-right and nationality, 1865–70* (London, 1974), p. 170).

In a subsequent conversation with Gathorne Hardy, it was suggested that Carnarvon himself should fill the post of leadership. But the Reform Bill crisis and the attitude of former colleagues still rankled. 'I told him', wrote Carnarvon in his diary,

> that the Party in the House of Lords had behaved to me with so much injustice and unkindness that though I had forgiven it I should not forget it and that whilst I would do as I was doing every real service in my power, I was not inclined to undertake the lead.[73]

Hardy afterwards wrote to Cairns, 'I thought you would like to know something of my talk with Carnarvon. I suppose his leading would not do. Indeed, in turn I do not think health or nerve would allow his taking it.'[74] At a meeting of peers at the Carlton on 26 February, Richmond agreed to be Leader.[75] Carnarvon was once again in the counsels of the Party and had promised to rejoin the front Opposition bench, to use his favourite phrase, 'with some rather curious feelings'. His sense of grievance was never much below the surface. After taking his seat on 28 February, he declared, 'Three years ago I deliberately resigned my seat on the bench, or at least on the Treasury bench. Since then I have been in exile below the gangway, always an object of dislike, sometimes attack, with many opponents and few friends.'[76] Salisbury, who had also sworn not to rejoin the front bench because of his dislike of Disraeli, also resumed his old position.

A family tragedy occurred shortly afterwards. Carnarvon's favourite cousin, Edward Charles Herbert, who was Secretary to the British Legation in Athens, together with three companions had set off for an expedition to Marathon. On 11 April, the men were seized by a gang of brigands, who demanded a ransom of £25,000, with a threat to kill if it were not forthcoming. Carnarvon on hearing the news informed his mother, 'We have been obliged to undertake for the whole sum if necessary [...]. It is a very serious matter and it <u>may</u> cripple me for several years to come, but I see no alternative.'[77] Carnarvon did not consider Herbert's life to be in danger, but was worried that he was

---

[73] Diary, 22 February 1870.

[74] Hardy to Cairns, 22 February 1870, quoted in E. Feuchtwanger, *Disraeli, Democracy and the Tory Party* (Oxford, 1968), p. 7.

[75] Richmond was reluctant to take on the position. He wrote to his mother the night before the meeting, 'I cannot bear the party to break up, and if the Peers who meet tomorrow at the Carlton wish me to lead I will do so, though very much against my wishes, habits, &c. I do not think I am up to it but I must do my best.' 25 February 1870, Goodwood Papers, 862.12.

[76] Diary, 28 February 1870.

[77] Carnarvon to Henrietta, 3rd Countess of Carnarvon, 15 April 1870: Herbert Papers, Hampshire Record Office, 75M 91/L21/49.

not strong 'or fitted for much roughing'.[78] Meanwhile, Herbert had written a long letter to Carnarvon headed 'A Brigand Encampment near Oropos, 19 April 1870'. In it, he mentioned that the brigands demanded an amnesty as well as a ransom for their release, but had warned the hostages that they would resort to extreme measures if their terms were not agreed. He went on,

> I told the captain on Saturday I wished to visit the Acropolis of Oropos, and consequently he took us up there, and it was a very strange sight to see all the Brigands doing a wild dance on the top and singing most monotonous Khept ditties. Next day Easter [Greek Palm Sunday] we marched into the village to Church, which seemed curious, but our band are very religious and I am sure would think it necessary to cross themselves very often before murdering us.[79]

The letter was never delivered, as the party were put to death two days later; the bloodstained letter was found in Herbert's pocket. The brigands had panicked when some of the Greek soldiers who surrounded them attempted to capture the group. It was rumoured that there was a connection between the Greek 'political men' and the tragedy, but this was not proven.[80] Carnarvon, who feared that this would be the outcome, wrote to a friend, 'This is a terrible story but hope that there was comparatively little suffering.'[81] Carnarvon arranged for the body to be brought back to England, accompanied by his friend Frederick Vyner. Carnarvon met the boat at Southampton on 16 May, and Herbert was buried at Burghclere, the parish church of the Highclere estate.[82] It had been a taxing time for Carnarvon: in late May, he told Lytton, 'I can hardly tell you [. . .] how greatly I have suffered during the last month. Even now I can scarcely bear to dwell upon the terrible picture of cruelty, treachery and suffering [. . .] it has been great pain, for poor Edward was to me like a younger brother.'[83]

Carnarvon's constitution was never strong and he suffered frequent breakdowns throughout his political career. In 1872, he had a severe illness from which he only slowly recovered. During his convalescence, he reflected on the nature of life and death as well as on his own religious beliefs in a book, *The Shadows of the Sick Room*, published in 1873.

---

[78] Carnarvon to Cranbrook, 20 April 1870: Cranbrook Papers, T501/262.

[79] E. Herbert to Carnarvon, 19 April 1870: Highclere Castle Archives, A/41.

[80] Clarendon to Carnarvon, 8 May 1870: Clarendon Papers, dep. c. 496.

[81] Carnarvon to Lady Vincent, 25 April 1870: Vincent Papers.

[82] J. Thorp, 'Murder near Marathon', *Hampshire Archives Trust Newsletter*, Autumn 1988, p. 12.

[83] Carnarvon to Lytton, 25 May 1870: Lytton Papers, Hertfordshire Archives and Local Studies Office, D/EK C36/47.

Freemasonry had played an important part in Carnarvon's life since he was a youth. He was initiated in February 1856 into the Westminster Keystone Lodge, which was intended as a London base for Oxford University Masons.[84] At that time, there was some friction between the Canadian Lodges, who wished to form their own Grand Lodge, and the Grand Lodge in London. Carnarvon was criticized for heading a faction in favour of giving the Canadian Lodges their independence and in reforming the Grand Lodge administration.[85] He became Provincial Grand Master of Somerset in a ceremony at Bath in 1869 and was made Deputy Grand Master of the United Grand Lodge of England in 1870. Four years later, he was installed as Pro Grand Master at the Albert Hall, and was given the honour of installing the Prince of Wales, later Edward VII, as Grand Master at the Royal Albert Hall in April 1875.[86]

Apart from attending ceremonies and presiding at Masonic meetings, Carnarvon had routine work to do, which could be heavy at times. In proposing the division of responsibilities between the Prince, himself, and Lord Skelmersdale, the Deputy Pro Grand Master, Carnarvon offered to take the main burden.[87] A matter that had caused Carnarvon much worry was that the Grand Orient of France had eliminated one of its fundamental rules, which formerly maintained a belief in God and immortality of the soul. A resolution by British lodges deploring this move came before the Council, over which Carnarvon presided.[88] The case was referred to a committee of inquiry, which led to a complete separation of the French lodges from those in England.

Another difficult situation had arisen in Australia. When Carnarvon visited that country in 1887–1888, he found that there were no fewer than four different rival Masonic constitutions in New South Wales. After consultation with the Prince of Wales, Carnarvon drew up a plan to conciliate the parties. Subsequently, the lodges agreed to become a single body, the United Grand Lodge of New South Wales.[89] Towards the end of his life, he obtained immense pleasure from presiding at the Great Meeting at the Albert Hall, when he presented an address

---

[84] *The Freemason*, 5 July 1890.

[85] Hardinge, I, pp. 222–226.

[86] A.F. Calvert, *The Grand Lodge of England, 1717–1917: being an account of 200 years of English Freemasonry* (London, 1917), p. 292.

[87] Carnarvon, Memorandum, 'Proposed arrangement for the future division of Masonic work between His Royal Highness, Lord Carnarvon and Lord Skelmersdale, 16 Feb. 1877': CP, TNA, PRO 30/6/4, fos 23–24.

[88] Diary, 30 November 1870.

[89] The Library and Museum of Freemasonry, London, Carnarvon file, p. 228. Carnarvon also attended Masonic functions in Melbourne: *Melbourne Argos*, 9 November 1887, p. 2.

to Queen Victoria on her Golden Jubilee, with the Prince of Wales in attendance. 'It was a really magnificent sight,' Carnarvon recorded in his diary, 'crowded as it was, with the masses of colour, the orchestra, the organ and the great gathering.'[90]

Colonial Secretary, 1874–1878

In March 1873, Gladstone failed to secure the passing of the Irish University Bill, which seriously undermined his administration. Carnarvon was congratulated by Disraeli for his fierce opposition to another piece of legislation, the Judicature Bill. 'I was in your House a good deal during the fatal events', he wrote, 'and more than once thought your eloquence and energy would have triumphed.'[91] In the general election of February 1874, the Conservatives were returned to office. Sir William Heathcote had received a letter from Disraeli stating, 'You and Carnarvon are the only two persons for whose political judgment I care.' In transmitting this surprising message to Carnarvon, Heathcote added, 'N.B. remember this when any little passing cloud leads you to doubt his high regard for a high opinion of you.'[92]

While Carnarvon was being urged by his friends to join Disraeli's government, Salisbury was reluctant to follow.[93] It was seven years since the two men had resigned from Disraeli's Cabinet, vowing never to work with him again. Lady Derby, Salisbury's stepmother, acted as an intermediary in enticing him back. Salisbury reported to her on 8 February,

> This morning Carnarvon appeared. We had a very long talk. He decidedly leans towards taking office. I tried to persuade him that we were not in the same boat, and that my refusing would not involve him doing the same. He pressed on me strongly that if I remained outside, I should be a perfect cipher – which is entirely true.[94]

The large Conservative majority at the general election meant that further opposition to Disraeli was useless. Carnarvon wrote to a fellow sympathizer at the time, 'I feel the helplessness to which one would be

[90]Diary, 13 June 1887.
[91]Disraeli to Carnarvon, 28 July 1873: CP, BL 60763, fos 14–15.
[92]Heathcote to Carnarvon, 11 February 1874: CP, BL 81078, fo. 116.
[93]Sir Stafford Northcote reported to Disraeli in 1872 that Carnarvon, like other Liberal-minded Tory peers, was 'very much alarmed at the possibility of a great attack on the land, suspicious of Gladstone and of an attempt to set tenants against landlords': Northcote to Disraeli, 23 September 1872, quoted in D. Southgate, *The Passing of the Whigs, 1832–1886* (London, 1962), p. 353.
[94]Cecil, II, pp. 43–44.

reduced outside the Government if one thought it right to criticise.'[95]
By 19 February, Salisbury had rejoined the Government, along with
Carnarvon. Both returned to the posts that they had held in the
previous administration: Salisbury to the India Office and Carnarvon
to the Colonial Office. With similar political tasks, Carnarvon and
Salisbury frequently communicated with each other. Carnarvon wrote
to Salisbury in August, 'You are very good to me to let me talk to you as
I do, often urging disagreeable things and making idle criticisms. But
it is the privilege of our long friendship and if it seems sometimes
unnecessarily capricious it really proceeds from my affection and
admiration for you.'[96]

Shortly before taking office, Carnarvon received a reassuring note
from his cousin Sir Robert Herbert, Permanent Under-Secretary at
the Colonial Office:

> I think I can guarantee that you shall not be overburdened by the work. You
> should not, I think, attempt to look at every little detail, as Lord Kimberley does,
> but you must adopt the more Granvillian system of giving the necessary amount
> of attention to the really important matters, and letting the Parliamentary and
> Under-Secretaries deal with the trivial ones.[97]

This advice was not easy to follow in practice. By September,
Carnarvon was complaining, 'Work follows me about everywhere,
almost every moment of time is occupied. It is indeed almost a wonder
to me how I get through 24 hours.'[98]

The Earl of Kimberley, his Liberal predecessor, had authorized
a reduction in the size of the Colonial Office staff, and there was
friction between Carnarvon and the Treasury over staffing and other
questions. Sir Henry Ponsonby, after a discussion with Carnarvon at
Balmoral, wrote to his wife,

> He seems to be at perpetual war with the Treasury, which he says is controlled
> by two or three very inferior clerks – and he is proud of his triumph in making
> the stamp office disgorge some thousands which they had got out of Colonial
> Governors for stamps on Commissions which he, Carnarvon, discovered was
> illegal.[99]

Carnarvon was popular with his staff and was wholly dedicated
to the conduct of colonial affairs. He was given a fairly free hand

---

[95]Carnarvon to Duke of Northumberland, 13 February 1874 (copy): CP, BL 60774,
fo. 108.

[96]Carnarvon to Salisbury, 5 August 1874: Hatfield House Papers, 3M/E.

[97]Herbert to Carnarvon, 9 February 1874: CP, BL 60791, fos 39–40.

[98]Carnarvon to Henrietta, 3rd Countess of Carnarvon, 26 September 1874: CP, BL 61044,
fo. 157.

[99]Ponsonby to Mary Elizabeth Ponsonby, 15 September 1875: Royal Archives, Add A/36.

in deciding colonial policy by Disraeli, whose main interest lay in the wider field of foreign affairs.[100] Two of Carnarvon's objectives were imperial expansion and federation, and he urged his Cabinet colleagues to re-establish imperial garrisons in the larger colonies. He made a number of errors in his judgements, much to the Cabinet's irritation, but his successes were praised by the public; it has been suggested that Disraeli was jealous of his Colonial Secretary's triumphs.[101] As he once wrote to Lady Bradford, 'I am extremely amused that, while all the Government are attacked in the metropolitan papers for their blundering, etc., little Carnarvon, who feeds the Radical press, is always spared, and really he is the only one who has made mistakes, and committed a series of blunders.'[102] Carnarvon claimed that Disraeli rarely read colonial material that he had dispatched, and that the Colonial Secretary was expected to 'make bricks without straw'.[103] Nevertheless, the Prime Minister generously praised Carnarvon for his involvement in his work. Disraeli wrote to the Queen in 1875,

> Lord Carnarvon was the first Colonial Secretary who opened his house and his castles to Your Majesty's Colonial subjects. They knew when they were in England they had a chief on whom they could rely as a friend, and his hospitality and courtesy effected immense good in Your Majesty's Colonial Empire.[104]

Carnarvon pursued a policy that encouraged closer ties between the colonies,[105] which, while retaining control of their internal affairs, at the same time had a good relationship with the imperial government and parliament. One of the unsolved problems presented to the new Colonial Secretary was the future of South Africa. There have been many interpretations of Carnarvon's South African policy: some writers have stressed the humanitarian aspect, others a search for a uniform native policy; it has also been seen as a strategy to protect the route between Britain and India;[106] and yet another view interprets it as a desire to develop a modern capitalist society following

[100] See C. Eldridge, *Disraeli and the Rise of a New Imperialism* (Cardiff, 1996), p. 46.

[101] B.L. Blakeley, *The Colonial Office, 1868–1892* (Durham, NC, 1972), p. 71.

[102] Buckle, *Disraeli*, V, p. 475.

[103] Minute, Carnarvon: TNA, CO 179/118.

[104] Disraeli to Queen Victoria, 25 January 1875: Royal Archives, J 53/142.

[105] But Shannon has pointed out that the new 'forward' policy in action, involving Britain in places such as the Gold Coast, the Malay States, and the Fiji Islands had in fact been recommended by Carnarvon's Liberal predecessor, Kimberley, and accepted by Gladstone's Cabinet: R. Shannon, *The Crisis of Imperialism, 1865–1915* (London, 1974), p. 107.

[106] For example, the refusal of Portugal to sell Delagoa Bay to Britain in 1875 upset Carnarvon's plan for securing strategic points on the route to India (M. Swartz, *The Politics of British Foreign Policy in the Era of Disraeli and Gladstone* (London, 1985), p. 21).

the discovery of diamonds there in 1867.[107] The annexation of the recently discovered diamond fields in Griqualand West highlighted the rivalry between English and Dutch settlers. In April 1875, Carnarvon ordered troops from Cape Town to quell a serious disturbance there. There were further difficulties with the Governor of the Cape and the High Commissioner of South Africa, Sir Henry Barkly, who lacked leadership in diplomatic dealings with the Orange Free State. Carnarvon had much sympathy for the native peoples of Cape Colony, Natal, and Griqualand West, because of their harsh treatment by the English colonists. In a move to pacify them, he reversed a sentence for high treason passed on a Kaffir chief, Langalibalele. Benjamin Pine, Governor of Natal, who had presided at the court, was subsequently recalled. Lord Derby at the Foreign Office had earlier written to Carnarvon, 'I have no doubt that the Chief with the long name ought to be detained for the present.'[108] In October 1874, Carnarvon requested Cairns, who was in attendance at Balmoral, to inform the Queen about 'the important subject of the abolition of West African slavery [. . .]. It has cost me a good deal of labour and some anxiety, but I am sanguine of success.'[109]

Carnarvon had criticized a federal solution in South Africa in 1859,[110] but now in office his attitude changed. The historian James Anthony Froude had, five years earlier in his rectorial address at St Andrews, proclaimed himself an imperialist. In 1874, Carnarvon sent him to South Africa (ostensibly on a health cure) to report back on the feasibility of such a scheme. In June the following year, Froude – who was not the most discreet of men – was sent as an official emissary of the British Government. His visit coincided with the receipt by the Cape Legislative Assembly of Carnarvon's despatch on Federation. The Assembly, in a defiant mood, turned down Carnarvon's proposals, which were greeted with ironic laughter.[111] Carnarvon withdrew his scheme in October 1875; a South African conference, held in London the following year with Carnarvon in the chair, was also a failure. 'Matters are moving faster in South Africa than most people here know', wrote Derby to Carnarvon at this time; 'The Dutch States – particularly the Trans Vaal – are seeking to enlarge their borders, and if

[107]R.L. Cope, 'Local imperatives and imperial policy: the sources of Lord Carnarvon's South African Confederation policy', *International Journal of African Historical Studies*, 20, 4 (1987), pp. 602–603.

[108]Derby to Carnarvon, 20 November 1874: Derby Papers, 920 DER (15) 17/2/5.

[109]Carnarvon to Cairns, n.d. but October 1874: Cairns Papers, TNA, PRO 30/51/8, fo. 74.

[110]K.N. Bell and W.P. Morell (eds), *Select Documents on British Colonial Policy, 1830–1860* (Oxford, 1928), pp. 191–194.

[111]H. Paul, *The Life of Froude* (London, 1905), p. 208.

possible to get down to the sea coast and *under existing circumstances* this would be extremely inconvenient'. Carnarvon suggested that 'we assert English sovereignty [. . .] the quicker the thing can be done the better'.[112]

Carnarvon believed that pursuing a more aggressive policy, with further annexation, would help to achieve federation. After the defeat of the Boers in 1876, Sir Theophilus Shepstone, Secretary for Native Affairs in Natal – a man in whom Carnarvon had the highest confidence – was dispatched to the Transvaal by the Earl. Shepstone was backed up by troops with the order to bring about annexation.[113] Carnarvon also told Heathcote, 'I really begin to hope that I may be able to annexe the Transvaal Republic before the meeting of Parliament.'[114] Sir Bartle Frere was dispatched as Governor of the Cape in March 1877 (with the hope that he would be the first Governor-General of a united South Africa), to find that Shepstone had already annexed the Transvaal. This move did not, however, bring about Carnarvon's original intentions. By August, the Cape Frontier War had broken out and the Zulus were now fighting the British rather than the Dutch. Lieutenant-General Sir William Butler, who participated in this campaign, later declared that 'these little movements [Shepstone and Frere's appointments], unknown and unnoticed at the moment of their occurrence, were in reality the spring-heads of the stream of events destined to plunge South Africa into a state of intermittent war for 26 years.'[115]

Carnarvon justified another annexation, that of Fiji in October 1874, superficially because of its need for 'an English government' but in reality for strategic reasons – the safeguarding of communications between Sydney and North America.[116] Meanwhile, when governors overstepped their jurisdiction, Carnarvon asserted his authority quickly and decisively. Such an example was that of Sir William Jervois, who was appointed to the Straits Settlements in February

[112]Carnarvon to Derby, 27 October 1875: Derby Papers, 920 DER (15).

[113]Carnarvon to Maj.-Gen. Sir Garnet Wolseley, 24 Sept 1876: Wolseley Papers; see also Carnarvon to Cranbrook, 20 September 1876: Cranbrook Papers, T 501/262.

[114]Carnarvon to Heathcote, 13 September 1876: CP, BL 61074, fo. 47.

[115]Sir William Butler, *An Autobiography* (London, 1911), p. 195. On 3 July 1878, Sir Michael Hicks Beach, Carnarvon's successor as Colonial Secretary, gave a gloomy account of disaffection in the Transvaal to the Cabinet: 'all lamented and blamed Carnarvon's annexation of it. Rising of Boers feared in a few months': C. Howard and P. Gordon, *The Cabinet Journal of Dudley Ryder, Viscount Sandon*, Bulletin of the Institute of Historical Research, Special Supplement no. 10 (London, 1974), p. 37. For a summary of Carnarvon's legacy in South Africa, see C.F. Goodfellow, *Great Britain and South African Confederation, 1870–1881* (Cape Town, 1966), pp. 148–150.

[116]B. Knox, 'The Earl of Carnarvon, empire, and imperialism, 1855–90', *Journal of Imperial and Commonwealth History*, 26, 2 (1998), pp. 57–58.

1875. In December of that year, Carnarvon informed the Queen of his 'disapproval of the wholly rash and insupportable act on Sir W. Jervois's part in the annexation of Barak'.[117] This had led to the assassination of the British resident and a native revolt. On Carnarvon's insistence, Jervois's policy was reversed.[118]

At the end of 1874, Carnarvon's wife, Evelyn, had given birth to their fourth child, but then became desperately ill. She died on 25 January 1875. A family friend, Lord Ronald Gower, wrote in his diary, 'Yesterday died Lady Carnarvon, in every sense a *grand dame*; her death a terrible loss to the poor husband.'[119] The effect on him was considerable. Derby, after dining with him, noted,

> I was struck with a change in him which I can scarcely describe. He talked incessantly in a rapid excited way which is new to him, except that he has done the same once or twice in cabinet. Lady Derby was impressed as I was by his manner; it seems as if since his loss he had thrown himself into work with a feverish activity, not quite healthy or natural.[120]

The Queen had expressed a wish to be godmother to the baby, who bore her name, and was represented at the christening by a lady-in-waiting, Lady Ely, bringing with her a locket with the Queen's picture in it.[121]

In November of that year, Disraeli offered Carnarvon the post of Viceroy of India, which Lord Northbrook wished to relinquish. As was often Carnarvon's practice on such an occasion, he drew up a lengthy memorandum listing the pros and cons of the proposition.[122] Disraeli informed Lady Chesterfield of the outcome: 'Carnarvon after three days meditation has refused the greater I [India]. It was the children and that only which prevented him.'[123] Disraeli omitted to mention that the post had already been turned down by Lord Powis and Lord

---

[117] Carnarvon to Queen Victoria, 14 December 1875: Royal Archives, P25/1. Jervois's insubordination infuriated Carnarvon. He described one of Jervois's despatches, which 'unquestionably had the merit of cleverness', as 'unscrupulous in argument, overbearing in tone and disingenuous in character'. Carnarvon filled the margins with exclamation marks and expressions such as 'Monstrous', ' Absurd', and 'An outrageous doctrine': C.D. Cowan, *Nineteenth-century Malaya: the origins of British political control* (London, 1961), p. 241.

[118] H.L. Hall, *The Colonial Office: a history* (London, 1937), p. 242.

[119] R. Gower, *My Reminiscences* (London, 1883), p. 107.

[120] Vincent, *Derby*, II, p. 252. Lady Derby reported to Carnarvon after his wife's death that the Queen had spoken 'very warmly and feelingly and seemed deeply interested. She feared you were ill and heard you were very thin, and wishes you would not do too much': W.A.H.C. Gardner, Baroness Burghclere (ed.), *A Great Man's Friendship: letters of the Duke of Wellington to Mary, Marchioness of Salisbury, 1850–1852* (London, 1927), pp. 26–27.

[121] Diary, 11 February 1875.

[122] Carnarvon to Disraeli, 5 November 1875: CP, BL 60763, fos 111–113.

[123] Zetland, I, p. 304.

John Manners. Another offer was made to Carnarvon eleven days later to replace the incompetent Ward Hunt at the Admiralty. After a considerable talk with Disraeli, Carnarvon told the Prime Minister 'that affairs at the Colonial Office were such and so critical that it would be very unfortunate *now* to remove me'.[124]

One piece of legislation in which Carnarvon was concerned was that relating to vivisection, on which he had strong views. As the only member of the Cabinet who showed an interest in experimental science and who was also an anti-vivisectionist, he introduced the second reading of the Cruelty to Animals Bill in May 1876.[125] He admitted the difficulties of the subject: 'On the one side there is a strong sentiment of humanity: on the other, there are the claims of modern science.'[126] Although strongly opposed by sections of the medical profession, the bill received Royal Assent in August, giving some form of regulation of vivisection.[127]

There was a further burden for Carnarvon to carry that he could not have anticipated when taking office. In October 1876, Disraeli had requested Salisbury to attend, as plenipotentiary, a conference in Constantinople of the signatory powers convened to deal with the relations between the Sultan and his Christian subjects. Carnarvon was asked to supervise the work of the India Office in Salisbury's absence, as well as his own departmental work. Salisbury had anticipated that the India Office commitment would involve little more than the signing of despatches once a week. In fact, the worsening famine in southern India presented many unforeseen problems. Carnarvon wrote to the retiring Viceroy, Lord Northbrook,

> I am not in a very easy position for I have fallen on evil times without warning or preparation and in necessary ignorance of all the details on which any Minister would have had time to learn. It is also not a sinecure to carry on two such Offices as the Colonial and the Indian.[128]

Carnarvon calculated that this extra work, which included presiding over the Indian Council, involved an extra four to five hours each day.[129]

---

[124]Diary, 18 November 1875.
[125]L. Williamson, *Power and Protest: Frances Power Cobbe and Victorian society* (London, 2005), p. 127.
[126]*Hansard*, CCXXV, 22 May 1876, col. 1002.
[127]J. Turner, *Reckoning with the Beast: animals, pain, and humanity in the Victorian mind* (Baltimore, MD, 1980), p. 91.
[128]Carnarvon to Northbrook, 12 January 1877: CP, TNA, PRO 30/6/15, fo. 76.
[129]Carnarvon to Heathcote, 18 January 1877: CP, BL 61074, fo. 68.

Although Disraeli's health had been stable during 1875, when he returned to London in the second week of January 1876 he suffered an acute seizure. Writing to Lady Bradford after chairing a Cabinet meeting on 18 January, he complained, 'I have been, and am a great sufferer. I have had the illness of a month crammed and compressed into 8 and 40 hours.'[130] The same evening, Carnarvon dined with Sandon, and they discussed the question of the Duke of Richmond becoming Prime Minister in the event of Disraeli resigning on account of ill health. Sandon, then Vice-President of the Committee of the Council on Education, who had been in bitter conflict with Richmond over educational legislation, recorded their conversation in a memorandum:

> We both agreed, notwithstanding personal regard for the person in question that such an appointment would be fatal to the Conservative Party, as he has no knowledge of the feeling of the Party, or sympathy with the people, or anything approaching to intellectual grasp, but we both agreed the danger of his having the position was a real one as H.M. may be favourable, and Lord Derby in the Lords to be afraid of the responsibility of the leadership. The Lord Chancellor [Cairns] is a sworn friend of the Duke of Richmond being of the same narrow political intellect or rather having the same want of it in *political* matters (not legal or oratorical in which the latter is no mean master) and it may be difficult in the House of Commons to decide between the pretensions of Cross and Northcote. The latter we both agreed was clearly pointed out for the lead.[131]

The Russo-Turkish War of 1877–1878 and Carnarvon's second resignation

By this time, events in Eastern Europe were beginning to overshadow other issues. A revolt in European Turkey, starting in Herzegovina, had broken out in the summer of 1875, and there were fears for the Christian population of the region. A much larger uprising in Bulgaria began in May 1876, resulting in many thousands of people, mainly Christians, being massacred. There was great concern in England that the Christian population of Constantinople was now in danger; as a result, the Cabinet sent a British squadron of ships to Besika Bay. Carnarvon's main worries, expressed in a later memorandum, were the irresolute attitude of Derby, the Foreign Secretary, and the pro-Turkish stance being taken by Disraeli, who in August moved to the House of Lords, taking the title of the Earl of Beaconsfield. Carnarvon claimed that Disraeli 'disliked the Christian cause from his Jewish

[130] Buckle, *Disraeli*, V, p. 489.
[131] Sandon, 'Memorandum: confidential for self', 18 January 1876: Harrowby Papers, 2nd series, lv, fo. 55.

sympathies,[132] and also in part from a political point of view and from the influence which the Court was now beginning to exercise upon him in the matter'.[133] Meanwhile, Gladstone roused public opinion by his pamphlet on the Bulgarian atrocities, stating that it was necessary to support Russia in the Christian cause. In a long private letter to Derby, written in 1876 but never sent, Carnarvon admitted, 'You know that my personal feeling is probably more anti-Turkish and pro-provincial (if I may coin the word) than possibly some of our colleagues.'[134] He was anxious not to push the country into going to war on the matter. He told his friend Lord Bath, 'Anything publicly said or done which seems to give support to Russia as against our Government (and unless the greatest care is taken this will be the appearance which any support is likely to have) will seriously cripple our power of negotiation and indirectly tend to war.'[135] He was disappointed that the conference at Constantinople failed to settle the Russo-Turkish dispute.

On the night of Salisbury's return, the two men dined alone. Salisbury, Carnarvon noted, 'appeared in talking over with me all that had passed, to have but one feeling – viz. a rooted belief in Disraeli's untrustworthiness, and a dread of the policy which he thought Disraeli intended to pursue'.[136] By 23 March 1877, Disraeli was attacking Carnarvon and Salisbury in Cabinet, accusing them of disloyalty. However, during the spring and summer, Carnarvon observed that Salisbury's relationship with Disraeli was changing and was more antagonistic towards Derby, who, like Carnarvon, was becoming alarmed at Disraeli's warlike language. Further, it seemed to Carnarvon that obvious pressure was being exercised by the Queen on Disraeli and individual members of the Cabinet. Even more alarming was Salisbury's support of the view now being put forward by members of the Cabinet that the fleet should be sent to Constantinople in the event of an attempted occupation of the city by the Russians. By July, the Cabinet was in disarray, with members changing their minds on the issue and threats of resignation. Carnarvon had formed an alliance with Derby on future action by the end of the month.[137] At the Cabinet

---

[132] For a discussion of the deep suspicion of Disraeli's Jewish sentiments at the time, see E. Feuchtwanger, '"Jew feelings" and realpolitik: Disraeli and the making of foreign imperial policy', in T.M. Edelman and T. Kushner (eds), *Disraeli's Jewishness* (London, 2002), pp. 193–195.

[133] 'Memorandum on the circumstances which led to my resignation in January 1878', September 1879: CP, BL 60817, fo. 29.

[134] Carnarvon to Derby, 24 September 1876 (copy): CP, BL 60765, fo. 115.

[135] Carnarvon to Bath, 27 November 1876: Longleat Papers.

[136] 'Memorandum on the circumstances which led to my resignation in January 1878', fo. 39.

[137] Diary, 3 August 1877; Vincent, *Derby*, II, p. 425.

on 15 August, the question again arose of possible action in the event of the Russians once more threatening to occupy Constantinople. During the subsequent discussion, Carnarvon dissented three times, against the rest of the Cabinet, on taking any action which would ally Britain with Turkey.[138] Adding to the difficulties was Disraeli's obvious physical deterioration. It was for this reason that he had left the Commons the previous August to sit in the House of Lords. Carnarvon observed in his diary for the 28 June, 'Disraeli in the House of Lords this evening looked like a corpse – his face drawn, his breath laboured, his arms and hands rigid, his whole appearance and attitude ghastly. Can he possibly last? And how will this extraordinary tragedy end?'

In October 1877, Disraeli met Lady Derby at Woburn and told her that 'he had six parties in the Cabinet – how could they be reconciled?'[139] Although this claim was somewhat exaggerated,[140] Lord Derby summed up the situation after the Cabinet meeting on 5 October: 'On the whole I class my colleagues as follows: For war: Beaconsfield, J. Manners, Beach, Cairns and Richmond. Against: Salisbury, Carnarvon, and in general, Derby. Undecided: Northcote, Hardy, Cross and Smith.' Following the defeat of the Turks at Plevna on 10 December, Disraeli proposed four days later to the Cabinet to place the armed forces on full alert and augment their number, to summon Parliament immediately, and to encourage mediation between the powers. The Cabinet met again on Monday 17 December. During the weekend, the Queen, in a remarkable public display of support for Disraeli, had paid a visit to Hughenden. The next Cabinet failed to make progress and Disraeli offered his resignation. The Queen wrote to the Prime Minister stating that she would never accept it.

Standing in the way of the Cabinet coming to an agreement was the opposition of Salisbury, Derby, and Carnarvon. After the meeting, it was later reported that Salisbury had changed his disposition towards Disraeli. Salisbury defused the situation by proposing that the Cabinet should meet the next day before any further action was taken. Subsequently, it was agreed as a compromise that the Cabinet should meet on 3 January 1878 and that Parliament would reassemble a fortnight later. Derby, too, sought appeasement. He requested a meeting with Disraeli before the Cabinet meeting of 18 December in the hope of arriving at a compromise. At the Cabinet meeting, Disraeli announced the change of heart of two of the three colleagues. Carnarvon now found himself in a minority, in judging that

---

[138] Memorandum, 'Note on the Cabinet of 15 August 1877', Disraeli to Queen Victoria, 15 August 1877: Royal Archives, B52/24.

[139] Mary, Lady Derby to Carnarvon, 26 October 1877, CP: BL 60765, fo. 137.

[140] Vincent, *Derby*, II, p. 442.

the occupation of Constantinople would be a *casus belli*. According to Disraeli, Carnarvon, 'who had hitherto been silent, screamed out that although he accepted these resolutions, begged it to be understood that their acceptance, on his part, involved no assent to any expedition to any part of the Turkish Empire or any alliance with the Porte'.[141] Disraeli wrote gleefully to Lady Bradford after the last Cabinet meeting two days later, 'The great struggle is over, and I have triumphed.'[142] His actions against the three reluctant peers had been successful, though it was Carnarvon's departure from the Cabinet that would remove the main obstacle to progress.

Before the meeting of the Cabinet in the New Year, Carnarvon received a South African commercial deputation at Highclere. He chose this occasion to announce his view that peace was of paramount importance, and that a repeat of the Crimean War would be insane. His speech was widely reported in the national press. On receiving a copy of it, Gladstone declared, 'Lord Carnarvon has manhood as well as integrity.'[143] Disraeli's reaction was somewhat different. He informed the Queen

> He has heard nothing yet of his disloyal colleague. Lord Beaconsfield would at once accept his resignation, if offered. Lord Carnarvon [. . .] was in his castle in the country, surrounded by a circle of literary parasites, chiefly contributors to the Liberal press [. . .]. Without consulting a single colleague, he delivers himself of all the fine phrases at Highclere, whereas, had he remained in London, like myself, and seen men and things, his speech might have been duller, but it would have been wiser.

At the Cabinet meeting, Disraeli delivered a blistering attack on Carnarvon, who attempted to defend himself and then offered his resignation. Disraeli, who requested the Queen to invite Carnarvon for an audience, 'as a personal favour to myself', telegraphed her immediately after the meeting, 'He (C.) has departed for Osborne, much excited.'[144] And Ponsonby, who privately sided with Carnarvon, reported the same day to the Queen, 'He evidently did not think that his speech would have been considered in an antagonistic light by the Government.'[145] At the interview, the Queen gave 'that foolish misguided and yet in his own department very able Lord C. [. . .] such a dressing down'.[146] The following day, having read the speech, she

---

[141]Buckle, *Disraeli*, VI, p. 206.

[142]Ibid., p. 207.

[143]Gladstone to Chamberlain, 3 January 1878: Gladstone Papers, BL 44125, fo. 2.

[144]Disraeli to Queen Victoria, 3 January 1878: Royal Archives, H 18/T6.

[145]Ponsonby to Queen Victoria, 3 January 1878: Royal Archives, B 54/40.

[146]R. Fulford, *Darling Child: private correspondence of Queen Victoria and the Crown Princess of Prussia, 1871–1878* (London, 1976), p. 275.

wrote to him, 'The Queen cannot refrain from <u>now</u> expressing her
deep concern that Lord Carnarvon should have allowed his personal
feelings (which she is bound to say SHE <u>cannot</u> understand) to find
vent in a speech to a Commercial Delegation [. . .]. It is (the Queen
must speak <u>strongly</u>) lamentable.'[147]

Allies in the Cabinet were few. Derby, while disagreeing with
Disraeli, was at the same time busy revealing Cabinet secrets to the
Russian ambassador, Shuvalov. Carnarvon had become increasingly
suspicious of Salisbury's attitude; he wrote to him after the Cabinet
meeting of 3 January, 'I not only do not wish you to leave me – if it
comes to this – but I doubt whether it is wise for you to do so. The point
is quite sufficient for one person to stand upon; but perhaps not large
enough for three.'[148] To the relief of the rest of the Cabinet, Carnarvon
withdrew his resignation, comforted by the knowledge that, privately,
other members shared his view that Disraeli was determined to form
an alliance with Turkey and to go to war with Russia. This suspicion
was made manifest at the Cabinet meeting of 9 January to discuss
the Queen's Speech, when Disraeli took a strong pro-Turkish line.
Carnarvon noted in his memorandum that this was the last occasion
when Salisbury acted openly with Derby and himself. Three days
later at the Cabinet, a letter from the Queen was read, urging them to
stand by the principle 'which we have declared that any advance on
Constantinople would free us from neutrality'. Only Carnarvon and
Derby opposed an expedition to Gallipoli, either with or without the
consent of the Sultan.

Carnarvon's standing with his colleagues became increasingly
precarious. After the speech to the South African delegation, which
had been widely reported, he was seen as the leader of the peace party.
His health deteriorated at this time, and he carried on business with
difficulty. Derby, too, was ill with overwork and nervous exhaustion,
and missed the two Cabinets of 14 and 15 January.[149] After the latter
meeting, where it was unanimously agreed (except for Carnarvon)
that the fleet should be ordered to Gallipoli if the co-operation of
Austria could be obtained, Carnarvon returned home, and wrote to
Disraeli with his resignation, to take effect when the order to the
fleet would be given. At the next day's Cabinet, it was stated that the
Government had been assured by Russia that their troops would not

---

[147]Buckle, *Letters*, III, p. 588.

[148]Carnarvon to Salisbury, 3 January 1878: Hatfield House Papers, 3M/E.

[149]Although Carnarvon added in his memorandum on the crisis, 'the report was
immediately set in circulation in the Carlton, and thence carefully disseminated through
every Conservative drawing room in London that he was suffering from drink':
'Memorandum on the circumstances which led to my resignation in January 1878',
fo. 76.

occupy Gallipoli, and on 18 January Disraeli replied to Carnarvon's letter, assuring him that the differences between them were bridgeable. Three days later in Cabinet, when the question of a defensive alliance with Austria was once more proposed, only Carnarvon and Derby opposed it. The order to the fleet to proceed to Constantinople was then drafted, and, on the following morning (23 January), Carnarvon's final letter of resignation was despatched: that same evening, Disraeli replied, accepting it.

Derby had spoken to Carnarvon after the Cabinet meeting, begging him to withhold his letter until the following day, while he wrote his own letter of resignation. On 25 January, orders were sent to the fleet to countermand the previous instructions. While Carnarvon had been outmanoeuvred by Disraeli, overtures were made to Derby in the form of offers of other government posts to persuade him to stay in office: the Prime Minister announced to the Cabinet on 27 January that Derby had withdrawn his resignation. This ploy was, for the time being, successful. 'I am not disappointed at Derby having failed at the last hurdle', Carnarvon wrote to his sister; 'I always knew that he would not take the leap. I told everyone else so.'[150] Interestingly, two years later, Salisbury told his nephew Arthur Balfour that he was puzzled at Carnarvon's resignation with Derby as 'they were the two members of the Cabinet who got on least well together. At one time (so the Lord Chancellor told me) Lord Carnarvon used to complain bitterly that Lord Derby was using every means of thwarting his policy and undermining his influence.'[151] On 4 February, Derby announced in the Lords that an armistice had been concluded. It was not until 27 March that he actually resigned. Cross wrote of Derby's speech, that it was 'very different from the tone in which Lord Carnarvon had announced his own resignation some weeks before'.[152]

Carnarvon later maintained that had he known that the counter order to the fleet would be given: 'I do not think it would have altered my decision.' Sensitive as ever about his public image, he continued, 'I was utterly weary of the oscillations of purpose, and very fearful that this prolonged and extremely unequal conflict would lead me into a position in which I would find myself seriously compromised and

---

[150] Carnarvon to Eveline, Countess of Portsmouth, 27 January 1878: CP, BL 61049, fo. 149. Carnarvon commented to Derby's wife, 'Different circumstances allow for different action and I will not say that Derby has decided otherwise than right. I have, as you know, never said a word to induce anyone to follow my example' (Carnarvon to Mary, Lady Derby, 27 January 1878: CP, BL 60765, fo. 161).

[151] Quoted in R. Harcourt Williams (ed.), *The Salisbury–Balfour Correspondence, 1869–1892* (Ware, Hertfordshire, 1988), p. 45.

[152] R.A. Cross, *A Political History* (Broughton-in-Furness, 1903), p. 50.

perhaps damaged in public character.'[153] The day after he resigned, Carnarvon made a personal explanation in the House of Lords. Derby considered that it was 'rather too long, and he unwisely brought into it his quarrel with Lord Beaconsfield three weeks ago, which betrayed personal feeling'.[154] The speech was not well received by his former colleagues. Carnarvon wrote to Sir William Heathcote, 'There is much discomfort but there is also great relief in having escaped the "net of the fowler."'[155] The following day, he met his successor, Sir Michael Hicks Beach, to discuss outstanding colonial matters, and then left for Highclere. His future political career, it seemed, was uncertain.

The reaction to his resignation, which was seen by many of his colleagues as an act of treachery, was soon manifest. On the day that he handed over his office to Hicks Beach, Carnarvon told his sister,

> it is curious to see how almost without exception all London Society is against me. All Conservatives – and many Whigs – and generally 'society'. This however really makes very little difference to me. I am older by many years than when ten years ago I took the step of resigning Office. I have passed through tumbles by the gate, of which any of those social and personal annoyances count as nothing.[156]

In February, Gladstone told a mutual friend, Sir Robert Phillimore, that he was anxious to meet Carnarvon. This took place on 14 February at Phillimore's house, both feeling that, if seen together, suspicions would be aroused. Phillimore's daughter wrote, 'I shut them up in R's room. Mr Gladstone entered saying, "Nicodemus by day [...]"'. They discussed the situation for nearly an hour.'[157] In May, Gladstone had a remarkable conversation with Carnarvon in which the latter, talking of his former colleagues, stated that he had 'lost faith in the words of many men'.[158] A few days earlier Carnarvon noted in his diary, 'Levée, the Prince of Wales there, curt but cold.'[159] In early June, he told Heathcote that 'the Cabinet had patched up their quarrels and the anger and violence of the Party finds a vent in much abuse of Derby and me. In the Clubs no words I hear are too bad for us.'[160]

Carnarvon was despondent at the animosity that was displayed. 'Old intimacies and even friendships will not stand the strain', he

---

[153]'Memorandum on the circumstances which led to my resignation in 1878', fo. 78.

[154]Vincent, *Derby*, II, p. 492.

[155]Carnarvon to Heathcote, 30 January 1878: CP, BL 61074, fo. 112.

[156]Carnarvon to Eveline, Countess of Portsmouth, 30 January 1878: CP, BL 61049, fo. 150.

[157]Diary of Charlotte, Lady Phillimore, 14 February 1878: Phillimore Papers, 75 M 91/514/2.

[158]W.E. Gladstone, Memorandum, 26 May 1878: Gladstone Papers, BL 44763, fo. 130.

[159]Diary, 17 May 1878.

[160]Carnarvon to Heathcote, 1 June 1878: CP, BL 61074, fo. 126.

wrote to Bath; 'scarcely any one has the true courage of his opinions or faith in the ultimate triumph of what is right [. . .]. Isolation is one of the most difficult of all to bear philosophically.'[161] There are some indications that Carnarvon was actively considering his own political position. Lord Acton, a Liberal, who became one of his friends, believed that 'Soon after his resignation, Carnarvon certainly wished to come over.'[162] The situation was hardly made more tolerable after Disraeli returned from the Congress of Berlin in July, bringing with him 'Peace and Honour'.[163] Nevertheless, Carnarvon was convinced that he had taken the correct course, and trusted that he would be judged by events.[164] He was suspicious when he was offered the governor-generalship of Canada in late February 1878, believing it to be 'some sort of trap'. Derby, on the other hand, was told by Disraeli of the offer and believed that it 'illustrates strongly one of the Premier's great merits, the entire absence of vindictiveness'.[165]

A return to extra-parliamentary pursuits

Carnarvon was able to find satisfaction in attending to other public and private duties. He had been elected a Fellow of the Society of Antiquaries in 1876, though his only published archaeological work in this field was his presidential address to the British Archaeological Association.[166] In April 1878, the Society reverted to the tradition of having a peer as President with the election of Carnarvon. He immediately proposed an ambitious programme of action. This included an archaeological survey of each county; a corpus of English charters; a new edition of Dugdale's *Monasticon*; editions of the pipe rolls, subsidy, and episcopal registers; lives of saints; town histories; and a complete catalogue of English seals.[167] This programme proved to be overambitious, but there were successes in other fields. An immediate problem was the controversial restoration of St Albans Abbey, especially the destruction of the nave roof. Carnarvon corresponded

---

[161]Carnarvon to Bath, 20 August 1878 (copy): CP, BL 60771, fo. 91.

[162]H. Paul, *Letters of Lord Acton to Mary, Daughter of the Right Hon. W. E. Gladstone* (London, 1904), p. 16.

[163]For Carnarvon's criticism of the treaty, see R.W. Seton-Watson, *Disraeli, Gladstone and the Eastern Question* (London, 1935), p. 499.

[164]See his lengthy 'Memorandum on the circumstances which led to my resignation in January 1878', in which he justified his actions.

[165]Vincent, *Derby*, II, p. 515.

[166]*The Archaeology of Berkshire: an address delivered to the Archaeological Association at Newbury, 12 Sept. 1859* (London, 1859). Carnarvon's correspondence on the matter is in Yale University Library, headed 'Berkshire Archaeological Society'.

[167]J. Evans, *A History of the Society of Antiquaries* (London, 1956), p. 349.

with the Earl of Verulam, chairman of the St Albans building committee, which resulted in modifications to the restoration.[168]

No legislative machinery then existed in Britain for the conservation of monuments dating from prehistoric times onwards. Sir John Lubbock, a Liberal MP, had introduced a bill in the Commons in 1877 to provide such safeguards. In the face of fierce opposition from landowners, the bill made slow progress in a reluctant House. A special meeting of the Society's Council was called on 17 June 1879 to expedite matters. Carnarvon announced that he consented to take charge of the Monuments Bill in the Lords, and was able to steer it through successfully. On 18 August 1882, the Ancient Monuments Protection Act became law. Meanwhile, although Carnarvon's proposed county-by-county archaeological survey by the Society was never realized, nevertheless it led to the establishment of an independent body, the Historical Monuments Commission, to carry out this task.[169] Carnarvon attended many of the Fellows' lectures, showing a keen interest in many topics. One lecturer who did not make a particular impression on him was Heinrich Schliemann, whose excavations at Mycenae between 1874 and 1876 had excited much public interest. A lecture on the topic was delivered by C.T. Newton, Keeper of Antiquities at the British Museum, at a meeting in May 1877, at which Schliemann was present; Carnarvon was not satisfied with Schliemann's explanations on many points that were raised.[170] Having served his full seven years as President, Carnarvon retired from the post in 1885.

On 31 October 1878, on his way to Edinburgh to give a lecture on imperial administration, he decided to call in at his mother's former home at Greystoke Castle, Cumberland. There he met his aunt and one of her daughters, Elisabeth Catherine, known as Elsie. He was instantly captivated by the beauty and intelligence of his twenty-two-year-old cousin, who was less than half his age. Despite some misgivings on the part of her mother, Elsie was consulted and agreed to marry Carnarvon. Exactly eight weeks later, on 26 December, Carnarvon and Elsie were married in Greystoke church.[171] The union produced two sons, Aubrey and Mervyn. Carnarvon wrote in his diary on New Year's Eve, 'I end this long eventful year as I never dreamt to close it, married for the first time for – what shall I say? – many

[168] Society of Antiquaries, Council Minute Book, 25 November 1878, vol. 8, fo. 173; P. Perriday, *Lord Grimthorpe, 1816–1905* (London, 1957), pp. 95–102.

[169] Society of Antiquaries, *The Presidents of the Society of Antiquaries of London*, Occasional Paper, 1945, p. 14. Carnarvon was an early member of the Commission.

[170] Diary, 31 May 1877.

[171] M. Fitzherbert, *The Man who was Greenmantle: a biography of Aubrey Herbert* (London, 1983), pp. 6–7.

years – enjoying a sense of repose and quiet.' But, always the pessimist, he added, 'How long will it last? What will be the next cloud?'[172]

Carnarvon as landowner

One of Carnarvon's tasks as a conscientious landlord was the administration and supervision of his considerable estates. In 1883, he held a total of 35,583 acres, consisting of 13,247 in Nottinghamshire, 12,800 in Somerset, 9,340 in Hampshire, 120 in Derbyshire, 68 in Devon, and 8 in Wiltshire (Bateman placed Carnarvon in the 'richest' category of landowners).[173] His great-grandfather, the first Earl, had inherited the principal seat, Highclere, from an uncle, Robert Sawyer Herbert. Pixton, in Somerset, an Acland family seat, was brought to the Herberts by the second Countess. Carnarvon's first wife, Evelyn, as heir to the sixth Earl of Chesterfield, added several large estates, including Bretby in Derbyshire, and Shelford in Nottinghamshire. Teversal, Kneeton, and Wellow, in Nottinghamshire, were acquired through the third Earl's marriage to Henrietta, daughter of Lord Henry Thomas Molyneux Howard; Teversal later became Elsie's home as lady dowager.[174] Christian Malford in Wiltshire, was purchased with the dowry of the first Countess.[175]

The income yielded by 1883 was £37,211 gross rental. This was not only agricultural land: the collieries in Nottinghamshire yielded over £23,000 a year in the 1870s. In 1888, Carnarvon recorded a visit with his wife to Bretby Colliery, where over 700 miners were employed.[176] A firm but fair landlord, he made improvements to the villages on his estates and undertook an extensive programme of church restoration after inspecting their condition. One striking example was in Nottinghamshire. He recorded in his diary:

> I went over to Nottingham to meet Wright [William Wright, agent, Teversal] there, visited the churches of Gedling, Burton Joyce, Carlton and Netherfield. Those at Burton Joyce, Carlton and Shelford are certainly among the best record of my reign on these properties and I never see them without satisfaction. They have been done and Burton Joyce is a little gem of its kind. Of all the

---

[172] Diary, 31 December 1878.
[173] J. Bateman, *The Great Landowners of Great Britain and Ireland*, 3rd edn (London, 1883), pp. 79, 495–496.
[174] The Molyneux estates remained in the Carnarvon family until her death in 1929, when they were sold at auction. See Molyneux of Teversal Papers, University of Nottingham, Department of Manuscripts and Special Collections.
[175] Royal Commission on Historic Monuments, *Principal Family and Estate Collections: family names A–K* (London, 1996), p. 80.
[176] Diary, 3 September 1888.

churches I have built – and practically it was rebuilt – it is to my mind the prettiest, not excepting Highclere.[177]

At Bretby, he threw open the Park on Wednesdays and Saturdays: 'The privilege seems to be appreciated and I have heard of no case of abuse.'[178]

By far the greatest worry for Carnarvon, as for many other landlords (particularly in the arable parts of south and south-east England), was the agricultural depression that transformed the rural economy from the 1870s. This came about by a combination of factors. The demand from the new urban areas for bread saw a spectacular rise in imports of cheap wheat from Canada and the United States, leading to the closing of many farms. A series of wet summers resulted in poor harvests, the worst one being in 1879. Writing at the beginning of that year, Carnarvon was unable to be optimistic about the future. He told Bath that even a remission of rents of 20 to 25 per cent would not save the situation. The high cost of labour was another important factor, increasingly so as villagers sought and gained employment in towns, where there were many opportunities.[179] Carnarvon believed that, unless some relief was forthcoming, large farms would not be able to go on, and that England was 'on the eve of a very great and bloodless revolution'.[180] In March, he calculated that some 3,000 acres of his land in Hampshire were in trouble and that they would be returning to grass. Four months later, he gave the figure as nearly 4,000 acres.[181] The picture was different in different counties: by September 1879, rents in Hampshire had been reduced by a quarter, while, in Somerset, Carnarvon reported that not only were there no requests for rent reductions but that there was still competition for some of his farms.[182] After one meeting with his principal tenants at Bingham, Nottinghamshire, in September 1879, Carnarvon rejected a permanent reduction of rent but agreed to double the amount of the current year's allowance, which represented 20 per cent of income. 'I hardly know how I shall be able to carry on matters in the future', he wrote in his diary. He found it easier to deal with his Nottinghamshire tenants than those in Hampshire 'who are terrible complainers for

---

[177] Diary, 14 September 1888. Others built were at Woodcote and Kneeton. See Carnarvon, 'Memorandum as to my stewardship of the property and my dispositions in regard to it', 18 October 1889: CP, BL 61054, fos 88–89.
[178] Diary, 1 September 1888.
[179] Carnarvon to Bath, 29 January 1879: Longleat Papers.
[180] Carnarvon to Eveline, Countess of Portsmouth, 17 March 1879: CP, BL 61050, fo. 96.
[181] Carnarvon to Heathcote, 3 July 1879: CP, BL 61075, fo. 40.
[182] Carnarvon to Bath, 28 April 1879: Longleat Papers.

less cause'.[183] By October, Carnarvon calculated that at least a third of all agricultural rents were lost.[184]

It was also necessary to look for economies in managing domestic affairs. On being asked to contribute to a memorial for John Ruskin, Carnarvon replied, 'At this moment and amid falling rents and bankrupt tenants and large farms on hand, claims multiply upon me so greatly that I had better draw within the narrowest limits at least any contributions to statues and memorials'.[185] One widely adopted solution to such financial problems was for owners to close or rent their country seats, either temporarily or permanently, or to take up residence abroad. In 1888, Carnarvon contemplated renting out Bretby on a short-term lease. He admitted 'that with three country homes [Highclere, Pixton, and Bretby] I felt the difficulty of doing justice to the different properties'.[186] However, as the future began to look more optimistic, he was not obliged to take this step.

Carnavon was aware, throughout the period of the agricultural depression, of the need for landowners to create a feeling of trust between themselves, their tenants, and their workers. In two articles that were published in the *National Review* in 1884 and 1885, Carnarvon, though anonymously, set out his views on the subject. In the first, entitled 'A word to country gentlemen by one of themselves', Carnarvon discussed the new political climate that existed following the Reform Act of the previous year, which had enfranchised most of the agricultural workers. He acknowledged that it had led to a changed relationship between the classes, but that old obligations remained. He pointed out that there was less likely to be civil unrest 'where the Squire and Parson had, in the past, done their duty by the people' and that, where there was severe distress among the agricultural labourers, the landlord should help out with wage reviews and provide cottage property. In the other article, 'Letters by Ruricola', the argument is described by an imaginary dialogue with a friend, Mr Miles Mannering of Durlestone Chase, a product of Oxford and a Tory MP. Obviously a thinly disguised mouthpiece for his own views, Mannering recommended that his squire, by judicious economies, would be able to provide for the cultivation of farms: for example, by a reduction in spending on the household, the library, and the stables, including his 'favourite four in hand', he would be able to provide funds for the cultivation of farms. He also recommended that the labourers

[183]Diary, 20 September 1879.
[184]Diary, 27 October 1879.
[185]Carnarvon to H.W. Acland, 13 June 1880: H.W. Acland Papers, MS Acland, d. 77, fo. 50.
[186]Diary, 6 September 1888.

should be entertained once a year, when the squire would 'address them in homely language with great good sense and kindness'.[187]

Another theme that ran through both articles was the need to counter the radical propaganda being spread by Joseph Arch, the champion of the agricultural workers, which was causing disaffection in urging them to support Liberal Party candidates and in encouraging unionization.[188] Carnarvon pointed out that 'The aristocracy of England are not the luxurious and selfish aristocracy of Rome [. . .] they can best discharge its duties in the interests of the nation, and not a class.'[189] He suggested that each parish and county should set up its own association or committee and provide speakers to point out the folly of their opponents. In the 'Letters by Ruricola', Miles Mannering gives a fictitious account of a visit to his village by Arch's supporters, who were given short shrift. Carnarvon sympathized with the labourers, who were 'sometimes out of heart' at the 'downward and dangerous tendencies of the times [. . .] but I cannot easily believe in any real antagonism of classes in England'.[190] He was fair-minded, too, at election times. When an enquiry was made whether his Somerset tenants could be canvassed by the Liberal candidate, Carnarvon assented, stating, 'I have never sought to put the slightest pressure on my tenants in Somersetshire or elsewhere.'[191] Nevertheless, Carnarvon was much exercised by the 'socialistic doctrines' that found ready acceptance among many of his workers.

Political isolation and rehabilitation

In politics, Carnarvon's reputation was not helped by his speech in the Lords on 26 July 1878, when he bitterly attacked the terms agreed to by Disraeli at the Congress of Berlin. The outcome of the Congress, which was to bring peace to Turkey and Russia, was widely regarded as a triumph and Disraeli was feted by the public on his return. Now

---

[187] Herbert, *Essays, Addresses and Translations*, II, p. 80.

[188] The National Agricultural Labourers' Union, formed in May 1870, was inspired by Arch. At a meeting held at Newbury, near Highclere, in July 1873, he told a large gathering, 'Whether for good or evil, he has probably a greater influence over an outdoor assembly than any other man in England' (quoted in P. Horn, *Joseph Arch (1826–1919): the farm workers' leader* (Kineton, 1971), p. 83). Advising a cousin against attending one of Arch's meetings, Carnarvon stated, 'Arch is apparently fast becoming more and more of a political demagogue and agitator, and those who sympathise with him will naturally lose influence and power of usefulness with the more moderate part of the country' (Carnarvon to H.W. Acland, 22 October 1872: MS Acland, d. 77, fo. 39).

[189] Herbert, *Essays, Addresses and Translations*, II, p. 51.

[190] Ibid., p. 81.

[191] Carnarvon to S. Lucas, 13 February 1879: CP, BL 60856, fo. 67.

stung by Carnarvon's criticisms, the Prime Minister was reported by *The Times* (29 July) as having complained to Cabinet colleagues that Derby and Carnarvon, after accepting Cabinet policy, failed in their responsibility to carry it out. In fact, Carnarvon hesitated to display any outward sign of disloyalty to the Party. In November 1879, he advised Derby to remain on the Government's side in the House of Lords, at least for the time being.[192]

At the end of the year, Carnarvon reviewed his own position in a long entry in his diary. He referred to the 'extreme bitterness' displayed towards him by Cabinet members, excepting Hicks Beach, Sir Stafford Northcote, and Sandon: 'All intercourse has ceased and hardly a letter ever passes.' He also doubted their political judgement and convictions. As London society and politicians had isolated him, he owed nothing to them and was free to consider his own course of action. Carnarvon then addressed a difficult question: his position should the Liberals regain office. While eschewing the radical element, he felt differently towards the Whigs, except on Church questions: 'Socially and intellectually, there are many bonds of union and much personal kindness has been shown to me by many of them.' As for Gladstone, Carnarvon had no apprehensions: 'There are things I regret and in which I disagree, but I have far more in common with him than with most living statesmen and I am perfectly convinced that the very Radical schemes with which he is credited are wilful misrepresentations, or absolute delusions.'[193] Carnarvon had one reservation about Gladstone returning as Prime Minister: he wrote in the margin of a letter in December 1878, 'Gladstone may possibly return but only for a time. This is the only point on which I doubt.' Weighing up all the arguments, he decided for the time being to remain on the Conservative benches.[194] When both Parties declared their policy a year later, he felt free to act 'as I may think best; politically I believe there is a road open to me in either direction'.[195]

Rumours of Disraeli's intention to retire after the next general election became stronger, and there was a likelihood of a Gladstone ministry being formed. In January 1880, Lord Granville sent Carnarvon a note inviting him to a parliamentary dinner, which he declined;[196] the offer was repeated in May, but again refused.[197] On the latter occasion, Carnarvon wrote, in reply to Granville, 'I wish you and

---

[192] Carnarvon to Derby, 27 November 1879: Derby Papers, 920 DER (15).
[193] Diary, 29 December 1879.
[194] Carnarvon to Herbert, 13 December 1878: CP, BL 60794, fo. 133.
[195] Diary, 29 December 1879.
[196] Carnarvon to Derby, 29 January 1880: Derby Papers, 920 DER (15).
[197] Carnarvon to Granville, 26 January 1880 (copy), 15 May 1880: CP, BL 60773, fos 131, 129.

the Government collectively well but I see no good reason for thinking I should do any good by changing my seat, which dining with you on the 19th would mean.' However, two events made the need for a firm decision urgent. On 7 March 1880, the dissolution of Parliament was announced, and Derby, as Carnarvon had anticipated, left the Party and joined the Liberals. Carnarvon, in the absence of a rebellion of the Conservatives against their leaders, decided to lend his support to what he believed would be best for the country, 'without regard to old political relationships'.[198]

Gladstone formed his new ministry, and it is possible that Carnarvon's decision to stay with the Conservatives was governed by his failure to be offered a post by Gladstone. Edward Hamilton, Gladstone's principal private secretary, later reported a conversation with Bath: 'He tells me he knows for certain that Lord Carnarvon was disappointed at not being asked to join the Government when it was formed [. . .]. His disappointment, has subsequently turned into very open bitterness against the Government.'[199] A month after Gladstone had taken office, putting a brave face on the matter, Carnarvon wrote to Heathcote, 'I assure you I am honestly and truly relieved and glad at the decision come to as to myself. I only feared that such a proposal might be made to me.'[200]

Carnarvon had seen little of Disraeli since leaving the Colonial Office, apart from a chance meeting at Lady Derby's, where he 'met the old gentleman on the stairs, shook hands with him as if he were a dear friend, and escaped'.[201] Nevertheless, he was invited to join the meeting of peers, over which Disraeli presided, at Bridgewater House on 19 May. After a long discursive speech by the Leader, Carnarvon spoke and was, in his own opinion, 'extremely well received and cheered [. . .]. My old position in the Party appears to have come back.' He had told Lady Derby before the meeting that he felt it his duty to attend: 'My only wish is to do what moderate amount of good there is to be done and as far as possible not to lose any old friend who may yet remain.'[202] A further step to reconciliation was taken by Disraeli in August. Carnarvon wrote,

Whilst in the House, D. wrote on a slip of paper the following: 'Do you think you could meet a few of our friends tomorrow morning at 11 o'clock at No. 1

[198]Carnarvon to Bath, 5 April 1880 (copy): CP, BL 60772, fo. 98.
[199]Diary, 3 February 1889; Edward Hamilton Papers, BL 48633, fo. 43.
[200]Carnarvon to Heathcote, 5 May 1880: CP, BL 61076, fo. 2.
[201]Diary, 21 May 1879.
[202]Carnarvon to Lady Derby, 15 May 1880 (copy): CP, BL 60766, fo. 89.

Seamore Place? Beaconsfield.' I nodded assent, and so in this brief fashion I once more returned to the counsels of the Party.[203]

This move did not come as a complete surprise to Carnarvon. Only a few days earlier, he had received a letter from Montagu Corry, Disraeli's principal private secretary, giving details of the proposed Conservative-front-bench tactics in Parliament in dealing with the Employers Liability Bill, due for its second reading. Corry commented, 'Lord B. writes me to say that he counts much on your presence and your aid in examining a Bill as difficult and important.'[204]

Carnarvon, shortly before this, had suffered a severe attack of what was diagnosed as gout. Accompanied by his family, he recuperated for over five months in Madeira. On his return, as the ship approached Plymouth on 9 April 1881, Carnarvon learned that Disraeli was dangerously ill. He died two days later. Carnarvon's tribute to him, contained in a letter to Cairns, was a somewhat muted one:

> It is the close of a strange and most singular career – the strangest of any in our time in England – and I doubt much if there is any one living who combines all the conditions for a faithful description and analysis of so singular a life and character. It is most probable I think that he will go down to posterity as a curious theme of speculation and controversy – such in a great measure as he has been doing in his life.[205]

Salisbury was appointed leader in the Lords and Northcote in the Commons. The choice of Salisbury, Heathcote reported to Carnarvon, depressed Northcote, who had preferred the Duke of Richmond.[206] Richmond meanwhile 'had pressed [me] personally and in a friendly way to return to the front Opposition bench and have done so'.[207] Pleased to be once more involved in the day-to-day detail of political life, Carnarvon took an increasing part in the Party's deliberations. Writing to Hardy (now first Earl Cranbrook) some three years later, he remarked, 'Cairns has been a good deal away and Salisbury and myself have been the only two survivors of the old Cabinet on the front Bench.'[208]

Carnarvon's rehabilitation to public life had recommenced when Disraeli offered him the chairmanship of the Royal Commission on Agricultural Distress in July 1879. It was certainly a subject close to his

[203]Diary, 24 August 1880.
[204]Corry to Carnarvon, 19 August 1880: CP, BL 60853, fos 38–39.
[205]Carnarvon to Cairns, 1 May 1881: Cairns Papers, TNA, PRO 30/51/8, fo. 12.
[206]Heathcote to Carnarvon, 7 May 1881: CP, BL 61076, fo. 159.
[207]Carnarvon to Heathcote, 6 May 1881: CP, BL 61076, fo. 156.
[208]Carnarvon to Cranbrook, 27 May 1884: Cranbrook Papers, HA3 T501/262.

heart, though he approached the offer with his usual caution, sounding out five different people – Spencer Walpole, the Duke of Somerset, Frederick Townsend, Gladstone, and Granville. After deciding to accept the post, he objected to the large size of the Commission (sixteen in all) and the calibre of the 'mediocrities of whom for the most part the list was made up', mainly tenant farmers and politically lightweight landowners.[209] Looking for deeper reasons for being offered the post, Carnarvon surmised to Granville, 'The chances of making a success of it were but small and in the event of failure the temptation to make a scapegoat of me would have been irresistible.'[210] Carnarvon's objections were resisted in the Cabinet and the post was given to Richmond. At the same time, Carnarvon received a letter from Hicks Beach offering him the chairmanship of another royal commission, on Colonial Defence, with the remit 'to inquire into the State of Defences of the most important Colonial Ports and Naval Stations, and the best mode of placing them in a thoroughly secure condition'.

Carnarvon had raised the matter of colonial defence in the House of Lords as early as 1862.[211] By the time Disraeli took office, imperial ports were largely undefended and no systematic plan existed for their defence by either the naval or military branches of the forces. When Carnarvon met Sir Gavan Duffy, recently prime minister of Victoria, Australia, at Highclere in late September 1874, they discussed the matter extensively, with a view to persuading self-governing colonies to co-operate in a joint scheme of military defence.[212] By 1879, the threats to security, especially from Russia and Germany, aroused fresh fears of military and naval unpreparedness, and in September a Royal Commission was appointed to examine the current situation. Carnarvon readily accepted the chairmanship and took a close interest in the composition of the body. The secretary was Captain Herbert Jekyll, Carnarvon's previous private secretary at the Colonial Office; there were three politicians – Hugh Childers, Sir Henry Holland, and Sir Thomas Brassey; the remaining places were filled by Sir Alexander Milne, General Sir John Simmons, and Robert Hamilton. Childers and Carnarvon were initially surprised at the large scope of the enquiry. All the evidence that was taken and the subsequent reports were strictly confidential and for the use of the Cabinet only. Carnarvon took great pains with the details of the enquiry, even

[209] Diary, 14 July 1879.
[210] Carnarvon to Granville, 1 August 1879 (copy): CP, BL 60773, fo. 119.
[211] Hardinge, III, p. 36.
[212] Sir R. Herbert to Carnarvon, 25 September 1874: CP, BL 60791, fos 125–127. Carnarvon also discussed the idea with Disraeli at Highclere four days later.

supervising the appointment of a secure shorthand writer and the arrangements for printing.[213]

With the general election in April 1880 and the return of a Liberal government, several Cabinet ministers expressed their concern about the continuance of the Commission. Gladstone believed it to be 'the most singular delegation of the duty and discretion of Government that I at the moment can remember'. Northbrook at the Admiralty pointed out the 'delicate and confidential arrangements in view of war' that were disclosed in evidence. The Duke of Argyll, the Lord Privy Seal, considered the Commission to be 'a dangerous Body and Lord Carnarvon's demand that it must have the support of Government makes it more formidable still'. Kimberley, the new Colonial Secretary, agreed and promised to see Carnarvon, with a view to reconsidering the instructions to the Commission.[214] When Kimberley met Carnarvon, he mentioned that the Government now wished to limit the inquiry to discussing with the colonies the arrangements for their homeland defence, leaving to the Government the larger questions of the defence of shipping routes, protection for the East, and the provision of coaling depots. Kimberley wrote to Gladstone after the interview,

> I saw Carnarvon. He showed himself averse to any limitation [. . .]. He told me that it was contemplated by himself and I suppose his brother Commissioners that their report, which we may expect next year, will recommend considerable expenditure. The question is whether we can interfere with the Commission. I am afraid we cannot.[215]

Gladstone suggested, hopefully, 'that we should give the Commission its tether, let it take its time and perhaps make itself harmless'.[216]

In fact, under Carnarvon's chairmanship, the Commission pursued its enquiries with great vigour. Carnarvon had undertaken visits to some of the naval fortifications around Britain from the time of the Commission's inception. By October 1880, a large amount of important evidence had been amassed,[217] which showed much disturbing information on the state of military preparedness.[218] One of the members, Milne, an experienced naval man who had twice

[213]Childers to Kimberley, 10 May 1880, Kimberley Papers, MS Eng. c. 4197, fo. 9.

[214]Kimberley to Gladstone, 16 May 1880: Kimberley Papers, MS Eng. c. 4197, fo. 17.

[215]Kimberley to Gladstone, 23 May 1880: Kimberley Papers, MS Eng. c. 4197, fos 34–35.

[216]Gladstone to Kimberley, 12 June 1880: Kimberley Papers, MS Eng. c. 4197, fo. 56.

[217]Carnarvon to Kimberley, 26 October 1880 (copy): CP, BL 60813, fo. 5.

[218]Carnarvon noted in his final report 'that many individual opinions were expressed to us in evidence on the understanding that they would not be published': Royal Commission into the Defence of British Possessions and Commerce Abroad, 1880–1882, third report (Ministry of Defence, War Office Library, 1976), p. 29.

been First Sea Lord, told Carnarvon after almost two years' work, 'How the First Lord of the Admiralty is to give satisfactory replies to the questions which will have to be put to him is beyond my comprehension, for we really have no Navy to match the requirements of a Naval War.'[219] The first report, thirty-two pages in length, was ready by September 1881, and Carnarvon sent a copy to Kimberley, adding, 'It deserves I think your attention, as it treats of serious and in every case urgent questions.'[220] The report dealt mainly with the Cape of Good Hope and troops in British Honduras. A second report followed two months later; it expressed concerns at the state of readiness of the Navy and the defence requirements of the Australian colonies. The third and last report, in July 1882, dealt with the defence of the major trade routes. The Commission concluded that direct communication should be maintained by British ships with all important parts of the empire; and, having observed the obsolete nature of the fortifications, it recommended that the United Kingdom and the colonies should work out a scheme to strengthen defences. Local garrisons were to be raised, in view of difficulties in providing sufficient British troops.[221] Four months later the Commission was wound up.

The papers and the reports were never published in full, and the records of the Commission were deposited at the Colonial Office. Jekyll, the secretary, told Carnarvon, 'The volume of 700 pages which you will shortly receive, though bulky, hardly conveys an idea of the labour it has cost.'[222] In pointing out to the Government the usefulness of the information and evidence that the Commission had gathered and the recommendations that it had made, Carnarvon proffered one further piece of advice: the need to establish a permanent central point of communication for the Colonial Office, the War Office, and the Admiralty. He wrote to Kimberley,

> I feel satisfied from my experience, both as a Minister and as Chairman of this Commission, that some such body – but permanent and probably fewer in number – would be of great public value. I believe indeed that it is, taking into account the working capacity of the departments and the character of the business concerned very necessary.[223]

[219]Milne to Carnarvon, 2 May 1881: CP, BL 60813, fo. 12.

[220]Carnarvon to Kimberley, 18 September 1881: Kimberley Papers, MS Eng. c. 4113, fo. 127. See also J. F. Beeler, *British Naval Policy in the Gladstone–Disraeli Era, 1866–1880* (Stanford, CA, 1997), p. 253.

[221]Royal Commission into the Defence of British Possessions and Commerce Abroad, 1880–1882, third report, p. 30.

[222]H. Jekyll to Carnarvon, 16 November 1882: CP, BL 60796, fo. 176.

[223]Carnarvon to Kimberley, 29 November 1882: Kimberley Papers, MS Eng. c. 4238, fo. 123.

Gladstone, however, failed to follow up the recommendations of the Commission. Carnarvon was bitterly disappointed. He observed in a speech in the Lords in the following year that the Reports had been 'consigned to the pigeon-hole'.[224] Salisbury established a Colonial Defence Committee in 1885 but it was allowed to lapse.[225]

The Franchise Bill of 1884

By the 1880s, the question of the extension of the franchise to rural labourers needed to be settled. Gladstone had introduced a Franchise Bill in the Commons on 29 February 1884 that would have given the vote to two million more people. A great weakness of the bill was that it made no provision for the redistribution of seats. As matters stood, Salisbury argued, the Liberals would have had the gift of forty-seven seats in the Commons. Although the Franchise Bill was approved by a large majority, it was strongly attacked in the Lords during its second reading on 8 July. Carnarvon, in an hour-long speech, argued that the Commons would become less and less 'a true mirror of the people in all its varied interests'.[226] Gladstone withdrew the bill, but warned that it would be reintroduced in the autumn. Its subsequent history and complex manoeuvrings can be traced in detail in the diaries, where it becomes clear that Carnarvon's part in the negotiations was a more substantial one than is normally believed.

Two days after Gladstone announced that Parliament would be wound up until the autumn session, Carnarvon visited Salisbury at his house in Arlington Street to discuss tactics. One suggestion was that a bargain should be made with the Government, allowing a franchise bill to be passed if, at the same time, a distribution bill was introduced.[227] Carnarvon, like a number of other Conservative peers, was becoming increasingly impatient at Salisbury's uncompromising attitude towards franchise legislation. Much to Carnarvon's annoyance, Salisbury rejected any hope of reconciliation with Gladstone at a meeting of Conservative peers on 15 July, and there was growing unease in the Party. Carnarvon confided to his diary, 'Salisbury has not the confidence of those who follow him or who are supposed to be his colleagues and advisers. The first he alarms by his supposed rashness. The latter he alienates by seeming to distrust them.'[228]

---

[224] *Hansard*, CCLXXVIII, 4 May 1883, cols 1831–1835.
[225] Shannon, *The Crisis of Imperialism*, p. 256.
[226] *Hansard*, CCXC, 8 July 1884, col. 378.
[227] Diary, 10 July 1884.
[228] Diary, 18 July 1884.

There were moves behind the scenes to expedite matters. In August, the Liberals appointed a Cabinet committee, consisting of Lord Hartington, Sir Charles Dilke, and Joseph Chamberlain, to produce a draft redistribution bill. The sudden appearance in the *Standard* on 10 October of a Government scheme for redistribution was construed as a willingness to seek conciliation. On 22 October, G.C.T. Bartley at the Conservative Central Office showed Carnarvon his own draft redistribution scheme, 'which proceeds on a distinct principle and has no Party taint about it'. Carnarvon believed that it could be a basis for further action. However, after a meeting at Northcote's, at which Salisbury and he were the only peers, Salisbury told Carnarvon that he was much opposed to Bartley's scheme.[229]

Carnarvon believed it was now necessary publicly to air his own views in order to break the apparent impasse. At a Conservative demonstration at Shoreditch Town Hall on 21 October, he put forward a plan to refer a distribution scheme to 'three or four impartial men who had the confidence of both parties'; the aim would be to produce a scheme free from any party bias and acceptable throughout the country.[230] There were a number of reasons why a settlement was becoming urgent. In Birmingham, Chamberlain had made speeches attacking the House of Lords for their 'arrogant and monstrous pretensions' in opposing the Franchise Bill, accusing that body of attempting to place the Commons in an inferior position. There had also been riots at Aston on 13 October, when a Conservative meeting was invaded by Liberal supporters and Randolph Churchill and Northcote had to run for their lives.[231] The Queen, too, was alarmed by Salisbury's 'momentous practical inquiry' whether, if the Lords were swept away, 'the Monarchy isolated and laid bare' would survive.[232]

Returning to Portman Square after the meeting at Northcote's house, Carnarvon was visited by Sir Henry Ponsonby on behalf of the Queen. Ponsonby had come to London to find some way out of the difficulties, because the Queen was 'extremely anxious about it'. She had already consulted Richmond and Cairns, as well as Salisbury, who 'had given no hope of compromise on his part'.[233] Ponsonby was attracted by Carnarvon's suggestion to set up a small inter-party group to examine the question and asked for the best way to proceed. Carnarvon advised him to contact Northcote and, if the latter was

---

[229] Diary, 22 October 1884.
[230] See *The Times*, 22 October 1884, p. 7.
[231] P.T. Marsh, *Joseph Chamberlain: entrepreneur in politics* (New Haven, CT, and London, 1994), pp. 174–176.
[232] E.D. Steele, *Lord Salisbury: a political biography* (London, 1999), p. 163.
[233] Diary, 22 October 1884.

agreeable, then to confer with Salisbury. Carnarvon added that his own name should not be mentioned to any of the parties. Ponsonby then telegraphed this information to the Queen. On 23 October, when Parliament assembled, the Queen's Speech briefly mentioned that a bill to extend the parliamentary franchise would be introduced. During the next few days, Carnarvon was active in sounding out some of the leading figures. He saw Richmond, who considered a joint understanding on the redistribution to be impracticable, and Hicks Beach, who, after initial scepticism, agreed.[234] Two days later, he wrote to Salisbury stating that he believed Gladstone was disposed to agree with his (Carnarvon's) plan and requesting that the letter should be shown to Northcote. The following day, 27 October, Carnarvon received a letter from Lord Norton, who acted as an intermediary, enclosing another letter from Gladstone, which 'appeared to invite some overture from us'.[235] Carnarvon then left Highclere for London that evening, after writing to Salisbury, Northcote, Hicks Beach, and Ponsonby to arrange a meeting.

The next day, he conferred with Northcote, after which the two men called on Salisbury, who agreed that Carnarvon should see Erskine May, the distinguished constitutional jurist; Carnarvon was anxious to know 'if Gladstone's letter meant business'. When Carnarvon called on May, the Earl offered to see Gladstone himself, but the Prime Minister replied that 'it was more prudent we should have no verbal communication which would be sure to be noticed'.[236] In the end, however, Carnarvon admitted that negotiations had not been advanced. Ponsonby, on being informed of this, wrote to his friend Lord Spencer:

> There are so many cooks engaged in bringing about an agreement that I am rather out of it. I hope they will succeed. Lorne, the Duke of Argyll, Peel, Lord Norton, Lord Carnarvon, etc, etc. H.M.'s last plan is that the two chiefs should meet and settle distribution between them. But imagine Mr G. and Lord S. being locked up together: nothing would be found but a beard and a pair of collars next morning.[237]

Salisbury's uncompromising attitude was causing Carnarvon much concern. In the Commons on 7 November, the Franchise Bill received

[234] Diary, 24 October 1884.

[235] See W.S. Childe-Pemberton, *Life of Lord Norton* (London, 1900), p. 260.

[236] Gladstone, through Lord Richard Grosvenor, the Liberal Chief Whip, nevertheless expressed himself as anxious that Carnarvon was not disposed to abandon his scheme: Erskine May to Carnarvon, 28 October 1884: Erskine May Papers, ERM/8/249.

[237] Ponsonby to Spencer, 1 November 1884: Spencer Papers. The same day, the Cabinet appointed Hartington and Dilke as official plenipotentiaries in the negotiations: D. Nicholls, *The Lost Prime Minister: a life of Sir Charles Dilke* (London, 1995), p. 147. Furthermore, some Conservatives were buoyed in their opposition to the Franchise Bill by the overwhelming by-election victory in South Warwickshire two days later: see Diary, 9 November 1884.

its second reading: a confrontation with the Lords seemed inevitable. Talking with Northcote on the state of affairs that day, Carnarvon reiterated the widespread belief 'that Salisbury is "riding for a fall" and is quite reckless as to the destruction of the House of Lords'.[238] At a meeting at Salisbury's house on 12 November, the day after the Franchise Bill had received its third reading, Salisbury was in favour of forcing a dissolution and of not assisting in any redistribution scheme. Only Lord John Manners and Rowland Winn agreed with him, Smith, Sandon (since 1882 the third Earl of Harrowby), Northcote, and Carnarvon dissenting.[239] Cairns, who arrived back from Balmoral too late for the meeting, would have sided with the majority. He told Carnarvon that the Queen was extremely anxious about the situation and had sent him a letter emphasizing both the importance of bringing about a meeting of leaders of both sides and also the risk of dissolution. Carnarvon wrote in his diary,

> We are undoubtedly in the midst of a very serious crisis; but assuming that we do not show too much anxiety to deal, which would probably induce Gladstone to raise his terms, I think we ought to settle the matter. Richmond, Cairns and I, reinforced as we now are by Sandon, are I think strong enough for the purpose.[240]

Suddenly, there was a new development. On the following day, the newspapers announced that the Government would make some statement on the franchise and distribution question. A meeting of Conservative peers at Salisbury's was called at midday. Carnarvon had surmised that their numbers would be limited; instead, it consisted of any who had held office in Disraeli's last administration. He was suspicious that this had been arranged in order to outnumber him and any other colleagues who were in favour of compromise. In the afternoon, Granville's statement in the Lords that the Government were willing to introduce a redistribution bill quickly changed the situation. Immediately after the House rose, there was a further meeting of Conservative peers, this time at the Carlton. Salisbury was still hostile to the proposals until Arthur Balfour interrupted the meeting with a memorandum from Gladstone setting out his own views. Carnarvon wrote, 'This, as Salisbury said, altered the case greatly, and we broke up.'[241] A Redistribution Bill was introduced into the Commons on 1 December and the Franchise Bill received the Royal Assent on 6 December. Carnarvon was pleased that his original

[238] Diary, 7 November 1884.
[239] A. Jones, *The Politics of Reform, 1884* (London, 1972), p. 194.
[240] Diary, 16 November 1884.
[241] Diary, 18 November 1884.

proposal for the two leaders to begin consultations, together with a small committee of the House of Commons representatives to keep them in touch with the negotiations, was adopted.

One aspect of the franchise question that Carnarvon believed that the Government had ignored, as he remarked in an adjournment debate in the Lords in July, was the question of female suffrage. He pointed out that many of the two million men now given the vote were 'illiterate, ignorant, and of very questionable character', but to exclude from enfranchisement a small sector of persons who were intelligent and possessed property was indefensible.[242] Carnarvon was congratulated on his speech by Lydia Becker, party agent of the National Society for Women's Suffrage, promising him that his stand would be reported in the *Women's Suffragette Journal*.[243] Shortly before the Franchise Bill passed through Committee in the Lords, Carnarvon once again spoke in favour of the vote for qualified women. Although the House agreed to the motion, no further action was taken.[244] Later that day, he was interviewed by Lilias Sophia Ashworth Hallett, who, together with Millicent Fawcett, had previously put forward an enfranchisement bill for unmarried women and widows. Hallett was accompanied by Lydia Becker, whom Carnarvon described as 'a rather grim and bespectacled lady of middle or any age'.[245] After being pressed by the two women to introduce a separate franchise bill in the Lords, he sought Salisbury's views on the matter. Salisbury, while remarking that women's suffrage 'was not in any sense a party question', offered only lukewarm support, and Carnarvon agreed that such a bill should originate in the House of Commons.[246] For his part, Carnarvon was cautious about the consequences of unlimited rights for women. At a house party at Canford Manor in Dorset, he described one fellow guest, 'a Miss Wentworth, a rather terrible specimen of the young lady of the present day, hardened into all the coarseness of a man's making speeches at Primrose (League) meetings, using very questionable language, etc etc. May Heaven protect us from these petticoat imitations of the other sex!'[247]

On 10 December, Carnarvon and Elsie were summoned to Windsor, together with Cairns and his wife, for dinner with the Queen. 'It is evidence', Carnarvon noted, 'of a reconciliation on her part after

[242] *Hansard*, CCXC, 8 July 1884, col. 381.
[243] Becker to Carnarvon, 21 July 1884: CP, BL 60832, fo. 102.
[244] *Hansard*, CCXCIV, 4 December 1884, cols 578–579.
[245] Diary, 4 December 1884.
[246] Carnarvon to Salisbury, 15 and 20 December 1884: Hatfield House Papers, 3M/E.
[247] Diary, 8 November 1884.

nearly six years of absolute silence.'[248] After dinner, the Queen talked
with frankness to Carnarvon about his part in the franchise question:

> She said something to the effect that she was aware that I had done my best to
> help matters to this conclusion [. . .]. It was a real personal pleasure to me to
> feel that the Queen was completely reconciled to me; for the alienation after
> so much kindness to me in former years pained me.[249]

Lord Lieutenant of Ireland

The many problems that Ireland had presented to successive British
governments for many years had remained unsettled. Gladstone had
been moving towards the notion of a measure of home rule as a means
of restoring peace to the country. His Lord Lieutenant in Ireland, Lord
Spencer, had come to the same conclusion. Writing in September
1884, Spencer had stated, 'Simple repression is not sufficient. We must
win the people over to our side [. . .] have begun with the Land Act, we
go on with the Franchise, we must carry a large and wide measure of
Local Government.'[250] The hated Land Act was due for renewal and
the Franchise Act had tripled the number of male voters in Ireland.
One stumbling block was the demand of Charles Parnell, the leader
of the National League, for an independent Irish parliament.

Carnarvon's own views differed from those of the majority of his
Conservative colleagues in favouring an experiment of home rule. He
told Derby as early as October 1879 that the Irish crisis was a result
of enormous misgovernment: 'It is not really reasonable that good
intentions and so somewhat tardy application of good government can
remove the accumulated evils of a detestable system of administration
extending over many generations.'[251] Drawing on his own experience
at the Colonial Office, he pointed out to Heathcote 'that there always
remained in store the alternative of governing by a more despotic
Crown Colony system than had been tried for many generations.
This is possible but it could not be permanent: we could not hold
Ireland as an English Poland.' Prophetically, he added, 'the policy of
repression would be certainly followed by a terrible reaction in the
opposite direction'.[252]

When Gladstone's ministry was defeated by a combination of
Parnellites and Conservatives in June 1885, Salisbury accepted office

---

[248] Diary, 8 December 1884.
[249] Diary, 10 December 1884.
[250] Spencer to E.G. Jenkinson, 18 September 1884 (copy): Spencer Papers.
[251] Carnarvon to Derby, 26 October 1879: Derby Papers, 920 DER (15).
[252] Carnarvon to Heathcote, 20 March 1880: CP, BL 61075, fo. 157.

but with a minority administration. In February of that year, Sir Charles Gavan Duffy, the Irish nationalist and colonial politician, had published an article in the *National Review* outlining procedures necessary for securing a peaceful settlement in Ireland. Carnarvon wrote enthusiastically to Salisbury supporting the scheme: 'For my own part [...] our best and almost only hope is to come to some fair and reasonable arrangements for Home Rule.'[253] Salisbury replied that he found Carnarvon's letter most interesting, but added, 'I am not hopeful, for I have been unable to think of any provisions which would answer the above requirements.'[254]

Three days after the fall of Gladstone's government, Northcote was sent by Salisbury to sound out Carnarvon on his opinion of Irish affairs. The latter was convinced that the settlement of the question would be central to the new government's actions. Carnarvon advised that thoughts of a coercion bill should be abandoned: if there was a renewal of outrages, then martial law should be introduced. He suggested that a military man should be sent as Lord Lieutenant, with General Wolseley as a possible candidate.[255] On the following day, Salisbury travelled to Balmoral and recommended to the Queen that Carnarvon should be appointed Lord Lieutenant of Ireland, stating that 'he was very clever and conciliatory, and popular wherever he went'.[256] No mention was made of this move at a meeting of the ex-Cabinet at Arlington Street on 15 June but, on the following day, Carnarvon was called by Salisbury and offered the Lord Lieutenancy with a seat in the Cabinet. According to Carnarvon, Salisbury said 'that there really was no one to whom he could look but myself'.[257] Carnarvon promised to consider the offer and, after consultation, accepted the post later that evening. His reluctance stemmed mainly from health reasons: 'The climate is particularly adverse', he wrote, and added, 'as a provisional and temporary appointment however, I would take and keep Office till after the next general election and the meeting of the new Parliament'.[258] He was congratulated on his appointment by a friend, who also warned, 'Accepting Ireland is really walking up the valley from a sense of duty only [...]. I trust you will escape all enemies, but you will come out of it with your hair white and your heart harder.'[259]

---

[253]Carnarvon to Salisbury, 5 February 1885: Hatfield House Papers, 3M/E.
[254]Salisbury to Carnarvon, 15 February 1885: CP, BL 60760, fos 22–23.
[255]Diary, 11 June 1885.
[256]Queen Victoria, Memorandum, 12 June 1885: Royal Archives, C36/420.
[257]Diary, 17 June 1885.
[258]Carnarvon to Salisbury, 16 June 1885: Hatfield House Papers, 3M/E.
[259]M. Townsend to Carnarvon, 18 June 1885: CP, BL 60770, fo. 228.

On 24 June, Carnarvon kissed hands with the Queen at Windsor. He was already involved in talks with many Irish officials in London, attended the first Cabinet on 26 June, and, on the following day, had an 'important conversation with Salisbury on Irish matters. I told him my ideas of dealing with different parties in Ireland, and he agreed.'[260] Accompanied by Elsie, Sir William Hart Dyke (the new Chief Secretary), and Jekyll, his private secretary, he arrived to a good reception in Dublin on 29 June. He was sworn in the following day. Carnarvon's first landing on Irish soil had occurred two years earlier, when he visited Canada. On the way, the boat stopped at Loch Foyle to pick up the mails. 'I cannot say that I was much attracted by what little I saw', he wrote. 'Very bad one storied cottages, poor farming in many parts, the police everywhere, armed and going about together in twos, a general look of poverty.'[261] He was pleased to learn from Sir Bernard Burke, the Ulster-born editor of *Peerages*, that he, Carnarvon, 'was the fifteenth Viceroy of Ireland of my own family, counting both sides'.[262]

The routine of a Lord Lieutenant was a hectic one. After being sworn in, Carnarvon returned for a Cabinet meeting in London – the first of many – on Friday 3 July, returning for his public entry on the following Tuesday. Domestic arrangements had to be settled. Eager to continue to live a normal life, Carnarvon surprised the household staff by bringing his children and establishment to Dublin before the outgoing Lord Lieutenant, Spencer, had managed to remove his own baggage and personal belongings.[263] His health was a continual worry, with attacks of gout that debilitated him. Shortly before leaving for Ireland, Carnarvon had been corresponding with his medical adviser, Dr Michael Grabham, on possible courses of treatment. Visits to spas and an opportunity to take the waters were now out of the question. Grabham remarked, 'I should not be dismayed to find that your recovery must be affected, even serving the causes and work and office.'[264] By September, Carnarvon was also suffering from kidney problems.

The expenses involved in accepting the post were formidable. Lord Spencer was warned before setting off for Ireland that the £20,000 salary would prove to be insufficient.[265] Carnarvon had hardly taken up the reins of government when he became personally involved in a serious crisis in the banking world. The Munster Bank, in which many

[260] Diary, 27 June 1885.

[261] Diary, 24 August 1883.

[262] Carnarvon, Memorandum, 'Lord Carnarvon's memoirs relating to his Lord-Lieutenancy', March–April 1886: CP, BL 60826, fo. 1.

[263] J. Caulfield to Spencer, 17 July 1885: Spencer Papers.

[264] Grabham to Carnarvon, 12 August 1885: CP, BL 60868, fo. 157.

[265] P. Gordon, *The Red Earl: the papers of the fifth Earl Spencer 1835–1910*, 2 vols (Northamptonshire Record Society, 1981 and 1986), I, p. 9.

farmers and tradesmen were shareholders and depositors, suddenly collapsed, causing widespread panic. The much larger Hibernian Bank was also involved and it was feared that the National Bank might be a similar victim if there were a second collapse. Carnarvon pleaded with the Government that they should intervene but the Cabinet refused to do so, instead sending out the Conservative banker Sir George Kellner to report back on the situation. It was customary for Lord Lieutenants to use the bank. Only four days before it suspended payments, Carnarvon had placed a large sum of money in his account there. Describing the situation to Harrowby, he stated, 'As to money matters, I believe we shall come out half ruined!! I am afraid that a great deal of my money in this wretched bank is gone!!!!'[266] Matters settled down after Carnarvon had interviewed a deputation of shareholders, and a reconstruction of the bank was attempted. Nevertheless, he was forced to sell his claims to a realization of assets of the company, at a loss of 25 per cent.[267]

A much larger issue, however, had occupied Carnarvon since taking office. Joseph Chamberlain, President of the Board of Trade in Gladstone's government, had earlier in the year put forward a plan for the extensive reorganization of the system of Irish local government, based on county boards and culminating in a central board (though not a parliament). The intention was to pacify the moderates in Ireland, isolate the extremists, and appeal to Irish voters in Great Britain, who were expected to hold the balance between the two parties in many constituencies.[268] Parnell's own plan for local government was sent to Chamberlain on 13 January. Although it went further than Chamberlain's, the latter did not dismiss it, as he considered it to be a possible basis for moving forward. The Liberal Party was divided on the local government plan and it was rejected by Gladstone's Cabinet on 9 May. Chamberlain's central board scheme was discussed at the first meeting of Salisbury's Cabinet on 26 June, but was held over 'for more knowledge'. (Strangely, Ireland was not mentioned by Carnarvon in his diary for that day.) On 4 July, at a meeting of the Cabinet, Carnarvon and the new Irish Lord Chancellor, Lord Ashbourne, had advised that renewing the Crimes Act was untenable, an opinion that was endorsed. Two days later, Carnarvon had 'a most important and private interview' with Justin McCarthy, the Parnellite leader, at the house of Howard Vincent, the first director of the CID and Conservative parliamentary candidate

---

[266] Carnarvon to Harrowby, 21 July 1885: Harrowby Papers, 2nd series, vii, fo. 128.

[267] Carnarvon, Memorandum: Harrowby Papers, 2nd series, viii, fo. 4.

[268] C.H.D. Howard, 'Joseph Chamberlain, Parnell and the Irish "central board" scheme, 1884–5', *Irish Historical Studies*, 8, no. 32 (1953), p. 327.

for Sheffield. In a previous conversation with Vincent, Carnarvon had expressed a wish for a meeting to be arranged with Parnell, indicating that he 'was anxious to go as far as I could go', though adding that he did not necessarily speak for the rest of his party.[269]

McCarthy believed that Parnell was in favour of a large measure of self-government 'not quite equal to that enjoyed by a State in the United States Union', and that he would prefer a gradual development in order the better to educate the people. Carnarvon pressed McCarthy about security against confiscation and for property, and was assured there would be no obstacle on the part of Parnell. The two men agreed that a face-to-face meeting between Carnarvon and Parnell would be useful.[270] That same afternoon, Carnarvon saw Salisbury, informing him of all that had happened. Salisbury, after stating that he was prepared to agree to provincial councils in Ireland but not a central one, remarked, 'I must stand aside, but you could carry it out.' Carnarvon replied, 'That, my dear Salisbury, is not practical. I can do nothing of the sort'. Carnarvon then asked, 'If we had not had this conversation would you still have wished me to undertake this task?' 'Yes,' replied Salisbury, 'because no one else could have undertaken it on [sic] in all the same way.' Carnarvon said, 'Very well, remember you pressed it upon me: but we must not have any divergences, and we must be perfectly frank with each other and have a complete understanding.'[271] Relieved at the outcome of the meeting, Carnarvon spoke in the Lords later that day, announcing that the Crimes Act would not be renewed and that a Land Purchase Bill would be introduced giving favourable terms to Irish landlords. He also hinted that moves towards home rule would be explored.[272] Carnarvon was aware of the views of the majority of his colleagues in the House: his statement 'was listened to with the deepest attention, but I do not think our Irish peers or for that matter most of our supporters really liked it', adding, 'It was hardly likely, I fear, they should.'[273]

By the following day, McCarthy confirmed that Parnell was willing for the meeting to take place. Carnarvon asked Ashbourne to sound out Salisbury's views on the situation. Ashbourne, the author of the Land Purchase Act, reported that the Prime Minister advised Carnarvon to do 'the minimum of writing' in fixing the meeting. Ashbourne left for Ireland after the Cabinet of 24 July, and discussed

[269] A.B. Cooke and J.R. Vincent, *The Governing Passion: Cabinet government and party politics in Britain, 1885–86* (Brighton, 1974), p. 273.
[270] Carnarvon, Memorandum, 'Conversation with Justin McCarthy', 6 July 1885: CP, BL 60829, fo. 74.
[271] Diary, 6 July 1885.
[272] *Hansard*, CCXCVIII, 6 July 1885, cols 1658–1662.
[273] Diary, 6 July 1885.

with Carnarvon both the future of Ireland and the proposed interview with Parnell.[274] Three days later, on the death of Lady Chesterfield, Carnarvon was summoned to England. At the same time, he telegraphed Salisbury that he wished the meeting to be held without witnesses, adding, 'I have spoken to Gibson [Lord Ashbourne] on the matter and he is in agreement with me.'[275] In the light of subsequent events, this change of plan was probably an error of judgement.[276]

Parnell proposed that the meeting should take place at Carnarvon's Portman Square house, while Carnarvon suggested that it should be at Vincent's residence, at 1 Grosvenor Square. In the end it was agreed that it should be held in a deserted Mayfair house, 15 Hill Street, at noon on 1 August. The meeting lasted just over an hour, after which Carnarvon drew up a memorandum to take to Salisbury at Hatfield, as previously arranged. A wide range of topics had been discussed: the protection of property, the possibility of a central board, the removal of Irish Members from the House of Commons if an Irish parliament were established, the question of a Land Purchase Bill, and the improvement of industrial resources.[277] Carnarvon assured Salisbury that no promises had been made to Parnell during the interview, and the Prime Minister was satisfied with Carnarvon's handling of the meeting 'apart from the question of its expediency'.[278] Two days later, a Cabinet meeting was held, which Salisbury had specifically requested Carnarvon to attend. To the latter's annoyance, no mention was made of Ireland. It had been agreed beforehand that the interview with Parnell was to be kept secret; Salisbury also decided not to inform the Queen of the meeting. Carnarvon then returned to Ireland.

From the start Carnarvon had adopted a policy of openness in his Irish dealings. Unlike his predecessor, Lord Spencer, he refused to have guards and escorts, and was confident of his acceptability to the Irish people. Carnarvon had talked with Edward Jenkinson, Under-Secretary for Crime, Ireland, on the matter, probably shortly after

---

[274] Hardinge, III, p. 174.

[275] Carnarvon to Salisbury, 29 July 1885: CP, BL 60825, fo. 47.

[276] Hart Dyke, Carnarvon's Chief Secretary, informed Carnarvon, however, the following year, when Parnell had disclosed that a meeting had taken place, 'I quite understand and appreciate your motive for not telling me, and of course I should have said don't!! as the fact of knowing it would at once have made it more or less hazardous' (Hart Dyke to Carnarvon, 16 June 1886: CP, BL 60830, fo. 44). A biographer of Salisbury claims that the Prime Minister was alarmed to discover that Gibson was not present at the meeting: R. Taylor, *Lord Salisbury* (London, 1975), p. 94.

[277] CP, BL 60829, fos 99–101.

[278] Cecil, III, p. 157.

taking office. Jenkinson was 'of opinion that I may dispense with them [an escort of soldiers and possibly even mounted police]. This corresponds with my own wishes, for I feel that the effect of an open trust will probably be good.'[279] Carnarvon's sympathy with the poverty of the people was shown by his desire to help them in practical ways. In the summer, he made a tour of the west coast of Ireland, beginning at Galway and ending at Sligo, during which he met a wide section of the population. In the autumn, he made a visit to the north, starting at Belfast. He was saddened by 'the most flagrant discreditable, and cruel disregard of the commonest duties of property'.[280] It particularly pained him that landlords in all parts of the country treated him with suspicion. Carnarvon wrote despondently, 'For once they had a Lord-Lieutenant – born and bred a landlord and full of landlord instincts and traditions, and who stood between them and their opponents – and yet they did their best to thwart him.'[281] He believed that this was largely due to his sympathetic attitude towards the Roman Catholic hierarchy, particularly in the field of education. One of his initiatives was the creation of a system of industrial schools run by clergy and nuns, which rescued many children from crime and poverty. He also encouraged the growth of much-needed technical education. On his western tour, Carnarvon realized the potential for a flourishing fishing industry, setting up a private subscription for the purchase of boats and equipment. He raised in Cabinet, as well as with Hicks Beach, the Chancellor of the Exchequer, the question of funding the various enterprises. Carnarvon blamed the lack of progress in stimulating these initiatives on Hicks Beach's parsimonious attitude. He noted, after one discussion with Hicks Beach on Treasury matters, 'A long and rather disagreeable talk with Beach, who is simply odious to do business with.'[282]

Overshadowing many of these restorative measures was the growth in strength of the National League and the high level of agrarian crime. Boycotting, murder, and the prevalence of secret courts were sponsored and encouraged by the League. Carnarvon believed that Spencer had missed an opportunity when the Land League was suppressed by allowing its successor to flourish. He calculated that, when he took office, the League had over 1,000 branches: by the time he left office, the number had grown to more than 1,250.[283] Another urgent problem that needed immediate attention was the

[279]Carnarvon to Sir Robert Hamilton, 25 June 1885: CP, TNA, PRO 30/6/56, fo. 12.
[280]'Lord Carnarvon's memoirs relating to his Lord-Lieutenancy', fo. 18.
[281]Ibid., fo. 7.
[282]Diary, 5 October 1885.
[283]'Lord Carnarvon's memoirs relating to his Lord-Lieutenancy', fo. 18.

reorganization of the police force. Its head, Colonel Robert Bruce, was persuaded by Carnarvon to retire, and the mode of selecting and appointing resident magistrates was changed, in order to counter cases of jobbing and patronage.

Apart from meetings with clergy, politicians, and officials, and receptions of deputations, there were many ceremonial and other duties. These included visits to schools, shipyards, and exhibitions. Carnarvon was expected to deliver many speeches: for instance, on his visit to Galway in August, at the first stop he received four addresses and he made four speeches.[284] Fortunately he was a fluent speaker, having no need to use notes, so this presented few problems.[285] However, his already weak constitution was undermined by the heavy burden of his day-to-day work. Lady Carnarvon informed Harrowby during the Munster Bank affair, 'Carnarvon has been very nearly crushed with all the business of this banking crisis.'[286] By 11 August, overwork had resulted in attacks of lumbago and rheumatism. Carnarvon was so ill that he was unable to walk and had to be carried upstairs to his bedroom.[287] He was also deeply anxious about the state of the country, as he told Cranbrook in September:

Irish matters are the first and last and middle thought of every day. Little as I ever dreamt of coming here, now that I am in Ireland I can think of nothing else, and my whole mind seems to me divided with deep pity for what I see on every side and anxiety as to the future. It is a most unhappy country, dowered – as in a fairy tale – with great gifts and great misfortunes. Very little is known or understood in England.[288]

In addition to his Irish responsibilities, Carnarvon's membership of the Cabinet entailed much travelling. For instance, on 7 October, Carnarvon received a message from the Queen requesting him to go to Balmoral after the Cabinet. He left Dublin with Ashbourne the following day, attended the meeting in London, and left the next day for Balmoral immediately afterwards. He returned to Dublin on 12 October.[289] He was doubtful about the value of attending Cabinet

[284]Diary, 17 August 1885.
[285]One official, Sir Henry Robinson, observed, 'He had the most marvellous knack of saying what sounded a very great deal but which when analysed amounted to absolutely nothing at all, and for an English statesman charged with the government of Ireland, I cannot imagine a greater gift': Sir H. Robinson, *Memories: wise and otherwise* (London, 1924), p. 76.
[286]Lady Carnarvon to Harrowby, 17 July 1885: Harrowby Papers, 2nd series, l, fo. 183.
[287]Diary, 10 August 1885.
[288]Carnarvon to Cranbrook, 2 September 1885 (copy): CP, TNA, PRO 30/6/54.
[289]Ashbourne Papers, A 25/1.

meetings: 'The attendance there matters one atom in 99 out of 100 cases and it is a long journey to undertake for so little.'[290] One of his main grievances was that, when he accepted the post, he was assured of the fullest support from Salisbury and the Cabinet: this promise was never kept. He later recorded,

> I was left entirely to my own resources and I could never obtain what I considered *essential* without a wrangle and often my own personal presence in London. The Treasury treated every application, though I wrote with my own hand explaining that the question was one involving the efficiency of the whole police force or the support of the Roman Catholic bishops, or the contentment of a disaffected district, just as if I were an inexperienced clerk in a Government Office.

Much of this animosity was directed at Hicks Beach himself:

> He was the very embodiment of red tape, and had not even the personal courtesy which I have found in every other Chancellor of the Exchequer with whom I have had to deal. An honourable and upright man, as I believe, he was one of the most disagreeable whom it has ever been my fortune to meet in business.[291]

Carnarvon reserved his main criticisms for the attitude of his Cabinet colleagues towards Ireland. The evidence clearly shows that on several occasions he requested that a full discussion of Irish policy should be held, but was frustrated to find that this was not granted.[292] No doubt this was largely due to Carnarvon's well-known views on home rule, which found little sympathy.

One of the colleagues to be the cause of much trouble was Randolph Churchill, Hicks Beach's friend. When Salisbury was forming his 1885 ministry, Churchill made it a condition of joining as Secretary of State for India that Northcote should no longer be Leader of the Commons and should be elevated to the Lords. He also wished to exclude Carnarvon as representing the old guard, but Salisbury had insisted on his own choice. Carnarvon's endeavours in Ireland were initially hampered by the behaviour of Churchill and Hicks Beach, arising out of the Maamtrasna murder case. In the previous year, Myles Joyce had been found guilty along with three others and hanged, through the evidence supplied by a fellow prisoner. Although there was some doubt about the verdict, Gladstone rejected all demands for an enquiry. When Salisbury's Cabinet subsequently endorsed Gladstone's decision, it seemed that the matter was closed. However, on 17 July, Churchill, Hicks Beach, and Sir John Gorst – all of whom had been members of the Fourth Party – strongly supported Parnell's

---

[290] Carnarvon to Ashbourne, 6 November 1885: Ashbourne Papers, A25/21.
[291] 'Lord Carnarvon's memoirs relating to his Lord-Lieutenancy', fos 1–2.
[292] Cooke and Vincent, *The Governing Passion*, p. 73.

motion censuring Spencer's actions. Most Conservatives, including Carnarvon, condemned this defiance of party policy.

By the middle of May, Churchill had established a rapport with Parnell. The former opposed the reintroduction of coercion in Ireland, favoured a system of local government similar to England, and called for an unarmed police force.[293] He differed from Carnarvon in opposing the notion of home rule to solve the country's problems. Churchill's closest Irish friend was Gerald Fitzgibbon, an outstandingly gifted and acerbic lawyer. They were of one mind on Ireland and had drafted an Educational Endowments Bill as part of Churchill's campaign for educational reform.[294] Fitzgibbon gleefully supplied Churchill with unflattering accounts of Carnarvon and his dealings with leading Irishmen. Referring to Carnarvon's recent visit to the north, Fitzgibbon wrote:

> The sunny climate of the West has been exchanged for wetter dullness by Lord Carnarvon, without any apparent loss of gushing power [. . .]. You saw that he promised when next he met his 'Royal Mistress' to tell her that his head 'thrilled with emotion' on hearing *God Save the Queen* in one room and for *God Bless the Prince of Wales* in another at St Enoch's Presbyterian National School.[295]

Carnarvon erroneously believed that Churchill was a supportive colleague. When he made his visit to the north, Churchill gave him useful advice on the state of the area.[296] Hearing of Churchill's intention to stay with Fitzgibbon at his home at Howth, Carnarvon invited the former to the Vice Regal Lodge; he arrived there on 1 October, Carnarvon finding him very amiable. During the course of a long discussion, Carnarvon stated his belief in home rule. At dinner, Churchill described to Lady Carnarvon his part in Northcote's departure as Leader of the Commons, and his joy at having ousted him. 'Indeed,' she wrote in her diary, 'his hatreds are not few or weak.' Churchill, however, praised Carnarvon 'and said the state of Ireland was quite marvellous to anyone who had seen it in former days'.[297] His

---

[293] In a biography of his father, Winston Churchill reported a conversation between Randolph Churchill and Parnell about this time, at the former's London home: "'There was no compact or bargain of any kind", Lord Randolph said to Fitzgibbon a year later, "but I told Parnell when he sat on that sofa [in Connaught Place] that if the Tories took office, and I was a member of their Government, I would not consent to renew the Crimes Act." Parnell replied, "In that case, you will have the Irish vote at the Elections."' (W.S. Churchill, *Lord Randolph Churchill*, 2 vols (London, 1906), I, p. 395.

[294] R.F. Foster, *Lord Randolph Churchill: a political life* (Oxford, 1981), pp. 229–230.

[295] Fitzgibbon to Churchill, 9 September 1885: Randolph Churchill Papers, Add. MS 9248/7/883.

[296] Carnarvon to Churchill, 18 September 1885 (copy): CP, TNA, PRO 30/5/4.

[297] Lady Carnarvon's diary, 2 October 1885: Herbert Papers, Somerset Archives and Record Service, DD/DRO/3/7.

real views differed markedly from Carnarvon's. He wrote from the
Vice Regal Lodge the same day, 'I trust it will not be [. . .] necessary to
show our hand about local government too much or to allude to Home
Rule at all [. . .]. The Nationalists [. . .] do not want us to do so.'[298]

Carnarvon appeared blissfully unaware of Churchill's machinations. The boycotting was widespread by the autumn and the
National League had increased in power; with the fall in prices,
the economic situation was causing concern. Carnarvon was seeking
Cabinet support for home rule as a possible solution but this was not
forthcoming. On 20 November, he had an important conversation
with Salisbury. The latter expressed the fear that if Carnarvon retired
now it would probably break up the Party. At the meeting, Carnarvon
produced a memorandum of the alternatives available for settling the
Irish question after the next general election.[299] He saw the Queen
on 26 November, when he discussed the situation with her. She gave
him a copy of Gladstone's memorandum on Ireland, which he had
drawn up in May, and asked Carnarvon for his opinion. While he
was guarded in his comments, she pointed out that there was great
danger in delaying finally dealing with the question, stating that
'a measure of self-government might now be given'.[300] Carnarvon
incurred Salisbury's wrath for expressing his own views to the Queen
before the Cabinet had pronounced on home rule.[301]

About this time, Churchill had learned, much to his astonishment,
of Carnarvon's secret meeting with Parnell in August. After consulting
Hicks Beach and Smith, and considering Carnarvon's memorandum,
Churchill wrote to Salisbury that the Party should remain opposed to
home rule: 'If that blessed man sets the signal for concession our party
will go to pieces [. . .]. Lord Carnarvon has it once more in his power,
as on two former occasions, to disintegrate, demoralise and shatter.'[302]

At the final Cabinet meetings of the year, on 14 and 15 December,
Carnarvon's memorandum on home rule for Ireland was once more
discussed: only Ashbourne supported him. Carnarvon, for his part,
produced another memorandum for the Cabinet, setting out the
terms for the conditions of his remaining Lord Lieutenant. The
formidable list included setting up a joint committee of both Houses
to consider the future government of Ireland, a working towards local
self-government, and a free hand for the Lord Lieutenant in dealing

[298] Quoted in Steele, *Lord Salisbury*, p. 187.

[299] Carnarvon, Memorandum, 'Conversation with Lord Salisbury', 23 November 1885:
CP, BL 60760, fos 78–80.

[300] Carnarvon to Queen Victoria, 26 November 1885: Royal Archives, D37/99.

[301] A. Ponsonby, *Henry Ponsonby, Queen Victoria's Private Secretary: his life from his letters* (London,
1942), pp. 199–200.

[302] Quoted in Churchill, *Lord Randolph Churchill*, II, pp. 21–22.

with the Treasury. These proposals were rejected by the Cabinet.[303] At the last meeting, he declared his wish to be relieved of his post but he was urged to stay on for the sake of Party unity.[304] The understanding was that he should be able to resign at the end of January. If the Government stayed in office after the general election (which had begun on 23 November), Carnarvon would continue to hold a Cabinet seat without portfolio.[305] When the results of the election were declared, the Liberals had 335 seats, the Conservatives 249, and the Irish Nationalists 86; Salisbury and the Parnellites together held the same number of seats as the Liberals, and the Conservatives could stay in office if they could rely on Irish support. The urgency for action was increased by the publication of the so-called Hawarden Kite leak (17–18 December), which was widely interpreted as a sign of Gladstone's conversion to home rule.[306]

Carnarvon had few regrets on the prospect of giving up the post. In October, he had told Sir John Macdonald, the Canadian premier, 'I certainly had no desire to come here. My affections were wholly given to my old Office, and there is at the moment so much Colonially that is deeply interesting to me.'[307] He was also worried about his wife's deteriorating health: 'She has not been well since she came here', Carnarvon informed Salisbury on 17 December.[308] Looking beyond the immediate

---

[303] Carnarvon also proposed a bill 'to promote the Extension of University Education in Ireland'. The draft bill, printed on 19 December, does not appear to have been discussed by the Cabinet. See 'University Education (Ireland) Bill', in Ashbourne Papers, B 25/6; Cooke and Vincent, *The Governing Passion*, p. 298.

[304] Salisbury to Queen Victoria, 14 December 1885: Royal Archives, A65/93. On the same day, Parnell wrote to Mrs O'Shea on the Liberal and Conservative Parties' attitude to home rule at the coming general election. She stated, 'I have not seen Lord C. [Carnarvon] and shall probably not arrange to do so for a week or two, as I wish to know how the other side is disposed first': K. O'Shea, *Charles Stewart Parnell: his love story and political life*, 2 vols (London, 1914), II, p. 29. She also told Gladstone on 10 December that 'Parnell was to see "Lord C." in a day or two': R.C.K. Ensor, *England: 1870–1914* (Oxford, 1936), p. 561. Henry Labouchere reported to Herbert Gladstone after a meeting between Carnarvon and John MacCarthy on 13 December, where they discussed Home Rule, 'Lord C. said that personally he was in favour of a large measure of Home Rule, but that he despaired of winning his party and some of his colleagues. He asked MacCarthy whether he thought that Parnell would accept an "Inquiry", during which the Conservatives might be educated. MacCarthy said that this would not do' (quoted in F. Callanan, *T.M. Healy* (Cork, 1996), pp. 134–135).

[305] Diary, 15 December 1885.

[306] Gladstone was influenced in his thinking by a memorandum written for Carnarvon in October 1885 by Sir Robert Hamilton, Under-Secretary, Dublin Castle: see J. Kendle, *Ireland and the Federal Solution: the debate over the United Kingdom Constitution, 1870–1921* (Kingston, Ontario, 1989), p. 42.

[307] Carnarvon to Sir John Macdonald, 2 October 1885: CP, TNA, PRO 30/6/65, fos 160–161.

[308] After Carnarvon's death, Ashbourne ventured another explanation: 'For his great wealth, I think he was unduly close, and I always thought that his principal reason for

present, Carnarvon had contacted his cousin at the Colonial Office, Sir Robert Herbert, to investigate the possibility of undertaking some 'important foreign mission'. Herbert advised that such a move would weaken Carnarvon's claim for a future return to office.[309]

The question of his successor as Lord Lieutenant now arose. Salisbury suggested Wolseley, a soldier much admired by Carnarvon, but the latter believed that such an appointment would be viewed by the Irish as a declaration of war: 'I doubt whether his employment to oppress Arabs and to reduce the Zulus would make his reception a warm one.'[310] In a letter to Carnarvon headed 'Measures for meeting rebellion in Ireland', Wolseley declared, 'Myself I don't believe in rebellion. Formerly Irish discontent was led by gentlemen of fighting families; now it is led by pork butchers and green grocers who will murder the country, but will never endanger their necks by an appeal to arms.'[311] In fact, Cranbrook was offered the post on 15 January.[312] On the following evening, Sir William Hart Dyke, Carnarvon's Irish Secretary, who had served him loyally, suddenly resigned. Salisbury then offered the post to W.H. Smith, mentioning that Hart Dyke had claimed 'that Carnarvon had never let him know anything that was going on'.[313] This was in contrast with Smith's relationship with his chief, noted five months later: 'Give me the opportunity some time and I shall be very glad to show how closely we were as colleagues and as friends.'[314]

The post of Irish Secretary was a crucial one because, as Salisbury pointed out, 'It is possible to go without a Viceroy by the help of justices, but it is not possible to go without the help of an Irish Secretary.' Churchill saw this as an opportunity to exert his influence on Irish affairs. He wrote to Salisbury about the Secretaryship, 'I think there are three men in the Government who would answer to the requirement of the position – Lord Cranbrook, Mr Smith and (please don't be shocked) myself.'[315] Subsequently, Smith accepted the post: the Lord Lieutenancy, meanwhile, remained unfilled for the remainder of the ministry.

resigning in January /86 (at the end of the 6 months he had originally named) was to escape all or any of the expense of the Dublin season, then about to commence' (A.B. Cooke and A.P.W. Malcolmson, *The Ashbourne Papers, 1869–1913: a calendar of the papers of Edward Gibson, 1st Lord Ashbourne* (Belfast, 1974), p. 26).

[309] Herbert to Carnarvon, 24 December 1885 and 9 January 1886: CP, BL 60795, fos 69–73.

[310] Carnarvon to Salisbury, 6 January 1886 (copy): CP, BL 60762, fo. 129.

[311] Wolseley to Carnarvon, 18 January 1886: CP, TNA, PRO 30/6/66, fos 275–276.

[312] A.E. Gathorne Hardy, *Gathorne Hardy, First Earl of Cranbrook: a memoir*, 2 vols (London, 1910), II, pp. 233–234.

[313] Salisbury to W.H. Smith, 17 January 1886: Hambleden Papers, PS9/104.

[314] Smith to Carnarvon, 9 June 1886: CP, BL 60830, fo. 40.

[315] Churchill to Salisbury, 16 January 1886: Randolph Churchill Papers, Add. MS 9248/1/134.

Carnarvon missed the first two Cabinets of the New Year (9 and 12 January) because of illness. On arriving in London soon afterwards, he was surprised to read a leading article in the *Standard* announcing his retirement later in the month, a fact that had obviously been leaked by an unknown person.[316]

One of the Cabinet's immediate tasks was to draft paragraphs on Ireland for the Queen's Speech. These included the introduction of a bill for the suppression of the National League, and a Land Bill. Carnarvon warned the Cabinet that legislation against the League would not be effective without a Crimes Bill. A sweeping Coercion Bill introduced by the new Irish Secretary, Smith, was planned for 28 January. However, the day before this, the Government were beaten in the Commons, following an amendment proposed by Jesse Collings regretting the omission in the Queen's Speech of benefits to rural labourers. Salisbury resigned the following day.

Despite Carnarvon's claims that his Lord Lieutenancy had been a successful one, there were many indications to the contrary. The Liberal MP Anthony John Mundella had visited Ireland the previous December and wrote to Lord Spencer, 'Since you left Dublin everything has fallen into chaos. There is no Government. [Sir Antony] McDonnell writes this morning that so far from the Government governing, Hamlet is left out of the play altogether.'[317] It was also observed that Carnarvon's trust in negotiations with Irish politicians and clergy was somewhat naïve, and that he lacked firmness in the administration of the country. Carnarvon, on the other hand, reflecting on his time in Ireland shortly before his death, defended himself in a bitter letter to Salisbury. In it he stated that his task had been an 'almost hopelessly difficult one. You had given up the Purchase Act and left me no adequate criminal law on which to depend – it was in truth requiring me to make bricks without straw.'[318]

The main legislation put forward by Gladstone was a Home Rule Bill, introduced on 8 April. It was more radical than that proposed by Carnarvon, who wished to challenge the Liberal leader, but he was bound by silence to Salisbury. By now, rumours were circulating in London about Carnarvon's meeting with Parnell the previous year. Carnarvon himself was probably one of the culprits, as he freely

---

[316] A previous Lord Lieutenant, the 7th Earl Cowper, who had resigned the post four years earlier in unhappy circumstances, wrote in his diary, 'Lord Carnarvon leaves suddenly. I fancy had a hint to go. No one reaps any credit from that wretched island' (Lady Katrina Cowper, *Earl Cowper, K.G.: a memoir by his wife* (London?, 1913), p. 629.

[317] Mundella to Spencer, 28 December 1885: Spencer Papers, BL 76927 (unnumbered).

[318] Carnarvon to Salisbury, 2 April 1890 (copy), CP BL 60760, fo. 148.

discussed Irish affairs with a number of friends and colleagues. On 6 June, for example, he disclosed his conversation with Parnell to W.H. Smith. In the closing hours of the debate on the Home Rule Bill, Parnell had revealed that he had had an offer from a minister in the last Conservative government of a statutory parliament in Ireland. Two days later, Carnarvon read in the *Pall Mall Gazette* that he was named as the minister who had made the offer. He consulted Harrowby, who, like Smith, urged him to remain silent. After a further article appeared, this time in the *Daily News*, Carnarvon telegraphed Salisbury of his intention to make a statement in the Lords that night. At a hastily arranged meeting between the two men, Salisbury reluctantly agreed that Carnarvon should speak, on condition that he took all the responsibility on himself for the Parnell meeting, and added, '"Pray make it [the statement] as dry as possible and without any sentiment," to which I replied that "I should be very short and simple but that I always eat my bread with butter": and so we parted.'[319] The speech was a plain account of the meeting, omitting any mention of Salisbury's prior knowledge, and Carnarvon disagreed with Gladstone's suggested solution for settling the Irish question. He recorded in his diary,

> It was listened to with the utmost attention, but with a frigidity on the part of my late colleagues that was curious. Not one of them said a word; nor when I sat down and remained sitting on the same bench for an hour and a half afterwards did anyone of them say a syllable to me.[320]

Gladstone had been defeated because of the defection of 94 members of his Party, voting with the Conservatives on the second reading of the Home Rule Bill on 8 June; Parliament was dissolved on the same day as Carnarvon's statement. Thenceforward, debate on the Parnell incident was conducted by newspaper correspondence. Letters from both Gladstone and Parnell alleging Salisbury's involvement appeared in the press. There was also correspondence between Carnarvon and Salisbury, the former anxious to clear his name, the latter cold and unfriendly in his replies. Finally, on 29 June, Salisbury reluctantly agreed that some sort of statement should be made and, in a speech that night to the Constitutional Union, he repudiated Parnell's claims. Two days later, Salisbury and Carnarvon met to discuss the contents and wording. Salisbury, who seemed friendly, had drafted the statement and invited Carnarvon's comments. It mentioned the differences between them as to home rule, and the fact that neither the existence nor contents of the meeting were subsequently disclosed

---

[319]Diary, 10 June 1886.
[320]Ibid.

to the Cabinet. It also confirmed that no action was taken as a result of it, and that Carnarvon had not resigned after any disagreement of opinion with his colleagues, but that he had from the outset indicated his intention to relinquish the post of Lord Lieutenant after the next general election. On the meeting itself, the phrasing was a little ambiguous. Even though Carnarvon had the opportunity to make amendments to the draft, there was no mention that Salisbury had approved of the meeting in the first instance, the document simply stating, 'In August, Lord Carnarvon gave me an account of his interview with Parnell.' Accounts of Salisbury's speech appeared in the press the following day, but the matter of the responsibility for the Parnell meeting was never publicly settled.

Politics from the sidelines

The general election resulted in an easy victory for the Unionists, with a majority of 118, the new parliament consisting of 316 Conservative seats and 78 Liberal Unionists as against 191 Gladstonian Liberals and 85 Irish Nationalists. On 20 July, Gladstone resigned. While the election campaign was still under way, Carnarvon had a long discussion with Sir Robert Herbert about the possibility of being offered a post by Salisbury in the event of his party being returned to power. Carnarvon was uncertain as to the wisdom of once more resuming his career: 'To accept would cure the seeming differences of opinion for the time: but if a break were afterwards to come it would be impossible ever again to mend the broken china.' On the other hand, he dreaded taking office again after having been in four governments and three Cabinets, preferring the freedom to pursue his own interests.[321] In a further discussion with Herbert it was agreed that it would be wiser to refuse.

Salisbury had also shown reluctance in resuming office. He twice approached Lord Hartington in the hope that he would head a joint Unionist government but without success. On 25 July, Salisbury wrote to Carnarvon from Osborne, stating that their differences on Irish matters would make it difficult for Carnarvon to be in a Cabinet that was largely resistant to that country's aspirations, adding, 'The country does not understand such *nuances*'.[322] Salisbury asked Carnarvon, though no longer in the Government, to continue his support. The same day, Carnarvon received a telegram announcing a meeting of the Party at the Carlton. He spoke briefly, expressing a wish that a strong

[321] Diary, 5 July 1886.
[322] Salisbury to Carnarvon, 25 July 1886: CP, BL 60760, fo. 116.

Conservative government should be formed, and that, apart from the Irish question, he would remain loyal to the Government. The speech was received in a friendly 'but not cordial' manner, according to Carnarvon, by the audience.[323]

An important change in the new Salisbury administration was the deposition of Hicks Beach as Leader of the Commons and the elevation of Randolph Churchill to the post. To Carnarvon, this news was unwelcome. He noted in his diary,

> I cannot forget my last conversation with R. Churchill, which was on his side as mad a one as I ever listened to from mortal lips and I am glad not to be tied to him as a colleague. Humanly speaking, I cannot see much probability of my being again in Office.[324]

This forecast proved to be correct.

Carnarvon was not impressed with the make-up of the new Government. He believed the replacement of Hicks Beach (now Chief Secretary of Ireland) as Leader of the Commons by Churchill to be an intriguing one. 'Randolph is as likely to make peace as to war when responsibility is put on him', he told Harrowby. 'Beach is happily relegated to a place where his rather unamiable qualities will do very well.'[325] Churchill's dramatic resignation from the Government four months later came as little surprise to Carnarvon.

One way in which he was able to show his continuing loyalty to the Party was by participating in the activities of the Primrose League. The League was the brainchild of Churchill and members of the Fourth Party who, from 1883, envisaged it as a vehicle for influencing Conservative Party organization. It was hoped to recruit a younger, active, and more democratic membership than hitherto; but, at the same time, the underlying motive was to strengthen Churchill's own position on the National Union Council.[326] Salisbury and Northcote reluctantly accepted the League. The Corrupt Electoral Practices Act of 1883 restricted the number of paid political helpers in constituencies at election time. However, by setting up a network of habitations throughout the country, each with a ruling councillor, assisted by knights and dames, the League could operate effectively. Two interesting features were the recruitment of women as well as men to spread the message, and the inclusion of a large working-class force by means of associate membership. Meetings were frequently

---

[323] Diary, 27 July 1886.
[324] Diary, 29 July 1886.
[325] Carnarvon to Harrowby, 13 August 1886: Harrowby Papers, 2nd series, lii, fo. 171.
[326] See Foster, *Lord Randolph Churchill*, pp. 128ff.

held on the estates of large country houses and were addressed by leading League members. There was also the incentive of a range of entertainments, from dancing and magic lantern displays to lectures, theatricals, and exhibitions.[327]

On 17 January 1884, Carnarvon had had a long talk with Northcote about Churchill and the state of Party organization at Conservative headquarters. Northcote was suspicious of Churchill's motives in supporting the League, having suffered from the manoeuvrings of the Fourth Party. Carnarvon, however, urged considerable changes in the organization as soon as possible. Northcote also showed him some papers concerning the new Primrose League 'which I think may have a great boom in some of the large towns'.[328] Clearly, the League's aims – 'to embrace all classes and creeds except atheists and enemies of the British Empire [and] the maintenance of religion and of the Constitution of the realm and the Imperial ascendancy of Great Britain' – appealed to Carnarvon.

He registered as a member of the Primrose League in November 1884,[329] and the Highclere Primrose Habitation held its first meeting on 1 June 1885. Carnarvon took the chair and his wife was elected as ruling councillor. Associates were to pay sixpence.[330] Lady Carnarvon recorded in her diary the same day, 'The first meeting of the habitation (which began at five) was interminable and lasted till after seven.'[331] Large-scale meetings were held in the grounds at Highclere, where a range of events were usually organized. Carnarvon described one such occasion:

> We had a Primrose Meeting of the Highclere and Burghclere Habitations, and a very successful one too. About five hundred members attended for the tea. The Highland Band played, the day cleared up from the showers of the morning, and after tea we all marched round to the east side of the Castle and then we made a few speeches after which we had a display of fireworks which gave the greatest pleasure. Many if not most of those present had never seen such a thing as a rocket or a squib [. . .]. Altogether it was a great success. There was not a single hitch or difficulty, first to last.[332]

Carnarvon's speeches were a central feature of these gatherings, and were widely reported. At a meeting the following year, he described one local feature, Beacon Hill, the prehistoric hill fort within Highclere

[327] J.H. Robb, *The Primrose League, 1883–1906* (New York, 1942), pp. 87–89.
[328] Diary, 17 January 1884.
[329] C.G. Hay to Carnarvon, 28 November 1884: CP, BL 60857, fo. 37.
[330] Diary, 1 June 1885.
[331] Lady Carnarvon's diary, 1 June 1885: Herbert Papers, Somerset Archives and Record Service, DD/DRU/3/7.
[332] Diary, 10 August 1886.

Park, where Britons had supposedly resisted the attacks of a wild horde of barbarians. Drawing an analogy with political opponents, Carnarvon urged Primrose League members to defend the English Constitution against 'all those who would bring desolation on the prosperity and honour of our common country (hear, hear)'.[333]

Carnarvon's real estate and investments

By the 1880s, with increasing ill health, Carnarvon was conscious of the need to put his affairs in order. His London properties had proved profitable. The house at 66 Grosvenor Square had been sold by him in 1872 for £14,500; in the following year he bought 16 Bruton Street (Lord Granville's house) for £29,000, 'a heavy sum but as houses go, not so very heavy'.[334] With a growing family, more space was needed, and house-hunting was resumed in 1881. 'The most absurd prices are constantly asked', he wrote.[335] They had hoped to buy Lord Suffield's house at 16 Grosvenor Street, but the negotiations had fallen through. Finally, in February 1882, they purchased 43 Portman Square, the residence of Lady Cardigan, for £17,000. The price was fairly modest as there was only a thirty-five-year lease, 'a considerable, very considerable, saving on the Bruton Street one'.[336] In addition, Carnarvon owned a property in St James's Square, which was worth some £50,000 by 1889.[337]

Taking into account the capital improvements that he had made on his country properties, particularly at Highclere and Pixton, the latter of which he practically rebuilt, Carnarvon calculated that his capital and income from his estates and overseas investments totalled about £273,000.[338] His pessimism about the political situation in England in 1884, particularly the growing radicalism in agricultural areas, the possibility of further franchise legislation, and other measures of the Liberal government, led him to draw up a memorandum for the guidance of Lady Carnarvon 'in the event of any serious trouble in coming times'. The extent of his fears for the collapse of institutions can be seen in his statement 'all the investments in Australia, Canada and the United States, such as Massachusetts Bonds, are, as you know,

---

[333] *Newbury Weekly News*, 4 August 1887.

[334] Diary, 25 February 1873. See also 'Papers relating to purchase of 16 Bruton Street in 1873': Highclere Castle Archives, Teversal 3/4.

[335] Diary, 30 June 1881.

[336] Diary, 28 February 1882.

[337] CP, BL 61504, fos 83–91.

[338] Ibid, fo. 91. Carnarvon's wealth at his death was £328,809. 0s. 4d.

intended as a nest egg against troublesome times and *out of England'*.[339] He also mentioned the contingency of his wife's need to 'flee across the seas'.[340] By the time of his death, he was in a more optimistic frame of mind about his finances.

The sale of Christian Malford for £190,000 had earlier given Carnarvon the opportunity to purchase property in Australia, which had great potential for investment. In August 1882, he had purchased 2,560 acres of land near Lake Macquarie in the county of Northumberland, New South Wales,[341] and he continued to look for further opportunities. The following April, Sir Robert Herbert told his cousin of an important proposition just made to him by Sir Julius Vogel, a former premier of New Zealand, and a colleague, the chairman of Messrs Wallis Landholding Company, to buy a block of one hundred square miles of land in West Australia at 2s. 6d. per acre. There were several blocks to be disposed of and Herbert suggested that he should buy one block and Carnarvon another for £8,000. On 23 April, Carnarvon decided to proceed with the purchase.[342] Within four months, the Legislative Council of West Australia had given Vogel a concession for the construction of a railway from Perth to a remote township, Eucla, six miles from the West Australian boundary with South Australia. The new line would pass very near the blocks purchased by them, and thus their value would be enhanced. Vogel's ambitious plan was for the establishment of a town on 3,000 acres of land given up by block-holders for this purpose. Trustees would be empowered to select sites for the town, which would be the property of the block-holders, who would thus be enriched.[343] Carnarvon bought a further one-tenth share in two more blocks, but he was uneasy, expressing 'perhaps unreasonable suspicion of Vogel's speculations'.[344] The capital sum to be raised was in the region of £300,000, and the aims of the Company were set out in the prospectus. The Company would also receive 12,000 acres of good land from the Government for every mile of railway constructed. One newspaper stated that Carnarvon was head of the syndicate and that a portion of the land was to be placed at the disposal of future immigrants who would settle and cultivate it.

Carnarvon's suspicions proved to be correct. The route chosen crossed long stretches of desert and difficult terrain; even more

---

[339] Carnarvon, Memorandum, 24 March 1884: CP, BL 61504, fos 74–75.

[340] A. Adonis, *Making Aristocracy Work: the peerage and the political system in Britain, 1884–1914* (Oxford, 1993), p. 284.

[341] Highclere Castle Archives, Teversal 2/4 (g).

[342] Diary, 23 April 1883.

[343] Herbert to Carnarvon, 20 Sept 1883: Highclere Castle Archives, Teversal 9/2.

[344] Carnarvon to Herbert, 1 November 1883: ibid.

serious was the report of a mining engineer, C.P. Lempriere, who was employed to survey the proposed line. He pointed out that the lack of water in the area was a major problem. Accordingly, the project soon collapsed. The extent of Carnarvon's financial losses is not known. A note that he wrote on the correspondence relating to the negotiations simply states, 'These papers are now of no importance. They refer to a property, Eucla, bought in Western Australia but soon sold again.'[345]

It is not surprising that, at a time when investment in Australia was being sought, there were inevitably many instances of sharp practice. Carnarvon was involved five years later in another fiasco. In November 1888, a Sydney newspaper announced 'among the men in distinct England who have selected Sydney as the spot for their investments are Lord Carnarvon, Lord Hindlip and Lord Rosebery, and one or two other prominent capitalists'. It claimed that the North Shore Company had purchased a thousand acres of North Sydney land, with an enormous frontage to the deep-water bays of Middle Harbour, which would be sub-divided into blocks. A suspension bridge for tramway and passenger purposes would span the bay; it would be built at a cost of £27,000 and would be the longest of its kind in Australia. English capital amounting to between three and five million pounds would be secured at 4 per cent and used to develop North Sydney.[346] Carnarvon had already purchased property in Sydney,[347] which was being managed by the local law firm of W.W. Billyard. His London lawyer subsequently wrote to Carnarvon that Billyard 'not only without your knowledge but really in the teeth of your instructions to the contrary, has used your credit and name to bolster up his Company in which he has speculated to a very large extent'.[348] Rosebery, too, was unaware of his involvement. Carnarvon accordingly ordered Billyard to remove his name from the list of shareholders.[349]

[345] Highclere Castle Archives, Teversal 9/2, n.d.

[346] 'Merry millions for Sydney', unnamed newspaper, November 1888: Highclere Castle Archives, Teversal 9/3.

[347] Valuation after Carnarvon's death. See file 'Australia, New South Wales, Sydney Property': Highclere Castle Archives, 1891–1898, Teversal 9/4.

[348] W.S. Foster to Carnarvon, 2 January 1889: Highclere Castle Archives, Teversal 9/3. Carnarvon's banking adviser in Australia had warned him earlier, 'Mr Billyard has lately been concerned with other speculation in a large land transaction. I understand that they bought an estate for a low price and resold it to a company at very great profit. Some unpleasant things have been said about it but I have not been able to discover anything that would justify me in making specific enquiries on your behalf' (Sir G. Verdon to Carnarvon, 12 September 1888: CP, BL 60802, fo. 35).

[349] Carnarvon to Billyard, 8 January 1889: Highclere Castle Archives, Teversal 9/3.

A more successful enterprise were his extensive property purchases in Perth, much of it in the centre of the growing city.[350] On hearing of Carnarvon's death in 1890, the Hon. John Forrest, an official at Government House, Adelaide, wrote to the new Earl that he had acted as a friend rather than a man of business in advising Carnarvon, 'as I believe the fact of his investing would do good for this Colony and I was anxious he should invest his money well'. Forrest had invested £18,500, producing rents amounting to £935 per annum.[351] Carnarvon had also been active in New Zealand, investing up to £25,000 in housing development and land speculation in Christchurch in 1883–1884.[352]

A home in Italy

Carnarvon's medical advisers recommended a warmer climate both for his health and as an escape from politics. While on holiday on the French Riviera and in Italy in early 1882, the Carnarvons found a suitable site at the fishing village of Portofino, on the Gulf of Genoa, near to that city. Now a well-known resort, it overlooks the Mediterranean with the Appenines to the north. Over the doorway of the house were carved the words *Reddens Deo gratias et redditurus*, 'the motto of my present and my future life'.[353] The house was completed after three years and named *Altachiara*, 'Highclere' in Italian. Carnarvon and his family took up residence for the first time in January 1885: it was there that he learned of the death of General Gordon at Khartoum. He corresponded regularly with a wide range of colleagues and, with a well-stocked library, found it an ideal place to write articles and books. It was there in April 1890, for example, that he finished the translation of *Prometheus*. Carnarvon once noted in his diary that he had read, *inter alia*, four large volumes of Hodgkin's *Invasion of Italy*, some Dante, and a quantity of other books. He was also able to revise his translation of the first twelve books of the *Odyssey*.[354]

A fortnight after arriving back in London after relinquishing the Lord Lieutenancy of Ireland in 1886, Carnarvon started out for

---

[350] See Western Australia, Perth Property 1888–96: Highclere Castle Archives, Teversal 9/7. In 1888, Carnarvon invested £10,000 in Perth housing property.
[351] Forrest to 5th Earl of Carnarvon, 7 August 1890: Highclere Castle Archives, Teversal, 9/7.
[352] See file 'New Zealand Property, 1883–4': Highclere Castle Archives, Teversal 9/1.
[353] Diary, 26 December 1888.
[354] Diary, 1 April 1887.

Portofino.[355] His firm views on Ireland and his enthusiasm for granting a greater degree of self-government were still an embarrassment for the Conservatives. This was increased in April after Gladstone introduced his Home Rule Bill, the Land Purchase Bill following just eight days later. Carnarvon was set to return to England towards the end of the month, but the receipt of two letters made him delay his departure. One was from Harrowby, who 'wrote strongly urging me not to return if possible till the Home Rule bill was disposed of', a sentiment which Salisbury also asked Harrowby to convey. The other, from Sir Robert Herbert, stated more directly that 'it would be a good thing if I were not in London just now with party spirit running so high'.[356]

In February 1887, the Carnarvons experienced a rare but severe earthquake, lasting four days, when there was panic and heavy loss of life, with widespread destruction. It began on Ash Wednesday, 23 February, when the family were awoken in the early hours of the morning; the whole house shook violently for one and a half minutes, and that was followed by several other shocks.

Perhaps the most worrying aspect of Portofino was the effect that the climate was having on Carnarvon's health. Herbert felt obliged to tell his cousin, 'Porto Fino is not the best place for you with an ailing throat, indicating that the fortress of the body is not impregnable to fever; and I shall be glad if you move northward rather sooner than you at present contemplate doing.'[357] Travelling to Portofino by train across Europe, sometimes with a family party of as many as twelve, was a major undertaking. There was, too, always the possibility that the holiday could be interrupted unexpectedly. One such occasion was in January 1889, when Carnarvon was called back on urgent county council business.

Colonial tours

Carnarvon had long wished to visit some of the colonies in order to be better informed on imperial questions. The pressure of work while he was in office had made this impracticable. In August 1883, he made a brief tour of Canada. He was able once again to make the acquaintance of Sir John Macdonald, the premier, and observe how the Canadian parliament was operating. Apart from the obligatory

---

[355] Crown Prince Friedrich Wilhelm, briefly Kaiser Friedrich III, recuperated at the villa in 1886. He died two years later. See K. Baedeker, *Northern Italy* (London, 1930), p. 269.
[356] Diary, 24 April 1886.
[357] Sir R. Herbert to Carnarvon, 17 April 1888: CP, BL 60795B, fos 166–167.

sight-seeing, Carnarvon attended to Masonic business, as well as informing himself of his Canadian investments.[358] Once out of office, a much more ambitious programme was undertaken in August 1887, with visits to South Africa and Australia. At Cape Town, where he arrived after a stormy passage, he met Sir Hercules Robinson, the Governor of New South Wales, who had negotiated the cession of Fiji in 1874, and travelled to Kimberley to see the diamond mines and attend a Masonic meeting. His last function in Cape Town was to be installed as Chancellor of the University on 29 September. He noted the vast unclaimed territories to the north of Transvaal, and believed that Britain should extend the British Protectorate to this area before other European powers took over the region.[359]

The brief South African visit was followed by a more extensive one to Australia, with a five-month tour during which Carnarvon was accompanied by Elsie. Starting at Hobart, he was greeted by Sir Robert Hamilton, his former Permanent Under-Secretary in Ireland, who was now Governor of Tasmania. He visited the colony's Houses of Parliament and, after receiving a vote of both Houses, followed the debate in the Council Chamber from a seat especially placed on the floor of the House.[360] Comparing the different Australian states, Carnarvon remarked, 'In South Australia it is a middle state between Tasmania and Victoria, less energy, intellect and movement than in Victoria, more than in Tasmania. I could not live in Tasmania satisfactorily, but I might, I think, find sufficient pabulum in South Australia.'[361] They next travelled to Queensland and Western Australia to see many of the famous beauty spots, and were back in Sydney on 24 January 1888 to witness the widespread celebrations for the centenary of the first English settlement. Carnarvon also attended an inter-colonial gathering of Australian governors.[362] Not the least important business was the meeting with the New South Wales Masonic members to settle the differences between the lodges.

Remaining political concerns

Stopping in Italy on his return journey in March 1888, Carnarvon read in the Italian papers an account of a Local Government Bill

[358] Diary, 6 September 1883.
[359] See Carnarvon's lecture, 'The Cape in 1888', in Herbert, *Essays, Addresses and Translations*, III, pp. 53–96; see also Hardinge, III, p. 274.
[360] Diary, 22 November 1887.
[361] Diary, 9 December 1887.
[362] Hardinge, III, p. 285.

that had recently been introduced in the Commons and had been warmly welcomed by the Liberal press. Carnarvon wrote immediately to Harrowby, 'I am afraid it means such a revolution of the existing system and is far more in accordance with the views of some of our Radical allies than with our own traditions. The *destruction* of our Quarter Sessions system ought not to come from our side.'[363] The bill provided for a reconstruction of local government, with elected councils exercising the functions so far undertaken by magistrates in Quarter Sessions. These included the management of county finances and the making and assessment of rates. Too late, many Conservative peers on the right of the Party bitterly complained of this revolutionary measure. Carnarvon spoke 'very strongly' against it on its second reading in the Lords on 31 July, deploring the destruction of tried and valuable institutions. He warned that 'it distinctly paved the way at no distant day, for a demand by the London County Council for the control of the Metropolitan Police'.[364] As ever, he was disappointed at the lack of support from his colleagues. He noted afterwards, 'The feeling of all or almost all on the Conservative side was evidently with me, but no one (as I expected) had the courage to follow in the same line.'[365]

For the first time, the electoral register contained the names of peers of the realm who were eligible to vote by virtue of being ratepayers. They were also eligible to stand for election as councillors and aldermen. Carnarvon was torn between the call of duty to stand for the Hampshire County Council and the need to preserve his failing energy. He had been appointed the Lord Lieutenant of the county in July 1887 and thus, he considered, he should put himself forward. However, there was, initially, a problem. As he wrote in his diary, 'One cannot canvass, one ought not to be opposed, one must not be beaten.' In October 1888, Carnarvon sought the advice of his predecessor in Ireland, Lord Spencer, who became chairman of the Northamptonshire County Council after standing as a councillor. Carnarvon, who was still wavering, did not believe that it was necessary for him to become chairman 'but as an outsider of all parties one may be of use as *amicus curiae* [disinterested adviser] in giving the first start to the Council'.[366] A week later, at a meeting of the Winchester Quarter Sessions, he announced his intention of standing for the new Council.

At Portofino in the new year he received letters from old colleagues urging him to return to advise on future Council tactics. 'There

[363] Carnarvon to Harrowby, 21 March 1888: Harrowby Papers, 2nd series, lii, fo. 176.
[364] *Hansard*, CCCXXIX, 31 July 1888, col. 923.
[365] Diary, 31 July 1888.
[366] Carnarvon to Spencer, 7 October 1888: Spencer Papers.

appears to be no one at this moment', he wrote, 'to take much lead or give much guidance.'[367] Although unwell, Carnarvon left Italy for England alone four days later, to chair (as Lord Lieutenant of the county) a preliminary meeting of the new Council, but was too ill to attend. He was co-opted as an alderman at the first formal meeting of the body on 1 April but was saddened to observe how different in character it was from the old Quarter Sessions:

> The 'outsiders' behaved well and showed no disposition to give trouble [. . .]. Many of the old members of the Court were there but a different spirit was moving the as yet not very articulate body; the elective and the representative idea has come and one felt oneself in contact with an entirely new creation.[368]

Carnarvon's views on the question of the reform of the House of Lords were somewhat different. While upholding the principle of a second chamber, he believed that some change was long overdue. When Rosebery issued a circular on the subject in December 1884, Carnarvon was the only member of the Conservative front bench to whom it was sent and he approved of its contents.[369] With the Conservatives once more in office, Salisbury half-heartedly took up the issue by promoting two bills: a Life Peers Bill and the Discontinuation of Writs Bill, the latter to give powers to expel so-called 'black sheep' from the House. Carnarvon was critical of the latter bill, calling the method whereby expulsion from the House was to be carried out 'quite the most clumsy that parliamentary wit ever devised'.[370] In an earlier motion on 11 March calling for a Select Committee, Rosebery had dismissed the provision for allowing a maximum of five new life peers a year as creating 'a mere zoological collection of abstract celebrities'.[371] The Life Peers Bill was dramatically withdrawn on its second reading on 10 July, shortly followed by the 'black sheep bill': 'I said a few words', wrote Carnarvon, 'in a sort of protest against this second bill being thus immolated and so matters came to an end.'[372]

The matter was revived early in the following year, on Carnarvon's initiative. Salisbury was at first 'a little nettled' that the question of the suspension or removal of black sheep from the Lords should once more be raised. He declined to bring in a bill but offered to support Carnarvon if he wished to do so. Accordingly, on 4 March, Carnarvon told Salisbury of his intention to introduce legislation. Carnarvon was

[367] Diary, 27 January 1889.

[368] Diary, 1 April 1889.

[369] Carnarvon to Rosebery, 24 December 1884 (copy), and Rosebery to Carnarvon, 6 January 1885: CP, BL 60855, fos 43–44.

[370] Diary, 18 June 1888; *Hansard*, CCCXXIX, 18 June 1888, cols 387–414.

[371] *Hansard*, CCCXXIII, 11 March 1888, col. 1567.

[372] Diary, 10 July 1888; *Hansard*, CCCXXIX, 10 July 1888, cols 871–872.

suspicious of Salisbury's apparent interest, recording, 'If I were to follow his advice [it] would probably go some way towards wrecking its chances.'[373] The debate on the second reading took place in a full House on 21 March. It provoked a lively discussion with Salisbury, who ended the debate by attacking it. Carnarvon refused to be deterred and insisted that the Lords should divide. The bill was lost by 73 to 14. Salisbury's actions were a disappointment to Carnarvon, even though they came as no surprise – 'another curious illustration of his falsity and untruthfulness. He is as false as he can be.'[374]

The relationship between Rosebery and Carnarvon, as mentioned above, had been a close one over their overseas financial initiatives. At a previous private meeting on 4 February 1889, the two men had had a long talk, first about New South Wales property matters, then about politics in general.[375] They were in agreement on the proposed reform of the House of Lords and also shared a strong belief in imperialism.[376] Rosebery became chairman of the Imperial Federation League, a non-political organization founded in November 1884, whose aim was to act as the focal point for imperial sentiment in Great Britain and to preserve and strengthen the unity of the empire on federal principles. Carnarvon became a leading member, together with other Conservatives such as W.H. Smith and Sir Henry Holland, and attended many of its meetings.[377]

Carnarvon's concern over Ireland did not diminish out of office. With the accession of Balfour to the post of Irish Chief Secretary, which led to a series of repressive legislative measures and the Plan of Campaign in retaliation, the chances of a peaceful settlement remained far away. Carnarvon was therefore pleasantly surprised when, in April 1889, he was approached by Fitzgibbon, on the prompting of Randolph Churchill, to discuss aspects of Irish self-government. This led to a meeting with Churchill himself three days later. Since his dramatic resignation from the Salisbury administration at the end of 1887, Churchill had been in the political wilderness; he now wished to re-establish a power base from which he could

---

[373]Diary, 4 March 1889.

[374]Diary, 21 March 1889; *Hansard*, CCCXXXIV, 21 March 1889, cols 333–343.

[375]Diary, 4 February 1889.

[376]The Earl of Selborne wrote from his home at Blackwood in Hampshire on 31 December 1884, 'The Colonial party here, also, is increasingly powerful and aggressive. Rosebery and Carnarvon both caress and flatter it': R. Palmer, Earl of Selborne, *Memorials: personal and political*, 2 vols (London, 1898), II, p. 132.

[377]Urging Carnarvon to join, W.J. Courthope stated, 'I feel strongly that the Conservatives are not so prominently represented in the direction of the affairs of the League as they should be' (Courthope to Carnarvon, 7 June 1886: CP, BL 60775, fo. 183). Carnarvon accepted the vice-chairmanship of the League in 1886: J.C.R. Colomb to Carnarvon, 11 November 1886: CP, BL 60811, fos 74–75.

challenge Balfour's hard-line policy. The 7 April meeting proved to be a fruitful one. Churchill suggested that they make a joint move in both Houses to highlight the state of Ireland and to recruit sympathizers. A memorandum was to be drawn up by them to be presented to Salisbury, stating their position. Carnarvon was sympathetic to this action but preferred initially to seek out the views of Hartington, now an influential and leading Liberal Unionist, and he offered to make the approach. Churchill, whose attitude towards Ireland had softened, told Carnarvon that 'he was willing to give everything short of a Parliament'.[378] Carnarvon was flattered by Churchill's attention, even postponing a planned visit to Germany to take the waters,[379] but at their next meeting was a little more cautious. He frankly told Churchill that his (Churchill's) unpopularity with the Government would be worse if he took over action either in Parliament or at public meetings and could be construed as jealousy of Balfour. Carnarvon counselled patience and the sounding out of possible supporters.[380] He was ill with a severe attack of gout for most of the remainder of April and was thus out of action. In mid-May, after a further discussion with Churchill, he helped to draw up a ten-point memorandum, listing the changes necessary in Ireland. They included the extension of local government, the need to develop Irish resources, and the gradual relaxation of control of the police, with responsibility being gradually handed over to the Irish authorities. The memorandum also pointed out the impossibility of maintaining the enforcement of the law under the existing system.[381]

Carnarvon arranged a meeting with Hartington on 24 May. As a former Chief Secretary of Ireland, Hartington listened sympathetically to the proposals. He did not give an immediate answer on the question of raising the issues in the Lords but, a week later, after consulting Chamberlain, he advised against the expediency of such action. At the same time, he agreed to help in recruiting friends 'privately and unofficially on active and conciliatory policy'.[382] Carnarvon informed Churchill of the outcome and it was agreed to follow Hartington's advice for the time being.[383] Churchill was away fishing in Norway and was later in France. They met at Highclere on 14 July, where they had a long conversation on European

[378] Diary, 7 April 1889.
[379] Carnarvon to Churchill, 7 April 1889: Randolph Churchill Papers, Add. MS 9248/23/3098.
[380] Diary, 2 April 1889.
[381] See CP, BL 60828, fo. 26; Hardinge, III, p. 246.
[382] Hartington to Carnarvon, 31 May 1889: CP, BL 60828, fos 18–23.
[383] Carnarvon to Churchill, 5 June 1889: Randolph Churchill Papers, Add. MS 9248/24/3170.

politics and the possibility of war between France and Italy. The main concern, however, was Churchill's forthcoming speeches at Walsall and Birmingham at the end of the month, when 'he intended to speak out, telling his audience that he could not speak freely in the House of Commons. I urged him to be very careful as to this, because he would have the House of Commons to deal with anyhow for another two years and that it was of no use to get quite angry with them.'[384] At Birmingham on 30 July, Churchill spoke out about Irish policy as agreed, but the impact was lost because of the lack of detail. Carnarvon wrote to Churchill congratulating him on the speech and agreeing with its content, 'with an occasional subtraction here and an addition there', though he voiced substantial differences with Churchill on his attitude towards Egypt.[385] Nevertheless, Carnarvon was aware of Churchill's capacity to use people for his own ends and his ability to flatter where necessary. In July, he summed up Churchill as follows:

> He is very clever – it is impossible to doubt this – and he has a very considerable attraction when he desires to put it out [. . .]. I fancy that he is so cut off from his old party and friends that he is really glad of a friend, though probably he would throw the friend over without much remorse if circumstances seemed to require it.[386]

In November, Churchill consulted Carnarvon regarding the offer of the post of ambassador to St Petersburg, which he hoped to receive from Salisbury. Carnarvon advised him to take it. By this time, the prospect of a working alliance between them on Ireland had faded, and there were no further serious political contacts with Churchill during the remainder of Carnarvon's life.

Carnarvon and the press

Carnarvon, like many of his political colleagues, was aware of the importance of the press in opinion formation. He kept in contact with some of the leading journal and newspaper editors, a tactic that roused some suspicions in the Conservative ranks. Disraeli's private secretary, Algernon Turnor, wrote to Ponsonby shortly after Carnarnvon's resignation in 1878, expressing the Prime Minister's concern at events in the Cape: 'The troubles commenced by Lord Carnarvon, who, he says, lived mainly in a coterie of Editors of Liberal papers who praise

[384] Diary, 14 July 1889.
[385] Carnarvon to Churchill, 1 August 1889: Randolph Churchill Papers, Add. MS 9248/24/3230.
[386] Diary, 14 July 1889.

him and drink his claret.'[387] While this is an overstatement of the case, it is true that Carnarvon was not always as discreet as he might have been. Invitations for weekends at Highclere were common; among the guests were J.T. Delane, editor of *The Times*, John Walter, the paper's proprietor, and Frederick Greenwood of the *St James's Gazette*. Carnarvon's correspondence also contains many acknowledgments from grateful editors, such as that from Edwin Arnold of the *Daily Telegraph* for the receipt of game and haunches of venison.[388] When W.T. Stead, editor of the *Pall Mall Gazette*, requested sight of a copy of the secret Colonial Defence Committee's recommendations, Carnarvon replied that he could not wholly refuse, finally capitulated, and sent the information.[389] Furthermore, the contents of confidential telegrams giving the news of the Turkish defeat near Bayazid during the Eastern Crisis were leaked to Delane.[390]

There was also pressure from editors to influence politicians' attitudes. During the crisis over the Franchise Bill in 1884, Stead asked for an interview with Carnarvon. 'He came', Carnarvon wrote afterwards in his diary, 'as far as I could judge mainly to urge on me the policy of some compromise as to the Franchise bill difficulty.'[391] On the other hand, when Carnarvon requested the editor of the *Standard* to advance a policy in a leader column he received a snub.[392] Shortly before Disraeli's death, Alfred Austin, then a leader writer for the *Standard* and later Poet Laureate, had a conversation with him, during which the idea emerged of starting a monthly journal that could promote various aspects of Conservative sentiment and opinion. Austin also suggested the creation of a club called the Cecil, after Salisbury, which was to be the nursery of the magazine. In June of that year W.H. Smith told Carnarvon that he had been

> endeavouring during the last two months to induce two of three business men possessing Capital to embark on an enterprise of a weekly penny newspaper, upholding Conservative principles for the classes who read *Lloyds*, *Reynolds* and the *Referee* [. . .]. I have failed to persuade any one man to attempt the work.[393]

---

[387]Turnor to Ponsonby, 13 May 1878, in Ponsonby, *Henry Ponsonby, Queen Victoria's Private Secretary*, p. 330. A different sort of link that Carnarvon had with the press was through T.H. Escott. The latter, after writing a favourable leader in the *Standard* on a speech by Derby, added, 'You may have heard of my name through my friend and relative, Lord Carnarvon' (Vincent, *Derby*, III, p. 174).

[388]CP, BL 60776–60780.

[389]L. Brown, *Victorian News and Newspapers* (Oxford, 1985), pp. 162–163.

[390]Carnarvon to Delane, 2 May 1877: CP, BL 60779, fo. 26.

[391]Diary, 16 July 1884.

[392]K. Jones, *Fleet Street and Downing Street* (London, 1920), p. 95.

[393]Smith to Carnarvon, 25 June 1881: Herbert Papers, Somerset Archives and Record Service, DD/DRU 2/82.

This was not Carnarvon's first involvement in such an enterprise. In 1866, he had approached Derby, then Prime Minister, with a scheme for 'a first class Conservative daily Paper' under the editorship of William Howard Russell, the editor of the *Army and Navy Gazette*. Derby was not in favour and the subject was dropped.[394] Salisbury was not enthusiastic either. He had for many years contributed to the *Quarterly Review*, where the basic assumption underlying the editorial policy was always Conservative.[395]

Nevertheless, in 1882 Salisbury agreed to Carnarvon's proposal to establish a Literary Committee as part of the Conservative organization; Northcote also gave his blessing. Austin and W.J. Courthope, the latter the author of a book on Alexander Pope, were appointed joint editors.[396] On 27 October, a meeting (with Carnarvon in the chair) was held at the Junior Carlton to launch the new Conservative monthly magazine and the Club. There were about forty people in the audience, including Hardy, Arthur Balfour, Lytton, and a good number of men of letters. Carnarvon urged that all Conservative clubs should be recommended to purchase it. Contributors were to be paid for their articles but not the editors.[397] The first issue of the new journal, named the *National Review*, appeared in March 1883. Its opening two articles were by Austin, on the history and principles of the journal, and by Carnarvon, entitled 'The First of March 1711', which compared the *Spectator* with the *National Review*.

Carnarvon became heavily involved in the running of the journal. In January 1883, he noted in his diary,

> Austin writes to me every day on the fortunes of the new periodical and my correspondence has consequently been largely increased by this. Having begun with the avowed intention of helping to launch the undertaking by presiding at the meeting last summer, I find myself more engaged in it than anyone else, except the two editors. I can only hope that it will succeed.[398]

After six months, the average monthly sale was about 1,300 copies, a reasonable start in the face of strong competition from other

[394]Diary, 21 May 1866.

[395]W.E. Houghton (ed.), *The Wellesley Index to Victorian Periodicals, 1824–1900*, 2 vols (Toronto, 1966–1972), I, p. 697. Salisbury wrote thirty-three articles in all for the *Quarterly*, averaging 15,000 words each, between 1860 and 1883: see P. Smith, *Lord Salisbury on Politics: a selection from his articles in the 'Quarterly Review', 1860–1883* (London, 1972), p. 5.

[396]Carnarvon wrote afterwards, 'The former I like rather less on further acquaintance. The latter gains very much' (Diary, 14 October 1884). Courthope resigned in 1887 on becoming a Civil Service commissioner: see A. Austin, *The Autobiography of Alfred Austin*, 2 vols (London, 1911), II, pp. 175–176.

[397]Diary, 27 October 1882.

[398]Diary, 11 January 1883.

journals.[399] However, it had begun with little capital, and more funds were required. Carnarvon wrote in January 1883 to Lytton, 'There is remarkable apathy even amongst those who attended the meeting. Their promises are melting into air.'[400] At a meeting between Carnarvon and Balfour in June 1884 it was agreed to approach twenty-five people to guarantee £50 each for three years: only Salisbury, Jersey, Percy, Cadogan, W.H. Smith, Balfour, and Carnarvon were subscribers.[401]

The range of topics and quality of contributions was impressive, however: by the end of the first year, there had been articles by Balfour, Hardy, Northcote, Henry Raikes, Salisbury, and Carnarvon. The last, finishing an article for the *Review* on the last day of 1883, noted that this was his fourth piece for the journal that year. Between March 1883 and July 1885, Carnarvon's writings appeared in no fewer than eleven issues.[402] Writing to Cranbrook in December 1884, he stated,

> I am confident that in a political point of view the *Review* is well worth this little risk [of a guarantee] – and much more. It is a standing contradiction to the calumny that the Party is too stupid to have a high Review. It is drawing in a good deal of young talent; it is educating those who need education.[403]

The *Review* continued to be published until 1960.

The final year

Carnarvon was surprised to receive a request from the Cape Government in March 1889 to accept the vacant governorship, if only on a temporary basis. Both Elsie and Robert Herbert were doubtful as to the wisdom of accepting it: Carnarvon's health was still precarious and there were some difficult problems confronting the incoming office-holder. His main concern, however, was that he could not count on the support of his former colleagues. 'If I were to be involved in difficulties, as very likely would be the case,' he wrote, 'Salisbury would, I imagine, be well placed to draw the net tighter round me.'[404] Carnarvon refused the offer, though the Cape Government made a

---

[399] S. Koss, *The Rise and Fall of the Political Press in Britain*, 2 vols (London, 1981–1984), I, p. 249.

[400] Carnarvon to Lytton, 3 January 1883: Lytton Papers, Hertfordshire Archives and Local Studies Office, D/EK C36/147.

[401] Carnarvon was reluctant to continue paying his subscription 'as in the case of other landlords, there never was a time when money was harder to find' (Carnarvon to Edward Stanhope, 23 December 1883: Stanhope Papers, Centre for Kentish Studies).

[402] Houghton, *The Wellesley Index to Victorian Periodicals*, II, p. 536–545.

[403] Carnarvon to Cranbrook, 28 December 1884: Cranbrook Papers, T501/262.

[404] Diary, 22 March 1889.

further approach to him in June of the same year. Ill health had laid him up since January. On 6 May, he once more resumed his many activities.[405] He had been persuaded, with some reluctance, to accept the chairmanship of one of the two Standing Committees of the House of Lords. Farrer Herschell, the Lord Chancellor in Gladstone's last two governments, had been elected chairman of the Law Committee, while Carnarvon took on the General Bills Committee. The work of the latter was onerous, spanning many different topics, such as the drink traffic in Africa, indecent advertisements, the sale of horseflesh, and smoke nuisance.

Carnarvon's spells of illness became increasingly frequent. At the end of 1880, when he was forty-nine, he had written, after a lengthy consultation with his physician, Dr Grabham, 'It seems to me as if I were hanging in a sort of borderland between health and confirmed valetudinarianism and if that is so and I were to become a real invalid, I doubt whether I should last very long.'[406] He tried various cures, including galvanism, courses of colchicum, resting in Portofino, taking the waters at Strathpeffer in Scotland, and driving in the country. On one occasion, he and Elsie made a rural ride to Hendon, Kilburn, and then Maida Vale.[407] Sudden attacks of gout were accompanied by heavy coughing and bouts of rheumatism. Even when he was pronounced fit to resume work, Carnarvon was pessimistic. As early as April 1881 he had remarked, 'I have a sort of warning, a Socratic demon in me, that my old strength is much altered.'[408] On a visit to Greystoke in September 1889, he was unable to move because of what he called his *corpus vile*.

The influenza epidemic of 1890 affected Carnarvon, Elsie, two of his sons (Aubrey and Mervyn), and most of the rest of the household, and a planned holiday to Portofino had to be postponed until March.[409] He contracted influenza once more while abroad and was still unwell when the family returned to England in May. On 14 May, he described his condition: 'I have had a really terrible time since Sunday – rheumatic gout, or rather gouty neuralgia – in one knee – pains in one side of my body everywhere – hopeless torment at night, unable

---

[405] One cause that he enthusiastically supported was the opening of churches on a regular basis in large towns: see Carnarvon to Archbishop Benson, 26 July 1888: Benson Papers, 60, pp. 24–25. He was also an active trustee of the British Museum.

[406] Diary, 4 December 1880.

[407] Diary, 9 May 1887.

[408] Diary, 2 April 1881.

[409] At the end of the month he wrote, 'I shall be very sorry to exchange the beauty and sunshine of this for the equivocal pleasures of an English spring' (Carnarvon to A.J. Mundella, 31 March 1890: Charnwood Papers, BL 70948, fo. 212.)

to sleep'.[410] A fortnight later, he told Sir Henry Acland, 'I have suffered more than I have ever suffered in my life.'[411] Although he had been generally unwell since the beginning of the year, Carnarvon planned to undertake a number of engagements. In February he agreed to act as chairman of the Archaeological Congress at Oxford in July, while in May he attended his last Standing Committee on General Bills. He dined with the Jeunes on 6 May; Randolph Churchill was a fellow diner and they had a 'very friendly' discussion on politics. Two days later, Carnarvon had a fainting attack and from then on was confined to his London house. A welcome visitor on more than one occasion was Gladstone. The conversation on 15 May centred round the sale of Lord Acton's library – consisting of some 80,000 books – following his bankruptcy. Carnarvon wrote after the visit, 'He [Gladstone] is extremely interested in the matter and threw himself with the intense earnestness of his whole nature into it – as if he had nothing else to think of.'[412]

Thirty years later, Carnarvon's medical consultant, E. B. Turner, gave an account to Elsie of her husband's discussions with him during his final weeks. When Turner broke the news that he was suffering from

> a disease to which there could be only one ending [. . .] [i]n no case have I ever been more impressed by the calm, steadfast courage, the resolution and perfect faith shown by one who, being practically under sentence of death, knew and thoroughly realised that fact [. . .] his only care and concern was for others.[413]

The daughter of one of his oldest friends, Sir Robert Phillimore, visited him on 29 June. 'Dear Lord Carnarvon,' she wrote

> quite prepared, waiting for the will of God, desirous to be of rest, happy in himself, saying at intervals, 'I am so happy.' Lady Portsmouth told all this to me [. . .]. He was not in pain but sinking and at 8 p.m. came a Telegram from poor dear Margaret that her father had passed away peacefully at 5.30 p.m.[414]

Conclusion

When Carnarvon was appointed as Colonial Secretary in Derby's government in January 1858, an anonymous leading politician wrote at the time:

---

[410] Diary, 14 May 1890.
[411] Carnarvon to Acland, 26 May 1890: H.W. Acland Papers, MS Acland, d. 86, fo. 30.
[412] Diary, 15 May 1890.
[413] Turner to Lady Carnarvon, 30 July 1921: CP, BL 61060, fos 229–230.
[414] Diary of Charlotte, Lady Phillimore, 29 June 1890: Phillimore Papers, 75 M 91/514/2.

A laborious student, and a finished scholar, his acquirements, to a great extent, made up for his want of originality, while a desire of success may compensate the absence of any striking ability. On the whole, he is a good average Minister, though his early succession to the peerage, and a shy supercilious demeanour, will prevent his achieving the foremost rank or becoming a party leader.[415]

His High Toryism was tempered by a strong conscience, which led to some of his more unfortunate political judgements. Lady Gwendolen Cecil, Salisbury's daughter, praised his character:

All that was not rare and delicate seemed to have been excluded from its composition. He appeared as the embodiment of the traditional knightly virtues; the polish of manner, the perfect courtesy, the scrupulous standard of honour were there; loyalty and courage, chivalry and generosity were salient characteristics. He was even fastidious on the point of honour – uncompromising in his condemnation of failure to reach the standard set.[416]

Carnarvon's two resignations from office when he was a member of the Cabinet were one manifestation of his independence of spirit, though Robert Blake's dismissal of Carnarvon as 'a priggish Puseyite much addicted to resignation' is not totally fair.[417] On leaving the Government in 1878, he told Salisbury, 'You know me of old and that once I have made up my mind on a question like this I am what friends will call obstinate and my opponents perhaps something worse.'[418] Queen Victoria, on hearing of Carnarvon's death, commented in her Journal, 'though not a good politician, he was a very clever, good and accomplished man'.[419]

Although Carnarvon's political manoeuvres made many of his colleagues wary of him, nevertheless he established a good relationship with a select few. Sandon, who had been at Oxford with him and had shared his adventures in the Middle East, was perhaps the one in whom Carnarvon could most readily confide. Northcote, too, was often in sympathy with his views, and Carnarvon's affection for him is clear in his *Times* obituary that followed Northcote's death in January 1887. While finding Ashbourne an admirable colleague as Irish Chancellor, he was unimpressed with his capacity to conduct official business.[420] From the time of his first meeting with Cross at Knowsley in December 1872, Carnarvon and he became political

[415]Quoted in Sir H. Drummond Wolff, *Rambling Recollections*, 2 vols (London, 1908), I, p. 258.
[416]Cecil, I, pp. 221–222.
[417]R. Blake, *The Conservative Party from Peel to Churchill* (London, 1970), p. 106.
[418]Carnarvon to Salisbury, 26 January 1878: Hatfield House Papers, 3M/E.
[419]Queen Victoria, Journal, 29 June 1890: Royal Archives, Z/408.
[420]Diary, 29 October 1886.

allies.[421] With time, however, the bond weakened. Similarly, Salisbury and Carnarvon were the staunchest of allies in the 1860s; by the end of Carnarvon's life, however, Salisbury had become an object of great bitterness. When, in 1876, the possibility of Disraeli's resignation seemed likely because of his ill health, Carnarvon discussed with Sandon some possible successors as Prime Minister. Both Cairns, the Lord Chancellor, and Richmond, the Lord President, were mentioned. Carnarvon agreed with Salisbury's description of Cairns, a self-made man, as 'the great spider',[422] though at the same time he admired Cairns's legal and oratorical skills; Richmond was described as 'being of the same narrow political intellect or rather having the same want of it in political matters'. Both were dismissed as unsuitable.[423] Hicks Beach, especially during Carnarvon's Irish viceroyalty was 'ungracious and ungenial and during my last tenure in office he was a thorn in my side'. At the same time Carnarvon admitted that 'with all his angularities and roughness of temper, I think he was upright and truthful'.[424] Carnarvon's dealings with Cranbrook had been cordial up to 1885, after which they deteriorated, much to Cranbrook's puzzlement.[425]

Carnarvon was complimentary about a number of leading Liberal members. As Colonial Secretary in 1858, he had appointed Gladstone to head a mission to the Ionian Islands; as the decades passed the two men, with many shared literary interests, became closer. In 1888 Carnarvon remarked, after dining with the G.O.M., 'I never remember to have seen him in greater form and not as sometimes used to be the didactic and monopolising the conversation, but giving and taking, and in fact very versatile and agreeable.'[426] He defended the judgement of Dufferin, the Liberal Governor-General of Canada, for his actions in 1874, stating, 'I am naturally disposed to see his merits rather than any past defects.'[427] He also admired Hartington 'for his straightforwardness and, in spite of his Cavendish taciturnity, a sense

---

[421] D.J. Mitchell, *Cross and Tory Democracy* (London, 1991), p. 48.

[422] Diary, 15 July 1875.

[423] Carnarvon, Memorandum, 'Confidential for self', 18 January 1876: Harrowby Papers, 2nd series, lv, fos 181–182.

[424] Diary, 8 March 1887.

[425] Cranbrook Diary, 30 June 1890, Johnson, pp. 772–773.

[426] Diary, 19 June 1888.

[427] Carnarvon to Lord John Russell (copy), 18 September 1874: CP, BL 60792, fo. 2. On becoming Colonial Secretary in Disraeli's second ministry, Carnarvon wrote to Dufferin 'a few lines to assure you how glad I am to have an old friend like yourself in Canada to depend upon in the rather difficult and delicate questions with which we have to deal' (W. Kiewiet and F.H. Underhill (eds), *The Dufferin–Carnarvon Correspondence, 1874–1878* (New York, 1955), p. 1).

of humour'.[428] More surprisingly, he was able to record, following a long conversation he had had with his implacable enemy, John Bright, shortly before the latter's death, that 'I felt glad that I could agree so well with the old man'.[429] When Lord Ripon, President of the Council in Gladstone's 1868 ministry, and a fellow Mason, was received into the Catholic Church in 1874, Carnarvon wrote him a supportive letter: 'Our relations as in everything else have been so steady and agreeable that you might, independent of all other reasons, depend on me.'[430] Farrer Herschell was also described as 'agreeable and reliable, and I am glad to know him better'.[431] Carnarvon met Chamberlain on only two occasions; in their public speeches they had often been critical of one another. After their second meeting, in 1886, Carnarvon noted that Chamberlain had been friendly but considered that 'there is an undercurrent, as it were, in the conversation or perhaps in the pronunciation which is a little vulgar: other wise there is not much to complain of so far as externals go'.[432]

In office, Carnarvon was probably overzealous in his anxiety to deal satisfactorily with the many problems facing a Colonial Secretary. Disraeli, who did not welcome involvement in the detail of colonial policy, complained to Lady Bradford at the end of 1875, 'Carnarvon is in Somersetshire and worries me to death with telegrams of four pages [on Perak]: he is a very clever fellow but the greatest fidget in the world.'[433] During Carnarvon's temporary oversight of the India Office in 1876 (due to Salisbury's mission to Constantinople), Lord George Hamilton, the Under-Secretary, was provided with first-hand experience of Carnarvon's working methods:

> There happened to be a good many questions that required prompt decision and, accustomed as we were to Salisbury's virile and prompt intellect, we were driven distracted by the endless queries, alterations and alternatives that beset every important proposition put before him. He was a high-minded and lovable gentleman with strong moral ideals, but not the stamp of man to deal with a crisis or to fall into the team work necessitated by our party system.[434]

The contradictions in his personality were well described by his friend, Lady St Helier: 'He was too chivalrous a man for the hurly-burly of public life, but with a certain gentleness of character combined with great firmness and absolute adherence to his own

[428] Diary, 23 September 1874.
[429] Diary, 27 March 1889.
[430] L. Wolf, *Life of the First Marquess of Ripon*, 2 vols (London, 1921), I, p. 350.
[431] Diary, 7 October 1888.
[432] Diary, 31 January 1886.
[433] Zetland, I, pp. 312–313.
[434] Lord George Hamilton, *Parliamentary Reminiscences and Reflections, 1886–1906*, 1922, p. 10.

opinion.'[435] On the other hand, he was influenced in his political judgements by the opinion of both his first and second wives, who were strong personalities. Lady Dorothy Nevill remembered Lord Ellenborough saying to her of Evelyn, after Carnarvon had made a particularly brilliant speech, 'She did it! She did it!'[436] Stanley, shortly to succeed as fifteenth Earl of Derby, wrote in his diary in July 1868, 'Another wrangle in the Lords [. . .] Carnarvon, the most bitter and vehement, though not very effective against ministers: it is said his wife pushes him on, being ambitious both of political and fashionable distinction.'[437]

Carnarvon's political views were those of an aristocratic Whig more than a party man, and they remained consistent throughout his career. A *Vanity Fair* portrait of him appeared in 1869, which, while exaggerated, is recognizably accurate:

> Lord Carnarvon is one of those honourable and impractical statesmen, whose honesty stands like a shining beacon to warn the political mariner off the fatal rocks upon which it is built. He believes in the original Tory creed which teaches the maintenance of the prescriptive privileges of the intelligent and propertied few as the best method of governing the poor and unintelligent many, and now that the creed has been solemnly buried by informed professors, he walks like a good and dignified political ghost among a backsliding generation.[438]

His views on Toryism were set out in a speech in 1882, in which he claimed, 'Three-fourths of the literary and four-fifths of the intellectual ability of the country are with us.'[439] Another observer believed that his disposition 'as a man of fine taste and ready sympathy, and naturally given to ideals [. . .] affected to some degree the quality of his statesmanship'.[440]

Among Carnarvon's main achievements was the establishment of a federal constitution for Canada, though he was frustrated at its failure in South Africa. Discussing South African matters with Shepstone in 1883, when in opposition, he observed, 'It is really sad to see how my whole policy, which, in spite of faction and opposition, was gradually ripening to a conclusion, has been torn up by its roots and destroyed.'[441] As a reasonably successful Colonial Secretary, Carnarvon was sad to observe towards the end of his life what he considered

---

[435] S.E.M. Jeune, Lady St Helier, *Memories of Fifty Years* (London, 1909), p. 265.
[436] Nevill, *Reminiscences*, pp. 140–141.
[437] Vincent, *Derby*, I, p. 335.
[438] *Vanity Fair*, 11 September 1869, p. 149.
[439] Address to the Newbury Working Men's Club, 30 September 1882: CP, BL 60856, fo. 138.
[440] T.R. Kebbel, *Lord Beaconsfield and Other Tory Memories* (London, 1907), p. 85.
[441] Diary, 27 May 1883.

to be the failure of his successors in the Office, particularly Hicks Beach ('priggish officialism'), Stanley ('let everything go'), and Holland ('incredibly weak').[442] Reluctantly accepting the poisoned chalice of the Irish viceroyalty, he made himself unpopular with his colleagues while being welcomed in Ireland. His greatest disappointment was his failure to find a successful solution for Ireland. As one Irish contemporary stated, 'He was supposed to be that contradiction in terms "a Tory Home Ruler", but he was only a high minded gentleman who made a genuine attempt to deal with the Irish problem'.[443]

His two resignations from office weakened his credibility within the Party, although he remained loyal when there were Liberal overtures to switch sides. Probably his greatest blunder was to resign over the Russo-Turkish conflict in 1878, though his value to the Party was recognized during the following years, when he returned to the Front Bench. Carnarvon, however, remained convinced that his actions were justifiable. He told Lord Grey five years later, 'I regret and always shall regret the mistake which, I think, Lord Beaconsfield made when I left the Government, for independently of the right or wrong of his policy it broke up the possibilities of a sober Conservative policy in home matters and it practically brought Gladstone into power.'[444] *The Times* neatly summed up Carnarvon's political life in its obituary of him:

> He was not born to lead in troubled times, but he was born to fill a prominent place in our complex society and to keep in touch with many and diverse interests; and now that he has gone the worst that can be said of him is that he was too conscientious for partisanship and too scrupulous for political success.[445]

---

[442] Carnarvon to Harrowby, 10 January 1888: Harrowby Papers, 2nd series, lii, fo. 174.
[443] C. O'Mahony, *The Viceroys of Ireland* (London, 1912), p. 293.
[444] Carnarvon to 3rd Earl Grey, 3 December 1883: Grey Papers, 80/9.
[445] *The Times*, 30 June 1890, p. 10.

MINISTERIAL POSTS HELD

Under-Secretary, Colonies
(PM 14th Earl of Derby

26 February 1858–11 June 1859
21 February 1858–11 June 1859)

Colonial Secretary
(PM 14th Earl of Derby

6 July 1866–8 March 1867
28 June 1866–25 February 1868)

Colonial Secretary
(PM Disraeli

21 February 1874–4 February 1878
20 February 1874–21 April 1880)

Lord Lieutenant, Ireland
(PM Lord Salisbury

27 June 1885–21 January 1886
23 June 1885–28 January 1886)

Forebears and siblings of the 4th Earl of Carnarvon

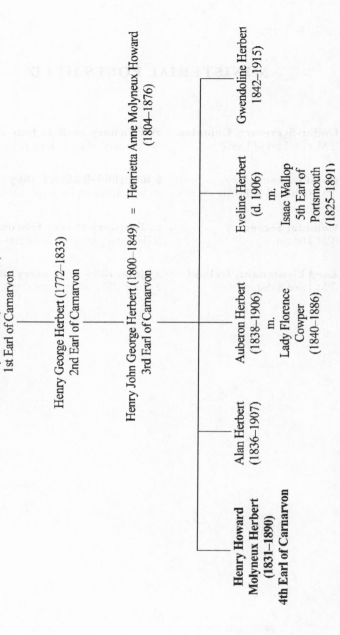

Henry Herbert (1741–1811)
1st Earl of Carnarvon

Henry George Herbert (1772–1833)
2nd Earl of Carnarvon

Henry John George Herbert (1800–1849) = Henrietta Anne Molyneux Howard
3rd Earl of Carnarvon   (1804–1876)

**Henry Howard
Molyneux Herbert
(1831–1890)
4th Earl of Carnarvon**

Alan Herbert
(1836–1907)

Auberon Herbert
(1838–1906)
m.
Lady Florence
Cowper
(1840–1886)

Eveline Herbert
(d. 1906)
m.
Isaac Wallop
5th Earl of
Portsmouth
(1825–1891)

Gwendoline Herbert
1842–1915)

Wives and children of the 4th Earl of Carnarvon

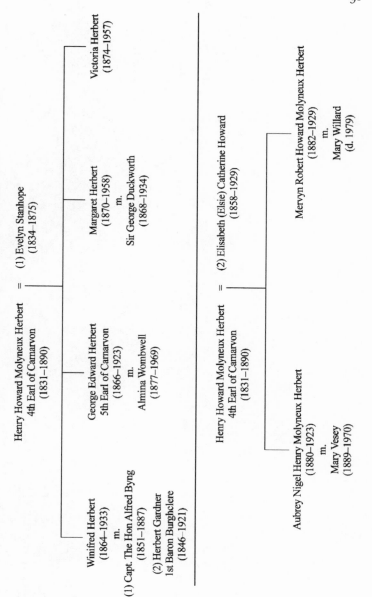

Henry Howard Molyneux Herbert
4th Earl of Carnarvon
(1831–1890)

= (1) Evelyn Stanhope
(1834–1875)

Victoria Herbert
(1874–1957)

Margaret Herbert
(1870–1958)
m.
Sir George Duckworth
(1868–1934)

George Edward Herbert
5th Earl of Carnarvon
(1866–1923)
m.
Almina Wombwell
(1877–1969)

Winifred Herbert
(1864–1933)
m.
(1) Capt. The Hon Alfred Byng
(1851–1887)

(2) Herbert Gardner
1st Baron Burghclere
(1846–1921)

Henry Howard Molyneux Herbert
4th Earl of Carnarvon
(1831–1890)

= (2) Elisabeth (Elsie) Catherine Howard
(1858–1929)

Mervyn Robert Howard Molyneux Herbert
(1882–1929)
m.
Mary Willard
(d. 1979)

Aubrey Nigel Henry Molyneux Herbert
(1880–1923)
m.
Mary Vesey
(1889–1970)

1857

Wednesday 16 September

During this Session I have become intimate with some persons of whom I knew comparatively little before. The Dunravens[1] I have seen constantly and a great intimacy has from peculiar causes grown up there.

I spent several days with Sir E. B. Lytton,[2] with whom I found many points in common. He has been very agreeable and I have known him better than I expected. Stanley[3] sought me out – for his character is so peculiar that I have always feared to be the first to make advances – this summer in London to propose various plans of foreign travel together. These, from the divorce bill,[4] the lateness of the Session and other reasons, fell through: but he subsequently paid me a visit of several days at Highclere, where I learnt to know more of him than any former occasion permitted.

Many old friends have married this year – Robert Cecil, Lothian, Shaw Stewart, H. Jenkinson, Egerton etc, but others such as Lygon and Sandon[5] I have often seen from their now being in Parliament. This concentration of those for whom I have a real affection has been

[1] Edwin Richard Wyndham-Quin (1812–1871), 3rd Earl of Dunraven (1850), archaeologist and antiquarian; and his wife, Augusta.

[2] Edward George Earle Lytton-Bulwer (1803–1873), 1st Baron Lytton (1866), novelist and statesman. Con. MP for Hertfordshire (1852–1866), Colonial Secretary (May 1858–June 1859). Among his many novels are *The Last Days of Pompeii* (1834) and *Rienzi* (1835).

[3] Edward Henry Stanley (1826–1893), 15th Earl of Derby (1869). Con. MP for Kings Lynn (1848–1869), Under-Secretary for Foreign Affairs (1852), Colonial Secretary (February–May 1858), Secretary of State for India (1859), Foreign Secretary (1868 and 1874–1878). Left Conservative Party in 1880; Colonial Secretary in Gladstone's government (1882–1885), Leader of Liberal Unionists, House of Lords (1886–1889).

[4] The Matrimonial Causes Bill, popularly known as the Divorce Bill, introduced in the spring of 1857 by Palmerston, would allow, for the first time, for a divorce to be obtained in a court of law. It was much opposed by the Church and Gladstone, but was eventually passed by the Commons on 25 August (see S. Walpole, *The History of Twenty-five Years*, 4 vols (London, 1904), I, pp. 94–105). Carnarvon spoke against the bill several times during its passage.

[5] Robert Arthur Talbot Gascoyne-Cecil (1830–1903), Viscount Cranborne (1865) 3rd Marquess of Salisbury (1868); Secretary of State for India (1866–1867, 1874–1876), Foreign Secretary (1878–1880), Leader of Opposition, House of Lords (1881–1885), Leader of the

a great source of pleasure during my London life [. . .]. If I live to the close of another 12 months, the comparison of that year with the past will be interesting and I hope useful to me.

When I review the last six or seven months as a whole and compare them with my first Session of Parliament in 1854 I do not think I am mistaken in supposing that I have made an advance. How far I am myself capable of doing more than I was able to do is another question: but even there I think there has been considerable progress and certainly greater self-confidence, the absolute condition to success in life. I have acquired *valent quantum* – a certain position in the House of Lords and generally, and though now exiled from all chance of office by adherence to a broken and mastless party I am expected, as I cannot avoid knowing, to succeed eventually; and this is no mean auxiliary to success. For myself I scarcely know whether to wish for success or not.

Conservative Party (1885–1902), Prime Minister and Foreign Secretary (1885–1886), Prime Minister (1886), Prime Minister and Foreign Secretary (1887–1892, 1895–1900), Prime Minister and Lord Privy Seal (1900–1902). William Schomberg Robert Kerr (1832–1870), 8th Marquess of Lothian (1841). Sir Michael Robert Shaw-Stewart (1836–1903), Con. MP for Renfrewshire (1855–1865). Henry T. Jenkinson, barrister, Carnarvon's cousin. Hon. Wilbraham Egerton (1832–1909), 2nd Baron Egerton (1883), 1st Earl Egerton (1897); Con. MP for Cheshire North (1858–1868) and for Cheshire Mid-division (1868–1883). Frederick Lygon (1831–1890), 6th Earl of Beauchamp (1866), Con. MP for Tewkesbury (1857–1863) and for Worcestershire West (1863–1866), Lord of the Admiralty (March–June 1859). Dudley Francis Stuart Ryder (1831–1900), Viscount Sandon (1847), 3rd Earl of Harrowby (1882); Con. MP for Lichfield (1856–1859) and for Liverpool (1868–1882), Vice-President, Committee of Council on Education (1874–1878), President of the Board of Trade (1878–1880), Lord Privy Seal (1885–1886). The majority of these were Carnarvon's Eton and/or Christ Church, Oxford contemporaries.

1858

Wednesday 24 February

I received a letter from Lord Derby[6] requesting me to call upon him between 5 and 6 in the evening. At that hour I found him in the library surrounded with heaps of papers and with Colville[7] sitting at the same table engaged in writing or copying for him. He came at once to the point and offered me the Under Secretaryship of the Colonial Office. I replied at once that I hoped he would allow me to speak quite frankly to him, that I felt the kindness which had made him propose the post, that I owed him gratitude for the encouragement and assistance which before now he had given me in the House of Lords and which had led me on in the first instance, that whatever he wished as regards office that I would do, that I placed myself entirely in his hands, but that I thought it was due to my strong feelings on one point to ask him the intentions of the Government as to Lord Palmerston's[8] Conspiracy bill.[9] Did they propose to take it up and carry it or to throw it over at once.

He replied that he could satisfy me on this head, that it was intended to write to the French Government to require an explanation of Walewski's Despatch and that having obtained an *amende* from the

---

[6]Edward George Stanley (1799–1869), 14th Earl of Derby (1851), Chief Secretary for Ireland (1830–1833), Colonial Secretary (1833–1834, 1841–1845), Prime Minister (1852, 1858–1859, 1866–1868). Derby had assumed office on 21 February.

[7]Charles John Colville (1818–1903), Lord Colville of Culross (1849), 1st Baron Colville (1885), 1st Viscount Colville of Culross (1902), Master of the Buckhounds (1866–1868), Whip, House of Lords.

[8]Henry John Temple (1784–1865), 3rd Viscount Palmerston (1802), Tory MP for Newport (1807–1811), for Cambridge University (1811–1831), for Bletchingly (1831–1832), and for Hampshire South (1832–1834), Con. MP for Tiverton (1835–1865), Secretary of State for War (1809–1828), Foreign Secretary (1830–1834, 1835–1841, 1846–1851), Home Secretary (1852–1855), Prime Minister (1855–1858, 1859–1865).

[9]The Conspiracy to Murder Bill had been introduced by Palmerston following the near assassination of the French emperor Napoleon III in Paris on 14 January 1858. The plot had been devised in England. Palmerston was criticized in the Commons for not replying to a despatch by Count Walewski, the French foreign minister, urging the Government not to allow abuse of the right of asylum. The Government were defeated by 234 to 218 votes and Palmerston resigned three days later, on 19 February (*Hansard*, CXLVII, col. 1847).

French Government he would then be able to proceed with the measure. I urged as quietly and deferentially as I could my strong objections to the bill, the decided repugnance to it on the part of the country, of the Conservatives themselves, and of the radical press at this moment inclined to support him. He answered, "I will not have a war with France", in a tone which made me decide to close the conversation and I rose to go expressing my regret that after sitting on his side and agreeing on almost every subject for the last three years I should now for the first time be unable to concur. He then seemed to soften and begged me not to decide at once but to think it over during the next day, to consult Lord Salisbury[10] "or better consult yourself," and if possible to join him, that he should be very sorry if on such an account he had not my support.

I left him and went at first to Sir William Heathcote[11] who is well aware of my views on the subject of this bill and who has entirely agreed with me from the first, and then to Lord Salisbury. He argued out the case with me, admitting that my view was a very strong one but always fell back on the fear of a quarrel with France, therein reflecting the feeling which influenced the Cabinet and probably emanates from Lord Derby. I dined at the Colchesters'[12] that evening and found the solution of the difficulty, for Walpole[13] and Eglinton[14] were both there. Both had heard of my objections and discussed the question with me and whether I should have felt that their wishes that I should join were sufficient to make me give up this scruple I hardly know. I think however that they would have fairly assumed that, after I had stated my difficulty, I should abandon the point, but Walpole overcame my doubts by at last assuring me that though the course which the Cabinet would pursue was not quite definite as yet, they did not intend to take up the bill but probably to appoint Committees of both Houses to consider if any and what alteration of the law should be made. This relieved my mind and when I found on the following morning that Sir W. Heathcote agreed in thinking that I ought to join Lord Derby I wrote at once an acceptance of his office.[15]

[10] James Brownlow William Gascoyne-Cecil (1791–1868), 2nd Marquess of Salisbury (1823), Lord Privy Seal (1852), Lord President of the Council (1858–1859).

[11] Sir William Heathcote (1801–1881), Con. MP for Hampshire (1826–1832), for Hampshire North (1837–1849), and for Oxford University (1854–1868). He was Carnarvon's guardian.

[12] Charles Abbot (1798–1867), 2nd Baron Colchester (1829), Paymaster-General (1852–1853), Postmaster-General (1858–1859).

[13] Spencer Horatio Walpole (1806–1890), Con. MP for Cambridge University (1856–1882), Home Secretary (1852, 1858–1859, 1866–1867).

[14] Archibald William Montgomorie (1812–1861), 13th Earl of Eglinton (1819), Earl of Winton (1859), Lord Lieutenant of Ireland (1852–1853, 1858–1859).

[15] Carnarvon to 14th Earl of Derby, 25 February 1858: Derby Papers, 920 DER (14) 163/5A.

Saturday 27 February

Commencement of official life. I found Stanley at the Colonial Office at 12 o'clock and we discussed all the necessary arrangements.

Monday 1 March[16]

During the whole of this week I have been engaged at the Colonial Office. At first pressure of work to keep pace with Stanley and to read the greater portion of what was supplied has been considerable. Under ordinary circumstances when work is slack I fancy that from 11 to 4.30 o'clock will not be at all too long.

I began official work with Stanley as my principal. I wrote to ask him his wishes on certain points and I received in reply a very cordial assurance in which he said that he was very glad to have me in his Office: and during the whole time that I served under him I found him very friendly. On one or two occasions I doubted his inclination to give me full opportunities for doing justice to myself, but I am now disposed to believe that what I mistook for an inclination to hold me back was in truth but an extreme caution on his part, joined to the love as far as possible of doing all the work himself. He was really indefatigable in his application to business and generally fair and patient in hearing all that was to be said on a subject, in intention just, not very rapid in conception or even in seeing the whole bearing of a case at a glance but singularly clear in his distinctions and statements when once he had considered the matter.

At times towards the close of his stay in the Colonial Office he talked freely to me on many subjects, gave me some of the credit for my own work and referred long and intricate cases to me to enquire into for him. He was certainly in point of capacity at the head of the Office, and I was surprised to find when he left so general a feeling of regret at his loss.

The work itself I find it harder to describe. At first, I thought it severe and heavy in character but the necessity which Stanley's rule imposed, of clearing each day's work off by the evening, was very useful to me. It compelled me to do something: and brought me regular habits which have been salutary both to myself and to the Office.

I was struck by the manifold character of the business – the great difference in the subject matter of the several colonies, the large questions of Government and principle which were constantly involved, and by the smaller proportion of insignificant detail than I had originally

---

[16]Carnarvon began this entry in March 1858 and continued it, without a new date, until later in the year.

expected. My position was an easy one, for before long I saw that Stanley was master of his work, and that if I chose to evade giving an opinion it was in my power to do so. Whilst therefore his superior workmanship raised my own standard – at least in estimation – the security which I felt in his not overlooking any point of importance may often have come in as the advocate of indolence and indecision.

Since then my position has materially altered and I feel it necessary now to understand and advise on every question which arises. I feel that my opinion is looked for and that it is important in its effect upon the ultimate decision. This too may have its advantages and disadvantages. Acting for myself and advising with the knowledge that in nine cases out of ten my advice will be taken, I am in danger of taking myself as my own standard instead of having a higher one continually before my own eyes: but on the other hand, I am under a greater sense of responsibility and under the necessity of forming an opinion on the several questions as they arise.

When Cardwell's Resolution in the House of Commons[17] fell to the ground it became necessary to fill the vacancy which Lord Ellenborough's resignation had created.[18] The negotiations were long and protracted. Gladstone[19] was again asked to join us and I believe that in his heart he desired it. Mrs. Gladstone[20] talked the matter over with me and made no secret of her wish that a junction should be effected. S. Herbert,[21] with whom I dined on the second night's debate in the House of Commons, though not so hostile to us as

[17] Edward Cardwell (1813–1886), 1st Viscount Cardwell (1874), Lib.-Con. MP for Clitheroe (1842–1847) and for Oxford City (1853–1874), President of Board of Trade (1852–1855), Chief Secretary for Ireland (1859–1861). The motion in the Commons, urging the House to abstain from expressing an opinion on the situation, was on 14 May (*Hansard*, CL, col. 686).

[18] Edward Law (1790–1871), 2nd Baron Ellenborough (1819), 1st Earl of Ellenborough (1844). Governor-General of India (1841–1844), four times President of the Board of Control (1828–1830, 1834–1835, 1841, 1858); resigned the latter post on 5 May 1858 for publicizing a despatch to Lord Canning, Governor-General of India, criticizing the latter's proclamation, without first consulting colleagues. See A.L. Imlah, *Lord Ellenborough* (Cambridge, 1939), pp. 251–261.

[19] William Ewart Gladstone (1807–1898), Con. MP for Newark (1832–1846), Peelite MP for Oxford University (1847–1865), Lib. MP for Lancashire South (1865–1868), for Greenwich (1868–1880), and for Midlothian (1880–1895). President of the Board of Trade (1841–1845), Colonial Secretary (1845–1846), Chancellor of the Exchequer (1852–1855, 1859–1866, 1873–1874, 1880–1882), Leader of the House of Commons (1865–1866), Prime Minister (1868–1874, 1880–1885, 1886, 1892–1894), Lord Privy Seal (1892–1894).

[20] Catherine Gladstone (1812–1900), daughter of Sir Richard Glynne of Hawarden Castle, Flintshire. For her interest in Indian affairs, see M. Drew, *Catherine Gladstone* (London, 1919), p. 145.

[21] Sidney Herbert (1810–1861), 1st Baron Herbert of Lea (1861). Con. MP for Wiltshire South (1832–1861), Secretary of State for War (1843–1846, 1852–1855), Colonial Secretary (February 1855, but resigned after a fortnight).

Mrs. Herbert wished to make him, was decidedly opposed. And so, after many attempts, and a reference to Sir James Graham,[22] the Gladstone negotiations broke off and Stanley was named Minister to the India Board. He was anxious, and felt the greatness of the task he undertook – and certainly, since he has been in Office, his conduct has shown remarkable ability and vigour. He wished me to accompany him to the India Board but Baillie[23] would not resign.

Stanley's removal from the Colonial Office[24] left a Cabinet seat at the disposal of the Government. Sir Edward Lytton was the choice. He had originally been offered office, and indeed he had long before been promised it, when Lord Derby undertook to form his Government. He had accepted it with great satisfaction: but within twenty four hours, the news came to London that his re-election would be opposed by Cowper,[25] or some Whig candidate if the Hertfordshire magnates would give him the necessary sum. This was at once communicated to Lord Derby, who, unfortunately as I think, instead of sending for Lytton or communicating with him personally, sent a message to him, saying that he could not expose the new government to the danger of a contest. Lytton of course withdrew, but he was very much annoyed, and when I dined with him a fortnight afterwards, he prophesied a speedy dissolution of the administration and denounced Disraeli's financial intentions. Now on this second and unexpected opening he curiously enough regained the office originally destined for him.

The change has been a very considerable one as affecting me: but I do not feel that I in any way regret it. I have found Sir Edward so thoroughly friendly, kind, disposed to treat me without jealousy or reserve and to place great confidence in me that working under him has been on the whole very pleasant. His speeches on colonial matters have been remarkably good but his powers of administration are by no means equal. He has no great capacity for business, or method in the small details and arrangement of the daily work, his ideas succeed each other when he takes up keenly any subject too rapidly and his plans undergo too many changes. But his views, when once he has a question fairly before him, are broad and in his sympathies he is far more human than Stanley, who sometimes seemed to have none, except his particular idol, "public opinion." Hayward[26] one day told

---

[22] Sir James Graham (1792–1861), Leading Peelite MP for various constituencies, Home Secretary (1841–1846), First Lord of the Admiralty (1852–1855).

[23] Henry James Baillie (1804–1885), Under-Secretary of State for India, previously Joint Secretary of the Board of Control until March 1858.

[24] On 4 June.

[25] William Francis Cowper (later Cowper-Temple) (1811–1888), Lib. MP for Hertford (1835–1863), Vice-President, Committee of Council on Education (1857–1858).

[26] Abraham Hayward (1801–1884), essayist and journalist.

me that, as a young man, Bulwer was very irritable and impatient – if so he has checked and greatly modified the tendency; for though now, occasionally he is quick in speech, it is not to any great extent.

I pointed out to Stanley in a minute of which he approved that the only logical and satisfactory mode of dealing with the abuses [of Chinese Coolie traffic] existing under the present system would be, to permit as now, but under somewhat more stringent regulations, the export of Chinese labourers to English Colonies, but to prohibit it absolutely – so far as English ships are concerned – to any foreign port.[27] Stanley concurred in this view and was prepared to bring in a Bill. When Lytton succeeded to the C.O. I brought the matter before him, and having obtained his assent and the permission, as time was pressing, to introduce it in the House of Lords, I took advantage of a motion of the Bishop of Oxford's[28] to make a statement as to the horrible abuses which do exist in the trade as carried out in English ships to Cuba. Lord Derby was fortunately absent from the House, being laid up with gout, and therefore I had my own way: but not, as may be supposed, much to the satisfaction of my friends on the Treasury Bench – and perhaps it was rather cool in me to take this sort of line *sponte mea*. However, it paved the way to the Bill – which a few days after, I introduced and passed almost without discussion through the House.[29] But on its arrival in the House of Commons a different fate was in store for it. It was at once attacked by the representatives of British shipping – who would, as Lytton once said to me, be ready to sell their grandmothers for a consideration – and after seeing deputations, and writing, and talking, and explaining, *usque ad nauseam*, we were obliged to withdraw the Bill in order to prevent it being rejected, on the ground of the lateness of the Session.

I succeeded in passing three larger measures, all of very considerable importance: 1. The Medical practitioners bill 2. The Local Government bill and the 3rd the bill for the establishment of civil government in the new Colony of British Columbia.[30] But my

---

[27] Although slavery had been officially banned in the British Empire since 1834, a system of indentured labour, employing 'coolies', akin to slavery, had been allowed.

[28] Samuel Wilberforce (1805–1873), Bishop of Oxford (1845–1869), Bishop of Winchester (1869–1873).

[29] Wilberforce had moved an Address for the production of correspondence between the Colonial Office and the Government of Hong Kong and between the Colonial Office and the Foreign Office on the subject of emigration from Hong Kong and China to the British West Indies and other possessions since 1 January 1856: see *Hansard*, CLI, 2 June 1858, cols 70–73, and cols 73–80 for Carnarvon's reply.

[30] An Act to Regulate the Qualifications of Practitioners of Medicine and Surgery; the Local Government Act; and an Act to Provide for the Government of British Columbia: all received the Royal Assent on 2 August 1858 (*Hansard*, CLI, col. 2369).

greatest triumph in the way of legislation was the *Jew Bill*[31] which passed under the name of Lord Lucan[32] but was my suggestion and framing in the first instance. When I now after the lapse of several months look back to this I do not regret having solved, as I may fairly say that I did solve, this question which was becoming an awkward and irritating one. Certainly I did good service to the Government by removing from their path a question which threatened to embarrass them during the recess and the next Session.[33]

The advantages of the measure were chiefly these. The bill, though logically perhaps inconsistent, yet admitted the Jews to Parliament whilst at the same time it saved the honour of the House of Lords. It was a compromise which after all under a constitutional Government is the only course when great powers in the State disagree. The Jews gained what they required though little more than what they practically had already obtained. Lord John Russell[34] and Bethell[35] and the troublesome party in the House of Commons were satisfied and at the same time the House of Lords gained two points – the admission of the Jew only to the House of Commons, and his admission not under a law but by a resolution necessarily renewable, if acted upon, every fresh Session of Parliament, and therefore liable to be rescinded if public opinion should change.

The solution, a simple one enough, had occurred to me whilst the bill was being agitated and one day after a conversation with Stanley who alarmed me as to the possible cause of disruption to the Cabinet which the question, if unsettled, contained, I determined to try my scheme. He was sceptical but I immediately propounded it to one or two Peers in the House and the next day I had a visit from Lord Lucan who asked me whether I objected to his undertaking the measure and whether I advised it etc. Of course I highly approved and we launched the measure to the infinite astonishment of Lord Derby, the Treasury Bench, the newspapers and the whole House. The only

[31] An Act to Provide for the Relief of Her Majesty's Subjects Practising the Jewish Religion; first reading, 7 June 1858, Royal Assent, 23 July (*Hansard*, CLI, col. 1967).

[32] George Charles Bingham (1800–1888), 3rd Earl of Lucan (1839), lieutenant-general (1858). Gave orders for the Charge of the Light Brigade at Balaclava in 1854.

[33] Derby allowed a free vote on the bill. Carnarvon warned the Prime Minister that he intended to support it (Carnarvon to Derby, 29 May 1858: Derby Papers, 920 DER (14) 163/5A).

[34] Lord John Russell (1792–1878), 1st Earl Russell (1856), Liberal statesman. Colonial Secretary (1839–1841), Prime Minister (1846–1852), Foreign Secretary (1852–1853), Cabinet without portfolio (1853–1854), Lord President (1854–1855), Colonial Secretary (1855), Foreign Secretary (1859–1865), Prime Minister (1865–1866).

[35] Richard Bethell (1800–1873), 1st Baron Westbury (1861). Lib. MP for Aylesbury (1851–1859) and for Wolverhampton (1859–1861), Attorney-General (1856–1861), Lord Chancellor (1861).

person discontented was old Lord Lyndhurst[36] and he could not get over his disgust at his favourite measure being at last taken out of his mouth and passed in a month and a half – and passed by Lord Lucan! I kept my counsel and though a few persons knew the hand which I had in it the majority were content to believe it to be Lord Lucan's and as he had the trouble of it I was in fairness bound to maintain silence on the subject.

The end of the Session at last arrived when all London was ill with the effect of heat and horrible smells and exhalations from the Thames. The fish dinner and Lord Redesdale's dinner[37] at Greenwich wound up our labours and London became a wilderness. I went for five days to the West of England and commenced a riding holiday with Mr Kent[38] through Cornwall but becoming alarmed at the reports in the newspapers of the state of affairs in British Columbia I went no further than Bude and returned to Downing Street and my work where I have been occupied ever since without interruption beyond Saturdays and Sundays in the country, mainly at home.

---

[36] John Singleton Copley (1772–1863), 1st Baron Lyndhurst (1826). Tory MP for Ashburton (1818–1820) and for Cambridge (1826–1827), Lord Chancellor (1827–1830, 1834–1835, 1841–1846).

[37] John Thomas Freeman-Mitford (1805–1886), 2nd Baron Redesdale (1830), 1st Earl of Redesdale (1877). Chairman of Committees and Deputy Speaker, House of Lords (1851–1886).

[38] John Kent (1807–?), private tutor to Carnarvon when at Eton.

1859

Friday 1 July

Since last I wrote the events of the Session, a change has taken place both as regard myself and the Government. We are no longer in Office though the length of the Session and the obstinacies of the new Ministry are matters of very considerable doubt and uncertainty. Palmerston is once more at the helm and the Tories though stronger as a party both numerically and from the prestige of a successful administration than they have been for many years, are again under the shade of opposition. It remains therefore only to note the main circumstances which have occurred up to the present date.

I spent with the exception of a few days in the country the whole summer, the whole autumn and the winter in London. Merivale[39] left England some time I think in October and Sir E. Lytton was chiefly at Knebworth. His health began to show signs of an incapacity to bear the ordinary amount of business and as Elliot[40] could only deal with the usual work and some few additional subjects the main pressure devolved upon me. This however was what I desired and I do not think that, from that time to the present, during which the general administration of the Office passed into my hands and rested practically with me, I have ever wished it to be otherwise. The experience has been greater than normally falls to the majority of men in my position, and I feel that I have gained considerably by it both in actual knowledge and in a greater sense of self-reliance.

It has also been my good fortune during these 9 or 10 months to steer clear of mistakes and to involve neither the Government nor Sir E. Lytton in any real embarrassment. For the last three months of Office, I may say that I alone managed the Office, as Sir Edward was too unwell to attend to any business and as Merivale was again absent in France: but during the autumn and winter, my usual plan of proceeding was to deal with all matters which I felt required an early settlement and either to refer to Sir E. Lytton only those affairs on which it was absolutely necessary that he should be informed or to refer them in such an advanced stage that there need be little or

---

[39] Herman Merivale (1806–1874), Permanent Under-Secretary for the Colonial Office (1848–1859) and for the India Office (1859–1874).

[40] Sir Thomas Elliot (1808–1880), Assistant Under-Secretary, Colonial Office (1847–1868).

no delay in securing their completion. Nevertheless, I have frequently felt that the responsibility which I thus assumed, though absolutely necessary, was a severe burden, and called for no slight exercise of tact and discretion towards him.

During the autumn, the Canadian, the Nova Scotian and the New Brunswick Ministers came to this country to discuss with the Imperial Government the schemes for a federation of the North America Colonies and the completion of the Intercolonial Railway.[41] The first of these, I soon ascertained, originated only in the necessities of local politics and of the Canadian Government who were trembling on the verge of dissolution: the second practically amounted to the demand for a large pecuniary contribution from the funds of this country to a great Speculation, which however useful and comprehensive in its objects was hardly worth £1,500,000 at our hands. Both questions were considered with care and attention and I have by me most of the confidential papers and minutes on which it was decided to decline a compliance with the several schemes. But there was this difference, that whilst a gift of money would be refused broadly on financial grounds, it was necessary to evade rather than refuse the proposal of Federation which rested on and could be argued only on political reasons.

An opening for this was fortunately found in the evident contrariety and interests on the part of several North American Colonies and the reluctance of Nova Scotia and New Brunswick to come into the proposal, afforded us the opportunity of shelving the question, which I think ought never to have been brought forward by Sir E. Head[42] in Canada without the express sanction of the Secretary of State as was undoubtedly the case.

Failing however as the Canadian Ministers did in the political objects of their mission, I do not think that they returned home altogether discontented. Sir Edward asked them to spend a few days with him at Knebworth and I afterwards invited them to Highclere where I fortunately succeeded in amusing and pleasing them. Cartier,[43] the Attorney-General and Prime Minister, Galt,[44] who represented the office of Chancellor of the Exchequer, and Ross,[45] were our

[41] For the list of ministers, see Hardinge, I, p. 123.

[42] Sir Edmund Walker Head (1805–1868), Lieutenant-Governor, New Brunswick (1847–1854), Governor-General, Canada (1854–1861).

[43] Sir George-Étienne Cartier (1814–1873), Member, Lower Canada Legislature (1848), Attorney-General, Canada East (1856), Prime Minister (1858–1862), Attorney-General (1864), Minister of Militia (1867–1873).

[44] Alexander Tilloch Galt (1817–1893), Inspector-General (1858–1862), Minister of Finance, Canada (1867–1872), High Commissioner in England (1880–1883).

[45] John Ross (1818–1871), Solicitor-General, Canada West (1851–1854), Leader and Speaker of the Legislative Council (1854–1856), Receiver-General (1858), President of the Executive Council and Minister of Agriculture (1858–1862).

guests and on the whole they were agreeably and easily disposed to be pleased with any civilities on our part. I subsequently asked the Nova Scotian Prime Minister, Tupper, and Smith and Fisher;[46] the New Brunswickers, to Highclere and succeeded also in pleasing them. I am indeed convinced of this, that a Colonial Minister in this country with sufficient tact and etc. might produce an influence on the minds of Colonists which as yet has had no precedent. Their experience of England where they know no one of any position and where they receive none of the courtesies and attention which can so easily be paid is very dull, and their knowledge of the Colonial Office where Merivale sees them and talks to them on little else than public business and where the Secretary of State can give them but five or ten minutes conversation is little less prepossessing in favour of the Mother Country. I have uniformly found that the little attention which I was able to show was repaid tenfold by the disproportionate gratitude which it called for and Sir Edward's particular felicity of expression in all his speeches on Colonial subjects far above the level of a vast majority of Colonial Ministers for many years past – produced a satisfactory impression. In this manner, the Canadian dinner at which we both were present was very successful. My speech which I was not myself disposed to rate highly, was certainly extremely successful and won considerable praise from Lytton.

But as the autumn wore on an important event took place in which I had some considerable share. Affairs for a long time past had been growing more and more perplexing in the Ionian Islands where the Grey–Seaton Constitution of 1849 was bearing the fruits of its impractical nature.[47] Sir E. Head had declared that it was "workable by human power" and Sir J. Young[48] with good temper and a general good disposition to do what was right by the Islands, was alike ignorant of the work to be done and incompetent to perform it, even if dictated by others. One error led to another and before long confusion became so inextricable that it was even then that the mistakes could only be

[46]Sir Charles Tupper (1821–1915), Con. Member, Legislative Council, Nova Scotia (1855), Prime Minister (1864–1867), member of the federal Cabinet (1870), Minister of Railways and Canals (1879–1884), Prime Minister of Canada (1896). Sir Albert James Smith (1822–1883), member of Executive Council, New Brunswick (1854–1862), Attorney-General (1861–1862). Charles Fisher (1808–1880), leader of the New Brunswick reform movement (from 1837), Prime Minister (1854–1861).

[47]Drawn up by John Colborne (1778–1863), 1st Baron Seaton (1839), Governor, Ionian Islands (1843–1849) and Sir Henry Grey (1802–1894), Viscount Howick (1807), 3rd Earl Grey (1845), Colonial Secretary (1846–1852). The constitution of May 1849 established a new system of government, allowing for freedom of election to the Assembly, voting by ballot, and the reduction of qualifications for the franchise.

[48]Sir John Young (1807–1876), Baron Lisgar (1870). Con. MP for Co. Cavan (1831–1835), Chief Secretary of State for Ireland (1852–1855), Lord High Commissioner, Ionian Islands (1855–1859); he opposed union with Greece.

corrected by some fresh person on the spot. I disagreed indeed with the view which Sir E. Lytton took of the course to be pursued and was in favour of more stringent measures than any which he would sanction but before long the matter passed beyond the stage of consultation and forced upon us the alternative either of recalling Sir J. Young or of sending some special Commissioner to enquire into the state of things, and suggest remedies and if necessary to act. Many names occurred to us but among others I suggested that of Gladstone.

I have become aware through R. Phillimore[49] earlier in the year that he was growing restless of inaction – at least, this was my inference – and that he was actually ready to accept the Embassy to Naples if, as was then the report, we were on the eve of renewing diplomatic relations with the Neapolitan Court. At that time I mentioned this to Malmesbury[50] as I considered it right that he should know it. He however only replied that relations were not to be renewed, but if they were, the sending of Gladstone after the course which he had adopted on Neapolitan affairs "would be a diplomatic impossibility". This therefore fell to the ground; but the wish to attach Gladstone to the Government and the Party remained strongly in mind as I had fair ground for supposing that if he were really willing to go as Minister to Naples he might not be indisposed to undertake a special Commission on the case of a nation or country where his sympathies were more warmly enlisted even than they were in that of Poerio and the Neapolitan prisoners.[51]

I accordingly proposed to Sir E. Lytton that he should write to him to make him the offer and etc; after much consultation it was decided in the affirmative and a note was despatched to Gladstone which found him on a visit at Lord Aberdeen's.[52] He wrote cautiously but came up to town and when night had fairly closed in a long November evening he made his appearance at the Colonial Office under the cover of the friendly shades. Two weeks or so then followed of endless explanations, conversations, interviews and letters and it

[49]Sir Robert Phillimore (1810–1885), Lib.-Con. MP for Tavistock (1852–1857), Judge, High Court of Admiralty (1867), created baronet (1883).

[50]James Howard Harris (1807–1889), 3rd Earl of Malmesbury (1841). Foreign Secretary (1852, 1858–1859), Lord Privy Seal (1866–1868, 1874–1876), Con. Leader in the House of Lords (1868).

[51]Carlo Poerio (1803–1867), politician, lawyer, and poet. Minister of Education, Naples (1848–1849); resigned, and then led parliamentary opposition to Ferdinand II. He was arrested and sentenced to nineteen years' imprisonment in chains. Gladstone's report in 1851, drawing attention to the inhumane conditions under which Poeiro and the other political prisoners were being held, caused an international furore.

[52]George Hamilton-Gordon (1784–1860), 4th Earl of Aberdeen (1801). Peelite Leader, House of Lords (from 1846), Prime Minister (1852–1855). For a fuller background of events leading to the offer to Gladstone, see Diary, 8 January 1884.

was to the astonishment of all London suddenly made known one morning in the papers that Mr Gladstone was to proceed as High Commissioner Extraordinary to the Ionian Islands.

When once the decision was taken all the steps preliminary to embarkation were rapidly hurried over. But scarcely had Gladstone left this country when a great catastrophe took place which disturbed all our calculations, nearly brought him back again to England, and certainly neutralised the object and intention of the mission. The confidential despatches and papers bearing on the various Ionian questions had been confidentially printed for our use, and one of the copies was seen, through the carelessness of the Librarian in the Library by an unprincipled friend, who stole the document and conveyed it to the *Daily News*, the Editor of which very much to his discredit gave it publicity in his columns.[53] The despatch was precisely the one which at that moment it was desirable should never see the light, and advocating as it did the abandonment of the Protectorate over the southern islands, it was supposed to give the key to Gladstone's mission, its publicity was attributed to design on the part of the Government, and the ferment and confusion which it created here, at the foreign Courts and in the Ionian Islands were very great. Gladstone unquestionably behaved well: for though his friends were indignant and chose to attribute every unworthy and fraudulent motive to the Government, urging him in letters to throw up the mission and to return, he at once stated his belief in our honesty and proceeded to his original destination.

In the due course of time he arrived there to meet an excited people in the Ionians who were persuaded that annexation to Greece was at hand in the persons of Sir John and Lady Young, who gave him no cordial welcome. The accounts of Mr A. Gordon[54] who accompanied G. as private Secretary, of the various encounters and especially among the ladies on either side were highly amusing: but Sir J. Young allowed himself, I think, in one or two instances, to be led too far by his wife. The great gravamen was that no accommodation was provided for Gladstone except two bedrooms and a dressing room!

Time, however, passed on. Gladstone examined and wrote voluminous letters and reports, a large part of which were printed confidentially and give a fair idea of the general course of the inquiry:

[53]Thomas Walker (1822–1895), editor of the *Daily News* (1858–1869) and of the *London Gazette* (1869–1885). See 'Mission of Mr Gladstone to the Ionian Islands', *Daily News*, 5 November 1858, p. 4. The despatch was published in the paper on 12 November.

[54]Arthur Charles Hamilton-Gordon (1829–1912), KCMG (1871), 1st Baron Stanmore (1893). Lib. MP for Beverley (1854–1857), Gladstone's private secretary (1858–1859), Lieutenant-Governor, New Brunswick (1861–1866), Governor of Trinidad (1866–1870), of Mauritius (1871–1874), of Fiji (1875–1878), and of Ceylon (1885–1890).

and step by step it became evident, as the matter developed still further, that Sir J. Young must be recalled and that Gladstone must take the Government of the Islands, provisionally at all events. Numberless points of difficulty arose in carrying this decision into effect. One of the most embarrassing was when Gladstone would not render himself ineligible for a seat in Parliament by accepting a place of emolument even though he did not accept the normal salary attached to the place. This difficulty was at last overcome by the "dodge" of appointing him Lord High Commissioner and delaying the moving of his writ for a new election to the last possible moment. As soon as the writ for a successor was appointed in the person of Sir H. Storks,[55] he was sent to Malta and instructed to issue a power to Gladstone to act as his deputy whilst he remained absent from the seat of his government.

This on the whole was tolerably successful and Gladstone was enabled to bring forward his proposals of reform, the outline of which he had communicated to us in his several reports and despatches. I for one did not agree in the scheme which he proposed and I doubt whether Sir Edward did not consider them misplaced and mistimed in several important particulars; but the difficulty of resisting Gladstone – who was on the spot exercising full powers and ready to turn upon us in England, supported as he would have been by a considerable party of friends and neutrals who would have agreed readily in saying or doing anything to embarrass the Government – was very great and where doubts might reasonably be maintained, I do not blame anyone for striking the balance of these doubts in favour of concurring with and thereby conciliating Gladstone.

I was however questioned by Lord Grey in the House of Lords as to the concurrence of the Government in their proposed reforms and was obliged to answer in the affirmative: on which Lord Grey fixed a day for the discussion of the whole question. I should have been glad to have had the opportunity of thus discussing the matter, inconsistent as the policy was, which I should have been obliged to defend with my own views: but after fixing and re-fixing the days on which the debate should take place it was at last finally deferred *sine die* at the request of Lord Derby who urged the public inexpediency of a discussion in Parliament at the present time. The question curiously enough was never raised in the House of Commons and scarcely had it blown over in our House when the news arrived that the Assembly had refused the offer which Gladstone had made them. I had had during the month before the meeting of Parliament the opportunity of saying a few words upon the subject at the Fishmongers' Dinner, but with the exception of that and of the short discussion in the House of Lords, nothing passed on the Ionian question.[56]

Opportunities of speaking on Colonial matters or indeed on any other matter were infrequent during the winter. Just before the meeting of Parliament, Lytton went to the Australian dinner and I went also. We both spoke but there was less interest than at the Indian meeting. Generally speaking the Australians are men of a lower calibre than the Canadians and the New Zealand Colonists, though intellectually of considerable power, are morally lower than the Australians. This at least has been the inference which I have drawn both from the legislation of the Colonies of Australia and New Zealand and from individuals with whom I have been brought into contact. The New Zealand Colonist is generally cleverer but he is shifty and unreliable, ready to take advantage of you whenever an occasion presents itself and withal very sensitive and even touchy.

During the autumn the Cabinet met very often and I was aware that they were engaged by means of a Committee of their members in framing a Reform bill. I had a general idea of the course which they were about to take and which on the whole was pretty nearly that which they finally adopted. But I felt sure at the time that they were falling into a mistake and I told Lytton as much. The mistake was the taking of such a man as Rose[57] into counsel. I told Lytton that I felt certain that if they trusted to him for figures and calculations they would be mistaken, for he was both sanguine and inaccurate. They, however, consulted him then and they consulted him again, I suspect, as to the dissolution: his opinion was, I know, wrong in the latter, and I believe it was equally incorrect in the former. With February, however, came Parliament and the first real question was Reform. Some few topics as to Jamaican Immigration[58] which the Anti-Slavery Society wished us to disallow and which I had infinite trouble in persuading Lytton to confirm, as to Ionian affairs, and as to the transfer of the Straits Settlement to the Colonial Office,[59] were discussed in the House of Lords, but no debate of importance took place. But with regard to Reform our position became immediately one of very great difficulty.[60]

[56] See *Hansard*, CLII, 17 February 1859, Carnarvon, cols 463–465, Grey, cols 463, 465–466. The Ionian Islands were evacuated and handed over to Greece on 2 June 1864.

[57] Sir Philip Rose (1816–1883), 1st Baronet Rose (1874), Conservative Party agent. He wrote to Disraeli on 12 August 1858, 'I had my first Reform interview with Lord Derby yesterday. It lasted for nearly *three* hours' (Buckle, *Disraeli*, IV, p. 182).

[58] The Jamaican Immigration Act, which had been framed by the Jamaican House of Assembly the previous year, encouraged immigration to the country. Stanley, then Colonial Secretary, had sent it back, but Carnarvon favoured the Act: *Hansard*, CLII, 8 February 1859, col. 170.

[59] Singapore. Resolution. *Hansard*, CLII, 10 March 1859, Carnarvon, cols 1605–1606.

[60] The 1859 Reform Bill left the borough franchise unchanged, reduced the occupation franchise in counties from £50 to £10, transferred the right of voting in regard to town

The debate came on and a junction between Palmerston and Lord John became manifest, and after very able speeches on both sides, the Government was left in a minority of thirty-nine. That the secession of Henley[61] and Walpole was the cause of this large defeat is certainly untrue; but I do not doubt that their secession and the general belief entertained on both sides that there would be no dissolution unless the majority should be a very slender one, contributed to the result. The decision to dissolve was taken on the following day; but not without much opposition and difference of opinion in the Cabinet. Lytton was particularly averse to the measure and when he told me of it afterwards, he went so far as to say that it was the most fatal step since Charles I dissolved his Parliament. Roebuck[62] also, whom I met at the Levée and took home in I my carriage as his own was not to be found, deplored the decision to dissolve, saying that we were ringing our death-knell. For my own part, I felt inclined to regret it also, and had I been in the Cabinet should, I think, have voted for a resignation. I was however otherwise determined and the General Election came on. We were not attacked in North Hampshire as the Whigs could not find one man who could be well put forward but in the Hundred of Cricklade whither I sent Auberon[63] to canvass for Mr Goddard.[64] Sir

freehold from counties to towns where freeholds were located, and did nothing to enfranchise the working classes. On 21 March, in a heated debate in the House, Russell moved an amendment on the bill's second reading. Supported by Palmerston, it was carried on 1 April by 330 to 291 votes. Derby did not resign but decided to fight a general election, which proved to be indecisive. Five days after a meeting with the Liberal Party on 6 June, which cemented the Russell–Palmerston alliance, the Government resigned; Palmerston became the new Prime Minister. See S. Walpole, *The Life of Lord John Russell*, 2 vols (London, 1889), II, pp. 302–309; H.C.F. Bell, *Lord Palmerston*, 2 vols (London, 1936), II, pp. 206–207; J.H. Harris, 3rd Earl of Malmesbury, *Memoirs of an Ex-Minister: an autobiography* (London, 1885), pp. 490–492.

[61] Joseph Warner Henley (1793–1884), Con. MP for Oxfordshire (1848–1871), President of the Board of Trade (1852, 1858–1859). Although it was inevitable that Henley and Walpole's dissatisfaction over the Reform Bill would lead to their resignation, they postponed taking this step, at Derby's request, until late February 1859.

[62] John Arthur Roebuck (1801–1879), Lib. MP for Sheffield (1849–1869, 1874–1879).

[63] Auberon Edward William Molyneux Herbert (1838–1906), Carnarvon's younger brother. Secretary to Stafford Northcote, President of the Board of Trade in Derby's 1866 administration, Lib. MP for Nottingham (1870–1874). Political philosopher and follower of Herbert Spencer. Beatrice Webb called him 'an enthusiast, a Don Quixote of the nineteenth century, who had left the real battle of life to fight a strange ogre of his own imagination – an *always immoral State interference*' (B. Webb, *My Apprenticeship* (Cambridge, 1979, facsimile of 1926 1st edition), p. 189.

[64] Ambrose Lethbridge Goddard (1819–1898), Con. MP for Cricklade (1847–1868, 1874–1880).

John Neeld[65] lost his seat.[66] On the whole we gained some thirty seats which was less than was necessary to retain us in Office.[67]

From this time Lytton, whose health gave way after a very brilliant speech on the Reform bill, withdrew entirely from any part either in the Cabinet or the Colonial Office. His nerves were for the time completely broken and the Doctors thought very ill of him. I had had for several months the chief management of the Office and therefore I found less difficulty in assuring the entire conduct of it, and perhaps all the more that Merivale left England for a month in order to bring back Mrs. M. from Nice.

Under ordinary circumstances there would probably not be very much to be done during such an interval as that which now passed. But there were many points of importance which Lytton had refrained from settling and then I determined at once to deal with, that if, as I expected, the result of Elections should be unfavourable I might hand over the Office clear of arrears to our successors. And this I succeeded in doing, for when the Duke of Newcastle[68] came to the Colonial Office he found nothing except the current business and that which could not by any effort on my part or the part of others be decided without further correspondence. Other matters also of very considerable consequence grew up during these two months with which I had to deal exclusively.

Of these the main affairs which, as far as I can remember that I decided are as follows:

1. *New Zealand Acts*
2. *Increase of Australia Squadron*
3. *Military Defence of the Colonies*
4. *Recall of Sir G. Grey[69] from the Cape.* This was necessitated against my will by Sir G. Grey's perverse disobedience.[70] Among other schemes

---

[65]Sir John Neeld (1805–1891), Con. MP for Cricklade (1835–1859) and for Chippenham (1865–1868).

[66]The election was on 30 April. Goddard headed the poll with 745 votes; Lord Ashley, the Liberal candidate, was second with 743. Neeld attracted only 712 votes.

[67]The new Parliament consisted of 353 Liberals and 302 Conservatives.

[68]Henry Pelham Fiennes Pelham-Clinton (1811–1864), 5th Duke of Newcastle-under-Lyme (1851), Secretary of State for War and the Colonies (1852–1854), Colonial Secretary (1859–1864).

[69]Sir George Grey (1812–1898), Governor-General of New Zealand (1845–1854, 1861–1867) and of Cape Colony (1854–1861).

[70]Grey's autocratic behaviour and public speeches and actions, although popular with the colonies, were condemned by Parliament and officials. He told the South African legislature in 1856, 'The Governor is, by virtue of his office, the Head of all the Departments. The Colonial Secretary, as far as his position has been defined, is merely the pen or mouth of His Excellency, acting by his orders, whatever his own opinions or advice may have been'

which his versatile brain continually produced he had propounded a general scheme for the reannexion of the Orange River Territory and the Boer Free States and their federation with the Cape and B. Kaffrania and Natal. We warned him at once on the 5th Nov. to take no further steps in the matter without our concurrence and instruction. This despatch he acknowledged and subsequent to the acknowledgement wrote again to say that he intended to bring the question before the Cape Parliament. We wrote again very strongly telling him that he had been directed to take no steps in the matter and that we required obedience on the part of a Governor. A month afterwards a formal deputation was received from him stating that he had made the proposal for federation to the Cape Parliament, and that he had advised them to arrange the preliminaries! It was in answer to this that I now wrote to express the disappointment of H. M. Government at this conduct. It had been impossible for me to see Lord Derby, whom I felt that I ought to consult on so serious a matter in Sir E. Lytton's absence, till within an hour of the time when the South African mail closed: and my despatch was written under very great pressure of time. On considering it subsequently I found to my satisfaction that I had not omitted any point and that it generally answered the purpose very well.

We waited for another month for the chance of further explanations from Sir G. Grey and then just before leaving Office we formally recalled him.[71] I was anxious that this should be done as to have left him in his Governorship after this formal disapproval would have seemed, and justly, to be an evasion of our responsibilities and a taking advantage of our position. Lytton offered the Governorship (£6000 per annum) to Sir John Lawrence[72] but he declined it and we left the place open when we withdrew.[73]

5. The next measure was hardly less if at all inferior in importance to those already noted. The *Newfoundland Fishery Question* had become

---

(J. Rutherford, *Sir George Grey, K.C.B., 1812–1898: a study in colonial government* (London, 1961), p. 295).

[71] Lytton to Carnarvon, 30 May 1859: see Hardinge, I, pp. 128–129.

[72] John Laird Mair Lawrence (1811–1879), 1st Baron Lawrence (1869), India Office (1859–1862), Viceroy of India (1863–1869).

[73] After the change of ministry, Grey was reinstated by the Duke of Newcastle, on the understanding that his scheme for the federation of South Africa should be abandoned, and that he would obey instructions issued by the Colonial Office. See G.C. Henderson, *Sir George Grey: pioneer of empire in southern lands* (London, 1907), p. 183.

a serious difficulty, threatening to compromise our relations with the French Government or with the Colony.[74]

6. *Change of Governors*

We made several changes in the Colonial administration which on the whole were advantageous. I say on the whole, because Wolff,[75] Sir E. Lytton's private Secretary, was too much taken by him into council in the distribution of Patronage, and whenever it was possible to intrigue and to make a bad appointment Wolff invariably recommended it. Nothing more surprised me than to see the influence which Sir E. Lytton allowed a man of such inferior mind and character to acquire.[76] For myself, I could not bear his presence and it always required a strong effort of self-command to be civil to a man whom I despised so heartily but whom I felt was from the power which he exercised on matters of patronage and misfortune to the public service. However *requiescat in pace* – he has obtained the grand success of all his intrigues and machinations in the office of Secretary in the Ionian Islands with a salary of £800 per annum.

The two best appointments were Sir B. Pine[77] to St. Kitts and Sir H. Storks to the Ionian Islands.

7. *Transfer of Straits Settlements to the Colonial Office*

8. *The Hudson Bay Company Question*[78] This was one of extreme difficulty and was indeed hardly possible for me to deal with in the absence of Lytton from the Office.

These were the principal points of importance with which I had to deal. The current work of each day I maintained at a fixed level, and when I left Office there were no arrears for our successors. On the whole the last year and a half, though often bringing with it fully as

[74] On the controversy with France over its demands to fish in the region see The Newfoundland Fisheries, *Hansard*, CLII, 10 March 1859, cols 1667–1676.

[75] Sir Henry Drummond Wolff (1830–1908), private secretary to Lytton (February 1858), Secretary to High Commissioner, Ionian Islands (1859–1864), Con. MP for Christchurch (1878–1880) and for Portsmouth (1880–1885).

[76] Wolff appreciated Lytton's relaxed approach to work, appointing 'gentlemen' rather than regular official subordinates 'not liking to trouble his official secretaries with work' (H. Drummond Wolff, *Rambling Recollections*, 2 vols (London, 1908), I, p. 178).

[77] Sir Benjamin Pine (1809–1891), Governor of Natal (1849–1856, 1873–1875), of the Gold Coast (1856–1859), of St Kitts (1859–1869), and of the Leeward Islands (1869–1873).

[78] The Hudson Bay Company had been granted a charter in 1670 for a monopoly of trade over the vast territories in the north of Canada. The Company's licence over the territory was due to expire in 1859, at the same time as the new colony of British Columbia was created. Shortly after leaving office, Carnarvon urged in the Lords that the privileges of the trading company should not be allowed to stand in the way of improved colonization and that the Government should provide means of good communication with Canada and British Columbia (*Hansard*, CLIV, 14 July 1859, Carnarvon, cols 1189–1193).

much work as I could dispose of, has not passed unpleasantly, so far as work can affect one's happiness, and I feel sure that I have gained a very considerable advantage from the experience which it has given me in the transaction of public business and from the very large authority and consequently responsibility which fell to my share. Lytton was in many respects a very agreeable principal in the Office except when difficulties arose and parliamentary opposition was threatened. Under ordinary circumstances I was left to the absolute disposal and management of the affairs of the Office, sending him as little or as much work as I pleased, and at such times the intercourse with him was really very delightful. He treated me with complete confidence and talked all matters over with me, and though he insisted generally on talking upon Colonial subjects – rather than general topics his conversation was equal to that of any man whom I have ever met. But when there was a question of a difficulty or an opposition in Parliament he seemed to lose his judgement. For the time he would be almost distraught and would be willing to sacrifice anything to conciliate a few second or third rate speakers in the House of Commons.

The fact clearly was that he had entered Office too late in life with his habits of mind and character formed and unadaptable to the new state of things, and this with his extreme nervousness and sensitiveness combined to make him quite unfit for the conduct of a large and weighty department. The wish to understand and to act rightly was there, and there was ample ability, but there was want of all training for the task and an absence of firmness to act upon what he easily saw was right. My intercourse with him was generally as I have said most agreeable but on one or two occasions when these difficulties arose, difficulties which were not more frequent with us than they had been to every other administration, we had differences of opinion.

In one instance, and in one only as far as I remember, there was an actual dispute. Lytton allowed himself to be carried away and spoke in terms which I did not consider that he had any right to use towards me. I told him so at once and after a coldness for two or three days he wrote to me begging my pardon and expressing his regret with so much real feeling and kindness that all was well again and I never thought more of the affair.

Lord Derby, who it was occasionally necessary for me to consult during Lytton's absence, I found patient and kindly. Disraeli,[79]

[79] Benjamin Disraeli (1805–1881), 1st Earl of Beaconsfield (1876). Con. MP for Maidstone (1837–1841), for Shrewsbury (1841–1847), and for Buckinghamshire (1847–1876), Leader, House of Commons, and Chancellor of the Exchequer (1852, 1858–1859, 1866–1868), Lord Privy Seal (1876–1878), Prime Minister (1868, 1874–1880).

whenever I met him, was only too civil, and of the other Ministers I saw little *officially*, as I preferred doing business with the permanent Under-Secretaries, who were generally more conversant with the details of each question as it arose.

[On the last page, Lady Carnarvon added: Lord Carnarvon's feeling for Sir E. B. Lytton was a sincere and affectionate one, and this expression of his judgement of Sir E.'s character was for himself alone.]

Saturday 3 March (London)

In the evening talked with Lowe[80] as to the Reform Bill.[81] He spoke of the Whigs as a party with bitterness and of the Govt. with the determination of destroying them if possible somehow. "If your party" he said "are only true the Govt. have not a chance". Anyhow he and some who act with him on his side of the House are decided to vote against the 2nd. reading.[82] He asked me to give him any information I could during the next few days.

I talked also a good deal with Delane,[83] who is only one degree less hostile to the Government. The burden of his conversation was "The crash must soon come, but are you on the other side ready. Have you made your arrangements to succeed?" He was all in favour of being free of Lord Derby as a leader.

Sunday 4 March

When at the Carlton this afternoon Bath[84] came up to me and imparted his apprehension that Disraeli intended to support the Government bill, alleging that Major Edwards[85] had a conversation with D. and that he (D.) had left on him the impression that he could not object to a £15 franchise in the counties and a £6 rating in the boroughs,

[80] Robert Lowe (1811–1892), 1st Viscount Sherbrooke (1880), Lib. MP for Kidderminster (1852–1859), for Calne (1859–1868), and for London University (1868–1880), Vice-President, Committee of Council on Education (1859–1861), Chancellor of the Exchequer (1868–1873), Home Secretary (1873–1874).

[81] For Lowe's manoeuvring at this time, see J. Winter, *Robert Lowe* (Toronto, 1976), pp. 217–218.

[82] Gladstone, then Chancellor of the Exchequer, announced that a Reform Bill for England and Wales was to be introduced on 12 March: *Hansard*, CLXXXI, 5 March 1866, col. 1503.

[83] John Thadeus Delane (1817–1879), editor of *The Times* (1841–1877), wrote to Bernal Osborne, 'Nobody in the Cabinet except Lord Russell and Gladstone have the least hope or desire of carrying the Reform Bill' (A.I.D. Dasent, *John Thadeus Delane, Editor of "The Times": his life and correspondence*, 2 vols (London, 1908), II, p. 166).

[84] John Alexander Thynne (1831–1896), 4th Marquess of Bath (1837). Ambassador to Lisbon (1858) and Vienna (1867).

[85] Possibly Henry Edwards (1812–1886), Con. MP for Halifax (1847–1852) and for Beverley (1859–1868), who favoured a reduction in taxes for the working classes.

I said I thought this was very unlikely. *Bath* however was in a great state of excitement and told me that he "held extreme, very extreme, opinions on religious matters and all that", but that he was ready to waive everything rather than allow the Government bill to pass.

He then asked me whether a meeting of Conservative Peers and Commoners could not be convened. I suggested that Lord Derby and Disraeli were the natural persons to organise such a meeting.

He said the D. of Richmond[86] might in default of the leaders be a person on whom "the party could rally" though he did not much like him personally. I said I did not think the D. of R [would] do anything in opposition to Lord Derby. He then said they must fall back on the D. of Rutland[87] to which I merely said he would find that impossible. He then declared that "if the worst came to the worst the Conservatives must go over to the Whigs, – much as he individually hated them – and make common cause against the Radicals."

I advised him finally to see Lord Derby and press him to call a meeting, for this can do no harm. Further, it will irritate Lord D. into resigning and provoke the crisis which should now come, or Lord D. will consent and discussion will do good.

Tuesday 6 March

Baillie-Cochrane[88] came to me tell me Walpole had told him that if the Government reform bill should be – what is now currently reputed – £20 in Counties and £6 rating in boroughs and the abstraction of one seat from 25 constituencies he could not oppose it.[89] If this is so and Walpole carries his intention into acts it is most serious. Henley would probably go with him and some 15 or 20 on our side. This will effectually paralyse Lowe, Elcho,[90] and some 40 or 50 on

[86] Charles Henry Gordon-Lennox (1819–1903), 6th Duke of Richmond (1860). President of the Poor Law Board (1859), President of the Board of Trade (1867–1869), Lord President of the Council (1874–1880).

[87] Charles Cecil John Manners (1815–1888), 6th Duke of Rutland (1857). Con. MP for Stamford (1837–1852) and for North Leicestershire (1852–1857).

[88] Alexander Dundas Ross Baillie-Cochrane (1816–1890), 1st Baron Lamington (1880), Con. MP for Isle of Wight (1870–1880).

[89] 'Lord Derby and Disraeli from their side are, I think, doing everything they can to wreck the ship' (Carnarvon to Sir William Heathcote, 6 March 1866: CP, BL 61070, fo. 150).

[90] Lord Francis Charles Douglas Elcho (1818–1914), 10th Earl of Wemyss (1883), Con. MP for Haddingtonshire (1847–1883). Elcho informed Lowe that day, 'I heard an alarming piece of intelligence last night. The weak and excellent Walpole considers himself pledged to a £6 rating and a £20 in the counties [. . .]. Horsman told me at dinner that he had heard Walpole was shaky. You must look after him' (Elcho to Lowe, 6 March 1866: Wemyss Papers, Letter 15, fo. 27).

the Liberal side whose accession to us depends upon our remaining united.

The extreme Radicals on their part will accept anything as an instalment and the H. of Lords is not now strong enough to stand out against a considerable majority of the Commons. The Conservative Party will again be split up, the Liberals will carry almost all the constituencies. I have written strongly to Sir W Heathcote pointing out the danger and urging him to use his influence with Walpole and to Denison[91] in the same sense with regard to Henley.

I somehow suspect both Disraeli and Lord Derby. They are both I imagine hampered by the supposed consequences of their Reform bill of 1859. Anyhow the state of things is very critical.[92]

Friday 9 March (London)

I have been for some days anxious as to the Reform bill or rather as to the course which the leaders of the Party are likely to take. Yesterday Lord Derby summoned a House of Commons meeting, talked chiefly about the Oaths bill[93] but also urged the policy of non-committal to anything on the 1st reading of the Reform bill. The meeting generally assented, but later in the day a private meeting was held in the H. of C. at which Disraeli, Northcote,[94] Cranborne, Sir W. Heathcote and Walpole agreed to speak in support of the Liberals who will attack the bill on Monday. This is as it should be.

Last night Lowe dined with us and after dinner I went with him into the whole question. Our conversation was a full and confidential one.[95]

He enumerated to me the names of a good many of the Liberals who are prepared to support him against the bill, amongst them the two

[91]John Evelyn Denison (1800–1873), Speaker, House of Commons (1857–1872), 1st Viscount Ossington (1872).

[92]The bill was introduced on 1 July 1859, but defeated before its second reading.

[93]Parliamentary Oaths Amendment Bill, introduced by Russell in the Commons on 6 April. The bill abolished all distinctions between religious creeds in the House of Commons; it received the Royal Assent on 30 April (*Hansard*, CLXXXII, 6 April 1866, cols 1322–1355).

[94]Sir Stafford Northcote (1818–1887), 1st Earl of Iddesleigh (1885). Con. President of the Board of Trade (1866), Secretary of State for India (1867), Chancellor of the Exchequer (1874–1880), Leader of the House (1876), Leader of the Opposition (1880–1885), First Lord of the Treasury (1885–1886), Foreign Secretary (1886).

[95]Lowe had written to Carnarvon on 8 March urging the meeting: 'Let us defeat the Bill and leave the future prospects of the Government to take care of themselves' (Lowe to Carnarvon, 8 March 1866: CP, BL 61070, fo. 55).

Grosvenors[96] whose adhesion is of the utmost consequence. He had not actually counted noses but relies upon not much less than 40 votes.

He wishes for two nights debate which with the Government so weak in debating strength will he thinks knock the bill to pieces, but his object is to get support in the way of speaking from our side.

Anyhow he and his friends are resolved to vote against the bill whether they get help or not from us. If indeed they were deserted by us "it would be a spectacle" to the whole of the country to see this band of 30 or 40 men fighting it out to the last: and he added that in such a case if they would not stop the bill against a combination of the two great parties in the State they could at least do the Conservatives a mortal mischief by stepping forward to maintain the position which they ought to defend.

The great principle on which they are prepared to stand is no lowering of the £10 franchise in boroughs. They will accept no compromise on this head.

He expressed a good deal of distrust of Disraeli, some little distrust of Northcote whom he called "dolose",[97] but said he could get on very well with Hardy.

We afterwards diverged into more general politics and discussed though with some reserve the possibilities of a combination of moderate Liberals and Conservatives. He described himself as "a Whig except in respect of family considerations": agreed with me when I said that we seemed to be passing into a new era in the political and parliamentary Government of the Country and admitted that the principal difficulties which a fusionist Government would have to deal with would be Church questions, though he did not think them insurmountable.

This morning I had a talk with Cranborne on some points raised by Lowe and have helped I hope to make matters safe for Monday night.

Saturday 10 March (London)

Our usual Saturday dinner.

Delane amongst others dined here. His opinion as to the state of Ireland is bad, as bad as can be. The whole people are in his view

---

[96]Richard Grosvenor (1795–1869), 2nd Marquess of Westminster (1845), and Hugh Lupus Grosvenor (1825–1899), Lib. MP for Chester (1847–1869), created 1st Duke of Westminster (1874).

[97]'Intentionally deceitful' (Latin).

(excepting of course the Orange party) entirely disaffected and incapable of being reconciled by any moderate change of government etc.

The only remedy which he could suggest and he owned it was an utterly revolutionary one would be to stop absenteeism by giving the alternative of a compulsory sale. It would be desperate but nothing short of this would produce any effect. However, it may be doubted in such a case whether the cure would not be worse than the original evil. Last autumn Irish landlords of the best kind and class told him that they could not count on the support of one single tenant.

In the evening I had some talk with Northcote as to the present state of things. He admitted the enormous difficulties of forming a government out of the present materials at our disposal. He began by admitting that Disraeli could not become the nominal leader and that Lord Derby was little likely to be in earnest. He went on to say that the Party would not follow Stanley, and that General Peel[98] had distinctly declared that he would neither take the lead nor serve under Stanley as leader. He said – and in fact gave me such strong reasons for what he said that I think he must be correct – that Disraeli had made real and repeated offers of ceding his claims wholly or partially and had told Lord D. in the autumn (which I knew of at the time) that the old combinations were impossible: but that Lord D. would not give up the existing arrangements. We were interrupted in our conversation but the upshot of Northcote's opinion is that when the crash comes as it shortly will in all likelihood Lord D. will give Disraeli carte blanche to form the H. of C. Government, that D. will offer Lowe and Horsman[99] places if they can bring over some 25 men and that Lord D. will try to obtain the cooperation of "Lord Westminster, Duke of Cleveland, Lord Lansdowne"[100] and possibly some few other Whigs.

Thursday 15 March (London)

I had a talk with Northcote as to the Reform bill. He is anxious and fears much that the Whigs will end after much grumbling by

---

[98] Gen. Jonathan Peel (1799–1879), Con. MP for Norwich (1826–1831) and for Huntingdon (1831–1868), Secretary of State for War (1858, 1866–1867).

[99] Edward Horsman (1807–1876), Whig MP for Cockermouth (1836–1852), for Stroud (1853–1868), and for Liskeard (1869–1876), Chief Secretary for Ireland (1855–1857). One of the founders, with Lowe, of the Cave of Adullam, in protest against the Reform Bill of 1866.

[100] Henry George Vane (1803–1891), 4th Duke of Cleveland (1864); Henry Charles Petty-Fitzmaurice (1845–1927), 5th Marquess of Lansdowne (1866), Under-Secretary of State for India (1880), Governor-General of Canada (1883–1888), Viceroy of India (1888–1894), Secretary of State for War (1895–1900), Foreign Secretary (1900–1905).

supporting the Government and that Lowe's and Horsman's party will when it comes to voting turn out much smaller than they anticipated.

Lord Derby's conduct is incomprehensible. He summoned the Party in the H. of C. to meet him the other day and talked to them about the Oaths bill. He then dismissed them with a promise that when the Government scheme was out he should hope to see them again. The bill comes out and Lord Derby summons the Party on Thursday 12 April at 12 o'clock on the very day when it is to be read the 2nd time. It is in part an insult to the Party, and they so felt it: for such was the expression of opinion that Taylor[101] went to Lord D. and in consequence a second circular appears today convening them for tomorrow!!

The result of my conversation with Northcote was a visit to me this afternoon by Disraeli, who discussed everything with great frankness. His hopes are founded in securing the adhesion of some of the great Whig Peers. It is a case he says for the intervention of Peers and the support of Lord Westminster or the Duke of Cleveland will determine many in the H. of C. "But it is," he added, "vain to expect or even to ask anything from Lord Derby. He would probably receive these great personages if they would come to him in St. James' Square[102] and offer him their allegiance but he will not take a single step towards them. *He knows nothing of the management of men.*"

After discussing various plans of action at length I undertook to try to deal myself with some of the persons in question. I intend to communicate personally with them and to put aside all party considerations treating it as a question which is so important as to be above all party.

I have this evening done something towards this. I sought out Lichfield[103] in the House and walked home with him. He is very much discomposed at the idea of Reform such as this and quite entered into my views. I urged on him the importance of securing the cooperation of some of the Whig Peers to put pressure on the Government to withdraw their bill. He promised to consider it well and to see as many as he could on the subject tomorrow evening.

Tuesday 20 March (London)

We have had a very anxious week of it with regard to Reform matters but this evening I think we really begin to see the light. Grosvenor[104]

[101] Thomas Edward Taylor (1811–1883), Con. Chief Whip (1859–1868).
[102] 10 St James's Square, Derby's London house.
[103] Thomas George Anson (1826–1892), 2nd Earl of Lichfield (1854).
[104] i.e. Hugh Lupus Grosvenor.

has given notice in the H. of C. of a resolution declining to discuss the Government Bill and the notice has been received I hear with loud cheers from both sides.[105] I have been in constant communication throughout the whole of this time with Lowe and Elcho endeavouring as far as it lay with me to facilitate matters. Both are thoroughly in earnest, but I cannot help thinking that Lowe is either a little jealous of Elcho or a little fretful with him on account of Elcho's greater nobility of character. It is however impossible not to like Elcho much the best. He is so thoroughly a gentleman and if he does ever make a mistake it is made in all honour and good faith.

Meanwhile I have persuaded Lord Shaftesbury[106] to move for a return of the male occupiers in boroughs at a gross estimated rental of from 10 to 7 who belong to the working class. This will give Lord S. the opportunity of declaring himself against the indiscriminate introduction of the lower element and will tell with great force on all the shop-keeping and Dissenting interest.[107] There is to be a debate upon his motion, not going into the merits of the bill: but I hope that a few well-chosen sentences from him will produce a great effect.

Wednesday 21 March (London)

Lord Shaftesbury gave up his motion. In part he was frightened at it and the possible consequences of it. In part he was worried with his Chancery law suit and so after putting his notice upon the papers he abandoned it. Lowe was of course very sarcastic upon this.

Sunday 25 March (London)

In the afternoon I took a long walk with Northcote round Kensington Gardens. We discussed past, present and future in politics. Northcote expressed his firm resolution not to form part of a

---

[105] *Hansard*, CLXXXII, 12 March 1866, cols 87–90. 'Carnarvon called and left a line to say he wished to see me', wrote Elcho to Lowe, 'and the sooner the better. I accordingly went to him tonight and had a long talk over the words more as suggested by you. The result is that it may be not only necessary but very desirable. Still it should be made to depend on Grosvenor's resolve as if he asserts it will not be necessary and had better be left alone. Carnarvon is therefore to ask Lord Ellenborough not to give notice. *That*, if the move is rendered necessary can be done later in the week' (Elcho to Lowe, 20 March 1866: Wemyss Papers, Letter 20, p. 36). Lowe told Carnarvon, 'I believe we shall get Grosvenor and if so I think we are safe' (Lowe to Carnarvon, 20 March 1866: CP, BL 60831, fo. 8).

[106] Anthony Ashley-Cooper (1801–1885), 7th Earl of Shaftesbury (1851), social reformer. Held junior offices under Wellington and Peel, but joined the Whig Party in 1847.

[107] Shaftesbury had been disillusioned with the Liberal ministry since Palmerston's death (see B.A.M. Finlayson, *The Seventh Earl of Shaftesbury, 1801–1885* (London, 1981), p. 468).

government which would not deal fairly with Church questions and said he was perfectly ready to take up his seat with Henley, Sir W. Heathcote and others on the back benches and to give a Conservative government every help but not to be party to any movement against the Church.[108]

In the afternoon later Elcho called and I talked much with him, *inter alia*, on the recent violent articles in the *Telegraph* which he tells me are written by Frank Lawley,[109] who is just as intimate with Gladstone as he ever was.

Wednesday [*sic*] 17 April[110] (London)

All through the last week or rather four days our prospects in the House of Commons have been growing brighter. The Government are moving heaven and earth to detach men but Grosvenor whom I met today is sanguine.

Beaumont[111] met me, talked much of the rascality of many of the liberals who though hating the bill are yet afraid to vote against it, assented to all that I said with regard to the necessity of a combination government and then informed me that he suspected that Gladstone intended on the night of the division to attempt a *coup de théâtre* by announcing that if the House would agree to the 2nd reading of the Reform bill[112] the Government would undertake not to proceed further with it till they had brought the Redistribution of Seats bill through a 2nd reading also and then proceed with both bills *pari passu*. It is so shabby a trick that it is likely. He wished me to communicate it to Lord Derby which I undertook to do.

He further told me that H. Herbert of Kerry[113] who is the O'Donoghue's[114] mouthpiece in the matter told him that the Irish

---

[108] See also Northcote's diary entry for his version of the meeting (A. Lang, *Life, Letters and Diaries of Sir Stafford Northcote, First Earl of Iddesleigh*, 2 vols (Edinburgh and London, 1890), I, pp. 256–258).

[109] Francis Charles Lawley (1825–1901), journalist and former private secretary to Gladstone, worked for the *Daily Telegraph* from 1865. See leaders in that paper, 22 March 1866, p. 6, and 23 March 1866, p. 4.

[110] The date should probably be Tuesday 17 April.

[111] Henry Frederick Beaumont (1835–1892), Lib. MP for West Riding of Yorkshire South (1865–1874) and for Colne Valley (1885–1892).

[112] The second reading of the Reform Bill was introduced on 12 April.

[113] Henry Arthur Herbert (1815–1866), Lib. MP for Co. Kerry (1847–1866), Chief Secretary for Ireland (1857–1858).

[114] Daniel O'Donoghue (1833–1889), MP for Tipperary (1857–1865) and for Tralee (1865–1885), founder of O'Donoghue Party.

members would vote against the bill if the Conservatives would promise to give them an Enquiry into the Irish Church, but that the Irish members the villains – thought that they were the masters of the political situation, and were prepared to use their advantage.

Monday 23 April (London)

Stanley breakfasted with me and we afterwards walked round Kensington Gardens. As we were returning – I had previously made up my mind to speak to him on the subject of possible change – I told what Lowe had said to me, how determined he was not to serve under Disraeli, how doubtful even whether he could serve with him, and that on the whole he seemed to me to be the one person possible who as much from position and character as from ability was able to centre in himself the different parties and interests. He expressed grave doubts as to his being able, even physically, to undertake the leadership of the House, to which I replied that he was in that position that a statement would often be accepted from him where an argument would be required from others. I then said that in proposing to him what of itself amounted to a dispossessing of Lord Derby of position he would of course acquit me of any disloyalty to him but that looking to all the [circumstances] and the critical character of the time I believed that what I suggested was the only course. He replied that his father and he quite understood each other on these points. I told him that I had told Northcote of my conversation with Lowe for him to communicate it to Disraeli.

He said to me something which implied that he thought himself unpopular with the Party, to which I answered that whatever might have been the feeling some time since I saw on every side in the Party signs of very great good sense and moderation and that several of the younger men had on several occasions of late expressed themselves quite ready to accept such an arrangement as his leadership because it offered an escape from the present great difficulties.[115]

Saturday 28 April (London)

The report today at the Carlton (which looks much like a hive of bees upset and ready to swarm) is that the Government are already

[115]For Stanley's recollection of this meeting see Vincent, *Derby*, I, p. 24.

out.[116] The report is founded on a statement to this effect said to be made by Childers to Sir E. Tennent.[117] It is said Sir G. Grey has gone down to the Queen to the Isle of Wight but one does not see what Sir G.G. can have to do with the matter in the present stage.[118]

There are three contingencies at least which are now possible:

1. A pure Conservative Government with Lord D. and Disraeli, undertaking to deal with Reform and leaning on the Lowe, Grosvenor and Horsman party, probably referring the question to a Commission and so gaining time and strength and reserving the chance of a dissolution.

2. A combination Government of Stanley and the Conservatives with a Whig adhesion might perhaps be made to extend somewhat beyond the Lowe – Horsman party.

3. A Combination Government of Whigs including and indeed starting from some members of the present Cabinet and of the Conservatives with either Disraeli or Stanley as leader in the H. of C., and Lord Derby waiving his leadership in the Lords: and either taking a seat without office in the Cabinet or standing aloof and giving a general support.

It is anyhow a critical state of things and I almost think that it would be better that the present Government should go on, get deeper into difficulties and make the split between themselves and the secessionist Whigs irremediable.

Friday 4 May

I have had great trouble and anxiety for the last four or five days in an attempt to bring about a conference between Grosvenor, Lowe,

---

[116]The Government had been challenged by the Opposition to postpone the second reading of the Reform Bill. After eight days' debate, the amendment was defeated by five votes, 318 to 313 (*Hansard*, CLXXXVIII, 27 April 1866, cols 152–155). Much weakened, the Government remained in office.

[117]Hugh Culling Eardley Childers (1827–1896), Lib. MP for Pontefract (1859–1885) and for Edinburgh South (1886–1892), First Lord of the Admiralty (1868–1871); Sir James Emerson Tennent (1804–1869), Permanent Secretary, Poor Law Board (1852), Permanent Secretary, Board of Trade (1852–1867).

[118]Grey wrote to Russell the following day, 'The Queen showed me your letter to her written after yesterday's Cabinet. The only way in which we have any chance of success in carrying the Reform Bill and the only way in which we can bring the question before the House is by placing the matter before the House in a complete form' (G.P. Gooch, *The Later Correspondence of Lord John Russell, 1840–1878*, 2 vols (London, 1925), II, pp. 345–346).

Horsman and Elcho and some of our friends.[119] There have been great difficulties on all sides – the Adullamites, as they are now commonly called, fearing that the report of any meeting should get abroad and lead to misrepresentation: but on the other hand fearing that Pakington,[120] Peel, and several more of our friends might also hear of it and take offence at the idea of what might seem to be a hole and corner meeting. Twice the scheme seemed on the point of succeeding: twice it broke down and ultimately it failed through the apprehension on Grosvenor's part that it might be known. I have had repeated conferences with Disraeli who has been perfectly frank and open, holding back nothing as far as I can see and being very sound as I think in his views of what is to be done.

The state of things is this. The Government feel themselves to be in a difficulty and Bouverie[121] under the guise of a neutral bystander is organizing with Whitbread[122] and some others a sham opposition to the Government in order to affront away from the Grosvenor and Lowe party any waverers and ultimately to lead them back home to this government. And his mode of accomplishing this is by throwing out proposals of a compromise which of course the Government would accept in Committee; that compromise evidently being the substitu-tion of £20 for £14 in the Counties and £8 for £7 in the boroughs, together with some boundary revision and the gift of some borough seats to the Counties in order to bribe the County members with them. This is a very dangerous game for us, because there are a good many people on our side who in their timidity and ignorance are so anxious to settle the question, as is now the cry, that they do not see that this is no settlement that it would only lead to further charges and that it is the policy of the Whigs and the ruin of the Conservative Party.[123]

[119]The previous day, Elcho had hoped to arrange a meeting between Carnarvon and leading members of the Cave, 'which I hope may lead to a satisfactory settlement of the Reform question next year. I assume that we are thinking of accepting an £8.00 compromise with a view to what is called getting the question out of the way in the present session' (Elcho to Carnarvon, 5 May 1866: CP, BL 60831, fos 14–15). When Elcho saw Hugh Grosvenor later the same day, the former considered it best 'not to go to your house, as he has declined a Conference with Bouverie and *his* friends' (ibid., fos 18–19).

[120]Sir John Somerset Pakington (1799–1880), baronet (1846), 1st Baron Hampton (1874). Con. MP for Droitwich (1837–1874), Secretary of State for War (1852) and for the Colonies (1858–1859), First Lord of the Admiralty (1866).

[121]Edward Pleydell-Bouverie (1818–1889), Lib. MP for Kilmarnock (1844–1874), President of the Poor Law Board (1855–1858).

[122]Samuel Whitbread (1830–1915), Lib. MP for Bedford (1852–1895), Lord of the Admiralty (1859–1863).

[123]Carnarvon set out his views in a lengthy memorandum to Derby: Carnarvon to Derby, 7 May 1866: Derby Papers, 920 DER (14) 163/5A.

Henley, Walpole, Cairns,[124] Pakington, Adderley,[125] G. Hardy[126] and some others seem to be bitten with the delusion. Of these however Walpole we have almost I think succeeded in convincing. Disraeli gave him a home thrust by pointing out that Bouverie who is looking to the Speakership – on which Walpole has always had a longing eye, was the author of this scheme – and all the others, if only they can be prevented from committing themselves, can with the exception of Henley I think be managed. They will go with their Party.

Stanley was the author in the bill of 1859 of the retention of the £10 borough franchise: he has always had a strong feeling in favour of adhering to this but the weak point in his character – his timidity comes out and as the difficulty of holding his own increases he begins to waver. Disraeli, however, is pressing him: and I have done my best in the same sense. Fortunately too the Lowe and Grosvenor Party have taken up most distinctly the policy of no compromise and postponement for this Session at all events.

Meanwhile, the Secessionists are in great difficulties. The four leaders are firm enough and they say that they can count upon some eight or ten more, but that for the remainder no dependence can be placed on them. The Government is tampering with them and with the large majority it appears to be simply a question of the amount of the bribe. That most miserable and despicable creature Beaumont – for really there is nothing else in plain truth to be said of him – is wavering and more than half prepared to go and this after all the fine speeches about honour and good faith which he made me ten days since!

Altogether it is a very critical state of things. We have much in our favour and against us the strong will of one man who seems to have all the cleverness, the violence, and the obstinate cunning of a madman – It is Gladstone alone who forces the Government and his party on.

---

[124]Hugh MacCalmont Cairns (1819–1885), Baron Cairns of Garmoyle (1867), 1st Earl Cairns (1878). Con. MP for Belfast (1852–1854), Solicitor-General (1858–1859), Lord Justice of Appeal (1866–1868), Lord Chancellor (1868, 1874–1880).

[125]Charles Bowyer Adderley (1814–1905), 1st Baron Norton (1878). Con. MP for Staffordshire North (1848–1871), Vice-President, Committee of Council on Education (1858), Under-Secretary of State for the Colonies (1866), President of the Board of Trade (1874–1878).

[126]Gathorne Gathorne-Hardy (1814–1906), Viscount Cranbrook of Hemsted (1878), 1st Earl of Cranbrook (1892). President of the Poor Law Board (1866–1867), Secretary of State for the Home Office (1867–1868), for the War Office (1874–1878), and for India (1878–1880), Lord President of the Council (1885–1886, 1886–1892).

Thursday 10 May (London)

Great shakiness in some of our own party on the subject of a supposed compromise with regard to Reform. They are disposed to substitute in Committee an £8 for a £7 and a £20 for a £14 franchise. This would be absolute.

After much discussion of the subject with various people feeling very anxious as to the course which has to be taken in the H. of C., I wrote a rather long letter to Lord Derby[127] and subsequently had back from him a reply agreeing so far with me that he said that the Government scheme if passed even though with modifications "would be the extinction of the Conservative Party for the next 20 years." Lord Russell is said to have formed pretty nearly the same opinion of his bill, for Lowe declares that he told someone that his bill "would prevent a Conservative Government coming into office for the next 20 years."

It is a very critical time in every point of view, but I hardly think that whatever the issue the Whigs as a Party are likely to enjoy 20 years of bearable supremacy.

Friday 11 May (London)

The great panic, a money crisis in the City, the most fraudulent and bankrupt firm of all – the Government – which most deserved to fail seems likely to go on.[128]

A meeting of Conservative H. of C. M.P.s. Much discussion but ultimately a good understanding and very tolerable unanimity. I hope it will last.[129]

Monday 21 May (London)

I called on Lord Derby in order to state the proposed scheme of a Conservative first class daily Paper under the editorship of Russell,

---

[127]'I feel afraid', wrote Carnarvon, 'that an acceptance of the government plan would be our ruin as a party' (Carnarvon to Derby, 10 May 1866: Derby Papers, 920 DER (14) 163/5A).

[128]So–called 'Black Friday', with the collapse of the bankers Overend and Gurney.

[129]Elcho noted, 'The situation is upon the whole not unsatisfactory. There has been amongst the Conservative members a danger of a selfish split between Town and Country each threatening to make its own terms with the enemy if occasion required it. This is, I hope and believe, at an end' (Elcho to Carnarvon, 11 May 1866: CP, BL 60831, fo. 24).

The Times correspondent and present editor of the *Army and Navy Gazette*,[130] and to endeavour to obtain from him an expression of general goodwill.

I told him that Russell proposed to raise the necessary funds by shares of £10 or £20 throughout the Country, that W.H. Smith[131] approves the scheme and will cordially go along with it, that Cubitt[132] and Edwards[133] have promised large subscriptions, that Delane is friendly wishing for a first class Conservative paper to stand between him and the penny Press and has offered to give him his accounts and every other information which can be useful, that the sub-editor of the *Saturday Review* is to be had, the best sub-editor in London, and that all that Russell needs is £2000 per an. for the next two or three years till the paper pays. He wishes to go thoroughly along with the Conservative Party but he will not pledge himself to a slavish allegiance on every point.

Lord Derby's answer was a string of objections.

First, he was not sure that it was desirable to have any paper which was or professed itself an organ of the Party.

Next, how would Russell go on Church questions? Would he be in favour of perpetual concession and sacrifice as soon as a pinch came?

Next, would not this injuriously affect the *Standard?*

Finally before answering he would wish to talk the matter over with Disraeli.

To this of course I could offer no objection though I am afraid that it will lead to some intervention on the part of the Rose, Baxter[134] and *especially Spofforth*[135] firm who will view this only in the light of opposition to the *Standard;* and will do everything to thwart it accordingly.

---

[130] *Army and Navy Gazette*, founded in 1860 by William Howard Russell (1820–1907), war correspondent for *The Times* (1854–1871).

[131] William Henry Smith (1825–1891), Con. MP for Westminster (1868–1885) and for Strand (1885–1891). Financial Secretary to the Treasury (1874–1877), First Lord of the Admiralty (1877–1880), Secretary of State for War (1885–1886), Chief Secretary for Ireland (1886), First Lord of the Treasury and Leader of the House of Commons (1887).

[132] George Cubitt (1828–1917), Con. MP for Surrey West (1860–1885) and for Epsom (1885–1892), 1st Baron Ashcombe (1892).

[133] John Passmore Edwards (1823–1911), newspaper proprietor and editor of the *Echo*, and philanthropist. Lib. MP for Salisbury (1880–1885).

[134] Dudley Baxter (1827–1875), member of the firm of solicitors Baxter, Rose, Norton & Co, Westminster, parliamentary lawyers since 1860. See H.J. Hanham, *Elections and Party Management: politics in the time of Disraeli and Gladstone* (Hassocks, Sussex, 1978), pp. 357–358.

[135] Markham Spofforth (1825–1907), principal Conservative agent for twenty years.

Saturday 9 June

Gladstone seems to be going out of his mind. Northcote has just told me that Gladstone's last passion is for Mrs Thistlethwayte.[136] He goes to dinner with her, meets her frequently, seems engrossed with her: and she in return in her preachments to her congregation exhorts them to put up in their prayers on behalf of Mr Gladstone's reform bill.

His manner in the H. of C. even is very extraordinary. When Stanley on Thursday night stated the object of his motion of postponement, Gladstone gave a half shriek and threw himself back on his seat as if he had been shot.

Mrs Gladstone the other day in her very simple manner said to someone that it was "a great pity that dear William returned home so angry as he often does."

Monday 17 September (Buxton)

I have had several anxious days and even weeks with regard to Canada and the threatened Fenian invasion.[137] Lord Monck's letters have been unsatisfactory.[138] At first denying and discrediting all ideas of danger – then a hasty telegram calling for reinforcements – then explaining the news of his requisition by a despatch in which he reiterates his own belief that there is no danger and yet gives way to the expression of alarm on all sides of him – a series of inconsistencies.

His information is very scanty – not nearly as much as I can glean from occasional Canadian papers. Meanwhile in the midst of all this he talks of returning to England to confer on the subject of Confederation, and it is only after repeated letters of mine in which I point out the impossibility of his leaving, and when matters seem coming to a head

---

[136]Laura Thistlethwayte, who lived with her husband in Grosvenor Square, and had been well-known in the *demi-monde*. Gladstone had met her after she experienced a religious conversion to a non-denominational ethical Christianity. She played an important part in Gladstone's emotional explosion in the autumn of 1869, when he was Prime Minister. See H.C.G. Matthew, *Gladstone, 1809–1874* (Oxford, 1986), pp. 157–158.

[137]Earlier in the year, Irish Fenians in the United States had made abortive attempts to invade Canada.

[138]Charles Stanley Monck (1819–1894), 1st Baron Monck (1866), Governor-General of Canada (1861–1868), had commuted the sentences after no further Fenian attacks materialized. See W.L. Morton, *The Critical Years: the union of British North America 1857–1873* (Toronto, 1964), p. 202.

as regards Fenianism that he writes to say that he must give up coming home – and writes as if we have been urging him to come![139]

Two days since (the 15th), I received a telegram stating that the Canadian delegates cannot arrive till the close of the Navigation on the same account. I wrote to Elliott desiring him to fix a day for the North Britain and the Nova Scotian delegates, and that I would come up to London to meet them.

So ends my second attempt to drink the water.

Monday 8 October (London)

Discussed Reform question with Bagehot.[140] He admits possibility of postponing question for a year or so but says it must be settled. He believes trimming of franchise in small boroughs would give them up to Conservatives, certainly in Devon and Cornwall.

Saturday 27 October (Highclere)

Walked with Disraeli in morning.[141] He then began on Reform. He said Cranborne was much against any bill: and had promised but not sent a paper of objections. He wishes to hold our hand till later when we shall see what is public feeling on many points, meanwhile consider it. He seems to be most in favour of resolutions and perhaps a Commission appointed by Parliament founded on the resolution. I stated some objections. He admitted them: but is obviously in an undecided state of mind, sometimes inclines to one side sometimes to another.

He suggested as a detail to omit all mention of reform in Queen's Speech, to lead the opposition to believe that they would move an amendment on Address and then just before moving Address to let the Secretary to the treasury announce that on a certain day the question of Reform would be considered. I objected to this as laying us open and as a dodge from which nothing could be gained and he seemed to assent to this view. He spoke of the difficulties of government and said he had never been in a majority.

---

[139] Carnarvon wrote two days before, 'I have nothing to communicate with regard to the Delegates now in England except that they are growing very impatient at the delay of their Canadian colleagues. I feel that in truth they are subject to great inconvenience both on public and personal grounds' (Carnarvon to Sir W.F. Williams, 15 September 1866: Williams Papers).

[140] Walter Bagehot (1826–1877), economist and journalist, editor of *The Economist* (1860–1877), author of *The English Constitution* (1867).

[141] Disraeli and the 2nd Marquess of Salisbury had arrived at Highclere the previous day.

Sunday 28 October (Highclere)

Walked to the lake with Disraeli [. . .]. He admired everything, the sun shining brightly and the trees flaming with autumn colours, and talked agreeably on all subjects *inter alia* Copernicus and Pythagoras and ancient astronomy.

I gave him Mansel's letter[142] to see on Reform. He was so struck that he asked to show it to Lord Derby and said if the Deanery of Norwich was still vacant he would do his best to get it for him.

Monday 29 October (Highclere)

Spoke to Disraeli before he left as to Sir W. Heathcote and a peerage in consequence of something which D. had said to Evelyn[143] the evening before.

Disraeli said Lord Derby was not inclined to give the peerage, that there was not money enough, and that many creations had been made.

I told him Sir W.H.'s health was doubtful that he might be obliged to resign the seat and that I should not advise him to sacrifice or risk his health.

Our Party all went.

Wednesday 31 October (London)

Our first Cabinet since end of Session. Mainly employed in discussion of reform.

The first question was whether reform should be ignored or dealt with and every one, however reluctantly, admitted it was necessary to attempt it.

On the whole the general feeling was in favour of resolutions a Commission and a bill. Lord Derby read a letter from Genl. Grey to him[144] an honourable and creditable one in which Grey stated the Queen's wish to have the question settled and her readiness to communicate with any political persons and to facilitate a concurrence

[142] Henry Longueville Mansel (1820–1871), formerly Carnarvon's tutor at Oxford. Professor of Ecclesiastical History, Oxford University (1866–1868), appointed Dean of St Paul's (1868), a post he had requested after the death of Revd George Pellew, which occurred on 13 October.

[143] Evelyn, Carnarvon's first wife (1834–1875), daughter of George Stanhope, 6th Earl of Chesterfield.

[144] Gen. Charles Grey to Derby, 28 October 1866 (copy): Gen. Grey Papers, Grey III/3.

if possible. He also read a memorandum drawn up by Lord Grey[145] advocating

1. a concurrence of parties for this object.

2. a concurrence proposed and made openly and to avoid all risk of it being thought an aristocratic cabal.

3. providing by resolutions.

4. a Committee of the Privy Council.

His resolutions were abstract but yet much to the point. He wrote apparently in a very friendly spirit.

Evelyn entertained Lowe at luncheon. He was very vehement on Reform and said that if we attempted he would oppose us to the utmost of his powers with at least ten of the Adullamite party. He declared we were judicially blinded as the aristocratic party in the French Revolution etc.

Thursday 1 November (London)

I had a talk with Northcote on Reform this morning. We are generally well agreed. If we bring forward any scheme it should be a well-considered and a bold one.

Thursday 8 November (London)

Cabinet on Reform

At first the discussion showed only great differences of opinion. Afterwards Lord Derby and Disraeli ground through a series of resolutions which no one much liked but to which the resistance was so fragmentary and uncombined that they were finally adopted.[146] Cranborne proposed two preliminary resolutions directed *totidem verbis* against the principle of numerical class ascendancy. John Manners[147] produced a series of general resolutions which were in part adopted. Pakington raised the question of a separation of votes in large towns into 2 classes according to some money qualification: but it found

---

[145] Henry, 3rd Earl Grey had sent the memorandum to Gen. Charles Grey, his younger brother, former private secretary to the Prince Consort and subsequently to the Queen, at Balmoral. The memorandum was given to Northcote for the consideration of the Cabinet. 'I fear', he wrote, 'that if adopted it will be with changes by no means calculated to ensure chances of success' (Journal, '1866 to end of the year': Grey Papers, C3/22).

[146] For details, see W.D. Jones, *Lord Derby and Victorian Conservatism* (Oxford, 1956), p. 299.

[147] Lord John Manners (1818–1906), 7th Duke of Rutland (1888). Commissioner of Works and Buildings (1852, 1858–1859, 1866–1868), Postmaster-General (1874–1880), Chancellor, Duchy of Lancaster (1886–1892).

no favour [...]. I raised the question of a preliminary commission to consider the whole question but was over-ruled on alleged impossibility of getting a fair commission. I also urged household suffrage accompanied by Conservative restrictions and safeguards, but was again overruled. Peel proposed adding $\frac{1}{4}$ to existing electors in every boro', but this was objected to.

I am not satisfied at the general result.

Friday 9 November (London)

Lord Mayor's dinner. I sat between Mr Disraeli and Stanley! The latter drank like a fish. He must have consumed more than 2 bottles of sherry alone.

Ld Derby's speech was excellent and the reception given to him was warm and cordial. The most popular minister could not have been greeted more warmly.

Monday 12 November (London)

Met Solicitor-General[148] at C.O. to consider case of Fenian convicts.[149]

Afterwards went to Lord Derby and settled to telegraph to Lord Monck to spare their lives but not announce commutation of sentences.

Tuesday 13 November (London)

Received deputation from Aborigines Society[150] at C.O. Adderley present, but I contrived to prevent him saying anything.

Cabinet 3.30

Several matters discussed.

1. I raised question as to Fenian convicts under sentence of death in Canada. Agreed to explain commutation, viz., 20 years, *in a despatch*, and probably want Lord Monck's explanatory despatch.

---

[148]Sir William Bovill (1814–1873), Con. MP for Guildford (1857–1866), Solicitor-General (1866), Chief Justice of Common Pleas (1866–1873).

[149]A Fenian force of 600 crossed from the United States to Canada. The leaders were captured and two of them, Lynch and McMahon, sentenced to death for high treason.

[150]Report of the Aborigines' Protection Society deputation to the Earl of Carnarvon, *The Times*, 14 November 1866, p. 7.

2. Stanley mentioned his answer to Seward's[151] letter to Bruce[152] claiming amnesty for these convicts.

3. Naas[153] apprehends much agitation in Ireland for next month. Three fresh ships are to cruise on Irish coast in case of any attempt at a landing [. . .].

Went afterwards with Disraeli to his room and discussed reorganisation of C.O.[154] He assents to the addition of a legal adviser but opposed M. Bernard[155] – a fair compromise.

Thursday 15 November

Cabinet

I brought forward my proposal for exchange of territory with French and Dutch on West coast of Africa. Cabinet agreed leaving me to settle details with Stanley.

Some discussion as to proposed meeting by Trades Unions on 3 December. Sir R. Mayne[156] called in.

Friday 16 November (London)

Cabinet

Lord Derby read a letter from the Queen complaining that she had not had enough information as to Fenian convicts under sentence of death in Canada or general proceedings of Cabinet. I received a similar letter with special reference to Canadian affairs through Genl. Grey[157] which I answered that evening by special messenger.[158]

Northcote brought forward his railway plans.

[151] William Henry Seward (1801–1872), US Secretary of State (1861–1869).

[152] Sir Frederick William Bruce (1814–1867), British diplomat, envoy to Washington (1865–1867).

[153] Richard Southwell Bourke (1822–1872), Lord Naas (1849), 6th Earl of Mayo (1867), Chief Secretary, Ireland (1852, 1858–1859, 1866–1868), Viceroy of India (1869–1872).

[154] Carnarvon had complained to Disraeli of the impossible burden of combining the role of under-secretary and legal advisor, and had suggested that Bernard should fill the latter role: Carnarvon to Disraeli, 9 October 1866: Hughenden Papers, dep. 100/1, fo. 15.

[155] Montague Bernard (1820–1882), Professor of International Law and Diplomacy, Oxford University since 1858.

[156] Sir Richard Mayne (1796–1868), Chief Commissioner, Metropolitan Police since 1850.

[157] Gen. Grey to Carnarvon, 15 November 1866: CP, TNA, PRO 30/6/44, fo. 72.

[158] Carnarvon to Queen Victoria, 16 November 1866: Royal Archives, P23/43.

Some further discussion as to Reform meeting on 3rd December. Sir R. Mayne attended and reported his interview with the deputation, who represent the numbers likely to attend at 200 to 300,000 men.[159]

Walpole is fast losing his head. He seems to grow feverishly nervous at the prospect of any row and his police are either ineffective or neglect to keep him informed. If there is a breeze we shall probably see a repetition of the mismanagement of last summer.

Tuesday 20 November

Cabinet

I mentioned arrival of delegates and it was understood that the sentences of Fenian convicts should be commuted to 20 years.

I showed Ld Derby my draft despatch on this subject to which he assented. Sent it on to Stanley.[160]

Tuesday 27 November (London)

Went to the Duke of Cambridge[161] and discussed question of succession to vacant Governorships. Told him that I should always be glad that military officers should succeed in the large free Colonies but that in many if not most of others it would only be just to Colonial Service to reserve places for them.

Dined with Phillimore and discussed the whole position personal and general with regard to the *Alabama* claims. I cannot say I feel satisfied either way.[162]

Cranborne opposed the reference of *Alabama* claims to arbitration very strongly, on ground that late Government had laid down denial so decidedly, that Lord Derby had in opposition denounced arbitration, that the questions were not such as any country ought to surrender

[159] In the event, only a little over 20,000 people turned out for the demonstration. It was held in the grounds of Beaufort House, Kensington. For a full report, see the *Annual Register 1866* (1867), pp. 188–191.

[160] Despatch for Lord Monck on Fenian convicts submitted to the Queen for approval, 21 November 1866 (Carnarvon to Queen Victoria: Royal Archives, P23/47; see also Carnarvon to Monck, 23 November 1866: Monck Papers, 27021 (3)).

[161] George William, Duke of Cambridge (1819–1904), Field Marshal (1862), General Commanding-in-Chief (1856–1895).

[162] A long-standing dispute between the United States and Great Britain was the claim that, during the American Civil War, Britain had built two ships for the southern states – the *Alabama* and the *Orestes* –which had subsequently been used for attacking and destroying American shipping. The matter was not resolved until 1871, when arbitrators decided against Great Britain and awarded substantial damages.

Fig. 2 'The Fathers of the Confederation', London, December 1866.
Carnarvon is standing on the left with Lord Monck, right. The seated figures
are the delegates from Canada, Nova Scotia, and New Brunswick.

to arbitration. He argued that we should conciliate no party and only
lower the country by such a course.

Some general discussion followed and I said that I agreed with
Stanley, because when as foreign minister he could not guarantee
peace and it had become a grave matter but that personally I found
on reference to Hansard that I had in opposition used language very
strongly against arbitration and I endeavoured to let the Cabinet
understand that I should have to consider my own position.

Finally decided not to offer special points for arbitration but to
suggest arbitration generally and to have Seward to say on what
points he wished to arbitrate.

Thursday 29 November (London)

Cabinet

Revised the draft on *Alabama* claims. Stanley inserted a few words
which much modified the character of it. It was understood, on my
asking, that it commits us to nothing beyond a general disposition to
accept arbitration without specifying any particular points [. . .].

After Cabinet talked to Cranborne about the *Alabama* claims and our despatch. He thought that I was not sufficiently committed by my speech in 1864[163] to make it necessary for me to resign. He was prepared to resign if the original draft had been agreed upon.

Monday 3 December (London)

The Reform meeting and Procession. They did not start from the Parade in front of the Horse Guards till 12.40. When once off they moved quickly.

Met Walpole at the Carlton – he seemed delighted with the mob, the rainy day and himself, but was in a nervous state.

Tuesday 11 December (Highclere)

Discussed various points in Confederation scheme with delegates.[164] They are much in favour of a nominated not elective Legislative Council. They will I think give up right of pardoning now proposed to be given to Lieutenant-Governors, and they expressed themselves anxious to make provincial Legislatures and Governments as municipal in character as possible.

Tuesday 18 December (Highclere)

Went up to town by first train.

Received Howe,[165] Annand,[166] and Macdonald,[167] anti-confederates at the C.O.

Howe managed his case with great skill and temper and impressed me much. He went away I think in good humour. If only the question

[163]United States, British and American Claims. Motion for Returns. *Hansard*, CLXXIII, 16 February 1864, cols 618–627.

[164]The conference with the Canadian delegates had opened on 4 December at the Westminster Palace Hotel, with Carnarvon in the chair. Three of the leading delegates – Macdonald, Cartier, and Galt – travelled to Highclere on 11 December for relaxation and further drafting of the British American Bill. They returned to London the following day (see D. Creighton, *John A. Macdonald: the young politician*, 2 vols (Toronto, 1952), I, p. 453).

[165]Joseph Howe (1804–1873), the Nova Scotian delegate, a passionate opponent of Confederation.

[166]William Annand (1808–1887), Minister, Nova Scotia Legislative Council, Prime Minister (1871). Opposed to British North American union.

[167]Sir John Alexander Macdonald (1815–1891), Attorney-General, Upper Canada (1854), Premier (1857), First Premier of the Dominion (1867), Leader of the House of Assembly (1856–1891).

is referred to the *people of N. Scotia*, not the Parliament, he is satisfied. It is an awkward question.

Thursday 20 December (Highclere)

Canadian delegates arrived 19 December. Macdonald went. He said that the conferences of the delegates would probably be over by Saturday. I told him that the two main difficulties which I foresaw were

1. the guarantee question – to which he said that they only wanted what Cardwell had promised.[168]

2. the position of the N. Scotian legislature. He said that any dissolution on this question would give a majority against Confederation and would postpone it for years. He said that Howe had so influenced the public mind on the subject that even he probably could not now restrain them.

Sunday 23 December (London)

Discussed various questions with Stanley [. . .]. He does not believe that we shall come to any agreement amongst ourselves or be able to do much in the House. He used to me many of Lowe's arguments against Reform derived from and through Lady Salisbury.[169] He was curiously indisposed to it. The only thing he said on which he was decided, was that if beaten we ought *not* to dissolve.

Tuesday 25 December (Highclere)

Discussed with Lowe [. . .]. On reform he strongly urges delay and caution. He would be very favourable to a franchise founded on £100, or even £50 income tax. It is an advantage to make income tax permanent for if it were abolished we should have a property tax immediately.

Confederation. He objected to guarantees but says truly that we are committed by the acts of our predecessors and may fairly say so. As to Confederation itself [. . .] his main objection is one to the whole

---

[168] Cardwell, Carnarvon's predecessor in office, on the subject of imperial defence.

[169] Mary Catherine, Marchioness of Salisbury (1824–1900), who married the 15th Earl of Derby in 1870, had met Lowe two years previously at Highclere. He was subsequently greatly influenced by her views. See Winter, *Robert Lowe*, p. 231.

scheme because it may increase rather than diminish the connection of North America with us.

He urges me strongly to represent to Lord Derby *Adderley's incapacity* and anyhow to wash my hands of all responsibility. Adderley, he said, is almost certainly to involve us in difficulties and probably serious ones. I am afraid he is right.

Wednesday 26 December (Highclere)

The Lowes, Bakers and Lady D. Nevill[170] went.

Lowe feels very bitterly the treatment which he has had from the Whigs. He said to me that there was nothing that he could not have had and that had not been offered short of the Governor-General of India *out of England*: but that the Cabinet was reserved exclusively for men of particular connection and family. Had he been a radical he might indeed have had it but for a man of moderate views the cabinet was closed. But if ever difficulties arose in Parliament, a hard committee to be carried through, then no one could do it as he could and the entire work was put upon him. I observed that whatever our faults as Party this exclusiveness was not one, to which he cordially assented. There is certainly no love lost on his side.

[170]Lady Dorothy Nevill (1826–1913), society hostess.

1867

Thursday 10 January (London)

Cabinet at 3. J. Manners and Northcote absent.

We began on Reform.[171] Lord Derby recapitulated all our previous steps and stated the position of the Cave declaring that the more he considered it the more clear he was that resolutions and a Commission offered the best and only chance. He then read over the resolutions which he and Disraeli had amended in some parts, and which were much improved, having acquired a more distinctive character. These were fully discussed and finally agreed to, various contingencies being considered. The plan of operations determined being this Reform to be mentioned in the Queen's Speech but so as to cover the bill, or Commission or resolution, no explanations to be given on the Address but on the following Monday. Then course to be explained and resolutions to be laid on table. Some interval must ensue and various large bills (Confederation *inter alia*) to be brought forward.

Pakington reported a commission received from A. Anson[172] on behalf of the Cave to the effect that they would have nearly as many men as last year, that they were quite staunch and ready to support us in anything, provided *that we do not attempt a strong reform bill*. This if correct is very important.

Some discussion on Canadian matters. France and Russia willing to support a scheme of local autonomy with a tribute if we join.

Friday 11 January

Had a conference at the Colonial Office with Sir E. Head on the H.B. Co. affairs [. . .].

Later saw Northcote and talked to him about the Reform resolutions. Subsequently I went over to the India Office and discussed them with Cranborne. With him I drew up some criticisms, some of

---

[171] Derby had written to Disraeli on 22 December 1866, 'Of all possible hares to start, I do not know a better one than the extension of household suffrage, coupled with plurality of voting' (Buckle, *Disraeli*, IV, p. 484).

[172] Augustus Henry Archibald Anson (1835–1877), son of the 1st Earl of Lichfield.

which he adopted, some of which I adopted, forwarding on the box with our comments.

Tuesday 15 January

Cabinet at 3
Walpole assigned reasons for delaying all attempts at a reform of the Metropolis on the ground that a Committee was sitting in the House of Commons [. . .].
Some dismay was occasioned by its being discovered that the resolutions on reform were circulating in a box without an envelope. It is clear that what I hear that Naas was one of the guilty persons.[173]

Friday 18 January (London)

At 12, Lord Monck came and for two hours we discussed Reilly's draft of Confederation bill.[174] Agreed that he should settle with Macdonald that I should meet the delegates next Wednesday.

Tuesday 22 January

Still very poorly.
In the afternoon at 5 p.m. Cartier and Langevin[175] came to discuss Confederation as regards Lower Canada. Sir F. Rogers,[176] Lord Monck, Adderley and Reilly (the draftsman) were present.
I explained the scheme but found unqualified opposition
1. On my proposal for the Legislative Council
2. On my distribution of these powers between the Central and Provincial Legislatures
3. On my proposal to place "civil right and property" open to concurrent legislation by Government and local legislatures, and

[173] Naas sent a memorandum the following day to Disraeli stating that he preferred to keep the franchise question beyond the competence of the Commission: F.B. Smith, *The Making of the Second Reform Bill* (Cambridge, 1966), p. 145.

[174] F.S. Reilly (1825–1883), professional legal expert, had produced the first draft of the bill.

[175] Sir Hector-Louis Langevin (1828–1906), Solicitor-General, Quebec Parliament (1864–1866), Postmaster-General (1866–1867).

[176] Sir Frederic Rogers (1817–1889), Permanent Under-Secretary at the Colonial Office (1860–1871), Baron Blachford (1871).

4. On Lord Monck's suggestion to put a check upon undue action of the General Legislature by passing all bills of a local character through a Committee composed of all the members of the Province affected.

The result of this is that I shall have certainly to withdraw my Committee plan, to leave the civil right to the exclusive action of the local legislatures and perhaps to make other changes.

Saturday 26 January

At 11 o'clock the British North American Association delegates came to me in Grosvenor St. to discuss Federation. Lord Monck, Adderley, Sir F.R. and Reilly present.

I commenced by explaining the bill of which I had sent a copy to each and pointing out the differences made in it from the Quebec Resolutions. Macdonald was in the main the spokesman for the rest.

The real point at which we were at issue was the constitution of the Legislative Council, they urging the nomination for life principle, I desiring to modify it. I was very firm about it, but we broke up to meet again at 3.30 at the C.O., but meanwhile to consider the matter.

The pardoning clauses were a matter of controversy [. . .].

On the whole, I am better today though I mend rather slowly.

Sunday 27 January (London)

In the afternoon Disraeli came to me, to talk over the Intercontinental Railway Guarantee. He had been in hope that somehow it might be possible to escape it but I undermined him. He is to receive from me early tomorrow the necessary papers and probably he, Stanley, Northcote and I shall have to settle everything as it is doubtful whether Lord Derby will be fit for any disruption that is not absolutely necessary [. . .].

We talked a good deal on the campaign now before us. He was in good spirits and even sanguine, anticipated a fight on the resolutions, but not before the beginning of March, and thought it probable that we should win then.

Monday 28 January

Meeting with the Delegates in the afternoon at the C.O.

I announced that I could not admit pardoning power in the bill and that I would consent to the Administrators of the Provinces being called Lieutenant-Governors, that there must be some guarantee that the first members of the Legislative Council should be fairly and impartially chosen. Lastly that I could not accept the life nomination principle for the Legislative Council.

A sort of sham fight than ensued between Macdonald and me which ended in his proposing that they should retire to consider the question.

Received an invitation from Osborne for tomorrow but decided not to go as I am not well enough.[177]

Tuesday 29 January (London)

Cabinet at Lord Derby's. He is better but still obliged to keep within doors.

We went through the Queen's Speech, discussing at great length the sentence on Reform. I suggested a slight amendment which was adopted.

Met the Delegates at the C.O. They gave in as to the constitution of the Legislative Council, suggesting a complicated but still an improved plan. I promised to consider it.

Gave Disraeli the memorandum drawn up by the Delegates on the Guarantee.

Friday 1 February

In the afternoon I went to Disraeli (in Downing Street) to talk to him about the Intercolonial Railway guarantee. He however soon threw aside the railway papers and opened the question of Reform. He told me that Baxter had calculated that household franchise would only give 820,000 persons and that a residential qualification of three years and a payment of rates would of course reduce this by about one third.[178] I discussed the question of a bill with him, subsequently reducing to writing in a letter to him my opinion on the matter.[179]

[177] Carnarvon was recovering from a severe attack of gout and was unable to walk: see Carnarvon to Gen. Grey, 20 January 1867: CP, TNA, PRO 30/6/144, fo. 126.

[178] The scheme, devised by Dudley Baxter, was based on the system of plural voting in parochial elections.

[179] Carnarvon to Disraeli, 2 February 1867: Hughenden Papers, 100/1. Reflecting on the letter in the light of subsequent events, Carnarvon stated, 'The system of separate and

Saturday 2 February

In afternoon received the Delegates' proposal on the Senate and circulated it amongst the Cabinet.[180]

A very bad influenza cold began.

In the evening we had a large dinner party – some of the Delegates, the Cranbornes, Lord and Lady Grey, the Cairns, Gathorne Hardy, etc. Afterwards to the astonishment of our guests Gladstone walked in. Hardy looked as if he would have fallen down in a fit.

Gladstone looked much aged and very ill.

Monday 4 February

Confined to the house during the day by a bad cold, but in the evening dined at Lord Derby's in Downing Street.

There were about 45 Peers – everyone in good humour at the Party being in office.

Speech[181] was much cheered when read, especially the part which alluded to Reform. The D. of Rutland asked whether "it was intended to pass the measure" to which Lord Derby said that "that must rest with the House of Commons", to which he added that no Government could hope to pass a reform measure without the co-operation of some opponents and that it did not rest entirely with us. This was much cheered.

The D. of Cambridge and the D. of Wellington[182] were both present. The D. of Buccleuch[183] told me that he had come there on purpose to give whatever support he could to the Government.

confidential communications which Mr Disraeli had carried on with each member of the Cabinet from whom he had anticipated opposition had divided them and lulled their suspicions whilst the pre-arranged decision of the interior Cabinet had so strengthened Mr Disraeli's hand that the individual in question stood in an isolated and therefore powerless position' ('Memorandum on Reform 1867', CP, BL 60831, fos 152–153).

[180]The Cabinet wished to alter the constitution of the Canadian Senate. The delegates accepted the principle, but proposed six additional members to the existing seventy-two and that the appointments should be approved by the Crown. Ten members of the Cabinet stated their options at the end of Carnarvon's memorandum on the subject. See Carnarvon, 'Confederation of the British North American Provinces', 2 February 1867: CP, TNA, PRO 30/6/109, fos 162–163.

[181]The Queen's Speech, to be read when Parliament assembled the following day.

[182]Major-Gen. Arthur Richard Wellesley (1807–1884), 2nd Duke of Wellington (1852). MP for Aldeburgh (1829–1832) and for Norwich (1837–1852).

[183]Walter Francis Scott (1806–1884), 5th Duke of Buccleuch and 7th Duke of Queensberry (1819). Lord Privy Seal (1842–1846), Lord President of the Council (1846).

Wednesday 6 February

Cabinet

[...] We next discussed Reform. Considerable divisions of opinion for the first time showed themselves on the question whether we should attempt actual legislation.[184]

Saturday 9 February

Cabinet at 3.

Discussed Reform Resolutions. The Resolution which alluded to Household suffrage was struck out to meet General Peel's very strong objection who had communicated with Lord Derby and evidently communicated his intention not to stay in the Government if the words were adhered to. I am inclined to think that it is for the best.[185]

Friday 15 February

Lowe came here in the afternoon and talked to Evelyn about our reform move.[186] He says that we have betrayed the country and the Constitution. But I still do not well see what else we could have done.

Saturday 16 February

Cabinet at which we discussed Reform. Disraeli began with a long speech congratulating us on being a "homogenous" and effective Cabinet, and then stated that the general feeling appeared to be against our resolution in favour of "plurality of votes", such plurality being understood to mean the gift of one vote to voters being £4 or £5 rating to £10, and two votes to all above £10. And he then proposed to submit his alternative plan of a plurality of votes in virtue of different franchises. He proposed 1. a £5 rating, 2. an educational franchise, 3.

[184]After a long discussion it was decided not to delay but to proceed by resolutions, prior to a bill.

[185]General Peel had threatened resignation on 6 February if the resolutions were not amended. Disraeli saw Peel two days later, telling Derby, 'I soothed him and it is all right' (Buckle, *Disraeli*, IV, p. 492).

[186]Disraeli had announced in the Commons on 11 February that the Government proposed to proceed by resolutions; the motion was agreed to (*Hansard*, CLXXXV, 11 February 1867, cols 214–219).

one for savings banks investments, 4. one in virtue of all payments of direct taxes. He showed by figures that the admission of artisans would be considerable – about 330,000 but that there would be an excess of about 60,000 on the other franchises. We all accepted this after some discussion as a very conservative measure: but Peel then announced his unconquerable aversion to all reform, for it amounted to this, and his virtual determination to leave us. A long and rather painful conversation ensued, but I am afraid he will go.[187]

Monday 18 February

In the morning called at the War Office and had some talk with General Peel as to his position with regard to the reform question.[188] He was evidently very unhappy at the alternative before him. He said on the day following to that at which the resolutions were read he wrote to Lord Derby stating insurmountable difficulty he felt.

Tuesday 19 February

Cabinet at 1.

Lord Derby began by saying that he approached the question of reform more hopefully than on any former occasion because
  1. General Peel had in the handsomest manner waived his objections to the plurality of votes paragraph[189]
  2. there was evidently in the House of Commons an intention not to oppose the resolutions as such. The Queen was prepared to do anything in her power to assist us and that she had expressed herself as believing that "the security of her throne was involved in the settlement of this question and if possible by her present advisers."

---

[187] After the meeting, Derby and Disraeli saw the Queen to seek her support and learn her attitude towards possible Cabinet changes. She agreed that the reform was more important than the loss of Peel (see Jones, *Lord Derby and Victorian Conservatism*, p. 304). Neither Cranborne nor Carnarvon had raised any objections to the scheme at the Cabinet meetings of 15 and 16 February (M. Cowling, *1867: Disraeli, Gladstone and revolution: the passing of the second Reform Bill* (London, 1967), p. 141).

[188] In a draft letter to the Queen, written possibly on that day, Disraeli stated that, besides the possible resignation of General Peel, there were more rumours that Cranborne might join him.

[189] Peel had called on Derby before the meeting and agreed to support Disraeli.

Lord Derby said that she had appealed to him in such terms that he felt bound to make every sacrifice and effort to stand by her.

We went into the question of plurality of franchises, residential qualification, amount of payment of direct taxes, which Disraeli proposed at 40/-s but Cranborne wished to stand at 20/-s.

In the evening I brought on the British North America Confederation bill for 2nd Reading. Spoke for $1\frac{3}{4}$ hours. My speech was, though long, generally liked in the House, but my voice was so weak I could hardly get through my task.[190]

Wednesday 20 February

The newspapers complimentary on my speech last night. Delegates who were present seem also entirely satisfied. Afterwards saw Macdonald. We had a nice dinner party. Club afterwards, talked much as to reform. It appears that the idea of our proposing household suffrage is afloat, that Gladstone is much alarmed by it and says that it ought not to be proposed by the Treasury Bench as it is an irrevocable step.

Thursday 21 February

Had a long talk with Cranborne in the gloom of the evening at the far end of the House of Lords library on the subject of the Reform question in the Cabinet. He is firmly convinced now that Disraeli has played us false, that he is attempting to hustle us into his measures, that Lord Derby is in his hands and that the present form which the question has now assumed has been long planned by him. On comparing notes it certainly looks suspicious. My own suspicions have for some time been roused in this direction though I hardly perhaps admitted them as fully as he did.[191]

The conclusion was a sort of offensive and defensive alliance on this question in the Cabinet, because if we are decided upon acting together we can almost beyond doubt prevent the Cabinet adopting any very fatal course. Constant communication resolved upon.

It is much to be regretted that we did not decide upon this before.

---

[190] *Hansard*, CLXXXV, 19 February 1867, cols 157–182.

[191] Cranborne sent the memoranda from Baxter, setting out the respective figures for likely borough householders and direct taxpayers. Cranborne was alarmed at Baxter's calculations for the immense increase in numbers in the latter category alone to 200,000 (Cranborne to Carnarvon, 22 February 1867: CP, BL 60758, fos 32–34.)

Saturday 23 February

A Cabinet in which Lord Derby brought forward Reform immediately. Disraeli recapitulated his figures which he assured us had been drawn up and tested by the "ablest statistician of the age". Lord Derby said that he must leave early and the business was hurried through. Then a bribery bill was introduced, barely read, and scrambled over, and lastly the scheme for the redistribution of seats was proposed.

The limit of disenfranchisement in boroughs is to be 7000 population and the limit of enfranchisement in counties to be 200,000. The four delinquent boroughs, Totnes, Reigate, Lancaster and Yarmouth to be absolutely disenfranchised which gives seven seats – twenty three seats to be gained from the boroughs in all thirty – of which fifteen to go to counties, fourteen to boroughs of 18,000 population by last census and one to University of London.

I objected to these enormous changes being thus introduced at the eleventh hour when it was impossible to consider them and Cranborne muttered his discontent in very audible tones. Excuses were made, the Cabinet generally was afraid to interfere and the various subjects were held to be settled.[192]

In the evening I met Hardy and told him that though I had submitted once I would not submit twice to such treatment.

Sunday 24 February

In the evening Cranborne came to me with some alarming calculations as to our reform scheme. It appeared that Baxter had only taken the totals and that the distribution of the new voters in the boroughs made 20,000 population would be such as to have the counterpoise (i.e. the direct taxpayers) not quite equal to the net additions made to each constituency. Thus a complete revolution would be effected in the boroughs. It seemed hardly possible to conceive an answer. We went over the figures repeatedly but always came to the same result.[193]

Cranborne then said he intended to send the figures to Lord Derby with his resignation. I persuaded him to give this up and to write to state the case and to request a Cabinet.[194] I undertook to concur with him.

[192] Nevertheless, Derby reported to the Queen that the scheme had been accepted by the Cabinet (Harris, *Memoirs of an Ex-Minister*, p. 627).

[193] See also Cranborne to Carnarvon, 24 February 1867: CP, BL 60758, fo. 36.

[194] For Cranborne's letter to Derby, see Cecil, I, pp. 233–234.

He returned home and I after a few mouthfuls of dinner drove down to Hardy's, laid the case before him and after arguing it some time persuaded him to come with me to Cranborne's where we again discussed the matter till nearly 11.[195] I then drove to General Peel's, found him in bed but begged that he should be awakened. He came down bare-legged and dressing-gowned, heard with unmistakable satisfaction my statement and declared that if either Cranborne or I left the Government he should at once resign.

Monday 25 February

By 8.30 I wrote to Lord Derby saying that I thought an explanation was necessary and that I concurred in asking for a Cabinet.

A Cabinet was in answer summoned to St. James's Square for 12.30. When I arrived there I found about eight or nine but Cranborne who had not received the summons did not arrive till past one o'clock. The stress of the controversy therefore fell upon me.

Lord Derby opened by saying that he had this morning received letters from Cranborne and me saying that on consideration we were unable to concur in the reform plan.[196] I then replied by stating the facts and by explaining that I did not dissent from the plan to which I had agreed but that the figures which had been produced required explanation. Till that was given I could not in conscience agree to a measure of which the whole character was altered.

Then ensued a very angry discussion. Disraeli did not attempt to deny the figures – he only said that there would be great variance in the boroughs in question and that the influence of land and wealth would be supreme. He at length went so far as to say that the bill had been assassinated. I immediately said that I objected to the use of such a word and others then interposed.

No attempt however was made to controvert the accuracy of our case. Whilst Disraeli was white as a sheet, Lord Derby was very angry, broke in repeatedly, using the strongest expressions of regret and dismay, etc.

Pakington seemed to lose his self-possession. He advised the Cabinet to go to the House and to announce the "unprecedented resignation of three Cabinet ministers at the last moment" and to throw themselves

---

[195] Carnarvon told Hardy 'that both he and Cranborne would resign if our measure went on' (Johnson, p. 31).

[196] Derby received Cranborne's letter early in the morning. He quickly sent it to Disraeli with a note: 'The enclosed, just received, is utter ruin. What on earth do we do?' Disraeli replied, 'This is stabbing in the back.' (See Smith, *The Making of the Second Reform Bill*, p. 155.)

upon the House. On this Peel (who had by this time openly joined me, Cranborne not having yet appeared) said, "By all means but that we should reserve to ourselves the right to tell our own story." On this the rest interposed. Finally Cranborne came and the discussion was renewed. At last when we had come to within half an hour of Lord Derby's meeting and the Cabinet had in fact dissolved, Stanley proposed as a compromise a £6 rating, but without any duality of voting.

Vehement discussion followed on this and it was only within five minutes of Lord Derby's meeting that it was finally decided to take the £6 rating so proposed!

I proposed to abide by the original proposal – household rating and plurality of votes and direct tax! but only to apply it to the larger boroughs. This would have been the best course I believe, but the Cabinet were naturally not much disposed to accept anything coming from me, and it was overruled.

None of the Cabinet stood by us. Peel, Cranborne and I were alone. Walpole sat in a corner of the room speechless. Naas who came late into the room could not make out what we were discussing and thought that we were considering the suspension of the Habeas Corpus Act.

It was altogether a very painful scene.[197]

Tuesday 26 February

A Cabinet at 2.

Great gloom and personal irritation prevailed. Cranborne and I said very little, General Peel nothing. Decided on Disraeli's proposal to withdraw the Resolutions and to undertake to introduce a bill in about a week's time.

Wednesday 27 February

Presented five of the delegates, Macdonald, Galt, Cartier, Tupper, Tilley[198] to the Queen. She was very gracious to them.[199] Lord Derby

[197]Carnarvon wrote to Derby, 'The position in which we are placed is almost desperate. I have no time to vary any proposed course of action and hardly even time to consult calmly upon what should be done.' For Derby's account of the meeting, see Derby to Queen Victoria, 25 February 1867: Royal Archives, F15/31. For Carnarvon's own version, see Carnarvon to Malmesbury, 25 February 1867: CP, BL 60831, fo. 88.

[198]Sir Samuel Tilley (1819–1896), Lib. leader, New Brunswick (1866), office-holder in Macdonald's ministries (1868–1873, 1878–1885).

[199]The British North America Bill had passed through the House of Lords the previous night.

had, I found, an audience with her before I had mine and his brougham was waiting there when I went away. The Queen said nothing to me as to the recent differences in the Cabinet and so on the whole I thought it best to say nothing myself.

At 3 there was a Court to which I also went. An obvious coldness on the part of almost all the members of the Cabinet towards me. There is I see plainly the greatest irritation.

Thursday 28 February

Saw Cranborne in the morning. It is clear that a strong pressure is to be put upon us. The papers are writing in this sense. Settled with him to consider terms of a letter to Lord Derby putting the causes of all our recent action on record.

In the afternoon in the House of Lords, the Duke of Buckingham[200] sought me out. He said that he could not agree in the present bill any more than I could in the former plan and that the only alternative was for Lord Derby to reconstruct his Cabinet. I said that I was perfectly willing and that I should be very glad to go and that I advised him to see Lord Derby and to tell him so.

Dined tête-à-tête with Evelyn. In the evening Lady Salisbury came in and talked over the state of affairs. To do her justice I think that she penetrated Disraeli's scheme in the latter part of the autumn.

Saturday 2 March

Replied to Lord Derby's letter[201] and said frankly that without an explanation to my objections I could not proceed with the Reform scheme. Saw Cranborne, talked matters over with him and sent off the letter.

Cabinet at 3 – a most painful scene. Lord Derby opened by a solemn speech recapitulating what had passed, declaring that the £6 rating plan was in his opinion impossible and inviting us to reconsider the original plan abandoned on Monday last. Cranborne, Peel and I then followed, stating that we could not accept the plan with the objections as to the smaller boroughs unanswered. I offered the alternative of a household franchise in boroughs over 25,000 population and a £6

---

[200] Richard Plantagenet Grenville (1823–1889), 3rd Duke of Buckingham and Chandos (1861). Lord President of the Council (1866–1867), Colonial Secretary (1867–1868).
[201] Carnarvon to Derby, 2 March 1867: Derby Papers 920 DER (14) 143/6.

rating in boroughs under that population. I argued this and proposed it more than once, but it was definitively negatived.

Then ensued a desultory discussion and at the end of this, it having been unanimously decided that the £6 rating scheme was impracticable, the question was formally put to each member of the Cabinet and Peel, Cranborne and I separately replied that we could not accept the plan. Lord Derby closed a red box with a heavy sigh and said, "The Party is ruined" and Disraeli added rather cynically "Poor Tory Party!" Peel, Cranborne and I left the room and so ended a most painful scene.[202]

Sunday 3 March

Lovaine[203] called in the afternoon to "congratulate" me on my resignation. He expressed himself ready to do anything and offers Northumberland House as a central place of meeting in case anything can be done to keep the Adullamites together.

Bagehot lunched here.

Monday 4 March

The morning papers were full of the schism in the Cabinet. I went down in the afternoon to the Office and a little before 5 received a note from Lord Derby asking me to come to him. I went there. He said that he had not been able to get the Queen's consent to my explaining the grounds of my retirement but that he proposed to deal very generally with the question and hoped that I should do so.[204] I said I had no wish to revive the past circumstances which could be of little satisfaction to anybody and that I should be general if it was necessary for me to speak.

[202]Derby wrote to the Queen afterwards that it had been impossible at the Cabinet meeting to obtain Cranborne's withdrawal of his intention to resign: 'If he had given way, both Carnarvon and General Peel would have waived their objections. Lord Carnarvon most reluctantly followed Lord Cranborne and General Peel, finding that unanimity was hopeless and felt that he was absolved from his undertaking to sacrifice his own personal feelings and opinions' (Buckle, *Letters*, I, p. 404).

[203]Algernon George Percy (1810–1899), Lord Lovaine (1830), 6th Duke of Northumberland (1867), Lord Privy Seal (1878).

[204]Carnarvon had written to Lord Grey the previous day on whether to take his place in the Lords 'when I am no longer, as I consider, a member of the Government' (Carnarvon to Grey, 3 March 1867: Grey Papers, 80/3). Grey advised him to be in the House 'whether I get the Queen's permission or not' (Carnarvon to Cranborne, 4 March 1867: Hatfield House Papers, 3M/E).

In the House Lord Derby made a *very* long statement. In his recapitulation of the past history he sailed very near the wind, especially when he said that the principles of the measure had been decided in the autumn by the Cabinet.[205] He did not say anything directly reflecting upon Cranborne and me and so in replying I said nothing. I spoke under great discomfort and embarrassment, and thought that I had made a terrible failure, but apparently not so to judge from the papers.[206]

Tuesday 5 March

Saw the Duke of Buckingham at the Colonial Office who succeeds me there and gave him some information on Colonial matters.

I took leave of all the heads of the different departments, who are apparently sorry to lose me. On the whole my tenure of office has been a satisfactory one.

Wednesday 6 March

Cranborne's speech was an excellent one – moderate and in good taste, a sufficient justification for us who seceded and yet no disclosure of the frequent change of policy in the Cabinet [. . .].[207]

Went down to the C.O. and explained to the D. of Buckingham all the leading questions with which he will have to deal. I gave him every information, not even withholding from him the amount of dependence he might place on Adderley.

In the evening Lady Salisbury looked in for an hour.

Friday 8 March (London)

Delivered up the Seals of the Colonial Office to the Queen at Buckingham Palace. She was smiling and gracious, said that she

---

[205] *Hansard*, CLXXXV, 4 March 1867, cols 1284–1289 and 1298–1300.

[206] Ibid., cols 1289–1291. Carnarvon wrote to Cranborne, 'Read in *The Times*, what happened last night in the Lords and let me know whether you think I went too far' (Carnarvon to Cranborne, 5 March 1867: Hatfield House Papers, 3M/E). Derby wrote the next day to the Queen, 'Lord Carnarvon went rather fuller in his personal explanations last night than he was warranted in doing: and by doing placed Lord Cranborne and General Peel in a difficult position' (Derby to Queen Victoria, 5 March 1867: Royal Archives, A35/45).

[207] *Hansard*, CLXXXV, 5 March 1867, Cranborne, cols 1347–1351. Carnarvon called it a 'masterpiece' (Carnarvon to Cranborne (copy), 6 March 1867: CP, BL 60761, fo. 24).

was sorry to receive them and hoped to have my services again on some future occasion. I expressed my great regret and sorrow and said I hoped that she was aware of the causes of my resignation. To this she assented. I said that I could not with credit to myself remain in the Cabinet and when that was the case I felt I could not serve her properly or be of use to my colleagues. She replied warmly to this that I was quite right. I then said that I trusted she had been made aware of my feelings and motives. She said yes but gave me no further encouragement to explain, so I made my bow and retired.

Horsman called to congratulate me on my resignation. Dined in the evening at the Stanhopes.[208] Met amongst others young De Grey.[209] He is a most promising fellow.

Saturday 9 March (London)

Horsman called on me to speak about Reform[210] and the present position of affairs. He was very eager and hot to do something. He said that Gladstone was dismayed at the prospect of household suffrage being proposed from the Treasury Bench, but that if ordered he would be obliged to adopt it.[211] The Whips he said feared that if the Government were allowed to dissolve on household franchise they would carry the Election and would probably go on for 4 or 5 years on "sensational legislation" with the support of Bright.

His object is 1st. to get a vote of want of confidence moved, which he said would be taken up immediately by the Liberals 2nd. not to allow if possible a dissolution. He wished me to collect two or three men of position on our side of the House to consult as to the state of affairs.

Afterwards I saw Sir W. Heathcote and Cranborne on the same subject. Very little comfort from either of them.

---

[208] Philip Henry Stanhope (1805–1875), 5th Earl Stanhope (1855). Under-Secretary of State for Foreign Affairs (1834–1835), Con. MP for Hertford (1835–1852).

[209] George Frederick Samuel Robinson (1827–1909), Viscount Goderich (1833), 2nd Earl of Ripon and Earl de Grey (1859), 1st Marquess of Ripon (1871). Secretary of State for War (1863–1866) and for India (1866), Lord President of the Council (1868–1873), Governor-General of India (1880–1884), First Lord of the Admiralty (1886), Colonial Secretary (1892–1895), Lord Privy Seal and Liberal Leader, House of Lords (1905–1908).

[210] On 4 March, Disraeli had announced that a Reform Bill would be introduced on 18 March.

[211] See Shannon, *Gladstone*, II, pp. 32–33.

Monday 11 March (London)

Lord Russell brought on his motion in the House of Lords[212] but very poorly.

Had some talk with the Duke of Richmond upon his joining the Government[213] and the present state of affairs. He is not happy I think but he said that he trusted in Lord Derby. I said that Lord Derby was entirely in Disraeli's hands. Afterwards wrote to him.[214]

Afterwards saw Sir W. Heathcote for a short time. It seems clear that nothing can be done till the Government state their views.

Wednesday 13 March (London)

Went to Gladstone's after dining at the Salisburys. Gladstone was evidently very anxious as to Reform. He said that he was not afraid of a low suffrage in the sense of redistribution because he had great confidence in the good sense of the people, but that a household suffrage would be a very serious, because inevitable, step.

Friday 15 March (London)

Lord Derby's meeting of his House of Commons supporters took place. The majority of the Party evidently swallowed the proposed measure with reluctance and disgust, but they did not fail in discipline.[215] Sir W. Heathcote was the only man of mark who expressed an unfavourable opinion. Lord Derby seems to have expounded his whole scheme which was much the same as that on which we seceded from the Government.

Sunday 17 March (London)

Bagehot lunched with us [. . .]. Phillimore called and walked for half an hour with him. Afterwards saw Sir W. Heathcote.

---

[212]Relating to electors in cities and boroughs: *Hansard*, CLXXXV, 11 March 1867, cols 1633–1643.

[213]Richmond was appointed President of the Board of Trade on 8 March.

[214]Carnarvon stated, 'I do not desire to make mischief or even give way to bitterness which I can hardly help feeling when I see the ruin to which he [Disraeli] brought a great Party' (Carnarvon to Richmond, 11 March 1867: Goodwood Papers, 822.7).

[215]The meeting, held in Downing Street to explain the Reform Bill to be introduced in the Commons in three days time, attracted 195 MPs (Buckle, *Disraeli*, IV, pp. 518–519).

Phillimore, when speaking of Gladstone, told me in confidence that so far from being a democrat in real sentiment he was staking out a "majorat" for his son with (as he believed) the prospect of a peerage. Curious!

Wednesday 20 March (London)

Dined at Northumberland House and had long conversation with Cairns who is very much alarmed at Reform prospects.

His scheme is £6 rating, a lodger franchise, a large redistribution of seats making 43 additional three-cornered constituencies (in all with the existing seven 50) and cumulative vote. He would make up his numbers by the 4 delinquent boroughs 12 new seats to the House of Commons and the remainder by political disfranchisements up to 16,000 population boroughs. His notion is that if such a scheme as this could be proposed to Gladstone, perhaps G. would accept it and that it might be carried by the Liberal Party on each side. I promised to try to see Cranborne on it.

Thursday 21 March (London)

Saw Cranborne early and talked whole question over. He sees no alternative but to turn out the Government if possible, to see Gladstone and communicate with him. He generally concurred with Cairns' plan.

I went to the National Gallery and spent 1½ hours with Cardwell and Boxall[216] over the pictures. Afterwards walked back to the Athenaeum with Cardwell and had a long and confidential talk with him on reform.

I broached Cairns' plan. Individually he had no objections to offer. He said that the bill to which he was a party last year of £7 rental went beyond what he liked, but he feared that the Liberals as a Party would not accept £6. They might perhaps take £5 rating with 3 cornered constituencies, voting papers, cumulative vote, etc. I said that it would be more difficult to obtain a considerable Conservative support on these terms. I gave him leave to mention all that I had said to Gladstone but to no one else. I distinctly said that it must be understood that in any such communication there was no intention on our part, i.e. Cranborne and mine, to intrigue and that office formed no part of our plans.

[216] Sir William Boxall (1800–1879), Director, National Gallery (1865–1874).

Saturday 23 March (London)

In the evening we had a large dinner party – Binghams,[217] Kimberleys,[218] General and Lady A. Peel,[219] Sir R. Peel,[220] Delane, young De Grey and some others.

Delane volunteered to tell me that I had "acted most wisely in resigning, that I had placed myself on a pedestal etc." It is disagreeable now that general opinion has declared itself in favour of our secession that the way in which people seem inclined to attribute it to great sagacity and appreciation of interests, when in fact it was a very disagreeable act which I certainly should not have done had I seen my way to any other course.

Reports flying about as to the possible retirement of G. Hardy and Walpole.[221] Both of them make no secret of their wish to be turned out.

Monday 1 April (Torquay)

Called on Cairns who is staying here and walked with him.[222] Talked much on Reform. He agrees with me in my estimate of persons and things except that he attributes Disraeli's conduct to his inveterate habit of deferring all decision to the last moment rather than to predetermined deception. He is quite aware that Disraeli did not forgive him for leaving the House of Commons but he equally clearly intimated that one cause why he left it was his disinclination to be obliged to defend a Reform bill which he foresaw would not be one of which he could approve.

He anticipates an evil fate for the Irish Church from a reformed House of Commons and he believes that the destruction of the Irish Church will be the first blow inflicted on the Church of England.

Wednesday 15 May (London)

Spent the afternoon at the Athenaeum at work.

Met Lowe in the afternoon. He is in despair at the Reform bill and the consequences which he says are inevitable. Everyone who has

---

[217] The Earl and Countess of Lucan.

[218] John Wodehouse (1826–1902), 1st Earl of Kimberley (1866), Lord Lieutenant of Ireland (1864–1868), Lord Privy Seal (1868–1870), Colonial Secretary (1870–1874, 1880–1882), India Office (1882–1885, 1886, 1892–1894).

[219] Lady Alicia Peel.

[220] Sir Robert Peel (1822–1895), 3rd Baronet (1850), Chief Secretary for Ireland (1861, 1865).

[221] In the event neither resigned, though, on 17 May, Hardy replaced Walpole as the Home Secretary.

[222] Cairns resigned as Attorney-General in October 1866 when he became Justice of Appeal.

money in his opinion ought to find some foreign investment for it. Here in England when once the working classes are in the ascendant taxation of the rich and a compulsory division of landed property will soon become the law.

On the other hand when dining at the Shaftesbury I met Delane and talked to him on the same subject. He is far more sanguine, says Lowe is in great danger of playing Croker's part in the Reform bill of 1832[223] and that he can well remember how only two years after that bill the Duke of Wellington was in power holding all the Offices, sending for Sir R. Peel out of Italy and receiving addresses of support from the great merchants of London. He anticipates in this case the disappearance of the Whigs (as a party) and the formation of an advanced Liberal and of a Tory party. I hope he is right.

Friday 24 May (London)

The Government have made a fresh surrender last night in Committee on the Reform bill. They have given 60 years leaseholders at a rent of £5 per annum votes in the Counties, swamping I imagine all property influences in many parts of the country.[224]

It is very alarming to see how thoroughly frightened at last are men of all parties – Whigs, Conservatives, Liberals. Nevertheless the Party still support the wretched impostor who is running them and the Country.

Tuesday 2 July (London)

Walked home from the House with Kimberley and had a curious conversation. He admitted that there was not a man on his side who liked Gladstone and who yet was prepared to follow any one else. He said that failing Gladstone there was absolutely no one capable of leading on their side. He looked forward with great apprehension to the meeting of a new Parliament and the advent of so many new and inexperienced members with such a leader as Gladstone, and he contemplated the probability that Disraeli might remain on in office for several years to come. Formerly he was one of the extremist Liberals in the House of Lords now he has become sobered into

---

[223]John Wilson Croker (1780–1857), friend of Peel, resigned as Secretary of the Admiralty in 1830; opposed the Reform Bill and resigned as MP on its passing. See M. Brock, *The Great Reform Act* (London, 1973), p. 216.

[224]*Hansard*, CLXXXVII, 23 May 1867, cols 991–1011.

Conservatism. He fears for the House, and is alarmed for the existence of the Church. He dreads a wild spirit of change taking possession of every one and destroying Lords, and Church and Monarchy all together.

Wednesday 10 July (London)

The Reform bill passed last night through Committee in the House of Commons. It passed in furious haste with hardly any debate.[225]

Had some talk with Cranborne and Sir W. Heathcote on the subject, but I am not sanguine of amending it much. Lord Stanhope today used as an argument against attempting any amendment that it would be well not to offend the new constituencies. It is altogether very sad.

Rode down to Holland House in the afternoon for a large party at which Royalties were as thick as blackberries from the Pasha of Egypt to the Princess Mary.[226]

Thursday 11 July (London)

Had a long talk with Lord Grey at his house on the course to be adopted in the House of Lords with regard to the Reform bill.[227] He showed me a long memorandum which he had drawn up containing proposals for amendments in favour of the cumulative vote in two-membered constituencies, of an increase of members for the University and Inns of Court which were to be obtained by grouping small boroughs, non-vacation of seats upon acceptance of office, and lastly to enable a peer on the death of his father to retain his seat in the House of Commons if he should so choose.

I objected to the two-membered constituencies and raised some objections as to the last; but as he said he should move it on the report which would avoid interference with the Committee I said no more. But I am certain that it is idle to attempt the cumulative vote except for the three-cornered constituencies and I do not think that the House

[225] Ibid., CLXXXVIII, 9 July 1867, cols 1264–1292.
[226] See *The Times*, 11 July 1867, p. 9.
[227] Earl Grey, during the debate on the second reading of the bill in the House of Lords on 16 July, sought to obtain more time for discussion (*Hansard*, CLXXXVIII, 16 July 1867, col. 1616).

of Lords are ripe for such a change as Lord Grey contemplates with regard to charities.

Saturday 13 July (Hatfield)

Spent the morning with Cranborne going through the Reform bill. Wrote afterwards to Lord Grey to urge him not to move the cumulative vote in *two*-membered constituencies.

In the afternoon, we went down to Hatfield.[228]

Tuesday 16 July (London)

Canvassed privately a good many peers on the Reform bill[229] and arranged a meeting at Lord Harrowby's[230] for Saturday next at 11 a.m.

Lord Grey gave up his plan for two-membered constituencies in favour of three-cornered ones.

Friday 19 July (London)

Lord Derby's meeting of Peers in Downing Street. He commenced by a long recapitulation of the history of Reform in which he dextrously but deliberately misrepresented Cranborne and myself on three points.

1. He said the Cabinet had been with the exception of General Peel unanimous in favour of household suffrage guarded by residence and personal payment of rates.

2. That when Cranborne and I wrote to him on the Sunday night we said that we were not ready to accept household suffrage.[231]

3. He expressed surprise at the shortness of our notice.

I followed him and replied to the 1st. by saying the Cabinet had not been unanimous, that they had only accepted household suffrage when accompanied by many other safeguards on the faith of certain explanations.

---

[228] He wrote the following day to Cranborne, 'Lord Salisbury is very anxious we should get together a meeting. I am not very sanguine: but the attempt is worth making and I have written to Percy to ask for Northumberland House' (Carnarvon to Cranborne, 14 July 1867: Hatfield House Papers, 3M/E).

[229] First reading of the Reform Bill in the Lords.

[230] Dudley Ryder (1797–1882), 2nd Earl of Harrowby (1847), Lord of the Admiralty (1827–1828), Secretary, India Board (1830–1831), Chancellor, Duchy of Lancaster (1855).

[231] See entry for 2 March 1867.

I replied to the 2nd by stating what had happened, that figures had been given us at the last moment and that they turned out to be untrustworthy and the counterpoises founded on them illusory.

I replied to the 3rd. by saying that we only had the scheme before us on Saturday night and therefore had but 24 hours in which to decide.

I stated what I thought of the bill and said that I should not debar myself from the honour of adopting any amendments. Proceeded to say in my own name and in that of any who agreed with me, whether present or absent, that attendance in that room was not to be held as any evidence of approval of any part of the bill and that we claimed absolute freedom of action in every stage of the measure.

Bath who was there said that I had made everything perfectly clear, but I am not sure myself whether I could not have done it better.

Lord Derby did not look very well pleased, especially at my concluding remarks.[232]

Saturday 20 July (London)

A meeting of Peers at Lord Harrowby's which I had organised for the purpose of considering the Reform bill – Lords Grey, Shaftesbury, Selkirk,[233] Bath, Hardinge,[234] Zetland,[235] Rivers,[236] Southampton,[237] Warwick,[238] Romney,[239] Amherst,[240] De Vesci,[241] Duke of Buccleuch,

[232]When Grey laid an amendment on the table in the Lords on 22 July, Derby remarked to Disraeli, 'I have immediately sent out as strong a Whip as possible, against it. But I learn that the whole of the Opposition will support him and he has been tampering, with the aid of Carnarvon, not unsuccessfully with our people' (Jones, *Lord Derby and Victorian Conservatism*, p. 316).

[233]Dunbar James Douglas Hamilton (1809–1885), 6th Earl of Selkirk (1820), Keeper of the Great Seal (1852, 1858–1859).

[234]Charles Stewart Hardinge (1822–1894), 2nd Viscount Hardinge (1856), MP for Downpatrick (1852–1856).

[235]Thomas Dundas (1795–1873), 2nd Earl of Zetland (1839), Grand Master of the Freemasons (1844–1870).

[236]Horace Pitt-Rivers (1814–1880), 6th Baron Rivers (1867).

[237]Charles Fitzroy Wriothesley (1804–1872), 3rd Baron Southampton (1810).

[238]George Guy Greville (1818–1893), 4th Earl of Warwick (1853), ADC to Queen Victoria (1878–1893). Warwick, described by Carnarvon as 'a very uncompromising opponent of the bill', was pessimistic about the wisdom of Grey pressing for amendment of the Reform Bill: 'In any event, he will be in a small minority, and unless the Whigs take it up as a party question to turn Lord Derby out, that minority will be small' (Warwick to Carnarvon, 21 July 1867: Grey Papers, 80/3).

[239]Charles Marsham (1804–1874), 3rd Earl of Romney (1845), Con. MP for Kent West (1844–1845).

[240]William Amhurst Tyssen-Amherst (1835–1909), 1st Baron Amherst (1892), Con. MP for Norfolk West (1880–1885) and for Norfolk South-west (1885–1892).

[241]Thomas Veasey de Vesci (1803–1875), 3rd Viscount of Abbeyleix (1855).

Lord Harrowby and myself. We talked the matter over and on the whole separated with something like a general understanding. Another meeting was fixed for Friday at 11 a.m., and a sub-committee appointed of the Duke of Buccleuch, Lord Harrowby, Lord Grey, Romney, Hardinge and myself to consider amendments and to meet at Lord Grey's on Tuesday at 11 a.m.

Had an interview with the Sultan[242] at Buckingham Palace, with some 40 or 50 others. His face is handsome and his eye good. Nothing passed beyond a bow and a shake of hand and a few words in Turkish which Fuad[243] who was with him always translated into *"enchanté de faire votre connaissance"*.

Monday 22 July (London)

Debate on 2nd Reading of the Reform bill in the House of Lords. Lord Grey broke down, partly from exhaustion, partly from a strange sort of confusion of mind as it seemed. I spoke about ten o'clock to a House that rapidly filled and which soon grew excited as I went on. It was altogether perhaps the most telling speech that I ever made in the House, though I do not think my best.[244]

Tuesday 23 July (London)

Debate resumed.[245] Lord Derby made a rather sharp attack upon me. He was obviously very angry at what had passed.[246] Every one else however seems to be pleased and a great many people have come or written to me to thank me for what I said.

Lord Shaftesbury made a very fine speech late and one which was even finer for its fearlessness.[247] He stated exactly what he knew of the working class and predicted the use which they would make of the power now transferred to them. In that speech he jeopardised the popularity of a life time but he rose incalculably in the opinion of every honest man. I can hardly say how much I respected him for it.

---

[242] Abdul Aziz I (1830–1876), Sultan, Ottoman Empire (1861–1876).

[243] Fuad Pasha (1814–1869), Grand Interpreter for the Porte (1852, 1855), Grand Vizier (1861–1866).

[244] *Hansard*, CLXXXVIII, 22 July 1867, cols 1838ff. Kimberley noted, 'Carnarvon was admirable' (A. Hawkins and J. Powell (eds), *The Journal of John Wodehouse, First Earl of Kimberley, for 1862 to 1912*, Camden 5th series 9 (Cambridge, 1997), p. 206.

[245] *Hansard*, CLXXXVIII, 23 July 1867, cols 1916–2033.

[246] Ibid., Derby, cols 2023–2031.

[247] Ibid., Shaftesbury, cols 1917–1934.

Friday 26 July (London)

My life is one ceaseless running to and fro consulting about this Reform bill, discussing amendments, and explaining to some stupid peer the meaning of some very simple proposition.

Monday 29 July (London)

House of Lords in Committee on Reform bill. I spoke in favour of the general principle of extending the redistribution scheme, but in opposition to Lord Halifax's motion.[248]
The spectacle of weakness and incompetency exhibited by the Government was pitiable. Lord Derby's absence, from gout, left them absolutely without the power of expressing an opinion upon any subject. They surrendered different points without one word of discussion and when asked once how they intended to vote the Earl of Malmesbury foolishly announced that the House would see when the division should take place. This raised such a storm that Malmesbury was obliged to apologise. Committee adjourned about 12 $\frac{1}{2}$ o'clock at night.

Tuesday 30 July (London)

The Committee again all night. We carried the representation of minorities moved by Cairns by a majority of nearly three to one. I spoke on it. This was the principal amendment.[249]
Adjourned about 12.30 again.

Wednesday 31 July (London)

All the morning spent over redistribution schemes with Hugessen[250] and at Lord Harrowby's where some seven or eight peers were present.

[248]Charles Wood (1800–1885), 1st Viscount Halifax (1866), a former First Lord of the Admiralty and a Liberal, proposed that there should be an increase in the number of representatives for the larger and more important constituencies (*Hansard*, CLXXXIX, 29 July 1867, cols 256–327; Halifax, cols 256–271, Carnarvon, cols 280–285). Cairns moved the amendment: Contents 124, Non-Contents 76.
[249]Ibid., cols 405–473.
[250]Edward Knatchbull-Hugessen (1829–1893), Lord of Treasury (1859–1866), Under-Secretary for the Colonial Office (1871–1874), 1st Baron Brabourne (1880).

Lord Sherborne[251] came but left on the ground of non-agreement with our views. The Duke of Buccleuch was there.

Thursday 1 August (London)

House in Committee on Reform bill. Lord Grey moved his amendment in favour of increased distribution of seats. I had drawn up the proposed plan of redistribution after consultation with K. Hugessen. Lord Grey made a long and poor speech on opening his plan, leaving people in entire doubt as to what he proposed.[252] I afterward re-stated his case as clearly as I could.[253]

Lord Derby came down to the House with his arm in a sling, looking very ill. He was irritable and evidently very angry, but he put on the screw by threatening to move to report progress in order to consult the Cabinet (as if he ever consulted any one but Disraeli!),[254] that men gave way and we were beaten by 12. Lord Shrewsbury,[255] Lord Amherst, the Duke of Buccleuch and several others who had attended our meeting at Lord Harrowby's did not vote or voted with the Government. Twelve voted with me.

It is a great chance lost.

Monday 5 August (London)

Came up by the early train with the Greys, Lowe, Cork[256] and A. Herbert.

In the House the Government gave up the amendment on the Lodger franchise (raising it to £15 from £12) which they had accepted with such unwise precipitation.[257] It was a very contemptible spectacle and I do not think that any one was edified on either side of the House. The bill passed the Report. Dined with Stanhope at the Carlton.

[251]James Henry Legge Dutton (1804–1883), 3rd Baron Sherborne (1862).

[252]*Hansard*, CLXXXIX, 1 August 1867, cols 526–539.

[253]Ibid., cols 565–571. Earlier in the day, Carnarvon wrote to Grey, 'You must remember that we have but a few hours tonight in which to put our views forward – and no time to inform men's minds. If we produce a reasonable and symmetrical scheme, the Government are not likely to be able to make much of an answer, especially if Lord Derby is absent' (Carnarvon to Grey, 1 August 1867: Grey Papers, 80/13).

[254]*Hansard*, CLXXXIX, 1 August, 1867, cols 565–571.

[255]Henry John Chetwynd-Talbot (1803–1868), 18th Earl of Shrewsbury (1856), Vice-Admiral.

[256]Richard Edmund Boyle (1829–1904), 9th Earl of Cork and Ossery (1856), Deputy Speaker, House of Lords.

[257]*Hansard*, CLXXXIX, 5 August 1867, cols 821–828, Lodger Franchise in Boroughs; amendment moved by Earl Russell, cols 821–822; motion agreed.

I stood godfather today to Cranborne's child.[258] The ceremony took place at All Saints. Lady Salisbury was godmother.

Tuesday 6 August (London)

Reform bill passed the 3rd. Reading, Lord Derby admitting in *ipsissimus verbis* that "it was a leap in the dark."[259] No Prime Minister ever before ventured to say such a thing. Lord Grey walked back from the House with me. He is very much depressed at the prospect before us – and with reason.[260]

Monday 12 August (London)

Lunched with the Sandons.
In the House of Lords we considered the Commons reasons of disagreement with our amendments of the Reform bill. Lord Derby made one of the most imprudent speeches I ever heard, a speech abusing and ridiculing the House of Commons whilst he was obliged to accept their conclusions.[261]
Afterwards in putting a question as to the Australian postal subsidy I had rather an unpleasant little wrangle with him. He interrupted me in so disagreeable a manner that it is possible that I replied rather more sharply than I should otherwise have done.[262]

Saturday 17 August (Highclere)

Sir W. Heathcote came over and I had some hasty talk with him on political matters. I threw out to him the doubt which I have recently

[258] Cranborne had invited Carnarvon to take on the task 'both for auld lang syne and political sympathy'. He added, 'I am sure it would have the effect of implanting some principles in the infant's mind. Shall we call him "Benjamin" in memoriam of this year's campaign or Ichabod?' (Cranborne to Carnarvon, 26 July 1867: Hatfield House Papers, 3M/E).

[259] *Hansard*, CLXXXIX, 6 August 1867, cols 930–952; Derby, cols 948, 950–951. At the end of the debate, Derby stated, 'No doubt we are making a great experiment and "taking a leap in the dark".' The bill was passed with only Lords Ellenborough and Selkirk against. The Royal Assent was given on 15 August. See also A. Hawkins, 'Lord Derby and Victorian Conservatism', *Parliamentary History*, 6 (1987), p. 254.

[260] Cranborne was equally pessimistic. He told Carnarvon, 'The best thing would be to settle some compromise at a Conference; but I feel that everybody was too weary to attempt it' (Cranborne to Carnarvon (copy), 9 August 1867: Hatfield House Papers, 3M/E).

[261] *Hansard*, CLXXXIX, 12 August 1867, cols 1306–1326; Derby, cols 1306–1316.

[262] Ibid., cols 1329–1332; Carnarvon, cols 1329–1330.

had whether under my present relations with Lord Derby I ought to retain the High Stewardship of the University.[263] He strongly urges the retention of it, even if my disagreement with Lord Derby were greater than it is. There was of course much force in all that he said, but I am not quite clear that under all and possible circumstances he would be right.

Saturday 21 September (Hatfield)

Reached Hatfield (from York) after rather a tiring day's journey. Found here the Queen of Holland,[264] the Clarendons,[265] Stanhopes, Cowleys,[266] one or two Dutch people and Subaroff, a rather pleasing Russian attaché. Stanley also came and came not in a pleasant humour. He has not yet recovered his temper and seems to resent my opposition to the Reform bill as a personal attack on himself. It is very absurd but I shall take no notice of it.

Lord Cowley is agreeable. Like every one else alarmed at the recent reform measures and citing all his foreign experiences in aid of his opinion. The Queen is very frank and easy to get on with so things do not drag much.

Sunday 27 October (Highclere)

Had a long talk with Cranborne as to political prospects. He is very hopeless of doing anything under present circumstances. At first his reasoning went almost to the utter uselessness of doing or attempting anything. Afterwards he agreed that it was our duty to go on and make the best of a very bad affair. He agreed with me that the only course which gave any hope of success would be the formation of some third Party as analogous as possible to the Peelites; but he said and truly that they were essentially a *central* party whilst our materials were likely to be drawn from an extreme side. In his opinion Lord Derby's death or retirement probably would offer the first opening for a redistribution and resettlement of parties.

---

[263]Appointed as High Steward of Oxford University on 13 October 1859, Carnarvon continued to hold office until his death.

[264]Sophie Friederike Mathilde (1818–1872), first wife of King Wilhelm III of Holland.

[265]George William Frederick Villiers (1800–1870), 4th Earl of Clarendon (1838), Foreign Secretary (1853–1858, 1865–1866, 1868–1870).

[266]Henry Richard Charles Wellesley (1804–1884), 1st Earl Cowley (1857), ambassador at Paris (1852–1867).

He had had advances made to him by Gladstone and J. S. Mill[267] which he has neither accepted nor rejected. His dislike of Disraeli was certainly not diminished. His view as to any future policy not to hold for a while untenable posts, but to decide clearly what we are to stand upon.

Tuesday 29 October (Highclere)

Cranborne and Sir W. Heathcote and I had a long discussion on the present political situation. The general conclusion arrived at was free criticism of the government and government measures, but no pronounced opposition to the Government as such, though we are all agreed that the main subject in view is the getting rid politically of Lord Derby's and Disraeli's supremacy. Cranborne does not rank Stanley very high. He has, he says, less influence in the House than he had and does not impress.

We talked a good deal about the Irish Church, but settled that it is not necessary now to indicate any particular course of action. The issue of the new Commission and the reasonableness of leaving the decision of so large a question to the new constituencies are adequate reasons for delaying all real action for another year. But we all lean towards larger measures.

The chief object should be no longer to defend untenable posts. It is even desirable to clear away all collateral questions that only raise dust and embarrass Parliament in coming to a decision. We ought to settle what we will not defend and that by which we intend to stand.

The English Church is a great problem, but even here Cranborne agrees with me that moderation on both sides is the doctrine now to be inculcated.

Sunday 10 November (Highclere)

Received a letter from Mayo[268] asking me to serve on a Commission which the Government are about to issue with regard to Primary Education in Ireland and to act as Chairman in place of Lord Rosse[269] who has just died.

---

[267]John Stuart Mill (1806–1873), author and Lib. MP for Westminster (1865–1868).

[268]Mayo to Carnarvon, 9 November 1867: CP, BL 60829, fo. 2.

[269]William Parsons (1800–1867), 3rd Earl of Rosse (1841), scientist and educationist, had died on 31 October. Carnarvon declined the invitation to chair the Commission on Irish Primary Education: see Diary, 12 November 1867.

Decided to go to Winchester to talk the matter over or rather the form of refusal with him.

Friday 29 November (Oxford)

Went down to Oxford [. . .] called on Dr. Pusey[270] and had some talk with him [on the Ritual question]. Liddon[271] especially dreads the effect which any legislation in this subject may have upon the minds of many persons who are already nervously sensitive on the question of State interference [. . .]. Nothing could be more moderate than both Pusey and Liddon. Both too see that the main danger at present lies in the possible ascendancy of the infidel party rather than the Low Church. The story which I have heard on this point from all at Oxford is concurrent and most melancholy. The younger tutors and masters seem in a great measure to be poisoned by Mill's philosophy and they of course poison the undergraduates with whom they are brought in contact. The educational system so far as philosophy is concerned seems to have become inverted since my day. Then Classical authors, Plato and Aristotle, formed the basis of instruction and were illustrated by Christian writers: now modern (not to call them Christian) writers like Mill are the textbooks and basis, illustrated by heathen writings. The result is a deplorable one. The main interest (Liddon says) centres in philosophy rather than classics the intellectual set of young men's minds in this direction – and the philosophy in vogue is already going far beyond that of Mill himself. It is a gross and coarse materialism in which all idea of free will is discarded.

[270] Edward Bouverie Pusey (1800–1882), Regius Professor of Hebrew, Oxford University since 1828.
[271] Henry Liddon (1829–1890), Vice-Principal, St Edmund Hall, Oxford (1859–1870), canon at St Paul's Cathedral and Ireland Professor of Exegesis, Oxford University (1870–1890). Both Pusey and Liddon were leading lights in the Oxford Movement.

1868

Monday 13 April (The Coppice)

I went to Phillimore's for the night. At Reading Station I was overwhelmed by the news of Lord Salisbury's most sudden death.[272] The result will be great and I am afraid very unfortunate. Cranborne's removal to the House of Lords though it will strengthen my hands wonderfully and be personally very pleasant to me leaves the Conservative Party without anyone to rally round. Disraeli almost becomes a necessity to them and I am afraid that it will drive them to him and strengthen him.[273] Politically matters look very gloomy to me.

Thursday 23 April (London)

We had a debate in the House of Lords on Church Rates. Lord Derby made as unwise and inconsequential speech for an extremely clever man as I ever heard. I followed him.[274]

Lord Derby took his seat just below the gangway immediately under me. He seemed disinclined to shake hands, so I thought it better to offer to do so. He answered I thought rather coldly and in an embarrassed manner, so having done my duty I left him afterwards alone.

Saturday 2 May (London)

Breakfasted at Grillions, dined at the Academy.[275] I was agreeably placed between Landseer[276] and Lord Clarendon. Lord C. spoke most gloomily of everything from political prospects down to public morals. We got upon the subject of the House of Lords and he said that he had recently spoken with Bright[277] on it. Bright said that he was most

[272]James Brownlow William Cecil, 2nd Marquess of Salisbury, died on 12 April at Hatfield.
[273]Disraeli had become Prime Minister on the resignation of Derby on 27 February.
[274]Compulsory Church Rates Abolition Bill, second reading. *Hansard*, CXCI, 23 April 1868, Derby, cols 1124–1127, Carnarvon, cols 1127–1129.
[275]Anniversary dinner held at the Royal Academy: see *The Times*, 4 May 1868, p. 10.
[276]Sir Edwin Henry Landseer (1802–1873), noted painter of animals.
[277]John Bright (1811–1889), Lib. MP for Birmingham (1857–1885), President of the Board of Trade (1868–1870), Chancellor, Duchy of Lancaster (1873–1874).

anxious to see the House maintain its position and influence, that he considered it essential that it should do so but that he every week received communications of the most radical kind for its reform. Life Peerages were the most moderate of their proposals.

Lord Clarendon spoke of Lord Derby. I said that though I had felt that his personal manner to me was unduly bitter and unfriendly that I should never forget his age and our past relations. Lord Clarendon said that as for that he considered that his speech last year in the House on Reform had "squared accounts", and he went on to say that Lord Derby never forgave and that if he could find out a tender point he would endeavour always to rub in salt.

Sunday 3 May (London)

Cranborne, or Salisbury as I must learn to call him, called this afternoon and I talked over several matters with him of consequence.

Monday 4 May (London)

Explanation in the House of Commons by Disraeli. At the end of the first half hour no one could tell whether he meant resignation or dissolution.[278] W. Harcourt[279] dined with us alone. We talked of Confederation and other matters amongst which he mentioned this curious fact, that Delane had told him that in November 1866 Disraeli had shown him (Delane) a copy of the Reform bill with a clause enacting household suffrage! And this at a time when Disraeli would not consent in the Cabinet even to the resolutions being printed for our use.

Friday 26 June (London)

I opened the Irish Church debate,[280] speaking I imagine for nearly an hour. The opposition were of course much pleased, a few, *very*

---

[278] The Government had been defeated on 30 April in the Commons on the Established Church (Ireland) Bill in Committee by 330 to 265. For Disraeli's statement, see *Hansard*, CXCI, cols 1694–1707.

[279] Sir William Vernon Harcourt (1827–1904), Lib. MP for Oxford (1868–1880), Derby (1880–1895), and Monmouthshire (1895–1904), Solicitor-General (1873–1874), Home Secretary (1880–1885), Chancellor of the Exchequer (1886, 1892–1895).

[280] Established Church (Ireland) Bill, second reading: *Hansard*, CXCIII, 26 June 1868, cols 4–19.

few, of my own friends like Hardinge were on the whole pleased, but the main body looked very annoyed. The Government seemed to feel particularly the attack on them. The House was crowded and very attentive. I think it was for me a good speech, though I suspect that in *manner* I was too bitter. In fact I was warmed up as I went on.

Salisbury's speech[281] was a very fine one, of a very high order in all respects, but it left open as I thought a dangerous point for the future in deliberately joining for the sake of present argument Ireland with England and in connecting more closely than I liked the fortunes and futures of the English and Irish Churches.

Saturday 27 June (London)

My speech of last night seems to have been very successful. The Government very angry and of course their supporters, but others pleased. Dined at the Duke of Cleveland's.

Last night found on my arrival a letter from Mayo challenging a statement that I had made in the House in my speech. I went to the Athenaeum to refer to Hansard and back files and then wrote my answer which is to go tomorrow morning.

Monday 29 June (London)

Debate renewed for the third night in House of Lords on Irish Church.[282] The Chancellor attacked me with very considerable bitterness and when I attempted to make a personal explanation at the end the Government and the back benchers were so furious that they positively shouted me down. I could not say what I wished.

It was the first time that I ever saw this in the House of Lords and proves how angry they are with me. No one from our side of the House except Rollo[283] voted for the bill. The bishops were all very cross. I did not get to bed till 4, when I reached Grosvenor Square with Somers[284] I still felt so heated and the morning felt so fresh and pleasant that I walked on with him to Hyde Park Corner.

[281] Ibid., Salisbury, cols 39–90.
[282] Ibid., cols 243–283.
[283] John Rogerson (1835–1916), 10th Baron Rollo (1852), Lib. peer, later Unionist.
[284] Charles Somers-Cocks (1819–1883), 3rd Earl Somers (1852), Lord-in-Waiting (1853–1857).

Thursday 3 December (Oakley – Highclere)

News of Disraeli's resignation.[285] Beach[286] received a circular from
D. stating it, and *The Times* had an article on it.[287]

As a matter of political tactics it is the wisest step I think that he
could take.

[285] At the general election, the Liberals came into office with 354 seats, the Conservatives
holding 272. Disraeli immediately resigned, together with his Cabinet, over Irish Church
disestablishment.

[286] Sir Michael Edward Hicks Beach (1837–1916), Con. MP for Gloucestershire East (1864–
1885) and for Bristol West (1885–1906), Chief Secretary for Ireland (1874–1878, 1886–
1887), Colonial Secretary (1878–1880), Chancellor of the Exchequer (1885–1886, 1895–1902),
created Earl St Aldwyn (1913).

[287] See *The Times*, 3 December 1868, p. 9.

1869

Thursday 7 January (Highclere)

At night after every one else had gone to bed I had a curious conversation with Delane. 1st. he told me on my enquiring it of him that it was true that he was shown in the winter of 1866 a printed draft Reform bill substantially founded upon the resolutions which were at that time kept in MS. in the Cabinet which Lord Derby and Disraeli would not put into print for fear of their becoming known, and which even they at first refused to circulate among the Cabinet. Was there ever such treachery? 2nd. The present Government are deliberating upon endowing the Roman Catholic Church and the Presbyterians with the money available of the Irish Church. They applied to Delane to help them, but he declined to do this. He looks upon it as good in itself but as a breach of public faith.

Thursday 28 January (London – Hatfield)

The Ritual Commission[288] again came down to Hatfield in the afternoon. Had a long talk with Salisbury.

Told him of my recent conversation with Delane (7th inst.) as to Reform bill. Attended to the report that he had promised his support to Cairns in the leading of the House of Lords. He said that Cairns had written to him offering to give up the lead to him, but that he had declined this (through inability to act with Disraeli), and told him that he should consider each question on its merits and would so far as he could support him. I suspect that the promise of support was rather strongly expressed and that he looks through Cairns, even from below

[288] A Royal Commission on Ritualistic Practices in the Church of England, 'to inquire into the varying interpretations put upon the rubrics, orders and directions', had been formed in June 1867. When Gladstone invited Carnarvon to join the Commission in December 1868, the latter wrote in his diary, 'Lord Stanhope wishes to discuss the Anathasian Creed, Venn and the Low Churchmen to alter the absolution of the sick, Stanley to throw down all dogmatic restrictions. It is very doubtful whether I can do any good, but it seems just possible that at this moment an attempt might be made to stop this dangerous opening out of every question and so though with great doubt, I have decided to accept' (Diary, 28 December 1868).

the gangway, to take great part in leading the Party. I expressed the hope that he had not identified himself with Cairns,

1st. because Cairns is the same now as Disraeli.

2nd. because Cairns on Church questions is absolutely unsound.

I told him that if he would come forward as leader of the House of Lords, even with the view of bringing about a deadlock and compelling a choice between himself and Disraeli, I would do anything I could; but that having no confidence in Cairns, Disraeli or any others of the late Government I would not support them, except in so far as each particular measure which they might put forward was good.

Saturday 24 April (London)

Three persons have spoken on political matters to me today in rather a curiously coincidental manner.

1st. B. Cochrane called for some lunch and afterwards retailed all his own grievances and those of the party with whom he comes in contact. The burden of it was the general distrust that has now succeeded to the former confidence in Disraeli and the wish to get rid of him and to see Salisbury and myself in some recognised position as leaders.

2nd. The Duke of Wellington whom I met at dinner opened the same subject, stating that Cairns was a failure as leader, that I had been badly treated but that there was only one wish that I would return to my place in the House and that moderate people had confidence in me particularly.

3rd. The Duke of Cambridge opened on the same line, deplored Cairns as leader[289] and urged strongly my return and Salisbury's to the Front Bench and Salisbury as leader. He said everything was going by the board in the House of Commons and that unless matters could be rearranged the worst results would follow. He looked however to getting rid of Disraeli – but that is the real difficulty.

Saturday 5 June (London)

Very far from well and obliged to send for Gull,[290] who pronounced that it was only a sort of nervous disturbance from one's work, and that a little care and rest would soon bring me round.

Salisbury called at 11 and though very poorly went with him to the meeting of Conservative Peers in St James's Square. It was very full.

---

[289]'His very pronounced Low Church proclivities coupled perhaps with a certain jealousy towards him as a newcomer prevented him from being popular there' (J. Bryce, 'Lord Chancellor Cairns', in *Studies in Contemporary Biography* (New York, 1920), p. 186).

[290]Sir William Withey Gull (1815–1890), physician to Queen Victoria (1887–1890).

Cairns began by a long and an able speech declaring that the only course to be taken with the Irish Church bill was to reject it,[291] and that there was no middle term. Salisbury followed in a very able speech, asking what next would follow on rejection and that as it was only a question of time and pressure he could not vote for its rejection. On the other side Lord Harrowby and various second rate speakers followed, then Lord Stanhope declared that rejection of bill would destroy all chance of getting better terms and on this Lord Derby made a very vigorous speech in his old manner, denouncing the bill in the strongest language and looking almost pointedly at me said that there was anyhow no individual who did not dislike and protest against every part of the bill and regard it as revolutionary and abominable.

On this after a few words from the Duke of Rutland I said that I could not assent to that uncompromising denunciation of the bill, but that I did object greatly to some parts (disendowment) which were repugnant to me and which were unjust and cruel to the Irish Church; that I was ready to join in amending this, but that I deprecated earnestly the rejection of the measure. I urged that such a rejection would be dangerous to the House as bringing it into collision with the Country; that the final result was inevitable; that the bill would then come to us without the powers of making amendments and would be then most injurious to the Church. I ended by pointing out that the times were critical, that the old constitutional forces were almost in suspense, that the House of Commons was more democratic: that the present crisis might be tided over and the Country recover its balance but that if a collision was provoked indefinite changes and disasters might follow.

Monday 7 June (London)

Very busy in the House on the subject of the Irish Church bill. Several Peers came to me to say that they should vote for the bill or that they should stay away.[292] Cawdor[293] and Delamere[294] both said this and others expressed themselves doubtfully.

---

[291] On 3 March, Gladstone announced that he proposed to introduce a bill to end the Established Church in Ireland.

[292] 'I have a list of 35 or 36 Peers already who will either stay or vote for the second reading of the Bill and I hope and believe it will grow' (Carnarvon to Salisbury, 7 June 1869: Hatfield House Papers, 3M/E).

[293] John Frederick Campbell (1817–1898), 2nd Earl Cawdor (1860), Con. MP for Pembrokeshire (1841–1860).

[294] Hugh Cholmondley (1811–1882), 2nd Baron Delamere (1855), Con. MP for Denbighshire (1840–1841) and for Montgomery (1841–1847).

Tuesday 8 June (London)

Again busy in the House.[295]

Had a communication with Granville.[296] Told him that I thought
it was possible to get rid of the majority though with difficulty but
that matters would be smoothed if any indication could be given
of a readiness on the part of the Government to consider *reasonable*
amendments.[297]

His reply was much as I expected – that of course the Government
could not offer this etc., but he intimated that any amendments that
could be devised which were plausible and which did not vitally affect
the bill or "re-endow" the Irish Church would not be objected to. He
hinted that some margin had been left in the bill with this object and
that Gladstone was really sincere in his wish to leave the Church as
well as he could, but not re-endowed. I said that the object of any
amendment would probably be to improve the pecuniary position
of the Church. He parted with, I think, the understanding that the
Government would offer no hasty or unfair objection to reasonable
amendments.

He expressed himself astonished at the folly of the move, and told
me in strict confidence of a certain letter that had been written to
Lord D. by —.

Thursday 17 June (London)

Irish Church debate again going on. Salisbury's speech was very
good and produced a great effect. Lord Derby's was a melancholy
spectacle of the failure of great powers.[298] Physically, oratorically,
mentally, there was a gulf between what he was now and had been a
few years ago. He could not resist, as usual, an attempt to fix some
sort of attack and misrepresentation on me, but I contented myself
with almost a simple denial. His last sentences were almost pathetic,
but he closes a career which on the whole I suppose has done as much

---

[295]The second reading of the Irish Bill took place that day: *Hansard*, CXCVI, 8 June 1869,
cols 1370–1391.

[296]George Leveson-Gower (1815–1891), 2nd Earl Granville (1846). Under-Secretary for
Foreign Affairs (1840–1841), Foreign Secretary (1851–1852, 1870–1874, 1880–1885), Colonial
Secretary (1868–1870, 1886).

[297]Granville wrote to Gladstone after the meeting, 'He is always oversanguine in this
matter' (Ramm, 1952, I, p. 27).

[298]Third night of second reading: *Hansard*, CXCVII, 17 June 1869, Derby, cols 18–41,
Salisbury, cols 81–98.

mischief to his Party and the House as can be reasonably achieved by any one man.[299]

Friday 18 June (London)

The close of the Irish Church debate. We divided at 3 in the morning and I walked home with Lyons.[300] The cool fresh air and the sun rising over the houses were pleasant after the heat and excitement of the debate. The majority of 33 was larger than we desired, but Bath, who acted as Whip for our *tiers parti*, was afraid of running it too close.[301]

Cairn's speech was tedious and the Chancellor's though good was not forcible.[302]

Thursday 24 June (London)

My 38th birthday. Time flies very fast and will I suppose fly faster as the hour glass empties. But personally everything has gone well with me.

Salisbury tells me that this morning he, Cairns and the two Archbishops settled the amendments and from what he says I think they are very moderate in character.

Saturday 26 June (London)

Visit from Lowe who said he wished me to understand the exact position of the Irish Church measure and the Government. They wish, he says, to give better terms and to endow the Roman Catholics and Presbyterians but they have sold themselves to the Voluntaries at the Election. They are bound to them and as a matter of *self-preservation*, for Government and Party, they can consent to nothing which is at variance with the terms of their compact. They would prefer to throw up the bill and to risk all chances of collision with the House of Lords etc. This applies to any amendments which would have the

[299] Derby apologized to Carnarvon the following day, 'I am glad to find that your opinion in favour of a "Free Church" did not go as far as I supposed' (14th Earl of Derby to Carnarvon, 18 June 1869: CP, BL 60765, fos 36–37). For Carnarvon's reply, see Carnarvon to Derby, 18 June 1869: Derby Papers, 920 DER (14) 163/5A.

[300] Richard Bickerton Pemell Lyons (1817–1887), 2nd Baron Lyons (1858), ambassador at Paris (1867–1887), 1st Earl Lyons (1887).

[301] Fourth night of the second reading, and the vote: Contents 179, Not-Contents 146. Carnarvon voted with the Contents.

[302] *Hansard*, CXCVII, 18 June 1869, Cairns, cols 267–301, Hatherley, cols 247–267.

Fig. 3 Earl of Carnarvon, *Vanity Fair*, 11 September 1869, by Carlo Pellegrini (Ape).

effect of an "amendment of error", as regards Roman Catholics, or a "re-endowment" as regards the Church. Nothing, he added, could exceed the tension and the pressure on the Government, and nothing but a new Parliament and one pledged to follow a particular minister as this is could have enabled them to go on. He wished, he said, that I should understand that the Government *could* not substantially alter the bill and that I should think well how far that ought to modify the course of the House of Lords.[303]

[303]Carnarvon informed Salisbury, 'This conversation is strictly private to yourself alone. Lowe begged that I would so consider it' (Carnarvon to Salisbury, 26 June 1869 (copy): CP, BL 60761, fo. 5).

In the later part of the day I had a rather curious confirmation of Lowe's conversation. I met Kimberley and walked with him for $1\frac{1}{2}$ hours discussing all subjects and amongst others the Irish Church bill. I alluded to the amendments and to test the matter said that they did not seem to me to be generally and in substance unreasonable except perhaps the one relative to the Ulster Glebes. He assented. So did Chichester Fortescue[304] later in the evening[305] whom I saw at the Duc d'Aumales.[306] But when I said the same thing to Clarendon, he implied very nearly to what Lowe had expressed. From which I drew the conclusion that Lowe and Clarendon being of the inner cabinet knew what course of policy would be but that Kimberley and C. Fortescue regard the matter as any one of the outer world would.

Tuesday 29 June (London)

Irish Church bill in Committee, a long night, only down to Clause 10, and rose about 12.30.[307]
In the middle of the day I received an invitation to a meeting of Conservative Peers at 10 St James's Square. Cairns made a long speech urging our unconditional adoption of six principal amendments and a further proposition to leave the surplus to the disposition of Parliament. I expressed myself doubtfully as to some of the points and declined to pledge myself as to the last and entirely new proposal without further consideration. I think that I was the only person who spoke in a semi-dissentient sense, but there were several in the room who seemed to agree with me.[308]

[304]Chichester Samuel Fortescue (1823–1898), created 1st Baron Carlingford (1874). Lib. MP for Louth (1847–1874), Under-Secretary for the Colonial Office (1857–1858), Chief Secretary for Ireland (1856, 1868–1870).

[305]Fortescue, as Liberal Chief Secretary, had discovered that there was no power in ecclesiastical law to compel an incumbent to build a glebe house, except where the net revenue of the benefice exceeded £100 per annum, or to spend two years' income on the house. Many had been built voluntarily. Fortescue devised a plan to give a half of the value of glebe houses free to the disestablished church. Gladstone did not approve of the plan, stipulating much greater punitive terms of purchase. See D.H. Akenson, *The Church of Ireland: ecclesiastical reform and revolution* (New Haven, CT and London, 1971), pp. 255–256.

[306]Henri-Eugène-Philippe-Louis d'Orléans, duc d'Aumale (1822–1897), elected to French Assembly (1871).

[307]Committee stage of the bill; Carnarvon was the last speaker in the debate: *Hansard*, CXCVII, 29 June 1869, cols 746–747.

[308]Salisbury wrote from Hatfield, 'We have done our utmost to conciliate those who will not be conciliated and can go no further with honour. I am not quite so despondent as you are, but undoubtedly we have a stiff struggle before us' (Salisbury to Carnarvon, 29 June 1869: CP, BL 60758, fos 65–66).

Thursday 1 July (London)

Irish Church bill again in Committee. I moved an amendment for compulsory commutation and 14 years purchase as in the case of Maynooth.[309] It was at the time a successful speech though this morning it seems badly reported. The House was quite full and very attentive. We carried it by 155 to 86, and the argument was entirely on my side.

Barrington[310] wrote to me as to Lord Derby, whom I saw a few minutes afterwards in the House. He shook hands and assured me that so far as he was concerned there was absolutely no ill feeling, so I hope that it may be so. I would wish to be in peace with him now that he is so broken.

Thursday 15 July (London)

Ritual Commission.
Called on Lord Derby and conferred with him as to the University Tests bill, agreed to move the previous question. The last time I was in that room was the morning of the famous "10 minutes Cabinet" when the Reform bill broke down.[311] Lord Derby was very much changed – voice, strength, mental power. He spoke of himself "as politically dead".

[Added subsequently]
It was a very curious interview and the last time that we ever met. At the end of it I expressed the hope that we were friends and Lord Derby quite assented. He tried to induce me to sign a protest as to the Irish Church which would have put me in a ridiculous position after the line I had taken but when I declined he said he was not surprised. We parted as friends and I never saw him again.[312]

Tuesday 20 July (London)

A general meeting of the Conservative Peers at 10 St James's Square. Cairns advised the meeting in the sense we had previously agreed on.

---

[309] *Hansard*, CXCVII, 1 July 1869, cols 869–943. St Patrick's College, a seminary that provided priests, had been disestablished in 1869 with compensation of £369,000.

[310] George William Barrington (1824–1886), 7th Viscount Barrington (1867). Private secretary to 14th Earl of Derby (1866–1868), Con. MP for Eye, Suffolk (1866–1880), Vice-Chamberlain of the Household (1874–1880).

[311] See entry for 4 March 1867.

[312] Derby died on 23 October.

One or two peers seemed not quite to like the retention of the Ulster Glebes, but as [no] one said a word, the meeting broke up, but when I came down to the House 2 hours afterwards I found the Ulster Glebes abandoned. It seems that a sort of mutiny had been extemporised at the Carlton against the retention of the amendment and that Cairns had given way – subject to the opinion of the Archbishop of Canterbury[313] – not very fair to the Archbishop as he thought and reasonably thought. The fact is that Cairns is weak and has very little hold on the party.

The debate on the Preamble was very hot. I never remember the temper of the House so keen on both sides. We divided and beat the Government by 78, a momentous division.[314] I think we had no alternative but the crisis is a very serious one. Is it like the first shot fired on Fort Sumter?[315]

Thursday 22 July (London)

A marvellous solution to the Irish Church bill entanglement, a compromise come to by Cairns and the Government and announced by Cairns in the House. Neither Salisbury nor I knew anything of it till put before the meeting of the House.[316] We owe it entirely to the division of Tuesday evening and in a great measure I think to Salisbury's uncompromising speech. On the whole we are well out of a great difficulty though the terms of the compromise may not be all that we might desire.

---

[313] Archibald Campbell Tait (1811–1882), Bishop of London (1856–1868), Archbishop of Canterbury (1868–1882).

[314] *Hansard*, CXCVIII, 20 July 1869, cols 235–343; Contents 96, Non-Contents 174.

[315] Fort Sumter, South Carolina, was attacked by the Confederates on 12–13 April 1861, marking the beginning of the American Civil War.

[316] For details, see Granville to Gladstone, 21 July 1869 (Ramm, 1952, I, p. 37).

1870

Friday 4 February (Hatfield)

Ritual Commission. Evelyn came up to London and we then went down together to Hatfield.

Salisbury in the evening before dinner came to my room to speak to me. He said that he had been repeatedly urged during the winter to change his seat, that he held out no promise on the subject but said that he would speak to me. A curious communication had also passed through Malmesbury from the Queen who is anxious "that the Opposition should reconsolidate themselves as the Government may any day break to pieces." This was said of course on the general subject and not on the change of seats. I promised I would think it over, meanwhile my impression on the whole being the same as his that it would probably be inadvisable to make the change now.

There are several reasons for this:

1. To go to Cairns' dinner is a move which will probably be commented on: to change seats afterwards will make the step a much more important one.

2. So long as Disraeli is the nominal leader it is unwise to put oneself in a position which implies a complete reconciliation with him. This might set him up.

3. It is a last card to be played out if the Government do anything very outrageous.

Salisbury declared that nothing would tempt him to serve again with D. He knew nothing more than I do of the leadership of the House of Lords, and supposed Stanley would probably take it. Lady Salisbury at dinner spoke more quietly than usual but with her customary dislike of Stanley.

Sunday 6 February (Hatfield)

After Church walked for some time with Cairns. Our conversation was very frank and friendly. He said he had no intention whatever of retaining the leadership, and he grounded this on the ground that he was receiving a pension for judicial work which was incompatible with political.[317]

He said that on the whole he thought Stanley was fittest to lead in the House: and that his very neutrality of temper on many subjects made him at present the fitter, that he only needed the requisite pressing.

He strongly argued that Salisbury and I should change over seats, on ground that the party was gone for the moment in the House of Commons, and that its principles could be best expounded from the House of Lords, that whenever a change of Government should come the choice of a prime minister must be from there, and that if the House of Lords led the House of Commons (i.e. Conservatives in it) would follow. He also said that Disraeli had given up all idea of again being prime minister.

I had in the evening a talk again with Salisbury on the subject, telling him what had passed and advising him to consider the whole matter carefully.

Monday 7 February (London)

Dined in the evening at Cairns' Parliamentary dinner, where he announced definitely his intention of resigning. Cadogan[318] made a speech in which he said that he hoped the leadership would not be settled in any small caucus, but he got little by his harangue. I suspect everyone knows his measure by this time. The Duke of Manchester[319] made an ass of himself and Malmesbury gave us a long rigmarole on the gravity of the position, otherwise everything passed off quietly.

Tuesday 8 February (London)

Meeting of Parliament. Cairns made a good, but as usual, too long a speech.[320]

The Duke of Richmond opened a conversation with me the object of which was to convince me that Salisbury and I ought to return to the front opposition bench. After the debate in returning home he renewed the subject. There is clearly a decided wish on it amongst the principal members of the party. They say – and it is doubtless

---

[317] Cairns invited Carnarvon to dinner on 7 February, the eve of the meeting of Parliament, to discuss his successor (Cairns to Carnarvon, 3 February 1870: CP, BL 60768, fos 16–17).

[318] Henry Charles Cadogan (1810–1873), 4th Earl Cadogan (1864).

[319] William Drogo Montagu (1823–1890), 7th Duke of Manchester (1855), MP for Bewdley (1848–1852) and for Huntingdonshire (1852–1855).

[320] *Hansard*, CXCIX, 3 February 1870, cols 16–40.

true – that the party looks all the stronger from the appearance of being undivided.

Saturday 12 February (London)

We had a dinner party in the evening [. . .]. Mr. Featherston and Mr. Dillon Bell,[321] the two New Zealand envoys, dined. Sandon, Cairns, the Hardys, the Stanhopes, also dined.

Cairns after dinner resumed the conversation as to the leadership in the Lords. He said Salisbury would be best, and repeated his belief that there need be little communication between the leaders in the two Houses: but failing him he thought Stanley was ready though not anxious to take it. I promised to talk once more to Salisbury on Monday and to tell him the result[322] and it was then agreed that we should have a meeting of all the Peers in town in order to consider and decide the question before the end of the week as he then leaves for Mentone.

Wednesday 16 February (London)

Wrote to Cairns a letter as to leadership of the House of Lords, which is entered in letter book.[323] Subsequently received a note from Colville asking me on Cairns' part to see him, my letter having crossed his. I saw him this afternoon: and told him that Salisbury had come to the conclusion that whilst Disraeli remained leader in the House of Commons, he could not take the lead in the House of Lords but that he would attend the meeting of Conservative Peers next Saturday or that if he could not attend I would be present and say as much for him.[324] I

---

[321] Dr Isaac Earl Featherstone (1813–1876) and Francis Dillon Bell (1826–1898) were sent to London to negotiate the retention of two British regiments and a loan of two million pounds towards public works. They went back to New Zealand with a loan of only one million pounds.

[322] Lord Cowley, who had been staying at Highclere, wrote to Lady Derby, 'Lord Carnarvon seems low and dispirited about politics. He evidently wants Cranborne [*sic*] to make it up with Dizzy, but despairs of bringing about a reconciliation. He is afraid that Dizzy will give the lead in the Lords to the Duke of Buckingham or Marlborough, I forget which, but it is pretty much the same' (W.A.H.C. Gardner, Baroness Burghclere (ed.), *A Great Lady's Friendships: letters to Mary, Marchioness of Salisbury, Countess of Derby, 1862–1890* (London, 1933), p. 238).

[323] See Carnarvon to Cairns, 16 February 1870: Cairns Papers, TNA, PRO 30/51/8, fo. 65.

[324] Carnarvon wrote afterwards to Salisbury, 'I am, as you know, sorry that matters cannot be so arranged as to admit of your taking the lead: be as it may, it may do after all perhaps best as it is' (Carnarvon to Salisbury, 16 February 1870: Hatfield House Papers, 3M/E).

distinctly said to Colville that Stanley if he took the lead, knowing as he does that he is not in accord with us on religious subjects, must in return for our support exercise forbearance on religious and suchlike questions, to which he quite assented.

Saturday 19 February (London)

Meeting of Conservative Peers at the Carlton. The Duke of Richmond proposed and Salisbury seconded the appointment of Stanley to Cairns' place. Salisbury was nearly late for the meeting and they asked me if he failed then to second.

Salisbury in doing this guarded himself and others by saying that whilst giving a support he could not pledge himself to an absolute adhesion on all points, especially those other than secular. Redesdale also put in a sort of caveat in the same sense and the Duke of Northumberland said that the events of two years since had induced him to break all allegiance to the party and to act with reference to his own feelings alone. Stanley was then accepted by the meeting which was not a very large one – about 50 or 60 – and the Duke of Richmond went to inform him but returned in 20 minutes saying that he was out having mistaken the hour. Lord Chelmsford[325] and Colville undertook to communicate with him, the Duke of Richmond leaving London. Cairns starts for Mentone this evening.

Monday 21 February (London)

Colville called to consult me as to the present difficulty. It seems that Stanley has positively declined the leadership, and has written two letters to Colville – one private and expressed in very good terms the other for the newspapers tomorrow morning more formal and dry and guarded. The substance in both was much the same. He rested the refusal on personal grounds, his inexperience of the House etc, his doubt whether he would be efficient in debate, the absence of those combative elements needed in a partisan leader and in the private letter the comparison which he thought he should provoke with his father.[326] Colville was at his wits ends what to do and felt the responsibility much.

---

[325] Frederick Thesiger (1794–1878), 1st Baron Chelmsford (1858), Lord Chancellor (1858–1859).

[326] Derby set out at length for his own consideration 'Reasons for accepting' and 'Reasons against accepting' (Vincent, *Derby*, I, p. 50).

I advised:

1. the calling together at an early day of a fresh meeting of Peers.
2. the consideration in the interval of a scheme to be recommended.

What that scheme should be is the difficulty. The Duke of Richmond he says has positively declared he will not accept the leadership.

Finally at his request I consented to go to Stanley and afterwards to meet him and Lord Chelmsford at the Carlton. I found Stanley in and was received in a friendly manner: I put the whole case before him, that failing him there was only Salisbury, that S. would not undertake it whilst Disraeli led in the House of Commons, that failing Salisbury the party might disband in the House of Lords and we might then lose our majority there.

I pointed out that some of his objections were not really weighty. He admitted and said that the truth was that the Party was out of office for years, that he thought it better for himself to keep himself clear, that during his father's life he had followed him, that now he saw no necessity for sacrificing himself, that he had some influence with the moderate Liberals and Whigs and intended to keep somewhat aloof. From Colville's account to me he had used somewhat different arguments to him. He then asked me whether I would not take the leadership. I said at once no, that I had no wish to mix myself up with it though ready and perhaps able to give useful support. In conclusion his mind seemed to be made up. I went on to the Carlton, met Colville and Lord Chelmsford and helped them to draw up circular for next meeting of Conservative Peers. Wrote to Salisbury and urged him to come up.[327]

I put to Colville and Stanley, both, that the obstacle to Salisbury leading was Disraeli, and suggested his retirement if he knew the case.

Tuesday 22 February (London)

Met Colville, Duke of Richmond and Malmesbury by appointment at Carlton to consider question of leadership. The Duke of Richmond declared strongly against taking lead himself, saying he knew his own measure too well to undertake it. I then saw Salisbury at their request and urged upon him the expediency on the whole of his taking it. I pointed out that 1. probability that if we drifted on thus we might lose our majority in the House of Lords 2. that if we did even assuming that

---

[327] With the changing situation, Carnarvon told Salisbury, 'There would be no reason why you should not take the lead in the House if Disraeli were out of the way' (Carnarvon to Salisbury, 21 February 1870: Hatfield House Papers, 3M/E).

the Whigs would ultimately join when property became imperilled we should see Church questions go hopelessly by the board. 3. that if he took it the understanding should be clear that he and we should act independently of Disraeli both now and in the future in the most improbable event of a change of government. He said it was too serious a matter to give an answer at once but he would write me his answer.

I next had a talk with the Duke of Richmond whom I strongly urged to take the lead if Salisbury would not. He grounded his great hesitation 1st on his doubt of his own power, 2nd on the dislike of the Duchess to his taking part in public matters. I promised him if he did lead my hearty support and help. I think he will take it if Salisbury does not.

Finally I had a conversation on the same subject with Hardy, than whom no one could be more friendly. His view was I was the best leader, failing Salisbury: and that though Disraeli was not popular in the House of Commons no such terms as I suggested would be practicable. I told him that the Party in House of Lords had behaved to me with so much injustice and unkindness that though I had forgiven it I should not forget it and that whilst I would do as I was doing every real service in my power, I was not inclined to undertake the lead.

Ritual Commission [. . .]. I walked up from the Ritual Commission with Walpole who curiously enough repeated what Hardy had said to me respecting my leading in the House.

Colville called on me in the evening to show me a letter from the Duke of Richmond in which he implied pretty clearly as he had to me that failing Salisbury he would screw himself up to the point and take the leadership. He said that he had no ambition and I believe him.*

[* but now that he has taken the place he likes it. Oct. 1870]

Thursday 24 February (London)

Received a long and carefully written letter from Salisbury deciding against taking the leadership.[328] I communicated the fact to Colville who asked me to write to Salisbury to beg him to propose the Duke of Richmond, which I did.

Saturday 26 February (London)

Meeting at the Carlton to settle the question of the leadership in the House of Lords. According to agreement Salisbury proposed

[328] Carnarvon was disappointed at Salisbury's decision: 'I admit all the weight of your argument whilst I cannot avoid regretting your conclusion' (Carnarvon to Salisbury, 2 March 1870: Hatfield House Papers, 3 M/E).

and Stanley seconded the Duke of Richmond who then said that understanding that the Party thought that at this juncture he would be the best person he was ready to make all personal sacrifices and to accept the post: but that he should need all support, and that he must make it his earnest and personal request to Salisbury and myself that we would change our places and move from below the gangway to the front bench by him. Salisbury in reply said that the request rather put him on the defence and that consequently he hoped no one would be offended if he said that his reason for having taken his seat there was that he was not prepared now or hereafter to act with Mr. Disraeli, but that with that explanation he would comply with the request and move.

I then followed and said that Salisbury's explanation covered my position but that I thought after what the Duke of Richmond had said I ought to express my own readiness to give him all the support in my power. That wherever I sat I hoped to render him any service that I could believing that he was in all respects the best leader: but that if he really looked upon a change of seat on my part as an evidence of personal regard for him and a wish to support him I could not refuse and would do as he desired. That I had little doubt that I should concur with him in his general views: but that in making this change of place he would not misunderstand me if I also reserved to myself all freedom of action should circumstances make it necessary. This is as nearly as I can remember what passed. Redesdale in the Chair. What I said was well received.

After the Duke of Richmond asked me to stay and to help him in drawing up a circular to the Peers which I did, and when we parted he thanked me in the heartiest manner for all that I had done, and in fact I know that as I could have prevented at any moment the present settlement of the question, so I have been the means of smoothing all the difficulties. Almost 50 Peers were present.

Monday 28 February (London)

Went down to the House and took my seat according to promise on the front opposition Bench – with some rather curious feelings. Three years ago I deliberately resigned my seat on that bench, or at least on the Treasury bench, since then I have been in exile below the gangway, always an object of dislike sometimes of attack, with many opponents and few friends. And now I return at the earnest personal appeal of the new leader of the party whom I probably as much as any man have helped to place there and apparently to the great satisfaction of the party. It is a curious piece of personal history:

and perhaps the end of the chapter is not yet. But I seek nothing, and if it comes as a matter of duty will refuse nothing.

Tuesday 28 June (London)

Fourth and last night of Committee on the Land Bill.[329]

Some conversation with Salisbury as to the course to be taken on the rejection by the House of Commons of a considerable part of our amendments. I am afraid we may have a breeze. He is keen for standing to almost all that we have carried and he says that the feeling in the back benches is that we shall be utterly discredited if we have any repetition of the compromise of last year.

He declared his intention in such case of leaving the front opposition Bench and resuming his old position of "fighting for his own hand." I said what I could to bring him to a somewhat more moderate view. At the same time from what Colville subsequently told me I suspect there is a good deal of feeling on the subject on the back benches, but then they have little responsibility and are sure to be vehement in such cases. I spoke cautiously and *confidentially* to the Duke of Richmond, who is sore with Salisbury it seems and said he was much disposed to push matters to extremities.

Friday 22 July (London)

In the afternoon a meeting of Peers at the Carlton to consider amendments or rather one amendment in the Irish Land Bill. The Duke of Richmond and Cairns proposed to agree to the House of Commons amendment and then Salisbury denounced it on the ground that it was an attempt of the House of Commons to coerce the Lords and that at any risk it should be resisted.

Some speeches were then made and I then said it was difficult to decide, that I disliked the principle of the bill and of the amendment so far as this latter could be called a principle, but that on the whole believing there to be little real principle in it, none for the future, and that the wording was such as to render it inoperative, I thought it better to agree to it. As regards a collision with the House of Commons, that I was quite ready to fight but on one condition, that we could choose our battlefield and the sense of the country to back us: but that in this case I thought the point was not one that would be intelligible and that for that reason we should only be defeated if we risked our

---

[329] The Irish Land Bill (*Hansard*, CCII, 28 June 1870, cols 1052–1088).

strength on it. What I said seemed to be accepted generally and the amendment was agreed to. Salisbury seemed a little put out I thought at the moment but afterwards in the House he supported me well.

In the House I introduced my Canadian motion with regard to the Volunteers. I was obliged to give up the division so there was some hesitation in our own back benches, some on genuine, some on foolish grounds.[330]

Tuesday 20 December (Pixton)

Heard from Bernstorff[331] who conveys the virtual refusal of the German authorities to give Gleissner the safe conduct for which I had applied.

I received also a very curious letter from H. Mayhew[332] with whom years ago I had a "misunderstanding" and who now writes to express his regret and offer his apology, which he says he is convinced is due from a study of my public career. Of course I have written a thoroughly hearty letter thanking him and saying that in some measure perhaps the cause of misunderstanding may have been mine.

This is the 4th reconciliation which I have had this year: Lord Derby, Cairns, Bath, Mayhew. A singular combination.

---

[330] Ibid., CCIII, cols 703–729, on the Canadian frontier volunteer militia.

[331] Count Albrecht von Bernstorff (1809–1873), Prussian Foreign Minister (1861–1862), ambassador at London (1871–1873).

[332] Henry Mayhew (1812–1877), joint first editor of *Punch* (1841), author of *London Labour and the London Poor* (London, 1851; reissued with additions 1861, 1862, 1864, 1865).

1871

Monday 1 May (London)

I see a horrible phaeton before me in the coming break up of the Government who seem bent upon self-destruction, and in the consequent struggle of the Conservatives to get back into office. It would be a very foolish attempt but some of them seem to be bent upon making it. Sandon began to talk to me of it this afternoon.

Sensible as he is on the subject, Beauchamp went to the point and asked me whether Salisbury would take office with Disraeli, and whether failing him I would. I cannot help thinking Disraeli has inclined him to sound me.

I said I thought Salisbury would not join and that my relations with him had been far too personal and intimate for me to separate my fortunes. He asked the grounds, and I said broadly that it was distrust of Disraeli that he had or he had seemed to trick us and that there could be no confidence in such circumstances with such a colleague, and that as a matter of fact his being in a different House enhanced the difficulty as one could exercise no control over him. I hope sincerely the Government will go on, but they are staggering about so wildly that they may go to pieces at any moment.

Thursday 20 July (London)

Pakington called on me to consult me on "a matter of great importance and difficulty". He explained that there are some 700,000 skilled workmen organized under a Council in London to which they give the utmost obedience, who have certain schemes of social reform. That they distrust the employers, and the radicals and the ordinary M.P.s, that they (mainly the Council) look to the House of Lords, that Scott Russell is President of the Council which consists of the highest class of workmen, that he proposed to Pakington three months ago the formation of a small committee of Peers to consider whether they could promote some of the legislation which these men desire. He showed me the programme which though strong does admit I think of being handled in a Conservative sense. He had consulted Disraeli who properly said he could not act but advised him to communicate with me. I promised to consider it and to give what help I could. It is a most serious affair for good or evil; the most serious that I have heard of for a long time.[333]

Gladstone's announcement in the House of Commons of the decision to proceed by warrant and to set aside the vote of the House of Lords on the Army Bill.[334] The same announcement was made by Granville evidently much against the grain. The Duke of Richmond did not speak at all up to the occasion, though it must be owned that it was very difficult to know what to say.[335]

Tuesday 25 July (London)

Saw Pakington in the morning on the subject of our conversation. Names agreed on, Derby, Salisbury, Lichfield, myself, Pakington, Hardy, J. Manners, Sandon. Northcote has been spoken to, but on the whole decided that if the number should be eight, he must be sacrificed. The House of Commons side of the Committee might be stronger.

After the business in the House of Lords met for consultation in Cairns' room, present, Cairns, Redesdale, Chelmsford and myself, Salisbury not being in the House. Discussed the amendment to be issued on Monday and agreed to a slight alteration to avoid a wrangle on the point of form. Afterwards Cairns raised the question of a revival of proxies for such a case as that of the Ballot bill. To my satisfaction the general feeling was against it on various grounds. I think it would be unwise.

Friday 13 October (Ostend)

A startling article in the *Telegraph* of today[336] which I have just seen as to what it calls our "secret treaty" with the working men. I am very uneasy about it.

---

[333] John Scott Russell (1808–1882), a marine engineer and inventor, conceived the idea of a Council of Legislation, consisting of Conservative peers, and a Council of Workmen, consisting of labour leaders, to agree on a programme of reform that would bring the labour leaders towards Conservatism. Apart from Carnarvon, Salisbury, Manners, Pakington, Northcote, and Hardy were so-called members.

[334] Army (Purchase System). The Royal Warrant. Government statement: *Hansard*, CCVIII, 20 July 1970, cols 16–23.

[335] Ibid., Granville, cols 2 and 10, Richmond, col. 6.

[336] 'The secret treaty', *Daily Telegraph*, 13 October 1871, p. 4.

Saturday 14 October (Tunbridge Wells)

Saw some more newspapers as to this "secret treaty" affair. It is very unsatisfactory and I cannot understand it.[337] Wrote Hardy, telegraphed to Hatfield and to my great relief found Salisbury was there. Retelegraphed to say I would come on Monday evening to see him.

Monday 16 October (Hatfield)

Went by myself to Hatfield and found Salisbury alone, all his family being on their way to if not in Italy.

Discussed this tiresome affair of the alleged secret "compact" with the working men. His opinion was against any collective action on our part by the publication of our memorandum or otherwise; but he much approved of my writing and getting Hardy also to write to *The Times* to give separate contradictions to the statements which have been made.

His conclusion was pretty much my own, that Pakington had mismanaged the affair in his conversations with Scott Russell and that there had been foul play on the part of some of the workmen. Later a letter arrived from Pakington to him speaking of his regret at the "premature publication of our plan"!! a sentence which though in accord apparently with his Address at the Social Science meeting[338] shows how little he appreciated our position or intentions. Altogether we have narrowly escaped burning our fingers, if indeed we do come out of the mess quite unharmed.

Thursday 19 October (London)

In the evening saw Salisbury and discussed the situation as regards this vexatious affair of the working men's resolution.

[337] Pakington had summoned a meeting of the Committee at the Carlton on 1 August. Carnarvon had attended, together with Hardy, Manners, and Sandon. Carnarvon was disturbed at the newspaper accounts of the negotiations. Singling out the *Daily News*, he told Sandon, 'The form in which it appears is a travesty of our resolutions as agreed at the meeting at the Carlton' (Carnarvon to Sandon, 15 October 1871: Harrowby Papers, 2nd series, ii, fo. 102). For details of the alleged agreement on a seven-point programme between peers and working men, see E. Feuchtwanger, *Disraeli, Democracy and the Tory Party* (Oxford, 1968) pp. 92–93.

[338] Pakington's presidential address at the Social Science Congress at Leeds on 4 October included a plea for legislation to improve the condition of the working classes in housing, education, and food. See *Transactions of the National Association for the Promotion of Social Science* (1871), pp. 1–21.

He is against any further letters or correspondence to the Papers if possible. If however there should be a very distinct challenge of facts by some one in a position to give such a challenge as Scott Russell it must be met by a denial and a publication of our memorandum; but he would far prefer to wait for Parliament if further explanations are needed.

He has begged me if it should be necessary to make any further disclaimers or statements to include him in anything that I may say for myself, which I have promised to do. He promised me a short memorandum in writing on one part of the question.

He, like myself, fears that Pakington has been very unwise to say the least of it. I suspect that he said to Scott Russell far more than he was authorised to say.[339]

Tuesday 24 October (Hemsted)

Spent a quiet day walking about with Hardy. In the evening came a telegram from Pakington saying that the "final form of statement settled yesterday evening" (i.e. at Hughenden whither Pakington, Sandon and I think Northcote were going)[340] and urging strongly Hardy to give his signature. He answered by saying that he would sign the August memorandum but not the statement in which I made him include me.

Settled with Hardy that if there should be any necessity to write again to the Papers on this subject we should not do so till after communication with each other.[341]

Friday 27 October (Highclere)

I see by the Papers that, as I expected, a kind of counter-statement is put forth by the Working Men's Council in answer to ours. It seems that Scott Russell has played fast and loose with both parties. Had a letter from G. Hardy on the subject.[342]

---

[339] Carnarvon informed Salisbury that Disraeli had advised Pakington to stay silent and that members should 'prevent the publication of anything purporting to be a collective statement' (Carnarvon to Salisbury, 20 October 1871: Cranbrook Papers, HA3, T501/262).
[340] 'The visit to Hughenden was amusing and pleasant [. . .]. We sat up till one o'clock' (Sandon to Lady Sandon, 24 October 1871: Harrowby Papers, 2nd series, xlv, fo. 80).
[341] Hardy noted in his diary on reading *The Times* on 25 October, 'The statement and memorandum appear quite unexceptionable and the leader in *The Times* so accepts them' (Johnson, p. 144).
[342] Carnarvon replied, 'Like you, I was satisfied on reading it that we were not open to attack' (Carnarvon to Hardy, 26 October 1871: Cranbrook Papers, HA3 T501/262).

1872

Monday 4 March (London)

I went up to town.

Called at Hardys. He tells me that there is a real move in Lancashire to put Derby at the head of the Party, that it was discussed at Burghley before the meeting, that it was declared to be necessary to tell Disraeli but that every one shrunk from doing this and that he refused.[343] That he doubts whether Disraeli knows it, that he believes Derby does not wish it, only wishes to return to the Foreign Office. Derby's late speech,[344] when I was ill, brought him thus forward. On leaving Hardy the first person I met in the Park was Disraeli with whom I stopped to say a few amiable nothings as to weather etc.

Saturday [*sic*] 21 April[345] (London)

Called on Lady Derby and had a good deal of conversation with her. She regretted that Stanley had been obliged to attend the Manchester meeting as it involved the recognition of Disraeli as head of the Party thereby removing what might be a useful check on him, viz. the sense that he was not inevitable.

She told me that the late Lord Derby seemed almost effaced from recollection at Knowsley, probably because he had so few sympathies with others.

She has the full sense of the great place which Stanley as Earl of Derby and Master of Knowsley fills in Lancashire. She said that when he went to Manchester they kept it a secret by which train he went lest his reception should interfere with that of Disraeli's. But she spoke very nicely and with much feeling on many subjects.

[343] At a meeting at Burghley House, Stamford, home of Lord Exeter, on 1 February, attended by Hardy and members of the Opposition Front Bench, there were only two dissenters to the view that Derby would make a more effective leader. The Chief Whip, Gerard Noel, believed that Derby's name alone would be worth 40 or 50 seats (R. Blake, *Disraeli* (London, 1966), p. 521). Carnarvon, who was unwell after the Scott Russell fiasco, did not attend.

[344] Address at the meeting of the Liverpool Conservative Working Men's Association on 9 January.

[345] This entry should be for Sunday 21 April.

Wednesday 11 December (Knowsley)

A long walk and talk with Wilson Patten.[346] He looks forward gloomily to the future, has no faith in the real conservatism of working men and believes that before long the old political questions will disappear in social controversies of a very dangerous kind.

He agreed with me as to the impossibility of Disraeli again taking the Prime Ministership with any success. He said he was convinced that Disraeli would not press it; that he had told him that he had gained all he cared for and implied that he would in every way make place for any better man.

Afterwards Lady Derby asked me to walk with her and I stirred the same question, saying that I believed Derby to be at this moment the best and the only man to lead. She then said that during last summer (at the time of the Thames Embankment bill),[347] a certain number of Conservatives (among them Cairns) had communicated with Disraeli and represented to him that he had better resign in fact, that he had expressed himself quite willing to do so and especially in favour of Derby, but that he did not think that a Prime Minister in the House of Lords was possible; that he had told this to Derby who had thereupon been more and more confirmed in his unwillingness to take the lead.

I then said something to raise the question as to the leadership in the House of Commons in the event of Disraeli failing. I said that Hardy was the only person. She then said this was not Derby's view and as good as intimated that he would not accept him as his lieutenant there. I then asked whom? and she to my great surprise suggested Cross as "our best man." I observed that this would be simply impossible; that however solid Cross might be, he had not by his antecedents or position the slightest chance with the body of the Party. If really she spoke Derby's opinion it was the most extraordinary view: but I suspect it was mainly her own.[348]

---

[346] Col. John Wilson Patten (1802–1892), Con. MP for Lancashire North (1832–1874), Chief Secretary for Ireland (1868).

[347] The Thames Embankment (Land) Bill was introduced in the Commons by the Chancellor of the Exchequer, Robert Lowe, on 8 March 1872 (*Hansard*, CCIX, col. 1742).

[348] Richard Assheton Cross (1823–1914), MP for Lancashire South-west, was a frequent visitor to Knowsley. When he called on Lady Derby in June 1872, she had used him to spread the word that there was no lack of communication between her husband and Disraeli. See D.J. Mitchell, *Cross and Tory Democracy* (New York and London, 1991), p. 48.

1873

Monday 5 May

Dined at Grillions and oddly enough I found myself within one seat of Disraeli. At first he wore his Egyptian sphinx-like face as if he saw and did not see me, but I thought that this was unnecessary and absurd and so I opened the conversation on a literary topic and we then talked in a very friendly, and so far as he was concerned, in a very agreeable way.

Sunday 13 July (London)

A very wet day, the rain falling in heavy semi-tropical showers. Had a long talk with Northcote in the afternoon mainly on the Persian question of Reuter's concession.[349] He was on the cautious side as I expected but able, clear and open to all fair argument.

Disraeli dined with us, the first time since our memorable schism in '68. Since then we have frequently met, but there has always been constraint. Lady Chesterfield[350] is really the authoress of this and on the whole, whatever the results, I am glad. He was very agreeable and we talked on general and indifferent subjects but after dinner the Judicature bill came up. He is or seems of opinion that it might even yet be thrown out and that Cairns is really at heart sick of it. I intimated a disposition if circumstances allowed of it and "if Cairns was not actually a consenting but an assenting party" to move to get rid of the bill on the ground that it was morally damaged, like indeed the Government. Disraeli caught at this, said he would speak to Cairns and it was understood that some communication should follow.

In conversation, Disraeli said a curious thing, speaking of the Duke of Richmond, "that he was entirely under Cairns' guidance." Curious

---

[349] Baron Paul Julius von Reuter (1816–1899), who founded the first news agency, had obtained a concession accorded by the Shah of Persia the previous year to be given absolute right to provide the country's transport, exploit mining potentialities, and have preference in producing manufactured goods. Details of the concession emerged only a year later. See *The Times*, 5 July 1873, p. 7.

[350] Anne Elizabeth Stanhope (1802–1885), wife of George Stanhope, 6th Earl of Chesterfield, and a confidante of Disraeli.

but quite true. He spoke too of Cairns with some light touch of criticism, as a very able lawyer but only a lawyer.

Tuesday 15 July (London)

Met Disraeli at the Carlton and talked about the Judicature bill. He was all in favour of extinguishing it in the House of Lords and on my *intimating* a readiness if all circumstances were favourable to move something to this effect he caught at it and said that he felt sure that Cairns would be glad if I did so, as Cairns felt himself in a false position by the course he had taken and would be glad to get out of it. Later however I saw Cairns in the House and opened the subject to him, explained that I thought there was a chance of postponing it for this year when it returned to us and put it to him. He admitted that he knew that many disliked it as I did but that he did not think it would be possible to deal with the bill in this way, that "the weak kneed" members of the Party would flinch and finally that he was so bound in honour as to be unable "to support" such a motion. I replied that I considered such a conclusion fatal and intimated that I should not proceed further with the matter though I did not disguise that I had always disliked the bill and the cessation of the judicial power.

I afterwards saw Dr. Ball[351] with whom I had had much previous conversation on the subject. He regretted it but did not dispute the course I had taken.

Tuesday 22 July (London)

Conference with Disraeli in morning on Judicature bill. He wrote to ask me to come to him or to propose to come to me.[352] I accepted the latter.[353] A curious interview in which he expounded what he believed to be Cairns's state of mind of the subject.

Conversation afterwards with Vernon as to Repton School scheme. I told him I could not consent to its abandonment this year.

[351] Dr John Thomas Ball (1815–1898), Attorney-General for Ireland (1868–1875), Lord Chancellor of Ireland (1875–1880).

[352] Disraeli had written, 'At half past 5 o'clock today, Lord Cairns had agreed to sanction the defeat of the measure, and pressed on me to ensure its being sent to your House if possible tomorrow. We arranged that the Rating Bill, which was to have been thrown out, should in consequence pass. Two hours afterwards, he sent for me and said all was at sea again, in consequence of the decided opposition of Lord Derby to the proposed course' (Disraeli to Carnarvon, 22 July 1873: CP, BL 60765, fo. 11).

[353] Ibid., fo. 12.

Thursday 24 July (London)

Judicature bill came on, and the result of all our conversations, communications etc. over the carrying of the Commons amendments with one or two exceptions. The truth is that Cairns and Richmond and Derby were all for them and even Salisbury would not vote. I spoke and I believe I spoke fairly being a good deal cheered by all our party and I turned a few votes, but after all we only divided 34 to 61, there being a good many pairs.[354]

Tuesday 7 October (Bretby)

Went out shooting with H. Lennox,[355] a fine day [. . .].

Disraeli made himself very agreeable. We talked freely enough of Political matters, though of course abstaining from reference to our old subject of division, and a great deal of literary questions where he is at home. His training as a trustee of the British Museum has given him knowledge on many of these matters.

He spoke, more to Evelyn than to me but also to me, of the late Lord Derby with little or no affection. He said he (Lord D.) had no softness or kindness of heart. Stanley, the present Lord Derby, was very different and his marriage had called out the kindlier parts of his nature. Frederick Stanley[356] he says is very attentive in his attendance in the House of Commons but needs pushing.

One of the most remarkable features in this remarkable man is the apparently total absence of personal rancour. He seems to have no feeling against those who have shown the greatest feeling against him.

He spoke of Salisbury and Hatfield in the language of a wholly indifferent bystander, allotting to Hatfield the preference over every other country house in England, oddly enough on the same grounds on which I have always said the same.

[354] *Hansard*, CCXVII, 24 July 1873, cols 886–898. Carnarvon told Disraeli afterwards, 'I am sorry for the result of Thursday night. We made the best fight we could and but for a singularly untoward combination of unlucky circumstances might have been successful' (Carnarvon to Disraeli, 26 July 1873: CP, BL 60763, fo. 13). The Judicature Act amalgamated the superior courts into two divisions, the High Court of Justice and the Court of Appeal.

[355] Lord Henry George Gordon Lennox (1821–1886), third son of 5th Duke of Richmond. Con. MP for Chichester (1866–1885), Secretary to the Admiralty (1866–1868), Commissioner of Public Works (1874–1876).

[356] Frederick Arthur Stanley (1841–1908), younger son of 14th Earl of Derby. Con. MP for Lancashire North (1868–1885) and for Blackpool (1885–1886), Civil Lord of the Admiralty (1868), Secretary of State for War (1878–1880), Colonial Secretary (1885–1886), President of the Board of Trade (1886–1888), Governor-General of Canada (1888–1893), succeeded his brother as 16th Earl of Derby (1893).

Friday 10 October (Bretby)

I took a long stroll with Disraeli through the Park. His conversation is of an agreeable kind – easy, with truth anecdote, occasionally a sparkle of genius, and often inclining to the dreamy not to say mystic. Anything of a poetical sort seems to attract him and his mind has much more *classical* culture than I had supposed. I fancy it has been obtained through German rather than English sources. Speaking of death he said to me "when the curtain falls I avert my eyes and dare not look beyond", and yet he acquiesced heartily when I said afterwards that it was far harder to disbelieve than to believe. He spoke of recent discoveries having given a real historical value to the Scripture records. It would be hard to say what are the limits of his religious belief.

1874

Tuesday 27 January (Bretby)

All England seems in a state of excitement. In a few days the election will begin.[357] I do not like either Gladstone's or Disraeli's addresses.[358] Gladstone offers a bribe of £5,000,000 in the shape of remission of tax and Disraeli at once caps it. It is what we said at the passing of the last Reform bill, that the Constitution would be put up to auction at each general election.

Friday 6 February (London)

Dined at the Derbys who were quite alone [. . .]. After dinner when alone Derby introduced the real question by saying he wondered whether either would have Office. I replied in joke and then he asked me if Salisbury in my opinion would join. I said I could not say but I inclined to think it was not hopeless. He then said something to effect that an offer anyhow would be made but it was a question how and whether it would be pressed. I said that though I could not answer for him I thought it was possible he might join, that as Derby knew it was owing mainly to me that some two or three years since he had come up from the gangway to the front opposition bench and that if there was a real anxiety to get him the attempt would be perhaps most likely to succeed if made in some measure at least through me. To this Derby cordially assented. He however expressed some doubt whether Salisbury was really worth a large price. I said I thought he decidedly was worth it, that whatever his present good intentions he must, if outside, soon become a critic and the involuntary leader of all that unappropriated balance of Conservative feeling in the House which though discontented and generally passive occasionally became a very difficult element. The upshot of the whole was that Office would

[357] Gladstone had informed his colleagues of his decision to dissolve Parliament on 26 January. The following morning, he issued his election manifesto. The move took Disraeli by surprise.

[358] Disraeli wrote to Lady Chesterfield, 'I agree with Carnarvon that Gladstone's Manifesto is very ill-written, but I do not agree with Carnarvon that it is not in his usual style. I think his usual style the worst of any public man' (Zetland, I, p. 49).

beyond doubt be offered to me, that it would be offered to Salisbury but whether as a mere form or as a reality was uncertain.

No one could be pleasanter or more like himself than Derby was.

Sunday 8 February (London)

In the afternoon had a long conversation with Salisbury who returned yesterday from France. I stated to him the great probability that an offer of office would be made to us, and then the objections to our acceptance with the counter-reasons for doing so. The objections were 1. that we could not really trust Disraeli. To this it might be said that one could trust the prime minister; that he is now in a different position as a minister with a majority from a fortune hunter in a minority, and that G. Hardy and Derby would be a sort of support if not guarantee against violent changes. 2. that it will be said that we are inconsistent. To this he attached little weight. 3. what is our duty? by standing aloof he must cause a split in the party and would certainly waste great power which he might politically otherwise exercise. *On the whole* I inclined towards acceptance. *On the whole* he leant the other way on two grounds. 1. that D. might play us a trick as before and that our last card of resignation was played out. 2. that we should be placed in a position of servitude, that it would be an act of submission and that he might then retaliate against us. Nothing could be kindlier or even more affectionate than his manner. He promised to consider the whole case, and he urged me repeatedly to remember that my case was not his, and that even if he did not join I might. Finally he said that if anything should be said he should do nothing without communicating with me.[359]

Monday 9 February (Bretby)

My conversation last night with Townsend[360] was singularly confidential considering our different political views but I believe him

---

[359] After the meeting, Carnarvon sent a note to Salisbury: 'I trust before going [to Bretby] how earnestly I hope nothing will separate our political relations. Our personal friendship cannot, I believe, be shaken by matters as those with which we are now dealing [. . .]. I dread the political separation and even the consequences of it' (Carnarvon to Salisbury, 8 February 1874: Hatfield House Papers, 3M/E).

[360] Meredith White Townsend (1831–1911), editor of the *Spectator* (1860–1898).

to have a real personal regard for me. He is anxious that I should take Office but either such Office as I held before or an absolute sinecure, nothing whatever like the Post Office, his argument being that this would look like an act of surrender. He thinks either the Colonial or India Office offer the best alternatives.

The Times article today hopes that Salisbury and I shall "condone the past and return," all which makes my return easier.[361]

Before leaving town I wrote to Salisbury earnestly hoping that we should not separate our fortunes and resting it on the ground of personal friendship and affection.[362]

Monday 16 February (Bretby)

Everyone seems half-crazed by the prospects and the uncertainties of a new Government, and everyone seems very hungry for places. The only two people who are doubtful and anxious as to accepting Office are Salisbury and myself and probably for this reason it will come to both of us.[363]

Tuesday 17 February (Bretby)

There is no doubt from *The Times* that Gladstone has resigned, but beyond this we know nothing. It is an interesting time but I own my own mind is doubtful and my heart rather heavy about Office.

---

[361] *The Times*, 9 February 1874, p. 9. In congratulating Carnarvon on his appointment as Colonial Secretary, Townsend stated, 'the success of the whole arrangement is the more important because to my savage annoyance your people are probably in for a generation' (Townsend to Carnarvon, 26 February 1874: CP, BL 60776, fos 3–4).

[362] Carnarvon reiterated his opinion from Bretby: 'I still incline on the whole (and it is a question to be decided on the balance of considerations) to my general view of yesterday' (Carnarvon to Salisbury, 9 February 1874: Hatfield House Papers, 3M/E).

[363] Heathcote had written to Carnarvon two days earlier, 'Salisbury, after a full discourse, gave way and I think the reason is that he is satisfied that it is right though his inclinations are still the other way' (Heathcote to Carnarvon, 14 February 1874: CP, BL 61073, fo. 21). Carnarvon had come to a similar decision, admitting, 'I am, as I think of the matter, often in many minds but I conclude on the whole [. . .] it is probably right to accept office' (Carnarvon to Salisbury, 16 February 1874: Hatfield House Papers, 3M/E). He proposed to stay at Bretby until he heard from Disraeli.

Thursday 19 February (London)

A very busy day.[364] Breakfasted with Salisbury and discussed everything. He had virtually given in his adhesion yesterday but on the understanding that he was in complete concert with me. He had written to me to that effect but the letter had missed me. He detailed all that had passed between Disraeli and himself and the conversation seems to have been almost the counterpart of that which I subsequently had with him. So I went to D.'s Whitehall Gardens and found him in. He was very friendly and civil and he explained himself on all points with entire frankness. He began by describing the composition of the Cabinet which he said he was desirous of reducing to much smaller numbers.[365] The Duke of Richmond to be supported by three Secretaries of State, Derby, Salisbury, and myself and the Chancellor, the Army and Navy to be in the Commons because they involved such long and detailed financial statements.[366] He dwelt on the necessity of getting rid of some who had belonged to the old Cabinet and the possibilities of some heartburnings etc. As to legislation I spoke of the possibility of some aggressive measure against the Ritualists being urged, and tho' I had no sympathy with them I should object to that and trusted that he would not sanction it. He entirely assented: and added that some private bills, such as Sandon's, on such subjects must be treated as "open questions". He desired all Church appointments to be shared by the several parties within the Church, those parties always being within certain limits.

Friday 20 February (London)

Long talk with William Peel as to private secretary. Afterwards a conversation with Duke of Richmond. He is very much distressed at not being War Minister which he says belongs to him almost by hereditary right: but he also behaved very much like a gentleman

[364]Disraeli had telegraphed Carnarvon the previous day to call on him in London 'on urgent business as soon as you can' (Disraeli to Carnarvon, 18 February 1874: CP, BL 60763, fo. 19).

[365]At Windsor, the Queen had stated her wish that the Cabinet should consist of twelve members, six from each House (Queen Victoria, Journal, 18 February 1874: Royal Archives, Z/380).

[366]Northcote as Chancellor of the Exchequer, Hardy at the War Office, and George Ward Hunt at the Admiralty. 'It will be equally pleasant and curious', Carnarvon observed, 'if our old Ch.Ch. [Christ Church, Oxford] generation find themselves all members of the same Government' (Carnarvon to Sandon, 19 February 1874: Harrowby Papers, 2nd series, lii, fo. 106).

acknowledging that there was good reason for having the War and Navy Offices represented in the Commons and saying that he was ready to take any or no office. But he added that the Presidency of the Council had always been his abomination and the place which he particularly desired to avoid. The Duke of Marlborough is very sore at being omitted. A very long conversation with Kimberley at the Colonial Office. He went through the affairs of each Colony for $2\frac{1}{2}$ hours and gave me the fullest explanations.

Saturday 21 February (London)

Went down to Windsor to kiss hands and receive the seals of the Colonial Office. We were cheered at Paddington and Windsor by a tolerably large crowd, favoured by the weather, safely whirled along in a saloon carriage by special, and went through the usual ceremony. It had, as on a former occasion, no special features. The Queen was in a very small room only just large enough to hold us and we knelt down (I thought that Hunt[367] would never succeed in recovering his legs when once he was down) and took various oaths, and kissed H.M.'s hand and turned and finally retired. The scene was like, and yet in many respects unlike, that which I remember seven years ago when Lord Derby was Prime Minister. Now it is Disraeli I hope all may go straight and well: but I have an uncomfortable feeling which is quite unreasonable but which I cannot shake off, a feeling of some coming trouble. In some ways this is perhaps well. It will at least restrain all undue satisfaction.

Sunday 22 February (London)

In spite of Sunday a busy day.

Hunt mentions an intention on part of some mad Captain to plant English flag on the Fijis, a troublesome question enough without this addition!

Conversation with Lady Derby. She assures me that Disraeli is entirely altered, cautious, disinclined to any innovation and disposed to go on quite quietly. "There is no chance of any mine" [*sic*]. Nor is there "any sign or risk of personal arrogance", still less "of any feeling of personal grudge". He has only put into his cabinet the best men whom he could find.

---

[367] George Ward Hunt (1825–1877), Con. MP for Northamptonshire North (1857–1877), Chancellor of the Exchequer (1868), First Lord of the Admiralty (1874–1877).

Tuesday 24 February (London)

I had a rather curious and not very satisfactory letter from Disraeli as to my new Under Secretary.[368] I showed it to Salisbury but he attached no real importance and showed me another of a similar kind to himself. This manner of writing is inherent, he says, in the man and though singular must not be taken for more than it is really worth.

Wednesday 25 February (London)

In the afternoon serious telegram from Sir G. Wolseley[369] announcing great battle. Heavy losses and apparent check of the whole force 15 miles from Cormassie. It seems very difficult to do anything in the way of reinforcements.

Cabinet

We discussed:
1. The telegram that had arrived.
2. Income tax. Northcote made a long statement to us pointing out that total abolition would involve a general revision of taxing system and balancing evils and advantages. The general feeling of the Cabinet was for ultimate abolition, Hunt and myself perhaps making the only two protests against it, but this abolition was more the result of our political situation in the House of Commons than anything else: nothing decided.
3. India. Salisbury does not anticipate as great distress as supposed, but proposes to ask for powers to take loan of £10,000,000 on Indian security.
4. Foreign policy. Derby says there is loose gunpowder about everywhere and Bismarck is very arrogant but hopes for the best.

Wednesday 4 March (London)

Cabinet

We talked for a short time as to:

---

[368]James Lowther (1840–1904), Under-Secretary for the Colonies (1874–1878). See Disraeli to Carnarvon, 24 February 1874: CP, BL 60763, fo. 20.

[369]Maj.-Gen. Sir Garnet Wolseley (1833–1913) was in charge of British troops on the Gold Coast during the Second Ashanti War. The capital, Kumasi, was captured on 5 February 1874 and King Koffee agreed to appoint commissioners to conclude a treaty. See Sir G. Arthur (ed.), *The Letters of Lord and Lady Wolseley, 1870–1911* (London, 1922), p. 18.

1. Ashanti War. Some question as to what should be said in Queen's Speech. I said it would be better to accept fact without going into history or reasons for it, which on the whole was generally adopted.[370]

2. Cairns announced bills on Register of Tithes and Judicature bill, including entire transfer of appellate jurisdiction from House of Lords. I opposed it, or rather said what I could against it, but when last year's bill passed knew the matter was sealed, and so it is. The only members of the cabinet who agreed at all with me were curiously enough members of the House of Commons.

3. Education – decided to say nothing about it in Queen's Speech.

4. Cross proposed his measures (he had talked them over with me before). Corn Law Amendment, Master and Servant Act and Conspiracy Law: agreed to issue a Commission on subject. Then discussion as to Licensing Act. All agreed some relaxation should be given (a) as regards London: question whether hour of closing should be 12.30 or 1. Anyhow the present power of exempting particular houses for the sake of theatres should be taken away as unfair (b) question whether there should be a distinction between large provincial towns and rural districts; the former ought not to close before 12, the latter might close at 11, but uniformity is very desirable.[371]

Wednesday 11 March (London)

A Levée which was wearisome.

A long talk with Magee[372] as to this new church bill of the Bishops and Archbishops.[373] His account of the matter is this. There are some things which are indifferent, some which are pronounced illegal. The first should be left to the discretion of the minister, as now. The second should be in the power of the Bishop and his Council to determine 1st, by restraining them, 2nd, by refusing to restrain, i.e. by sanctioning, that is by exercising a coercive and a dispensing power. He admitted there would be a difficulty in defining the illegal, but then

---

[370] For Carnarvon's policy on Gold Coast affairs, see J.D. Hargreaves, *Prelude to the Partition of West Africa* (London, 1963), pp. 170–174.

[371] In their election manifesto, the Conservatives had indicated more freedom for licensed victuallers on the sale of strong drink. Cross, the Home Secretary, who was in charge of the bill, disappointed their expectations.

[372] William Connor Magee (1821–1891), Bishop of Peterborough (1868–1891), Archbishop of York (1891).

[373] The Public Worship Regulation Bill 'on the present state of the laws regulating Divine Service in the Church'.

all legal tribunals would remain and all sources of appeal and redress continue to be available.[374]

I spoke to Hardy on the subject. Saw at the Colonial Office Dr Featherstone and Sir W. Grey[375] who goes to Jamaica on Tuesday.

Thursday 12 March (London)

Cabinet

We considered Queen's Speech.[376] The only question whether we should allude to a bill for regulation of relations of landlords and tenants. It was finally decided in the negative. Nothing else of importance.

Entry of Duke and Duchess of Edinburgh in a snowstorm which afterwards became a sea of mud; but all passed off well and the Queen was said to be unusually smiling and pleased.[377]

Saturday 21 March (London)

Cabinet to discuss Budget.

Agreed:

1. to adjourn local taxation as a whole to next year, but to double contribution to Police expenses = £600,000.

2. reduce Income tax by 1d = £1,540,000 this year, leaving about £200,000 for next.

3. make some further exemptions in small incomes, probably exempt completely under £150, and deduct £150 from incomes under £500.

4. repeal sugar duty = £2,000,000. It was a great question whether it should not be ½ tea duty instead.

5. probably repeal Brewers' licenses, about £450,000.

6. probably take off Passengers' tax, £500,000.

7. repeal horse duty = £480,000.

---

[374] For an account of the meeting, see Magee's letter to Carnarvon in J.C. MacDonnell, *The Life and Correspondence of William Connor Magee*, 2 vols (London, 1896), I, p. 2.

[375] Sir William Grey (1818–1878), Lieutenant-Governor of Bengal (1866–1871), Governor of Jamaica (1874–1877).

[376] *Hansard*, CCXVIII, 19 March 1874, cols 22–25.

[377] Prince Alfred, Duke of Edinburgh, had married Princess Marie Alexandrovna, daughter of Czar Alexander II, in St Petersburg on 23 January. They had arrived back at Gravesend the previous day (*The Times*, 12 March 1874, p. 8).

5 and 6 to be considered, and meanwhile a sub-committee appointed to consider a railway bill. Salisbury, Northcote, Cross. Northcote estimates surplus at £5,400,000.

Saturday 28 March (London – Highclere)

Detained in the Cabinet and came down by last train. Cabinet had discussed

1. Budget. Last Cabinet we had almost come to conclusion to appropriate the surplus as follows:

2d. off tea duty (= ⅓ tax) about	1,100,000
Locomotion – horse duty and railway	1,000,000
Police	600,000
Brewery licences	400,000
1d. off income tax about	1,500,000
	4,600,000

But Northcote said the surplus was going too fast as to be embarrassing; accordingly the question of the abolition of the sugar duties was reviewed, and finally we agreed though Hunt, J. Manners, Salisbury and I were *on the whole* disagreeing and Hardy only barely convinced. But I then urged that something more should be done for local taxation and after some debate it was agreed that Northcote should consider whether Lunatic Asylums could not be given. Disraeli offered this and I and others said it was a very reasonable proposal.

2. Some questions as to Sir G. Wolseley and Captain Glover.[378]

Disraeli announced all that had passed as to the Archbishops threatened Ecclesiastical Legislation. With the exception of Derby the entire Cabinet was opposed. Cairns expressed himself decidedly against. The matter was left with us to meditate on it.

Monday 30 March (London)

Came up, met Sir M. Beach in train. Vote of thanks to Army and Navy in both Houses. I never heard anything poorer

[378]Capt. John Hawley Glover RN (1829–1885), who had served in Lagos, achieved widespread popularity in Britain for his part in the second Ashanti War. He raised a force to assist the commander, Wolseley, much to the latter's annoyance. Carnarvon praised him for his actions and invited him to Highclere. See Lady E.R. Glover, *Life of Sir John Hawley Glover* (London, 1897), pp. 220–221.

than the speeches in the House of Lords. It was a farrago of such abominable and slipshod commonplace that I felt absolutely ashamed.

I gave a short explanation of the state of things on the Gold Coast but Lord Grey introduced the subject in such a manner as obliged me to be very brief.[379]

Thursday 9 April (Highclere)

All these unsatisfactory rumours as to Lady C. and Disraeli and his visit to Bretby have, as I have long been expecting, come into print.[380] There is a contradiction in the *Morning Post* but put in by whom I cannot say. The expression "ridiculous" clearly indicates that it does not proceed from him.

Saturday 11 April (Highclere)

A very serious harvest of Colonial difficulties and anxieties approach.
1. Fiji annexation
2. Very serious difficulties on the Natal frontier
3. Zulu trials and suppression of the insurrection
4. New Guinea annexation looming in distance
5. Gold Coast settlement.[381]

Wednesday 15 April (London)

Cabinet

1. *Settled the Budget.*[382] Hunt announced that he may have to come for a supplementary vote to make good deficiencies in the Navy. There

---

[379]Vote of Thanks to Forces in Ashanti War: *Hansard*, CCXVIII, 30 March 1874, Grey, col. 394, Carnarvon, cols 394–398.

[380]Disraeli was at Bretby from 1 to 11 April.

[381]Carnarvon told Disraeli, 'I am afraid that there are one, two or three large Colonial subjects ripening so fast that I shall have to trouble the Cabinet with them at an early date' (Carnarvon to Disraeli, 11 April 1874 (copy): CP, BL 60793, fo. 24).

[382]In his Budget speech in the Commons the following day, Northcote acknowledged Gladstone's economical management of the Ashanti War (see Lang, *Life, Letters and Diaries of Sir Stafford Northcote*, II, pp. 59–62).

was a rather general protest against expensive reconstruction, but he said that he did not want more than he needed.

2. *Annexation of Fiji*. I explained that the Commissioners had exceeded apparently their powers, but that I believed annexation would be inevitable ultimately though I did not much like it.[383]

3. *The South African difficulty*. Krater award and infringement of it by South African State. I found the Cabinet very timid, and not unnaturally, at the prospect of possible hostilities. I explained as much as I could and promised to circulate papers.

4. *Honours and rewards to Captain Glover and his officers*. Here the Cabinet misled by precedent decided against any money grant to him, an unwise decision which it is quite possible they will be obliged to retract.

Thursday 16 April (Osborne)

Wrote to Disraeli as to Glover.

The Duke of Edinburgh, Prince Leopold and Princess Beatrice[384] are here, a sort of home party, very little ceremony and rather interesting in that way. The Queen was in better spirits, and more animated than I ever saw her, laughing heartily at anything that amused her.

She asked much after my Mother, reminded me that she had first known me when I was quite a child and she was Princess Victoria, and finally went into fits of laughter over the story of Lady Chesterfield's supposed marriage with Disraeli.[385]

She is much interested as to Fiji, but alarmed at the idea of annexation, mainly I think on the ground of the barbarous customs prevailing there, particularly strangulation of widows. The Duke of Edinburgh is very anxious that we should get the islands.

[383] Two Commissioners, Commodore J.G. Goodenough RN and F.L. Layard, HM Consul in Fiji, had been appointed to report on 'various questions connected with the Fiji Islands'. A telegram received from them recommended that Fiji should become a colony. Carnarvon informed the Lords on 20 April 'that it was not very acceptable for the Commissioners to take such a step on their own responsibility' (*Hansard*, CCXVII, cols 909–911).

[384] Prince Leopold, Duke of Albany (1853–1884), youngest son of Queen Victoria; Princess Beatrice (1857–1944), youngest daughter of Queen Victoria, married to Prince Henry of Battenburg (1885).

[385] See account of meeting in Carnarvon's letter to his mother, Henrietta, 3rd Countess of Carnarvon, 17 April 1874: CP, BL 61043, fo. 146.

Monday 20 April (London)

I am anxious as to this South African difficulty between the Transvaal Republic and the Batlapin tribes. It looks very awkward and may easily grow into a very serious difficulty.

Saturday 25 April (Highclere)

A long and busy day and a Cabinet.

We discussed railway reforms, coming finally to no conclusion, and Scotch Patronage. Salisbury and Hardy and Duke of Richmond were in favour of abolishing it, giving compensation to Patrons and right of election to Assembly. I threw out some doubt as to how far English Church patronage would be involved in such a decision, but the general feeling was in favour of the measure. The Duke of Buccleuch was to be consulted.

We talked a little about the Archbishops' bill. Salisbury urged it to be an open question. Disraeli wisely pressed on us if possible to come to an understanding among ourselves and finally we agreed to press the Archbishop to defer the Second Reading of the bill till at least it had been discussed in Convocation.[386]

Wednesday 29 April (London)

Cabinet

Discussion of miscellaneous and not very important questions, except Hunt's recent alarmist speech on the Navy, evidently a silly affair for after making a great fuss about the deplorable condition of affairs, he is content to take only £150,000. The Cabinet agreed to give him this.

Thursday 30 April (London)

Interview and conversation with Froude[387] as to his journey to Australia.[388] It may I think have some useful results. When I mentioned

[386] The week before, the bishops, meeting at Lambeth, had submitted a new Public Worship Regulation Bill. It was introduced in the Lords on 20 April and, because of Cabinet divisions, was subsequently sent to a Cabinet committee (Buckle, *Disraeli*, V, pp. 321–322).

[387] James Anthony Froude (1818–1894), historian, editor of *Fraser's Magazine* (1860–1874), literary executor for Thomas Carlyle.

[388] In the event, it was another decade before Froude visited Australia.

to him some of the difficulties as to a satisfactory joint action in naval matters by the colonies and ourselves, he said it was a curious reproduction of some of the difficulties in Irish and English history.

Saturday 2 May (London)

Academy dinner, not as dull as sometimes as Hardy, Northcote and I were sitting together. The speaking was very poor with the exception of Disraeli's speech, which was a curious and highly wrought specimen of fine art – mosaic in its structure and pervaded by a dry humour and cultivation of thought, altogether a remarkable effort.[389]

Sunday 3 May (London)

A long walk round Kensington Gardens with Froude, discussing first his proposed journey to Australia, afterwards general matters.

Derby previously had spoken to me on this journey to the effect that he found the expense might be too great for him, £800 for the journey plus £1000 lost to him by cessation of literary work.

I held out to him some hope that I might be able to manage some help in the way of a grant if he undertook the mission as a public matter. He was, as I have always found him, very delicate in regard to personal interests.

Thursday 7 May (London)

Lord Blachford's bill passed second reading.[390]

Saw Grant and settled I think as to Porchy[391] and his Latin labours with Mr. Middleton.

Granville whom I met in the evening was talking of Palmerston's way of doing business at the Foreign Office. He used, he said, to devote himself to one or two particular subjects for which he cared and to allow the rest to take care of itself.

---

[389] See *The Times*, 4 May 1874, p. 8.

[390] Colonial Clergy Bill, second reading: *Hansard*, CCXVIII, 7 May 1874, Blachford, cols 1804–1805, Carnarvon, cols 1805–1806.

[391] George Edward Stanhope Molyneux Herbert (1866–1923), Viscount Porchester, Carnarvon's only son by his first marriage; later 5th Earl of Carnarvon (1890).

Saturday 9 May (London)

Cabinet

The first part was taken up in discussing the Archbishops bill. The subcommittee reported, and Cairns read the objections (and proposals) with regard to it. Then ensued a curious scene for Salisbury had to interrupt him at every passage and to say that it was not a correct representation of the Committee's opinions. In fact Cairns had so manipulated each proposition as to give it a different sense. I have only once before seen Cairns so upset and annoyed and that on a similar occasion when he misrepresented me in the House of Lords. The Cabinet was against him and Disraeli was quite fair and straightforward: and the conclusion was to leave us all free to speak as we pleased but I think with a general agreement to assent to nothing which would not be *a really fair compromise*. The subcommittee were Salisbury, Richmond, Cairns, Hardy and Cross.

Sunday 10 May (London)

Disraeli dined with us. I never knew him more agreeable or full of conversation and anecdote. The languor and lassitude so common to him was gone and he looked ten or twelve years younger. He gave a very curious account of his first acquaintance with Bismarck in England at a ball at the Russian Embassy, just at the time when B. had been summoned to Prussia to form a Government.[392] Bismarck sought him out and said he wished to know him and then went on to say that he was going to Prussia to form the Government and that after weighing this and that policy he went there with the intention of "making Prussia a Kingdom", a curious anticipation, curiously realised.

Monday 11 May (London)

The Archbishop's bill, a very late sitting. Shaftesbury's speech very good and vigorous, considering him to be in his 73rd year; The

---

[392] In May 1862, Bismarck was appointed ambassador at Paris. He came to England to see the Crystal Palace and also to meet Gladstone and Palmerston. According to Disraeli, Bismarck told him, 'I shall declare war on Austria, dissolve the German Confederation and subjugate the middle and smaller states and give Germany national unity under the control of Prussia'. On 23 September he was in Berlin and, at the age of forty-seven, was appointed Prime Minister of Prussia. See W. Richter, *Bismarck* (London, 1964), pp. 75–76.

Bishop of Peterborough brilliant, personal, extremely clever, very unepiscopal and ungenerous to a man like Shaftesbury. Salisbury rather embarrassed at first from I think his speaking for the Government, afterwards very able and weighty, the Archbishop of Canterbury able and oratorical but bitter and showing much mental irritation.[393]

Saturday 16 May (London – Hampstead Marshall)

Cabinet

Nothing very important till we came to the Archbishops bill. Agreed that Cairns' proposal for one lay judge to be appointed should be offered to Shaftesbury to propose to take the place of the proposed machinery; also that Salisbury's article of comprehension should be offered to the Bishop of Peterborough to propose. The only difference on this head is that Cairns wishes to limit the toleration to the Eastward position of the Celebrant during the Consecration prayer, we desire to tolerate it during the whole service. Disraeli and indeed I think all the Cabinet leant to this view. On the whole things look well, but the insertion of the Athanasian creed will cause a great deal of opposition among the High Church.

I understand it to be agreed that we should act freely as individuals but also give our support as individual members of the Government to these proposals.

I told the Cabinet my Gold Coast supplementary vote would probably be about £30,000.

Wednesday 20 May (London)

Dined with the Derbys at the Foreign Office. It was a fine sight. The Emperor of Russia was there, Schouvaloff,[394] Adlerberg[395] and some others. I had not much talk with any of them, except Soltikoff, an admiral, who sat by me. I tried to bring him on to French and

---

[393]Public Worship Regulation Bill, second reading: *Hansard*, CCXIX, 11 May 1874, cols 2–65.
[394]Count Petr Andreievich Shuvalov (1827–1889), Head of Secret Police (1866); he arranged the marriage between Alfred, Duke of Edinburgh and Alexander II's daughter, Marie.
[395]Count Aleksandr Adlerberg (1819–1889), Second Secretary to Shuvalov.

German affairs but he had had, so Lord A. Loftus[396] said, his *mot d'ordre* and would not speak.

Tuesday 2 June (London)

Cabinet

First part of time spent in discussing course of action to be taken on a resolution as to Mr. O'Keefe.[397] It was a difficulty whichever way it was decided.

Agreed to adjourn on the Endowed Schools Commissioners bill.

Interview with Mr. Daldy, Secretary to Copyright Association, as to Copyright bill.

Long interview with Gregory[398] as to Ceylon matters.

House of Lords sat late over Scotch Patronage bill.[399] I dined with Derby [. . .] and he then took the opportunity of saying what Lady Derby has now twice said to Evelyn, that he foresaw that before long it was likely that I should have to take his place at the Foreign Office. I made no answer and I certainly do not desire it for I could see many difficulties and objections.

Saturday 6 June (London)

Cabinet

Long discussion on Endowed Schools bill. Afterwards the question was raised as to the proposed appropriation by the War Office of the new buildings intended for the Colonial Office and Home Office. Hardy made a poor case for the War Office, only saying that the present quarters were too small and were "pestilential" and that the new buildings were more than the Colonial Office required.

I replied urging: 1. utterly bad state of the War Office buildings into which it is proposed that we should go. 2. the original intention

---

[396] Augustus William Spencer Loftus (1817–1904), Secretary of Berlin Legation, attended Czar Alexander II on his visit to London (1874), Governor of New South Wales (1879–1885).

[397] John O'Keefe (1827–1877), Lib. MP for Dungarvan (1874–1877), supporter of home rule.

[398] Sir William Henry Gregory (1817–1892), Con. MP for Dublin (1842–1847), Lib.-Con. MP for Co. Galway (1857–1871), Governor of Ceylon (1871–1876).

[399] Church Patronage (Scotland) Bill, second reading: *Hansard*, CCXIX, 2 June 1874, cols 809–846.

of Parliament and the Acts by which the place is allocated to the Colonial Office and the impossibility of reviewing this. 3. the original planning and grouping of the Colonial Office with all its subordinate departments in the new buildings. 4. the new offices of the Colonial Agents placed near. 5. the connection of the Foreign Office and Colonial Office and necessity of having them together.[400]

I absolutely protested and refused my consent, and with so much vigour that no one really offered me any opposition. It was accordingly agreed that the new buildings should remain as always intended for the Colonial Office and Home Office and that a Committee should be appointed to consider what can be done for the War Office. Cross supported me but very feebly; perhaps he was quite satisfied when he saw that I had it my own way. Hardy was a little bit annoyed but this was natural.[401]

The singular part of the matter was that I am convinced from what then passed as well as from what I have heard elsewhere that the whole affair had been planned and plotted, between the Duke of Cambridge and H. Lennox, that Disraeli had been got over and the Duke of Richmond, and possibly someone else. My extremely decided tone probably stopped the intrigue going on. Derby was absent. It is altogether a curious story.

Wednesday [*sic*] 16 June[402] (London)

Replied to Kimberley as to the Zulu insurrection.
Serious news from Canada. An envoy is on his way from British Columbia to appeal against Railway policy of Dominion Parliament.[403]

[400] The old Colonial Office building in Downing Street had been condemned in 1837. A new block in King Street, designed by Sir Gilbert G. Scott to accommodate the Foreign Office, the India Office, and the Colonial Office, was sanctioned in 1868. The Colonial Office transferred to its new site in 1876. See B.L. Blakeley, *The Colonial Office, 1868–1892* (Durham, NC, 1972), pp. 18–19; E. Walford (ed.), *Old and New London: a narrative of the history, the people and its places*, vol. 3 (London, 1876), pp. 392–393.

[401] Hardy at the War Office attempted to lay claim to the Colonial Office building. Before the Cabinet meeting, Carnarvon offered to discuss the matter with Disraeli, having already talked to Hardy (Carnarvon to Disraeli, 6 June 1874: Hughenden Papers, 100/1, fo. 46). Hardy recorded, 'Carnarvon was very hot on the subject' (Johnson, p. 209). Carnarvon moved into the new building in January 1876.

[402] This entry should be for Tuesday 16 June.

[403] A condition of British Columbia joining the Confederation in 1871 was a subsidy towards construction of a Pacific Railway within ten years. Lord Dufferin, the Governor-General, wanted Macdonald's resignation, but it was not until November 1873, after a vote of severe censure was passed in Parliament, that he resigned. Alexander Mackenzie was appointed

A very temperate protest also came to hand from Sproat, Agent to British Columbia.[404] After consideration I went over to Disraeli and explained the case. He heard it all and seemed to understand it perfectly, I then read him a telegram which I proposed to send at once to Canada, volunteering arbitration on the request of both parties and on the understanding that the arbitration should be conclusive.

He entirely agreed to it and to all that I said and saw no other prudent course open. I proposed to telegraph at once to which he assented, and I suggested whether I should bring it on in Cabinet, to which he said he thought there was no need for this; that he concurred with me and would take the full share of responsibility with me. I accordingly telegraphed.

Thursday 18 June (London)

Cabinet

Main discussion on course to be taken as to Archbishop's bill and his application for "renewal of letters of business to Convocation granted by late Government to consider rubrics." No one knew much of letters of business except myself, but the Cabinet decided to renew the grant. Cairns to announce tomorrow.

Derby announced Congress of Brussels. Agreed to send an envoy there on distinct understanding that rules of maritime warfare are not discussed. This was a point evidently overlooked by the Foreign Office.[405]

A very heavy day. Saw at the office Bishop of Capetown,[406] Bishop of Melbourne,[407] Revd. O. Crosse,[408] Dr. Hamilton[409] as to the 33 and the Prince of Wales.

---

as the new prime minister by Dufferin. See A. Lyall, *The Life of the Marquis of Dufferin and Ava*, 2 vols (London, 1905), I, pp. 224–227; W.L. Morton, *The Critical Years*, pp. 275–277.

[404]Gilbert Malcolm Sproat (1834–1913), agent to British Columbia (1872–1876).

[405]The conference, attended by all European countries, was intended to create firm guidelines based on an international code 'to improve the laws and usages of warfare'.

[406]Revd W.W. Jones, Bishop of Capetown.

[407]Revd Charles Perry, Bishop of Melbourne.

[408]Revd Oland Crosse, Vicar of St John the Baptist Church, Pawlett, Somerset since 1827.

[409]Dr John Hamilton (1809–1875), surgeon to Queen Victoria (1874).

Friday 19 June (London)

Answer from Canada declining arbitration from Mackenzie,[410] the Prime Minister, an ignorant and shortsighted fellow, in the absence of Dufferin[411] who would doubtless have dealt with the matter differently.

Saw Horsman at Colonial Office on Straits Settlements as to India Emigration and afterwards as to Scotch Patronage bill on which I made an unwise step, which I am afraid was owing as much to temper and personal feeling as to want of judgement. I hope that no harm will come of it.

I mentioned what had happened on this subject to Derby, Salisbury, Hardy and very generally to Northcote.

Saturday 20 June (London)

Some conversation with Northcote and Salisbury as to Endowed Schools bill.[412] Settled that the existing Commission should be continued Roby[413] only being removed. He is to be provided for in this way. Malcolm[414] is to be removed to the Colonial Office as Assistant Under Secretary and his place to be filled by Roby.

Afterwards a good deal of conversation with Salisbury 1. as to his own health. 2. as to the future of the Government in the event of Disraeli failing. His view is that we should insist on Hardy leading in the House of Commons and on a certain mode of dealing with Church

[410] Alexander Mackenzie (1822–1892), first Lib. Prime Minister of Canada (1873–1878).

[411] Frederick Temple Blackwood (1826–1902), Earl of Dufferin (1871), 1st Marquess of Dufferin and Ava (1888), Under-Secretary of State for India (1864–1866) and for War (1866), Chancellor, Duchy of Lancaster (1868–1872), Governor-General of Canada (1872–1878), ambassador at St Petersburg (1879–1881) and Constantinople (1881–1884), Viceroy of India (1884–1888). Dufferin, who was on a ten-day fishing holiday when Carnarvon's telegram was sent, displayed a more favourable attitude towards Mackenzie. He informed Carnarvon, 'the poor man never dreamt of adopting a disrespectful tone [...] and Mackenzie is not a statesman. When he first took office he was so anxious to disparage Macdonald and his predecessors that he could not refrain from denouncing in wild and ill considered terms [...] their general Railway policy' (Dufferin to Carnarvon, 9 July 1874: Dufferin Papers, D 1071/41/2, fo. 222).

[412] The Endowed Schools (Amendment) Bill introduced into the Commons on 14 July 1871 was aimed at abolishing the Endowed Schools Commission, a body set up by the previous Liberal government. The Commissioners were charged with altering the trusts of and settling schemes for endowed schools. See P. Gordon, *Selection for Secondary Education* (London, 1980), pp. 39–42.

[413] Henry John Roby (1830–1915), formerly Secretary of the Endowed Schools Commission (1869–1974) and Commissioner (1872–1874). Lib. MP for Eccles (1890–1895).

[414] William Rolle Malcolm (1840–1923), Assistant Under-Secretary at the Colonial Office (1874–1878).

questions. 3. He said he knew of no one to be Foreign Secretary in the event of Derby being Prime Minister but myself. This corresponds with what I know to be Derby's view, but I fought against it I doubt it suiting me, and I see very great objections to it.

Wednesday 24 June (London)

My birthday, and in keeping with this strange year we have had on Midsummer day heavy storms of rain at intervals and even hail. How time flies; how little one can foresee; how little one does of the work which should be done. I sometimes doubt whether as the years roll on, the horizon is contracting or widening.

Cabinet. We discussed Endowed Schools bill and we came to a fresh conclusion again. We decided to keep the old Commission providing for the retirement of Roby by giving him Malcolm's place at the Board of Trade and Malcolm coming to the Colonial Office, and adopting the other general provisions of the bill. Discussed Archbishop's bill and agreed that Cairns should make a critical (and I specially added and *colourless*) statement of its present condition. The Duke of Richmond very anxious to get it entirely into Cairns' hands, but I think I shall say something myself during the discussion.[415] The Duke of Richmond and Sandon certainly do not agree very well.

A long conversation with Froude at the Colonial Office, relative to his secret mission. I explained what I wished him to give his attention to in South Africa, specifying three subjects in particular:

1. generally Federation
2. relations of Free States and Nations and ourselves
3. Natal in reference to recent insurrection. Agreed on this head that if necessary I should write to him and appoint him a Commissioner to enquire on the spot.[416]

Agreed that he should have £1000 from Secret Service money, to which Derby and Disraeli have both agreed.[417] He expressed himself

---

[415]The third reading of the Public Worship Regulation Bill took place the following day, when Carnarvon spoke in support of it: *Hansard*, CCXX, 25 June 1874, cols 400–402.

[416]By the following day, Froude had several reservations about undertaking the task. He wrote to Carnarvon, 'I don't like the notion of mixing myself up in this Cape Commission unless in a distinct capacity [. . .]. I shall say frankly that I was collecting information which I should probably communicate to you and no suspicion would attach to me. At the Cape especially, even with nothing in writing about me to Sir H. Barkly, I shall feel like a Spy. I have paid no attention to internal Cape politics, and no one will be able to guess what induced me to meddle with them' (Froude to Carnarvon, 25 June 1874: CP, BL 60798, fos 12–13).

[417]Derby to Carnarvon, 22 June 1874: CP, BL 60765, fo. 69.

as fully and entirely satisfied in this respect. Settled that he should proceed very soon and go first to the Cape and then if he had time go on to Australia, but that Cape was first and urgent consideration.[418]

Wednesday 8 July (London)

Cabinet, entirely occupied with question as to Fiji.[419]
Finally settled to decline the conditional cession, but not to refuse an absolutely unconditional one: to telegraph this to Sir H. Robinson[420] and to send him out as a supreme Commissioner for the purpose of taking the opinions of King, chiefs, natives and whites in Fiji.

Saturday 11 July (Hatfield)

Cabinet at 1

Discussion on course to be pursued with Religious Worship bill. Disraeli described state of feeling in House of Commons as passionate for the bill and that unless the Government either gave facilities or undertook next year to bring in a measure it would be forced by its own supporters. At first I doubted this but Hardy acknowledged its truth and I have had since corroboration. After much discussion it was settled to give Wednesday or Thursday for conclusion of Second reading and to offer facilities for going into Committee on Friday. Hardy and Northcote were in favour of staving off legislation this year and promising a bill next; Salisbury strongly against, and so the matter was decided. I came away feeling uncomfortable about the whole matter and seeing that any course that is taken is bad. It is a choice of evils.[421]

---

[418] Froude, in writing to Carnarvon on the latter's appointment, had contemplated a visit to Australia and New Zealand to see 'whether there is any possibility of drawing them closer to us'. In reply, Carnarvon suggested that, first of all, Froude should visit South Africa 'and give the Government what help he could to understand the condition of affairs there'. See W.H. Dunn, *James Anthony Froude*, 2 vols (Oxford, 1961–1963), II, p. 390.

[419] Carnarvon had asked Montagu Corry, Disraeli's private secretary, if the Cabinet could discuss Fiji, and attempt to settle the question 'as I am to be questioned on the subject in the Lords this week' (Carnarvon to Corry, 6 July 1874: Hughenden Papers, dep. 100/1, fo. 58; see also Vincent, *Derby*, II, p. 174).

[420] Sir Hercules Robinson (1824–1897), Governor of Ceylon (1865–1872) and of New South Wales (1872–1879).

[421] The adjourned debate on the bill took place on 15 July, when it was read a second time: *Hansard*, CCXXI, cols 14–89.

Friday 17 July (London)

I made my statement about Fiji in the House. It seemed well received and Kimberley made a very fair speech in reply.[422]

The opposition to the Public Worship bill has entirely collapsed and Gladstone has been obliged to withdraw his resolutions. His own party are open mouthed against him and say that he has set up the Government for a fresh term of office. He certainly has not played his cards well, though at the same time the clergy will be generally angry with us for supporting the bill.[423]

Monday 20 July (London)

Cabinet, to discuss Endowed Schools bill.

Northcote proposed a clause to throw open the governing bodies under the old 19th clause of Endowed Schools Act to Dissenters. Salisbury opposed this strongly on the ground that we should destroy the character of the bill. Sandon was called in and he strongly defended the proposal. I argued for Salisbury's view and finally a compromise clause drawn by Cairns was agreed on, which Sandon was to announce. It was a curious but not satisfactory Cabinet.

We carried this clause through though we were a small minority, Salisbury, myself, Hardy and J. Manners. There were signs of concert and combination and pre-arrangement, and Disraeli showed all that curious desire of going with the House of Commons, and of manipulating them which has always distinguished him.

Saturday 25 July (Highclere)

A letter from Salisbury announcing a very "unpleasant Cabinet"[424] yesterday. He had been absolutely beaten on all the points in the

---

[422]On the cession of Fiji to the British Crown: *Hansard*, CCXXI, 17 July 1874, Carnarvon, cols 179–189, Kimberley, cols 192–195.

[423]Gladstone fiercely opposed the principle of the bill on the grounds of its spiritual absolutism. See Gladstone to Granville, 7 May 1874, in Ramm, 1952, II, pp. 451–453. He countered with six resolutions, but withdrew them on 16 July (see J.P. Parry, *Democracy and Religion: Gladstone and the Liberal Party* (Cambridge, 1986), pp. 414–416).

[424]Salisbury wrote from the India Office, 'I am very glad you were out of it for it would have annoyed you and done your health no good—and your presence would not have retrieved the day. We were too thoroughly overmatched' (Salisbury to Carnarvon, 25 July 1874: Hatfield House Papers, 3M/E). Disraeli dropped the controversial clause on retaining the Church character of an endowed school. See Diary, 28 July 1874 for Carnarvon's discussion with Salisbury on the bill.

Endowed Schools bill which he had tried to carry, even Hardy voting against him. He said he "felt himself in a very disagreeable position though it was too small a matter on which to resign", altogether very unsatisfactory. I telegraphed in general terms and wrote more fully, agreeing entirely that it was not a question on which a resignation was possible. I regret that I was not there for I might have prevented the discussion becoming disagreeable as I plainly see it was.

Later, Lady Chesterfield received a letter from Disraeli. I did not see it, but she said that he had said that the Cabinet was a "most critical one," "that he was sorry that I was absent," but that "he hoped all would be well."[425]

Tuesday 28 July (London)

Had some conversation with Salisbury as to the last Cabinet. It seems that Disraeli in stating the question of the Endowed Schools bill to the Cabinet said that he desired to consult Hardy particularly, whose position was difficult, and Salisbury "in a less degree" or words to that effect. I said that I thought this could only have proceeded from awkwardness, for that he had generally shown him marked consideration and that if he had meant anything offensive it would have been too offensive a speech. Salisbury on the whole agreed, but he is evidently annoyed.

We afterwards got into larger questions and I advised him not to speak on the bill when it comes up. I urged him not to give anyone the pretext for saying either that he had been beaten on a point where he had tried to win or that he was impracticable.

Spoke to Derby about the Fiji labourers and the payment of their wages and back passages. He was mightily discomposed at my statement.

Saturday 1 August (Highclere)

Cabinet

All the first part of the time occupied in the discussion of the Queen's Speech. On the whole a general agreement. I drafted a paragraph on the Gold Coast which was accepted.[426]

---

[425]'Carnarvon was much wanted today in the most critical Cabinet of the session. However, all has ended well apparently' (Zetland, I, p. 117).

[426]See Queen's Speech: *Hansard*, CCXXII, 5 February 1875, col. 4.

Afterwards some debate as to the Endowed Schools bill. Salisbury objected to a clause proposed but got little support. I then interposed and finally after some discussion it was left to Cairns to draft.[427]

Afterwards I stated the difficulty of the labourers in Fiji and proposed to take powers to pay their wages and back passages, putting a mortgage to the same amount on the estates of the planters. A good deal of opposition to this proposal, and it would have been shelved but that I said I could not have it put aside but that I must request that it could be considered fully, that the responsibility was first with me, afterwards, with them.

Finally, the Cabinet was settled to meet again on this subject next week.

Tuesday 4 August (London)

Saw Cairns, to whom I have given the Government of Queensland.[428] He seemed very grateful and looked better in health [...].

Debate in the House of Lords as to Commons Amendment on Archbishops bill. I spoke against the amendment giving an appeal to the Archbishops from the Bishops discretion. Bishop of Winchester[429] made a good speech against it. Salisbury also, but he spoke with too much warmth, the result however to my surprise that one had a majority of 12.[430] Richmond and Cairns voted in the minority. After speaking I saw Hardy and had some talk with him on the subject. He is evidently very much out of spirits, spoke rather sadly of the way in which he had been treated by his own friends and of the anger of the Queen at his having said that she was not the head of the Church. Altogether these Church subjects are likely to give us a great deal of trouble and possibly to break us up as a Government.

[427]The Endowed Schools (Amendment) Bill received the Royal Assent on 5 August.

[428]William Wellington Cairns (1828–1888), Governor of Queensland (1874–1875). He was Hugh Cairns's half-brother.

[429]Edward Harold Browne (1811–1891), Bishop of Winchester (1873–1890).

[430]*Hansard*, CCXXI, 4 August 1874, Salisbury, cols 1231–1232, Winchester, cols 1234–1238, Carnarvon, cols 1242–1245, Cairns, cols 1246–1249. Contents 32, Not-Contents 44.

Wednesday 5 August (London)

A long and very important conversation with Salisbury in prospect of possible changes of Government during the Autumn. It was agreed that we neither of us should accept anything without consultation. We both were of opinion that on the whole Derby would be the best head of the Government, that Richmond was impossible because so hopelessly ignorant and incompetent, that the question of the Foreign Office was an extreme difficulty and that the acceptance of it was equally repugnant to both of us, that individual questions would be dangerous but that everything was too uncertain here to decide on any course. I urged him again very earnestly to prune down the strength of his expressions and to give no occasion to people to call him intemperate. He accepted it all in the kindest and best part.

Oddly enough he had scarcely gone when he sent me a note from Disraeli to him, apologizing for some expressions that he (D.) seems to have used this afternoon in the House of Commons as to Salisbury.[431] I suspect D. had not recovered his temper, and that the decision of the House of Commons was still doubtful. Subsequently they accepted our amendment of last night.

Cabinet on Fiji matters postponed.

Thursday 6 August (London – Highclere)

Certainly nothing can be worse or more offensive than Disraeli's speech on Salisbury. Not one expression but a succession of sentences, each one worse than its predecessor. Salisbury came to me and talked matters over and settled to make an explanation in the House which he did and with complete success. Cairns asked me what Salisbury thought, whether he was much annoyed. I said no, that he was above being annoyed at such a thing but that it was impossible not to feel the extraordinary nature of the proceeding.[432]

---

[431] See *The Times*, 6 August 1874, p. 6, and The Public Worship Bill, third reading: *Hansard*, CCXXI, 5 August 1874, Disraeli, cols 1354–1360. Salisbury wrote to Carnarvon afterwards, 'To show you how much I have improved in style under your teaching, I enclose my reply to a strange note I received from D. What impertinences he has been saying about me I cannot conceive' (Salisbury to Carnarvon, 5 August 1874: CP, BL 60758, fo. 139). Carnarvon replied, 'You are very good to let me talk to you as I do often say disagreeable things and make idle criticisms' (Carnarvon to Salisbury, 5 August 1874: Hatfield House Papers, 3M/E).

[432] There was considerable speculation at the time that the three main Conservative rebels – Salisbury, Carnarvon, and Hardy – would have to resign. See J. Bentley, *Ritualism and Politics in Victorian Britain: the attempt to legislate for belief* (Oxford, 1978), p. 74.

I discussed everything again with S., and afterwards had a talk with Hardy. When I told him that I knew that Disraeli had sent a message to V. Harcourt assuring him of his readiness to offer him office he was overwhelmed.[433]

I too have had my cause of complaint. This morning I received a letter from M. Corry[434] saying the Cabinet was put off indefinitely and that "D. added that it was impossible to make any advance under present circumstances as regards Fiji." The impertinence and folly and absurdity of the proceeding at first irritated me greatly. I came down here determined to ignore this intimation and telegraph to Robinson to make the necessary advances.

Saturday 8 August (Highclere)

Froude, Delane, V. Harcourt, Dean of Westminster[435] and some others came.

Harcourt very agreeable socially. He makes no secret of his liking for Disraeli, his wish that he could exchange leaders and his acting in concert with him. He is evidently looking to a coalition and in fact hardly disguises it. He says that Gladstone is evidently bent next session on advocating Home Rule and disestablishment, and that he for one will not follow him there. He told me a curious story of Disraeli. It seems that he was talking to him of Lowe and that D. sneered at Lowe, on which Harcourt said that after all his speeches in the House of Commons had carried the House with him. To which D. replied that he had made Lowe, for that after the first of Lowe's speeches he had seen the importance of it, though his own party "who are not very intelligent" had not been alive to it, and he had accordingly placed members in different parts of the House with instructions to cheer Lowe at the proper passages, and that this had made his reputation. An extraordinary story! How much truth is there in it? Harcourt evidently believed it.

[433]See Diary, 8 August 1874. Harcourt had made a damaging speech on Gladstone in the Commons debate on the Public Worship Regulation Bill the previous day (see A.G. Gardiner, *The Life of Sir William Harcourt*, 2 vols (London, 1923), I, pp. 276–277).

[434]Montagu William Lowry Corry (1838–1903), private secretary to Disraeli (1866–1881), created 1st Baron Rowton (1881).

[435]Arthur Penrhyn Stanley (1815–1881), Dean of Westminster (1864–1881).

Sunday 9 August (Highclere)

Received an answer from Disraeli, leaving everything to my management and withdrawing all attempts at restricting my discretion, a very civil but a very sphinx-like epistle.[436]

Monday 14 September (Gedling)

Hamilton[437] from the Colonial Office came, a pleasant comprehending youth. Shot with him and Mr. Wright.

In the evening the Chandos Leighs[438] and Sheffield,[439] who looks very ill. Sheffield told me a curious story of Foreign Office blundering. It seems that Derby was on the whole prepared that General Sir A. Horsford[440] should sign the protocol of the Brussels Conference and that he allowed a despatch to this effect to be drafted and signed. It was then submitted to Disraeli who declared himself strongly against such a signature. Meanwhile the despatch had gone back to the Foreign Office and instead of being pigeonholed and cancelled, was by mistake forwarded to Brussels and presented to Sir A. Horsford. Thus we were committed to the signing of the Protocol – the very opposite of what we intended.

Saturday 19 September (Gedling)

Our party broke up and Orlando Forester[441] returned from Bretby where Disraeli is much laid up with bronchitis.

D. has given up going to Ireland, being finally decided, it seems by a letter from Derby dissuading him on the ground of the political risks

---

[436]i.e., allowing Carnarvon discretion on Fiji affairs. Disraeli to Carnarvon, 8 August 1874: CP, BL 60763, fos 39–42.

[437]Lord George Francis Hamilton (1845–1927), Con. MP for Middlesex (1868–1884) and for Ealing (1885–1906), Under-Secretary of State for India (1874–1878), Vice- President, Committee of Council on Education (1878–1880), First Lord of the Admiralty (1885–1886).

[438]Gilbert Henry Chandos Leigh (1851–1884), Lib. MP for Warwickshire South (1880–1884).

[439]Henry North Holroyd (1832–1909), 3rd Earl of Sheffield (1876), diplomat (1852–1856), Con. MP for Sussex East (1857–1865).

[440]Gen. Sir Alfred Horsford (1818–1885), the British delegate to the Conference, had been given strict orders to refer every point to the Government. After the report was received, no further action was taken to implement it.

[441]Revd and Hon. Orlando Forester (1813–1894), brother of Lady Chesterfield and Lady Bradford. Rector of Gedling, Notts, of which Carnarvon was patron. Disraeli had recently appointed him Canon Resident and Chancellor of York (Blake, *Disraeli*, pp. 685–686).

or *the necessity of being in good order for the discussion of measures in Cabinet in November.* He (O.F.) replied "Compulsory education". I suspect that but for me he would have said "religious questions" and lastly, to my surprise, he said something about "home rule", adding that M. Corry thought that it was quite possible to handle some of these questions in such a way as to be agreeable to all parties.

I believe that this must be the result of some conversation or other at Bretby and that Disraeli is as usual scheming and that he is more than ever in M. Corry's hands. Meanwhile he is certainly ill and apparently has been very low and depressed as to himself. It is quite possible that he may not get through the winter, and already Derby like the heir expectant is beginning to dictate terms and take powers. It is altogether very disagreeable. I see nothing in the future which is likely to be satisfactory – unbelief in religion, trimming in Parliament, cowardice in national policy.

Saturday 26 September (Bretby)

We came on here in the afternoon.[442] Found Disraeli better but looking very ill, and I think extremely low and depressed about himself. He had been out for a short airing for the first time. His gout is still bad, though I suspect not yet fully developed, and he has remains of a severe bronchitis. He seemed very glad to see me and declared that he had hardly heard anything of any of his colleagues except Derby. He began by telling me what had been done at the Foreign Office, 1st. recognition of Spain. 2nd withdrawal of minister from Papal Court and transfer of the whole business to Paget.[443] 3rd He gave me an account of the extraordinary blunder as to the Brussels Protocol.

He then went on to talk of what we must do on our meeting in November, saying that it was of no use merely to meet to ask each other how we had spent the holidays, that it was necessary to have our views as to legislation etc. ready. I expected something serious and large after this and remembered the hints as to Reform in '57: but he proceeded to say that Cross, in whom he had great confidence, had promised to consider some scheme as to dwellings for working classes, that he had not asked him what his plan was but that he believed that

---

[442]Carnarvon, who was at Gedling at the time, told his mother, 'I am obliged to go to Bretby today as Disraeli is there and it is a matter of consequence to me to see him on various Government business' (Carnarvon to Henrietta, 3rd Countess of Carnarvon, 26 September 1874: CP, BL 61044, fo. 157).

[443]Sir Richard Horner Paget (1832–1908), Con. MP for Somerset East (1865–1868), for Mid-Somerset (1868–1885), and for Wells (1885–1895).

he was maturing it. And there he stopped, adding I think somewhat as to sanitary reforms. He went on however to the Judicature Bills, reminding one that he had always disliked the removal of the power from the House of Lords, and saying that there would be no real opposition from Cairns on the subject. I think that he is anxious here for a modification of Cairns' bill of last session.

Something was then said as to the Religious Worship Act, and I said that it would not come into operation till July and that then no-one could say without further experience how it would work. To this he assented, and he gave me the impression that he did not contemplate any movement in this direction. I told him that the clergy was still sore, to which he assented.

He said he had heard once from Salisbury and that nothing could be more friendly.

Tuesday 29 September (Bretby)

Had a good deal of conversation with Disraeli on Colonial subjects. I broached to him my ideas of a fusion of the St. Michael and the St. George in the Order of the Bath. He agreed in it, said it ought to have been done when the St. Michael and St. George was revived, but that it would need much consideration and care and should be dealt with as a whole.

I explained also to him my notions as to a scheme of joint Colonial Defence, military and naval. He entered into it very warmly and added that I should have his heartiest support. He said that he wanted to send "the bearskin" back again to Canada to reassert the visible sovereignty of the Empire.

Wednesday 30 September (Bretby)

I have I think seen more of Disraeli and got a greater appreciation of him than ever before. There is no doubt as to his genius and his breadth of view. He detests details and always looks to the principle or rather the *idea* of any question. He is in fact unable to deal with details. He does no work. For many days past he has not put pen to paper. M. Corry is in fact Prime Minister and on the whole does not manage amiss or above much his power. He is in private life amicable.

Saturday 17 October (Highclere)

Telegram of annexation of Fiji received.[444] Wrote to Disraeli as to
Gold Coast slavery matter, saying I would need a naval force on the
Coast.[445]
Very hard day's work.

Wednesday 21 October (Highclere)

A great deal of navy business settled with Herbert[446] as far as possible.
1. Fiji matter, the proposed staff 2. Natal, course of proceedings
3. Canada Cables Act 4. British Columbian despatch: stands
over.[447]

Tuesday 27 October (Highclere)

The Salisburys came. He is looking better, but has little news having
just returned from France. We talked over matters generally. The only
point which he suggested was as to the course to be taken on the
Report of the University Revenues. There are two courses assuming
that we take action, which we both think desirable:
1. to draw the bill and to provide for their distribution
2. to enable the Universities to redistribute.
I am in favour of the 2nd and so was he, a plan for allowing
Convocation to appoint 3 Commissioners, each College, as its turn
comes on, 3 Commissioners, and the Crown 3 Commissioners, might
give, I think, a safe body.

[444]Robinson sent a telegram on 30 September stating that the King of Fiji had signed an
unconditional cession of the country. It was not received until 16 October. See Hardinge,
II, p. 134; Carnarvon to Disraeli, 17 October 1874 (copy): CP, BL 60763, fos 52–53.

[445]Carnarvon also wrote to Ward Hunt at the Admiralty requesting naval support: 'I have
seen my way towards the abolition of Slavery on the Gold Coast' (Carnarvon to Ward Hunt,
18 October 1874: CP, TNA, PRO 30/6/5, fo. 25).

[446]Robert George Wyndham Herbert (1831–1905), Colonial Secretary for Queensland
(1859), first Premier of Queensland (1860–1865), Permanent Under-Secretary for the
Colonies in London (1871–1892), KCB (1882), Agent-General, Tasmania (1893–1896).

[447]'I have just telegraphed to Carnarvon. He seems very busy annexing provinces to the
Empire' (Disraeli to Lady Bradford, 18 October 1874, in Zetland, I, p. 161).

Saturday 31 October (Highclere)

Colenso[448] came to confer on Natal matters. I found him very reasonable in conversation at least.

His recommendations, to sum up everything briefly, are:

1. Amnesty to Langalibalele tribe.[449] They are scattered and in hiding and would at once return.

2. Give them power to take service for 3 years with white settlers. Government to guarantee the contract, and with their wages to buy up land as individual holdings.

3. Patili tribe to go back to location but to give to each man a separate creation. There should be no power to sell to any Englishmen, only natives.

4. He agrees in view which I urged on Shepstone,[450] viz. to substitute white magistrates for Chiefs, but to make the change as gradual and gentle as possible.

5. To release the Chief, but not to imprison him. He has suffered enough, and Maritzburg prison is crowded and unhealthy. It will be enough to put him under surveillance.

6. Question arose under whose care: he again repeated his offer of taking charge of him. I said that if I could release him it must be without creating prestige of local government, to which he assented.

7. He advised a Durbar to be held every year in order to tide over transition period as the Chiefs do not come under Legislature.

8. He promises all co-operation that he can give in smoothing matters and he recognizes my great difficulties in dealing with the matter.

[448] John William Colenso (1814–1883), Bishop of Natal (1853–1863) and of Cape Town (1863–1883).

[449] Langalibalele, a Kaffir chief, had defied a Natal firearms registration order. Pine, the governor, decided to make an example of him, ordering the destruction of the chieftain's land stock. Captured by the Cape Mountain Police, Langalibalele was tried in a special court presided over by Pine himself and sentenced to banishment. This move was approved by Sir Theophilus Shepstone, Secretary for Native Affairs, and the Natal colonists. Colenso came to England in late September, to urge Carnarvon to ensure that justice was done to Langalibalele (see G.W. Cox, *The Life of John William Colenso,* 2 vols (London, 1888), II, pp. 389–392). After their first meeting, Carnarvon confessed, 'I was not prejudiced in his favour but I am bound to say that he did his part fairly well. His arguments were all reasonable and his facts fairly stated' (Diary, 5 October 1874).

[450] Sir Theophilus Shepstone (1817–1893), Secretary of State for Native Affairs, Natal (1856), Administrator of the Transvaal (1877–1879) and of Zululand (1884).

Thursday 12 November (London)

Cabinet

Disraeli is certainly very poorly. The gout and bronchitis combined have pulled him down greatly and I own to great misgivings.

He began by a strong appeal to Hardy and Hunt in consequence of Northcote's serious financial statement to consider if a reduction between them of some £500,000 were possible; and both declared themselves unable to reduce a shilling. Hunt said that anyhow he had looked to at least 3 years to set things straight in consequence of the wholesale reductions of the late Government.

We then discussed the proposed bill for the Government of the Metropolis. Cross explained it and proposed to indicate some reforms that might be made in the Government as apart from the City, leaving the City alone. Finally agreed to oppose the bill *in toto* and to hold out no hope of dealing with other parts of London. There was a very divided opinion as to the fact whether any change there would be an improvement.

Public building Northcote explained there would be in this year £500,000 surplus, next year deficiency of £700,000 and if things were unfavourable, the total deficiency would be about £900,000. We would have to keep income tax as permanent tax and as at present and probably get £1,000,000 on spirits. Under these circumstances *it seemed* to be agreed not to commence purchase of land for War Office and new buildings which would cost £2,000,000 and with the buildings £3,000,000.

Arctic Expedition Agreed to give grant for this. This year £40,000, next £36,000, next £22,000, next £13,000.

Question of Game Decided to postpone bill.

Landlord and Tenant Decided to introduce a bill and Committee appointed, Duke of Richmond, Malmesbury and Hunt.

Endowed Schools Commission Agreed to wait to see what new Commissioners do, i.e. to do nothing at present.

Saturday 14 November (London)

Cabinet

We discussed:

1. *Workmen's dwellings* Cross proposes a bill on principles of Glasgow, Edinburgh and Liverpool Acts, also appropriation of land *near* but not quite part of Battersea Park. He is to prepare a bill.

2. *University Revenues* Disraeli to write to the Vice Chancellors, to ask for their proposals.

3. *Sanitary legislation* Sclater Booth[451] who was called in says there is enough power already given by Act of last year.

4. Bills as to pollution of Rivers and Adulteration of Food to be prepared.

Immediately afterwards I received a telegram from Dufferin asking me to intervene by commuting sentence on Lepine.[452] This is a serious matter. Talked to Northcote as to this, as to probable financial difficulties regarding Griqualand and as to the Endowed Schools scheme remaining.

In the morning I saw the Prince of Wales as to his Grand Mastership and Masonic matters. He told me he had consulted the Queen before accepting and though she was not fond of Masonry she had agreed to it.[453]

Sunday 15 November (London)

There is this great satisfaction in doing business with Disraeli that whilst he never worries or interferes unnecessarily he has the imaginative faculty which enables him to apprehend the true state of the case in its broad outlines from a distance far more truly than the dull matter of fact politicians that one ordinarily deals with.

The Queen had just written to him on the Greville *Memoirs*, very indignant at what she called "the indelicacy the indiscretion and the ingratitude" of them, a very royal alliteration.[454]

I had a long conversation with him and an interesting one. Among other things he discussed the late Lord Derby and said he had neither sympathy nor heart. He spoke of and rated much higher the present Derby.

---

[451] George Sclater-Booth (1826–1894), Con. MP for Hampshire North (1857–1887), President of the Local Government Board (1874–1880), 1st Baron Basing (1887).

[452] Dufferin to Carnarvon, 12 November 1874: Dufferin Papers, D/1071/H1/3, fo. 80. Ambroise-Dydime Lépine, a Canadian accused of committing a murder in 1873, had been sentenced to death a few weeks earlier. The French Catholics were demanding commutation and caused a government crisis.

[453] The Prince had been promoted Grand Master of the Order in England in 1874, and became Past Master on the resignation of Lord Ripon in September 1875 (S. Lee, *King Edward VII*, 2 vols (London, 1925–1927), II, pp. 291, 568).

[454] Charles Cavendish Fulke Greville (1794–1868), Clerk of the Council in Ordinary, author of *A Journal of the Reigns of King George IV and King William IV*, edited by Henry Reeve and recently published.

Tuesday 17 November (London)

Cabinet

1. *Irish bills* Dr. Ball gave as his opinion as to course to be taken. He enumerated 3 questions: a) Judicature bill on which he said nothing. b) Jury bill, the introduction of which he considered very important. An English bill has to be prepared and it is a question if the Irish should not follow on a line similar to it. c) Peace Preservation Acts. He says that Ireland is very tranquil, little crime, but they ought apparently to be renewed. Nothing agreed but a report to be prepared.

2. A bill as to explosives discussed.

3. Agreed that in January we should decide on Master and Servant bills, Irish legislation and Workmen's dwellings.

4. I explained the following Colonial questions a) British Columbia controversy b) Lepine's case, in Canada and Riel c) Natal difficulty. There was a good deal of objection to an Act of Indemnity. d) Eyre's Pension, great dismay at this idea of a bill, but I left it so that I consider myself to do as I please.[455]

Dined at the Derbys. Schouvaloff was there, plausible and agreeable, but as false, I doubt not, as most other Russians.

Thursday 19 November (London)

Cabinet

Disraeli asked me to explain Natal question. I did so, much discussion and questioning, but the only point which the Cabinet had was a great fear of any legislation. They all dread the House of Commons, as I think, very unnecessarily.

Finally it was agreed that I should go on with all my preliminary measures, write my despatches, take steps for recall of Pine, appointment of new Governor, etc. but reserve question of legislation and mode of release of Langalibalele till January.[456]

[455] Edward John Eyre (1815–1901), Governor of Jamaica (1864–1866). Eyre put down a riot at Morant Bay, killing and wounding many people. As Colonial Secretary in 1866, Carnarvon condemned the methods used by Eyre to quell the insurrection. See B.A. Knox, 'The British Government and the Governor Eyre controversy', *Historical Journal*, 19 (1976), pp. 888–894.

[456] Derby wrote after the Cabinet, 'The governor, Sir B. Pine, to be recalled' (Vincent, *Derby*, II, p. 183).

Friday 20 November (London)

Cabinet

1. Aggravated outrages. Cross read opinion of Judges, etc. as to flogging – large preponderance for it.

2. Adderley produced bill as to unseaworthy ships, differing mainly from Plimsoll's in that survey should not be universal but only on suspicion.[457]

3. Northcote proposed for consideration a scheme of co-organisation, main principle being to transfer roads, poor law, education and sanitary business to an elective Board, leaving to Quarter Sessions judicial, prisons and Lunatic Asylums. A new valuation bill would be necessary. General feeling was against it.

4. At the end of the meeting suddenly like thunder in a clear sky, a storm broke. Cairns spoke of the Judicature bill and the transfer of appellate jurisdiction in it from the House of Lords. Richmond then very pointedly said he hoped that he should not be put in the position he was in last year. He looked at me and soon after repeated it and so pointedly that I took it up and said that my position was such that I had not voted for it, that I did not care to oppose my colleagues but that the strong part which I had taken against this part of the bill in '73 made it impossible for me to do otherwise. Then Cairns joined in and the discussion took rather a disagreeable character. On which Salisbury took up my defence and said that it was monstrous to endeavour to tighten the bonds of party discussion to try to force me to vote for what I had openly opposed. I said something implying it was not impossible for me to vote for it. Cairns said something (I could not say what) about his honour, and the matter closed rather disagreeably but I think with the understanding that I should certainly not give way, and that we should reconsider the actual question of the transfer in January.

As we broke up Richmond came up and said I had misunderstood him in thinking he alluded to me and somewhat apologised. Cairns was also much in the same line. My strong impression however, and Salisbury's, that it had been concerted between them. Disraeli I think did not anticipate it and was annoyed. No one else was prepared for it. Came down to Hatfield and found Lyons there.

---

[457]Samuel Plimsoll (1824–1898), Lib. MP for Derby (1868–1880), a vigorous campaigner for the compulsory survey of merchant shipping and the creation of a load line. An Act of 1873 had failed to meet Plimsoll's demands. Sir Charles Adderley, an incompetent President of the Board of Trade, promised further legislation. See N. Jones, *The Plimsoll Sensation: the great campaign to save lives at sea* (London, 2006), pp. 131–135.

Sunday 22 November (Hatfield)

I have had a good deal of conversation with Lyons, amongst other things on the disagreeable question of a possible removal of Derby from the Foreign Office. The subject came up in conversation and I thought it then to talk it over with him as an old friend and one whose opinions could well be trusted. He was strongly in favour of my taking the Foreign Office should the necessity arise.[458] I put it to him whether a foreign policy was really possible for this country. He thought it was though he admitted that we were now living on our prestige and that without stronger armaments our position was hardly one of security. Still he thought it was possible to have a certain voice in European affairs. His points were:

1. No programme at first. It only hampers. Let the policy be ascertained by the acts done and gradually.

2. Absolute veracity in smaller trifles, so as evince entire confidence in every word.

3. Conciliation and personal attention to foreign ministry.

4. Private correspondence with our own Ministers abroad.

Salisbury and Lady S. seem to me to have made up their minds that he would not take the Foreign Office and that I ought in such case to do it. But *absit omen*.

Tuesday 24 November (London)

Had a long conversation with Shepstone as to Natal matters; I think that I have now settled all the main points and that my despatch may go out on Friday week.[459] I heard that the first meeting of the Chiefs on the West Coast of Africa had been held and that the announcement of slave dealing had been made. It is a great step made and I trust all things will go right.[460]

---

[458] At the end of the year, Derby wrote to Lyons, 'I cannot make head or tail of French internal politics, and presume that most Frenchmen are in the same condition' (T.W. Legh, Baron Newton, *Lord Lyons: a record of British diplomacy* (London, 1913), p. 326).

[459] Carnarvon sent a draft to the Queen of his despatch proposing a conditional pardon for Langalibalele, following 'a very unfavourable judgement and the unquestionably wrong and illegal procedure at Natal' (Carnarvon to Queen Victoria, 28 November 1874: Royal Archives, O32/24).

[460] Carnarvon announced in the Lords that the Gold Coast Governor, G.C. Strahan, was instructed to carry out this policy of the abolition of slavery. He wrote to the Queen, 'Every slave will be at liberty to leave his master without assigning any cause for so doing' (Carnarvon to Queen Victoria, 26 November 1874: Royal Archives, P24/128). The

Saturday 28 November (London)

I called at Disraeli's. He was still too ill to see me, but I found Cairns there who made a very long face when I came in, and shaking his head, said that he was afraid that Disraeli was very ill. I am myself afraid that it is so, and I wrote a few lines to Corry to advise him to come up. I am very sorry for D. alone, untended, uncared for in the midst of his external power and fancied prosperity. Vanities of vanities. I sometimes doubt whether we are not on the immediate verge of great changes.

Derby came up to town this evening.

Monday 30 November (London)

Plots and intrigues of all kinds are going on upon the supposition that Disraeli cannot last. I dined at the Royal Society, where I had to return thanks for the Government,[461] and returned with Salisbury. Much conversation with him on the point. We are agreed to prevent Richmond stepping in to the place, and it would all be easy enough but that Cairns is clearly pulling the strings. Cairns is a born plotter and of course he would not dislike having Richmond for Prime Minister, as a very flexible and docile puppet.

Tuesday 1 December (London)

Important conversation with Salisbury as to the present intrigues going on in favour of Duke of Richmond.[462] He showed me a letter which he had written on our conversation of last night to Derby urging him in the event of Disraeli's retirement to take the Prime Ministership. It stated the case most clearly as against Richmond,

---

Gold Coast would be annexed and made a Crown Colony independent of Sierra Leone. Carnarvon had been persuaded by philanthropists to abolish slavery. See Hargreaves, *Prelude to the Partition of West Africa*, pp. 171–172.

[461] 'Anniversary meeting of the Royal Society', *The Times*, 1 December 1874, p. 7. Carnarvon was elected Fellow on 8 April 1875.

[462] Before the meeting Carnarvon had told Salisbury, 'I fear we are on the verge of changes, but *I see my way to combinations that might in the end strengthen us. Nil desperandum*' (Carnarvon to Salisbury, 30 November 1874: Hatfield House Papers, 3M/E).

urging that he was simply incompetent and that a totally incompetent Prime Minister must lead to anarchy in the Cabinet and contempt out of it. He proposed (in this letter) that he and Derby and I should refuse to serve under Richmond and that this would settle the matter. I entirely agreed.

Interview with Colenso at the Colonial Office. I told him all that I proposed to do in Natal, exacting from him a promise that what I said should be in the strictest confidence. He promised. I told him everything and he then thanked me for all the consideration which I had given to the case and said though he might have preferred that things should be in some respects different he accepted the decision as entirely just and right and promised a loyal support to everything and that he would sanction and allow "no party triumph." Finally, I undertook to effect a personal reconciliation between him and Shepstone.

Saw Shepstone and settled this also.

Wednesday 2 December (London)

Effected a reconciliation between Colenso and Shepstone. They met in my room and shook hands. The Bishop showed a great deal of feeling. Shepstone seemed to be also much affected but in what precise way I cannot be sure.

I gave Shepstone his parting instructions and hinted that I hoped that he might obtain some recognition of his service (i.e. K.C.M.G.) I held out the hope to him yesterday of an increase of salary. He leaves London tomorrow.

Grand Lodge in the evening where I was installed Pro Grand Master. It was a very full attendance.

Thursday 3 December (London)

I announced to Gordon at the Colonial Office that he would be Governor of Fiji. He is an odd fellow for after having desired and almost asked for it he hardly seemed pleased when I told him. However I think this was probably only manner and that he will do well.

Salisbury came over to me to show me an answer from Derby in which he accepted the situation and said that Richmond would not succeed.[463] The curious fact of this matter was that he added that the information that Richmond was likely to put forward was entirely new to him. But had not Lady Derby said anything to him after all she said to me?

[463]Derby agreed with Salisbury. In his diary, Derby wrote, 'I am inclined to think that Salisbury's aversion to the notion of having Richmond for chief is due to the fact that the Duke is entirely under the influence of Cairns. S. [Salisbury] being a strong high churchman, fears nothing more than that Cairns, who is low, should virtually make bishops and guide ecclesiastical policy: he would prefer a neutral, like myself, whom he might hope in some degree to guide' (Vincent, *Derby*, II, p. 184).

1875

Tuesday 12 January (London)

Steady progress all through the day, more and quieter sleep, food, general repose. I trust now all will go well.

Cabinet

1. *Statement of foreign policy by Derby*
a) Proposals for a renewal of Brussels Conference. Russia, Prussia, Austria all in favour of a Code to regulate warfare, smaller powers against it. He proposed and we all agreed to decline Conference.

b) He described state of Spain. It is true that Bismarck proposes to have recognition on the removal of suspension of Protestant newspapers. German ambassador had spoken to Derby which, whilst he would be glad of all toleration, could not agree to found recognition on such a condition. Recognition for a while suspended.

2. *Colonial* – some explanations as to Gambia exchange.[464]

3. *Financial* – a very strong pressure put on Hunt by Cairns (supported by Derby slightly and by Salisbury) to reduce his proposals for Navy. Northcote estimates his surplus at £80,000 but War Office need addition of £350,000

Admiralty	250,000
Education	200,000
	800,000

Hunt on whole held his ground though he showed signs of yielding. I gave him some support by opposing the proposal to cut down the squadrons and to leave unbuilt the 7 unarmoured ships which are needed.[465]

---

[464]A proposal to exchange Gambia for French territory – a move which would have simplified Gold Coast administration.

[465]See Vincent, *Derby*, II, p. 189.

Wednesday 10 February (London)

Cabinet

1. Natal and Cape affairs. I stated the case and they agreed that I should write as I proposed to Cape.[466]

2. Landlord and Tenant bill.

3. Sandon called in and gave explanations as to Compulsory Education.[467]

4. Sclater Booth gave some explanations as to his Sanitary measures.[468]

Tuesday 30 March (Bournemouth)

Drove to see Cairns, who was very cordial. His new house is a strange building, semi-ecclesiastical in appearance which is not exactly what I should have expected. Settled to ride with him Thursday 2.30.

We discussed *inter alia* Judicature Bill and he told me his proposal, viz. to complete the Supreme Court, keeping it as a Court of First Appeal and leaving House of Lords as Court of Second Appeal for United Kingdom for the present and to take time to consider how to proceed. He said the House of Lords had never been so strong in Law Lords and never had had so small an amount of arrears, in fact none. He had proposed this at the last Cabinet when I was absent and all (except Derby) had agreed. I agreed.

Monday 19 April (London)

The Queen, from what Salisbury says – he has just returned from Osborne – does not like the Prince of Wales proposed visit

---

[466]The previous night, Carnarvon wrote to Hardy, warning of possible trouble in the Cape, 'I must bring the matter before the Cabinet tomorrow. It would be of very great advantage [...] if another Regiment should be allowed to stop at the Cape, if only for the next three or four months' (Carnarvon to Hardy, 9 February 1875: CP, TNA, PRO 30/6/12, fo. 33). On 16 February, Carnarvon had appointed Wolseley to act as a special commissioner for six months in Natal (see Carnarvon to Disraeli, 16 February 1875 (copy): CP, BL 60703, fo. 78).

[467]The Elementary Education (Compulsory Attendance) Bill was defeated on its second reading in June. In Sandon's Act of 1876, employers were unable to hire youths under ten years of age. Parents were also obliged to ensure that their children received sufficient elementary instruction.

[468]Sclater Booth obtained an amendment of the sanitary laws in 1874 to strengthen his department's powers.

to India, especially without the Princess. She fears his getting into scrapes.[469]

Sunday 25 April (London)

A good deal of conversation with Lady Derby who gave me many details. At her wish I agreed to speak to Derby on the general subject.

A long conversation with Froude in the afternoon as to South African matters. He very much likes my draft despatch concerning the Conference of Representatives of different States, and indicating Confederation as an ultimate object.[470]

Monday 26 April (London)

The storm has blown over. Disraeli told me he had pressed the Queen strongly and had told her that unless she assented "matters could not go on". He said that no one ever told Her Majesty the truth except himself which was very hard on him. I replied that it would in such case have the charm of novelty. Saw Lady Derby afterwards.

I received from Sir J. Ferguson[471] this evening some old papers left apparently in an old cabinet in Park Street when the house was sold, and when I opened them I found amongst them written on the subject of my then approaching marriage. How strange it seemed to re-read them.

Saturday 8 May (London)

Cabinet

Derby read over his telegram to Odo Russell[472] desiring him to give the Emperor of Russia strong support in pressing peace upon

---

[469]Princess Alexandra wished to accompany her husband but, as Derby pointed out, 'whether she goes or not, the P. is sure to run after women' (Vincent, *Derby*, II, p. 203).

[470]After Froude returned from the Cape in February 1875, Carnarvon concluded that a conference made up of the colonies should be held. Sir Henry Barkly, Governor of Cape Colony, was to be chairman and Froude would be Carnarvon's representative. See Dunn, *James Anthony Froude*, II, pp. 412–413.

[471]Sir James Ferguson (1832–1907), Con. MP for Ayrshire (1854, 1857–1865) and for Manchester North-east (1885–1906), Permanent Under-Secretary at the Home Office (1867–1868), Governor of South Australia (1869–1870) and of New Zealand (1870–1875), Postmaster-General (1891–1892).

[472]Odo William Leopold Russell (1829–1884), 1st Baron Ampthill (1881), diplomat, Assistant Under-Secretary at the Foreign Office (1870), ambassador at Berlin (1871–1874).

the Emperor of Germany.[473] The Cabinet concurred – an important move. It pledged us to three things:
1. affirmation that French do not meditate war.
2. strong support of peace through Emperor of Russia.
3. an offer of co-operation to Austria and Italy.

An interview with President Burgers of the Transvaal Republic.[474] He does not seem to me a very able man, and he appears overcome by his civil reception here, his invitation to the Foreign Office tonight and his dinner with me on Monday. Froude was present. I told him that without going into the past, and that probably as in all quarrels there was fault on both sides, I hoped now we might arrive at a good understanding and that it was for the interests of both parties that we should do so. I indicated Confederation as the ultimate object, subject only to securities being taken for the natives, which I said would be I knew consistent with his views. He seemed to reciprocate but to be rather overwhelmed by the attention that he is receiving.[475]

Sunday 9 May (Windsor)

I came down here in the afternoon and after a short talk with General Ponsonby[476] I had a long interview with the Queen. A very large part of it was devoted to purely personal matters and she was kinder than kind [. . .].[477] Afterwards she went to foreign affairs, and we discussed the telegram to Odo Russell.[478] General P. had warned me that she did not originally think it strong enough and that she wished a similar notice to be given to the French. I reassured her as to the first and pointed out that as yet the French had done nothing to

---

[473]Alexander II met Wilhelm I in Berlin the following day.

[474]Thomas François Burgers (1834–1881), President of the Transvaal (1872–1877).

[475]At a further interview on 11 May, Carnarvon gave Burgers a copy of his despatch concerning the proposed conference. Burgers, according to Carnarvon, 'approved of every word and that he would give me every support and assistance in his power' (Diary, 11 May 1875).

[476]Maj.-Gen. Sir Henry Frederick Ponsonby (1825–1895), private secretary to the Queen (1870–1895).

[477]Carnarvon's wife, Evelyn, had died on 25 January, as a result of complications following childbirth. The Queen wrote in her journal after the meeting, 'Saw poor Lord Carnarvon, who was very much affected in speaking of his terrible loss and who looks thin and ill, but is touchingly resigned. He spoke of his wife, a rare character and great love of her home life' (Queen Victoria, Journal, 9 May 1875: Royal Archives, Z/381).

[478]See previous entry.

require a caution. She then urged strongly the desirability of writing a private letter to the Emperor of Russia whilst at Berlin urging him to support the cause of Peace. I was cautious supposing Derby was not very favourable to this but she proposed to make the letter *personal* in its character and on family subjects winding up with the hope etc. To this I own I can see no objection. Accordingly at her wish wrote at once to Disraeli stating her desire, requesting a telegram and a F.O. messenger to take it. Late in the evening after the letter was gone Ponsonby showed me a letter of Disraeli in which he said, "Derby will not hear of" a private letter etc. But this must be his mode of expression and it applied to a more formal communication than the one now proposed.

Wednesday 12 May (London)

1. Peace Preservation Act, question how long House of Lords should sit to pass it.
2. Vivisection, decided to issue a Commission.[479]
3. Question as to payment of entrance money at Aquarium and Zoological on Sundays.[480]
4. Salt's bill.[481]
5. Some desultory talk as to Local taxation.

Whit Sunday 16 May (Cowes)

Much conversation with Froude. Amongst other questions discussed:
1. Possibility of restoring one part of Griqualand to Transvaal State, the other part to be taken over by Cape Government. It will be a

---

[479] A Royal Commission on the practice of subjecting live animals to experiments for scientific purposes, chaired by Lord Cardwell, was established on 22 June 1875 and reported on 8 January 1876. See E. Hopley, *Campaigning against Cruelty: the hundred year history of the British Union for the Abolition of Vivisection* (London, 1998), pp. 4–5.

[480] Much public criticism had been generated over a recent legal decision that meant that the Brighton Aquarium and other places of public amusement could not be open on Sundays for money. The situation was saved by a government bill that was hastily passed through Parliament.

[481] Thomas Salt (1830–1904), banker, Con. MP for Stafford (1859–1865, 1869–1880, 1886–1892), Parliamentary Secretary to the Local Government Board (1876–1880), created Baronet (1899). Salt took a great interest in the Friendly Societies Bill, which reached the Committee and Report stages on 13 May, and received its third reading on 22 July: *Hansard*, CCXXIV, *passim*.

delicate and difficult matter to manage having reference to my earlier despatches, all which I have urged on him.

2. Place of meeting for Conference. Port Elizabeth or Grahamstown, probably not Natal.

3. Request of Burgers to be allowed 2 delegates to the Conference: Froude advises.

4. Question as to Chairmanship of Conference in the failure of Sir H. Barkly[482] and Sir A. Cunynghame.[483] He advises Sir G. Wolseley.

Saturday 29 May (London)

Cabinet

The first part of time was occupied by discussion on state of business. It will be I believe impossible to carry through all we have announced and some bills must be sacrificed. Judicature, agricultural holdings and the new Labour bills were decided to be essential to keep.

A long discussion on these two bills. They were finally agreed to.

Salisbury – despatch as to the Gaekwar's deposal was agreed to. I had given him previously a paper full of criticisms.[484]

Walked home with Cross and talked over the state of public business.[485]

My large official dinner, 42 persons, but how sad to remember its anniversary last year when we were just getting into the house and making all our arrangements.

[482] Sir Henry Barkly (1815–1898), Governor and Commander-in-Chief, British Guiana (1848–1853), Capt.-Gen. and Governor of Jamaica (1853–1856), Governor of Victoria (1856–1863), of Mauritius (1863–1870), and of the Cape of Good Hope (1870–1877).

[483] Lieut.-Gen. Sir Arthur Augustus Cunynghame (1812–1884), Commander-in-Chief, Cape Colony, Natal, and St Helena (1874–1878), Lieutenant-Governor of Cape Colony (1877–1878). His vigorous campaigns against the Kaffirs are described in his *My Command in South Africa, 1874–78* (London, 1879).

[484] See Salisbury to Carnarvon, 29 May 1875: CP, BL 60761, fo. 125. Earlier in 1875 the Gaekwar of Baroda was alleged to have tried to poison the Resident, Colonel Robert Phayre. A commission, consisting of three British and three native members, disagreed, and a not guilty verdict was returned. Lord Northbrook, the Viceroy, nevertheless ordered his deposition, a move which the Cabinet later endorsed. See B. Mallet, *Thomas George, Earl of Northbrook* (London, 1908), pp. 92–96.

[485] Particularly the Vivisection Commission and the Master and Servants Bill (Carnarvon to Cross, 27 May 1875: Cross Papers, BL 51268, fos 99–109).

Sunday 30 May (London)

Long walk with Northcote in the afternoon. The conversation turned on the contingency of Disraeli's failure of health which Northcote represents as being very great in the House of Commons.

He made the old suggestion that no one could take the Foreign Office but myself, and I gave him much the same answer that I have given to others formerly.

Wednesday 9 June (London)

Cabinet

1. Prince of Wales visit to India.[486] Further discussion as to expenses. Sir B. Frere[487] estimated expenses at £250,000 at which there was a general howl of dismay and derision in the Cabinet. The general opinion was that £100,000 was amply sufficient. The question as to presents remains still unsettled.

2. Some discussion as to Agricultural Holdings bill.

3. Probability of war with Burmah. Salisbury seems to think this likely. Resolution in Parliament will be needed in such case under the Act which allows action to be taken by Indian Government only in certain cases of which this is not one.

I gave a dinner to a number of Colonists this evening, but after the Cabinet there arrived a most serious telegram from Sydney announcing the death of not less than $\frac{1}{4}$ of whole population of Fiji from measles. It is too horrible, but unhappily it is possible to give very little real help or relief. The ignorance and folly of the people led them to refuse all medicine.

Sunday 27 June (Windsor Castle)

I came down to Windsor by an afternoon train and having ample time I walked down to Eton with Lord Cowley whom I met in the train. The old place looked very pretty and very much like itself. As we reached it Chapel was coming to an end and a crowd of boys poured out. The playing fields were in all their beauty of shadowy tree and

---

[486]Carnarvon was involved because the itinerary included a visit to Ceylon (Lee, *Edward VII*, I, p. 377).

[487]Sir Henry Bartle Frere (1815–1884), Governor of Bombay (1862–1867), Governor and High Commissioner, Cape Colony (1877–1880).

glittering river and a good many recollections came before me as we wandered through them.

In the evening after dinner had a good deal of conversation with the Queen. She was very amicable and kind as usual, and desired me to bring all the children to see her at Windsor. Afterwards I settled this with the Duchess of Roxburgh.[488] The matter on which the Queen was most interested was the Vivisection Commission and when she found how much I had thought about it she spoke out most fully. She mentioned to me the name of Lister the Edinburgh[489] surgeon as strongly opposed to the practice.[490]

Friday 2 July (Windsor – London)

I took down all the children, Mrs. Mayson and the nurses to Windsor to see the Queen. Nothing in every way could have been kinder or fuller of the most delicate and pretty consideration for me or for them. They were, poor darlings, rather frightened and shy, but the Queen was so kind that they finally lost their fright and became at home and very much interested. She and Princess Beatrice and Prince Leopold were there and after luncheon we came to them in the corridor. She talked to each of them in turn and ended by making to all of them a little present. She asked Margaret[491] whether she had yet learnt French, knowing how tiresome she is, poor dear, in not trying to speak, and she knew that it was Winifred's birthday.[492] She was very kind to Mrs. Mayson who admitted afterwards she was very much frightened. Altogether they all returned – Margaret with her doll which after the Queen had given it she offered to restore and when she found that restitution was not necessary, expressed her satisfaction very loudly – extremely pleased.[493]

[488] Susanna Stephanie Innes-Ker, wife of 6th Duke of Roxburgh.

[489] Joseph Lister (1827–1912), Professor of Clinical Surgery, Edinburgh University (1869–1877), pioneer of antiseptic surgery.

[490] Carnarvon subsequently brought forward a bill on 22 May 1876 'to prevent Cruel Experiments on Animals'. It received its third reading in June after much opposition. See Carnarvon to Queen Victoria, 21 June 1876: CP, TNL, PRO 30/6/2, fos 298–299.

[491] Lady Margaret Herbert (1870–1958), Carnarvon's second daughter from his first marriage.

[492] Lady Winifred Anne Herbert (1864–1933), Carnarvon's eldest daughter.

[493] Carnarvon's mother reminded him of her children's visit to Windsor many years previously to see the Duchess of Kent: 'You had all practised so carefully, walking out of the room backwards, that she was exceedingly amused, and specially at *your* addressing her with a profound bow and "Yes, Your Royal Family."' (Henrietta, 3rd Countess of Carnarvon to Carnarvon, 29 June 1875: CP, BL 61044, fos 17–18).

Later I went to the Queen of Holland by appointment and had a long conversation with her. She was very kind and talked much to me of former times.

Saturday 3 July (London)

Cabinet

1. Prince of Wales' visit to India again. Sir B. Frere and the Prince say they want £100,000 this year and £100,000 perhaps next. The fact is that Sir B. Frere wishes to be magnificent and the Cabinet, with the exception of Northcote, is parsimonious. Finally settled that £40,000 be taken this year for Admiralty expenses, leaving a small surplus for next year, and £60,000 to be given for presents and every other expense.

2. Northcote announced the returns of the quarter to be satisfactory, showing a surplus of £900,000. But supplementary estimates will come out of this and they are heavy. He estimates them at not less than £300,000 and Prince of Wales tour £100,000 – £400,000, leaving about £500,000. But this greatly again depends on harvest, etc.

3. Labour Laws – some discussion: agreed to adhere to bills.

4. Some discussion also as to other questions but Disraeli now protests that all we can do is to carry out bills and I see evident signs of an approaching massacre of innocents. Nothing controversial can be admitted.

Wednesday 7 July (London)

Cabinet

1. Prince of Wales, as to his suite. The Queen desires someone of position and character to go. No one answering to this can be found.[494]

2. Mulhar Rao, the Gaekwar, desires to see his solicitor on private business. Northbrook[495] objects. Salisbury has overruled the objection,

---

[494] The Queen objected particularly to the inclusion in the party of Lord Charles Beresford and Lord Carrington. After a stormy interview with Disraeli in Downing Street, the Prince was eventually allowed to name them in the party of eighteen men accompanying him (see P. Magnus, *King Edward the Seventh* (Harmondsworth, 1967), pp. 173–174). From the outset, Victoria had given 'a very unwilling' consent to the Prince of Wales's visit (Queen Victoria to Disraeli, 17 May 1875: Hughenden Papers, dep. 78/3, fo. 267).

[495] Thomas George Baring (1826–1904), 2nd Baron Northbrook (1866), 1st Earl Northbrook (1876), Under-Secretary of State for War (1861, 1868–1872), for India (1861–1864), and for

but the solicitor is to state his business and the interview is to be in the presence of a third person. This seems quite reasonable.

3. Trades Union meeting, and some discussion as to accepting Lowe's resolution on the Labour bills. Agreed to adhere generally to the bills with a slight amendment by Cairns.

4. Lord Stanhope's[496] motion as to Irish Peerage.[497] Cairns to reply to it and mainly on technical grounds.

5. Sir J. Whitworth's[498] wish to vest the entire reversion of his whole property (£650,000) in the Nation for the benefit of Science and Art. He makes provision for his wife and a few distant relations.

Presided at the Boys' School Festival at Alexandra Palace, 800 present, rather a bear garden, but the enormous sum of £12,700 collected with more to come in.[499]

Wednesday 14 July (London)

Cabinet

1. Prince of Wales visit to India. Disraeli told us with much energy of zest and language that he had had an interview with the Queen for a full hour on this subject and that was most interesting; that the Prince of Wales had grown in his demands, that the whole state of affairs had altered since it was first mooted and that the Government was thereby placed in a very false position. That some persons (meaning some of the Royal family) had suggested to him that he would take a detachment of Guards with him and even some of the Horse Guards, which of course was utterly repugnant to the Queen's views. That there were two courses (1) that he should go as "the proclaimed representative of the Crown" which the Queen would not hear of and which would cost at least £500,000, (2) "as the guest of the Viceroy" in which case the £60,000 proposed would be a very handsome allowance. That he proposed tomorrow to state the case and advised that we should adhere to the second. To this we all assented. I shrewdly suggest that there is really far less difficulty both

the Home Office (1864–1866), Viceroy and Governor-General of India (1872–1876), First Lord of the Admiralty (1880–1885).

[496] Hon. Edward Stanhope (1840–1893), Con. MP for Mid-Lincolnshire (1874–1885) and for Horncastle division (1885–1895), Vice-President, Committee of Council on Education (1885), President of the Board of Trade (1885–1886), Secretary of State for War (1887–1892).

[497] Motion to relinquish the prerogative of and power of creating future peers of Ireland: *Hansard*, CCXXV, 7 July 1875, cols 1210–1213, Cairns, cols 1214–1224. The motion was withdrawn.

[498] Sir Joseph Whitworth (1803–1887), Manchester steel manufacturer.

[499] 'The Royal Masonic Institute for Boys', *The Times*, 8 July 1875, p. 5.

with the Prince and the Queen than is supposed. Agreed to this, and also to resist Fawcett's[500] motion to put all expenses on Imperial funds.

2. Discussion as to Labour Laws.

[Remainder of entry deleted.]

Thursday 15 July (London)

My cold very bad but I dined with Salisbury and Lady S. alone. After dinner we got upon the old question of political eventualities on Disraeli's retirement. He is evidently very apprehensive that Derby will either fail in courage or that the Queen will, from his strange habit of making himself disagreeable to her, pass him over and that Richmond will succeed. There is I am afraid only too much fear of this, but it is very hard to see how it is to be avoided. "The great spider," as Salisbury calls C[airns] is working for this and Salisbury has almost a superstitious fear of him.

Saturday 17 July (Hatfield)

Went down there with Winifred and Porchy and Mrs. Mayson. There were the Gladstones, the Edward Talbots[501] and one or two of the family. The children have been extremely happy, racing about the house and dragging each other up and down the Gallery on a bear skin.

I have had a good deal of talk with Gladstone who seems to me somewhat softened and quieter since I last saw him to talk with, now nearly a year ago. Theology and ecclesiastical controversy are the subjects on which his mind is mainly moving. I spoke to him also of Pembroke[502] and Lady P.

It has cost me something to go anywhere again – indeed each new thing that I do seems an effort – and Hatfield particularly has many

[500] Henry Fawcett (1833–1884), Lib. MP for Brighton (1865–1874) and for Hackney (1874–1884), Postmaster-General (1880–1884), Professor of Political Economy, Cambridge University from 1863.

[501] Revd Edward Stuart Talbot (1844–1934), First Warden, Keble College, Oxford (1869–1888), Vicar of Leeds (1889–1895), Bishop of Rochester (1895–1905), Bishop of Southwark (1905–1911), Bishop of Winchester (1911–1923), cousin of Salisbury. His wife, Lavinia (1848–1939), was one of the daughters of George, 4th Baron Lyttelton and Mary Glynne. For a description of the Talbots, see B. Askwith, *The Lytteltons: a family chronicle of the nineteenth century* (London, 1975), pp. 171–172.

[502] George Robert Herbert (1850–1895), 13th Earl of Pembroke (1862), Under-Secretary of State for War (1874–1875), brother-in-law of Talbot.

memories which are very saddening to me. The real and indeed the main charm is to see the enjoyment of the children and particularly of Winifred who enters into the whole history and great interest of the place. She is a very remarkable child in many ways and is growing more and more a companion to me.

Monday 19 July (London)

Returned to town having a narrow escape being run away with down the hill at Hatfield to the station. Happily no evil result, for the children were with me.

A discussion in the House of Lords[503] on the Coolie question in which I think I stated the case fairly on the whole.

A rather curious conversation with Lady Derby as to the future eventualities. Several conclusions to be drawn.

1. that Derby is aware of his danger as regards Richmond's competition with him.

2. that he is so weak that he will make no fight for himself and that he is virtually prepared to serve under Richmond, a man whom he despises and dislikes.

3. that he would wish to throw the whole burden of opposition on Salisbury and myself.

4. that they cannot decide on a Foreign Secretary. Lyons was mentioned but they know he cannot speak. She said to me, "You know, it would never do to move you in the midst of all your Colonial work."

5. She is aware of Cairns' views, and had had evidently some conversation with him.

Wednesday 21 July (London)

Cabinet

A long discussion as to public business. Disraeli proposed to sacrifice the Agricultural holdings bill to the Merchant Shipping, but with the exception of Hardy the feeling of the Cabinet was all in favour of

---

[503] *Hansard*, CCXXV, 19 July 1875, cols 1637–1640. The supply and transport of Indian and Chinese coolies, and the terms and conditions of their employment in foreign colonies, was a longstanding interest of Carnarvon. A royal commission on the subject was appointed and Carnarvon subsequently issued twenty-seven recommendations to governors on the regulation of such traffic.

the Agricultural holdings.[504] This was agreed to and a meeting of the House of Commons called for tomorrow in order to explain to them and persuade them to assist the Government.

Monday 26 July (London)

Cabinet at 2 to discuss what steps should be taken as to Plimsoll and the Merchant Shipping Bill. Disraeli declared that "something must be done" and finally a short provisional bill was agreed on.[505] Adderley was told to his amazement that he must announce it tonight. It was altogether a piece of panic legislation, not very creditable to any of us, whether we liked or disliked it.

Tuesday 27 July (London)

Plimsoll again, more discussion on the proposed bill. It is far from satisfactory. We are legislating to meet a supposed popular demand without any real knowledge of the subject or prospect of doing any good by it. It is a sorry proceeding, the worst thing I think we have as yet done.

Met Gavard who announced the French Government accepts the proposals as to the Gambia[506] and that as the Assembly rises on 4 August, some announcement would be made through Papers, etc. This led to much negotiation, etc. Northcote, Derby, Disraeli. It is altogether rather awkward to be driven into a corner.

[504] The Agricultural Holdings Bill, to give legal recognition to tenants' rights, received the Royal Assent on 13 August.

[505] On 24 June 1874, Plimsoll had promoted a Shipping Survey Bill to strengthen the existing legislation, but it was defeated by three votes in the Commons on its second reading in June 1874. It was announced that the Merchant Shipping Bill would not be proceeded with. Plimsoll created a scene in the Commons, using terms such as 'cheats' and 'liars'. For an eye-witness account of the incident, see R.H. Dana, *Hospitable England in the Seventies: the diary of a young American, 1875–1876* (London, 1921), pp. 28–29. In order to dampen growing public and political opposition, an Unseaworthy Ships Bill was introduced by the Government in July 1875.

[506] Meeting with Charles Gavard, first secretary to the French ambassador, on the proposed exchange of West African territories.

Friday 30 July (London – Cowes)

Cabinet

We only discussed Plimsoll and our temporary Merchant Shipping Bill and the discussion was not edifying.[507] It was clear that a bill was to be carried and the question of details was too long and too difficult to bear much consideration. But after all this merely the way of all Cabinets that have ever been or ever will be.

After the Cabinet I came down here and got on board my yacht, so worn out and exhausted that I slept soundly.

Sunday 1 August (Osborne)

In the afternoon came on from Cowes in the yacht and anchored off Osborne, and walked up to the house where I dined and slept. There were only Princess Louise and Lorne,[508] Prince Leopold and Princess Beatrice, so it was purely a family party, with extremely little form or restraint and everyone full of fun and the love of amusement. Altogether a pleasant picture.

The Queen was in good spirits and as usual extremely kind. She talked much of the Prince of Wales's visit to India and expressed anxiety as to his health, saying that he had not recovered from his illness entirely and was not of the constitution to bear great heat.[509] I told her of Gregory's letter to Meade[510] in which he had advised March as the time for Ceylon but that Fayrer[511] and Charsley[512] were both decidedly in favour of early part of December, and that I had impressed strongly on Fayrer the necessity of speaking plainly. She agreed in all and spoke very sensibly on the whole subject and with great moderation.

I spoke generally as to the Gambia exchanges.

[507]The Unseaworthy Ships Bill received its second reading in the Commons that day: *Hansard*, CCXXVI, 30 July 1875, cols 225–267. It received the Royal Assent on 13 August.

[508]John Douglas Campbell Lorne (1845–1914), Lib. MP for Argyllshire (1868–1878), married Queen Victoria's fourth daughter, Princess Louise (1871), Governor-General of Canada (1878–1883).

[509]See Carnarvon's detailed memorandum to the Queen on possible health hazards: Carnarvon to Queen Victoria, 27 July 1875: Royal Archives, T/6.

[510]Sir Robert Meade (1835–1898), Assistant Under-Secretary at the Colonial Office (1871–1892), Permanent Secretary at the Colonial Office (1892–1896).

[511]Sir Joseph Fayrer (1824–1907), Surgeon-General and Professor of Surgery, Medical College, Calcutta (1859–1874). He accompanied the Prince of Wales on the Indian tour.

[512]William Parker Charsley (1824–1881), former Principal Medical Officer, Ceylon.

Wednesday 11 August (London – Southampton)

Cabinet. Thank God our last.

1. *Col. Baker's case* A letter from the Queen strongly urging his dismissal for the honour of the Army and general example. Decided to "gazette him out".[513]

2. Instructions to Capt. Murray from Board of Trade as to new Act respecting unseaworthy ships, as to duties, etc. of officers at the several ports. I pressed on Cabinet necessity of appointing men of character and position. The general position was accepted but they were in too much haste to get over their business to settle anything.

3. *Office of Works* Galton's resignation announced. Pension of £1,000 to him agreed to.[514]

4. Circular as to Civil Service. I put in my protest, but otherwise accepted, as to last clause.

5. Northcote stated the expenditure of next year will be increased by about £2,000,000, without allowing for any increase in Army or Navy.

6. *Legal questions* Cairns proposed a departmental or Treasury Committee to consider (financially) the departments of the Irish Courts with a view to judicial changes. He proposed also to give some help to Sir H. Thring.[515] He asked Hunt to reconsider the new system as to a diminution of competition. Derby was very keen for competition.

7. Cross proposed to sell waste land at Balfour Park for artisans' dwellings under the new Act. Agreed to.

8. Sir G. Wolseley despatch requiring troops, etc. in Natal.[516] I stated to the Cabinet, enquired and finally it was agreed that 1. the £20,000 for annual advance to the Colony should *stand over* for the present. 2. the regiment of 840,000 in Natal should now remain there. 3. the question of a battery of mountain guns should be settled by Hardy and myself between this [*word omitted*] and November, pending or subject to arrival of Sir G. Wolseley. 4. the question of a Company of Engineers should be left to Disraeli, Hardy and myself in the same way.

---

[513]Col. Valentine Baker (1827–1887) had recently received a one-year prison sentence for assaulting a young woman in a train. See *London Gazette*, 2 August 1875.

[514]Douglas Galton (1822–1899), Director of Public Works since 1869.

[515]Sir Henry Thring (1818–1907), Parliamentary draftsman, counsel to the Treasury (1869), created Baron Thring (1886).

[516]On 1 April, Wolseley had replaced the dismissed Benjamin Pine, Lieutenant-Governor of Natal, to restore order in the country.

Came down to Southampton with G.[517] and came on board the
Aloma.[518]

Sunday 12 September (Balmoral)

A Presbyterian Service in the dining room in the morning, three-
quarters of an hour long including sermon. The prayers were, though
extemporary, much formed upon the model of the Prayer book, and
sometimes the actual words employed. The sermon was good and at
the end very pretty in thought. The preacher was a Mr. Lees,[519] an
educated man and incumbent of Paisley, one of the few good livings,
I believe.

Later I took a walk with Prince Christian,[520] who is sensible and
agreeable. We talked a good deal of Bismarck and Germany and later
Princess Christian in a long conversation deplored to me in very strong
terms the animosity felt against us in Germany. But they both agreed
in this, that the tone of our Government was considered in Germany
to be much firmer than formerly and that we were consequently all
the more respected. Prince Christian confirmed the fact to me of the
existence of ill feeling between the Crown Princess, who is thought to
be very English, and Bismarck: and this he said possibly accounts for
some of Bismarck's hostility to England, who is *extremely* personal to
his policy. Of the animosity in Berlin there can be no doubt.

Later the Prince of Wales walked into my room and sat some time
talking of his Ceylon and Indian journey. He was rather vexed, in
his very good-humoured way, at a supposed opposition to his going
to Ceylon and he asked me if I thought Gregory was unwilling to
receive him. I told him that Gregory was certainly poor and was
paying off his debts,[521] but it is clear to me that Birch[522] has behaved

[517] Lady Gwendoline Herbert (1842–1915), Carnarvon's younger sister.

[518] That same day Carnarvon told Ponsonby, 'I am very tired out with London work, and
the smell of bad drains at the corner of every street, and an atmosphere from which all the
oxygen seems to have been exhausted' (Carnarvon to Ponsonby, 11 August 1875: CP, TNL,
PRO 30/6/2, fo. 19).

[519] Revd James Cameron Lees (1834–1913), preacher, Paisley Abbey (1859–1879), chaplain
to Queen Victoria (1881–1901).

[520] Prince Christian of Schleswig-Holstein (1831–1917), married Princess Helena, third
daughter of Queen Victoria (1866).

[521] Gregory's financial position was already precarious. This was made worse by the fact
that governors of colonies receiving a royal visit were expected to provide hospitality out
of their own pockets. For the Prince, Gregory reluctantly purchased carriage horses from
Australia and imported wines and cognacs in quantities sufficient 'to float an ironclad'
(B. Jenkins, *Sir William Gregory of Coole: the biography of an Anglo-Irishman* (Gerrards Cross,
Buckinghamshire, 1986), p. 245).

[522] Sir Arthur Birch (1837–1914), Colonial Secretary, Ceylon (1873–1876), Governor of
Ceylon from 1876.

ill and has put himself forward in a very improper and self-seeking manner. I did what I could and had much conversation with Knollys,[523] William Russell and General Ponsonby, and in the evening, with the Queen.

Monday 13 September (Balmoral)

A long conversation with the Queen mainly as to Prince of Wales visit to India. The two points on which she was most earnest were (1) the addition of Lord Aylesford to the Party, which she had only heard rumoured, and to which she not unnaturally objects[524] (2) the desire of the Princess of Wales to go to Copenhagen for a considerable time. She showed me a letter of the Prince of Wales to her, strongly urging it and saying how disappointed the Princess would be and she said that she had reluctantly consented to a compromise, that the Princess should go for Christmas, but that it was an affair for the Government also to speak upon and if this was objected to she would do the best she could "to fight it".

The Prince, she said, had in this as in some other points of a similar kind, secured her consent almost without her knowing it. In all she said, much of which was so private that I do not like putting it down even for my own guidance, she spoke with extreme good sense and feeling, and impressed me again as she has often done before.

Afterwards there was a ball of gillies, etc. at which the Prince of Wales and others from Abergeldie were present. I had a good deal of conversation with Knollys and finally told him that if at any time in India there should be any matters over which he desired to write privately to me he might do so, and I would communicate with Salisbury. He was very grateful and afterwards the Prince thanked me.

The ball was very picturesque. The Queen in excellent spirits danced several times with the grandchildren and the Prince of Wales.

---

[523] Francis Knollys (1837–1924), Baron Knollys (1902), 1st Viscount Knollys (1911). Private Secretary to the Prince of Wales, later Edward VII (1870–1910), Joint Private Secretary to George V (1910–1913).

[524] Heneage Finch (1849–1885), 7th Earl of Aylesford (1871), known as 'Sporting Joe', was a personal guest in the Prince's party. In February 1876, while in India, his wife announced that she was eloping with another of the Prince's friends, Lord Blandford. For the subsequent scandalous events, see G. St Aubyn, *Queen Victoria: a portrait* (London, 1991), pp. 471–473.

Thursday 16 September (Balmoral)

I received this afternoon from the Queen a private letter to her from Duckworth (the clergyman going with the Prince)[525] urging the importance of doing nothing whilst in India to shock feeling by a disregard of the Sunday. The Queen accompanied this by a letter to me wishing me to speak to the Prince of Wales as from myself on the subject.[526] I undertook to do so as I dine at Abergeldie.

I asked the Prince accordingly to give me five minutes after dinner and then after discussing some other points connected with his visit I urged this as from myself as of importance. He took it remarkably well and said that he was quite prepared to avoid everything that could reasonably give offence. Of course it might under particular circumstances be necessary to travel, etc. but as the rule he would not hold durbars or have any great public ceremonies which could be construed into a disregard of the day. He talked to me a good deal on foreign affairs, the attitude of Germany and the German Press; and finally on leaving I promised to come up to London to see him off and to take leave of him, which seemed to please him.

General Ponsonby and I met with Prince and Princess Christian [...]. I wrote to the Queen on my return a brief report of my conversation with the Prince of Wales.

Friday 17 September (Balmoral)

Rode out by myself towards "Carndavan" and attempted to strike across the hills but was stopped by the boggy ground which seems very shaky. I got back and on my return found that it was perhaps as well that I did return. The Prince and Princess of Wales dined here, a somewhat curious scene, for at 9 p.m. the rest of the Abergeldie Party arrived saying that the Prince had not come back from deer stalking and the Princess was waiting for him. Half-past 9 came and no Prince; then the Abergeldie Party were sent to dinner and the Queen, the Christians, Princess Beatrice, Lady Churchill[527] and myself

[525]Canon Robinson Duckworth (1834–1911), Fellow, Trinity College, Oxford (1860–1876), Canon of Westminster Abbey (1875–1911), and friend of Lewis Carroll (he appears as the Duck in *Alice in Wonderland*).

[526]Ponsonby remarked to his wife, 'Carnarvon is in a funk [...] as to whether he should let the Prince go at all' (Ponsonby to Lady Ponsonby, 15 September 1875: Royal Archives, Add. A36/963).

[527]Lady Jennie Churchill (1851–1921), wife of Lord Randolph Churchill, whom she married in 1874.

waited counting the minutes in the drawing room and trying to make conversation on indifferent subjects. At last when the Queen was evidently becoming a trifle anxious, the sound of wheels was heard and the Prince arrived.

He had gone on too far and had lost his way. The Princess and his clothes were sent for from Abergeldie and finally he came into dinner which was unusually long, not eating until nearly 11 o'clock. The Queen showed to great advantage in this little domestic anxiety, and when the Prince did appear, sat on through this protracted dinner (which she cannot bear) with the greatest good humour, chatting away on every subject.

Sunday 19 September (Balmoral)

Service at the Kirk at Crathie, a very dreary and desperate affair. How the Scotch nation can hear this sort of thing I cannot tell. It perhaps however accounts for some of their defects. I can understand how poor Mary Queen of Scots must have hated Knox and his ecclesiastical colleagues.

I had a long conversation with the Queen in the evening, first on the Prince of Wales and Ceylon, etc. I submitted to her the draft of my confidential despatch to Gregory which they approved. She mentioned also to me her wish that 14 December, the anniversary of Prince Albert's death, should not be made the occasion of any great public show or pageant. This I undertook to do and wrote to Gregory a private letter on the subject. Next we wandered off into a general conversation on various matters, amongst others the character of some of the Prime Ministers. I told her of my recent conversations with Gladstone. She mentioned to me that no doubt a great speaker, he was lengthy and not very clear on paper, which is perfectly true. Whilst speaking of the late Lord Derby I said plainly my opinion of him, that he was hard, ungenerous and by nature cruel. She said that this would have surprised her but that she had of late heard much that agreed with this, and she went on to repeat a saying of the Prince Consort that the turf was not a good school but always seemed to have some taint behind it. This led me on to say something as to Derby, the present man and though it is clear that he is not a very great favourite I thought her manner of speaking of him was kind. I said (which is the truth) that I attributed a good deal of his apparent shyness and dislike of society to his early education with a father who did not, I think, behave well to him and to whom he always showed great respect. We spoke a little of Disraeli. She asked me also whether I thought anything was likely to come of his visits to Bretby. I said I thought not and that the real centre of attraction was Lady Bradford.[528]

Sunday 3 October (Highclere)

Much conversation with Northcote on Government affairs.

1. He is equally anxious as I am as to the Slavery instructions issued by Admiralty. They may be right in law but they are against all policy.[529] After much conversation we both wrote to Disraeli urging him to summon a meeting of those of the Cabinet who are in the South to consider what should be done.[530] I wrote to Salisbury also to explain.[531]

2. He tells me that at the end of the Session Disraeli wrote to Adderley virtually dismissing or superseding him at the Board of Trade yet ever since nothing has been done.[532] Adderley does not go near the Office, no preparations are being made to carry out the Act as to unseaworthy ships and all is confusion!

3. Much talk as to the future. We both of us see and admit that Disraeli is fast failing, that Derby is on the whole the best successor: but we are agreed as to his defects, his increasing shyness, his dislike of religion, his dislike of all royal persons. We are equally agreed that a mere figure-head for the chief of the Government would be an utter mistake. I said that in some respects I should be glad to retire. He said this would be a great mistake, as that independently of my own office, it would be impossible to fill the particular position which I occupy in the Government. He then said he always looked to me to take the Foreign Office. I said little on this except that a complete reorganisation of the Office would be necessary.

---

[528] Selina Louisa Bridgeman (1819–1894), wife of Orlando George Charles Bridgeman, 3rd Earl of Bradford.

[529] The Circular on Fugitive Slaves was issued by the Admiralty on 31 July. It countermanded previous instructions and stated that slaves on board Royal Navy ships in territorial waters should be given up to their owners if requested.

[530] Carnarvon to Disraeli, 5 October 1875: Hughenden Papers, dep. 100/1, fos 18–19. See also Carnarvon to Derby, 4 October 1875: Derby Papers, 920 (DER 15) 16/2/4.

[531] Replying from France, Salisbury admitted, 'I was as much startled as you at the Admiralty circular. I cannot conceive who drafted it' (Salisbury to Carnarvon, 5 October 1875: CP, BL 60758, fo. 162).

[532] See Buckle, *Disraeli*, V, pp. 364–365.

Thursday 7 October (Highclere)

Long talk with Greenwood.[533]

1. Asked his opinion as to cession of Gambia. He does not seem afraid of any misapprehension if the matter is properly explained, that it is an exchange rather than cession, and that it can be justified on trade grounds.

2. Discussed New Guinea and explained proposed answer. He said he thought nothing could be better.

3. Talked about the Slavery instructions issued by the Admiralty.

He is quite clear that the only thing to be done is to cancel them as a mistake. Any explanations would only lend to set them up, and give ground to belief that they had been considered and adopted deliberately; He said that the only reason why more had not been said or done was the general belief that it was all a mistake and that it was far better to "avow carelessness than error of judgment".

Long conversations with Sir G. Wolseley yesterday and today on Natal and Cape matters, the business part of which I have noted elsewhere.

As regards Sir H. Barkly he believes that it is only wise to remove him, that he cannot, whatever he may say, really give me support such as is necessary in this crisis. He advises the Duke of Manchester!!!

To my objections he repeats his belief that the Duke would answer with Froude by him and that his rank would carry so much weight that he would secure the end in view. I asked him whether he would go. He did not actually decline, but he represented several difficulties:

1. Sir A. Cunynghame, who is his senior.
2. Military contingencies abroad.
3. Doubt as to his success unless Delagoa Bay question can be solved. I think he might be induced to go, but he would not go very willingly. His repeated statement is that Delagoa Bay is the key of the whole question of Confederation.

Friday 15 October (Highclere)

Northcote and Lady N. came. His budget of news was considerable.

---

[533] Frederick Greenwood (1830–1909), editor of *The Queen* (1861–1863), of the *Cornhill Magazine* (1862–1868), and of the *Pall Mall Gazette* (1865–1880), founder of the *St James's Gazette* (1880).

1. After much pushing and persuasion Disraeli had agreed to offer the Board of Trade to Cave.[534] Cave wishes for Cabinet: but his looking to the relative positions of Sclater Booth and Beach is impossible. Adderley on the other hand is to be offered the headship of the Civil Service Commission with £2,000 per annum as a new and third Commissioner. This I told Northcote was in my opinion a very doubtful proposition. It would not really save Adderley's fall and it would be open to grave objection.[535]

2. Northbrook has written to announce his resignation of India after the Prince of Wales's visit.[536] It will be very difficult to know how to fill up this great office. I urged strongly that the fact should not be mentioned at present. Something passed between us as to whether I should take it: but Northcote said that I could be very ill spared, which at this moment I believe to be true, and that a reconstruction of the Government would become necessary. He thought Richmond must go – so it would rid us of many difficulties and be no real loss, but I doubt his going.

3. Disraeli had screwed himself up to writing a letter to Hunt as to the *Vanguard* case.[537]

Northcote's general estimation of the position of the Government was little altered.

Thursday 4 November (London)

Cabinet

1. *Slave trade Circular* Cairns proposed to withdraw and substitute another set of instructions and this was finally agreed to: a Committee of Cabinet appointed consisting of him, Derby, and Hunt to draw up fresh rules. I suggested that before publicly promising fresh rules it would be nice to draw them and see if they would stand criticism, but

---

[534] Sir Steven Cave (1820–1880), Judge-Advocate-General and Paymaster-General since 1874, resigned because of ill-health in December 1875 and was sent on a special mission to Egypt. Carnarvon told Derby, 'Cave, I believe [is] the best man in every way. He knows too the office and the subject' (Carnarvon to Derby, 12 October 1875: Derby Papers, 920 (DER 15) 17/2/5).

[535] In the event, Sclater Booth remained at the Local Government Board and Adderley at the Board of Trade until August 1878.

[536] Northbrook had written to Salisbury at the India Office on 15 September asking him to lay before the Queen his request to resign his office in the spring of 1876.

[537] HMS *Vanguard* had sunk off Iceland after a collision with HMS *Iron Duke* on 1 September. A controversial court martial cleared Admiral Tarleton, who was in charge of the squadron, and relieved Lieutenant Evans, who was on watch on HMS *Iron Duke* at the time of the collision, of responsibility. The Admiralty later reversed the decisions, causing offence to public opinion.

Disraeli was against any delay, and Cairns said he did not doubt being able to draw them. Agreed to issue a notice in the Papers.

2. *Vanguard minute* Hunt justified the minute, but the feeling of the Cabinet was against him and two real objections were expressed: 1. that it was not right to dismiss Lt. Evans of the *Iron Duke* without trial. 2. that it was wrong not to put Admiral Tarleton[538] on his trial. Generally the Cabinet was very forbearing to Hunt *personally* though the feeling that he had blundered was clear. Duke of Richmond alone showed some desire to attack him and make the worst of the case. The evil of all this is that Hunt is losing all influence and that any proposal which he may make, even in good will, will not be accepted.

3. *Brighton aquarium* Cross said that £3,000 penalties had been incurred by the Co. He proposed to remit them. Agreed.

4. *Alberta and Mistletoe Collision*[539] Hunt explained Admiralty private enquiry, and after discussion it was *on the whole* agreed that Capt. Welch should take the *Queen* over on 14 inst.

Friday 5 November (London)

This morning I received to my great surprise a letter from Disraeli in extremely handsome terms offering and indeed pressing me to accept the Governorship General of India.[540] I answered by requesting a few days to consider.[541] It is a very grave question in all respects public and private, but it is mainly on this latter head that I doubt. I have spoken privately to Herbert, Northcote and Salisbury. All three will be sorry to lose me and all three I think can advise well. I have written to Eveline and I have spoken to G. [Gwendoline] poor dear who was upset at the idea. The not least painful part of the matter is my Mother's health. I can hardly hope to see her again if I go, barring all accidents to myself.

Cabinet

1. Board of Trade and unseaworthy ships. Present staff ineffective and corrupt. 5 more surveyors needed, agreed to appoint them. Committee of Cabinet appointed to consider bill.

[538] Sir John Walter Tarleton (1811–1880), Vice-Admiral (1875), retired 1879.

[539] On 18 August, the Royal yacht *Alberta*, with the Queen on board, collided with a schooner, the *Mistletoe*, in the Solent, leading to two deaths. An Admiralty court of inquiry had exonerated the *Alberta*. This incident greatly distressed the Queen. On a visit to Balmoral shortly afterwards, Carnarvon observed, 'Dined with the Queen who after dinner could talk of little else than the *Mistletoe* collision' (Diary, 11 September 1875).

[540] Disraeli to Carnarvon, 5 November 1875: CP, BL 60763, fos 108–109.

[541] Carnarvon to Disraeli, 5 November 1875: Hughenden Papers, dep. 79/1, fo. 200.

2. Foot and mouth disease. Disraeli suggested slaughtering all foreign cattle. Cabinet generally against this.

3. I received Ceylon telegraph as to Prince of Wales and cholera.

4. I explained as to murder of Resident at Perak.[542] Settled that I should have troops if needed.

5. I told Cabinet that a confidential paper on Gambia issued to one of them had got into the market. Everyone of course was innocent.

6. Settled to buy land in George Street.

7. Gunboats for China, agreed to postpone decision till end of November. Derby said he "could not guarantee peace".[543]

Saturday 6 November (Highclere – London)

Cabinet

1. Cairns' plan as to Appellate Jurisdiction of House of Lords, on whole accepted. I urged it, said be soon drafted, but Cairns much demurred to it. I guarded myself by saying that all depended on phraseology. Disraeli repeated several times that the tribunal should be brought as much as possible into close contact with House of Lords.

2. Civil Service changes recommended by Northcote, nothing settled.

3. Sir M. Beach's letter proposing great amount of Irish legislation, found little favour.

4. *Vanguard* reported to be hopelessly sunk. The divers cannot bear weight of water.

I saw Gull and consulted him as to India. He thinks that in point of health I can bear it and that in fact the winter would do me good: but, he is very strong against my overworking, also he thinks it far better that I should stay 2 or 3 years rather than 5 or 6. The children may go out for 3 months with safety. But he says that it is a very great sacrifice that I am making, and in almost all points of view it is. He examined me carefully and said that organically all is right.

I came down here, and I have tested Dolly and Mrs Mayson with the secret. It was indeed necessary to do so, for I required their advice.[544]

---

[542]James Wheeler Woodford Birch, British Resident, was murdered on 2 November. See P.L. Burns, *The Journals of J.W.W. Birch, First British Resident to Perak, 1874–1875* (Kuala Lumpur and London, 1976), pp. 36–37.

[543]Relations with China had deteriorated following the assassination in February of Augustus Raymond Margary of the Chinese consulate service and the tardiness of the Chinese government in agreeing to Britain's demand to establish a trade route across China from Burma.

[544]Carnarvon wrote to Disraeli on 8 November declining the post (Carnarvon to Disraeli, 8 November 1875: Hughenden Papers, dep. 79/1, fo. 208).

Wednesday 10 November (London)

Cabinet

1. *Rising in Perak* decided that the 300 men should go at once to Hong Kong and that Viceroy should be requested to hold 1,000 men and artillery and mountain gun in readiness and select an officer to take command.[545] The general feeling of the Cabinet is strong in favour of sending sufficient men to suppress the rising. There is an understanding that the expense will have to fall on English Treasury. Telegram agreed to and sent.

2. Some discussion as to *Claremont and New Forest*.

3. Old proposal of last session to stop creation of *Irish Peers* will be revived next session. Discussion on this. Cairns disposed to give way. Disraeli denounced it as a violation of Act of Union. But this was violated in the Irish Church. General feeling of Cabinet that the movement in House of Lords would be too strong to resist.

4. *Burial Acts*. Cross undertook to have a bill prepared.

5. *Sclater Booth* called in and expounded generally a plan for formation of a county board to deal with highways and perhaps some other questions.[546] Settled that he should draw up his scheme. He proposes bills on pollution of mines, and on valuation (for counties?).

Thursday 11 November (London)

Cabinet

1. Heard just before the Cabinet that 300 men this morning sailed from Hong Kong for Penang and that General Colborne had gone with them. This is too bad thus to force himself into the command; the Viceroy had selected at the request of the Cabinet General Ross to take the command. I stated all this to the Cabinet and urged them to let me send Colborne back on *political grounds*. To this they greatly demur on the old notions of red tape and routine, Colborne being by experience, age, character, ability, temper, unfitted to command and Ross being specially selected. The question is postponed to tomorrow,

[545] Telegram detailing troop movements, Carnarvon to Ponsonby, 10 November 1875: Royal Archives, P24/170. Sir William Jervois (1821–1897), the High Commissioner, had issued a proclamation annexing Perak, contrary to Carnarvon's and the Cabinet's approval: this led to an uprising. On 7 December, a British force attacked a stockade, killing between sixty and eighty people. The commanding officers were Major-General Francis Colborne (1817–1895), commander in Hong Kong and the Straits Settlements, and General Sir John Ross (1829–1905), commander of the Laruf Field Force, Malay Peninsula from 1875.

[546] A Highways Bill was introduced in April 1876 but failed in July.

and meanwhile I have written to the Duke of Cambridge a very hasty letter urging him to support Ross.[547]

2. Sir M. Beach called in. He said he had revoked proclamations in two Counties and directed Police to watch effect, and that if report should be satisfactory he proposed to proceed to revocation. He declares Ireland to be growing quieter every day, but that the North is restless on subject of land and tenant right. He names bills for next Session a) Judicature, b) Prisons, c) Juries, d) Lunatic Asylums.

3. Proposed to consider Enclosures question tomorrow.

Saturday 13 November (London)

A terribly hard day's work beginning with a conference with Northcote and J. Manners as to Cartwright's[548] proposal for a line of steamers from Ireland to Nova Scotia to do the voyage in 5 days, and railway across Canada and 12 days clear to Japan.

The best part of the day spent on Perak. Settled with Salisbury to await Jervois' answer before sending final orders to India to send off the troops. I am utterly disenchanted with Jervois. I believe he is getting up a little war of annexation but I am nearly powerless to stop it. At this distance I cannot take the responsibility of refusing the troops if he persists in calling for them.[549]

I am nearly worn out: for the last week I have hardly had half an hour to myself. The work has been overwhelmingly hard.

Sunday 14 November (London)

Dined with the Derbys. She did not know of the offer of India to me till Friday evening when Disraeli for the first time told

---

[547] The Commander-in-Chief of the Army, the Duke of Cambridge, informed Carnarvon, 'I wrote to [General Sir Richard] Airey to suggest that *Gen. Colborne* should be *ordered* to have command' (Duke of Cambridge to Carnarvon, 12 November 1875: CP, TNA, PRO 30/6/14, fo. 187). On 12 November, the Cabinet decided to leave Colborne in charge (Carnarvon to Duke of Cambridge, 12 November 1875: Royal Archives, Add. E1/747).

[548] Sir Richard John Cartwright (1835–1912), Canadian Finance Minister (1873–1878), acting Prime Minister (1897, 1907).

[549] Carnarvon to Jervois, 13 November 1875 (copy): CP, BL 60761, fos 137–138. On the same day, Carnarvon informed the Queen that he had written to Jervois on three successive days for 'clear and full explanations of his intentions and objects, without a reply' (Carnarvon to Queen Victoria, 13 November 1875: Royal Archives, P24/175). Salisbury commented, 'A more unsatisfactory explanation of a war I never read' (Salisbury to Carnarvon, 13 November 1875: CP, TNL, PRO 30/6/10). Matters were made worse by the breaking of the telegraph wire between Madras and Penang. Carnarvon remarked, 'It deprives me of all real control over Jervois who will now, I presume carry out his annexation scheme' (Diary, 15 November 1875).

Derby.[550] He talked much after dinner on many things. I see that she dreams of an old Whig or Liberal combination under Derby as a Premier, but I told her that there was little chance of any but a few discontented men who would only bring themselves, no followers.

Tuesday 16 November (London)

Again a wonderful proposal to me. Northcote came to me to tell me that Disraeli is in very great difficulties not only as to the Board of Trade but as to Hunt, that Cairns is constantly pressing on him Hunt's incapacity and that he himself feels a change is necessary: that Disraeli is at his wits ends and that the only solution that he can think of is for me to take the Admiralty. This however is not a proposal and may not become one but is merely the present outcome of his state of despair at the circumstances. I said that it took me entirely by surprise and that of course *if necessary* I would do anything I could in England to make matters work but that it was altogether a serious change. The desire on Disraeli's part (if it came to that point) seems to be quite genuine. He really does not know exactly where to turn.

The Duke of Cambridge came to me at the Colonial Office to talk about Perak.[551] I read him the telegrams, etc. and then I pressed most strongly on him the question of increasing the troops in Natal.

Wednesday 17 November (London)

Cabinet

1. Derby announced that he had received from a private informant news that the Khedive[552] was in difficulties and was preparing to sell his shares (bought at £7,000,000 – worth £4,000,000) to the French

---

[550]Lady Derby had written two days earlier, 'I know the secret – but only this evening. Robert told Stanley yesterday. You can't think how well I diplomatised last night to discover if S. knew anything' (Lady Derby to Carnarvon, 12 November 1875: CP, BL 60765, fo. 98). Disraeli had consulted Salisbury about Northbrook's successor from the outset. Lady Derby asked Disraeli as early as 5 November if there was any truth in the rumour about Northbrook's resignation (Buckle, *Disraeli*, V, p. 436).

[551]Following the meeting, the order was given to increase the force to 3,000 men, including two regiments of Indian troops (Carnarvon to Ponsonby, 16 November 1875: Royal Archives, P 25/1).

[552]Ishmael Pasha (1830–1895), Khedive of Egypt (1867), deposed in 1879.

Société Générale.[553] He telegraphed to Stanton[554] who confirmed the news. Disraeli put the question what we could do and it was carried at once by a sort of whirlwind of argument that Derby would telegraph immediately to say that we would buy if terms could be settled. There was no difference of opinion though it should be said that Cairns, Salisbury and myself with Derby were the only persons who said anything. This suggests a rather serious inference, by the way.

2. I gave the latest accounts of Perak.

3. We discussed Education. *General* feeling in favour of doing something for the Union Party and Schools.

I received this morning a letter from Disraeli asking me to come to him after the Cabinet. I accordingly went and he at once with very little preface said that Hunt had blundered to such an extent that it was necessary to make a change and – would I take the Admiralty. A good deal of conversation ensued of which the following cover the main points.

1. I urged that I could not whilst ready to give any help act ungenerously to Hunt. He charged himself with this and said he could make it pleasant!!! to him.

2. I warned him he would be removing a successful minister from the midst of successful work into other work where success was at least very uncertain.

3. I said that I thought it might be a great mistake *from Government point of view* to remove Hunt.

4. That if I did go I should need, I was sure, an entire change of persons at the Admiralty. To all this he merely replied that a change ought to be made and that he felt sure I could be successful.[555]

I asked to consult Salisbury and Northcote. Salisbury entirely agrees with me, but admits the difficulty of my persistently refusing.

Thursday 18 November (London)

I had a considerable talk with Disraeli as to his offer of the Admiralty. I said 1) that affairs at the Colonial Office were such and so critical

---

[553]The Suez Canal was completed in 1869 by Ferdinand de Lesseps (1805–1894). Of the 400,000 ordinary shares of the canal, the Khedive held almost half. Frederick Greenwood, editor of the *Pall Mall Gazette*, informed Derby on 15 November that the bankrupt Khedive was about to sell his shares to a French company.

[554]Gen. Sir Edward Stanton (1827–1907), agent and Consul-General of Egypt.

[555]Carnarvon, as was his practice when decisions had to be made, drew up a memorandum stating the pros and cons of accepting. See 'Memorandum as to Admiralty', 17 November 1875: CP, BL 60763, fos 119–121.

that it would be *very unfortunate now* to remove me. 2) I urged that it was premature to move Hunt, that he had declared he could defend himself and had appealed to Cave; that it would be regarded as a sacrifice of him, etc. 3) I urged as strongly as I could that he should at least wait till the meeting of Parliament, when if matters were in a satisfactory state I would reconsider the matter 4) that if I did then undertake the Admiralty I should need both a change of persons and probably a change in the constitution of the Office, that as far as I knew the First Lord had not sufficient independent power. He denied this and said that Hunt had declared that he was "Lord Paramount". He listened rather gloomily like a man unconvinced but the final conclusion I understood to be that it should all stand over. One very curious thing occurred. He said the Duke of Richmond had called on him and declared the party in the House of Lords was becoming unmanageable through annoyance at Hunt's blunder. I said at once, "I do not believe a word of it". He said that "the managers of the Party" had so informed Richmond. I asked who? He said probably Colville. I replied, "All I know that Colville last summer did not conceal his strong opinion of the complete mismanagement of the Party by the Duke of Richmond."

Cabinet

1. Suez Canal question. Stanton had telegraphed that Viceroy would not sell his shares without giving us notice and that he would give us the option of purchasing. On discussing the matter further, great doubt as to the nature of the shares arose. No shareholder can have more than 10 votes, which is a serious drawback.
2. Education.

Friday 19 November (London – Munden – Watford)

Cabinet principally engaged in discussing the new regulations to Queen's ships in place of the condemned Slavery Circular. Cairns had drawn them and as usual with great ingenuity; but there were still many expressions that would have brought down much opposition. Some of these we succeeded in removing but it is very doubtful whether our wisest plan would not be to withdraw the instructions altogether. Even these amended instructions are open to severe criticism and will do the Government no good. However the majority of the Cabinet are in favour of issuing them. Meanwhile the Law Officers object to them and they must be heard on the subject.

I came down here to Sir H. Hollands.[556] The Northcotes, R. Herbert and Venables[557] the only other people. I have heard a good deal from Holland who sees many of the House of Commons people at the Carlton as to Hunt. There *does* seem to be a much stronger feeling than I thought as to his incapacity but it is hard to say exactly what it amounts to.

Monday 22 November (London)

Cabinet

1. Fresh telegram from Singapore and long despatch: a letter from Sir W. Jervois with the proclamation, announcing the virtual annexation of the Province, an outrageous act. Told the Cabinet and proposed to censure Sir W. J. but not to change horses crossing the stream.

2. *Suez Canal* affair. The matter seems to have got out of our hands for the moment. *Virtually* agreed to leave the question in Disraeli's hands, to buy the shares if he gets the chance.

3. *Slavery Circular.* Amended copy. Law Officers objection considered, and Cabinet agreed to over-rule them. I tried to get them to soften them down still more and warned them that the whole question was as delicate and dangerous as possible, but they went on with evident misgivings and finally decided to issue them at once.

4. Sclater Booth's proposals for highway boards and Company organisation – nothing actually decided.

Wednesday 24 November (London)

Cabinet

Very long sitting. 3 hours. One half at least as to Suez Canal affair. Cabinet of opinion that the Khedive's shares should be secured so far as possible. Agreed to advance him the money supposed to be required should that appear to be the only mode of action.

---

[556] Sir Henry Thurstan Holland (1825–1914), Con. MP for Midhurst (1874–1885) and for Hampstead (1885–1888), Financial Secretary to the Treasury (1885), Vice-President, Committee of Council on Education (1885–1886), Colonial Secretary (1887–1892), 1st Viscount Knutsford (1895).

[557] George Stovin Venables (1810–1888), journalist and barrister. Contributed to the *Saturday Review* (1855) and *The Times* (1857–1888).

I read telegram just received from Sir. W. Jervois. Opinion of Cabinet was strong that Sir W. J. has behaved ill. Wrote to the Queen afterwards.[558]

Law Officers objections to the Slavery Circular considered and set aside, the Circular finally amended and agreed (though somewhat against my view and Salisbury's) to issue it at once.

Question raised by Hunt as to asking for tenders for the raising of the *Vanguard*: agreed to. Also as to retaining counsel in the case of the *Mistletoe* Coroners Jury: agreed.

Thursday 25 November (London)

Cabinet

1. Suez Canal. Disraeli announced a new phase. It is no longer a question of advancing money on the Khedive's shares but a distinct offer on his part to sell for £4,000,000 with interest at 5 per cent till at the end of the 19 years the shares become free from the mortgage on them and become our absolute property. We telegraphed at once to accept the offer.[559]

2. I read the last telegram from Sir. W. Jervois which Disraeli declared to be very "pernitical",[560] and I told the Cabinet what I proposed generally to do in the way of announcing Sir W. J.'s last despatches [. . .].

A very singular paragraph appeared in the *Post* stating Hunt's resignation and H. Lennox's probable appointment to the Admiralty. Who can have inspired it?[561]

---

[558] 'Sir W. Jervois must of course be disapproved for an act which, intentionally or not, is subordinate in the highest degree' (Carnarvon to Queen Victoria, 24 November 1875: Royal Archives, P25/5).

[559] Disraeli triumphantly wrote to the Queen, 'It is just settled: you have it, Madam. The French Government has been out-generaled' (Buckle, *Disraeli*, V, p. 448). Carnarvon wrote at length to Disraeli four days later, urging that the government 'pause before we make a gratuitous offer to share the advantage we have secured with others' (Carnarvon to Disraeli, 29 November 1875: Hughenden Papers, dep. 100/1, fo. 124). He also told Heathcote, 'We firmly believe the value of the move was moral and political rather than financial' (Carnarvon to Heathcote, 26 November 1875: CP, BL 61074, fo. 4).

[560] The telegram was sent by Carnarvon to Disraeli before the Cabinet meeting (Carnarvon to Disraeli, 25 November 1875: CP, BL 60763, fos 122–124).

[561] In fact, Ward Hunt remained at the Admiralty until August 1877. Lord Henry Lennox (1821–1886), Disraeli's protégé, proved a failure as First Commissioner of Works and left the Government in August 1876. For an example of Lennox's incompetence, see Lord Redesdale, *Memories*, 2 vols (London, 1915), II, pp. 683–684.

Friday 26 November (London)

As usual a very busy day – what days are not? – but at 3 p.m. I got the telegram (in circulation) announcing that the bargain with the Khedive was completed:[562] and at 5.15 I met Delane who asked me if it was true and gave me all details. The Khedive must have communicated them at once. I telegraphed the news to Disraeli who is at Windsor.

Tuesday 30 November (Highclere)

A hard day's work. Heard from the Prince of Wales through Knollys asking us "advice and assistance" as to his money affairs in India.[563] I wrote to Salisbury at once and I think the request for an increase of money with which to make suitable presents is really very reasonable.[564] His progress through India has become a great state affair.

Thursday 2 December (Highclere)

Evidence keeps pouring in to shun the general belief in poor Hunt's incompetency at the Admiralty. I believe it is in a certain degree unreasonable, though I do not think he is a strong man for the post; but everything that goes wrong will be more or less credited to his account.

Thursday 16 December (Highclere)

Northcote and I had much conversation on many subjects. There are a good many clouds on the horizon and I see that he expects a stormy and a disagreeable session. Our chief change is probably in ourselves and in the happy-go-lucky fashion in which most things arrange themselves.[565]

---

[562]'You will have seen this morning that the cat is out of the bag and that the Papers have heard of our financial operation' (Carnarvon to Hardy, 26 November 1875: CP, TNL, PRO 30/6/12).

[563]The Prince and his party left for India on 11 October and landed at Bombay on 8 November. From there he travelled to Goa and Ceylon, reaching Colombo on 1 December.

[564]Carnarvon to Salisbury, 30 November 1875 (copy): CP, TNA, PRO 30/6/10, fos 73–74. Parliament had allowed £52,000 to be spent on the Prince's transport and another £60,000 for personal expenditure, including gifts to native rulers.

[565]See Northcote to Carnarvon, 18 December 1875: CP, TNA, PRO 30/6/7, fos 107–108.

Sandon and Richmond have had a rather serious quarrel, on the old subject. Richmond treats S. as a mere under Secretary and indeed with hardly the attention which most chiefs would pay to their under Secretaries, and S. says (and here reasonably enough) that he stands in the House of Commons on a different footing. It seems the quarrel went so far that S. was on the point of resigning. It was made up, but Richmond's ungracious manner and want of tact, and Sandon's sensitiveness will, it is likely, bring about at no distant time some fresh collision.[566]

Much talk also as to the Admiralty. I cannot but see that the shadow of that office grows more and more visible and though I shrink from it I suspect that I shall have to take it. Curious fate!

Heard from Lytton who has had the offer of India. His letter was very characteristic, very much pleased, very anxious to accept, but held back by certain considerations of health which he set forth to me. I wrote to him to encourage him to undertake it.[567] It was curious that he should write to me for my advice.

---

[566]In November, the Cabinet decided to undertake legislation on compulsory education. Richmond, the Lord President, insisted that he should introduce the bill in the Lords. Sandon, his Vice-President, was equally adamant that he should introduce it in the Commons. Disraeli had to intervene and the bill was dropped. To Sandon's satisfaction the bill was accepted by the Cabinet on 2 February 1876. See P. Gordon, 'Lords President and Vice-Presidents of the Committee of Council on Education: personalities and policies, 1856–1902', in D. Halpin and P. Walsh (eds), *Educational Commonplaces: essays to honour Denis Lawton* (London, 2005), pp. 164–167.

[567]Carnarvon to Lytton, 16 December 1875: Lytton Papers, Hertfordshire Archives and Local Studies, D/Ek c 36/47. Edward Robert Bulwer Lytton (1831–1891), 1st Earl of Lytton (1880), was offered the Viceroyalty on 13 December, after the post had been refused by the Earl of Powis, Manners, and Carnarvon. Lytton accepted on 5 January 1876. Derby doubted the wisdom of the appointment on account of his 'weak health and a dreamy absent habit of mind' (Vincent, *Derby*, II, p. 265).

1876

Monday 22 May (London)

A Cabinet

Disraeli brought before us the state of our Naval force in the Mediterranean at the present junction and stated the combined strength of French, Russian, Italian, Austrian ships – exclusive of 4 German ships ordered there – to be 19 ironclads, 215 guns and 9,380 men. Our force on the other hand stands at 7 ships, 72 guns, 2,774 men. He said probably this storm will not blow over, and that the allies will solve the problem forcibly. He proposed at once to increase our force, suggested the substitution of a stronger man for Elliot[568] at Constantinople and hinted at our seizing the Turkish fleet which is strong and consists of 27 ships and even Constantinople *if necessary*. The Cabinet were rather startled at these large proposals, and some discussion of a curious kind ensued. Finally we agreed to increase the Squadron by 3 more powerful ironclads (and to push on the commissioning of the *Thunderer* and some others).[569]

After Cabinet I went home to consider my speech on the Vivisection bill which I brought on in the evening. The House went with me and the Second Reading was safe enough.[570]

I returned home and dined at 10.30.

---

[568]Sir Henry Elliot (1817–1907), ambassador at Constantinople (1867–1876), British representative at the Constantinople Conference (1876), ambassador at Vienna (1877–1884).

[569]Disraeli had so far been reluctant to allocate funds to increasing the strength of the Navy. In November 1875, two outstanding naval men, Sir Alexander Milne and Sir Phipps Geoffrey Hornby, warned the Government of the need for a shipbuilding programme to provide 'the bare necessities of war'. Ward Hunt agreed. In the Cabinet debate on the estimates, Northcote, then Chancellor of the Exchequer, turned down the request for six more cruisers without even informing the Admiralty Board. See N.A.M. Rodger, 'The Dark Ages of the Admiralty: pt. II, change and decay, 1874–1880', *The Mariner's Mirror*, 62 (1976), pp. 36–37.

[570]*Hansard*, CCXXIX, 22 May 1876, cols 1001–1013.

Tuesday 30 May (London)

Incessant work all day. I never left off except to eat and to go for half an hour to the dentists. In the afternoon I had an hour and a quarter again with President Brand,[571] Malcolm present. I doubt if we made much way; the man is so incurably obstinate, narrow and dull, but we did not come to a break down of the negotiations as at one moment seemed likely.[572]

Later in the evening came the startling news that the Sultan is deposed and his nephew Mourad proclaimed. This is the 4th Sultan in my time – three of whom I may say I have seen – old Mahmoud, Abdul Medjid, Abdul Aziz and Mourad.[573]

---

[571] Jan Hendrik Brand (1823–1888), President of the Orange Free State (1864–1888).

[572] Carnarvon had met Brand a fortnight previously to discuss the Griqualand West question. The annexing of this territory by Britain in 1871 was badly received by the Boers. Carnarvon wished to know if Brand would welcome handing over the territory to the Orange Free State (Carnarvon, 'Memorandum of conversations with President Brand, 8 May 1876': CP, TNA, PRO 30/6/23, fos 95–99). The matter was settled on 13 July, when it was agreed that Britain would retain the diamond fields while the Orange Free State received financial compensation and minor redefinition of its frontiers.

[573] Mahmud II (ruled 1808–1839); his eldest son, Abdul Majid (ruled 1839–1861); his younger son, Abdul Aziz (ruled 1861–1876); and Murad, son of Abdul Majid, who was appointed Sultan of Turkey on the deposing of his uncle on 30 May and was deposed himself in August of the same year.

1877

Wednesday 3 January (London)

In the evening I presided in Grand Lodge and carried in a very triumphant way my proposal to establish in perpetuity two life boats in record of the Prince of Wales's return from India.[574] It was undoubtedly a successful speech, as it convinced a divided and rather reluctant body.

But I had bad news from India. Sir L. Mallet[575] came to me and gave me the details of the threatened scarcity in India. There is fault I think with the Foreign Office, and fault with the Government of India. I telegraphed to Lytton for more information – and I wrote to Lord Beaconsfield to ask for a very early Cabinet.[576] It is I fear a very serious case.

Thursday 4 January (London)

A very hard day's work.[577] This terrible Indian famine threatens to absorb all my time even if I had not the Colonial Office on my hands and plenty of other business. It looks very bad.

I spoke to Rowe[578] as to the contemplated mission to Dahomey and told him that if he went he must be successful, that his capture or death would not only be the loss of everything to himself but would jeopardise the whole policy on the West Coast. He understood all, and is so cool and courageous a fellow that I am ready to trust him: but I suspect Derby will be too timid to run any risk even though I offer to bear 5/6 of it.

[574] The Prince had landed at Plymouth on 11 May 1876.

[575] Sir Louis Mallet (1823–1890), Permanent Under-Secretary for India since 1874.

[576] Carnarvon to Disraeli, 3 January 1877: Hughenden Papers, 100/1, fo. 192.

[577] Carnarvon learnt of the 'extremely serious calamity which is impending in Bombay and Madras' on 3 January (Carnarvon to Sir George Hamilton, 6 January 1877: CP, TNA, PRO 30/6/15, fo. 52).

[578] Sir Samuel Rowe (1835–1888), Governor of Sierra Leone and the Gambia (1877–1881) and of the Gold Coast (1881–1884). He was an ambitious and energetic ex-army surgeon, who favoured acquiring territory for fiscal reasons.

Wednesday 10 January (London)

Took the Chair at the Indian Council in the India Office. I found the Council disposed to be harmonious. I explained the position and had the Department despatch on the famine read, appointed a famine Committee and referred the Department to them appointing a fresh Council for tomorrow.[579] It is an unwieldly body to manage and as yet I have had no experience of it. Today however there was no difficulty. It is a curious episode in one's life to find oneself the really active Minister at the same time of two such departments as the Colonial and India Offices: but it remains to see how I can do it. It has added much to my work and must add.[580]

I met Disraeli in the street and walked for half an hour with him. He was apparently in an amiable mood and spoke well of Salisbury, but this (perhaps I am uncharitable) may have been said with the personal object of letting me know or repeat it. I do not set much on this.[581]

Saturday 13 January (Highclere)

Worse accounts again from India. On the public works of Bombay there are 300,000 persons and on the State of Madras the incredible number of 1,250,000!! This only reached me late this evening. I hope to be in London again on Monday and must take some further steps though I really hardly know what they should be.[582] I have written privately to Northbrook on the subject.[583]

[579] For an account of the Council's deliberations, see Carnarvon to Lytton, 11 January 1877: Lytton Papers, India Office, BL, MSS EUR/E 218/10, II, Letter 23.

[580] Describing his 'double burden' of the India and Colonial Offices, he told his sister, 'It is strange how heavy work seems always to gravitate towards me' (Carnarvon to Lady Gwendoline Herbert, 7 January 1877: CP, BL 61054, fo. 5).

[581] Carnarvon gave a full account of the meeting to Salisbury but did not repeat Disraeli's comments on him (Carnarvon to Salisbury, 10 January 1877: CP, TNA, PRO 30/6/10, fos 105–107).

[582] Carnarvon sent a despatch on 12 January to Lytton, raising questions concerning the purchase of grain by the government of Madras and the employment of labourers on public works by the government of Bombay (CP, TNA, PRO 30/6/3, fos 156–158; see also Carnarvon to Queen Victoria, 13 January 1877: Royal Archives, N33/32). Nevertheless, he had qualms about Derby's telegram of 12 January to Salisbury stating that 'no language is to be held that can pledge the Government to enforce these proposals at a later date' (Carnarvon to Disraeli, 14 January 1877: Hughenden Papers, dep. 100/1, fos 194–195). See P.L. Brumpton, *Security and Progress: Lord Salisbury at the India Office* (Westport, CT and London, 2004), pp. 82–84.

[583] Carnarvon to Northbrook (copy), 12 January 1877: CP, TNA, PRO 30/6/15, fos 75–76.

I received late in the afternoon a telegram from Salisbury. It took me some time to decypher it and reply but I succeeded in doing both in time for the last train.[584]

Wednesday 17 January (Windsor Castle)

A very busy morning, almost entirely occupied with Indian work, a long conversation with Maine.[585] His is a singularly clear intelligence and not merely on abstract or legal subjects, but on high political matters [. . .].

After dinner I had a long conversation with the Queen. I told her as much as I could of the Indian famine but her thoughts were in Turkey[586] and not in India and so I soon gave this part of the subject up.[587] I found her very Turkish. She said she felt for the way in which they had been treated, the spirit that they had shown and the recollection that we had in former times fought for and with them. I reminded her of the Bulgarian horrors. She disbelieved many, thought others exaggerated and that the Bulgarians had been equally guilty. It was clear that she had moved in this respect considerably forward since my last conversation with her, and I thought I could trace distinctly Disraeli's influence. I said enough to show my own feeling but did not of course argue it further.[588] She seemed to be entirely satisfied with Salisbury but had heard that Lady S. had talked too freely and foolishly. She was angry with the Opposition, but admitted that Granville had been cautious and Hartington[589] had not behaved ill, but she did not agree

[584] Salisbury to Carnarvon (copy), 13 January 1877: CP, BL 60761, fo. 191.

[585] Sir Henry Maine (1822–1888), had been legal member of the Governor-General's Council in India (1862–1869), then first Professor of Jurisprudence, Oxford University (1869–1877). See W. Stokes (ed.), *Sir Henry Maine: a brief memoir of his life . . . with some of his Indian speeches* (London, 1892).

[586] On the Conference of European powers then in session in Turkey.

[587] See Queen Victoria's Journal, 17 January 1877: Royal Archives, Z/384.

[588] 'The news from Constantinople looks very bad [. . .]. The only thing that can be done is to press the Turks strongly and to make them feel that they really have no support from us [. . .]. The Prince does not like my "ideas" on this subject and Derby does not answer when he disagrees with a letter' (Carnarvon to Northcote, 16 January 1877: Iddesleigh Papers, BL 50022, fo. 202).

[589] Spencer Compton Cavendish (1833–1908), Marquess of Hartington (1858), 8th Duke of Devonshire (1891). Lib. MP for North Lancashire (1857–1868), for Radnor (1869–1880), for North-east Lancashire (1880–1885), and for Rossendale (1885–1891), Chief Secretary for Ireland (1871–1874), Secretary of State for India (1880–1882), Lord President of the Council (1895–1903), President of the Board of Education (1900–1902).

much when I included Forster[590] in this praise. She said he was not a man of the world and did not understand foreign affairs.

Thursday 18 January (London)

The best part again of my day has been spent on Indian affairs [. . .].

Later I called on Lady Derby and found her in. I had a long and very friendly talk on all subjects. Two or three things resulted:

1. It is quite clear that Derby is sore at my constant opposition (which as I explained is inevitable and is really more loyal than silent antagonism would be) in the Cabinet.[591]

2. We are in a state of tension. She expects the Cabinet to break up. Derby cannot bear opposition. Disraeli she thinks if now thwarted may take the Garter and retire and Derby will retire with him.

3. When Disraeli lately told us that the Russian Ambassador had intimated that his Government desired the withdrawal of Sir H. Elliot and on that statement I and others at once agreed that Elliot could not be withdrawn she said that *the statement was false*. She repeated this more than once.

Thursday 8 March (London)

I dined with Froude to meet Tennyson.[592] I naturally wished to know him and he was good enough to say that he wished to know me. On the whole I think we were mutually satisfied. His conversation has very little of the poet in it: or at least there is more of the "Northern Farmer" than the "Lady of Shalott".[593] He shows little sign too I should say of

[590]William Edward Forster (1818–1886), Lib. MP for Bradford (1861–1886), Vice-President of Committee of Council on Education (1868–1874), Chief Secretary for Ireland (1880–1882). After visiting eastern Europe (including Bulgaria and Turkey) in the autumn of 1876, Forster denounced Turkish atrocities but raised objections to British intervention. See T. Wemyss Reid, *Life of the Right Hon. W.E. Forster*, 2 vols (London, 1885), II, pp. 160–164.

[591]Carnarvon had urged Derby to accept General Ignatiev's proposals to offer Turkey reduced terms at the Conference of Great Powers (Carnarvon to Derby, 10 December and 14 December 1876: Derby Papers, DER (15), 17/2/a). Richard Millman has claimed that Carnarvon was being used as a spy in the Cabinet by Salisbury. The latter telegraphed Carnarvon on 13 January that he 'would need to control the Foreign Secretary for there to be any hope of Turkish acceptance' (R. Millman, *Britain and the Eastern Question, 1875–1878* (Oxford, 1979), p. 227).

[592]Alfred, Lord Tennyson (1808–1892), Poet Laureate (1850), succeeding Wordsworth, 1st Baron Tennyson (1884).

[593]'Northern Farmer Old Style', humorous and dramatic poem in North Lincolnshire dialect published 1864. 'The Lady of Shalott' appeared in 1832.

historical reading or knowledge which surprised me: but there were glimpses of his metaphysical studies in what he said, but generally he was straightforward and simple and fair and I liked what I saw of him in the two or three hours' talk. There was no one else as Froude had asked him alone. He began on the subject of Colonies and Colonial Government and said he heartily agreed in my administration of them.

Wednesday 14 March (London)

Usual day of work. I attended Lowe's Sustentation of Incumbents Fund [. . .].

A conversation later with Lady Derby as to D.'s manner, a delicate matter to discuss, and one impossible but for her perfect straight forwardness and the fact that she is so old a friend. I said of course nothing that possibly hurt her as regards D. but I also said that I thought that on the whole it was best not to say anything to him or to force any renewal of friendly relations on him: but I leave it all to time. I am not myself very sanguine.

Thursday 15 March (London)

Dined with Rosebery at the St. James's Club: and then was with him admitted as a member of the Society of Antiquaries, where I listened to a wondrously dull discussion on an old charter which had turned up at Dover and another old Bull of the reign of Henry VII.[594]

Just before going out to dinner I received in a circulation box a telegram from Lyons saying that Ignatieff[595] was coming to England immediately and was to go on Saturday to Hatfield. It is most singular and I can hardly believe it. Only a few days ago Salisbury agreed that it would be a great mistake if Ignatieff were to come to London and it is clear that his going to Hatfield would identify Salisbury with him and his Russian policy. It is altogether inexplicable, and I doubt if there is truth in it.[596] On returning home I found that Salisbury had

---

[594] *Proceedings of the Society of Antiquaries of London*, 2nd series, 7 (1879), pp. 162–163.

[595] Gen. Nikolai Pavlovich Ignatiev (1832–1908), Russian diplomat. Ambassador at Peking (1860) and at Constantinople (1864–1878).

[596] On 1 March, the day that peace was declared between Turkey and Serbia, Russia decided to send Ignatiev on a mission to European capitals to co-ordinate the Great Powers' views on the Russian protocol, giving conditions as to the Porte for Russian disarmament (Millman, *Britain and the Eastern Question*, p. 155).

THE AWKWARD SQUAD
(SEE BLUE BOOK)

SERGEANT. "On your Eastern Question—Right-about-turn!" COMPANY OFFICER (aside). "Ah, they always *were* slow at their 'facings!'"
SERGEANT (to himself). "Must get 'em round somehow!"

Fig. 4 'The Awkward Squad', *Punch*, 24 February 1877, by Sir John Tenniel, depicting the differences within the Cabinet on the Eastern Question. The Sergeant represents Lord Derby and the Company Officer, Disraeli. Carnarvon is the fourth figure from the left.

called here at 7.45: but having to dine early I had gone. Probably he called to give some explanation.[597]

Sunday 18 March (Hatfield)

Ambassadors, Northcote, Cross, Bourke,[598] Hartington, Bath, Goschen,[599] altogether about 35 or 40 persons – and on the whole

[597] Lady Salisbury later that day wrote to Carnarvon, 'The Ignatieffs have just telegraphed to our great surprise that they are coming to Hatfield on Saturday. Do pray by the memory of our ancient friendship come and meet them. We are in despair' (Lady Salisbury to Carnarvon, 15 March 1877: CP, BL 60759, fo. 2). Carnarvon agreed to join them (ibid., fo. 79).

[598] Robert Bourke (1827–1902), MP for King's Lynn (1868–1886), Permanent Under-Secretary at the Foreign Office (1874–1880, 1885–1886), Governor of Madras (1886–1891), created Baron Connemara (1887).

[599] George Joachim Goschen (1831–1907), Lib. MP for City of London (1863–1880) and for Ripon (1880–1885), Independent Lib. MP for Edinburgh East (1885–1886) and for St

everything well and handsomely done. As to the two chief guests Madam I. [Ignatieva] was certainly very pretty and is still good looking. She is agreeable, light in hand, speaks English very well and is extremely taking. He is very anxious to please: but I doubt if I quite like him. He talked to me some time this morning in a torrent of voluble French but the sum total of his conversation was reiterated assurances of his honesty and sincerity. At last I hardly knew how to answer him. This and the repeated statement that England and Russia had in the East few interests at variance comprised all he said. But he is doubtless clever and has evidently great energy.

I had a long and important conversation with Northcote as to the recent difficulty in the Cabinet respecting Elliot. He admitted and said that Derby's temper was becoming impracticable, that Disraeli seemed to be now entirely under Derby's influence, that matters could hardly go on as they now are and that the situation was growing dangerous and very disagreeable to all of us. The truth is that yesterday's Cabinet has been very useful in bringing matters on to a decisive issue. It has also perhaps cleared away that which was once a matter of extreme probability and which has always been a contingency – the succession of Derby to the Prime Ministership. I think this is almost disposed of. I doubt now if Salisbury would serve under him – I do not think I could – and if we both withdrew, *as things now stand*, it would make such an event almost impossible.[600]

Good Friday 30 March (Highclere)

I wrote to Northcote on the singular article in the *Pall Mall*,[601] put in evidently by official inspiration and saying that the signing of the protocol was due to causes operating within and without the Cabinet, in other words advertising our differences. It seems to me an unjustifiable and unprecedented proceeding on Derby's part.[602]

George's, Hanover Square (1887–1900). Contributed to formation of Liberal Unionist Party, President of Poor Law Board (1868–1871), Chancellor of the Exchequer (1886–1892), 1st Viscount Goschen (1900).

[600]Elliot, who was strongly pro-Turk, had come under pressure to resign. Disraeli and Derby wished to keep him; Salisbury opposed Elliot's return to Constantinople. At the Cabinet of 17 March, Derby threatened to resign if he was overruled (Vincent, *Derby*, II, p. 383). Elliot was replaced by Henry Layard, who was also pro-Turk, on 31 March.

[601]'The English Government and the protocol', *Pall Mall Gazette*, 28 March 1877, pp. 1–2. Carnarvon remarked that 'I can hardly recall anything like it, for it is a distinct announcement of the difference of opinion', and he believed that 'for weeks past the *Pall Mall* has been ostentatiously the F.O. organ' (Carnarvon to Salisbury, 30 March 1877 (copy): CP, BL 60761, fo. 207).

[602]Carnarvon wrote to Northcote about the Cabinet meeting of 28 March, the day the Cabinet agreed to sign the protocol: 'The extraordinary address which Disraeli made as on

Saturday 7 April (Highclere)

I have had a tolerably quiet evening here by myself and I have done a good deal of work. I think I begin to see how to deal with my South African Confederation question.[603] One of my greatest difficulties in office is that I have really no time for any quiet or deliberate thought. Everything has to be decided on the spur of the moment, and either it must be decided by a sort of instinct or on the advice of those whose judgement I think I can trust and who have had more leisure to look into the case. Everything too at home naturally and necessarily is referred to me and if I do not listen to every question from the children's dresses to the cooking of the dinner I know all would go wrong. At the same time it is fair to admit that the head servants are excellent, have really good judgement, and honestly try to spare me in every way.

Monday 16 April (London)

Walked home from the House with Salisbury and he told me that tomorrow evening he is to have a conference with Disraeli on foreign affairs. It shows that D. feels we have come to a serious stage and as Salisbury thinks it means business. Also it means that D. does not mean to break with us just now: but we are on hollow and slippery ground. Salisbury's notion is that we must take the harbour in Crete, erect Crete into a republic undertaking for her the management of her *foreign* affairs, and on the whole as I understand him not to let Russia get hold of Constantinople.

[? Saturday 5 May (London)]

[Page torn away] [. . .] was understood at the last Cabinet. He is so averse to taking any decided step that even when matters are thought to be decided he leaves them open. Some discussion ensued but I doubt if he will take any real action.

I called at Lady Derby's before the Cabinet as she leaves England today for a month. I had as usual a most friendly talk. She says she can

the disturbers of the unanimity of the Cabinet and which was obviously directed against Salisbury and myself, the things which *I know* to have been said out of the Cabinet on the same theme. Derby's intemperate conduct even in the ordinary relations of daily life – and this new method of advertising our differences in the newspapers – all this seems to me to be full of danger and if it were to be carried much further would threaten our existence' (Carnarvon to Northcote, 30 March 1877: Iddesleigh Papers, BL 50022, fo. 210).

[603] Carnarvon had sent Disraeli the proofs of the revised Confederation of South African Colonies and State Bill two days earlier (Carnarvon to Disraeli, 5 April 1877 (copy): CP, TNA, PRO 30/6/11, fos 189–190).

do no more[604] and that she hopes that peace is now in the ascendant, but I do not think that she believes much in the stability of affairs. She would not, I suspect, be astonished if during her absence Derby retired from office, a contingency which at times has been in view. Meanwhile he has recovered all his serenity as far as I am concerned, and is very affable again.

At the Academy dinner tonight I sat next to Hardy and talked much with him. He is angry with Disraeli's appointment of Thorold[605] as the new Bishop of Rochester, and certainly his way of speaking of the Prime Minister does not imply any great confidence in him on any subject. Gladstone spoke with singular eloquence at times, and Northcote in a wholly different and in a lower strain spoke well.

Monday 7 May (London)

Last night I received the news of the annexation of the Transvaal. On the 12th ult. it seems Shepstone after exhausting all other means told the Transvaal Government that he would wait no longer and acting on my general instructions he declared the territory to belong to the English Crown. It is a step which I think has no precedent for many a long year but I think it is right and it will anyhow mark my tenure of office.[606] *The Times* gives a friendly but cautious approval and one or two other papers write in the same sense.[607] I expect that the foreign Press will criticise in no friendly manner; and just at this moment it might be well to be spared this, but it cannot be avoided and on the whole it is enough for me if this Country generally approves. But for the war in the East which absorbs everything else it is an event

[604] War between Russia and Turkey had broken out on 24 April.

[605] Anthony Wilson Thorold (1825–1895), Bishop of Rochester (1877–1879), Bishop of Winchester (1890–1895).

[606] In sending his 'hearty congratulations' to Shepstone in carrying out the task, Carnarvon added, 'The work has been admirably done; and I rejoice to think that the hope which I expressed to you just before you sailed has been so well fulfilled' (Carnarvon to Shepstone, 30 May 1877 (copy): CP, TNA, PRO 30/6/23, fo. 16). For Shepstone's reply, see Shepstone to Carnarvon, 23 July 1877: ibid., fos 30–33. Cornelis Uys has pointed out that Carnarvon gave Shepstone no official instructions except in a vaguely worded Royal Warrant, while in private letters impressing on Shepstone the urgency for acquiring the Transvaal. 'The reason for this is obvious. His private epistles could not be published in parliamentary papers, nor could be used against him by his political opponents, trusting in Shepstone's loyalty to him. He evidently calculated that should the mission be a failure, Sir Theophilus would have to bear the full brunt, while he himself would not be jettisoned by the British nation. On the other hand, should the annexation be an unqualified success, he and his friend Wolseley would share the kudos with the Special Commissioner' (C.J. Uys, *In the Era of Shepstone* (Lovedale, 1934), p. 265).

[607] See leading article on the annexation, entitled 'South African Republic', *The Times*, 7 May 1877, p. 9.

which would have created a good deal of discussion. Derby from a few words that he said evidently does not like it: but it is in opposition to everything that he approves and so I am not surprised. As to the rest of my colleagues they hardly seem to know much of it, except of course Salisbury is evidently amused at the whole transaction.

At the Levée today d'Harcourt[608] told me privately, saying that he wished to tell me but that he had mentioned it to no one but Derby, that the Prince of Wales whilst in Paris had talked in a very injudicious way of the present war, saying that Russia had planned all this for a long time and that Germany probably intended to take the first opportunity of attacking France.

Thursday 31 May (London)

In the evening I took the Chair at the Society of Antiquaries to hear Newton deliver a lecture on the date of the Mycenae discoveries.[609] Schliemann was there but he did not make much head at an explanation of the several points raised. Newton was very clear. I summed up, but I doubt if I did it as well as I ought to have done.[610]

Friday 3 August (London)

I had some conversation with Lady Derby on recent events in the Cabinet. Derby had written to her before our alliance to say that he was extremely anxious and that affairs were more critical than they had as yet been: but now he was satisfied at the result and at the support which I had given him and which he seems to have appreciated. She was astonished at Salisbury's change of position and frequently recurred to it, saying she could not understand it.[611] Her general notion however was it was the result of his visit to Osborne and that the Queen had impressed him with her new ideas. It seems to have been Disraeli's notion that if he could be sure of Salisbury,

[608] Georges, Marquis d'Harcourt (1808–1883), French ambassador at London (1873–1879).

[609] C.T. Newton, 'On the discoveries of Mycenae', *Proceedings of the Society of Antiquaries of London*, 2nd series, 7 (1877), pp. 236–247.

[610] Ibid., pp. 247–250.

[611] Carnarvon later noted that it was at the Cabinet meeting of 21 July that 'Salisbury to my astonishment, expressed himself in favour of sending the fleet to Constantinople in the event of the Russians effecting an entrance in Constantinople. A few days afterwards he admitted that he had since been in conversation with Disraeli on the subject' (Carnarvon, 'Memorandum on circumstances which led to my resignation in January 1878': CP, BL 60817, fos 67–68).

he might count upon me, and if this was so all this must have been a great disappointment to him.

Monday 10 September (Highclere)

Derby has I find written a draft on the subject of Turkish atrocities but the draft when sent to Balmoral was disapproved. It came back to Disraeli who of course was in favour of assuming the Russians to be equally guilty, and since then it has been tinkered and patched and apparently has not yet gone.[612] Pauncefote[613] says that Serbia is entirely in Russian hands and only awaiting orders. Greece is much in the same position.

Tuesday 30 October (Highclere)

The Transvaal Delegates came down here for lunch before returning to London. Old Kruger[614] is a curious and really an interesting specimen. He illustrates, I take it, perfectly the Dutch "Dopper Boer"[615] – obstinate, narrow, rough, unlettered, prejudiced: but shrewd, not untruthful, homely and except as regards natives by no means unkindly. He looked at Margaret as she sat by me at luncheon with evident admiration and watched her as she moved about. But his chief admiration was for the stables and the horses: and when I had a breaking-in bit put into the mouth of one of the horses and a dumb jockey placed on the animals back he was extremely interested.

Both he and Jorissen promised to do all they could to influence their countrymen for good and to serve the Queen faithfully on their return.[616]

---

[612] Both Disraeli and the Queen had put pressure on Derby to take action. The Queen insisted that he not only protested against Russian atrocities but that he should appeal to other Powers to declare war against Serbia. See Millman, *Britain and the Eastern Question*, p. 322.

[613] Sir Julian Pauncefote (1829–1902), Assistant Under-Secretary at the Foreign Office since 1876.

[614] Paul Kruger (1825–1904), the Vice-President, and his political adviser, Dr Edward Jorissen (1829–1912), who made up the delegation, arrived in England at the end of July. They requested a plebiscite on some form of self-government for their country.

[615] Dopper or Canting Church, an evangelical body that strictly adhered to the decrees of the Synod of Dordrecht, 1618–1619. No hymns except psalms were sung by worshippers.

[616] See 'Memorandum of final interview of delegates with Lord Carnarvon in the library of the castle, 30 Oct. 1872', in Carnarvon's handwriting: CP, TNA, PRO 30/6/48, fos 214–216.

General Summary of Cairns' resolutions, 18 December [page missing][617]

1. Parliament to meet on the earliest day (7 January) and a vote of credit to be taken.

2. A despatch to be framed founded on the communication of 8th June to us by Russia which indicated the terms of peace which Russia would accept under certain circumstances, asking Russia whether we may communicate these terms to Turkey without expressing an opinion upon them.

3. Supposing that a vote is taken for increased armaments and that peace is not made and that Russia is not giving satisfactory assurances and that she continues to advance on Constantinople, that we should occupy the Gallipoli end of the Straits.

4. That the consent of the Sultan should be asked for this, but that if it is refused we should consider whether we should not take it by force.

5. That our objects are "British interest", the conclusion of the war and some other generalities which I could not take down.

6. That we do not propose an alliance with Turkey beyond what circumstances render necessary (this being the sense of the passage though the words used were different), that we do not intend to encourage her to continue the war and some other similar generalities.

[617]The fall of Plevna to the Russians on 9 December had increased the risk of war. At the Cabinet of 14 December, Disraeli had put forward three proposals: an immediate summoning of Parliament, a vote to increase military forces, and a proposal to act as mediator to the warring parties. The Cabinet meeting ended indecisively. At a further meeting on 17 December, Disraeli stated that he would resign. Cairns proposed a Cabinet the following day, at which he introduced a modified version of Disraeli's proposals. There was general consent to these views. 'The great struggle is over', Disraeli reported two days later, 'and I have triumphed' (Buckle, *Disraeli*, VI, p. 207).

1878

Thursday 31 January (London)

My successor, Sir M. Beach, is appointed. He called on me and I gave him all the information that I could.[618] The principal subjects on which I spoke were:

1. Governors – Dufferin suggesting Buckingham as successor to Phayre[619] – Hardwicke who wants a Governorship.[620]
2. Honours – G. Cross for Sir F. Williams[621] and C.M.G. for Captain Haig.[622] Knighthoods for Barry and others.
3. Sir A. Cunynghame's affair.
4. Malta – Revd. H. White.[623]
5. Mauritius and Bishop Scarisbrick[624] promised that if he saw his way to an increase in the Roman Catholic clergy I would support.
6. Fiji – explained Gordon's position. Some additional help is possible.[625]
7. West Coast – advised a parliamentary grant.
8. Gold Coast – called special attention to the Gold Coast Corps.
9. Hennessy at Hong Kong needs a careful eye.[626]

---

[618]Carnarvon told Disraeli earlier in the day, 'I think it will be of some advantage to my successor to talk to me. I can tell him many things in conversation which may be of value and which it is not easy to express in writing' (Carnarvon to Disraeli, 31 January 1878: Hughenden Papers, dep. 100/1).

[619]Sir Arthur Purves Phayre (1812–1895), Governor of Mauritius (1874–1878), was succeeded by Sir George Ferguson Bowen (1821–1899), who had been Governor of Victoria since 1873.

[620]Charles Philip Yorke (1836–1897), 5th Earl of Hardwicke (1873), known as 'Champagne Charlie'. Con. MP for Cambridgeshire (1865–1873), Master of the Buckhounds (1874–1880), declared bankrupt (1881).

[621]William Fenwick Williams (1800–1883), Baronet (1856), Lib. MP for Calne (1856–1859), Commander-in-Chief, Canada (1859–1865), Governor of Nova Scotia (1865–1867), Governor of Gibraltar (1871–1876).

[622]Capt. Arthur Balfour Haig (1840–1925), Equerry to the Duke of Edinburgh (1864–1880).

[623]Revd Henry White (1830–1890), Chaplain-in-Ordinary to the Queen (1870–1873).

[624]William Benedict Scarisbrick (1828–1898), Bishop of Mauritius (1872–1887).

[625]One of Gordon's tasks as Governor, ordered by Carnarvon, was to settle the many outstanding land claims. Gordon's enlightened policy towards the native Fijians caused much worry. See J.K. Chapman, *The Career of Arthur Hamilton Gordon, First Lord Stanmore* (Toronto, 1964), pp. 205–208.

[626]Sir John Pope-Hennessy (1834–1891), Governor of Hong Kong (1877–1882).

10. Barbados going on well.

11. Straits – needs watching: described Robinson.[627]

12. Canada – British Columbia difficulty.

13. Dwelt particularly on Herbert's merits and capacity and advised him to spare H. in every way.

Wednesday 13 February (London)

Came up and found London in great political excitement, Derby's probable resignation in everyone's mouth.[628] I received a private letter from Sandford[629] telling me that the tail of the Party at the Carlton is furious against him, that a meeting of some 25 members has been held and that on Saturday a much larger one will be held to turn him out or to compel him to take a stronger line.

I had a long talk with Lady Derby in the evening. Poor thing, I am very sorry for her for she had courage enough to have made him act on former occasions and now she plainly sees that he has lost ground and is sinking in public opinion. Meanwhile I am sure that he must be suffering extraordinarily as he finds himself driven on to measures which are intended to lead to war. Salisbury, I suspect, is driving on the coach recklessly, and Lady D. did not scruple to say (as others are indeed saying) with a view to the Foreign Office. What a spectacle as regards the man whom I respected so much. Some things which I have heard (past doubt) are almost incredible. Amongst them I find that during Derby's illness Disraeli took the opportunity of offering Austria the help of subsidies and that Austria having before rejected the offer has since expressed herself ready for them. This looks like action at last on her part.

Meanwhile nothing is known of the fleet, where it is. Pender,[630] it seems, offered the Government for £2,000 to lay a line for temporary use. A Committee of the Cabinet considered the proposal and declined

---

[627]William Cleaver Robinson (1834–1897), Governor of the Straits Settlements (1877–1879).

[628]The British Fleet had been ordered through the Dardanelles for a third time in three weeks. Derby gloomily wrote, 'There must be an end to the *imbroglio* within the next few months; if not, it will make an end of me' (Millman, *Britain and the Eastern Question*, p. 389). Carnarvon informed Bath, 'I hear that after the last Cabinet Derby said, "Things are looking graver than ever." This for what it is worth' (Carnarvon to Bath, 11 February 1878: Longleat Papers).

[629]Sir Francis Sandford (1824–1893), Assistant Under-Secretary at the Colonial Office (1868–1870).

[630]Sir John Pender (1815–1896), pioneer of submarine telegraphy and Lib. MP for Wick district, Linlithgowshire (1872–1885).

it on the ground of expense!!! I went to the Cosmopolitan in the evening. Everyone very civil but only one subject of conversation.

Thursday 21 February (London)

Late in the afternoon called on Beach at the Colonial Office to give him what advice I could on various Colonial matters [. . .]. At the close of our conversation he said he hoped I should not think it was an impertinence but he felt strongly that the British Columbia difficulty was very threatening, that it was extremely difficult to settle it, could I be persuaded to undertake the settlement? I said it took me by surprise, that if I remembered rightly the Canadian Parliament would meet shortly, that some proposal would then be made and that I hoped a solution would be found, but that Dufferin's term of office did not expire till after June, that no one was more competent than he to settle it, and that of course I could not do anything to set him aside. I saw, I said, little chance of the necessity arising for my intervention, but that "without prejudice as lawyers say" I would not refuse to consider the matter if the question should come up, but it must be understood that it could under no circumstances be other than a temporary mission, undertaken (if at all) to give him help in a peculiarly difficult affair.[631]

In the House of Lords we had some communications from Derby.[632]

Saturday 23 February (Battle)

The accounts from the East look very threatening. There will probably be an outcry here and a fresh outburst of the war feeling. We are very close to the edge of the precipice and I am very fearful that we shall go over. The Government I fancy are making great efforts to prepare for it. I hear of 20,000 horses being bought and a good many ironclads etc. It looks very bad.[633]

---

[631]The financial and administrative obstacles to the completion of the Canadian Pacific Railway had caused much friction between the government and the Columbians. It was not until 1881 that the contract was finally sanctioned, and a further seven years before the line to Vancouver City was opened.

[632]The Eastern Question. Movements of the Fleet. Conference. Questions: *Hansard*, CCXXXVIII, 21 February 1878, cols 43–45, Derby, cols 44–45.

[633]At the Cabinet meeting on 21 February, Layard's telegram was received, reporting a Russian demand that the Turks should surrender their fleet. In the event of this not being carried out, Russia would occupy Constantinople. The Royal Navy was put on high alert.

Tuesday 26 February (Highclere)

I hardly know what to think of the news. On the whole I believe it looks peaceful in spite of the warlike declamations of the *Daily Telegraph*.[634] The Russian demands are very high, and exorbitant, and this will raise a strong feeling against them which may help to war or may induce Russia to retreat before taking up an unalterable attitude. The whole situation, from the outside, looks very perplexing.

Thursday 28 February (London)

Came up, had a long talk with Gladstone.[635] His ability, memory, energy surprise me and with them all there is a singular simplicity and even humility of character. In talking to him, when there is nothing to excite or divert him, one feels how very superior he is to the mass of politicians. His obvious and certain desire is to do that which is right, and the moral atmosphere of his society is the exact reverse of that of Disraeli. He said and truly that it is difficult to know what the Government mean – on the one hand Derby's declarations are more or less satisfactory:[636] on the other these announcements of Lord Napier[637] taking the command and suchlike seem to point to war. Gladstone said he could not at present see even a pretext for war.

Sunday 10 March (Highclere)

I find from Lady Abercromby that the Queen is very much out of humour with me, and this I suppose will be the case for a long time at

---

[634]In a leader headed 'Russo-Turkish War', the newspaper encouraged the Government to 'take every precaution' to discourage the serious encroachment of the treaties of 1856 and 1871: *Daily Telegraph*, 26 February 1878, p. 4.

[635]Carnarvon commented afterwards, 'I do not know that it came to much. What he mainly wanted to hear was as to the course to be pursued by Disraeli and perhaps I was useful to him' (Carnarvon to Bath, 1 March 1878: Longleat Papers).

[636]A view not shared by several members of the Cabinet: 'all our eight heads of hair stood upright on reading the account of Derby's conversation with Shuvalov on the subject of the possible seizure of a Turkish island' (Northcote to Disraeli, 27 February 1878: Hughenden Papers, dep. 107/1).

[637]Gen. Robert Cornelis Napier (1810–1890), 1st Baron Napier of Magdala (1868), distinguished soldier in Indian, Abyssinian, and Chinese campaigns. Commander-in-Chief, India (1870–1876), Governor of Gibraltar (1876–1882).

least to come. It seems that at my last visit to Osborne[638] when I had such an extraordinary scene with her before dinner she was greatly put out at dinner. I noticed indeed that she was a little ruffled but I talked on just the same as usual and fancied that she had recovered herself, but this it seems was not the case.[639]

Disraeli appears to be more and more in her confidence on all subjects, public and private alike. This I hear on all sides from those who know the relations and I do not doubt it. One of the strongest evidences of his power over her is his inducing her to write to Leaders of Opposition. I *suspect* she has written to Forster of late and that he has not been able to resist. It is clear that many of these men, Cross and Northcote particularly, are quite powerless and surrender or suppress their opinions under this royal pressure.

Wednesday 13 March

I had a long conversation with Lady Derby. I see that there has been a great deal of fighting in the Cabinet, and that Derby has maintained his ground by stubbornness and his old plan of "wet-blanketting" each proposal as it is made. She said that he felt absolutely alone and missed me much.

Salisbury I fancy is very violent in language.

As to the Canadian offer, it seems clear that it was made by arrangement with Disraeli. It did not come from Beach alone and it was therefore I think somewhat of a trap. Derby was it seems astonished when Disraeli announced to him that there was some chance of my taking the Governor Generalship!!! and naturally – but it shows how far the matter had gone.[640]

---

[638]On 3 January, Disraeli sent a telegram at 2.20 p.m. that day to the Queen, 'I have brought the Speech of the Colonial Secretary before the Cabinet today. He has departed for Osborne much excited' (Royal Archives, H18/T6).

[639]Carnarvon, after his resignation on 24 January, had offered to attend for an interview with the Queen. She informed Ponsonby, 'The Queen does certainly not wish to see Ld Carnarvon, who finds sympathy with no one for his selfish conduct – leaving his Post at such a moment' (Queen Victoria to Ponsonby, 17 January 1878: Royal Archives, L14/30).

[640]According to Hardinge, II, p. 339, on 10 March, Carnarvon was asked by the Government 'to undertake a mission to Canada'. Lady Derby had previously written to Carnarvon, ' I thought the offer of Canada had been made and almost accepted. Stanley certainly understood so' (Lady Derby to Carnarvon, 10 March 1878: CP, BL 60765, fo. 171).

Friday 22 March (London)

I dined at Carlingford's and had some various conversation.

1. Hartington thinks it probable that there will be further and important discussion as to the Treaty between Russia and Turkey, the text of which appears in today's papers.

2. Borthwick[641] declared that he believed there would be war. He dwelt on the probability of collisions between the Fleet and the Russians.

3. Lady Waldegrave[642] believes in war. I asked her why? and she said Disraeli told her so. Lady W. is a Jewess and though the fact that Disraeli said this proves nothing yet it is an indication.

Trutch[643] of British Columbia called on me and I gave him leave to refer to me any application to Bench.

White also called on me and explained all his Malta and Savoy difficulties.

Saturday 23 March (Babraham)

Before coming here I called on Lyons who is at Norfolk House. Our conversation was short, but it leaves in my mind the distinct impression that he is very little hopeful as to the results of the Congress, if a Congress[644] there is, and that he feels anxious as to war. In the *Pall Mall* this afternoon there is another of the special articles written as if to prepare everyone for war;[645] altogether the outlook is not promising. Bath tells me that he had a conversation with Lady Salisbury, who says that the Russians are extremely anxious and indeed obliged to get their troops away from Constantinople on account of illness. This may be so, though probably exaggerated, and if it is so, the Government are, I doubt not, taking advantage of it to press their demands on Russia.

[641] Algernon Borthwick (1830–1908), proprietor of the *Morning Post* since 1876.

[642] Frances Elizabeth, Countess Waldegrave (1821–1879), whose fourth husband was Lord Carlingford, a leading Liberal politician. A great society hostess, she was on very friendly terms with Shuvalov. See O.W. Hewett, *Strawberry Fair: a biography of Frances, Countess Waldegrave, 1821–1879* (London, 1956), p. 256.

[643] Sir Joseph William Trutch (1826–1904), Surveyor-General of British Columbia (1864), Lieutenant-Governor of British Columbia (1871–1876).

[644] Russia had agreed to hold a Conference of the Great Powers in Berlin to reconsider the Treaty of San Stefano signed in March, which ended the Russo-Turkish war.

[645] 'The treaty from an English point of view', *Pall Mall Gazette*, 23 March 1877, p. 1: 'Is it possible an English Government can formally allow to Russia, along with the Armenian territory which the treaty gives her possession this fatal right of protectorate over the rest? We say that to do so may be possible, but that it would be a blunder absolutely criminal.'

I came down here to the Cadogans.[646]

Monday 1 April (London)

I had made an appointment with Townsend and had a long talk with him on arriving. He believes that it is war beyond doubt and Schouvaloff also believes this: Salisbury goes to the Foreign Office, Hardy to India Office and Stanley to War Office.[647] Townsend says that there will be very great defection of the Liberals in the House of Commons, that they fear for their seats, and that a large part of the middle class who before were all in favour of peace have now been converted to war. It is a very bad look out. I dined with Phillimore. Gladstone is very strong on the subject but beyond this I heard nothing.

Thursday 4 April (London)

Dined at the Ripons. After dinner talked to Bylandt[648] who does not believe in war, but he seems to found his belief on our Government withdrawing or modifying Salisbury's circular despatch. That despatch has in its own line and way had a very great success, but it seems to me a fatal document, for it places the Russian Government in the dilemma of yielding or fighting.

I had some talk with Derby this afternoon.[649] He was very friendly and after a good deal of conversation he agreed to speak and speak early on Monday. He recapitulated to me his speech and if he says it as he said it to me it will do very well.[650] My fear is that when it comes to the point he may water it down: at the same time, I think he is nettled by F. Stanley's appointment,[651] by the stories circulated of himself, by Salisbury's taking his place and by the general circumstances. I shall not therefore be surprised if he makes a good speech. It seems that the

---

[646] George Henry Cadogan (1840–1915), 5th Earl Cadogan (1873), Under-Secretary of State for War (1875–1878) and for the Colonies (1878–1880), Lord Privy Seal (1886–1892), Lord Lieutenant of Ireland (1895–1902).

[647] The Cabinet changes, following Derby's resignation on 27 March, were announced on 2 April.

[648] Charles Malcolm Bylandt (1818–1893), Dutch diplomat.

[649] Derby reported, 'Carnarvon [...] low in spirits [...]. He does not understand the complete change of opinion on Salisbury's part within a year; nor do I, except through female influence. Lady Salisbury has always, since Constantinople, desired to be at the F.O. and has not concealed the wish' (Vincent, *Derby*, IV, p. 2).

[650] *Hansard*, CCXXXIX, 8 April 1878, Derby, cols 789–801.

[651] Frederick Stanley had been appointed Secretary of State for War on 2 April, the same day that Salisbury was appointed Foreign Secretary.

reason of his resignation was a sudden proposal, which was carried unanimously, for the annexation of Cyprus and the landing of English troops "at some point on the Syrian Coast" (probably Scanderoon)[652] without the consent of the Porte. This scheme was (like so many other schemes) suspended. Meanwhile however military preparations are going on as though for an expedition somewhere.

Wednesday 10 April (London)

A long talk with Lady Derby in the morning. We spoke much of Derby's speech and she said that was now a break with the party and "There is nothing for you both but to look to some Liberal alliances." I said, "It is the fault of the present Government that they drive us away by their conduct, but I intend to keep myself very free as regards the future." The family discord, if that is not too strong a word, with F. Stanley and the Salisburys is a cause of pain.[653]

In the evening I met the Derbys again and the Gladstones at dinner with the Abercrombys.[654] Mr. Gladstone said incidentally that Lady Salisbury was in high spirits at having the Foreign Office.

Tuesday 14 May (London)

I had an important conversation with Derby as to the present. He feels very keenly his recent treatment and all his old distrust and distaste to the Conservatives as a party have returned to him. It is small wonder. He said to me that the present creed of the Government seemed to be High Church, High prerogative and High taxation. He is resolved himself to keep himself clear of all ties, that he is free now, and that though he is not anxious to be back in Downing St., he will have clearly no reluctance in taking office again if the proper opportunity arises. I was unable to agree with him on all this, except as regards the "High Church" part of the matter, saying that I too felt myself quite free and proposed to reserve myself for the various contingencies that might arise. There was a tacit but unexpressed understanding that we should as far as possible act together. He spoke

---

[652] Port, formerly named Alexandretta, in North Syria. For details of the proposed operation, see J. Headlam-Morley, *Studies in Diplomatic History* (London, 1930), pp. 203–204.

[653] Derby wrote in his Diary on 15 May, 'In afternoon, talk with M. as to whether any overture should be made to C.S. [Constance, Frederick Stanley's wife] of whose unfriendly language and conduct we have more evidence than enough' (Vincent, *Derby*, IV, p. 15).

[654] Sir Robert William Duff Abercromby (1835–1895), Commander, RN (1865), Lib. MP for Banffshire (1861–1893), Lib. Whip (1882–1885), Governor of New South Wales (1893–1895), and his wife, Louisa.

of Salisbury as one who would not get on with anyone else in the Cabinet. I suspect this is prompted by the recollection of Salisbury's treatment of him which certainly was in my time often disagreeable and which I imagine afterwards was much more so.

Sunday 26 May (London)

Townsend dined with me, full of information as usual [. . .]. A very curious piece of news which, as he said, he ought not have known and which of course is perfectly private, but which entirely agrees with all that I think probable. The telegraph desk (at Osborne or Windsor) wrote to his brother the other day saying that if the public generally knew the messages which passed from the Queen to Lord Beaconsfield, there would "be an end to the monarchy," or something equivalent. This very likely – Townsend had seen the letter.[655] Another volume of the Queen's diary is in preparation, and in it she says, "William III was a very great ruler but Prince Albert was a greater." Theodore Martin[656] has persuaded her to omit this.

Monday 17 June (London)

The agreement between the English and Russian Governments, which was published in Saturday's papers, will do the Government harm.[657] Lord Grey, who walked down to the House with me, said it was "disgraceful", mainly however because on the 8th. of this month it seems he asked Salisbury if there was any truth in the statement which had appeared in the *Globe* that Bessarabia was to be given to Russia, and that Salisbury had begged him not to ask any question as the Government were doing all they could to preserve it to Roumania, – but now that it appears that on the 30th May they had signed this

[655] Gladstone had a conversation with Carnarvon the previous day and made a note of the latter's observations: 'It has happened repeatedly that Cabinet Ministers have been sent to her to receive "wiggings" from the Queen which as he [Carnarvon] said is their affair and fault, if they allow it to impair their independence, but communications have from time to time been received by the Cabinet warning it off from certain subjects and saying she could not agree to this and not agree to that' (Gladstone, Memorandum marked 'Secret', 26 May 1878: BL, Gladstone Papers 44763, fo. 130).

[656] Sir Theodore Martin (1816–1909), who prepared *The Life of His Royal Highness the Prince Consort*, 5 vols (London, 1874–1880), for Queen Victoria. See St Aubyn, *Queen Victoria*, p. 250.

[657] The text of the Anglo-Russian Convention dealing with Bulgaria and Batoum, largely the work of Salisbury and Shuvalov at the Congress of Berlin, was leaked by Charles Marvin, a clerk at the Foreign Office, to the *Globe*. It appeared in the newspaper on 14 June. See C. Marvin, *Our Public Offices* (London, 1879), p. 203.

document and yielded up the point. It certainly was a very shifty answer, and it is only one more of the many things of late which place Salisbury in a very new light. We had a very curious scene in the House later, Richmond being questioned whether the agreement was authentic or not and declining to give a distinct answer.[658]

Wednesday 19 June (London)

An interesting dinner at Escotts.[659] I met amongst others Yates,[660] Chamberlain[661] and R. Earle.[662] Yates is not unlike what I expected, a rather coarse, rough, shrewd man. Chamberlain with a good deal of refinement both of manner and mind, and great moderation of language, but I doubt whether there is as much force of character as he has been credited with. Amongst other things he described himself in the course of conversation as a radical but as no revolutionist, and as having been greatly alarmed at the risks which war with a divided public opinion would entail on the older and settled institutions of the country. He said he did not believe that there was much socialism in any class and he praised the singular absence of envy in all classes of Englishmen. He attributed this to the fine graduation of one class from or into another. Earle struck me as much older than when I knew him and as having gone through a great deal of trouble or illness, I do not know which. I do not know whether I like him or whether he is a man to be trusted; he is certainly clever.

Conversation ranged over many subjects, chiefly political. All agreed that the publication of the Agreement had made a great difference in the situation, and all agreed that Salisbury's political position was much damaged.[663] The general impression I see is that he has calculated on Disraeli's speedy demise, and that now that D.

---

[658]The Eastern Question. The Congress – Alleged Agreement between Russia and England: *Hansard*, 17 June 1878, CCXL, Richmond, cols 1569–1572.

[659]Thomas Hay Sweet Escott (1844–1924), journalist, editor of the *Fortnightly Review* (1882–1886).

[660]Edmund Yates (1831–1894), editor of *The World* from 1874.

[661]Joseph Chamberlain (1836–1914), Lib. MP for Birmingham (1876–1886), Lib. Unionist MP for Birmingham West (1886–1914), President of the Board of Trade (1880–1885), President of the Local Government Board (1886), Secretary of State for the Colonies (1895–1903).

[662]Ralph Anstruther Earle (1835–1879), former private secretary to Disraeli (1858), Con. MP for Berwick (1859) and for Maldon (1865–1868), Parliamentary Secretary to the Poor Law Board (1866–1867).

[663]See C. Howard and P. Gordon, *The Cabinet Journal of Dudley Ryder, Viscount Sandon*, Bulletin of the Institute of Historical Research, Special Supplement No. 10 (November 1974), pp. 25–33.

is physically to all appearances much better he finds himself in much difficulty. Yates thinks D. is at the height of his success. He seems, I think, to anticipate a very considerable success from the Congress and an early dissolution.

Monday 1 July (London)

Came up by early train. Greenwood, with many other guests, came to lunch. He was shy and nervous at first, but Eveline's geniality soon dissolved this and he became happier and talked freely. There is evidently a plan for a President at Constantinople, a protectorate of a great part of Asia Minor, a treaty with Russia to respect as final the new Armenian boundary (such treaty probably to be more or less taken note of by the Congress), and perhaps an annexation of Cyprus or some territory near Aleppo contemplated. There is also an Anglo-Austrian agreement, but he thinks that this has already broken down and failed.

Afterwards I went to a meeting on the Armenian claims in the Jerusalem Chamber, the Dean of Westminster in the chair.[664] I spoke and rather more strongly on the Eastern question than I have yet spoken, but was warmly received. The meeting was extremely friendly. I think it was successful.

Monday 8 July (Hurstbourne)

This evening I received a telegram from R. Herbert telling me that Cyprus is to be taken over and G. Wolseley to go out as first governor;[665] and a few hours afterwards I read in the *Daily Telegraph* the announcement not only of this but of a defensive alliance with Turkey and a protectorate of Asia Minor.[666]

---

[664] Meeting of the Anglo-Armenian Committee, where Carnarvon moved a resolution for the creation of a separate Armenian Province.

[665] Salisbury and Disraeli had secretly negotiated with the Sultan the cession of Cyprus to Britain in return for a defensive alliance with Britain. It was signed on 4 June. Because of the publication of the Convention in the *Daily Telegraph*, the Cabinet decided to announce details of it in both Houses of Parliament (Johnson, p. 378). For the full text of the Cyprus Convention, see C.W.J. Orr, *Cyprus under British Rule* (London, 1918), pp. 35–41.

[666] 'England and Turkey: a defensive treaty', *Daily Telegraph*, 8 July 1878, p. 5.

It is a tremendously large measure of policy, a *casse-cou politique*, proving at least Disraeli's absolute ascendancy over his Cabinet. It alters all my plans and I must give up Devonshire for the present.[667]

Tuesday 16 July (London)

This afternoon Disraeli made his triumphal entry into London. I hear it was a considerable affair – nosegays, a vociferatory crowd, carriages, red cloth etc.[668]

Lady Derby called here to tell me that Derby wishes to speak after Granville on Thursday. I at once assented. She told me among other things that Derby had written to F. Stanley to tell him that he must not depend upon him at the next Election, in other words, that Derby's influence would be against him. A fraternal conflict is not a pretty sight, but it must be admitted that F.S. deserves this.[669]

Disraeli and Salisbury returned this afternoon, receiving an ovation from a very motley assemblage, Salisbury completely effaced by Disraeli and patronised by him, a very curious spectacle, and how different in everything from Salisbury's return from Constantinople when Lady Derby drove down to the station to receive him and he came and dined alone with me in Bruton Street. How wonderful are all these revolutions of the wheel of Fortune. The political future is as strangely uncertain as it can be. The Whigs are in a state of disintegration; it is very much the result of their hatred of Gladstone.

Friday 26 July (London)

Came up to town by early train. Saw Bath who has lately provided with all information, political and social.

Rosebery[670] brought on his question as to the Secret Anglo-Russian agreement. He spoke with very considerable ability and though he is not popular in the House, he is certainly very clever.[671] Salisbury's

---

[667] Carnarvon's subsequent disillusionment with the Convention is described in D.E. Lee, *Great Britain and the Cyprus Convention Policy of 1878* (Cambridge, MA, 1934), p. 145.

[668] Disraeli had signed the Treaty on 13 July. He arrived back in London three days later. See Buckle, *Disraeli*, VI, pp. 345–346.

[669] See Vincent, *Derby*, IV, p. 31 for further details.

[670] Archibald Philip Primrose (1847–1929), 5th Earl Rosebery (1868), Under-Secretary of State at the Home Office (1881), Lord Privy Seal (1885), Foreign Secretary (1886, 1892–1894), Leader of the Liberal Party (1894–1896), Prime Minister and Lord Privy Seal (1894–1895).

[671] *Hansard*, CCXLII, 26 July, 1878, cols 344–351.

answer was a vindication of his own veracity, but it was not successful though clever: he avoided all the broader parts of the question.[672] I then spoke. The House was not in a very sympathetic condition but they listened with a great deal of attention, the Government Bench evidently not liking my criticisms. I cut short a great deal I had intended to say, but perhaps I said enough. I hope so.[673] Bath spoke, in parts with a good deal of ability but as usual unequally.[674] The Government made no reply and the evening generally I should say was a damaging one to them.

In *The Times* of today my correspondence in the Middlesex magistrates case appears. It is not pleasant reading for the Government; one or two people spoke to me of it.[675]

Friday 9 August (Highclere)

A lovely day. We had tea at the Lake.

How curiously Disraeli has thrown his spell over everyone. My Uncle,[676] in walking down to the Lake, got on the subject of politics and entreated me not to abandon my own side to join the Liberals, showing that this is a subject which is sometimes under discussion in Liberal Society. He then went on to talk on this matter but in such a way as to show me that on the whole he sympathised far more with Disraeli's policy than with that of the Opposition. Later Fan[677] began eulogising the annexation of Cyprus.

The truth is the Liberal Party are desperately demoralized and broken; the leaders have lost all courage and I suspect all heart and faith in themselves. Bryce[678] told me the other day that Forster, and someone

[672] Ibid., Salisbury, cols 332–339.

[673] Ibid., Carnarvon, cols 359–366.

[674] Ibid., Bath, cols 371–381.

[675] At the end of June, Carnarvon had been offered the chairmanship of the Middlesex Court of Quarter Sessions, a post previously held by Salisbury. On learning that ten magistrates had formed a committee to secure another candidate, Carnarvon immediately declined. See 'Middlesex Sessions', *The Times*, 26 July 1878, p. 10.

[676] Not identified.

[677] Possibly Frances G. C. Herbert (d. 1885), Carnarvon's cousin.

[678] James Bryce (1838–1922), 1st Viscount Bryce (1914), lawyer, historian, and statesman. Professor of Civil Law, Oxford University (1870–1893), Lib. MP for Tower Hamlets division (1880–1885) and for Aberdeen South (1885–1906), Chancellor, Duchy of Lancaster (1892–1894), President of the Board of Trade (1894–1895).

else whose name I forget, said to him that they did not anticipate a return of the Liberals to Office for 15 years. If they really think this they are for the present gone as a party.

Sunday 1 September (The Moult)

A lovely day. In the afternoon I took a long walk with Froude and I sat up late into the night after dinner in conversation with him. He is a very interesting character and one with which I have only come into close, perhaps intimate contact, during the last three years. His own sorrows and mine perhaps made the first tie[679] and then his mission to South Africa brought us into very confidential relations. I have found him to be entirely trustworthy, to be on many subjects very much in sympathy with myself and replete with ability, information and mental elasticity. At times, as recently when in rather confidential moods and relations, he betrays an almost weariness of life, but at other times he is extraordinarily fresh and elastic, entering into almost every occupation and interest. Physically he is very fresh, swimming, walking and shooting: mentally he turns from one subject to another with great rapidity and ease. He is now writing a *Life of Julius Caesar* and I see how his mind is constantly working on it.[680]

Monday 14 October (The Coppice)

I found Phillimore brimming over with the Afghan question,[681] but he is looking at it only from the International Law side and though I think the Government have set the principles of International Law at defiance as they have every other principle I do not think either that the Ameer can be treated exactly as the independent sovereign of a European country nor do I believe that English people are prepared

---

[679] Froude's wife had died in February 1874.

[680] Published as *Caesar: a sketch* (London, 1879).

[681] On 3 August, the Cabinet had agreed that the Ameer of Afghanistan should accept a British mission to Kabul, and dismiss the Russian mission already there. On 8 September, Lytton sent troops under Gen. Sir Neville Chamberlain to enforce these demands but was halted at the Khyber Pass. Hardy, now Cranbrook, as War Minister, favoured Lytton's initiative. Salisbury had in fact earlier written to Cranbrook, requesting him to stop the mission. See M. Lutyens, *The Lyttons in India: an account of Lord Lytton's Viceroyalty, 1876–1880* (London, 1979), p. 133. On 26 October, the Cabinet agreed to an ultimatum being given to the Ameer unless the British mission was accepted. As no reply was received, troops were ordered to advance on 20 November.

so to treat him. To my mind neither the politics nor even the morality
of the question require such a course on our part. But the position
of affairs is very serious. I have heard from Townsend on the subject
and I do not doubt his information – Lytton says that two years ago
(at least) he had secret instructions to seize Afghanistan or a part of
it, that he took steps accordingly and that now when he was ready
for the blow he has been stopped by the Home Government. But
apparently the Home Government have only delayed action for a
while and are prepared to go on this rash enterprise in the spring
of next year – Salisbury it is said telegraphed to Lytton to delay and
that he (Salisbury) "*could/would* utilise the six months in Europe", an
extraordinary telegram, but one which T. assures me was sent. Lytton
is however very angry at the counter order and has been proclaiming
his dissatisfaction right and left.

It is a question perhaps whether Salisbury knows of these secret
instructions. I think he must have known them, for it is hardly possible
that Disraeli and Lytton could alone have been cognizant of such
a matter. But if so, what falseness on the part of Salisbury to the
principles of action which he was always announcing, and to me
personally when in repeated conversations he professed to tell me
everything as to Indian politics, etc.

Sunday 8 December (London)

A long and important talk with Townsend as to the general state of
politics and as to my own individual position. I am not seeking, I do
not desire to return to Office just now. I should prefer to be a while
quiet and have a little home rest, and my vote and speech tomorrow
night will be given without any personal views, but the Liberals are
talking of a Coalition government and at dinner where T. was a few
days ago, with Gladstone, Childers, Mundella[682] and some others there
were five who said they could accept such a ministry of which I was
the head. All this is I think most chimerical and unlikely, as unlikely
as anything could be, but it is important just so far as it shows that I

---

[682]Anthony John Mundella (1825–1897), Radical MP for Sheffield (1868–1885) and
for Sheffield, Brightside division (1885–1897), Vice-President, Committee of Council on
Education (1880–1885), President of the Board of Trade (1886, 1892–1894). Sharing
Carnarvon's views on the Eastern Question, Mundella had regretted Carnarvon's
resignation earlier in the year, calling him 'our watchdog in the Cabinet' (W.H.G. Armytage,
A.J. Mundella: the Liberal background to the Labour movement (London, 1951), p. 182).

am trusted and liked and believed in sufficiently for such a purpose by
some of the leading men on the Liberal side. Tomorrow night will be
a step and a very distinct one I think to take me over to the Opposition
side, and I asked T. how he thought I should be received wherever I
did, or do, go. He said he had no doubt most warmly: that my position
was fully understood and had been.[683]

[683]A vote of censure by the Opposition in both Houses on Government policy had been
fixed for 9 December. The Liberals were confident of success, particularly in the Lords.
Carnarvon was received '*on the whole* with less unfriendly exhibition than I expected' (Diary,
9 December). The next day, the Government triumphed in the Lords by 210 to 65. A
week later, Disraeli wrote whimsically to Lady Chesterfield, 'The name of the new party:
A.B.C.D. party, Aberdeen, Bath, Carnarvon and Derby!!!' (Zetland, II, p. 198).

1879

Tuesday 25 February (London)

I dined with Lady Abercromby alone and heard a great deal from her that was interesting to me. The Queen, when she told her that I had made a speech in support of the Government and the Zulu War,[684] said, "Oh, but you know it is his war." This is another indication of the line that Disraeli has taken. He has, I think it is clear, laid the responsibility of the war on me as the result of my annexation of the Transvaal.[685] Salisbury is, I hear, in much favour with the Queen, and Lady S. is perpetually retailing all sorts of gossip and scandal to the Queen. What is really bad, she tells frequent stories against the Derbys. This is only what I believe she did last summer in London but it is not the less odious.

Thursday 20 March (London)

Some talk with Derby on the Zulu debate on next Friday. He put the case very clearly against Frere.[686] I told him of my personal difficulty in condemning Frere and he was evidently not surprised. So we parted with an understanding on the subject.

---

[684]See Carnarvon's speech in the House of Lords on 13 December: *Hansard*, CCXLIII, cols 1064–1068.

[685]Sir Henry Frere, Governor of Cape Colony and High Commissioner of South Africa, was convinced that confederation in South Africa could be achieved only when the power of the Zulu chief, Cetewayo, was broken. Frere therefore issued an ultimatum to him on 11 December 1878. British forces under Lord Chelmsford entered Zululand on 6 January 1879 and were heavily defeated at Isandhlwana sixteen days later (see A. Lloyd, *The Zulu War 1879* (London, 1973), pp. 67–73). Disraeli, like the rest of the nation, was deeply shocked, and took to his bed. Carnarvon, however, stood by Frere 'as I do not expect that he will have a very warm defence at the hands of the Government' (Carnarvon to Heathcote, 21 February 1879: CP, BL 61074, fo. 211).

[686]Carnarvon told Heathcote, 'My disposition is to say what I can in defence of Frere and not to attack the Ministry' (Carnarvon to Heathcote, 23 March 1879: CP, BL 61075, fo. 9).

Tuesday 25 March (London)

Zulu debate in the House. I spoke to a thin house as it was close upon 8 o'clock when I began, but a very attentive one. On the whole I was tolerably satisfied when I ended with what I had said and the way of saying it, and Bath and Enfield[687] who were there told me that they thought it was quite a good speech, if not better, than they had heard me make. I was about an hour.[688]

Monday 19 May (London)

Derby wrote to propose to come to me to discuss Frere's despatch in yesterday's papers which seems to suggest the abandonment of the Transvaal.[689] I said I should be happy and he came – to argue strongly that the annexation had been an experiment, that it had failed and that it was desirable to give the Government help in getting rid of the bad bargain. My answer generally was that I felt sure that we should soon hear more fully from Frere in explanation of this despatch; that though I was prepared to accept changes and withdrawal of policy if necessary, yet that I thought this was particularly a case for great caution and for no hurry, and one too in which it is quite fair to let the Government find their own way out of the difficulty in which they have placed themselves or been placed. I afterwards wrote to him again in much the same sense. But it is quite clear to me that it would be a very foolish thing for me at all events to take the initiative. If I

---

[687] George Henry Byng (1830–1898), Viscount Enfield (1860), 3rd Earl of Strafford (1886). Lib. MP for Tavistock (1852–1857) and for Middlesex (1857–1874), Parliamentary Secretary to the Poor Law Board (1865–1866), Under-Secretary of State at the Foreign Office (1871–1874).

[688] A resolution in the Lords condemning Frere's ultimatum leading to war and stating that the conduct of affairs should be taken out of his hands, was lost by 61 to 159 votes (*Hansard*, CCXLIV, 25 March 1879, Carnarvon, cols 1645–1657, Kimberley, cols 1670–1678). Frere later wrote to Carnarvon, thanking him for 'your noble defence of me in the House of Lords [. . .]. We have all been like the crew of a ship in a hurricane – so hard at work saving the ship from foundering that I have barely time to keep the official log' (Frere to Carnarvon, 7 May 1879: CP, BL 60797A, fo. 109).

[689] Carnarvon wrote to Derby the next day, 'After seeing you I learnt that the Government are not aware whether the despatch published in the *Standard* is accurately given or not' (Carnarvon to Derby, 20 May 1879: Derby Papers, 920 DER (15)). Headed 'The Boer memorial to the Queen', the despatch set out the substance of a meeting with the Boers six miles from Pretoria, at which a memorial was presented stating that 'their [the Boers'] independence was unjustly taken away from them by the Act of Annexation'.

must accept the abandonment of the annexation, I am anyhow not the person to propose it.[690]

Tuesday 27 May (London)

I made an enquiry in the House as to the relations of G. Wolseley to the present Lieutenant-Governors of Natal and the Transvaal.[691] It is clear that he is sent out in a military capacity rather than a civil one though his appointment does two things: supersedes Chelmsford and gives a very decided buffer to Frere. I almost expect Frere now to resign.[692]

I made a short speech on a Malay question afterwards brought forward by Stanley of Alderley.[693]

We dined at the Goschens, met the Gladstones and Childers amongst others.

Friday 27 June (London)

Later I brought up my Armenian case in the House of Lords. Elsie[694] and Winifred went into the Peeresses' Gallery to hear. I think my statement was fair enough. Salisbury's reply was in argument very weak, and the ground he took up in the repudiation of all responsibility in Asia Minor was extraordinarily inconsistent with all that was said

[690]Derby commented after the meeting, 'I always doubted the wisdom of the policy of annexation, & assented to it reluctantly. It was a mistake, & one for which Carnarvon as colonial secretary is primarily responsible' (Vincent, *Derby*, IV, p. 127).

[691]South Africa – Natal and the Transvaal. Appointment of Sir Garnet Wolseley as High Commissioner: *Hansard*, CCXLVI, 27 May 1879, Carnarvon cols 1329–1330.

[692]The Cabinet decided on 19 May to replace Frere and Chelmsford, though the Queen was reluctant to consent. Chelmsford was sent back to England. On 27 May, Disraeli wrote to the Queen on the Cabinet deliberations of the previous day, 'It was with much difficulty that Lord Beaconsfield secured the arrangement, that Sir Bartle Frere should remain as High Commissioner of the Cape Colony and its dependencies. These are more than 1,000 miles from the seat of war' (Buckle, *Disraeli*, VI, p. 432).

[693]Henry Edward John Stanley (1827–1903), 3rd Baron Stanley of Alderley (1869), orientalist and diplomat. The motion introduced was 'Concerning the rights of succession following the death of the Sultan of Johore': *Hansard*, CCXLVI, 27 May 1879, Stanley of Alderley, cols 1341–1346, Carnarvon, cols 1347–1348. The motion was brought on by Stanley, 'that strange animal compounded of foolishness and mischief' (Diary, 15 May 1879).

[694]Elisabeth Catherine Howard (1856–1929), first daughter of Henry Howard of Greystoke Castle and Charlotte Long, married Carnarvon in December 1878. She was Carnarvon's first cousin, and twenty-five years younger than him.

last year as anything that was ever said in Parliament.[695] It was a most strange speech, to which Morley[696] and Granville both gave a very good answer. What is the meaning of it? Did Salisbury in Cabinet object to the English Protectorate and now, when in difficulty, go back to his old opinions? Disraeli has not been in the House the last two nights. One way or another I think the Government are failing.

Friday 11 July (London)

This evening Mr. Corry met me after the Committee as I was going into the House and asked for a few minutes conversation. He then asked me from Lord Beaconsfield whether I would be willing to undertake the Chairmanship of the Commission moved for the other evening by H. Chaplin[697] on the agricultural distress, its causes, etc.[698] I said it was a very large and important matter and must take a little time to consider. I promised an answer by Sunday afternoon.

Tues 15 July (London)

A debate in the House of Lords on the Vivisection bill[699] introduced by Lord Truro.[700] Beauchamp's tone offended me much and I attacked him rather severely for it.[701]

[695]Treaty of Berlin–Armenia: *Hansard*, CCXLVII, 27 June 1879, cols 811–830. Carnarvon referred to the articles in the treaty that promised improvements and reforms by the Turks in the treatment of Armenians (ibid., cols 811–819). Salisbury, in reply, 'repudiated any responsibility for the acts of the Turkish Government' (ibid., cols 820–826).

[696]Albert Edmund Parker (1843–1905), 3rd Earl of Morley (1864), Lord-in-Waiting to the Queen (1868–1874), Under-Secretary of State for War (1880–1885), Chairman of Committees, House of Lords (1889–1905).

[697]Henry Chaplin (1840–1923), Con. MP for Mid-Lincolnshire (1868–1896) and for Wimbledon (1907–1916), Chancellor, Duchy of Lancaster (1885–1886), President of the Board of Agriculture (1889), President of the Local Government Board (1895–1900), 1st Viscount Chaplin (1916).

[698]An archetypal Tory squire, Chaplin found himself, as a member of the Royal Commission on Agricultural Distress, resisting the efforts of the Radicals to set up peasant proprietors in place of landlords. See E.H.V.T. Stewart, Marchioness of Londonderry, *Henry Chaplin: a memoir* (London, 1926), p. 161.

[699]Cruelty to Animals Bill, second reading: *Hansard*, CCXLVIII, 15 July 1879, cols 419–436.

[700]Charles Robert Wilde (1816–1891), 2nd Baron Truro (1855).

[701]Ibid., Truro, cols 419–422, Beauchamp, cols 422–426. Carnarvon pointed out the need for new legislation because the 1876 Act had undergone so many changes in the Commons during its passing that it was deprived of its effectiveness (ibid., cols 433–434). The second reading was resolved in the negative.

Friday 25 July (Highclere)

I received a letter from Northcote in answer to my last long recapitulatory communication[702] saying that the Government were grateful to me but that they perceived the difference of opinion was wider than they had at first thought and that they would look to some other arrangement.[703] Northcote's letter was very friendly and I wrote him back a few lines in a very friendly tone saying that I thought the Cabinet were quite right in their decision. And I am also very glad to be spared the work [. . .].

I suspect that they desired more of me than I was prepared to give. In one of his letters Disraeli spoke of the difference of opinion between us not only as to the composition but as to the *duties* of the Commission. Did this mean that he wished it to be worked in a class and sectional interest?[704]

Oddly enough with this letter of Northcote's came one from Beach, knowing of course of the breakdown of these negotiations, asking me to take the Chair of a smaller Commission to consider the various military and naval stations abroad, their defence, the mode of defence, the way in which the expense should be divided, etc.

Wednesday 30 July (London)

Beach called on me in Bruton Street to communicate with me as to the Colonial Defence Commission of which he wishes me to take the Chair. He was satisfactory in all he said. He proposes to make the Commission one perfectly fair as regards political parties, Childers, Brassey, myself, L. Simmons, Milne, Barkly. I raised some objection to Milne and Barkly, the first as not adequately representing the modern and scientific view of things, the second as not conferring any real strength on us, and I suggested Holland as a very useful addition, to which he agreed. I also said that I must have Jekyll, to which he

---

[702] Carnarvon had objected to the proposed size of the Commission – fifteen members in all – as well as its composition, 'consisting mainly of tenant farmers with a few politically lightweight landowners' (Carnarvon to Heathcote, 24 July 1879: CP, BL 61075, fo. 51).

[703] The chairmanship of the Commission was offered to the Duke of Richmond, who accepted it. There were twenty members. The report of the Commission was issued in 1882. See F.M.L. Thompson, *English Landed Society in the Nineteenth Century* (London, 1963), p. 309.

[704] Ever suspicious of Disraeli's motives, Carnarvon asserted, 'The chances of making a success of it is very small and in the event of failure making a scapegoat of me would have been irresistible' (Carnarvon to Granville, 1 August 1879 (copy): CP, BL 60773, fo. 119).

assented, as Secretary. Subject to all this, I accepted.[705] I should on the whole have preferred not to have this particular task imposed but I hardly know how to decline.[706] I seem to live in a vicious circle of Royal Commissions but it cannot be helped.

Friday 8 August (London)

I went up to town by myself.

Beach called on me in Bruton Street to discuss and settle the question of the Colonial Defence Commission. It was agreed that the Commission should consist of myself as Chairman, Childers who has accepted, Brassey, Sir L. Simmons, Sir A. Milne, Sir H. Barkly and Holland, if he will serve, with Jekyll as Secretary. The whole affair passed off in a very quiet and friendly manner. But Beach's manner (I can hardly say why) gives me the notion that he is not on the most perfect terms with his colleagues or some of them.

Afterwards a long conversation with Bath who has just returned from his Bulgarian tour, which is still entirely in his mind. He is very bitter against the Government and especially against Salisbury and said to me that he would support even Arch[707] if he could damage the Government and take away from them a seat.

Later I urged the case of the India Museum in the House of Lords, but got an unsatisfactory reply from Hardy.[708] That august body was *in extremis*, scarcely anybody on the Opposition benches and an appearance of more than usual sleepiness and inactivity.

---

[705] Thomas Brassey (1836–1918), Lib. MP for Hastings (1868–1886), later publisher of *Brassey's Naval Manual*; Gen. Sir John Lintorn Arabin Simmons (1821–1903), Inspector-General of Fortifications, War Office (1875–1880); Sir Alexander Milne (1806–1896), Junior Naval Lord, Admiralty (1866–1868, 1872–1876); Sir Henry Barkly; Sir Henry Thurstan Holland; Capt. Herbert Jekyll (1847–1932), private secretary to Carnarvon at the Colonial Office.

[706] Informing Derby of his acceptance as chairman of the Commission, Carnarvon wrote, 'It is a much smaller affair [than the Royal Commission on Agricultural Distress] involving nothing but a moderate amount of trouble' (Carnarvon to Derby, 31 July 1879: Derby Papers, 920 DER (15)). This analysis turned out to be wrong.

[707] Joseph Arch (1826–1919), Organising Secretary and President of the National Union of Labourers (1872), Lib. MP for Norfolk North-west (1885–1886, 1892–1902).

[708] Carnarvon protested at the impending break-up of the India Museum, set up over 100 years previously by the East India Company: *Hansard*, CCXLIX, 8 August 1879, cols 491–492. Hardy commented on Carnarvon's wish to keep the collection together, 'I [. . .] found plenty to do until the House met at the I.O. [India Office] – Carnarvon did not do much as to India Museum' (Johnson, p. 419).

Thursday 14 August (London)

I went up by myself by an early train and took the Chair at an unofficial and informal meeting of the Colonial Defence Commission at the Colonial Office. We discussed preliminaries and I subsequently talked over the results of our discussion with Beach, who, I am bound to say, improves on acquaintance in business. He is I think straightforward and devoid of all shiftiness and he seems to me to be rather wide in his ideas on political matters, and to think more of what is desirable in a Colonial or Imperial than a party point of view. Jekyll, who is Secretary of the Commission, will take notes of all that passes and I therefore need not record it here.[709]

Thursday 13 November (Pixton)

A very heavy post [...]. An important letter from Derby informing me that he had taken his name off the Carlton and giving me his reason, viz. that the "logic of events" in Lancashire had been irresistible and had compelled him to this.[710] I answered him at some length for it was a letter needing a reply.[711]

Monday 29 December (Pixton)

In view of present events and of future contingencies it may perhaps be well, if only to clear my mind, that I should endeavour to put down very briefly what I conceive my political position to be.

I. The Position

(1) There has been extreme bitterness during the last two years towards me by many of the Cabinet and their supporters. All intercourse has ceased and hardly ever a letter passes. The only members of the Cabinet with whom I seem to be on anything like friendly terms are Sandon and Beach, perhaps Northcote.

---

[709] General principles were discussed by the Commission. It was agreed that India should be excluded from their deliberations, that the Commission should handle the self-governing colonies with tact, and that more information was needed on the state of Australian defences. The Commission gave priority to the need for secrecy and a guarantee that their reports would be for the Cabinet only. See D.M. Schurman, ed. J.F. Beeler, *Imperial Defence, 1868–1887* (London, 2000), p. 86.

[710] Derby to Carnarvon, 11 November 1879: CP, BL 60766, fos 76–77. At the same time, he withdrew from local Conservative organizations.

[711] Carnarvon to Derby, 13 November 1879: Derby Papers, DER (15).

(2) As regards political opinion I have long been conscious that I am considerably in advance of all the Government. They might perhaps concede as much as I should but it would be under pressure and not from any conviction. This of itself is not enough to prevent my acting with them. In many Conservative Cabinets there have been individuals by conviction much more Liberal than their colleagues. There are advantages and disadvantages in such conditions which need not be discussed here.

(3) With the general body of the party there is no necessary cause of quarrel. They distrust me and dislike me, but would gladly accept me or anyone else amongst their leaders if it suited party purposes. But a different question arises with regard to the Leaders. I do not trust them *politically* as regards neither convictions nor sound judgement. But this may be said of many other possible Cabinets and the amount of confidence which I should be ready to place in any conceivable Cabinet would after my past experience be limited. But the worst part of the business is that I cannot trust the most important section of the present Cabinet, *personally* as men. I think Beach is straightforward and there are some others whose word like his I would accept in all ordinary transactions, but there are some who are absolutely and as I know by experience, are [*sic*] perpetually intriguing either with or against each other. My offences in their eyes have been great, and after what has passed my political honour and certainly comfort would not be safe unless there were an infusion of some new and purer elements upon which I could count.

(4) But it may be said that there is not enough in this to call for a complete alienation from the party. The answer to this is that the party so far as London politicians and London society are concerned, have completely drawn aside from me. They have endeavoured to mark their displeasure sometimes by personal isolation, sometimes by petty spite. I at least, owe them nothing, and am free to consider my own course of action without the slightest reference to them.

As regards the party generally, the old principles whatever they were worth are gone. The Conservatives have become Tory Democrats avowedly appealing to a combination of the Crown and Populace. What policy they have is flashy and dangerous. They have found out the dangerous secret of appeal to the warlike spirit of the non-tax paying part of the community, and they are such bad financiers that there is a serious risk of permanent mischief.

II.

(1) The question is hardly less difficult when I come to consider my position with the Liberals in office. In a really Radical Government I could have no confidence, or hope, or sympathy. It is very different

as regards the Whigs. With them I have always had many friendly
relations. Socially and intellectually, there are many bonds of union
and much personal kindness has been shown me by many of them,
as indeed by many more advanced Liberals when I have been thrown
over by my supposed friends. Except in Church questions I probably
agree with the Whigs as much as I do with any party and I have
indeed some points of sympathy with some of the best of the more
advanced Liberals. It may easily become a question how a public man
may do most good whether in supporting a Conservative or Liberal
Government. Nothing would be more dangerous I believe than a shift
of the whole political ballast of property towards the Conservative
side. It would be a repetition, but a much more dangerous one, of
what occurred in Mr. Pitt's day. There is a strong tendency already
in this direction and a risk that the Whig or moderate liberal party
should become unduly weakened. It is perhaps possible to render the
greatest service to support and so restrain a Liberal Government.

(2) Gladstone may be an important factor in the future political
arithmetic. To me he is not a cause of apprehension. There are
things I regret and in which I disagree, but I have far more in
common with him than with most living statesmen and I am perfectly
convinced that the very Radical schemes with which he is credited
are wilful misrepresentation or absolute delusions. If I am wrong in
this I have no pretence to understand character and am absolutely
unfit to do another stroke of public work. My belief is that the
Conservative and cautious side of his character largely exceeds the
Liberal and the impulsive side. His political errors are those of a
generous temperament and an unduly strong morality. His merits are
perfect simplicity and truthfulness of character.

III.

(1) What position shall I take up when Parliament meets? Derby
having to all intents and purposes, if not openly, joined the opposition,
my impression is that it will be wise to retain my present seat, to watch
events and not to attack the Government unnecessarily. With the
general election change must come. Both parties must declare their
policy and it will now be time enough for me to take a more decided
course. Morally I feel quite free to act, as I may think best; politically
I believe there is a road open to me in either direction.

1880

Tuesday 24 August (London)

I came up to town for the Employers' Liability bill[712] and a question on Cape affairs which I had intended to ask, but which I found had never been placed on the Orders of the day in consequence of the House not sitting yesterday. I spoke however on the Employers' bill. Whilst in the House D[israeli] wrote on a slip of paper the following "do you think you could meet a few of our friends tomorrow morning at 11 o'clock at No. 1 Seamore Place? Beaconsfield". I nodded assent and so in this brief fashion I once more return to the councils of the Party, a curious little episode.

Wednesday 25 August (Highclere)

In the morning I attended the meeting at 1 Seamore Place (Rothschilds)[713] and found about 9 or 10 others – members of the late Cabinet, D. of Buccleuch and Aveland[714] – summoned I conclude for the Hares and Rabbits bill.[715] The greatest part of the time was

[712] Second reading: *Hansard*, CCLV, 24 August 1880, cols 1989–1991. Although Carnarvon believed that employers should be held responsible for accidents to their employees in certain circumstances, he added, 'The masters had a great deal to answer for in the past, and now the men tried to get more than they were entitled to.'

[713] Ferdinand James de Rothschild (1839–1898), Baron Rothschild (1874), Lib. Unionist MP for Aylesbury (1885–1898). Carnarvon and Disraeli differed on the reason for Carnarvon's presence at the meeting (see entry for 24 August). Disraeli wrote to Lady Bradford, 'Today I had my late colls. Duke of Buccleuch, Bradford, Aveland and Carnarvon! The latter will surprise you. It was at his own request!' (Buckle, *Disraeli*, VI, p. 588).

[714] Gilbert Henry Heathcote-Drummond Willoughby (1830–1910), 2nd Baron Aveland (1867), 1st Earl of Ancaster (1892).

[715] The Hares and Rabbits Bill, later the Ground Game Bill, was intended to redress the position whereby the relative value of sporting rights was the liability of the landlord. Under the bill, the tenant could recover a portion of the poor rate from the landlord. The debate on the second reading was due to take place on 1 September. Carnarvon told Cranbrook, 'I shall not come up on Monday [30 August]. If I were to come I must vote with Redesdale and I do not desire to place myself in needless opposition to the advice which Disraeli has given' (Carnarvon to Cranbrook, 28 August 1880: Cranbrook Papers, HA3 T501/362). Both the Ground Game Bill and the Employers Liability Bill received the Royal Assent on 7 September.

occupied in discussing the Employers' Liability bill: and it was finally settled that Disraeli should move that the bill should be limited (like the Ballot Act) in its operation to two years. It was a fair and friendly discussion. Afterwards we began to discuss Hares and Rabbits. I was on the whole in favour of rejecting it on 2nd Reading, and was ready to move the rejection but Disraeli was afraid of it. On the whole there is so great unawareness that I think there will be no opposition. I believe they are wrong but I do not think that it matters very greatly.

Thursday 26 August (London)

I came up again for the Committee on the Employers' Liability bill. I found a large muster in the House and we had an animated debate in which I spoke a good many times, but there is little or no report in the papers of what passed.[716] The Duke of Argyll made two or three of the best speeches I have ever heard from him, because they were very quiet and well reasoned.[717] Kimberley made an indiscreet admission of which I took advantage.[718]

[716] Carnarvon spoke four times in the debate: *Hansard* CCLVI, 26 August 1880, cols 61, 62, 67–68, 79.

[717] George Douglas Campbell (1823–1900), 8th Duke of Argyll (1847), Postmaster-General (1855–1858), Secretary of State for India (1868–1874), Lord Privy Seal (1880–1881). Ibid., cols 69–71, 82–85.

[718] Carnarvon took Kimberley to task for his statement that 'the Bill was introduced in the interest of the workman alone. Was the Bill intended to apply only to one single class in the community?' (ibid., cols 67–68).

1881

Saturday 16 April (London)

Called again at Lord Beaconsfield [*sic*] to enquire and had a talk with Barrington.[719] He told me a characteristic story of Disraeli, when very ill, if not at quite the worst stage. The Queen wrote a letter to him about himself[720] but at that time as no one was allowed to see him but the doctors: so Barrington, to whom it was sent under flying seal, handed it to the doctors to read. Whereupon Disraeli insisted on seeing Barrington, who found him with the letter crushed up in his hand, and refusing to allow it to be read by the doctor. He said, "I have sent for you as the only person in the house who is a Privy Councillor and who ought to read this to me" – very curious and characteristic, with some humour but on the whole more reality.

He has been, Barrington told me, very anxious to know his state, repeatedly asking if the doctors thought that he would die, and was in danger. Every sort of nostrum has been sent or suggested, the last being a proposal to put a two foot long pipe down his throat as a certain and infallible cure! There is a very wide interest in and anxiety about him, and each time I have been there I have seen a crowd round the door, waiting and watching.

Lansdowne, seeing the windows open as he passed the house, called to see me and we had some talk on political matters, particularly the Irish land bill.[721] He dislikes it much, but his tone is that of a man who thinks it must pass. Lowe, whom he had previously met, said to him, "You ought to be thankful it is no worse." He believes that Bright and Chamberlain are now the governing spirits in the Cabinet.

Easter Day 17 April (London)

Called at Disraeli's and saw Barrington. Disraeli seems to be holding his ground but it is clearly very precarious. I heard a story of him today

---

[719]Barrington had been acting as Disraeli's private secretary in the absence of Corry.

[720]The Queen wrote on 3 April from Osborne (Blake, *Disraeli*, p. 747).

[721]The bill was introduced by Gladstone on 7 April to meet the demands of the Land League for the 3 Fs – fair rents, free sale, and fixity tenure. For the bill's background, see P. Bew, *Land and the National Question in Ireland, 1858–82* (Dublin, 1979), pp. 145–151.

which I believe to be true. The Queen sent during a previous part of his illness to propose to come to see him, to which he said, "No – no – do not let her come. She only wants to send a message by me to Albert." It sounds like him.

Townsend dined here – very agreeable. He says that all sorts of intrigues are going on amongst the Conservatives as to the succession to the leadership, and of the three, Richmond, Cairns, Salisbury, he believes Richmond has the best chance. But his name is unknown in the large towns, he has no real ability and Townsend quickly added he is weighted with four dukedoms – one he inherits, one that he covets, one that he has stolen and one that he does not like.[722]

Tuesday 19 April (Hampton Lodge)

This morning I had a telegram announcing the death of Lord Beaconsfield at 4 a.m. It is a large character disappearing off the stage, great qualities, coupled doubtless with great faults, but a man who will be a puzzle and a subject of wonder. I am personally very glad that I returned in time to call and to send him a message. I wrote a few lines to Barrington in which I said that I hoped that he had found an opportunity of conveying my message to Lord B.[723]

Wednesday 20 April (Hampton Lodge)

Received two letters of some consequence – one from Cairns enclosing a copy of his late speech on Transvaal matters,[724] written evidently with the strongest desire to be friendly to which I replied at once in the same friendly tone,[725] the other from Gladstone, asking me to serve on the new Commission to consider the ecclesiastical laws.[726] To this I think I must reply in the negative.[727] I have not time for more work of this kind: the defence Commission is quite enough for me and will not be an easy task. The letter is not a very satisfactory one. It is a formal one with Gladstone's signature but copied out by a clerk giving

[722]Charles Henry Gordon-Lennox was 6th Duke of Richmond, Duke of Lennox, Duke of Aubigny, and Duke of Gordon.
[723]Carnarvon did not attend Disraeli's funeral at Hughenden because of a severe cold (Diary, 26 April 1881).
[724]*Hansard*, 31 March 1881, CCLX, cols 264–278.
[725]Carnarvon to Cairns, 20 April 1881: Cairns Papers, TNA, PRO 30/51/8, fos 121–125.
[726]Gladstone to Carnarvon, 20 April 1881: CP, BL 60773, fo. 17.
[727]Carnarvon to Gladstone, 23 April 1881: Gladstone Papers, BL 44469, fo. 144.

no information as to objects, number, chairman, etc. This looks like a large body like what I remember the Ritual Commission was.

I have heard from Barrington saying that he did give Lord Beaconsfield my message, the last indeed that he communicated to him. I am glad.

Thursday 12 May (London)

Barrington asked me when in the House whether I would give my name to the Committee forming to consider a public memorial to Lord Beaconsfield,[728] and I assented. I had rather the request should not have been made, but being made I did not like to refuse.

My estimate of his character is not at all affected by the exaggerated and sometimes most false and absurd eulogies; but I think him as I have long thought, a man of genius who from public service is entitled to an honour which he shares with others, also eminent for public work. My difference with him was confined to one question of policy (for other questions grew out of the first) and but for that one I should have gone on with him, I conclude, to the end of his government. My name therefore on the Committee is a sign that there was no personal ill will or quarrel and I think will be so understood.

Saturday 28 May (London)

A very long conversation with Northcote, ranging over many of the most important of present and pressing questions – the state of feeling in the country, House of Commons, London – the action of the Whigs as regards the Irish Land bill[729] – who make furious noises but who are terrified beyond measure at it being supposed that they have formed a cave and who are therefore totally unreliable – the threatening of Free trade and Protection lines in the towns and as he tells me in some parts of the country – and lastly many matters which occurred after I left the Cabinet. Amongst these he explained to me his apparent want of sincerity in the House of Commons, when he let them adjourn for the Easter (or Whitsuntide) holidays with the idea that there was nothing fresh to be done or in contemplation and the next day the news of the Indian troops being sent to Malta appeared. It was all owing to Lytton, who was certainly as bad a Governor-General as

---

[728] In Westminster Abbey.
[729] Land Law (Ireland) Bill, committee stage, second night: *Hansard*, 27 May 1881, CCLXI, cols 1464–1524.

could well be. But Northcote really was not untruthful, though he could not afterwards explain.[730]

Monday 20 June (London)

A meeting at Northcote's to consider course and amendments on Irish Land bill. Present, Northcote, Salisbury, Stanley, Smith, Sandon, J. Manners and Gibson.[731]

We discussed and settled various questions of detail on the bill, then some discussion as to Transvaal, then some conversation as to Tunis affair. Smith and some House of Commons members said the wish there was that something should be authoritatively stated to the effect that nothing further had been said or promised to France as to Tunis than that which had appeared in the parliamentary papers. Salisbury stated distinctly that nothing further had passed, but he did not seem very anxious that any discussion should take place.[732]

Househunting again.[733]

Tuesday 5 July (London)

Heavy day's work at the Commission.[734] We examined Northbrook who gave some remarkable evidence, admitting that the French Navy was very nearly equal to ours and in some classes of ships actually superior.[735] He evidently was not quite easy.

---

[730] In March 1878, because of the threat from Russia, Disraeli ordered Lytton to send 7,000 native troops to Malta. When Parliament adjourned on 15 April, the next day it was announced that Indian troops were to be despatched to the island. See Lutyens, *The Lyttons in India*, pp. 122–123.

[731] Edward Gibson (1837–1913), 1st Baron Ashbourne (1885). Con. MP for Dublin University (1875), Attorney-General for Ireland (1877–1878), Lord Chancellor of Ireland (1885, 1886–1892, 1895–1905).

[732] French imperialistic aspirations led to troops being sent to Tunis in April. On 12 May, the Treaty of Bardo appeared to have successfully settled the matter but, by June, the activity of rebel forces led to an army of occupation being despatched.

[733] Carnarvon's London house at 14 Bruton Street had been sold on 11 June. 'It is a relief to be free of it for it is an enormously expensive house to maintain and I have no pleasant recollections of it' (Carnarvon to Heathcote, 20 June 1881: CP, BL 61076, fo. 183).

[734] Imperial Defence Commission.

[735] Northbrook told a colleague three months later, 'The late Government let the shipbuilding go down too much, and I am trying to set it right as well as I can without asking for any serious increase in the estimates' (Mallet, *Thomas George, Earl of Northbrook*, p. 202).

Fig. 5 Earl of Carnarvon at his desk in his study, Highclere Castle, *c.*1880.

Attended also an ex-cabinet meeting at Northcotes, but I was not able to stay for more than a short time. Dined in the evening at the Northcotes.

Thursday 21 July (London)

Heavy Commission day, the last sitting except one, to wind up our present business in August, after which we adjourn to probably the end of October or beginning of November.

In the House of Lords I had a long talk with Shaftesbury, who was in a very cheerful mood, and told a variety of anecdotes, amongst others this which he had had from Palmerston. When Prince Albert was yet alive he was perplexed as to what he would do to instil into the mind of the Prince of Wales "a greater sense of reserve," and accordingly determined to send him to the Holy Land, which was done.[736]

Monday 1 August (London)

Elsie and I came up for the second reading of the Land bill.

A long debate in the House. It was good but to my mind not so good as many a debate which I have heard there or as good as it should have been for the occasion. The consciousness that it was to a certain extent a sham fight and that there would be no division weighed on every speaker and affected the speech. In particular I thought Salisbury was below his best level, but for some time past I have thought him less good than formerly. I had told him I would speak or not as I was wanted and as there were many speakers I remained silent. Perhaps I may say something on the third.

Dunraven's speech[737] was a curious see saw, Lansdowne's was good.[738]

Monday 8 August (London)

I went up alone but with our departing guests, leaving Elsie at Highclere. The House of Lords received the report and took the third reading of the Irish Land Bill, and on this last I made a speech which was answered by Granville, who looked very ill, barely recovered from a very severe fit of gout. It is remarkable how his presence seems to strengthen the Government. During his absence they have been weaker than weak, Kimberley sometimes losing temper, Carlingford extremely feeble and the Chancellor[739] much too forensic to be forcible. But Granville seems to give at once a new character to the discussion and makes himself felt. The debate which followed was not a very vigorous one.[740]

[736]The Prince, accompanied by his tutor, landed at Jaffa on 31 March 1862 and spent five weeks touring scriptural sites.

[737]Windham Thomas Wyndham-Quin (1841–1926), 4th Earl of Dunraven (1871), Under-Secretary of State for the Colonies (1885–1886).

[738]Land Law (Ireland) Bill, first night: *Hansard*, CCLXIV, 1 August 1881, Salisbury, cols 254–270, Lansdowne, cols 277–301, Dunraven, cols 320–333.

[739]Sir Roundell Palmer (1812–1895), Baron Selborne (1872), 1st Earl of Selborne (1882). Lib. MP for Richmond (1861–1872), Attorney-General (1863–1866), Lord Chancellor (1872–1874, 1880–1885).

[740]*Hansard*, CCLXIV, 8 August 1881, Carlingford, 1170–1179 *passim*, Selborne, col. 1176, Kimberley, col. 1177, Carnarvon, cols 1180–1186, Granville, cols 1186–1188. Third reading agreed to.

Tuesday 9 August (London – Highclere)

I had a very busy morning [. . .] and finally got to Northcote's by
11.30 for a private caucus there, to discuss the course to be taken as to
our Amendments on the Land bill.

Present Gibson, Salisbury, Smith, J. Manners, Sandon, Northcote,
D. of Northumberland and self. Salisbury declared himself determined
to vote for his own amendments when they came back from
the Commons. I doubt whether the rest, except the D. of
Northumberland, quite liked the uncompromising temper of
Salisbury's line of proceeding but they assented. No one believes that
Gladstone will dissolve, the worst they anticipate is an adjournment of
Parliament to October to resume the discussion of the amendments, if
one cannot come to an agreement. But the most serious contingency
is the coming winter in Ireland and Salisbury seems here to be alive
to this and to be prepared for a falling away in the House of the Irish
landlords. Portarlington[741] last night showed what may be expected in
this quarter.[742]

Saturday 13 August (Highclere)

Yesterday morning Elsie and I went up to town by the early train,
in pouring rain [. . .]. A little after 2 I went to the Peers meeting at
Salisbury's.[743] It was fairly attended. Salisbury made a rather combative
speech which was a good deal cheered. No one offered any expression
of a different opinion and I came to the conclusion, though not without
surprise, that the very large majority present agreed with him against
compromise. It is true that he spoke of resisting the Commons' view
with some idea of coming afterward to an agreement but he did not
disguise that notion of an agreement was thus conceding entirely to
our amendments. Cairns who was sitting by me evidently did not
agree in what Salisbury said but neither he nor I said anything. He
felt it as difficult I think from his position as I did from mine to seem
to oppose.

In the House matters opened badly and they went from bad to
worse. Salisbury's words and manner were hard and unconciliatory,

[741] Seymour William Dawson-Damer (1832–1892), 4th Earl of Portarlington (1889), Con.
MP for Portarlington (1857–1865, 1868–1880).
[742] Speech on the Land Law (Ireland) Bill, in favour of the measure: *Hansard*, CCLXIV, 9
August 1881, cols 1188–1189.
[743] Gladstone had rejected the majority of the Lords' amendments to the bill, which were
considered in the Commons between 9 and 11 August. The Peers' meeting was called to
consider the Commons' amendments.

and we reinserted all our amendments by the force of numbers without an attempt to come to any compromise or common line.[744] As the evening went on a good many peers spoke to me – Bathurst,[745] Jersey,[746] Clinton,[747] Cadogan, (and Shaftesbury and Bath very strongly) deprecating the course pursued and expressing great alarm. Then Northcote, Gibson, Cross, Smith came into the House and talked to me in the same strain saying that the House of Commons was getting into a great ferment, that the Speaker[748] was anxious and that the results would be very unfortunate. I only agreed too well in all they said; but I found myself in an awkward position. However after some conversation with Cairns who deprecated Salisbury's line of action very strongly I said something to Salisbury to warn him that there was great dissatisfaction. At first he was incredulous or affected to be so; then he showed that he did not like it, but having said so much I left the matter to work.[749]

This morning I attended another private meeting at Northcote's where I found all the H. of Commons members very seriously alarmed, believing that we are in the midst of a very grave crisis. The risks are that the Government may dissolve (unlikely) or resign, or adjourn the consideration of the bill for two months, or drop the bill which without exception they thought fraught with the direst consequences in Ireland. All of them also were evidently impressed with the idea of Salisbury's headstrong, reckless, tendencies, and determined to resist them, but they seemed not much to like this part of the matter. The D. of Northumberland, Cairns and I were the only three Peers present. We very soon got into the discussion and I strongly represented the feeling of dissatisfaction afloat amongst the Conservative Peers and with all the others urged a reasonable compromise on the different aspects of continuing. Salisbury was very stiff and did not actually promise to give up anything but he found every one against him and we broke up with the understanding that

---

[744] *Hansard*, CCLXIV, 13 August 1881, cols 1612–1706.

[745] Allen Alexander Bathurst (1832–1892), 6th Earl Bathurst (1878), Con. MP for Cirencester (1857–1878).

[746] Victor Albert Child-Villiers (1845–1915), 7th Earl of Jersey (1859), Governor of New South Wales (1891–1893).

[747] Charles Henry Rolle (1834–1904), 20th Baron Clinton (1866), Under-Secretary of State for India (1867–1868).

[748] Henry Brand (1814–1892), Speaker of the House of Commons, noted in his diary, 'Still much excitement on the possible or rather probable disagreement with the Lords on their amendments on the Land Bill.' He wrote to Gladstone the same day, impressing on him the advantage of an adjournment as compared with a prorogation in the event of continuing disagreement (Brand, Diary, 13 August 1881: Brand Papers, BRA/2/11).

[749] Carnarvon did not speak in the debate.

Gibson should at once try to effect a transaction with Herschell[750] on Clause 8 and that we should endeavour afterwards to compromise the other points of difference. He also consented to call another meeting of Peers on Tuesday, and we are to meet in private conclave on Monday at 2.30. But he has agreed to all this most reluctantly and I am afraid he is disposed to avoid any real concession if he can. He is I much fear justifying all the predictions that have been made of his impracticability on violence. We are on the edge of a collision of the two Houses. Cairns gave very prudent and conciliatory counsel.

Monday 15 August (London)

I came up by myself leaving E. at Highclere and drove at once to Northcote's, where we had another ex-cabinet meeting.[751] It was a meeting in which every one was in favour of coming to terms with the Government and H. of Commons except Salisbury who was I thought very stiff.[752] The differences between him and Cairns showed themselves at one moment very strongly. For Cairns defined the functions of the H. of Lords in such a crisis as this as of a body to suspend, debate, modify but not veto questionable legislation, to which Salisbury took very decided exception in language which showed a good [deal] of pent up personal feeling. I found myself obliged to express myself distinctly in favour of compromise; but it was very plain that my comments were not much relished. It is hard to say on what understanding we parted. Salisbury wished to have one and I think his desire now as from the first is to engage in a struggle *à outrance*. It is very unwise and his harsh unconciliatory manner in the House has done I think a great deal of mischief. It has stirred up a very bitter feeling to him which makes it all the more difficult to arrive at any common conclusion in such a case.

Lansdowne wrote to me at Highclere imploring me to do my best to promote moderate counsels and he called on me in Bruton St. with the same view on my arrival there from the station.

---

[750] Sir Farrer Herschell (1837–1899), Lib. MP for Durham (1874–1885), Solicitor-General (1880–1885), 1st Baron Herschell (1886), Lord Chancellor (1886, 1892–1895).

[751] Cranbrook, after the meeting on 13 August, stated, 'His [Salisbury's] insolence to Northcote has been disgusting' (Johnson, p. 480).

[752] See Report of Reasons for Disagreeing to certain of the said Lords Amendments: *Hansard*, CCLXIV, cols 2009–2011. Kimberley commented on this, 'Lord Salisbury [. . .] was rash in his proceedings & what was much worse, insolent in tone & manner. He ran a dangerous and unnecessary risk of provoking a serious collision between the Houses which was only averted by the admirable skill and calmness of Gladstone' (Hawkins and Powell, *Journal of John Wodehouse, First Earl of Kimberley*, p. 324).

Tuesday 16 August (Highclere)

Gladstone in the H. of Commons last night made a succession of very conciliatory speeches and gave up a variety of controversial points.[753] The Radical wing were furious: but they had to submit and the result was a triumph for the H. of Lords. I was however not without alarm for Salisbury's manner and language had been so harsh and uncompromising that I was afraid that he might insist on all the amendments we had made and refuse all compromise. I called on Northcote in the morning and found him laid up with a bad cold in bed; but I talked over the situation and he undertook to see Salisbury. At 2.30 we had a meeting of Conservative Peers in Arlington St. and then there was no doubt as to the feeling of the party. Everyone was jubilant, delighted to have escaped from the collision which some few were prepared to face but which all dreaded especially as we could escape with honour. Salisbury himself advocated a complete acceptance of Gladstone's terms and everyone who spoke urged strongly the same view.[754]

It is a success, and a success due in a great measure to standing firm, but we have also steered very near the shoals and if Gladstone had been unbending we should have incurred a great defeat. We have been in great danger: and I do not think that the policy will safely bear repetition.

The matter being now concluded I came down here by the last train to the surprise and satisfaction of Elsie and the children.

---

[753]Brand had met Gladstone and Forster, the Irish Secretary, joined later by Harcourt and Thring, in Downing Street on 15 August to discuss the Lords' amendments. Both Gladstone and Forster, Brand considered, were moderate. Brand recorded later, 'Gladstone exhibited remarkable tact [in the Commons] in carrying his amendments through the House: and by 2 a.m. we reported the amendments with reasons to the Lords' (Brand, Diary, 15 August 1881: Brand Papers, BRA/2/11).

[754]The Lords met at 5 p.m. and accepted the concessions made by the Commons: *Hansard*, CCLXIV, 15 August 1881, cols 1929–1998. Hicks Beach wrote to his wife on 16 August, 'I fancy the Land Bill is all settled by this time; the Lords have decidedly scored – the whole tone of the debate in the Commons last night, particularly Gladstone, was as different as possible from what it has hitherto been. Salisbury said the other day that as we had to deal with a madman in Gladstone, it was necessary to have a madman on the other side, and he offered himself for the purpose – the result has certainly shown that he was not far wrong' (Lady V. Hicks Beach, *Life of Sir Michael Hicks Beach*, 2 vols (London, 1932), I, p. 201).

Wednesday 17 August (Highclere)

I wrote a long letter to Whitbread[755] on the subject of the Commission and of my resignation after our meeting in October or November. I enclosed it to Jekyll.

[755] Samuel Whitbread and Robert, 3rd Earl of Camperdown (1841–1918), both former civil lords, and firm Liberals, had been added to the Defence Commission in August 1880, after Gladstone was returned to power.

1882

Sunday 26 February (London)

I received a note from Northcote asking me to attend a small ex-cabinet meeting. I went to his house by mistake and was summoned as from there to Salisbury's where the meeting was. Present Salisbury, Northcote, Cross, Smith, J. Manners and Gibson.

We had before us a letter from Gladstone to Northcote proposing to give him an idea of what he, Gladstone, intended to say, that he should express great anxiety to avoid dissension between the Houses and hinting though in a very tortuous manner that if the Committee of the House of Lords would exclude all enquiry into the "judicial administration" of the Land Act he (Gladstone) would drop his vote of censure.[756] Northcote's answer saying that the Committee was now appointed and that he was sure that anything which the Government desired to have avoided would be avoided was also shown. After some discussion the matter was left there. It appeared that Salisbury had had some communications with Granville, but not in writing, and that they had come to nothing owing to the fact that Granville would not or could not define "judicial administration". It is obvious that these words might be made to cover about everything comprised in the Land Act.[757]

So it ended. At the close when the others had gone I had some conversation with Salisbury and suggested my idea of some kind of Literary Committee as part of our party organisation.

Monday 27 February (London)

House hunting all the morning and very tiring work.

---

[756]The Lords set up a committee to inquire into the working of the Land Act after a debate on 24 February: *Hansard*, CCLXVI, cols 1501–1502. Gladstone protested that it was too soon to decide if the Act was a success.

[757]In fact, Granville had informed Salisbury on 25 February that the Cabinet would accept the proposed committee but not one sitting judicially on the administration of the Act by the Commissioners (Granville to Gladstone, 26 February 1882: Ramm, 1962, I, p. 346). The report, a scheme for land purchase, was very much a landlords' scheme. See J.L. Hammond, *Gladstone and the Irish Nation* (London, 1938), pp. 257–258.

In the evening at the House. There is evidently a good deal of dissatisfaction and apprehension at the chance of a collision between the two Houses. But there always are a great many who are very timid whenever there is a risk of any trouble.[758] It was so last year in the Irish difficulty. Lamington, Alington,[759] Shaftesbury (who is always very anxious) and several others began to talk to me in this strain. I drove home with Salisbury who does not seem to be at all alarmed. Gladstone had a meeting of the Liberal Party this afternoon and it does not seem to have been altogether unanimous, but one or two men of weight, like Whitbread, urged a support of the Government.

Cairns in the House.

Wednesday 15 March (London)

In the afternoon an important meeting at Northcote's. Present Salisbury, Cairns, Gibson, R. Winn,[760] Smith, Cross. Questions discussed:

1. Course to be pursued as to the Clôture resolutions,[761] generally understood to close debate if possible on Monday week 27th.

2. Serious discussion as to course to be pursued with regard to revival of the Coercion Act.[762] Salisbury very strong on the anomaly and impropriety of keeping men shut up indefinitely without trial. Most of us however very indisposed to take any step to enable Government to say that we had made their system of coercion impossible, which they would immediately do.

---

[758] Heated debate in the Commons on the Resolution on the Operation of the Land Law (Ireland) Act, first night: *Hansard*, CCLXVI, cols 1729–1798.

[759] Henry Gerard Sturt (1825–1894), 1st Baron Alington (1876), Con. MP for Dorchester (1847–1856) and for Dorset (1856–1876).

[760] Rowland Winn (1820–1893), Con. MP for Lancashire North (1868–1885), Lord of the Treasury (1874–1880), created Baron St Oswald (1885).

[761] Clôture was a process for bringing a parliamentary debate to a rapid end. It was introduced in the Commons in 1881 to overcome the delaying tactics of Irish members over the Coercion Bill.

[762] The Protection of Person and Property (Ireland) Act, more popularly known as the Coercion Act, which came into law on 2 March 1881, gave the Government wide powers of arbitrary arrest and detention. It was strongly opposed by the Irish members. After forty-one hours of debate in the Commons, the Speaker declared a closure, much to the surprise of the House. See T.P. O'Connor, *Memoirs of an Old Parliamentarian*, 2 vols (London, 1929), I, pp. 172–173.

3. Smith to give notice of a resolution to extend the purchase clauses in the Land Act of last year in such a way as to enable occupiers to become owners and to be just to landlords.

Afterwards attended Grand Lodge where the Prince of Wales made his motion as to the recent attempt on the Queen's life.[763] He did it extremely well, in a very crowded and enthusiastic Lodge. I seconded the motion. My speech was very well received.[764]

We afterwards dined at the Loyd Lindsays.[765] Old Lord Overstone[766] was there, feeble in walking power but as fresh as possible in mind.

Tuesday 25 April (London)

A very busy day beginning with a meeting of the ex-cabinet at Northcote's. Present, Northcote, Smith, J. Manners, Stanley, Cross, Cairns, Cranbrook, Salisbury, Gibson. The discussion was confined entirely to Smith's motion on the Purchase Clauses of the Land Act, and Smith gave us a general notion of what he proposed to say. Cranbrook was opposed to the whole thing. Whether any agreed with him I do not know, for no one said so: perhaps some doubted.

Friday 5 May (London)

A meeting of our old Cabinet at the Carlton to decide as to what should be done.[767] The motion originally drafted by Beach and revised by Cairns agreed to [. . .]. Advised Salisbury (who consulted me) against a debate at present on Irish policy.

[763] An attempt to assassinate the Queen had been made by a deranged man outside Windsor Station on 2 March. See E. Longford, *Victoria R.I.* (London, 1964), p. 446.

[764] A meeting at Queen Street, especially 'summoned to express the sentiments of the craft at the attempt upon the life of Her Majesty' ('The freemasons and the Queen', *The Times*, 16 March 1882, p. 10).

[765] Robert James Loyd-Lindsay (1832–1901), Con. MP for Berkshire (1865–1885), created Baron Wantage (1885), a prominent Freemason.

[766] Samuel Jones Loyd (1796–1883), 1st Baron Overstone (1849), economist and banker, Whig MP for Hythe (1819–1826). Overstone was Lindsay's father-in-law.

[767] The meeting followed on from one at Salisbury's the previous day. Hicks Beach was to call on Gladstone on 8 May to submit the Government's Irish policy to Parliament's scrutiny.

Sunday 7 May (London)

Horrible news this morning – poor Fred Cavendish cruelly murdered in the Phoenix Park close to the Lodge.[768] I got at breakfast a note from Salisbury asking me to meet him and others at Northcote's at 2.30. On arriving there we heard first for consideration a letter from Gladstone offering to accept Gibson's amendment of a ⅔ majority in the case of the Clôture, which after discussion was agreed to. Cross was the only one who was not favourable – all the others I think considered it a good bargain. Then we talked a good deal of this horrible murder. It was decided that Beach should not go on with his motion but that it should be accompanied by an intimation that we withdraw only on the understanding that the Government would act with vigour, and that we should instruct also that we are ready to give the Government every possible support in legitimate objects.

I walked away with Salisbury and thought him out of spirits and very much depressed, perhaps physically. He talked more than he has ever done in his old manner, community of danger strengthening the bonds between those who are acting together. I said to him what I said indeed to the others, that in my point of view this is rebellion, and I can see practically only two alternatives, either Irish Independence or very stern repression.

Later I called at the Phillimores. He was much shaken, and even he evidently condemns the Government, though he makes the best case he can for Gladstone. Later some talk with Froude and Lowe, interesting but very few details are known.

Thursday 15 June (London)

A meeting at Northcote's. Most of us, except Sandon, Beach, Duke of Northumberland present. We discussed little except the Arrears bill.[769] On the whole a general disposition to fight it, and an equally general belief that it will not do to put much trust in the Irish landlords.

[768] On 7 May, news came through of the murder of Lord Frederick Charles Cavendish (1836–1882), the newly appointed Chief Secretary for Ireland, and Thomas Burke, his under-secretary, in Phoenix Park, Dublin. See J. Bailey (ed.), *The Diary of Lady Frederick Cavendish*, 2 vols (London, 1927), II, p. 325; T. Corfe, *The Phoenix Park Murders: conflict, compromise and tragedy in Ireland, 1879–1882* (London, 1968), pp. 184–188.

[769] The Arrears Bill was aimed at Irish land holdings valued at £30 and under. Where the tenant paid one year's arrears and could demonstrate an ability to pay more, the Government would pay the landlord half the arrears and the rest would be cancelled. The money for the scheme was to come from the Irish Church Fund and the Exchequer.

In the House Salisbury made a very vigorous attack on the Egyptian policy of the Government.[770]

Thursday 13 July (London)

A heavy day at the Commission but we are now very near to the end of our work. Meanwhile very terrible telegrams have come in from Alexandria. The town is in flames, the convicts are released and the Christians and Europeans have been massacred almost to a man. There has been no such picture of horror since the burning of Paris.[771]

In the afternoon a Garden Party at Marlborough House. Every one was talking of these horrors, which seem to multiply upon us and (not unnaturally) we go on in the usual course marrying and giving in marriage and eating and drinking whilst the flood is rising round us.

Friday 14 July (London)

Our last formal meeting of the Defence Commission. It has lasted nearly three years, has often been very hard work, sometimes a matter of a good deal of anxiety, often of much difficulty. But we have completed it and I think the work will on the whole stand the test of examination.

Friday 21 July (London)

A meeting of the Peers at Salisbury's as to the Arrears bill. He made an able and very clear speech, saying that between the two views, against the Second Reading and for the bill, he advised amending it in committee in order (a) to make the application a joint one from landlord and tenant (b) to include in the "aspects" the tenant right.[772]

[770] At the end of May, ironclads had been sent to Alexandria and Port Said to protect British lives and property. Riots and massacres took place in Alexandria, resulting in the deaths of fifty Europeans. Salisbury suggested that the British fleet should take action against the perpetrator, Colonel Arabi (see Shannon, *Gladstone*, II, pp. 298–301). For Salisbury's speech, see *Hansard*, CCLXX, cols 1217–1220.

[771] After the Egyptian authorities had refused to dismantle the forts commanding Alexandria harbour, the British fleet bombarded the positions. This was followed by the burning of the city, and serious disorders took place. See P. Knaplund, *Gladstone's Foreign Policy* (New York and London, 1935), pp. 184–185.

[772] After the meeting, Salisbury wrote to Cairns, who was abroad, that two colleagues had sent messages voicing their opposition and that there was only one speaker at the meeting

The meeting was unanimous in agreeing to this except Leitrim[773] who made a dissentient and not very wise speech.

Thursday 27 July (London)

A long discussion over the Arrears bill.[774] I sat all the evening expecting to have to speak and taking notes: but the debate grew thinner and thinner and finally expired, so that any speech from me was unnecessary. I was the only one besides Salisbury on the Front Bench of the old Cabinet. Richmond and Cairns both absent – not quite right I think.

Friday 4 August (London – Highclere)

Two important conversations with Cairns and Salisbury [. . .]. My conversations with Salisbury and Cairns were on the subject of our amendments on the Arrears bill.[775] When I came into the writing room first Abergavenny[776] drew me aside in great excitement and told me he feared a split in the party if Salisbury persevered in insisting on the amendments. Then Barrington spoke to me in much the same line. On going into the House the first words I heard Salisbury say to Lathom[777] were "I will not eat dirt," so I knew pretty well what was going on. I talked a good deal to him and found him very determined – then he left the House and I had some conversation with Cairns, who said that he from the first had disliked the course taken, that he was in favour of compromise, that he "had a delicacy" in saying all this to Salisbury but that I could do well to use any influence I might have by representing all this to him. I said I thought he had much

who demurred to the amendments as being too strong. 'They, however, consented to my proposals, I pledging myself that, if they forbore to oppose the second reading and carry these amendments, I would, in any event, vote for them to the end' (Cecil, III, p. 52). The bill was read for a third time the same day.

[773] Robert Bermingham Clements (1847–1892), 4th Earl of Leitrim (1878).

[774] Arrears of Rent (Ireland) Bill, second reading: *Hansard*, CCLXXII, cols 1919–1957.

[775] On 31 July, Salisbury had moved his amendment in the Lords. It was agreed to by 169 to 98 votes, as well as a second amendment, by 120 to 45. Derby wrote in his diary, 'The two Houses are now committed to opposite opinions on this bill, & it is certain that the Commons will not give way on the main points at issue. What is to come next?' (Vincent, *Derby*, IV, p. 451).

[776] William Nevill (1826–1915), 1st Marquess of Abergavenny (1876), Conservative Party manager.

[777] Edward Bootle-Wilbraham (1837–1898), 2nd Baron Skelmersdale (1853), 1st Earl of Lathom (1880), Lord Chamberlain of the Household (1885–1886, 1886–1892, 1895–1898).

better talk it over with Salisbury: but on S. coming in again I told him all that had passed, and the two had some talk afterwards but not I imagine to much purpose. I understood from Cairns that he would not take any open part in dissenting but I doubt if he will vote for the amendments.[778]

It was finally settled that there should be a Peers' meeting on Thursday morning before we consider the amendments in the House.

All this is very unsatisfactory. Salisbury's notion is that the House of Lords had best fight both to show themselves a formidable power and to arrest the habit of compromise which is sapping their moral courage: my doubt is, and it is only a doubt, whether the field of battle is well chosen.[779]

Thursday 10 August (London)

Two very busy and anxious days. Came up to London with Elsie and first saw Northcote.[780] I questioned him as to his opinion on the course we ought to take upon insisting on our amendments. He was very divided in mind as to the policy of the matter but he was quite clear that as regards the House of Commons our men there would not vote again in support of our amendments. Smith he said was of much the same opinion and this in his mind was the great difficulty of the situation.

From him I went to Salisbury who seemed in a very reasonable mood, but his mind evidently made up to fight. I told him that Cairns was leaving London, and I mentioned one or two other depletions and I said that I anticipated a very small majority if any in support. He admitted the risk of this but seemed more sanguine than I quite understood.

The next day, Thursday, we had a meeting of Peers in Arlington Street, nearly 100. A large number spoke after Salisbury but except

[778] Carnarvon told Cranbrook, 'I much fear a desertion in a large body of our men or so large an abstention as to give us a very small majority. Either would be a great blow' (Carnarvon to Cranbrook, 5 August 1882: Cranbrook Papers, HA3 T501/262).

[779] Carnarvon's pessimism deepened in subsequent days. To Cairns he declared, 'I am extremely anxious that if possible you and he [Salisbury] should find a common ground of agreement as to the course to be taken. No evil could be so great for the Party as that the leader in the House of Lords should seem at variance with those whose opinion is regarded as is yours' (Carnarvon to Cairns, 8 August 1882: Cairns Papers, TNA, PRO 30/51/8, fo. 28). Cairns left for Scotland on 9 August 'and thus avoid[ed] the possibility of being a dissentient if present' (Cairns to Carnarvon, 9 August 1882: CP, BL 60768, fo. 54).

[780] Salisbury's amendments were rejected in the Commons on 8 August. The final vote of the Upper House was arranged for 10 August and the Peers' meeting was held at Salisbury's that morning.

Inchiquin[781] not one was in favour of insisting on the Amendments. I indeed spoke very strongly in support of Salisbury himself, said that I thought that *on the whole* it would be safer to fight than to retreat and that I should certainly vote with him and Cranbrook, whilst indisposed to insist, also spoke strongly for Salisbury. Richmond on the other hand headed an attack on the amendments and Salisbury went out of his way to inform them that Cairns differed from him. The sense of the meeting was so strong that Salisbury at last asked them to divide and it then appeared that about three fourths were against him.[782] He was evidently very much annoyed and later in the afternoon in the House announced that he had been beaten by an overwhelming majority of his own friends, giving an unfortunate appearance of temper.[783] He had no doubt great cause to complain of the change of the opinion on the part of the peers, but he also need never have nailed his colours to the mast in the earlier stages and even now might have retreated without the appearance of a quarrel with his friends. It was a bad business and will damage him and all of us, in the future.

Sunday 13 August (London)

Much interesting talk with Northcote particularly on recent events, which he much deplores. He said to me that he had greatly regretted Salisbury's great disinclination to meet in private conference to talk over matters and ascertain the views of each other. He seems to have founded this disinclination on the fear that we should be known to meet; but what did or does this matter? No one knows what we say or decide on.

The real reason is doubtless a different one, and is to be found in Salisbury's belief that he is more independent by avoiding consultation: but I do not myself think that this is the result.

[781] Edward Donough O'Brien (1839–1900), 14th Baron Inchiquin (1872), Lord Lieutenant of Clare (1879–1900).

[782] Salisbury described the meeting to his wife. 'Carnarvon and Cranbrook said they would vote with me, but – This went on for some time. At last I begged them to divide – those who were for resistance to one side and those who were against it to the other [. . .]. In all about twenty supported me. On the other side there were sixty. Of course, in this state of things it was useless going to a division of the House' (Cecil, III, p. 54).

[783] Instead of a division in the Lords, a voice vote was taken, with Salisbury, Carnarvon, and Cranbrook being among the few peers to call out 'Not-Content' (see A. Roberts, *Salisbury: Victorian titan* (London, 1999), p. 270; *Hansard*, CCLXXIII, cols 1328–1343).

1883

Tuesday 7 August (Highclere)

I went early to the House where we had a long debate on the Agricultural Holdings bill. I spoke and voted for it. Richmond was very keen for it, Salisbury spoke against it but did not vote, Elcho's speech was very dismissive, Carlingford's feeble.[784]

Friday 10 August (London)

All night in Committee on the Agricultural Holdings bill.[785] I moved several amendments etc but mine were all harmless. I cannot say as much of the other changes introduced. I regret much the party character given to the attack on the bill and Salisbury lent himself too much to it. Richmond who was very fair about it and who I think understands the bill was in despair on the subject and lamented bitterly over the whole proceedings. But it was all to little purpose and the bill was treated with a roughness which was from my point of view unfortunate. Legislation is, I admit, very bad and may possibly lead to mischief but when once that has been considered it is worse than idle to attack the bill with amendments which are for all practical purposes useless and which will give the Liberals the power of saying the bill is wholly illusory.

Tuesday 14 August (London – Highclere)

I went up to town for the report of the Agriculture Holdings bill and I took the opportunity of talking freely to Salisbury on the subject urging him strongly not to sacrifice the bill for the sake of amendments which were really useless. I assured him that if we came in Office we

---

[784]The Tenants Compensation Bill, or Agricultural Holdings (England) Bill, rewarded tenants making improvements on their holdings by obtaining compensation from their landlords. Second reading, *Hansard*, CCLXXXII, Carlingford, cols 1796–1803, Elcho (Wemyss), cols 1803–1807, Richmond, cols 1818–1824, Salisbury, cols 1831–1835; Voting: Contents 55, Non-Contents 9. The bill was sent to the Committee of the Whole House.
[785]Ibid., CCLXXXIII, cols 5–51.

could not pass a more moderate bill ourselves and that it was playing the Radical game to upset this measure.[786]

Sunday 18 November (Highclere)

I walked about with Froude this afternoon. He was as usual very agreeable and his remarkable powers of memory and his inexhaustible store of information struck me much. I thought him in rather a melancholy mood. He said that he thought that when once he had finished his life of Carlyle[787] he would not write again. He said that it had been a terrible task imposed on him by Carlyle to undertake these papers,[788] and that Carlyle's own feeling was to make atonement by his public exhibition of his own faults and weaknesses for the wrongs which he thought he had done his wife. He said that he was doubting whether or not to insert two characters of Gladstone and Disraeli which Carlyle had drawn. The former Carlyle detests: the latter he did not like. I told him that as he was certain to meet a good deal of censure he might as well accept the whole and not omit that which would be very interesting. He laughed in his comical fashion and agreed. We afterwards happened to talk of Charles Kingsley,[789] and he told me, which was new to me, that the last two or three years of his life C. K. was always wishing for death. At that time he was once fishing somewhere with Henry Cowper,[790] who overheard him say to himself almost with every cast of his fly, "I wish I were dead, I wish I were dead." Froude estimates Kingsley most highly as a poet.

[786] Ibid., cols 439–447. After attending the debates on the bill, Carnarvon left for Canada on 22 August.

[787] Thomas Carlyle (1795–1881), Scottish writer and historian.

[788] Froude, as Carlyle's literary executor, by the will of 1873 was given the task of writing the *History of the First Forty Years of Carlyle's Life* and *History of Carlyle's Life in London*. The first two volumes were published in March 1882 and the second two in October 1884. See Dunn, *James Anthony Froude*, II, pp. 471–480.

[789] Charles Kingsley (1781–1860). His declining health and mental obsessions are described in S. Chitty, *The Beast and the Monk: a life of Charles Kingsley* (London, 1974), p. 225.

[790] Henry Frederick Cowper (1836–1887), second son of 6th Earl Cowper, Lib. MP for Hertfordshire (1865–1885).

1884

Wednesday 9 January (Coppice – Highclere)

Poor Phillimore was much pleased to see me. He remains much the same, the mind very clear.

I talked over with Phillimore the old story of Gladstone's appointment to the Ionian Islands in 1858 as both he and I were interested in it.[791]

I was Under Secretary at the Colonial Office and Lytton was Secretary of State. He consulted me very much on all matters and I did a great deal of the office work, being left greatly my own master.

The Ionian Islands at that time gave us extreme trouble and Lytton asked me to advise him what to do. On reflection I advised him to send out a Special Commissioner of eminence and ability to take charge of the Islands and to recommend a new course of policy if such could be found. He asked me whom I recommended, and I said that I thought it not unlikely that looking to the nature of the work and his then political relations with other political persons and parties, Gladstone might be induced to accept it. He was at first surprised and perhaps disinclined, then, on talking it over became enamoured with the idea and at his wish I made some attempts to ascertain what Gladstone's feelings would be if the proposals were made to him through Phillimore. Phillimore communicated with him, and G. received the overtures, and the way being thus prepared, Lytton made a distinct offer to him which he accepted, to the amazement of every one.

Gladstone's practice at this time was one of great freedom from party and my hope was that this temporary connection with our Government would have become a permanent one. So far as Lytton was concerned there was no obstacle. He was thoroughly and perfectly loyal. Nor as far as I knew was there any real difficulty on Lord Derby's part. The barrier was Disraeli. Lytton repeatedly told me this himself.

[791] The idea originated with Sir Robert Phillimore, a Judge of Admiralty Court (1867–1883), who suggested that Gladstone should be sent as a commissioner to negotiate some disputes with the Neapolitan government. Carnarvon took up the idea, translating it to the Ionian Islands. See above, p. 5; Shannon, *Gladstone*, I, p. 363.

He also told Phillimore, with whom he was in communication, that Disraeli had said, "The place with its classical aestheticism suits him (G.) very well. Now that we have got him down, let us keep him down". These words were reported to Gladstone and he was furious and on his return to England came back with feelings of anger and irritation against the Government, though he always expressed himself (both to me and to others) as entirely satisfied with the good faith of Lytton in the whole transaction.

My own belief is that it was a turning point in Gladstone's political career and that but for Disraeli it *is possible* he might once more have found his way back to the Conservative side.

Tuesday 4 March (London)

I came up for a conference at Northcote's as to the course to be taken on the Reform bill.[792] Present Northcote, Salisbury, Cairns, Cranbrook, Smith, Stanley, J Manners, Richmond and R Winn. Settled that J. Manners should give notice to oppose it on Second Reading on ground of it being an incomplete scheme.[793]

Afterwards discussion as to time to be taken with regard to the Supplementary estimates – about £500,000 – on account of Egyptian expedition.[794] Settled that Stanley should move a resolution against giving future supplies without some new Statement of Government policy. I wished for some few additional words expressive of our readiness to give whatever may be necessary etc. and Cairns agreed with me; but the others preferred the terms as proposed.

Saturday 15 March (London – Highclere)

A meeting at Salisbury's, present: himself and Northcote, Smith, Cross, J. Manners, Stanley and myself. Northcote much pressed in

---

[792] Gladstone had introduced the Representation of the People Bill on 28 February: *Hansard*, CCLXXXV, cols 106–134.

[793] Manners spoke in the Commons later that day: 'That this House declines to proceed further a measure having for its object the addition of 2,000,000 voters to the electoral body of the United Kingdom until it has before it the entire scheme contemplated by the Government for the amendment of the representation of the people' (ibid., col. 490).

[794] In November 1883, an Egyptian army of 10,000 troops under an English officer, Colonel William Hicks, was annihilated by the Mahdi in the Sudan, which was under Egyptian rule. The Government decided, in January 1884, to send out Major-General Charles George Gordon (1833–1885) to Khartoum to report on the best means of evacuating Egyptian garrisons. By 12 March, the Mahdi's forces were closing in on Khartoum and telegraphic connection with the town was severed.

House of Commons by our own friends to declare a policy as to Egypt.[795] Salisbury much against it on the ground that we really know nothing of the feeling of foreign nations and might if called on to take office find ourselves in a difficulty. Agreed to press the Government for information but to do little more.

Smith anxious to move for a secret Committee on the defences of the country which are dangerously insecure. He is alarmed also at the notion of what we should have to do if we were to come into Office. Salisbury deprecated this *much* now and in the midst of all the Egyptian difficulties.

Tuesday 22 April (London)

In the afternoon I questioned the Government as to the position of General Gordon in Khartoum and the measures which, if any, they would adopt. Granville in his reply was very spiteful and cat like, but also very dextrous [...]. Salisbury seemed poorly. I told him what it has been long on my mind to say, that I feel sure that he is over-exerting himself and doing more work than he can or anyone can accomplish.

Friday 9 May

Poorly most of the day with cold caught at Peterborough.

Salisbury came to see me in the afternoon and sat and talked with me some time on various matters. Very pleasant. The Randolph Churchill[796] difficulty is at an end by R.C. knocking under. There will I think be trouble later, but for the present at all events we can get on with an united front.[797]

---

[795]Northcote spoke in the debate on Egypt at a Saturday meeting of the Commons on events in the Sudan: *Hansard*, CCLXXXV, 15 March 1884, cols 1717–1720, 1726–1727. Hartington, Secretary of State for War, had announced that no news had recently been received from Major-General Sir Gerald Graham, in charge of a relief force (ibid., cols 1651–1652).

[796]Lord Randolph Henry Spencer Churchill (1849–1895), Con. MP for Woodstock (1874–1885) and for Paddington South (1885–1895), Secretary of State for India (1885–1886), Chancellor of the Exchequer and Leader of the House (1886).

[797]Churchill, then chairman of the National Union, hoped to take control of the Conservative organization. This ambition was made public by him on 3 May. A reconciliation was effected six days later.

Saturday 10 May (London)

A meeting at Salisbury's of the two front benches to consider the question of how to deal with the Franchise bill.[798] There was remarkable unanimity. It was decided *nem. con.* to reject the bill on the Second Reading, and though no agreement as to the particular mode in which this should be done there was an evident inclination that it should be on the lines of J. Manners' resolution, viz. that the measure is an incomplete one [. . .].

I walked home with Stanley, who said to me that he considered our present position "neck or nothing". Northcote thinks it just possible that the Government may be in a minority if the Irish members vote against them, but I cannot think this very likely.

Tuesday 13 May (London)

Edward Grey[799] to breakfast to discuss Emigration matters and the Charity Organisation Society.

Afterwards a meeting at A. Balfour's[800] to consider the position of the *National Review*. Settled to call a private but larger meeting.

Afterwards in the House of Lords I fired another shot into Granville as to the proposed Conference.[801] I was followed by Cairns and Salisbury and on the whole the discussion was I think a useful one.[802]

Saturday 17 May (London)

We had a large dinner party this evening at which were the Salisburys. She was sitting next to me and said that in the event

[798]The bill entered the committee stage in the Commons on 1 May. The first day of the debate was 6 May (*Hansard*, CCLXXXVII, cols 1484–1548).

[799]Sir Edward Grey (1862–1933), recently succeeded as 3rd Baronet at the age of twenty-two, private secretary to Sir Evelyn Baring in July and, in October, private secretary to Childers, the Chancellor of the Exchequer; Lib. MP for Berwick-on-Tweed (1885–1916). See G.M. Trevelyan, *Grey of Fallodon* (London, 1937), p. 22.

[800]Arthur James Balfour (1848–1930), Salisbury's nephew. Con. MP for Hertford (1874–1885) and for Manchester East (1885–1906), Secretary of State for Scotland (1886), Chief Secretary for Ireland (1887–1891), Leader, House of Commons (1891–1892, 1895–1902), Prime Minister (1902–1905), 1st Earl of Balfour (1922).

[801]On 1 May, Gladstone had announced the setting up of a conference of European Powers to tackle the problem of Egypt's growing economic decline by changing the Law of Liquidation. See Knaplund, *Gladstone's Foreign Policy*, pp. 195–197.

[802]Egypt. The Proposed Conference: *Hansard*, CCLXXXVIII, 13 May 1884, Carnarvon, cols 150–154, Granville, cols 154–155, Cairns, cols 155–158, Salisbury, cols 159–161.

of our coming in, R. Churchill must have something but that the great object was to keep him far from English or Irish affairs – an Undersecretaryship in the Colonial Office or India Office, anything better than Home Office or Ireland. I said I doubted if he would be content with this.

She said that Lytton wished for an Embassy. I said "I suppose Paris?" to which she replied, "Yes," and that this would solve a great difficulty as he was not wanted for the Cabinet. She spoke of Cross and W.H. Smith as "Marshall and Snelgrove" rather contemptuously. It was all said in the tone of a person who wished the old relations to be considered to be entirely restored. I of course was very friendly – listened – but nothing more.

Wednesday 18 June (London)

I called with Elsie on old Lord Albemarle[803] to wish him joy on his birthday and on the anniversary of Waterloo day of which he is now one of the few survivors. What a change in the world and the history and position of England since the 18 June 1815.

Dined at the Duke of Cambridge's. My next neighbour was Cairns who told me the following anecdote, which old Lord Lyndhurst told him of his father.[804] Copley was painting a picture of Sir Edward Knatchbull and his wife Lady K. but there came a pause in the sittings and at the end of the time Sir Edward Knatchbull appeared and said that he had had the misfortune to lose Lady K. and the satisfaction of finding another wife, and that on consultation he had decided to ask Copley to substitute the second Lady K. for the first and to introduce the first as an angel in one corner of the picture. Copley acceded and the picture proceeded on the same lines. But then came another break in the sittings and once more Sir Edward appeared and told the same story. The second Lady K. had died but he now proposed to substitute for her the third and to place the second in the opposite corner of the picture as a second angel. After discussion Copley agreed to this: the picture was so altered, and so it remains to this day.[805]

[803] George Thomas Keppel (1799–1891), 6th Earl of Albemarle (1851). At the age of sixteen, he had been an ensign at Waterloo.

[804] John Singleton Copley (1772–1863), 1st Baron Lyndhurst (1827), Lord Chancellor (1827–1830, 1834–1835, 1841–1846); son of the portrait painter, John Singleton Copley (1735–1815).

[805] Sir Edward Knatchbull, 8th Baronet Knatchbull (1758–1819), twice a widower, with ten children. Copley's labours lasted from 1800 to 1802. Rejected by the Royal Academy, the portrait was eventually destroyed. See J.D. Prown, *John Singleton Copley in England, 1774–1815* (Cambridge, MA, 1966), pp. 360–372.

Thursday 19 June (London)

A meeting of peers at Salisbury's – Cairns, Cadogan, Colville, Lathom, Bury,[806] Beauchamp, Abercorn,[807] to consider the Franchise Bill. Decided to make it two nights' debate, that Cairns should open it and that I should speak first on the second night.

Tuesday 1 July (London)

A very busy day. Soon after 11 a hastily convened meeting at Salisbury's to consider whether I should give up my vote of censure this evening in consequence of what occurred last night in the House of Commons.[808] Present Salisbury, Cairns, Richmond, Northcote and myself. I was rather disposed to go on, but the general feeling was the other way and so it was decided. As soon as this was settled we adjourned upstairs for a general meeting of the Conservative Peers to explain our course as to the vote of Censure on Egyptian affairs, and to decide as to what we should do on the Franchise Bill. With the exception of Jersey and perhaps Norton, the meeting was unanimous for the rejection of the bill on the Second Reading. Cairns' amendment was submitted and agreed to, but with one or two improvements, which in my opinion were really great amendments.

We had scarcely disposed of this when we had another meeting at Salisbury's of the House of Commons' Cabinet and Bruce to consider what course should be taken in the House of Commons as to reversing the vote of censure there (Cairns and Richmond were absent from this meeting). It was finally settled that no steps should be taken with this view.

Then on to the House of Lords where Cairns gave notice of his resolution on the Franchise bill[809] and I put a question to Granville to

---

[806] William Coutts Keppel (1832–1894), Viscount Bury (1851), 7th Earl of Albermarle (1891), Under-Secretary of State for War (1878–1880, 1885–1886).

[807] James Hamilton (1811–1885), 2nd Marquess of Abercorn (1818), 1st Duke of Abercorn (1868), Lord Lieutenant of Ireland (1866–1868, 1874–1876).

[808] Edward Walter Hamilton (1847–1908), Gladstone's secretary, wrote in his diary for 30 June, 'The Egyptian vote of censure [on the terms of the agreement with France] came to an unexpected collapse this afternoon. With the smallest hint beforehand, Mr Goschen challenged Mr G.'s resolution for postponing the Order of the Day, and so successfully was the challenge taken up by the Liberal Party that they succeeded in overpowering the Government Front Bench and the Tories [by 190 to 148], and refused to allow the postponement for which Mr. G. was bound to ask' (Bahlman, II, p. 646; see also *Hansard*, CCLXXXIX, cols 1689–1702).

[809] Cairns's motion objected to 'a change in the constitution of the electoral body of the United Kingdom': *Hansard*, CCLXXXIX, 1 July 1884, col. 1770.

ask if he adhered to Gladstone's statement, in which case I should not press my motion.[810] It was not altogether an easy matter to extricate ourselves well from the position which it had been determined to give up: but I hope I did it sufficiently well to leave the Party on satisfactory ground.

Friday 4 July (London)

Salisbury ill and obliged to go to Brighton. I hope nothing serious [...].

Jersey called on me to consult me as to the Franchise Bill. He much fears and dislikes the course taken and would prefer that we should read the bill a second time and then amend it in some way so as to secure it not passing without a redistribution bill also passing. He speaks, I am afraid, the feeling of a good many and I fear that though little was said in opposition to Salisbury the other day at the Peers' meeting there was no inconsiderable number who remained silent because they lacked the courage to express their opinions. If so this silent dissent will come out in some disagreeable form.

I have myself some doubt as to the wisdom of the course decided on, but it is, I fear, too late now to vary it unless circumstances give us some chance. But I was influenced in my judgement by the very strong opinion of almost all our House of Commons people – Smith, Cross, J. Manners and particularly Gibson, whose opinion I am inclined to accept. All said the same thing and represented the feeling of the Party as unanimous and most strong. Their opinion was that the House of Lords must withstand the bill if redistribution was not given and that they would not be worth keeping if they flinched from their duty.

Monday 7 July (London)

The debate on the Second Reading of the Franchise Bill began, but to my mind it was hardly on the level befitting the occasion. Cairns' speech was able, but I have heard many abler from him and in the beginning of it was I think too lawyer like. The Duke of Argyll was on the whole the best, and as the evening drew on the argument and the speaking seemed to me to flag.[811]

---

[810] Egypt (Terms of the Agreement with France), 'that the terms of Agreement will not lead to the establishment of tranquillity and good government in Egypt': ibid., cols 1770–1774.

[811] Representation of the People Bill, second reading, first day: *Hansard*, CCXC, 7 July 1884, Cairns, cols 112–125, Argyll, cols 125–134.

Tuesday 8 July (London)

I moved the adjournment last night and began this evening. I spoke for an hour and on the whole and for me I think I spoke fairly well. What I said was well received and many of our people were much pleased and afterwards thanked me for it.[812] Salisbury's speech was very good: as an Electioneering manifesto it was excellent and was full of hard hitting. Derby's speech in answer to mine was fair and well reasoned, but badly delivered, the Chancellor was dull and Granville was *scratchy* and nothing more.[813]

But the die is cast and we are now in the open sea of war, and we must see what comes of it.[814]

Thursday 10 July (London)

Gladstone has announced that the business of the Session will now in consequence of our vote in the Lords be wound up and an autumn Session called and the Franchise Bill sent up to us again.[815]

After the House I went to Arlington St. and begged Salisbury to give me a few minutes to talk to him on the general state of affairs. I explained to him that in my opinion there were but two courses:

(1) to make a "transaction" with the Govt. on the redistribution question and that this would be done by allowing them to pass the Franchise Bill in October without delay or difficulty in the House of Commons and by then laying at the same time a Redistribution Bill which one would give a fair consideration.

(2) to lay out a plan of campaign for the autumn and counter organise and agitate in the great towns, meeting the agitation against the House of Lords. In this case I said that I was convinced that it was necessary to come to terms with R. Churchill, that however unsatisfactory a character he might be, he had acquired such an influence that it was impossible to go on in the present condition. Salisbury replied that he was going to France till the middle of September, that he preferred to leave the Radicals to agitate and to allow a reaction to set in and that R.C.'s "malignity" towards Edward

---

[812]Ibid., cols 375–389. Derby judged that Carnarvon's speech was 'thoughtful & in parts able, but rambling and discursive, as if he rather wished to say all that was in his mind about reform rather than to argue the question actually before us' (Vincent, *Derby*, IV, p. 686).

[813]*Hansard*, CCXC, 8 July 1884, Derby, cols 389–402, Selborne, cols 443–455, Salisbury, cols 455–469, Granville, cols 469–476.

[814]The Government was defeated on the Franchise Bill by 205 to 146 on Cairns's amendment motion.

[815]*Hansard*, CCXC, 10 July 1884, cols 692–693.

Stanhope was such that whilst that lasted he could not act with him
or words to that effect.

Friday 11 July (London)

I was astonished and much annoyed at the report of Gladstone's
speech in the morning's papers in which he announced an overture
to Salisbury and rejected by him, of which I had heard nothing. The
want of confidence seemed great.[816] I saw Northcote and Richmond
and talked everything over with them, finding them in considerable if
not in entire agreement. If the proposal has been made in bona fides,
I think something could be made of it and certainly it ought not to
have been in any way snubbed. Salisbury's opinion is dead against
any compromise and he wishes, too much, I think, to fight.

Saturday 12 July (London – Syon)

The extraordinary scenes last night in both Houses put a different
light on matters. I by accident was not in the House of Lords
and though I heard of the fracas, I only saw the account this
morning. There has been something like wilful misrepresentation on
Gladstone's part. Granville, I take it, was not to blame, beyond the fact
that he was not careful enough.[817] It is however difficult to reconcile
the whole affair with complete truth and fair dealing.

Wemyss called on me partly to consult me, partly to show me the
notice as to the Franchise bill which he has sent to the Papers.[818] I
told him at once that his notice meant the cancelling of our vote of
last Tuesday and that I did not see how any who had voted then for

---

[816]In the Lords, there was a bitter exchange between Granville and Salisbury and Cairns
concerning an overture made by Granville to leaders of the Opposition on 8 July with
a view to coming to terms with them. The understanding was that the meeting was a
confidential one, but Gladstone was unaware of this and referred to it at a Liberal Party
meeting at the Foreign Office, reported in the Press on 11 July. For Gladstone's explanation
in the Commons, see *Hansard*, CCXC, 11 July 1884, cols 832–838. Salisbury told Carnarvon,
'How outrageous of Gladstone to try and make political capital of confidential talk between
Granville and Cairns. It makes all such communications impossible for the future' (Salisbury
to Carnarvon, 11 July 1884: CP, BL 60759, fo. 139).

[817]Neither Granville nor Cairns would give way in the debate on the Franchise Bill,
constantly interrupting each other. For an amusing account of this incident, see H.W. Lucy,
A Diary of Two Parliaments: the Gladstone Parliament, 1880–1885 (London, 1886), pp. 429–430.

[818]Wemyss gave notice on 14 July that he would move a resolution that the Lords should
continue with the Franchise Bill providing that a redistribution bill was introduced in the
autumn: *Hansard*, CCXC, 14 July 1884, cols 873–874.

Cairns could now vote for him. He seemed disappointed, talked about altering it, and appeared alarmed at the general position of affairs.

Monday 14 July (London)

To the Conservative Central Association and a talk with Bartley[819] on the position of matters, the organisation of the campaign in the autumn, the meetings of the working men in different places and parks, etc.[820] Afterwards an important conversation with Greenwood as to the Franchise bill. He made a suggestion which falls in entirely with my own views and which I communicated to Salisbury, Richmond and Cairns: and on which I afterwards wrote again to Salisbury, offering to move in it if he liked in the House.[821]

Afterwards a discussion in the House on the French *Recidiviste* question in which I spoke.[822] Granville was very much nettled at some of my remarks, oddly enough, for I intended them to be conciliatory. It is curious that I seem to exercise a sort of irritating effect on him.

Tuesday 15 July (London)

A stormy, agitating day. At 12 we had a meeting of Peers and House of Commons at the Carlton, Salisbury in the Chair and Northcote with him.

Salisbury not favourable to conciliation, Wemyss defended his motion[823] supported by Jersey, Ravensworth[824] in a rather weighty speech and Lansdowne and Ritchie[825] speaking for Tower Hamlets.

---

[819] Sir George Christopher Trout Bartley (1842–1910), principal agent, Conservative Central Office (1883–1885), MP for Islington North (1885–1906).

[820] Carnarvon addressed meetings supporting the Lords' stance on the Franchise Bill between 25 July and 13 September at Osterley Park, Tredegar, Penrhyn, Highclere, Newbury, Nostell Priory, Teversal, and Hedsor Park.

[821] Carnarvon to Salisbury, 14 July 1884: Hatfield House Papers, 3M/E.

[822] On the proposal to increase the number of recidivists sent to the Western Pacific, a proposition of much concern to Australia: *Hansard*, CCXC, 14 July 1884, cols 876–882.

[823] Resolution on the Representation of the People Act, to be introduced on 17 July. Wemyss had given notice on 14 July (see *Hansard*, CCXC, 14 July 1884, cols 873–874).

[824] Henry George Liddell (1821–1903), 2nd Earl of Ravensworth (1878), Con. MP for Northumberland South (1852–1878).

[825] Charles Thomson Ritchie (1838–1906), Con. MP for Tower Hamlets (1874–1892) and for Croydon (1895–1905), Home Secretary (1900–1902), Chancellor of the Exchequer (1902–1903), 1st Baron Ritchie (1905).

On the other side Sir G. Elliot,[826] Chaplin in a good speech, H. Dyke[827] in another, and Northcote who went with Salisbury though in more moderate tones. There were many speakers. I did not speak, having risen but not being called, and not caring to do this again I said nothing more. Salisbury afterwards came to the House and made a somewhat awkward excuse, the fact being that *I think* he did not wish me to speak, not being quite sure whether I might not say something in the direction of conciliation. This is foolish, but very much like him and is only likely to oblige me to do it in the House.[828]

Later in the House there was curious excitement and very considerable dissatisfaction with Salisbury. He is getting the character of making what are called "intemperate" speeches and the House has a dread of being led in to scrapes. I can see it plainly and have repeatedly warned him but it is of little use, and with all his ability he will end by making some great mess.

St. John Brodrick[829] came to me with the report of a conversation with Dilke[830] and Goschen and indirectly of Gladstone, Harcourt and Childers. I sent on the papers to Salisbury saying I felt it my duty to do so.[831]

Wednesday 16 July (London)

A long conversation with Stead, Editor of the *Pall Mall*,[832] at his request. He came as far as I could judge mainly to urge on me the policy of some compromise as to the Franchise bill difficulty. I replied that we would gladly agree to any which provided for the consideration of the Redistribution bill also during the autumn. He said that would make us masters of the situation and he urged all the usual arguments as to agitation, the certainty that the House of

---

[826] Sir George Elliot (1814–1893), Con. MP for Durham North (1868–1880, 1881–1885) and for Monmouth (1886–1892).

[827] Sir William Hart Dyke (1837–1931), Con. MP for Kent West (1865–1868), for Mid-Kent (1868–1885), and for Dartford (1885–1906), Chief Whip and Secretary to the Treasury (1874–1880), Chief Secretary for Ireland (1885–1886), Vice-President of Committee of Council on Education (1887–1892).

[828] See A. Jones, *The Politics of Reform, 1884* (London, 1972), p. 160.

[829] William St John Brodrick (1856–1942), Con. MP for Surrey (1880–1885).

[830] Sir Charles Wentworth Dilke (1843–1911), Lib. MP for Chelsea (1868–1886), President of the Local Government Board (1882–1885).

[831] Carnarvon to Salisbury, 15 July 1884: Hatfield House Papers, 3M/E. The 'Memorandum of conversation between Brodrick and Dilke' is reprinted in Hardinge, III, p. 105.

[832] William Thomas Stead (1849–1912), editor of the *Pall Mall Gazette* (1883–1890).

Lords would be destroyed etc. I said that if we must fight I thought it was best to fight at once: and that was not a bad ground. Our conversation lasted two hours, most friendly, *absolutely confidential*, and at times interesting. If it did nothing else it left us with probably friendly feelings on both sides, a good prelude to the conflict. He mentioned several things, that Gladstone was the most inclined to be Conservative, that Granville was obsolete and incompetent and must soon go, that any other Redistribution Bill must be worse for us, that the Conservatives in the provinces would not fight, that the agitation would be great, that it would be accompanied by misrepresentation.

Thursday 17 July (London)

I had a letter from Salisbury this morning written in a generally moderate vein.[833] In the House in the evening he was as usual more combative. Part of the case he states very well; but he did not make the offer which I hoped he would make and which I firmly believe would have put him in a better position for fighting.[834] However the die is now cast. We are in for a struggle and it remains to be seen how the House will fight, what is the strength of the Radical caucus and what the power of Convocation in the country.

Friday 18 July (London)

After the fatigue and anxieties of the week today was rather a rest. The fact too is now decided – we must fight and we have nothing to do but to prepare for it. I had a talk with W.H. Smith who is anxious but reasonable.

One thing is very clear to me. Salisbury has not the confidence of those who follow him or who are supposed to be his colleagues and advisers. The first he alarms by his supposed rashness. The latter he alienates by seeming to distrust them. There is a general feeling among them that he will not really consult them, that he is too secretive. Time will show but I am afraid that with all his great gifts he will be a failure and may even do mischief.

---

[833] 'I hesitate to urge adjournment *now* very strongly – not on account of this question – but on account of the atrocious precedent it would make for helping forward obnoxious bills in future years' (Salisbury to Carnarvon, 17 July 1884: CP, BL 60759, fos 149–150).

[834] *Hansard*, CCXC, 17 July 1884, Salisbury, cols 1368–1373.

Tuesday 30 September (Greystoke)

We had a prosperous journey and arrived here in good time. Salisbury was in the same train going down to speak at Glasgow,[835] so I travelled with him between Rugby and Crewe. We had time for a full conversation on many subjects, and we discussed everything I think of consequence, Franchise agitation, foreign matters, Plan of Campaign, on the meeting of Parliament,[836] Ireland. He contemplates a renewal of Irish outrages this winter, not a pleasant anticipation. We discussed also the state of the House of Lords and some possible reforms which might be made. It was indeed on the whole the most undisturbed and satisfactory conversation which I have had with him for some time. He seemed well.

He told me of a sort of compromise through Argyll but the compromise was an unreal one and I see that he still remembers and resents the public use which Gladstone tried to make out of the private negotiations with Cairns and Granville at the end of last session on the Franchise Bill.

Friday 10 October (Ravenstone)

I got the news of this extraordinary revelation in the *Standard* of the Government's scheme of Redistribution – most astonishing.[837] I cannot resist a suspicion that it came from Chamberlain through E.[838] to the *Standard*.

Monday 13 October (Hams, Birmingham)

Elsie, Aubrey[839] and I came on here to Norton's.[840] On arriving in Birmingham which was in a political ferment, we found Station and

[835]Salisbury spoke at two meetings in Glasgow and then made further speeches in south-west Scotland (see *The Times*, 1 October 1884, p. 5).

[836]Carnarvon, writing of the conversation, remarked, 'I found that he agreed with me that it was important not to allow the House of Lords to be adjourned to long intervals, as during our last autumn Session, but to ventilate the different large questions which are pending' (Carnarvon to Cranbrook, 9 October 1884: Cranbrook Papers, HA3 T501/262).

[837]'The Redistribution Bill: the Government scheme', *Evening Standard*, 9 October 1884, pp. 2–3. The paper stated, 'We are now enabled to lay before you the complete details of the Government plan, in their present shape'.

[838]The identity of this person is not known.

[839]Aubrey Nigel Herbert (1880–1923), Carnarvon's elder son by his second marriage. Served in diplomatic service (1903–1905), then travelled extensively throughout the Turkish Empire. Unionist MP for Somerset South (1911–1918).

[840]Carnarvon and Elsie stayed at Hams Hall, Lord Norton's residence (W.S. Childe-Pemberton, *Life of Lord Norton* (London, 1909), p. 263).

Streets crowded. Northcote (and I think R. Churchill) arrived at about the same time and were received with great acclamations. It is to be a great demonstration and the Radicals are attempting to break it up by violent means.

Tuesday 14 October (Hams, Birmingham)

Last night there was a disgraceful attack made by the Liberals under the guidance of the Caucus upon the Conservative meeting in Aston Park. It was planned and organised and conducted with much ruffianly violence.[841] Today when I went into Birmingham everyone was full of it, and matters were so doubtful that I would not let Elsie go with me. Everything however at the Conservative banquet passed off quietly and the outrage of last night was the text on which we all more or less preached.

R. Churchill spoke remarkably well. His speech, which was apparently carefully prepared and written on several sheets of paper, was disfigured in parts by some personalities and violences, but in its general character it was extremely good and delivered very well. He had evidently modelled himself on Disraeli. The phrases are often imitations of him and he has even caught some of the intonations of his voice. But taken as a whole the speech impressed me with its ability.[842]

Wednesday 22 October (London)

An important conversation with Bartley at the Conservative Central Office.[843] He showed me his redistribution scheme, which as far as I have examined or understand it I like. It proceeds on a distinct principle and has no Party taint about it – all this most confidential.

---

[841] At the meeting, the platform was stormed by rioters, and Churchill and Northcote, who were to have publicly shaken hands, had to flee for safety (see T.H. Escott, *Randolph Spencer Churchill as a Product of his Age* (London, 1895), pp. 261–264). Hamilton attributed the rioting to a number of Liberal supporters at the meeting who were wearing Gladstone badges (Bahlman, II, p. 706).

[842] The banquet was held at the Exchange Assembly Rooms, Birmingham. Churchill's address was entitled 'Our Constitution' (*The Times*, 15 October 1884, p. 6).

[843] Bartley believed that 'the Scheme as put forward by the *Standard* is one which is so unfair in its operation, that it is quite out of the question our accepting it. It is based on no general principle whatever and shows signs of Party prejudice in every detail' (Bartley to Carnarvon, 11 October 1884: CP, BL 60832, fo. 30).

After this to a meeting at Northcote's where Salisbury and I alone represented the Peers, all the rest House of Commons, among them G. Hamilton, Bourke, R. Churchill, Dyke, Winn etc. I walked away with Salisbury and said something to him as to the redistribution scheme of Bartley. He is much opposed to it evidently: and as I understand wishes to fight on "without showing our hand." I do not agree in the wisdom of this. I doubt if we can continue to do this much longer.

On my return to Portman Square whilst writing I was told that Sir H. Ponsonby wished to see me. He was at once shown in, and he told me that he had seen the suggestion which I threw out yesterday that it was much to be wished that the Redistribution Scheme could be referred to 3 or 4 impartial men who had the confidence of both parties;[844] that he was now in London endeavouring to find some way out of present difficulties as the Queen was extremely anxious about it.[845] He told me that she had seen Richmond and that he and Cairns had been consulted, but that they could throw no light on the matter: that she had communicated with Salisbury that he had given no hope of a compromise on his part; that he had come to me and wished for my opinion in perfect confidence, undertaking that it should go to no one but the Queen.

I replied that I had only two objects in view:

(1) that I should do or say nothing which directly or indirectly could be thought to be acting behind the backs of those with whom I was acting

(2) that I considered it and always had considered it my duty to give any information or advice in my power to the Queen and to place myself absolutely at her command where I felt I could serve her.

Our conversation then continued. I told him that I had not spoken unadvisedly, that it was my deliberate opinion that a redistribution scheme, without any party taint would be drawn up on some fixed principle which both sides might accept and which would work out fairly and adequately. As to the four men who could enjoy the confidence of all sides, it was far more difficult to find them.

He asked me what he should do, and on the whole I advised him to talk to Northcote, and if he made way with him then to Salisbury; but I added that it would I thought be best to keep my name out of

---

[844] At a speech to the Hackney Conservative Union on 21 October, Carnarvon stated that, in his opinion, 'if the scheme of redistribution were submitted to a body composed of a few men on each side, who had the confidence of their respective parties, a settlement of the question might be arrived at' (*The Times*, 22 October 1884, p. 7).

[845] Ponsonby had told the Queen on 22 October, 'Lord Carnarvon in his speech said that four independent men might be found to settle it. Why should this not be tried?' (Buckle, *Letters*, III, p. 554).

it. But it would also be best for him to speak from the Queen and not from himself.

I said I doubted whether there was sufficient endeavour on the Government side to make this practicable. He also doubted. He excluded the violent men like Chamberlain and probably Dilke; but he said that Gladstone was very uneasy, very anxious and that he thought that he would agree to any fair compromise if it could be found. The advantage he said of my suggestion was that it was not a compromise but something in which the representatives of both parties would agree.

He left me to telegraph at once to the Queen to inform her generally of what had passed with me and to ask her to empower him to speak to Northcote.

I offered on my part to see him again if he would need it and to do anything in my power.

Thursday 23 October (London)

I received a letter from Sir H. Ponsonby telling me that he had met the "Secretary of one of the ministers" who told him that the suggestion of mine of a reference of the Redistribution question to some impartial persons had attracted attention and that some committee were passing [sic]. I am afraid however that nothing will come of it.[846] There is a general feeling and desire for more compromise. It is unmistakable. Richmond has talked much to me this evening in that sense and several of the more moderate men have said much the same, but I fear that Salisbury is very obdurate. We had a meeting of our old Cabinet this morning, but we did little beyond discussing the Queen's Speech. Richmond and Cairns were there but they go back to Scotland tomorrow.

The debate in the Lords was nothing remarkable. Salisbury's speech was good humoured, but hardly I thought up to the mark, Granville's below it. I followed but only on South African matters. Derby replied most fair, but the debate was on a rather dull level. Argyll spoke for

---

[846]Carnarvon immediately replied, 'The question is – first, are there a few individuals who sufficiently have the confidence of parties to undertake the task? Second, who are of sufficient fair temper to do the work? I have no doubt as to the second: I do not feel sure of the first, though on the whole I believe not, for such "righteous men" might be found' (Carnarvon to Ponsonby, 23 October 1884: Royal Archives, C50/12). More optimistically, he told Bath, 'If there be any merit in it, it is this – that there is no surrender or concession on either side. It is a common agreement, not a compromise which means concession' (Carnarvon to Bath, 23 October 1884 (copy): CP, BL 60772, fo. 102).

a few minutes and well in favour of coming to an understanding, but his was really the only speech in that sense.[847]

Richmond told me in strict confidence that he and Cairns had pressed on Salisbury the following proposal – that we should read the Franchise bill a second time then suspend it, then the House of Commons pass the Redistribution bill, and that on that being passed we could at once dispose of the Franchise and then proceed to the Redistribution. I said I doubted if the Government would agree to this bargain and I suggested a joint understanding as to Redistribution. This he thought impracticable.

Friday 24 October (London)

A very long conversation with Michael Beach on the Franchise and Redistribution question. I explained to him my whole view of the present position and my reasons for desiring to come to some good settlement of the matter if practicable. He started by replying that he was not much afraid of anything that would be done and that almost any reform of the House of Lords would be an improvement, and he doubted the practicability of my suggestion of a reference of the redistribution scheme to 4 impartial outsiders. But he ended by I think coming very much to my view and he said that he should call on Salisbury and without mentioning me urge these points on him and he proposed if necessary to come down to Highclere to talk again to me. It was a long, important and interesting conversation, and impressed me favourably with his clear and rather vigorous capacity.[848]

Tuesday 28 October (London – Highclere)

I have had a busy and anxious time the last two or three days which I propose to recapitulate as clearly and as briefly as I can. Raikes[849] and

---

[847] Parliament reassembled that day. Debate on the Queen's Speech: *Hansard*, CCXCIII, 23 October 1884, Salisbury, cols 16–27, Granville, col. 27, Carnarvon, cols 27–32, Derby, cols 34–39, Argyll, cols 41–43.

[848] Hicks Beach's views on franchise reform were somewhat in advance of the rest of the Party. With Churchill's encouragement, Hicks Beach suggested to Salisbury and Northcote that he should approach Hartington in confidence to discuss matters. See Hicks Beach, *Life of Sir Michael Hicks Beach*, I, p. 217.

[849] Henry Cecil Raikes (1838–1891), Con. MP for Cambridge University (1882–1891), Postmaster-General (1886–1891).

Sir Erskine May[850] spent Sunday here and I talked much with both of them on the present critical juncture and without explaining to them what had passed between Ponsonby and myself. I talked much on the feasibility of coming to some understanding with the Government by means of some such expedient of a conference as I indicated in my speech at Hackney. They both from different points of view seemed to be of much the same opinion as myself. On Sunday night I wrote a very full letter to Salisbury explaining my views and saying that I believed Gladstone was disposed to meet us on my suggestion of a conference. I requested Salisbury to communicate this letter to Northcote. Raikes took it with him to London on Monday morning.[851]

On Monday in the afternoon I received a letter from Norton enclosing one from Gladstone in which he commended and seemed to accept my suggestion and appeared to invite some overture from us in accordance with it.[852] This appeared a singular confirmation of my letter to Salisbury and I decided to go up to London that night, writing to Salisbury and Northcote and Beach and Ponsonby to appoint meetings.

On Tuesday morning I received a letter from the Duke of Argyll urging me to endeavour to arrange matters.[853] I then went to Northcote, read him copy of my letter to Salisbury as S. had not yet communicated it to him, showed him Gladstone's letter to Norton and explained everything.

He was I think much struck, agreed generally with me and we both went together to Salisbury whose brougham was at the door and who did not seem much pleased at the communication or desirous of going into the matter. He listened however to me and I told him of Ponsonby's communication, of the feeling of some others and of Gladstone's letter to Norton. Northcote supported what I said and Salisbury agreed that I should go to May and ascertain whether Gladstone's letter meant business.

I went on to May whom I found at home. I informed him of the substance of Gladstone's letter. He had not seen it tho' Gladstone showed it him immediately afterwards, but he said that Richard Grosvenor[854] had talked on Monday evening to him very earnestly as regards my suggestion, R. G. speaking, as I understood, Gladstone's

[850]Sir Thomas Erskine May (1815–1886), Clerk of the Commons (1871–1886), an authority on parliamentary procedure. Created Baron Farnborough (1886).

[851]Carnarvon to Salisbury, 26 October 1884 (copy): CP, BL 60832, fos 166–168.

[852]Norton to Carnarvon, 24 October 1884: CP, BL 60832, fos 40–41. See also Gladstone's reply to Norton, 24 October 1884: ibid., fo. 42.

[853]Argyll to Carnarvon, 26 October 1884: CP, BL 60832, fos 43–46.

[854]Richard de Aquila Grosvenor (1837–1912), 1st Baron Stalbridge (1886), Lib. MP for Flintshire (1861–1886), Liberal Unionist from 1886.

opinions. May asked if I would see Gladstone myself; I agreed provided that Gladstone asked me to do so and that it was understood that I represented only myself.[855]

May went to Gladstone, was absent for about an hour and returned saying 1st that Gladstone thought on the whole it was more prudent we should have no verbal communication which would be sure to be noticed and might lead to misunderstanding and 2ndly that he thought that the individuals who according to my suggestion should meet to confer upon Redistribution should not be accredited by the Government but should meet voluntarily thus casting upon them the initiative and the responsibility of action. I replied that I feared this would make my scheme at all events impracticable as no one whose character and position commanded weight would care to thrust themselves into a situation which under the best of circumstances was most difficult. Gladstone as I understood proposed that these gentlemen thus coming voluntarily together should agree if possible on some principle of Redistribution and would then communicate it to the Government who would then give it every consideration. 3rdly Gladstone avoided, as I understood, any distinctive answer to a further suggestion I had made through May for adding a suspending clause to the Franchise Bill.

From May's I went to the Carlton and had a long talk with Beach to whom I showed Gladstone's letter to Norton and to whom I also explained all that was essential in that which had passed. Beach is more anxious than I am to fight but he feels the situation critical and on the whole is disposed I think to agree with me. He told me that he was thinking of communicating personally and on his own responsibility with Hartington, Northcote and Salisbury being aware of this. I encouraged him in this.

From this I went to Ponsonby, told him again all that was essential in that which had passed. He said the Queen was most anxious to effect a settlement and had urged the Duke of Argyll to come up to London.[856]

Thence I went to Northcote, found him in, told him everything and with him went on to Salisbury to whom I announced that my mission had been fruitless. Salisbury said he expected this, but was evidently

---

[855] When May saw Gladstone on 28 October, Edward Hamilton noted, 'Mr. G. gave Sir T. May every assurance of a disposition for peace; and though he thought it might hardly be proper for him to see Lord Carnarvon behind (as it were) the back of the Tory leaders, he sent Lord Carnarvon friendly messages of encouragement' (Bahlman, II, p. 719).

[856] Salisbury told Ponsonby that day that the Lords should read the Franchise Bill a second time and then wait for the Redistribution Bill to come up from the Commons. See Cecil, III, p. 118.

much relieved, and then with great cordiality discussed Dunraven's motion on Fair Trade for Thursday week.

Friday 31 October (London)

These difficult and vexatious negotiations continue. Elsie and I came up to London yesterday afternoon in consequence of a letter most confidential which I received from Herbert[857] telling me that a friend of the Government had called upon him knowing our intimacy to offer to show me and any friends whom I might name the Government Redistribution scheme. Northcote, Richmond and Beach were specially mentioned as persons to whom I was free to communicate this but it was also requested that in the present stage I would not make any communication to Salisbury.[858] This placed me in a singularly awkward position.

On arriving in London I followed Northcote to the H. of Commons [and] told him briefly the circumstances but found him too busy to be able to attend. This morning I talked to him freely and told him that I proposed to write in reply that if I was free to communicate the offer to Salisbury and any others with whom I am acting I would at once do so. I then went on to the Colonial Office where I found [Sir Robert] Herbert[,] ascertained from him in confidence that the anonymous negotiator was Lord Reay[859] and I then wrote a letter to Herbert as I had proposed.

On returning to the Carlton I found Beach and communicated what had passed in the strictest personal confidence. He was very angry at the terms of the proposal saying that it was not a bona fide one. I differ with him there. It is absurd diplomacy to attempt to exclude at any stage Salisbury from a knowledge of such negotiations, but I believe it arises in part from a genuine apprehension of him and his supposed intentions. After a time he quietened down and gave me details of his conversation with Hartington to whom he seems to have explained all the principles which he thought ought to govern a Redistribution Bill and in which I think I agree with him. Hartington's view was for

---

[857]Auberon Herbert to Carnarvon, 29 October 1884: CP, BL 60795A, fos 9–10.

[858]Replying to Herbert, Carnarvon stated that he reserved the right to inform Salisbury of the letter, as well as Northcote and two or three other political friends (Carnarvon to Herbert, 31 October 1884 (copy): CP, BL 60795A, fo. 15).

[859]Donald James Mackay (1839–1921), 11th Baron Reay (1876), Governor of Bombay (1885–1890).

a much more limited and a Whig scheme. Beach wished for a larger and I think on the whole a safer measure.

After Beach I saw W. H. Smith and in the same strict confidence talked over the whole question. He agreed entirely in what I had done and I think looked at the matter from my point of view. He is not anxious to come to terms unless those terms are good, but he thinks that we ought not to reject a good bargain if one can be struck merely on the chance of what a Dissolution can bring us if taken on the existing Franchise.[860] Winn on the other hand with whom I have had a long conversation today is so despairing as to an election on the new Franchise that he would not accept any Redistribution Bill however favourable. He believes that it means the hopeless break up of the party and Cameron of Lochiel[861] tells me that the lowering of the Franchise in Scotland means the loss of every single seat. Akers Douglas[862] who helped to work out Bartley's scheme is rather more hopeful but he says that the Redistribution scheme published in the *Standard* when worked out was seen to be the most unfair and would have been fatal in many parts to us.

In the evening of Friday between 6 and 7 Herbert called and gave me verbally and in writing Reay's answer to my letter – and a singular answer it was. He said that circumstances had somewhat altered, that the bill was in fact not yet drafted, but he suggested (from the Government or Gladstone) that I and my friends should propose *our* redistribution scheme to the Government. I at once said that I thought the negotiations were at an end, but that I would see Northcote and Salisbury. The next morning (Saturday) I saw them both. Northcote agreed with me in my estimate of the whole transaction and was I think rather sorry at the failure of the negotiations: Salisbury evidently very much pleased.[863]

In the afternoon Elsie and I returned to Highclere.

[860]For Smith's views on the bill, see E.A. Douglas, 3rd Viscount Chilston, *W.H. Smith* (London, 1965), pp. 183–184.

[861]Donald Cameron of Lochiel (1835–1905), diplomat.

[862]Aretas Akers-Douglas (1851–1926), MP for East Kent (1880–1885) and for St Augustine's (1885–1911), Opposition Whip (1883–1885), Government Whip (1886–1892), Home Secretary (1902–1905), 1st Viscount Chilston (1911).

[863]Carnarvon had been in communication with leading Liberal peers on 29 October. In reply to a lengthy letter from Carnarvon, Granville wrote, 'I can answer for Gladstone in being sincerely anxious for an adjustment, provided it is compatible with his responsibility to the Liberal Party, with regard to the legislation he has undertaken' (Granville to Carnarvon, 31 October 1884: CP, BL 60773, fo. 139). To Argyll, Carnarvon declared, 'My efforts so far have been fruitless, but I am not without hope that some understanding may ultimately be built on them. The door is still open' (Carnarvon to Argyll, 1 November 1884 (copy): CP, BL 60832, fo. 70).

Thursday 6 November (London)

Debate in House of Lords on Dunraven's motion for a joint Committee on agriculture and trade. It was not a discussion worthy of time and place. Dunraven did not handle his subject well. Sandon spoke with force but only in a party point of view and I know that I was not particularly good.[864]

Dined with the Greenes, met Waddington,[865] Goschen, Foster, Froude, Reay. Had a great deal of conversation with Goschen as to the present situation. His great fear is that in any redistribution scheme the "middle class" should be trampled out of existence by the Tory democracy on the one side and the Radicals on the other. I agree, but they are a timid body which will not speak out for themselves.

Gladstone's speech in moving the Second Reading of the Franchise bill was extremely moderate and conciliatory and a very large part of it was written out.[866] Goschen told me this and Northcote repeated it to me.

Friday 7 November (London)

A talk with Northcote as to the position of affairs.[867] We talked freely and I went so far in personal confidence to tell him that there is a most widespread belief that Salisbury is "riding for a fall" and is quite reckless as to the destruction of the House of Lords.[868] He admitted it, but said that the Government disliked him so much and were anxious to damage him that he believed they would with that view accept

---

[864]Motion for a Select Committee jointly with the House of Commons 'to inquire into the condition of the work and commerce of this country': *Hansard*, CCXCIII, 6 November 1884, Dunraven, cols 1044–1060, Harrowby, cols 1070–1073, Carnarvon, cols 1076–1079. The motion was withdrawn.

[865]William Henry Waddington (1826–1893), French diplomat, Minister of Foreign Affairs (1877), ambassador at London (1881–1893).

[866]*Hansard*, CCXCIII, 6 November 1884, Gladstone, cols 1121–1129. The bill was carried by 372 to 232.

[867]Behind the scenes, on 31 October, Queen Victoria had suggested a bipartisan conference consisting of Gladstone, Salisbury, and Northcote. Salisbury accepted but Gladstone hesitated on the grounds that discussions were already under way between Hicks Beach and Hartington. See C.C. Weston, 'The royal mediation in 1884', *English Historical Review*, 77 (1967), p. 306.

[868]John Fair has pointed out that Carnarvon's remarks were less to do with a challenge to Salisbury than concern over the future of the House of Lords and perhaps more. Richmond told Carnarvon on 31 October, 'If the House of Lords is to be tinkered and the hereditary principle interfered with, it is not a very long step from the Throne' (J.D. Fair, 'The Carnarvon diaries and royal mediation', *English Historical Review*, 106 (1991), pp. 105–106.

worse terms for themselves as to re-distribution. But he knew that what I have said is the feeling all round and he admitted that it was very disastrous.

Cleveland seems to be elected President of the U.S., which as far as one can see is likely to be the best issue of the controversy.[869] On the other hand the cholera appears to be in Paris and I suppose we shall have it here.

Politically the tide at this moment seems against us. The pending Elections are likely to be a failure, and Fawcett's death[870] removes one moderate and upright man from the Government.

Tuesday 11 November (London)
[House of Lords]

The Franchise bill has passed so swiftly through all its stages that will be with us on Thursday.[871] Granville proposed to put down the Second Reading for next Tuesday, being less than a week. Salisbury objected strongly. G. very suave, S. very rough. Salisbury afterwards spoke to me about it and I said I thought it would be a pity to divide on such a point as to whether the bill should be taken on Tuesday or Thursday, and at last Salisbury agreed in this. But at first he let Granville understand that he should probably divide. It would have been a pity.

I am afraid the chances of a compromise or an understanding are fading away. The South Warwickshire election has excited some of our men.[872] The Duke of Argyll told me that he had been talking to Chaplin who was very hot to get rid of the bill altogether. Impossible. We have gone too far on the road of change.

Meanwhile there is great trouble brewing among the Scottish crofters, and all the airs of demagogism and agitation are at work there to fan the fire. There is a proclamation put out by some anonymous person inciting to the burning and destroying of the landowners' property.

[869]Grover Cleveland, the Democratic Party nominee, was elected after a turbulent campaign (see P. Nevins, *Grover Cleveland: a study in courage* (New York, 1932), pp. 156–188).

[870]Henry Fawcett, Lib. Postmaster-General since 1880, had died on 6 November. For an assessment of his career, see L. Stephens, *Life of Henry Fawcett* (London, 1886), pp. 450–456.

[871]*Hansard*, CCXCIII, 13 November 1884, cols 1463–1553.

[872]The South Warwickshire by-election on 9 November resulted in the capture of a former Liberal-held seat for the Conservatives: Sampson Lloyd, the Conservative candidate, obtained 3,095 votes; Lord William Compton, 1,919. Compton told Sir Edward Hamilton that his 'crushing defeat' was mainly due to 'the dislike of farmers to the enfranchisement of their labourers' (Bahlman, II, p. 730).

Wednesday 12 November (London)

A meeting at Salisbury's to consider what should be done as to the
Franchise Bill.[873] A good deal of discussion. Salisbury's view was not
to help, if possible, any redistribution and to compel a dissolution,
and with him agreed J. Manners and R. Winn. Against that view and
in favour of coming to terms if good ones can be had were Cross,
Smith, Sandon, Northcote and myself. Nothing definite was settled
except that the proposal to postpone the Committee to some distant
time should not be made, as Salisbury suggested, *immediately* after the
Second Reading but in the usual course, when the bill comes on for
Committee. This was undoubtedly the opinion of the majority but
perhaps this was not distinctly agreed to.[874]

Friday 14 November (London)

Conversation with Northcote as to the state of affairs. It seems
that Beach's negotiations are still in progress, or at least have not
broken down. Northcote is desirous of some compromise and would
like if possible that the Government should announce an intention
to introduce a redistribution bill in the House of Commons as soon
as we have passed the Second Reading of the Franchise bill in the
Lords, and that on this we should put our Committee to say, a
fortnight or to give time to see the nature of Redistribution, proceeding
with the Committee rather gradually, to give time for discussion of
Redistribution in House of Commons. This I think a very good idea,
my only doubt is whether it is practicable. It depends first on the
Government, secondly on Salisbury: the former are doubtful, the
latter very doubtful.

In the evening we dined with the Jeunes[875] and went to see *Hamlet* at
the Princess. It was very poorly played to my mind, not a single actor

---

[873] The second reading was to be in the Lords on 18 November.

[874] After the meeting, Salisbury wrote to Carnarvon, 'On the whole I come to the conclusion
that it would be wisest, as you suggested, to let the bill pass through the second reading in
the ordinary way on Tuesday, and take the division on going into Committee on Thursday.
The words to that effect will go out tonight, the arrangement was of course made with the
assent of Granville' (Salisbury to Carnarvon, 12 November 1884: CP, BL 60760, fos 3–4).

[875] Francis Henry Jeune (1843–1905), judge, created Baron St Helier (1905), and Lady Mary
Jeune (1849–1931), society hostess (see E.F. Benson, *As We Were: a Victorian peep show* (London,
1930), pp. 284–286). The following year, Lady Jeune played a part in helping to set up the
meeting between Carnarvon and Parnell on 1 August (Lady Jeune to Carnarvon, 22 July
1885: CP, BL 60822, fo. 125).

or actress of any power, and it proved to me that with all his faults Irving is in a rank far above his competitors.[876]

Saturday 15 November (London)

A long conversation with Greenwood as to the Franchise Bill. He too agrees that the time for negotiation is come, but that secret negotiations would be a mistake, except as to particular details in the redistribution plan, because if a joint bill could be agreed on by the Government and Opposition it would have to be forced on Parliament and would be bitterly objected to both by Radicals and Irish. There is much sense in this: but the fact is that Parliamentary Government is nearly at an end. It has lost all its old vital power.

Sunday 16 November (London)

In the afternoon I had a long and most important conversation with Richmond who arrived in London this morning with Cairns from Scotland about 4 a.m. He discussed the whole situation and I think we are perfectly agreed on everything of any consequence.

He is most anxious as to the crisis, much annoyed at the joint meeting of members of both Houses at the Carlton on Thursday which he says is an attempt to coerce the Lords by noisy members of the House of Commons, very much disturbed at Salisbury's attitude and supposed intentions, anxious to open private communication with the Government, and resolved at any price not to allow the hope of compromise to break down.[877] The Queen is *extremely* anxious on the matter and he read me a really important letter from her to him which she had sent to him by Ponsonby at Perth as he was on his way South. She is very desirous of bringing about a meeting of the leaders on both sides, and is extremely alive to the risks of a dissolution at present. We are undoubtedly in the midst of a very serious crisis; but assuming that we do not show too much anxiety to deal, which would probably induce Gladstone to raise his terms, I think we ought to

---

[876]Wilson Barrett (1846–1904), actor-manager of the Princess's Theatre (1881–1886), took the leading role. Henry Irving (1838–1905) had long been celebrated for his interpretation of the part.

[877]Carnarvon had arranged to meet Salisbury at midday on 17 November. Meanwhile, he warned Salisbury, 'I am afraid that your joint meeting of the two Houses on Thursday is not popular with many peers; and even if no open dissatisfaction is expressed, I doubt if the results will be good. You can learn more of the feeling by enquiry but it is, I think, even now worth considering whether anything can be done to give them the sense of a somewhat free and more independent discussion of the course which they will pursue' (Carnarvon to Salisbury, 16 November 1884 (copy): CP, BL 60960, fos 6–7).

settle the matter. Richmond, Cairns and I, reinforced as we now are by Sandon, are I think strong enough for the purpose. But I foresee that matters may be very disagreeable.[878]

Sir John A. Macdonald dined with us in the evening, alone, and we had some interesting conversation. One of the principal subjects was Ireland. I asked him how far his opinions had altered since we last spoke on it, and how he believed it could be governed. He said "by 'thorough', by Strafford's policy."[879]

But I said, "It is impossible, impossible under your present Parliamentary system."

He said "It is very difficult, and for this reason, that you are in a transitional state. You have neither the stability and permanence of an aristocracy nor the force of a democracy. A democracy may coerce Ireland, for there is nothing so hard and corrupt as a democracy when a dominant race in its dealings with a subject one".

I asked him who in his opinion would hereafter stand out as the greatest minister since 1832. He said Palmerston. Lord Derby had not had office long enough; Gladstone would be killed by the record of his own speeches and the "swamp" of words. Lord John Russell was already forgotten.

He first came to England in 1842 in the "great rally of Conservatism" and there saw and heard Peel, O'Connell[880] and Mr. Stanley. He seems to have been a good deal attracted by Lord Derby, then and afterwards, and spoke of him as "a great Patrician."

Tuesday 18 November (London)

We have had an anxious two days, ending however in a most successful and satisfactory compromise. On Monday morning

---

[878] When the Hartington–Hicks Beach discussions broke down, the way seemed clear for a meeting between Salisbury and Gladstone. As Gladstone was now willing to come to some understanding, Ponsonby informed the Queen on 15 November that he had talked to Richmond and Cairns (at Perth station that day, on their way to London) as she had requested, in order that they might persuade Salisbury to negotiate with Gladstone (F.E.G. Ponsonby, *Sidelights on Queen Victoria* (London, 1930), pp. 274–276). Salisbury, for his part, told Northcote on 13 November that there would be no easy passage for the Franchise Bill unless the Commons first sent up a Redistribution Bill (Salisbury to Northcote, 13 November 1884: Iddesleigh Papers, BL 50020, fo. 91).

[879] Thomas Wentworth, 1st Earl of Strafford (1593–1641), despotic Lord Deputy of Ireland (1633–1639). The previous year, Carnarvon had visited Canada and stayed with his old friend John Macdonald, the Leader of the Canadian Conservative Party. In discussing the Irish question, Macdonald expressed 'drastic and almost Cromwellian views' (Hardinge, III, pp. 92–93).

[880] Daniel O'Connell (1775–1847), MP for Dublin, Kilkenny, and Co. Cork, 'The Liberator', who supported Catholic emancipation in 1805.

the Papers announced that the Government would make some declaration on the subject of the Franchise and Redistribution question,[881] and at 12 some Peers met at Salisbury's. I had understood it was to be a very small and private meeting, instead of which it was composed of all the Conservative Peers who had held *any* office in the late Government – Bury, Beauchamp, Mount Edgcumbe,[882] Cadogan, Colville, with the addition of Northcote. Anything so unfit to discuss a delicate question like this in the actual crisis of the case it is impossible to conceive. I felt it at once, and Richmond afterwards said to me that he could not but perceive that it had been constituted in order [to] overbear Cairns, himself, myself, etc.[883] I fully believe it was so designed, but it did not answer, for the general feeling was that in the face of this announcement it was impossible to take up a fighting attitude and that we must defer our decision till after the declarations of ministers. Nothing however could be more hostile to compromise than Salisbury's attitude.

When the House met Granville made his announcement and with studied conciliation of language and manner. Salisbury merely replied by asking a question and the matter dropped.[884] Immediately after the House rose our same committee of the morning reassembled at the Carlton. The prevailing feeling was all in favour of an acceptance of the Government's proposals, and so strong was it that I was afraid of too much eagerness being shown. Salisbury came last, and his first words were all hostile. He insisted on it that the Government evidently meant to make our acceptance of the Franchise Bill a condition precedent on their showing us their Redistribution scheme. I said I thought this mot unlikely and advised some private communication to clear up the case, but while we were arguing and while Salisbury was very adverse to the proposals there came Arthur Balfour and his memorandum, which was afterwards read in the House and which set the matter

---

[881] *The Times*, for instance, announced that 'Lord Granville in the House of Lords and Mr Gladstone in the House of Commons will today make a public declaration of the basis on which they are prepared to proceed with reference to the Franchise and Redistribution Bills' (*The Times*, 18 November 1884, p. 9).

[882] William Henry Edgcumbe (1832–1917), 4th Earl of Mount-Edgcumbe (1861), Lord Chamberlain (1879–1880), Lord Lieutenant of Cornwall (1877–1917).

[883] Cairns and Richmond, strong advocates of reconciliation, nevertheless received Salisbury's permission after the meeting to talk to Granville (Richmond to Queen Victoria, 17 November 1884, in Buckle, *Letters*, III, pp. 575–576). Gladstone, in his speech later to the Commons on 17 November, as an act of reconciliation had offered either a conference or a Redistribution Bill on the lines discussed with Northcote, and that a second reading in the Commons could take place simultaneously with the passing of the Franchise Bill into Committee in the Lords (*Hansard*, CCXCIII, 17 November 1884, cols 1820–1824).

[884] *Hansard*, CCXCIII, 17 November 1884, Granville, cols 1806–1809, Salisbury, col. 1809.

372 1884

right and showed that the Government did not mean to set a trap for us. This, as Salisbury said, altered the case greatly, and we broke up.[885]

On Tuesday morning we had a meeting of our ex-Cabinet only at the Carlton where this point was made still clearer by further communication, so a conciliatory policy of meeting the Government was agreed on. After this we digressed into considerable discussion as to the principles of Redistribution. Beach *very* strong as to his own view in favour of single-membered constituencies, John Manners equally strong as to the fatal effects on the Conservative Party by the co-operation on Redistribution to which we are now pledged. Salisbury on the other hand now that he is compelled to accept this course seems inclined to accept it pretty heartily. Cairns suggested that the two leaders should go into consultation with the Government and that behind them there would be a small Committee, mainly House of Commons men, to advise them and keep them in relation with the Party. It is a good suggestion and is really almost identical with what I originally proposed in my abortive negotiations through Sir E. May.

After this the mixed meeting of Lords and Commons at the Carlton followed. It was singularly harmonious, the feeling of all being one of great satisfaction at this conclusion to an awkward business. Chaplin, though still anxious to get a dissolution, professed complete satisfaction.

In the House of Lords later Salisbury's speech, though not perhaps quite as conciliatory as it might have been, was good – and so ends the first stage of this question.

Wednesday 19 November (London)

In the evening we dined at the Jeunes where Northcote was. He begged me to draw him any suggestions as to redistribution, which I promised to do.

---

[885]Before the Carlton Club meeting, Salisbury despatched his nephew, Arthur Balfour, to Gladstone, seeking reassurance whether the pledge to pass the Reform Bill '*is* or *is not* to predate an agreement with regard to the provisions of the Redistribution Bill'. Acting through Hartington's private secretary, Reginald Brett, Gladstone replied in a conciliatory manner. An inter-party conference would safeguard Salisbury's position. See J.D. Fair, 'Royal mediation in 1884: a reassessment', *English Historical Review*, 88 (1973), p. 111. The Franchise Bill was given its second reading later in the day: *Hansard*, CCXCIV, 17 November 1884, cols 1–10. There was also some unease on the Liberal benches at the settlement. Arthur Elliot reported a dinner party conversation hosted by another Liberal MP, Leonard Courtney: 'Courtney like other people were taken aback by the novelty of Ministers and Opposition jointly bringing forward the Redistribution Bill: a course of action which effectively destroys any influence from the House at large before the measure' (Elliot, Diary, 19 November 1884: Minto Papers, MS 19511, vol. 10, pp. 75–76).

Monday 24 November (London)

I went to the House but there was no business of consequence. On returning to Portman Square, I had a long and interesting talk with Stead. He believes nothing to be yet settled as to naval expenditure, the Cabinet probably deciding it this week![886] He tells me that Gladstone and Salisbury get on very well in conference on the Redistribution matter and that all Gladstone's liking for Salisbury has returned.[887] Meanwhile Salisbury has summoned us to a small meeting next Wednesday to consider redistribution, so I think it all looks like a settlement. He mentioned to me a curious speech of Gladstone's yesterday indicating his Conservatism. G. was reviewing the last half century of Liberal legislation and he pronounced it be very remarkable, but wound up by saying that it was so remarkable that it now left nothing to be done.[888]

Wednesday 26 November (London)

A meeting of our ex-Cabinet at Salisbury's. He and Northcote were there to explain the course of negotiation and to get our consent and agreement to what they proposed to do.[889]

They read the memorandum of the proposed Government distribution bill which is in many respects like that which appeared in the *Standard*, perhaps is in essentials the same. They seemed to have not effected much in the way of alteration. Single membered constituencies appear to be about the only point on which the

---

[886] Stead, greatly concerned at the Liberal government's policy of reducing the vote on naval expenditure, wrote an article, 'The truth about the Navy', for his journal, the *Pall Mall Gazette*. It was later reprinted as a pamphlet and had a significant impact on public opinion. This led to an increase in the naval vote.

[887] On 22 November, Salisbury and Northcote met Gladstone, Hartington, and Dilke, President of the Local Government Board, with no minutes taken. A written compact known as 'the Arlington Street Compact', agreed between Salisbury and Dilke, was concluded on 28 November. See S. Gwynn and G.M. Tuckwell, *The Life of the Rt. Hon. Sir Charles Dilke*, 2 vols (London, 1917), II, pp. 74–75.

[888] Edward Hamilton reported after one meeting between the two men, 'Mr. G. was in great spirits [. . .]. He said the discussions were intensely interesting and carried on in great humour. Lord Salisbury, who seems to monopolise all the say on his side, has no respect for tradition. As compared with him, Mr. G. declares he is himself quite a Conservative' (Bahlman, III, p. 741).

[889] Carnarvon wrote to Salisbury later the same day, 'It seems to me of the highest consequence that the Redistribution Bill should be as far advanced at once as to have the Speaker out of the Chair on this side of Christmas' (Carnarvon to Salisbury, 26 November 1884: Hatfield House Papers, 3M/E).

Government are disposed to yield, minority voting being absolutely refused and grouping of towns strongly objected to.

Single membered constituencies and a good boundary Commission appear to be about all that can be got.

We agreed, everyone thinking it better not to break off the negotiation, and we consented though unwillingly to an increase of the total number of the House.

Ireland is to stand at the number of 100, and Scotland to get an addition of 10 or 13 members.

It is not satisfactory, but it is probably all that can be had and matters might be much worse; but one thing strikes me painfully, viz. that no one seems to have any knowledge or intelligent forecast of what will be the result of all this. It is another leap in the dark.[890]

In the evening I dined at the Empire Club at a dinner given in honour of Sir John Macdonald. He made a long speech which would have been a very good one if it had been a little more condensed, but it was too diffuse. Salisbury, Derby, Kimberley and I spoke.[891]

Tuesday 2 December (London)

Meeting of both Houses at Carlton. Salisbury made an able statement of his and Northcote's negotiations with the Government, describing the duty as a "repulsive" one, but claiming credit for considerable success.[892] It was most coldly received and a good deal of protest was entered by Chaplin, Raikes and some others. Ritchie on the other hand endorsed it all. But taking everything into account the Party seemed to me to behave very well, though many were under sentence of death there was nothing said that was unbefitting. It is a great question how it will all turn out. It may be the end of the old historic "Country Party" and sometimes I fear that it is, but it is the direct outcome of '67.

Later an important statement by Northbrook as to the Navy. I replied for our front bench as no one else knew anything of the

---

[890]After earlier hearing Gladstone's report to the Cabinet on the proposed conference between the two parties that day, Carlingford wrote, 'Very promising and near an agreement, but it is accepting the great change of the almost general introduction of the system of single member electoral districts instead of groupings which the Conservative chiefs began by proposing' (Carlingford, Diary, 19 November 1884: Carlingford Papers, BL 63692, fo. 254).

[891]*The Times*, 27 November 1884, p. 7.

[892]Gladstone had introduced the Redistribution Bill on 1 December: *Hansard*, CCXCIV, cols 372–385.

matter, the Admirals who spoke not saying much but what they said was much to the point.[893]

Thursday 4 December (London)

The Franchise bill passed through Committee in House of Lords. There was little discussion.[894] I said a few words on the subject of the female franchise,[895] and was afterwards interviewed by Mrs Hallett and Miss Becker, a rather grim and bespectacled lady of middle or any age.[896]

Dined at the Jeunes. She tells me that Chamberlain is much annoyed and dissatisfied at the Redistribution bill, which is good.

Monday 8 December (Highclere)

This afternoon as I returned from riding a telegram was put into my hands containing an invitation to Elsie and myself from the Queen to Windsor. It is evidence of a reconciliation on her part after nearly six years of absolute silence. I shall be curious to see whether when we meet everything falls back into the old lines and she gives me at once all the old confidence, or whether the meeting is to be a purely formal one, the step perhaps to other communications, but for the moment nothing more. I saw all the best side of her 7 or 8 years ago, and I have nothing to learn now: but if I can be of any use she may, as she must have known, command me now as always. I think it possible my communications with Ponsonby some weeks ago may have led to this overture.

---

[893]The State of the Navy: ibid., 2 December 1884, Northbrook, cols 395–414, Carnarvon, cols 414–422.

[894]Ibid., 4 December 1884, cols 572–594. Carlingford wrote the following day, 'To the House of Lords, and saw the Franchise Bill passed without a word, with a few cheers from our side – a historical event' (Carlingford, Diary, 5 December 1884: Carlingford Papers, BL 63692, fo. 254). It received the Royal Assent on 6 December.

[895]*Hansard*, CCXCIV, 4 December 1884, cols 578–579.

[896]Lilias Sophia Ashworth Hallett (1844–1922), who with Millicent Fawcett was responsible for campaigning for a bill to enfranchise unmarried women and widows; Lydia Ernestine Becker (1827–1890), agent for the Central Committee of the National Society for Women's Suffrage. See E. Crawford, *The Women's Suffrage Movement* (London, 1999), pp. 46, 260. Carnarvon received a warm letter of thanks from the Central Committee for his supportive speech (CP, BL 60832, fo. 107).

Wednesday 10 December (Windsor Castle)

In the afternoon Elsie and I went to Windsor. Only Cairns and
Lady Cairns were invited besides ourselves. The rest of the party was
composed of the Ladies in waiting and equerries etc.

The Queen was most gracious, it was an entire renewal of the old
manner and apparently feeling, just as if the last six years had gone
by and as if all cause for offence with me was entirely blotted out.
She talked to Elsie after dinner for a considerable time, and evidently
with great kindness, about the children and herself, and all kinds of
people and things; and when after dinner she talked with me she went
with all her old frankness into a conversation on the recent agitation
and the recent conference. She said something to the effect that she
was aware that I had done my best to help matters to this conclusion;
but I said that the greatest service of all had been rendered by her, at
which she was pleased, though it certainly is no more than the bare
truth. It was a real personal pleasure to me to feel that the Queen was
completely reconciled to me; for the alienation after so much kindness
to me in former years pained me.

1885

Thursday 5 February (Porto Fino)

Wrote an important letter to Salisbury and one to Sir G. Duffy.[897]

Friday 6 February (Porto Fino)

I received this morning a telegram from Herbert to say that "Khartoum has fallen and Gordon probably killed".[898] It is bad news and may lead to the gravest consequences in the East. The delay may jeopardise the whole expedition. It is very sad as regards Gordon and it is only too likely.

Monday 23 February (London)

Meeting at Salisbury's to arrange terms of note of censure in House of Lords,[899] and afterwards general meeting of the Peers. The last was a poor concern. A good many spoke but not one said anything worth hearing.

---

[897] Following a meeting with the Irish nationalist Sir Charles Gavan Duffy (1836–1903) at Highclere in October 1884, Carnarvon urged Duffy to put down his ideas for a Conservative Party settlement for Ireland. Duffy drew up a memorandum and wrote an article for the *National Review*. Entitled 'An appeal to the Conservative Party' and signed 'An Irish Conservative', it was published in February 1885. Carnarvon enthusiastically supported Duffy's ideas and told Salisbury, 'For my own part [. . .] our best and almost only hope is to come to some fair and reasonable arrangement for Home Rule' (Carnarvon to Salisbury, 5 February 1885 (copy): CP, BL 60760, fos 18–21). Salisbury, replying to Carnarvon's 'most interesting letter', was not encouraging. 'It is possible', he wrote, 'that such a scheme as you hope for may be devised which would give all requisite guarantees for the interests which we are bound in honour not to abandon, and yet would satisfy the separatist feeling. I am not hopeful, for I have been unable to think of any provisions which would answer the above requirements' (Salisbury to Carnarvon, 18 February 1885: CP, BL 60760, fos 22–23).

[898] Gordon, Governor-General of the Sudan, was murdered by the Mahdi's forces on 26 January, after a siege lasting 317 days and two days before relief forces arrived. See J. Marlowe, *Mission to Khartum: the apotheosis of General Gordon* (London, 1969), pp. 289–291.

[899] Deploring the failure of the Sudan expedition and the abandonment of the Sudan after military operations, Carnarvon had a conversation with Salisbury in the House three days earlier and wrote afterwards, 'A vote of censure in our House is decided on, he says, rather against his opinion. I think it is a mistake' (Diary, 20 February 1885).

In the House I made a short speech on the Colonial offer of military assistance.[900]

Tuesday 24 February (London)

A meeting of the two Houses at the Carlton and an important one, the real object being to protest against the feeble wording of Northcote's vote of censure. I was extremely sorry for Northcote, for he must have felt it. It was an unusual chorus of condemnation and unfortunately his speech had not been of a nature to redeem the charge of feebleness. The result of the meeting was to virtually make Salisbury the Head of the Party. This has been fast approaching, but I look upon the meeting today as decisive. Salisbury showed a great deal of ability as usual, and he was not at all ungenerous, but it was nevertheless a rather painful scene to me. Northcote has filled a position for which he was never really fit. His virtues and his defects were equally against him and in some respects he is too much of a gentleman for the circumstances of his time.

Friday 27 February (London)

Vote of Censure again.[901] I resumed it on our side. I was not myself satisfied with my speech, but I suppose it was fairly adequate as several people came up to praise it to me, which they would hardly have done had I really failed in it.[902] Granville and I had a scrimmage over one part of it. He has grown very irritable.

Salisbury's reply was very powerful, but with too much ceremony as regards Derby, whom he cannot bear, and to whom he never fails to show his dislike.[903]

Saturday 28 February (Pixton)

The Government have only a majority of 14 in the Commons. What a downfall – and how just a punishment.[904]

It is a great question now what they will do. The general idea is that they will go on and probably break up soon. It is a terrible prospect to succeed to such a heritage of blundering and misfortune and I shudder at the idea of a return to Office.

---

[900] The Australian Colonies: *Hansard*, CCXCIV, 23 February 1885, cols 1013–1014.

[901] Debate on the failure of the Sudan expedition, second day.

[902] *Hansard*, CCXCIV, 27 February 1885, cols 1526–1539.

[903] Ibid., cols 1590–1594. The House divided: Contents 189, Not-Contents 68.

[904] Ayes 288, Noes 302.

Thursday 9 April (Pixton)

This evening after dinner we had the news of the apparently unprovoked attack by the Russians on the Afghans, and the defeat of the latter.[905] It is very serious news and it determined us to go at once to Highclere and then on Monday to London. And so ends our holiday and our return to politics – alas! But the whole public prospect seems to me darker than it has ever been in my life time.

Monday 13 April (London)

I called at the Colonial Office and saw Herbert on my way to the House of Lords. At the House Cranbrook appeared having just returned from the West Indies, much restored I think and hope in health. He brought me home in his brougham and I had some pleasant talk with him. He gave me some details as to poor Cairns's death[906] which was peaceful and happy.

Thursday 7 May (London)

I was attacked this morning by a sudden fit of gout. I was perfectly well, was at the House and made a short speech on a small bill,[907] walked home and in walking felt a sudden pain in my foot. Since then it has been increasing and the foot is swollen though not very red.

A very curious and confidential communication made to me in the House of Lords by an old friend on the other side. It was made with a very friendly purpose, and the next week will show whether the information is correct.

Tuesday 9 June (London)

At the station the astonishing news of the Government defeat met me.[908] Justice is at last satisfied in Gladstone's downfall, but scarcely.

---

[905]The Russians had been gradually encroaching on Afghanistan, bringing near the prospect of war with Great Britain. On 30 March, Russian forces attacked Penjdeh, entirely unexpectedly and without provocation, heavily defeating the Afghans (see Sir G.F. Macmunn, *Afghanistan from Darius to Amanullah* (London, 1929), pp. 213–214). For the events leading up to the Penjdeh crisis, see K. Bourne, *The Foreign Policy of Victorian England, 1830–1902* (Oxford, 1970), pp. 41–44.

[906]Cairns had died on the 2 April.

[907]Friendly Societies Act (1875) Amendment Bill, second reading: *Hansard*, CCXCVII, 7 May 1885, Carnarvon, col. 1818.

[908]On the Customs and Inland Revenue Bill, second reading, the Government was defeated by 264 to 252, a majority of twelve: *Hansard*, CCXCVIII, 8 June 1885, cols 1514–1517.

I feel about him as Jeremy Taylor[909] said of the robber who had committed sacrilege and slept beneath a crumbling wall. His moral and political crimes deserve a severer penalty.

Reached London and found Elsie at the station, waiting for me.

Wednesday 10 June (London)

Great excitement and agitation here over the news, the Carlton I hear like a swarm of bees. Sandon dined with me last night and we had a long and a most pleasant conversation, mainly on the chances of a Conservative Government and the line to be adopted. We agreed extremely well.

I saw Gull this morning. He prescribed for me and said that he thought I was nearly well. At the same time I do not feel strong.

Thursday 11 June (London)

Northcote sent me yesterday evening a message by Lady N: that he was anxious for some conversation with me and offered to come and see me.[910] I said I would not hear of this but would come to him and this morning I called on him and had a considerable conversation on the present state of affairs. It was mainly to ask my opinion on the situation, and the main points in our talk were these:

1. He expressed some doubt as to whether the Liberal Government was at an end and whether we were bound to take office. I said I believed they were at an end and that however disagreeable, doubtful and dangerous it was our plain duty to take office – for the party and for the country.

2. I said that this being clear I thought the whole course and policy of a Conservative Cabinet were involved in their mode of dealing with Ireland, that my view was to throw the responsibility and blame on the Government for placing them in such a position, and that I was disposed to advise giving up all attempt to pass a coercion bill, to

---

[909] Jeremy Taylor (1613–1667), Bishop of Down and Connor (1660–1667), Vice-Chancellor, Trinity College, Dublin (1661–1667), ecclesiastical writer and literary genius.

[910] The previous evening, Northcote had been summoned by Salisbury to a meeting at which Hicks Beach was also present. Salisbury's scheme was that he would be Prime Minister and Foreign Secretary, with Northcote as First Lord of the Treasury and Leader of the Commons. Northcote noted in his diary, 'The more I think of the heads of Salisbury's scheme, the less I like it' (Lang, *Life, Letters and Diaries of Sir Stafford Northcote*, II, p. 211).

appeal to whatever Irish good sense and good feeling there might be, to send as Lord Lieutenant a military man and indicate that if there was a renewal of outrages we must fall back on Martial Law, and to promise that in the meantime the Conservative Government would consider the whole state of affairs in Ireland with a view to a new course of policy. I suggested Wolseley.

Friday 12 June (London)

Salisbury has gone to Balmoral. I heard this in a letter this morning from Northcote and half an hour afterwards saw it in the papers at breakfast.[911] I have been thinking a good deal since then on the contingencies likely to arise from this. My impression now is to this effect that it will probably be the duty and on the whole the interest of the Conservative party to take office; that it is possible that a Conservative Government may pull through successfully and even gain considerable credit (by a short administration as it most probably will be); but that the dangers are great and that the key of the position at this moment is Ireland. If they can preserve peace and order there without coercion and announce the intention of giving a policy there, without at present giving details which would only provoke opposition, they may perhaps achieve a considerable success. If they are obliged to have recourse to coercion they will provoke antagonism, damage their policy when they come to it and possibly fail. This is how it strikes me.

I shall *myself* go into Office, if I must do so, with a heavy heart: for I foresee many personal difficulties and disagreeables, but I am resolved as far as I can make it a matter of duty and in Elsie particularly I have the greatest help. Her steady judgement and true affection are more than I can describe.

Monday 15 June (London)

A meeting of our ex-Cabinet at Arlington Street to consider the state of affairs. Present – Richmond, J. Manners, Smith, Cross, Sandon, Beach, Salisbury, Cranbrook, Gibson, George Hamilton and myself. R. Churchill was not there and Stanley was in Lancashire.

---

[911]Northcote to Carnarvon, 11 June 1885: CP, BL 60760, fo. 40. The Queen recorded after the interview, 'Lord Salisbury arrived at 20 m. to 5 pm. (New govt.). Lord Carnarvon for Lord Lieutenant of Ireland who he thought very clever and conciliatory and popular wherever he went' (Queen Victoria, Memorandum, 12 June 1885: Royal Archives, C36/420).

Salisbury began by reading a telegram from the Queen dictated by him to Gladstone saying that he (S.) would be quite ready to take office etc., the other from Gladstone saying that the late Government were precluded from considering whether they would return to office or not. The telegram on S.'s part was certainly not guarded enough and might seem to indicate too much readiness to take office. This was noticed by Beach, who had evidently had some communication with S. before S. went to Balmoral and who said this telegram was not in accordance with what had been settled between them. This was not a pleasant beginning, and it was succeeded by an equally uncomfortable disclosure as regards R. Churchill. For something having been said as to him I urged the importance of taking him into the Cabinet. Salisbury then said that R.C. had declined to enter it unless certain members were excluded, and this he (S.) would never listen to. He spoke with great warmth. Beach then gave his explanation of the matter which was a different one, viz., that R.C. would not join unless there was a reconstruction of the Cabinet. This however I did not understand till afterwards G. Hamilton explained to Sandon, and me that R.C. had said that it was impossible for Northcote in his state of health to lead and that this was the change meant. And this unfortunately is too true. It is absolutely essential that a change should be made here. Northcote is so frail that he often remains torpid, I am told, during part of the afternoon sitting.[912] In essentials R.C. is right: but he made this case to Salisbury in a way to provoke him and irritate and there is a good deal of ill feeling, and it is not clear to me that the Cabinet will be formed after all – though I think it will.[913]

The points that I urged strongly were:

1. that it should be made clear that we accepted office only as in the last resort.

2. that we should not take it as a mere intermediary Cabinet *d'affaires*, but must make our mark: for that reason we must do something beyond merely passing Supplies.

---

[912] As understood by Northcote, the changes included a peerage for himself and the exclusion from the Cabinet of Richmond, Cross, Carnarvon, and Manners (see Cooke and Vincent, *The Governing Passion*, p. 264). Churchill was later appointed to the India Office.

[913] Lady Knightley, the wife of a veteran Conservative MP, commented on the situation two days later, 'Sir Stafford is shunted and goes to the Upper House [as First Lord of the Treasury]. Perhaps it is as well but I am *very* sorry for him' (P. Gordon (ed.), *Politics and Society: the journals of Lady Knightley of Fawsley, 1885 to 1913* (Northamptonshire Record Society, 1999), p. 59).

3. that we ought to exact some pledge from Gladstone to help in passing Supplies and to give us all Government time in the H. of C.

4. with regard to Ireland we are most of us apparently in favour of going on without coercion till the new Parliament but I urged a strong Lord Lieutenant, an indication that we did not intend to tolerate disorder, putting Irishmen in every office, and a statement that in the new Parliament, we should consider the whole state of Ireland.[914]

Wednesday 17 June (London)

We have had a very busy two days. On Tuesday whilst driving round the Regents Park with Elsie I was overtaken by R. Cecil[915] and asked to come at once to see his father. I found Salisbury in[916] who at once plunged in and with some personal compliments asked me to undertake the Lord Lieutenancy with a seat in the Cabinet. I made no answer at first, but then said that it certainly was not a post which I in any way desired, but that if he thought it necessary on public grounds I would consider it and give him my answer that evening. He said that there really was no one to whom he could look but myself. I said that if I did take it, it must be on the understanding that I should accept it as a temporary and provisional office for the next few months only to carry the Government over a crisis.

I returned home and communicated with Sandon, Herbert (and McCraw[917] on the question of expense which is a serious consideration), and at last late in the evening I wrote my acceptance to Salisbury stating the grounds on which I consented.[918] Sandon was really kindness itself. If he had been my brother he could not have done

---

[914] For details of the discussion, see Harrowby's 'Note for Ex-Cabinet meeting at Salisbury's June 15th/85': Harrowby Papers, 2nd series, lv, fos 195–197.

[915] Edgar Algernon Robert Gascoyne-Cecil (1864–1958), Viscount Cecil of Chelwood (1923), third son of Salisbury.

[916] At Arlington Street.

[917] James McCraw, Carnarvon's financial adviser and agent.

[918] After his meeting with Salisbury, Carnarvon wrote, 'I must ask you to understand that I cannot retain permanent office in Ireland, if the result of the General Election should be favourable towards us; and amongst many reasons for this is that the climate is particularly adverse to me as a matter of health. As a provisional and temporary appointment, however, I will take and keep the Office till after the General Election or the meeting of the new Parliament' (Carnarvon to Salisbury, 16 June 1885 (copy): CP, BL 60760, fos 48–49). As Lady Carnarvon stated, 'He finally decided he could not refuse' (Lady Carnarvon, Diary, 16 June 1885: Herbert Papers, Somerset Archives and Record Service, DD/DRU/317).

or said more and his advice was most valuable. He came no less than 3 times during the day and evening to confer with me.

Thursday 18 June (London)

I have had a great deal of business already in connection with this Irish affair. Several conversations with Gibson who is very quick and clear and will be I hope a pleasant colleague.[919] A long talk today with Col. Bruce the head of the Irish Constabulary,[920] a very long conversation with M. Beach who is clear and able though I think rather rigid.

Friday 19 June (London)

Applications of every kind and for every sort of place pour in upon me, and when it is useless to ask for a paid place the request is for an honorary one. It is a curious sight. Meanwhile it is very doubtful whether or no we shall really come in. Salisbury has shown me some correspondence between him and Gladstone through the Queen, in which I am bound to say I think G. has rather the best, and which taken as a whole throw doubt over the results. Still my impression would be that ultimately we shall come in.

Saturday 20 June (London)

We were all summoned to Arlington St. this afternoon, but I did not get my summons in time for the beginning of the discussion. It was a serious question to consider Gladstone's last reply to Salisbury's communications. It was a well drawn letter, dwelling on the absence of any remark by Salisbury in the previous letters as to the "spirit" in which Gladstone professed himself ready to act, and then concluding by saying that he and his late colleagues could not bind or compromise the liberties of the House of Commons, which no one had asked them to do.

As far as I could gather, coming late, the general feeling was one of regret that Salisbury had in a previous letter asked for precise pledges

[919] Gibson had been appointed as Lord Chancellor of Ireland. Salisbury had more problems with the Chief Secretaryship. He informed Carnarvon, 'There is considerable doubt about the Ch. Sec. Stanhope, Ridley, Chaplin, Dyke, have all been mentioned' (Salisbury to Carnarvon, 19 June 1885: CP, BL 60760, fo. 57). Hart Dyke was eventually appointed on 28 June.

[920] Col. Robert Bruce (1825–1899), Inspector-General, Royal Irish Constabulary until 1885.

of cooperation in money matters,[921] but that as he had asked them and the request had been met by a flat refusal, the matter was almost at an end. At the same time they agreed that notice should be taken of the part of G.'s letter in which he complained that he had not been met in his "spirit".

I think myself that the correspondence will not read well. Whatever the cause, Salisbury has hardly been up to his mark. His letters have not been as clear, vigorous, effective as they should be, whilst Gladstone's have been unlike himself, brief, clear and well written. I think some other pen than his must have drawn them.

Sunday 21 June (London)

No news and no change as far as I know in the position of the negotiations. Salisbury is I believe at Hatfield and the only person with whom I have talked is Sandon. He thinks, and I am *inclined* now to do, that the communications will come to nothing and that we shall have a Liberal Government patched up. He thinks that Salisbury is not anxious to take Office, Randolph Churchill very anxious, Beach not eager for it, Gibson anxious and this I believe to be a true diagnosis. For my own part I believe the matter really rests with Salisbury and the tone of the letter in which he replies to Gladstone. In my opinion he has been worsted in the correspondence as yet: but he has it in his power to make a very good final reply either in the way of accepting office or of breaking off all further communications.

For myself, apart from all public considerations, I shall be very much pleased to see Ireland vanish out of sight, and if it does I think that Elsie and I shall within the next ten days start for Schwabach. I am much better, but still far from strong and this change may set me up.

McCraw came and had a long talk with me on Ireland and *I think* I see my way more clearly here on the financial part of the question.

Monday 22 June (London)

A long waiting day of suspense, and some feeling of anxiety and wish that the question of Office or no Office should be settled one way or the other. This evening however Sandon came across and his news seems practically to decide it as I have from the first expected it would

---

[921]On 19 June in the Lords, Salisbury refused to proceed with the final stage of the Redistribution Bill. Both Houses adjourned until 23 June. A further communication was received by Gladstone on 20 June from Salisbury, through the Queen, demanding Liberal support in allowing the Budget to press for an 8d. income tax (Bahlman, II, p. 890).

be, viz., that we take Office. The Queen has really by her vigorous sense decided the question as she last autumn decided our fight over the Redistribution and Franchise Bills and little as I am disposed myself to enter on the work of Ireland I believe the decision will be best for the Country.[922] For, apart from all other considerations, if we fail there is a great chance that Chamberlain and the Radicals may somehow form a government which would be Radical in its general character. I hear that the Irish members are well disposed towards us and to me, that they will not give trouble during the winter and that their hatred of Spencer[923] is so great that they are inclined to be civil to me. I hope it may be so, as it may render my task easier.

Wednesday 24 June (London)

My birthday – how different from what I had imagined it would be. I look forward to my new Office with great anxiety and doubt as to the future. We went down to Windsor, the usual course of kissing hands being followed. A large crowd at Paddington and Windsor cheered us as they will probably cheer our successors. The Queen looked well and much pleased at being free of her old Ministers.

In the morning I had a long and interesting conversation with Cardinal Manning[924] at the Archbishops House at his request. I have made elsewhere a note of what passed.

Also during the day important conversations with Jenkinson[925] the head of the criminal department as to Irish matters, and also with Spencer, who was very frank and open in all his communications,

---

[922] Manners, who became Postmaster-General in the new Government, attended a meeting at Salisbury's together with Hicks Beach, Richmond, and Cranbrook, 'to read and discuss a letter from the Queen in answer to Salisbury's communication of Saturday. In it H.M. begged us not to desert her, pointed out that Gladstone's language was susceptible of a favourable interpretation, and offered to express in a letter to be made public that she attached that meaning to his letter.' Ponsonby, acting as a messenger between the two leaders, brought the crisis to an end. Manners wrote, 'The Rubicon is therefore passed, and we are virtually in office' (C. Whibley (ed.), *Lord John Manners and his Friends*, 2 vols (London, 1915), II, pp. 212–213).

[923] John Poyntz Spencer (1835–1910), Viscount Althorp (1845), 5th Earl Spencer (1857). Lord Lieutenant of Ireland (1868–1874, 1882–1885, 1886), Lord President of the Council (1880–1882), First Lord of the Admiralty (1892–1895).

[924] Cardinal Henry Edward Manning (1808–1892), joined Roman Catholic Church (1851), Archbishop of Westminster (1865–1892), Cardinal (1875), Member, Royal Commission on Housing of the Poor (1885). Manning told Carnarvon that the Irish bishops were in favour of union with England, and of local government in the provinces, but not of a central parliament (see Hardinge, III, pp. 161–162).

[925] Sir Edward George Jenkinson (1835–1919), Irish civil servant, Lord Spencer's private secretary (1882–1885), Assistant Under-Secretary for Police and Crime in Ireland (1882–1886).

some of them were very important. It has been a very hard and harassing day and I was obliged to send to the Archbishop an excuse on the ground of overwhelming business.

Thursday 25 June (London)

A hard day's work.

McCraw and Col. Caulfield[926] all the morning settling details as to the Household, which promises to be expensive in spite of all pruning and reducing. A Commission in House of Lords. Forster to consider some points of private business and Trench[927] in the evening, who discussed some Irish questions. He is against the removal of the Crimes Act.

I hope I shall get hardened to my work. At present I seem to feel it more than I should.

Friday 26 June (London)

Cabinet

Our first Cabinet. First question our position as to Afghan and Russian boundary.[928] It appears that there is only a small part of the line on which there is now any controversy, but that the whole line (R. Churchill says) is worthless both in a military and political point of view. Lumsden's line was a good one, this is of no use.[929]

Next question whether the troops which have already evacuated Dongola should be stopped in their further retirement. Smith to get information.[930]

A long talk with Jenkinson as to secret police, conspiracies etc. Afterwards he gave me his own views as to ultimate government of Ireland. His notion is – and it is worth considering as a principle – a *gradual* adoption of Home Rule.

---

[926] Lieut.-Col. John A. Caulfeild, formerly Spencer's Comptroller of the Household.

[927] H. Cooke Trench, Irish land agent, son-in-law of Sir William Heathcote.

[928] On supporting the Afghan claim to the head of the Zulfiqar Pass, the most southerly point reached by the Russians.

[929] Lieut.-Gen. Sir Peter Lumsden (1829–1918), member of Council of India (1883–1893), British Boundary Commissioner, Afghanistan. Gladstone looked for a compromise with Russia and opened negotiations in London on the general line of the frontier. Lumsden was put in an invidious position and asked to withdraw from the Commission, expressing himself with some force. See W.K. Fraser-Tytler, rev. M.C. Gillett, *Afghanistan: a study of political developments in central and southern Asia*, 3rd edition (London, 1967), pp. 165–166.

[930] In reply to Smith, now Secretary of State for War, Wolseley ordered the rearguard not to leave Dongola (Wolseley to Smith (Wolseley No. 324), 26 June 1885: TNA, PRO WO 33/4 Pt II, p. 413).

Saturday 27 June (London)

A very busy day, and I went to bed tired out.

Amongst others I have talked a good deal to Howard Vincent,[931] who is very cordial, and anxious to be of help. I think that he may be very useful from his personal knowledge of Irish things and men.

An important conversation with Salisbury on Irish matters. I told him my ideas of dealing with different parties in Ireland, and he agreed.

Monday 29 June (Ireland)

Elsie and I started by the 7.15 a.m. train, Dyke and Jekyll accompanying us, and Stafford and Rachel[932] and Herbert coming to the station to see us off. A prosperous journey and easy crossing.[933] On landing at Kingston I was received by rather a large assemblage and much cheered: and on reaching Dublin we passed through the streets with a good many marks of respect. No show of opposition anywhere except that some groups did not take off their hats as we passed. On the whole the reception was generally good.[934]

Tuesday 30 June (Ireland)

I was today sworn in before the Lords Justices as Lord-Lieutenant; Lieutenant-General of Ireland, a scene with many historic memories hanging about it and striking – perhaps still more striking if it is, as it may be, the last occasion of the kind. The troops drawn up in the Castle Yard, the scene in the Council chamber and Throne room to receive the descendant of Sir H. Sidney[935] made a curious and to me an interesting picture.

---

[931] Sir Charles Edward Howard Vincent (1848–1908), first Director, Criminal Investigations Department, Metropolitan Police (1878–1884), Con. MP for Central Sheffield (1885–1908).

[932] Edward Stafford Howard (1851–1916), Lib. MP for Cumberland East (1876–1885) and for Thornbury (1885–1886), Under-Secretary of State for India (1886, in Gladstone's government). Howard was Elsie's brother, and had married Lady Rachel Campbell in 1877.

[933] For an account of their arrival, see *Freeman's Journal*, 30 June 1885, p. 5.

[934] The two short ceremonies are described by Lady Carnarvon in her Diary, 30 June 1885: Herbert Papers, Somerset Archives and Record Service, DD/DRU/3/7.

[935] Sir Henry Sidney (1641–1704), Secretary of State (1690–1691), Lord Lieutenant of Ireland (1692), 1st Earl of Romney (1694).

Wednesday 1 July (Ireland)

A great deal of business, long conversations and conferences with Sir R. Hamilton,[936] Gibson the Lord Chancellor, and the Law Officers on the non-renewal of the Crimes Act.

I held another Privy Council to swear in Gibson and give him the great Seal and Purse.

Saturday 4 July (London)

A hard day's work.[937] We had a Cabinet at which we did a good deal of business, much of it Irish. I laid before them the state of Ireland as regards crime and made them understand that it is a serious, most serious experiment that we are trying in not renewing the Crimes Act and set before them the balance of advantage and disadvantage. It was agreed *not* to renew it. I also got their consent to allude to a Land Purchase and a Labourers Bill in my statement on Monday.

Conversation with Jenkinson, mainly as to the police protection to be given to Spencer for some time. He does not like it, but I said I thought it was necessary up to a certain extent arranged. A very important letter from Cardinal Manning which I answered.[938] Also a visit from Gavan Duffy. I agreed to his making some enquiries from certain parties, but only from himself and keeping me and my name altogether out of it.

Sunday 5 July (London)

The stars seem to be fighting in their courses for me and unless any accident arises a prospect really seems opening. A very important occurrence to me this thro' H.V.[939] for a meeting tomorrow privately

[936] Sir Robert George Crookshank Hamilton (1836–1895), Permanent Secretary to the Admiralty (1882–1883), Permanent Under-Secretary for Ireland (1883–1886), Governor of Tasmania (1886–1893).

[937] Carnarvon left Ireland early the previous night, arriving in London 'between 6 and 7, very tired' (Diary, 3 July 1885).

[938] Manning had impressed upon Carnarvon 'the danger of interference' in the appointment of a new Catholic Archbishop of Dublin, since William Walsh, President of Maynooth College since 1881, was given the post by Pope Leo XIII. See V.A. McClelland, *Cardinal Manning: his public life and influence, 1865–1892* (London, 1962), p. 185.

[939] Howard Vincent.

at his home with J.M.[940] It may produce nothing but it looks very like something substantial.[941]

Chamberlain alas is likely to go head over heels into the mud. He is going to Ireland in a very bitter mood; which is likely to set up the Irish feeling against him. I hear on all sides that my refusing all military escort has produced a very good effect.

Monday 6 July (London)

A most important and private interview with Justin McCarthy at Howard Vincent's of which I have elsewhere kept a note.[942] Our conversation was very friendly and promises to lead to considerable results. I told everything to Salisbury and this led to a very serious talk with him.

He said he individually was prepared to go to the extent of provincial councils in Ireland but not a Central one: that he thought it likely many in the Party would be ready to accept very forward views but that he would not play Peel's part in 1829 or 1845. He then said "I must stand aside, but you could carry it out." I said, "That my dear Salisbury is not practical. I can do nothing of the sort"; and I added "If we had [not] had this conversation would you still have wished me to undertake this task?" He said, "Yes, because no one else could have undertaken it in all the same way." I said, "Very well, remember you pressed it upon me: but we must not have any divergence, and we must be perfectly frank with each other and have a complete understanding." I think he was frank.

In the House I made my statement.[943] It was listened to with the deepest attention, but I do not think our Irish peers or for that matter most of our supporters really liked it. It was hardly likely, I fear, they

---

[940]Justin McCarthy (1830–1912), writer, Irish MP for Longford (1879–1886), Leader of the Irish National Party (1890–1896).

[941]According to Vincent, at a dinner at Portman Square with Carnarvon and his wife at the end of June, he had been asked for his opinion on the state of Irish affairs. Vincent replied that 'I had always felt that although any rapprochement with the Irish leader [Parnell] was difficult and dangerous [. . .] it was a mistake to keep them entirely at a distance and not to endeavour to see if any arrangement could be made with them [. . .]. The Viceroy was taken with the idea, and in subsequent interviews asked me to see if a meeting could be arranged between him and Parnell.' Vincent wrote to McCarthy to set up a meeting. See S.H. Jeyes and F.D. How, *The Life of Sir Howard Vincent* (London, 1912), p. 177.

[942]See 'Conversation with J.M', CP, BL 60829, fo. 74.

[943]Carnarvon: Government position on Irish affairs: *Hansard*, CCXCVIII, 6 July 1885, cols 1658–1662.

should. Gibson (Lord Ashbourne) said it was quite right. I expect that it will tell in one direction if not in the other.[944]

Wednesday 8 July (Ireland)

A very hard day's work of all kinds but a ride in Phoenix Park later, the weather much finer.

An interview with Dr Walsh,[945] the Archbishop of Dublin, and Father Molloy.[946]

The Archbishop first had a private interview in which he pressed

(1) Some provisions in our Land Purchase bill.
(2) Some enquiry into Spencer's action in Maamtrasna case.[947]

To the first I expressed myself favourable, to the latter I said we could not enter into this question.

Afterwards a long talk over the Queen's College and higher education, Sir R. Hamilton being present.

Later some important talk with the Chancellor on state of affairs and our own future policy. He fears some trouble from M. Davitt.[948]

Saturday 11 July (Ireland)

This week has been a very hard one in point of business, much letter writing, and much talking. It is remarkable how all government of the whole country unites in the Lord-Lieutenant. I do not understand how in former times the business was carried on with men who only amused themselves and played at royalty.

Monday 13 July (Ireland)

Received two deputations at the Castle, one from Trinity College, the other from the Irish Academy of Arts.[949] I made them both speeches

---

[944] 'If you can hear at the Carlton or elsewhere what is thought, especially by Orangemen, of my statement, will you send me one word' (Carnarvon to Harrowby, 6 July 1885: Harrowby Papers, 2nd series, iv, fo. 16).

[945] Dr William Joseph Walsh (1841–1921), Archbishop of Dublin and Primate of Ireland (1885–1921).

[946] Father Gerard Molloy (1834–1906), Rector, University of Dublin (1883–1906), Commissioner, Inquiry into Educational Endowments, Ireland (1885–1894).

[947] See below, p. 393, n. 960.

[948] Michael Davitt (1846–1906), Irish Nationalist imprisoned for treason in 1870 and released seven years later on 'ticket of leave', MP for Meath North (1892), for Cork North-east (1893), and for Mayo South (1895–1899).

[949] Carnarvon told Ashbourne, 'My deputations passed off well enough, like this generally uproarious day is, I hope, passing' (Carnarvon to Ashbourne, 13 July 1885: Ashbourne

instead of the ordinary formal replies and on the whole this seems to be best liked.

In the afternoon I had a visit from and conversation with Dr Delany[950] the head of University College as to the general question of higher education. What struck me most was the evident intention of one day assailing the endowments of Trinity College. What his reason for disclosing this so plainly I do not quite know. It may have been to induce me to come to some arrangement complete and final. It has been on what is said to be Bismarck's principle – speaking the truth in order to deceive. He is no doubt a clever man, and a good representative of the Jesuits; but I did not take as much liking personally to him as Molloy and some others whom I have seen. His relations with the Bishops were evidently not perfect.

I wrote to H.V. enclosing a letter for J.M.,[951] this being the result of a conversation with the Chancellor who has been to London and has talked to Salisbury and who agreed to my writing but recommended the minimum of writing.[952]

Thursday 16 July (Ireland)

A day of great anxiety and work. The failure of the Munster Bank threatens to be most severe and to assume still larger proportions.[953] I summoned over Vernon[954] and with him and Hamilton spent a great part of the night in discussion as to what should be done. We finally agreed on a plan of a Government guarantee of one half deposits and current accounts. I made up my mind to exclude myself from all advantages in the case. But I fear that my own loss may be considerable, and anyhow the inconvenience is very great.[955]

Papers, B25/6). Ashbourne, for his part, reported that 'the University men were greatly pleased at your reception of the Deputations' (Ashbourne to Carnarvon, 13 July 1885: CP, TNA, PRO 30/6/58, fo. 123).

[950] Revd Dr William Delaney (1835–1924), President, Catholic University College, Dublin since 1883.

[951] 'It would be a pleasure to meet [Parnell] at the end of this month or quite at the beginning of next' (Carnarvon to McCarthy, 13 July 1885: CP, BL 60829, fo. 79). McCarthy's account of subsequent events are described in his *Reminiscences*, 2 vols (London, 1899), II, pp. 110–114.

[952] Ashbourne wrote to Carnarvon afterwards, 'He [Salisbury] is in favour of the minimum of writing and thinks it best for some friend to *say*, rather than write, a reply to the effect that you would be glad to have a chat with your correspondent when next in London' (reproduced in Hardinge, III, p. 174; the original letter cannot be traced).

[953] This refers to the undermining of the already weak Hibernian and National Banks. A director of the Bank had embezzled £70,000 and then disappeared.

[954] John Edward Vernon (1816–1887), Director of the Bank of Ireland (1867–1885).

[955] Carnarvon had put £3,000 of his own money in the Bank (Carnarvon to Salisbury, 17 July 1885 (copy): St. Aldwyn Papers, D2455 PCC/78).

Friday 17 July (Ireland)

This banking crisis is most grave. All the morning has been spent in considering it and writing on the subject. I conferred with Vernon who acts for the Bank of Ireland and agreed to recommend the guarantee of one half of the deposits and current accounts if the Bank of Ireland would advance another £200,000 to the Hibernian to tide this latter over the difficulty. It may save them.

I took the responsibility and did so, telegraphing and writing fully.[956]

It is now 6.30 p.m. and I have just seen Hamilton and the crisis seems for the time abating in severity. I spoke to a deputation on the subject and what I said seems to have produced rather a quieting effect. I only hope that my words will not be taken in too large and favourable a sense. They were guarded and I talked them over with Hamilton just before saying them.

Saturday 18 July (Ireland)

Shaw the M.P.[957] called to see me on the banking crisis. After consultation I declined to see him and Hamilton saw him in my place noting all that passed.[958]

The reports of last night's debate on Parnell's[959] motion are to hand.[960] As regards Beach's speech I cannot complain, assuming the line adopted to be right.[961] Randolph Churchill was I think unfortunate

[956]After the Cabinet meeting of 18 July, Cranbrook wrote, 'Then Carnarvon & his guarantee of deposits. Consternation, but refusal to support means dethronement & no one wanted that so our hand is forced into unknown liabilities without knowledge of assets because the Irish are "emotional" & cannot take care of themselves! Oh dear' (Johnson, p. 569).

[957]William Shaw (1823–1895), Lib. MP for Co. Cork (1874–1885) and chairman of the Munster Bank; declared bankrupt (January 1886).

[958]Hamilton, Memorandum, 18 July 1885: CP, TNA PRO 30/6/63, fo. 18.

[959]Charles Stewart Parnell (1846–1891), Nationalist MP for Co. Neath (1875–1880) and for Cork City (1880–1891), imprisoned in Kilmainham Gaol (1881–1883), Leader of the Nationalist Party (1880–1890).

[960]Parnell's motion condemned the actions of Lord Spencer in 1882 for sentencing to death two alleged murderers at Maamtrasna. Despite the fact that the Conservatives (in opposition at the time) had supported Spencer's action, Randolph Churchill, now a Minister, attacked the former Lord Lieutenant. For Parnell's motion, see *Hansard*, CCXCIX, 17 July 1885, cols 1064–1085. For a first hand account of the events see W.S.J.F. Brodrick, Earl of Midleton, *Records and Reactions, 1856–1939* (London, 1939), pp. 61–65.

[961]Hicks Beach and Sir John Gorst had supported Churchill and Parnell in the debate. Four days earlier, Hicks Beach had requested Carnarvon to re-examine the evidence of the Maamtrasna case, but had counselled caution. See Hicks Beach to Carnarvon, 13 July 1885: CP, TNA, PRO 30/6/57, fos 148–151; Carnarvon to Hicks Beach, 15 July 1885: St Aldwyn Papers, D2455 PCC/78.

in requesting Parnell to withdraw. It implied a fuller inquiry than is desirable. Anyhow the load left on my shoulders is heavy.

Later in the afternoon came a telegram from Salisbury saying the Cabinet were alarmed at my proposals as regard the banking crisis (which I of course expected) but assenting to any promise I had given or action taken [. . .].[962] The effect of my short speech to the Deputation seems to have been very great.

Jenkinson arrived. He is anxious as to some Fenian outrages which are in course of preparation and which may be expected in about 6 weeks.

Sunday 19 July (Ireland)

I think this has been the hardest day I have yet had.[963] It has been impossible to go to church and I have been all day from breakfast to dinner time writing, telegraphing, consulting on this Bank business. Sir G. Kellner[964] arrived, a capable financier I think and a strong Conservative, charged with the fears and anxieties and communications of the Government in London. He and they thought that we had been precipitate and unwise in our action here, but he had not been long in the house before he changed his mind and admitted that there was little room for taking any other course. However, after much discussion I modified my line to this extent that I got the Bank of Ireland (through Vernon) to make their advances to the "Hibernian" being backed and guaranteed by the Government instead of letting the Government guarantee in the first instance. It really comes to the same thing, but the Government is not made a prominent figure in the transaction.[965]

Hamilton, the Solicitor-General, Gibson (Ashbourne's brother),[966] Kellner, Vernon were with me nearly all day.[967]

---

[962] 'They look with serious apprehension on the precedent which proposed action for the future' (Salisbury to Carnarvon, 18 July 1885 (copy): Hatfield House Papers, 3M/E).

[963] Carnarvon told Harrowby, 'The crisis is politically far more serious than is understood in England and the question must not be too closely measured by prudent and official rule' (Carnarvon to Harrowby, 19 July 1885: Harrowby Papers, 2nd series, lii, fo. 123).

[964] Sir George Welsh Kellner (1825–1886), Assistant Paymaster-General in Chancery (1884–1886). Kellner had been selected by the Cabinet on 18 July to help Carnarvon (Hicks Beach to Carnarvon, 18 July 1885: CP, TNA, PRO 30/6/63, fo. 13).

[965] Carnarvon remained pessimistic: 'What I have done and said has *so far* arrested the ruin', he informed Ashbourne, 'but the run on the Hibernian is considerable, and I do not feel sure that we shall succeed in keeping it up' (Carnarvon to Ashbourne, 19 July 1885: Ashbourne Papers, B 25/9).

[966] John George Gibson (1846–1923), Solicitor-General for Ireland (1885–1886, 1886–1887), Attorney-General for Ireland (1887–1888).

[967] Carnarvon to Hicks Beach, 19 July 1885: St Aldwyn Papers, D 2455 PCC/70.

Fig. 6 Earl of Carnarvon with his elder son by his second marriage, Aubrey Herbert, aged five, 1885.

Monday 20 July (Ireland)

This morning I received a deputation from the shareholders of the Munster Bank. It was large, important and had representation from many parts of the South. They asked for a loan to revive the bank. I was obliged to tell them that Government could not do this and to indicate what might be done. Sir G. Kellner quite agreed afterwards in what I said.

Matters today look perhaps slightly better: but the deputation were evidently disappointed. With sanguine Irish natures they had anticipated some great Government intervention. Sir G. Kellner is very reasonable and satisfactory to deal with, Beach and Smith in

London less so. They look at things from an English or Scotch point of view.

Tuesday 21 July (Ireland)

Matters again gloomy today. Sir G. Kellner has gone to London. I felt he would be more useful there. I received two deputations at the Castle. Elsie went over a hospital and seems to have charmed everyone by what she said and did.

I had also a conversation with Father Molloy as to the Educational Endowments Bill and the course to be taken on the Linen College Estimates. I arranged for a meeting between him and Dyke.

Wednesday 22 July (Ireland)

A very important conversation with Duffy, of which I have kept a memorandum elsewhere.[968] He and Lady D. lunched here. His letter to me appeared in the *Freeman's Journal*, an able paper, and likely I think to produce some effect, very complimentary to me personally.[969]

Received also a telegram in cypher from Salisbury, saying the Cabinet were averse to touching the Queen's Colleges question and were to sit on Monday in case I can attend. I am not surprised, but at the same time it is a cardinal point in my Irish policy. If no undertaking is now given to consider and deal with the question I shall lose the whole support of the Roman Catholic clergy and with it all chance of keeping the country quiet and holding the extreme people in hand. Further, the change will very soon be made, and it will be made in such a way as to leave Trinity College unguarded. By making an arrangement now I hope Trinity may be saved.[970]

Tuesday 28 July (Ireland)

I had to receive an address at the Zoological Gardens [. . .].

---

[968] Carnarvon, 'Memorandum of conversation with Sir C. G. Duffy, 22 July 1885': CP, BL 60825, fo. 38.

[969] 'The price of peace in Ireland', *Freeman's Journal*, 22 July, 1885, pp. 5–6.

[970] The Queen's Colleges were established by Robert Peel in 1845 to provide higher education in Ireland. They consisted of three institutions – Belfast for Presbyterians, and Cork and Galway for Roman Catholics. Sir Robert Hamilton had suggested a careful reconstruction of these colleges (Hamilton to Carnarvon, 9 July 1885: CP, TNA, PRO 30/6/58, fos 122–128).

Afterwards on my return home I had a long conversation with the Chancellor, who has returned.[971] He gave me an interesting account of all that had gone on in the Cabinet since he had left Ireland and we finally had a long, unreserved and important talk as to the future prospects of legislation for Ireland and as to a certain [action] of which I had spoken to him and in which he concurs. It was an important talk.

Friday 31 July (Bretby – London)

A mournful, melancholy day.[972] Spent all through the morning in assuming new responsibilities and giving instructions. Alas! what a crowd of sad memories are called up. The funeral was less painful than I expected [. . .].

Reached London in time to dine with Herbert at the Travellers' and heard from him some news, and later had a visit from H. Vincent and settled everything as tomorrow.[973] He is a most willing ally, and has offered to go through Ireland for me to collect opinions.

Saturday 1 August (London – Hatfield)

This afternoon at 15 Hill Street I had a remarkable meeting and conversation the details of which I have noted elsewhere.

Later I came down to Hatfield with Salisbury, with whom I have had much and serious conversation. Personally I think everything is right, politically, I see some very black clouds ahead. S.'s relations with Beach and R. Churchill are also not satisfactory. He says Beach is under the control of R.C., and that though this latter is manageable as regards India, he is very hard to control or guide in home matters. He repeated that he thought we should be out with the Elections and that his position was so disagreeable he did not care for himself, but that he thought the House of Lords would be in an intolerable situation.

I talked long and anxiously with him as to Irish matters. He entirely concurred in the line that I am pursuing in Ireland, though he reverted to his gloomy anticipation of what would ensue on the Dissolution.[974]

---

[971] Ashbourne had travelled to Boulogne on 25 July and arrived back in Dublin on 28 July (Ashbourne to Carnarvon, 25 July 1885: CP, TNA, PRO 30/6/56, fos 184–186).

[972] Lady Chesterfield, Carnarvon's mother-in-law by his first marriage, had died on 27 July.

[973] Carnarvon told Vincent that, because of business connected with Lady Chesterfield's death, he would be able to meet Parnell earlier than expected (Carnarvon to Vincent (copy), 29 July 1885: CP, BL 60829, fo. 48).

[974] The meeting with Parnell lasted one and a quarter hours. See Carnarvon to Ashbourne, 1 August 1885: Ashbourne Papers, B25/12 (reproduced in Hardinge, III, pp. 178–181).

Sunday 2 August (Hatfield – London)

A great deal of conversation with Salisbury as to Irish affairs. I drew up and showed him a memorandum of my "conference" of yesterday. He accepted it all.[975]

I returned to London in the evening and dined with the Harrowbys, which was very pleasant after all the worry and fatigue of the last few days.

Monday 3 August (London)

An extremely busy day. A long talk with Jenkinson on Irish police matters and on a recrudescence of dangerous Fenianism which is threatening.[976] He urged me to take all reasonable precautions as to myself and I promised I would do so.[977] I also later saw Dyke and gave him the caution and requested Jenkinson to see that he had a detective attached to him.

Lunched with Lady M. Charteris[978] who talked much of poor Lady Chesterfield and Bretby matters.

Then a Cabinet at which strange to say Salisbury whether from forgetfulness or some other cause never asked me to say anything as to the state of Ireland. I had nothing to propose or to ask for a decision, and so I did not raise the question and at last the time came for the House of Commons and the Cabinet broke up. Curious! The Cabinet was understood to be summoned for the purpose of hearing my opinion on Irish matters and I had staid on in London after consultation with Salisbury in order to explain. Very curious![979]

I dined at the Travellers' with Herbert and left by the night mail, Jekyll and Mrs. J. accompanying me.

[975] Before leaving for Hatfield the previous evening, Carnarvon wrote to his wife, 'Randolph [Churchill] has done as much as anyone to upset my Irish policy by making people think that he was ready to intrigue with the Irishmen and make any concession to them' (Carnarvon to Lady Carnarvon, 1 August 1885: CP, BL 61054, fos 42–43).

[976] See Jenkinson's lengthy letter to Carnarvon, 5 August 1885: CP, TNA, PRO 30/6/62, fos 1–12).

[977] Carnarvon set out his proposed rearrangement of the police and divisional magistrates to Cross, the Home Secretary (Carnarvon to Cross, 4 August 1885: CP, TNA, PRO 30/6/64, fos 24–25).

[978] Lady Margaret Charteris, daughter of 2nd Earl of Glengall.

[979] Later the same day, Carnarvon described the original plan for the Cabinet: 'He [Salisbury] had spoken to me of what I was about to say and had in certain measure arranged it with me' (Carnarvon to Harrowby, 3 August 1885: Harrowby Papers, 2nd series, lii, fo. 137).

Monday 17 August (Galway)

A prosperous journey to Galway,[980] considerable crowds at the stations. I got out and walked about at most of them. The people very respectful.

We reached Galway by 2.30, and found a great concourse at the station and of its kind very representative. Mr. Hallett the High Sheriff was the principal person, but with him all the respectable and propertied class. We adjourned to a large hall room close to the station and there I received 4 Addresses and made 4 speeches.

Wednesday 19 August (Kilkerran and Clifden)

Landed at Kilkerran and drove about with Father Flanary. We went into many cottages, some of the poorest I have yet seen; earthen floors, hardly any windows, only one room in which the cow and the children and the old mother were the principal occupants. One old woman who was born before /98 came out and shook hands with me and wished me a long life. Some of the expressions they use are pretty. The man wished me "a long life and a happy death," and when at Clifden I was entirely mixed up with the crowd, I heard some one near me say in answer to something which had been said by a neighbour, "We are his guards."

Our visit to Clifden was a great success. The people welcomed me with green boughs and acclamations and the reception was the most cordial and sympathetic that we have had. After we had seen the Convent, the whole appearance of which was most satisfactory, and driven about we had a great collection of people in front of the Hotel or Inn. Major d'Arcy made me a long speech of welcome and I then got on a chair and made the best reply I could. It was a curious scene and rather a comical one in some ways. I imagine that I am the first Lord-Lieutenant who has harangued with much applause an Irish crowd on a chair in the market place.

Thursday 20 August (Westport – Achill)

We landed after some misadventures from the blowing up of part of the boiler of the steam launch, were met by Lord John Brown, Lord

---

[980] Accompanied by his wife and daughter, Carnarvon made a tour of south and west Ireland from 17 to 22 August. He was the first Lord Lieutenant to visit this district. The itinerary included the Arran Islands, Kilronan, Clifden, Belmullet, and Sligo. See 'Viceregal tour in the West: Lord Lieutenant in Galway', *Freeman's Journal*, 18 August 1885, p. 5.

Sligo's brother and agent,[981] the High Sheriff, Mr. Livingstone, the principal merchant and Chairman of Harbour Commissioners etc. All went off well and we had a very good reception. Several addresses were presented and as I stood under the trees beside the river and the crowd all round me I replied to them all in one speech [. . .].

We went on to the Convent, that had the industrial girls school. Everything satisfactory. The nuns besought me to certify the school for more, I think 20 or 30. Lord Sligo has been a great benefactor and has given land and help on every occasion. His house and park are great features, whilst Croagh Patrick, where St. Patrick exorcised the serpents, towered up above everything.

Thence to Achill, the details of which I have noted elsewhere. Most horrible housing of human beings near the seacoast, a Protestant colony beyond. But the colony and Mission of which it is a part would have done better had they first brought light and cleanliness and decency into these savage abodes before preaching a propaganda of religion to them. It was to me a melancholy, miserable scene.

Saturday 22 August (Sligo – Vice Regal Lodge)

A great success to crown the whole expedition. The whole population turned out, a very large crowd welcoming us on our landing and cheering continuously. Colonel Cooper[982] as Lieutenant of the Cr: was there with two carriages, the Mayor and all persons, R.C. and Protestant, of any rank. A succession of addresses in the Town Hall followed and then we drove after some other places to the Convent and Industrial School, where the Bishop Gillooly,[983] received us. Everything was as friendly as it could be, and after more speeches etc. we dined at the Convent with the Bishop. It was a most successful day and on our way back to Dublin we had an oration at the large stations, at Boyle being presented with an address by Col. King Harman[984] and a large assembly. We arrived here at 10 p.m.

Saturday 5 September (Vice Regal Lodge)

It is very hard work to keep abreast with all the business, which is very multifarious.

[981] Lord John Thomas Browne (1824–1903), brother of George John Browne, 3rd Marquess of Sligo (1820–1896).

[982] Col. Edward Henry Cooper (1827–1902), MP for Co. Sligo (1865–1868), Lord Lieutenant of Co. Sligo (1877–1902).

[983] Laurence Gillooly (1819–1895), Bishop of Elphin (1858–1895).

[984] Col. Edward Robert King-Harman (1838–1888), Con. MP for Co. Sligo (1877–1880), for Co. Dublin (1883–1885), and for the Isle of Thanet (1885–1888), Lord Lieutenant for Co. Roscommon (1878–1888).

The work is very interesting and extremely varied; but it is hardly possible without spending a great deal of time over it to write down every day a faithful record of what passes, interviews with important people consume much time.[985] I do not do much in writing as at the Colonial Office. I hardly ever write a minute: and dictate a great many letters.

Tuesday 29 September (Vice Regal Lodge)

A conference on convict matters and the choice of Galway as the place. Present: Du Cane[986] from England, Chief Justice Morris,[987] Dyke, Hamilton, Charles Bourke[988] and myself.

A vexatious letter also from Beach as to Treasury matters. He is very tape-bound and official; and apparently is trying to save money by small economies in questions of important policy.

Friday 2 October (Vice Regal Lodge)

I had yesterday a long and interesting talk with R. Churchill.[989] He gives one the idea of being frank in saying what he thinks, and it seems to me as if Salisbury was gaining an influence with him. He showed me a letter from S. to him entering at some length into the present position of foreign affairs and evidently written for the purpose of pleasing him. Randolph in speaking to me of S. said that he was an enigma to him, that at times S. was so open and intelligible that at another time he dropped a veil over his thoughts.

He told me another thing which I had certainly never heard before, viz. a story that Disraeli was the real father of Dufferin, and he declared that when he was in India and saw much of Dufferin, D. said and did many things which indicated or bore secret evidence to the relationship. Curious!

---

[985]'Irish matters are the first and last and middle thought of every day [. . .]. I can think of nothing else' (Carnarvon to Cranbrook, 2 September 1885: Cranbrook Papers, HA3 T501/262).

[986]Sir Charles Du Cane (1825–1889), Chairman, Board of Customs (1878–1889).

[987]Michael Morris (1827–1901), 1st Baron Morris (1889), 1st Baron Killanin (1900). Lib. MP for Galway (1865–1867), Solicitor-General for Ireland (1866), Attorney-General for Ireland (1866–1867), Judge of Common Pleas for Ireland (1867–1887), Lord Chief Justice of Ireland (1887–1889).

[988]Charles Fowler Bourke (1831–1899), Chairman, General Prisons Board, Ireland (1878–1895).

[989]Churchill had arrived in Dublin the previous day and was staying with Hugh Holmes, the Irish Attorney-General.

I see in today's papers Lord Shaftesbury's death, another of my old friends gone.[990] I knew that he could not last long. He was a contemporary of my father's at Christ Church.

Monday 5 October (London)

Long conversation with Salisbury at Foreign Office.[991] I explained the whole Irish position, and told him the only solution in my opinion.[992] He said that before coming into Office Sir M. Morris had painted Ireland to him nearly the same colours. He reminded me of his own opinion. I said I had not forgotten, and that for my part I desired to avoid all division or difference in the party.[993]

Then talk with Herbert as to Ireland, Jekyll, etc. Then a long and rather disagreeable talk with Beach, who is simply odious to do business with. All on Treasury questions.

Finally long talk with Sandon as to Ireland. He quite agrees with me.

Tuesday 6 October (London)

A most important Cabinet. It was almost entirely occupied with Irish matters.[994] I made a very long statement of about $\frac{1}{2}$ hour, Ashbourne followed confirming me and G. Hamilton confirmed all my facts. My suggestions and indications of future policy found no real supporter, some expressed opposition. I note the general statement elsewhere. I believe I made my own position clear and understood.[995]

I dined afterwards with R. Churchill, Ashbourne, Lytton, W. H. Smith (who has I think grown very intent and rather dull), Beach,

---

[990] Shaftesbury had died on 1 October.

[991] Carnarvon had crossed over from Ireland on 3 October in preparation for the first Cabinet since the summer, on 6 October.

[992] Carnarvon had previously written to Harrowby, 'I have told Salisbury that I wish to see him on Monday [5 Oct]. Perhaps my greatest difficulty lies with one section of the landlords who think the Government is bound to keep them no matter how harsh they themselves may be' (Carnarvon to Harrowby, 28 September 1885: Harrowby Papers, 2nd series, lii, fo. 45).

[993] On 30 September, Salisbury – who was to make a major policy speech at Newport on 7 October – told Carnarvon that he 'should be glad for any material for the defence of our Irish position. Can you bring with you on Monday anything to show that 1) Boycotting went on vigorously while the Crimes Act was still in existence. 2) That its present prevalence could not be materially checked if the Crimes Act were still in existence' (Salisbury to Carnarvon, 30 September 1885: CP, BL 50760, fos 69–70).

[994] For details, see Hardinge, III, pp. 192–195.

[995] Cranbrook commented, 'Carnarvon's picture of Ireland was in the gloomiest of colours [. . .]. His remedies almost none & present action, though all that the law allows, does not promise much' (Johnson, p. 576).

who never has much to say, Rothschild and some others. R.C. is
extremely civil.

Thursday 8 October (Highclere – London)

A great deal of business of all kinds, public and private. We came
up to London and found piles of letters and red boxes.

The Queen is very anxious to see me.[996] I have had telegrams and
letters from Ponsonby and a further pressing letter through Northcote:
but I cannot. I must go back to Ireland tomorrow even though it
involves a journey to Balmoral from there next week.

Friday 9 October (London)

Cabinet, a good many miscellaneous subjects discussed, foreign,
Indian, home, Stead's prosecution, Skye crofters, some Treasury
disagreements between me and Beach in which the Cabinet decided
at once for me, etc. No Colonial question.

Afterwards I walked up to the Carlton with Salisbury and lunched
there with him. I showed him my memorandum of what I said on
Tuesday in the Cabinet about Ireland and asked him whether it
seemed to him quite correct. He said it was and suggested I could add
to it what Cranbrook had said.

Afterwards a rather interesting conversation with R. Churchill, who
told me a curious story as to the Duke of Connaught's wish to be
Commander-in-Chief in Bombay.[997]

Later Elsie and I and Esmé[998] left by night train for Ireland, a good
passage.

[996]'The Queen feels very anxious about Ireland and would be very glad to have seen
Lord Carnarvon before he returned to Ireland' (Queen Victoria to Salisbury, 6 October
1885: Buckle, *Letters*, III, p. 700). Carnarvon excused himself from going to Balmoral to talk
particularly on boycotting (Carnarvon to Queen Victoria, 8 October 1885: Royal Archives,
D37/94).

[997]Arthur William, Duke of Connaught and Strathearn (1850–1942), third son of Queen
Victoria. He followed an army career and, as a major-general, commanded a brigade in the
Egyptian expedition of 1882 and fought at Tel-el-Kabir. See Sir G. Aston, *His Royal Highness
the Duke of Connaught and Strathearn: a life and intimate study* (London, 1929), pp. 124–130. The
wish to be Commander-in-Chief in Bombay was never granted.

[998]Sir Esmé William Howard (1863–1939), Carnarvon's brother-in-law by his second
marriage, diplomat (1885–1892), Consul-General to Crete (1903–1906), 1st Baron Howard
of Penrith (1930).

Tuesday 20 October (Vice Regal Lodge)

A long conversation with Capt. Slack and Capt. Plunkett[999] with Sir R. Hamilton on the state of affairs in their districts. The account is not good as [to] boycotting. They do not recognise as yet any improvement.

Afterwards a conversation with Harrel.[1000] No special cause for anxiety at present: but there is no doubt that the old bad lot in Dublin are supplied with money, just enough to help them. It is probable that they are being held in reserve for whatever may be needed.

Monday 26 October (Vice Regal Lodge)

A very good natured letter from the Queen through Sir Henry Ponsonby releasing me from my journey to Balmoral and saying she will expect me at Windsor instead, when she goes there. A great relief.

We paid a visit to the rooms of the Royal Academy, a fine Library and collection of very valuable MSS. and books, and a magnificent collection of old Irish silver and gold ornaments. It is exclusively Irish, with no foreign admixture and is a most remarkable one.

Saturday 7 November (Vice Regal Lodge)

A considerable conversation with Gibson on future policy. I explained my view of the situation and its extreme danger and difficulty. He admitted it all, but argues for a staving off policy in the hopes that the Irish Parliamentary Party will be unable to hold together above one session.

Thursday 19 November (London)

I had a long and interesting conversation with Cardinal Manning on Irish matters. I have made a note elsewhere of it.

Saw Dyke who is rather sanguine as to Election prospects and the *Pall Mall* has a strange article prophesying very great Liberal reverses and a strong Conservative reaction. A conversation also, later, with Greenwood, which I have taken a note.

<hr />

[999] District magistrates.
[1000] Sir David Harrel (1841–1939), Chief Commissioner, Dublin Metropolitan Police (1883–1893).

Friday 20 November (London)

I had a long and very important conversation with Salisbury this morning, the details of which I have noted elsewhere.[1001] It was personally very friendly, in substance it has left me no option as to the course to be pursued if the Government come out unharmed from the Elections. But he is evidently in very indifferent health and there may be several unexpected and strange endings to his political prominence.

We lunched afterwards with Lady D. Nevill – F. Leveson[1002] there, very Granvillian in tone and manner.

Saturday 21 November (London)

Conversation with Herbert on my own case and later with Dyke on the position of affairs. He says that the parliamentary prospects are brightening all round, that there has been a great improvement in the last ten days and that almost anything is possible. On the other hand he describes the mental condition of the Party as regards Ireland as one of Cimmerian darkness. They know and understand nothing, hate the subject, but hate still more a proposal to make any change.

A long business talk with Mr. Roberts.[1003] Nothing can be worse than the agricultural outlook.

Monday 23 November (Windsor)

A talk with Jenkinson on his own position, salary etc, on which I wrote a long letter to Ridley[1004] to be communicated to Beach.[1005]

[1001] Salisbury met Carnarvon at Arlington Street at midday to discuss the consequences for the Government if the latter should retire after the next general election. Carnarvon offered to waive his retirement if Salisbury was willing either to set up a Joint Committee of both Houses to consider the future government of Ireland or to establish an Educational Council for Ireland and a fuller measure of self-government. See Carnarvon, Memorandum, 'Conversation with Lord Salisbury', 20 November 1885: CP, BL 60760, fos 73–77.

[1002] Edward Frederick Leveson-Gower (1819–1907), Lib. MP for Derby (1846–1847), for Stoke-upon-Trent (1852–1857), and for Bodmin (1859–1885).

[1003] J.D. Cramer Roberts, Carnarvon's London agent and financial adviser.

[1004] Sir Matthew White Ridley (1842–1904), 5th Baronet Ridley (1877), Viscount Ridley (1900). Con. MP for Northumberland North (1868–1885) and for Blackpool (1886–1900), Under-Secretary to the Home Office (1878–1880), Financial Secretary to the Treasury (1885–1886), Home Secretary (1895–1900).

[1005] Jenkinson, of whom Carnarvon thought highly, had had an interview with him on 31 August about his future position. It emerged that Cross had no opening for him in a permanent position at the Home Office (Cross to Carnarvon, 3 September 1885: CP, TNA PRO 30/6/62, fo. 20). After Jenkinson saw Hicks Beach at the end of the year, Carnarvon warned Hicks Beach, 'It is simply impossible for the Government to give up the machinery

Afterwards an important conversation with Salisbury as to myself and Irish matters. I gave him to read a long memorandum which I had drawn up since I last saw him.[1006]

Later Elsie and I came to Windsor. The Queen most kind and gracious. She kissed Elsie and talked with her for some time about Ireland after dinner, and before dinner I had a long audience. For the first time she made me sit down as she was sitting, a sign perhaps that she is not quite as strong as she once was; but in other respects she looked very well. In the evening after dinner came a telegram from Hamilton announcing the murder of a caretaker in Co. Cork. I trust it is not the beginning of a new series.

Tuesday 24 November (Windsor)

An interesting morning in the Library with Mr. Holmes the Librarian[1007] who showed us the miniatures. Later an interesting conversation with the Queen and an important one. I explained to her my position and the agreement with Salisbury.[1008]

Wednesday 25 November (London)

The first returns out of the General Election. We have undoubtedly done well. We have lost few and won many seats and we are exactly equal with the Liberals.

of which Jenkinson is the head [. . .]. We shall probably have very serious trouble before long and it would be nothing short of madness to weaken in any way the one agency that exists for the detection and prosecution of gross political crime' (Carnarvon to Hicks Beach, 30 December 1885: CP, TNA, PRO 30/6/62, fo. 45). Hicks Beach replied, 'I do not think it is my business to settle Jenkinson's case' (Hicks Beach to Carnarvon, 3 January 1886: Hatfield House Papers, 3M/E). In the end, the Home Office dispensed with Jenkinson's services. See C. Townshend, *Political Violence in Ireland: government and resistance since 1848* (Oxford, 1983), pp. 196–197; S. Ball (ed.), *Dublin Castle and the First Home Rule Crisis: the political journal of Sir George Fottrell, 1884–1887*, Camden 5th series 33 (Cambridge, 2008).

[1006] CP, BL 60780, fos 78–80.

[1007] Sir Richard Rivington Holmes (1835–1911), Queen's (and King's) Librarian, Windsor Castle (1870–1906).

[1008] Carnarvon found the Queen 'very much alive to the whole subject' of self-government for Ireland. At the meeting, she showed him Gladstone's memorandum of 25 May, setting out the options relating to Irish policy. See H. Gladstone, *After Thirty Years* (London, 1928), p. 395; Shannon, *Gladstone*, II, p. 360. Carnarvon replied two days later (Carnarvon to Queen Victoria, 26 November 1885: Royal Archives, D 37/99). Salisbury wrote to Ponsonby on 29 November expressing his disapproval of Carnarvon giving the Queen his views on Ireland: 'These opinions of Lord Carnarvon have been mentioned at the Cabinet and they were repudiated by all the Ministers who spoke.' The Queen subsequently informed Salisbury that she had invited Carnarvon to give his views. Salisbury did not mention the incident to Carnarvon. See A. Ponsonby, *Henry Ponsonby, Queen Victoria's Private Secretary: his life from his letters* (London, 1942), pp. 199–200.

Elsie and I came to London, lunched with Mrs. Jeune and travelled to Dublin in the evening.

Saturday 5 December (Vice Regal Lodge)

The Liberals have drawn very much ahead. This morning they were close upon a majority of 50 as against Conservative, excluding the Irish.

Thursday 10 December (Vice Regal Lodge)

The anniversary of my poor father's death.

Dyke returned from England. He tells me he urged on Salisbury the expediency of our retiring from Office as soon as we can,[1009] and that S. said he thought it would be the best thing for us to be out of it.[1010]

Friday 11 December (London)

I came over by myself, a very smooth passage and a good journey. Met Herbert at the Travellers' and dined with him.

He is, after hearing the whole case, clearly of opinion that on all grounds, personal, financial, political, it is best for me to claim my release under Salisbury's engagement with me and my letter of 16th June.[1011]

[1009] Hart Dyke's statement hardly tallies with a conversation he had the following day with Ashbourne, who reported, 'A long talk with Dyke today. He thinks that it would disadvantage our friends, and particularly the great towns which supported us, if we resigned before the meeting of Parliament' (Ashbourne to Carnarvon, 11 December 1885: CP, BL 60857, fo. 104).

[1010] At the general election, the Liberals won 334 seats, the Conservatives 290, and the Irish Nationalists 86. Thus the Conservatives could continue only with Irish support. Carnarvon pointed out to Salisbury, 'We must govern by and through the Irish, and unless we are ready to come to some understanding with them, they will play us off against the Liberals, and reduce us to the sorest difficulties' (Hardinge, III, pp. 203–204).

[1011] Carnarvon had come over from Ireland the previous day to lobby for home rule in the Cabinet on 14 December. Before leaving Dublin, Carnarvon wrote to Harrowby, 'I have found the copy of my letter to Salisbury which I wrote on the acceptance of Office, as you will remember greatly at your suggestion and with you, and I am delighted at it. It really seems as if it had been written in exact anticipation of present circumstances: and is so full and emphatic that if made public, it must, I think, carry conviction that I am retiring in accordance with a long formed conclusion without any reference to present questions' (Carnarvon to Harrowby, 10 December 1885: Harrowby Papers, 2nd series, lii, fos 153–154).

Saturday 12 December (London)

I had a talk with Cranbrook and explained all my own position. He is disturbed, and wishes me much to stay on, fearing my retirement may break up the Government. This I said I would not permit and though the difficulty is considerable I do not see that it need come to such an issue.[1012]

Sunday 13 December (London)

In the afternoon I went to Hatfield and had a very long conversation with Salisbury [. . .].

He was very friendly, deplored my retirement, but professed his inability to turn any of his colleagues out to make room for me, which of course I said I was the last person to desire. At the same time he was he said most anxious to find some mode of convincing everyone that there was no discord of opinion, so at last I said feeling that if I did not suggest something he had no resources and that unless I really persuaded him to let me go he might never get a successor, that if he liked I would take a seat in the Cabinet without a portfolio at all events for the present. He immediately caught at the idea, said it was an excellent one and seemed so much pleased at it that I am obliged to believe that he really was very sorry to lose me. So now I trust that matters are in a fair way of settlement.

Monday 14 December (London)

Long discussion [with Salisbury] as to resignation at once or meeting Parliament at once but to challenge a vote of confidence before the Address, a strange and novel proceeding, suggested by Beach and R. Churchill.

Then a discussion on Ireland, the result of which was that the Cabinet would do nothing and announce no policy, but they would not debar themselves from proceeding later by Committee, if circumstances should favour this. Lastly my retirement, in accordance with my letter of last June 16th. to Salisbury mentioned by him. He said he much regretted it, but it was part of an engagement; but that he had offered me and that I had accepted a seat in the Cabinet without

---

[1012] Cranbrook wrote in his Diary, 'I cannot help seeing that the burden of it and of dealing with the Irish question is really at the bottom of it. I told him that he wd upset the Coach for who would take his place in the existing circumstances' (Johnson, p. 584). Carnarvon told his wife, 'I have had neither letter or telegram from Salisbury [. . .]. I have been kept in suspense' (Carnarvon to Lady Carnarvon, 12 December 1885: CP, BL 61054, fo. 46).

portfolio. A good deal of discussion etc., Gibson much regretting. At last I promised to consider it again to see if I could hold on till the vote of confidence was taken.[1013]

Dined at the Jeunes and had a long and interesting conversation with Goschen. His whole notion as to Ireland consists in giving next to nothing and coercing. It is the view of most of my colleagues only more vigorously thought out and expressed.

Tuesday 15 December (London)

Cabinet

A long talk again on Ireland. The Cabinet will do nothing and they only say that if and when a great change comes it must be done by other hands.[1014] I had some talk with G. Hamilton afterwards who I think sees all the danger of this course but is bound by family and local traditions to resist it. Gibson (the Chancellor) generally supported me but all the rest of the Cabinet, some of whom I know agree with me, remained dumb, a curious but usual feature in Cabinets on such occasions.

My own position was made clear. I have agreed at their urgent wish to waive my immediate retirement and to stay on till the vote of confidence is disposed of, the understanding being that I should anyhow be free by the end of January. If the Government then fell we fall together. If they survive I retire but take a seat in the Cabinet without portfolio.[1015]

Left for Ireland this evening.

Monday 21 December (Greystoke)

After travelling all night, Elsie, Vera and I with Esmé arrived in the early morning. A wonderful change in the feeling of the air, here so keen and bracing, in Ireland is relaxing and soft.

[1013]Salisbury sent an account of the proceedings to the Queen. 'The Irish question was then considered [. . .]. Lord Carnarvon expressed his earnest desire to retire from office, in accordance with an understanding entered into with him when he took it. The feeling of the Cabinet however was that at this moment such a retirement would be misunderstood and he was strongly pressed to remain' (Salisbury to Queen Victoria, 14 December 1885: Royal Archives, A63/93).

[1014]Carnarvon presented his highly secret Irish University Bill but no action was taken on it (Cooke and Vincent, *The Governing Passion*, p. 293). He commented to Harrowby, 'I regret and shall always regret that they make no effort – if only to feel their way towards a settlement of this question [. . .] but a Cabinet is like a Council of War, it is very timid' (Carnarvon to Harrowby, 18 December 1885 (copy): CP, TNA, PRO 30/6/55, fos 144–145).

[1015]Carnarvon to Queen Victoria, 15 December 1885: Royal Archives, C37/1.

Thursday 24 December (Greystoke)

Elsie's attack was bad yesterday, today I am thankful to say she is much better.

I have not yet heard anything from Salisbury as to the Vice Royalty. He has become a very bad correspondent.

Sunday 27 December (Greystoke)

Yesterday I wrote to Salisbury as to my successor: this morning I have heard from him, and on the whole satisfactory.[1016]

[1016]Carnarvon to Salisbury, 26 December 1885 (copy): CP, BL 60702, fo. 118. Salisbury's reply has not been traced.

1886

Friday 1 January (Vice Regal Lodge)

The beginning of the New Year; and politically it opens darkly. We as a Government are entering on a course of policy which can only end in failure and may lead to great disaster; and on the other hand I have the deepest distrust of everything which Gladstone will do. Self pervades the whole of his course; but I expect that as death does not come to those who court it, so we shall stay on to follow the unreasoning impulses of men who are wholly ignorant of the facts of the case.

R. Churchill came here to luncheon on his way back to England. We talked for fully two hours and the conversation was very interesting; but I cannot say that I derived comfort from it.[1017] He is very clever and ingenious and has many far reaching thoughts; but he is over-rash and if he guides the chariot of the Sun he may easily set our English world on fire.

He has an attractive side to his character and is open to the influences of counsel and prudence, but—.

Thursday 7 January (Vice Regal Lodge)

I had two conversations today curiously opposite. Capt. Slack, after reporting the state of his district, told me that I am extremely unpopular with the landowners in the South and on pressing him for the reasons he gave me three:

1. My speech in the House of Lords just before coming over here.

2. My seeing the Mayor of Limerick in my bedroom when I was too ill to see him elsewhere, and my "civility" to the Nationalists.

[1017]The following day, Churchill suggested to Salisbury that Lord Wolseley should succeed Carnarvon as Lord Lieutenant (Churchill to Salisbury, 2 January 1886: CP, TNA, PRO 30/6/55, fos 165–166). Churchill had also discussed with Carnarvon the possibility of the latter writing a paragraph in the Queen's Speech on Ireland. Carnarvon, on reflection, wrote to Churchill, 'I doubt, with my ideas of policy, I am the best person to compose the paragraph' (Carnarvon to Churchill, 3 January 1886: CP, TNA, PRO 30/6/55, fo. 173).

3. My speech at Belfast where after impressing on the tenants to be reasonable I told the landlords to be forebearing.

On the same day old Sir P. Keenan[1018] with whom I had a long conversation as to the future of Ireland said, "One thing I can say that since Your Excellency came to Ireland I have not heard one unkind word spoken against you."

Two curiously opposed speeches made to me on the same day, and both I doubt not correct, but expressing the opinion of different classes.

Wednesday 13 January (London)

Elsie and Margaret and Esmé and I came over today. On the way I saw in the *Standard* the statement in the leading article announcing my retirement at the end of the month.[1019] It is worded in the most friendly terms, and it seems to me to come at a most opportune moment for me. The sky was looking dark. I can plainly see the symptoms of a dead set being made at me: circumstances rather favour it, and I might easily be placed in the position not of retiring according to a bargain with Salisbury and in accordance with my own wishes, but of being forced out of office on the ground of having failed. At this moment comes this statement which places everything in the pleasantest light to me personally and relieves me I hope from all risks of a breach with the Government and Party.

On arriving in London I wrote to Salisbury, but I found that he had gone down to Osborne.

A long talk with Herbert over the whole position. On the whole he agrees with me that it will be perhaps best that S. should for a while stand aloof from the Government, opposing in the House of Lords, and supporting them but not joining.

Thursday 14 January (London)

All or almost all the papers are writing of my retirement in fairly friendly terms, and none of them suggest that it is through a difference of opinion that I am going. Nevertheless these times are personally

[1018] Sir Patrick Joseph Keenan (1826–1894), Resident Commissioner of National Education, Ireland.
[1019] 'The retirement of Lord Carnarvon', *Evening Standard*, 13 January 1886, p. 8.

unpleasant and it will be satisfactory when the whole matter is concluded, if it is well concluded.

Friday 15 January (London)

Cabinet

A remarkable Cabinet[1020] which began by a reference to the recent announcement in the *Standard* as to myself with an assurance that I thought it well to give that I of course knew nothing of it.

Then we discussed Irish matters, and a very curious discussion it was. R. Churchill proposed that within the next few days before the meeting of Parliament, we should proclaim the National League, arrest all prominent persons, seize the officers of the League and their papers and apply to Parliament for an indemnity. This extraordinary proposal was accepted by the majority of the Cabinet, Cranbrook,[1021] Harrowby, Smith, Cross and several others. Salisbury opposed it and I said that I really could not carry out such a measure, and so ultimately we destroyed the absurd suggestion. Since then I have reason to think that R.C. himself only used it as a sort of feint to cover all proposals, but it was very curious to see how many of the Cabinet swallowed it eagerly.[1022]

The question remains, and this must be discussed tomorrow, whether in the Queen's Speech an intimation will be given that the Government will apply for fresh powers to put down the League.

Saturday 16 January (London)

Cabinet

A preliminary meeting at the Irish Office of Lord Ashbourne, the Attorney General, Dyke, and myself. We discussed the Queen's Speech and the proposed paragraph on Ireland. Ashbourne under

[1020] The Cabinet had met on 12 January with Carnarvon in Ireland. Parliament assembled on 15 January and adjourned until 20 January.

[1021] Cranbrook had received a letter from Salisbury in the morning, offering him the Lord Lieutenancy, but turned it down (A.E. Gathorne-Hardy, *Gathorne Hardy, First Earl of Cranbrook: a memoir*, 2 vols (London, 1910), II, pp. 253–254). Churchill sent Salisbury next day further suggestions for filling the post, including Cranbrook, 'W. H. Smith and (please don't be too shocked), myself' (Churchill to Salisbury, 16 January 1886: Hatfield House Papers, 3M/E).

[1022] See Carnarvon's lengthy letter to Salisbury, written after the Cabinet meeting: Hatfield House Papers, 3M/E.

the influence of present public opinion hot as any Orangeman for the assertion of most extreme measures.

Afterwards a Cabinet in which there was a great discussion as to whether there should be an intimation in the Speech of an intention to ask for powers to suppress the League, or only that the Government may ask for such, or no mention at all of it. The Cabinet could not agree and it was adjourned to Monday.

I afterwards saw Salisbury and settled (1) that I could not stay for the debate on the opening of Parliament but return to Ireland and wind up, (2) that I did not see any advantage at present of my taking a seat in the Cabinet without Office. He agreed to this and added that if the Government should go on there must be reconstitution and that he could then offer me some Office.

He said Cross was very weak, that Hamilton was also weak.

Sunday 17 January (London)

Elsie and I went to St. Paul's, a refreshing service after all the anxieties and worries and work of the last few days [. . .].

Dyke called this evening, to tell me he had just put his resignation in Salisbury's hands.[1023] Poor fellow, he is sore and out of spirits; for he considers that the attacks on him in the Papers have been got up for the purpose of driving him out; and he is convinced that they have been inspired by some of his colleagues. It is not pleasant to think this; but I suspect that he is not very wrong. But for the opportune publication of my retirement in the *Standard* I feel sure that a dead set was commencing against me in the Papers, proceeding possibly from a different source but practically much the same in effect.

Monday 18 January (London)

Cabinet and my last, I conclude, held at the Foreign Office. The Irish paragraph in the Speech finally settled, containing a clause against Home Rule and one against the National League. I took this opportunity of warning the Cabinet that this would be accepted as a declaration of War, that the National League differed from previous organisations in this that all the Irish members belonged to it, and that the R.C. clergy were now identified with it. I warned them that

---

[1023]Hart Dyke had informed Salisbury after the Cabinet meeting on 16 January 'that he did not want to go on as Irish Secretary – Carnarvon had never let him know anything that was going on' (Salisbury to W.H. Smith, 16 January 1886: Hambleden Papers, PS9/104).

a mere bill for the suppression of the League would not suffice: but that there must be a Crimes Bill and a pretty strong one too, and that if they were wise they would set about its composition at once.[1024]

Our parting was very friendly and I hope that I go out in the comparative odour of sanctity. But I welcome my release greatly.[1025]

Friday 22 January (Vice Regal Lodge)

The debate on the Address is interesting. Salisbury's reference to me was a handsome one, and there was no personal or hostile criticism of me as far as I saw.[1026]

Gladstone's speech was evidently an entire change [from] his original purpose: but he left open more back doors of escape. Parnell's was a very striking one, the best I have ever read of his, compressed force and moderation.[1027]

In the evening I had a telegram from Salisbury[1028] saying that he was sorry in the pressure of yesterday not to have announced Smith's appointment[1029] and that Cranbrook goes to the War Office.

Saturday 23 January (Vice Regal Lodge)

A horribly cold day, snow or sleet and rain.

Elsie distributed the prizes in a very cold room for some window gardening and neat cottages, and I made a short speech.

[1024] Lady Spencer, wife of the previous Liberal Lord Lieutenant, commented to her husband on the situation, 'It is curious to read all the papers and see how completely it [the Government] allowed that the attempts to govern without a Coercion Bill have failed. There *never* was so disastrous a policy' (Lady Spencer to Lord Spencer, 20 January 1886: Spencer Papers).

[1025] Carnarvon left by night train to Dublin.

[1026] Salisbury stated, 'It is impossible to exaggerate the care, benevolence, the tact, the skill which my noble Friend [the Earl of Carnarvon] brought to bear on the task of executing the message of reconciliation of which he announced in this House that he was the bearer' (*Hansard*, CCCII, 21 January 1886, col. 66).

[1027] Ibid., Gladstone, cols 100–120, Parnell, cols 151–160.

[1028] CP, BL 60762, fo. 132.

[1029] Carnarvon wrote immediately to Smith, remarking on the latter's 'great self-sacrifice' in accepting the post and offered to discuss matters with him (Carnarvon to W.H. Smith, 22 January 1886: Hambleden Papers, PS9/114). Smith crossed over to Ireland on 23 January (W.H. Smith to Carnarvon, 22 January 1886: CP, TNA, PRO 30/6/53, fo. 231). Cranbrook filled Smith's position at the War Office.

In the evening I gave a large state farewell dinner in uniform, 37 present. I had asked 50 but the others could not come.[1030]

A rather disagreeable controversy with the Chancellor (Gibson) as to my giving a P.C. ship to Monroe the late Solicitor General and now Judge of Land Court.[1031] He was overbearing and impertinent and so I was obliged to meet his opinion by a very distinct and clear refusal. He has a great deal of the typical Irishman in him.

Sunday 24 January (Vice Regal Lodge)

W.H. Smith, the new Chief Secretary, arrived and came here. Our meeting was very cordial and I had a very long conversation with him.[1032] I spoke to him with the fullest unreserve and told him everything that I thought would be of the smallest use.

I hope I have settled Jekyll with him as Private Secretary. It is apparently arranged that as soon as the debate in the House of Commons permits, a new Lord Lieutenant should be appointed, but that till then I should retain the Office nominally.

Monday 25 January (Vice Regal Lodge)

A deep snow, very cold, and unusual weather for Ireland.

My first and last Levée, I expected there would be a very small attendance owing to the horrible weather, the absence of many in London and political agitations. But it was a large one, 530 attended.[1033]

I thought there were comparatively few peers or great landowners.

I held a Privy Council to swear in A. Kavanagh,[1034] a curious and strange spectacle.

[1030] One leader writer commented on Carnarvon's impending departure, 'Beyond doubt, more regret is felt for his departure than pleasure was experienced for his incoming [...]. The character of his Government was greatly affected by his own personality. But he was handicapped too heavily to allow of his doing any substantial or memorable good' (*Freeman's Journal*, 25 January 1886, p. 4).

[1031] John Monroe (1839–1899), Solicitor-General for Ireland (1885), Judge of the Land Court (1885–1895).

[1032] Smith told his wife, Emily, 'I am here, very cordially and hospitably entertained by Lady Carnarvon who seems delighted at the chance of receiving me' (W.H. Smith to Emily Smith, 24 January 1886: Hambleden Papers, A/1064). Carnarvon, for his part, had stated to Salisbury, 'I think Smith's appointment a very good one' (Carnarvon to Salisbury, 22 January 1886: Hatfield House Papers, 3M/E).

[1033] *The Times*, 26 January 1886, p. 5.

[1034] Arthur MacMorrough Kavanagh (1831–1889), Con. MP for Co. Wexford (1866–1868) and for Co. Carlow (1868–1880), Lord Lieutenant of Co. Carlow (1880–1889).

Tuesday 26 January (Vice Regal Lodge)

Smith left by evening boat for London having been recalled for the purpose of proposing on Thursday a bill for the Suppression of the National League and another measure for the settlement of the Land question. I do not think he much likes his task, and he returns to London very much altered in his opinion after hearing all that he has heard from me and others during the last two days. He is a very honest, straightforward, sensible, moderate man, but I doubt his being very successful with his new charge.[1035]

We held our Drawing Room, the first and last, a large one of over 600, though the weather was very bad. Altogether successful, a rather pretty pageant [. . .]. It is just as well to have thus put a finish on everything.

Wednesday 27 January (Vice Regal Lodge)

Whilst we held our Drawing Room last night, the Government were beaten[1036] and I received late a telegram from Salisbury saying they had unanimously agreed to resign.[1037]

Thursday 28 January (Ireland – Holyhead)

We have made our formal and final departure and the Vice Royalty of seven months is closed. It began with a remarkably warm reception

[1035] Smith was sent to prepare a report on the need for a Coercion Act, in contrast to Carnarvon's attempt to rule by ordinary law. Smith believed that further legislation was necessary (see Douglas, *W.H. Smith*, p. 204). Smith had informed his wife, 'The Carnarvons are very kind and do all they can to make things pleasant for me, but it is dreary work and would be unendurable if it were not necessary' (W.H. Smith to Emily Smith, 25 January 1886: Hambleden Papers, A/1065).

[1036] On 26 January, Hicks Beach gave notice in the Commons that Smith would introduce a Coercion Bill 'for the purpose of suppressing the National League' on 28 January, to be followed by an enlarged Land Purchase Bill. The same day, Jesse Collings (1831–1920), Radical MP for Ipswich (1880–1886), introduced an amendment on the subject of 'three acres and a cow', on which the Government were beaten by 330 to 252 votes (Fourth night of the debate on the Queen's Speech: *Hansard*, CCCII, 26 January 1886, Hicks Beach, cols 525–529). See also J. Collings and J.L. Green, *Life of the Right Hon. Jesse Collings* (London, 1920), pp. 182–191.

[1037] 'Cabinet unanimously resolved to resign: am communicating now to the Queen, she is very reluctant to accept' (Salisbury to Carnarvon, 27 January 1886: CP, BL 60762, fo. 133). Carnarvon replied, 'Many thanks for your telegram. I anticipated the decision and have no doubt that it is quite right' (Carnarvon to Salisbury, 27 January 1886: CP, TNA, PRO 30/6/55, fo. 235).

and it ended with a demonstration quite as cordial. The day was lovely, a bright sun shining, the streets were lined from the Castle to the Station with troops and police, a large escort [...] preceded and followed us. Bands at intervals as we passed played God Save the Queen, and there was a very large crowd all the way. As we passed there was a general uncovering of heads and a great deal of cheering, with many cries of God bless, and God speed you, May you live long, Come back to us, etc. I think the feeling was mainly personal, though a part no doubt due to my supposed leanings to Irish self government. But there is great warmth of heart.

When we arrived at the station, a special train took us down to the special steamer and with us went Prince Edward,[1038] Lady Ailesbury[1039] (who as usual turned up a day or two ago) the Hamiltons etc. Here a large crowd followed us to the boat cheering and wishing us God speed, and one poor woman as we steamed away threw herself on her knees to pray for us. It was a striking scene, almost a bit of history; the cheering and the sympathetic crowd, the friends and staff who I believe were most sorry to lose us, the bright scene, the salute of the guns, perhaps more like the departure of Lord Fitzwilliam[1040] last century than anything else.

Before we left the Castle we had a sort of informal Levée of those friends who came to say goodbye to us.[1041]

It is curious how many friends we seem to have made, some of one view, some of another, in politics. The old Provost of Trinity, Redington,[1042] Hamilton, Major King-Harman, Mahaffy,[1043] all representing very different classes of opinion on these troublesome Irish questions.

And so ends the task which when I accepted it seemed to me so full of danger and so utterly impossible. The dangers which I anticipated have not confronted us. The difficulties we have had to meet have been different from what I expected. What I have done has been also different from what I had planned to do. I return with feelings far apart from that with which I went but with this feeling above all others, that I have been wonderfully and most mercifully guided in

---

[1038] Prince Wilhelm August Eduard (1823–1902) served in the British Army for fifty years and commanded forces in Ireland.

[1039] Lady Maria Elizabeth Ailesbury, widow of the 1st Marquess of Ailesbury.

[1040] William Wentworth Fitzwilliam (1748–1833), 2nd Earl Fitzwilliam (1756), Lord Lieutenant of Ireland (1795), recalled after three months because of his support for Roman Catholic emancipation.

[1041] 'The departure of Lord Carnarvon', *Freeman's Journal*, 29 January 1886, p. 5.

[1042] Christopher Talbot Redington, Commissioner on Poor Relief and mining royalties and education.

[1043] John Pentland Mahaffy, Professor of Ancient History, Dublin since 1869.

everything by the great Ruler and disposer of all things, who through all my life and all my want of faith has never abandoned me. I may say now as I have constantly said like Sir J. Astley[1044] in the Civil Wars, "Lord if I forget thee, yet do thou remember me."

Saturday 30 January (London)

I was busy all the morning with Forster[1045] and Roberts. In the afternoon Sandon called. The Cabinet seems to have been on the edge of dissolution after the last meeting at which I was present, a catastrophe which would have not only been ridiculous but which would have damaged them for many a long day. It seems that after that last Cabinet at which I was present some violent counsels again prevailed and it was decided to take some very immediate measure against the National League, but that Beach declared he would not agree to do this then, that in a fortnight's time he expected some justification would be given and that he would not move without this. Whereupon a complete disagreement ensued and the Cabinet was on the point of breaking to pieces, was adjourned to Monday and that in the interval Salisbury and one or two others patched it up. The Queen's Speech was agreed to in the terms ultimately adopted and so it ended for the time.

I gather that there was and is much bitterness against Beach, and also some anger with Salisbury for not having stated to the Cabinet the fact that I had bargained to go to Ireland only for a time. Altogether there appears to be a good deal of irritation with many persons and on many subjects: but this is the usual concomitant of the dissolution of a Cabinet.

Salisbury I suspect is far from well. I hear he is going very soon to Mentone.

Tuesday 16 February (Porto Fino)

A speech of R. Churchill's in Monday's paper in which he refers to me.[1046] It is not easy to frame a given number of sentences which are

[1044] Sir Jacob Astley (1579–1652), Royalist, major-general in the king's army, and later imprisoned.
[1045] William S. Forster, Carnarvon's solicitor.
[1046] In a speech to his Paddington constituents on 13 February, Churchill claimed that, on the eve of the meeting of Parliament in January, 'that most estimable and nobleman, Lord Carnarvon, threw up the Government of Ireland' (*The Times*, 15 February 1886, p. 10).

more inconsistent with fact, but it is not of course desirable to take any notice of them. And yet when last he talked to me in Ireland he said to me that the Government were under deep obligation to me and had I chosen to say in public what I had said to him and the rest of the Cabinet on Irish matters, I could, he said, have destroyed the Government at once – !!! And now compare that with his speech.

Tuesday 23 February (Porto Fino)

In the evening papers of Saturday, which arrived today, is a statement with regard to Parnell and communications having passed between him and me, which may lead to some explanations. I wrote to Herbert on the subject and to Hamilton.

Saturday 6 March (Porto Fino)

A disagreeable and awkward letter in Thursday's *Daily News* with regard to myself, signed X.[1047] I do not however think that it would be wise to take any notice of it.

(1) Anything I wrote from here might cross or be crossed by some letter from someone else. It is very disadvantageous to enter into newspaper correspondence when abroad.

(2) Whilst abroad I am not obliged to be thought to see the *Daily News*.

(3) If I must reply it had best be at the end of all attacks and rejoinders that I may make if possible one clear answer to cover everything.

I wrote to Herbert much in this sense.
I also wrote to Eveline about Irish matters. I have for some time been intending to do this in consequence of one from her.

Monday 8 March (Porto Fino)

The political aspect in England is very stormy. Gladstone's scheme is evidently very thoroughgoing. R. Churchill is violent, but I should not be surprised to see him go right round at a very short notice.

[1047]The letter quoted another letter sent by Churchill to an Irish priest claiming that Carnarvon had stated 'that the Conservative leaders had in November 1885 honestly made up their minds to try what they could to introduce Home Rule in Ireland' (*Daily News*, 4 March 1886, p. 5).

Meanwhile allusions continue to be made to me. In the House of Commons both Gladstone and R. Churchill quoted me in different senses. It looks as if anyhow we are in for a great fight.[1048] But perhaps Gladstone can tie up his land scheme and his home rule proposals so closely that the Irish landlords who are frightened and selfish may compel the House of Lords to accept both. As they say here when I ask them of the weather, "*Ché lo sa?*"

I finished the version of the first 4 books of the *Odyssey* today.

Thursday 25 March (Porto Fino)

In the *Pall Mall* received today to my surprise I saw quoted in one of the short articles an extract from a recent private letter of mine to Stead on the state of politics.[1049] It was no betrayal of any confidence for there was nothing to identify it with me though it was said to be by a Conservative ex-Minister who rendered important public service at former times, or something to that effect.

Sunday 11 April (Porto Fino)

The English papers came today with the report of Gladstone's speech introducing his Home Rule Bill. Whatever may be the expediency or misfortune of the policy the ability of the speech and the extraordinary effort in a man of past 77 years old cannot be gainsaid.[1050] I can see Sir R. Hamilton's hand in a good deal of the plan, and it is impossible also not to see a large amount of Conservative intention in the general outline. Coupled with the Land Bill, of the details of which we know nothing, yet it cannot be said to be a very revolutionary

---

[1048] Maintenance of Social Order (Ireland), committee stage: *Hansard*, CCCII, 4 March 1886, cols 1919–1998.

[1049] The note began, 'An esteemed Conservative correspondent of high rank, who has rendered distinguished service to the State, sends this lugubrious account of the political position and prospects' (*Pall Mall Gazette*, 22 March 1886, p. 3).

[1050] Government of Ireland Bill, first reading. For Gladstone's speech, see *Hansard*, CCCIV, 8 April 1886, cols 1036–1085. Lasting three and a half hours, it set out an ambitious programme for settling the Irish problem. The imperial parliament at Westminster would deal with foreign policy, defence, customs and excise, and religious institutions, with concessions to Ireland on certain matters (see P. Magnus, *Gladstone: a biography* (London, 1963), pp. 353–354). Edward Hamilton called it 'the most notable day probably in the annals of the present Houses of Parliament [...]. My first impression drawn from a sort of pulse-feeling of the House is that though the Bill may be and probably will be read a second time, it will be scotched and killed in Committee or undergo a most radical amendment' (Bahlman, III, p. 34).

measure, in one sense of the word, though of course involving great change. Trevelyan's speech[1051] reads extremely poor. Parnell evidently as friendly as he dares to be to the proposal.

Monday 12 April (Porto Fino)

A great storm is breaking in England over Gladstone's Home Rule proposals. It is clear that I ought not to be later than 28th. in England, though what my position should be I cannot yet tell. There has been a meeting of our late Cabinet at Salisbury's and I see my absence is commented on and explained by the fact that I am in Italy at the same time, but I have not had one line from any of my late colleagues. Since I have been abroad indeed, the only one that has written is Sandon.

Saturday 17 April (Porto Fino)

The state of feeling in England on Irish matters is a strange one.[1052] It is for the moment a coalition of Conservatives, Whigs and a certain number of Radicals, which is remarkable. It is I think anti-Irish and perhaps also it is anti-Gladstone for there has been a fire smouldering for a long time against him which till now has not dared to break out. This is certainly the case with a part of the Press. Almost everyone seems to be carried away by the general feeling; but whether it will last remains to be seen. If Irish outrages commence it is perhaps possible it may, and in that case be followed by severe repression.

Saturday 24 April (Porto Fino)

This morning I received two letters which made us make a complete change of plans. We had arranged to start on Monday: we now decided to postpone our departure for a week.

The two letters were from Harrowby and Herbert. Harrowby wrote strongly urging me not to return if possible till the Home Rule bill was disposed of, one way or the other, in the House of Commons, and conveying me a message from Salisbury to that effect – and Herbert,

---

[1051] Sir George Otto Trevelyan (1838–1928), Lib. MP for Tynemouth (1865–1868), for Hawick (1868–1886), and for Glasgow, Bridgtown division (1887–1897), Chief Secretary for Ireland (1882–1884), Chancellor, Duchy of Lancaster (1884–1885), Secretary of State for Scotland (1886, 1892–1895). For his speech, see *Hansard*, CCCIV, 8 April 1886, cols 1114–1124.

[1052] After four nights of debate, the Government of Ireland Bill completed its first reading in the Commons.

though expecting us back and promising to come and dine quietly at once to talk anything over, wrote in much the same sense, evidently thinking it would be a good thing if I were not in London just now with party spirit running so high. On consideration it seemed impossible to stay away so long as the time when the second reading of the bill would be affirmed or negatived; but we thought that we might take another week, and so we decided.[1053]

Saturday 1 May (Highclere – London)

Short as my time has yet been in England[1054] I can see how all engrossing is this Irish question. Everyone from the Inspector at the Railway to the country gentleman whom I met on the road came up at once to talk to me about it, all dead against the bill.

Tuesday 4 May (London)

Several more or less important conversations.

1st. with Sandon. I told him of my intended attitude as to the Irish bills, but I could see that his apprehension was that if I said that I had ever thought a settlement to be possible it might create some schism. I do not think this and I do not see how I can avoid saying what is really no secret. He said to me in reference to the message which he had lately conveyed to me from Salisbury that Salisbury was unwilling to write it to me himself but had begged him to do so. I asked him why? He did not give any very clear answer but merely said S. did not wish to write. The message was advising me against coming back until the Irish bill was through the Second Reading. I do not understand: if Sandon correctly apprehended Salisbury, why was he unwilling to write himself?

2. Conversation with Captain Ross,[1055] who had seen the Pope and had laid before him and his private Secretary and one or two of the Cardinals the state of affairs in Ireland and the relations of the Irish

---

[1053]Carnarvon replied to Harrowby that there were 'some very important and serious property questions on hand which no one can deal with but myself to attend to in England. This will I hope enable me to tide over in silence (which I quite recognise to be the best thing) the time between my return and the 2nd reading of the Bill in the H. of C.' (Carnarvon to Harrowby, 24 April 1886: Harrowby Papers, 2nd series, lii, fos 166–167).

[1054]Since 30 April.

[1055]Capt. John Foster George Ross-of-Bladensburg (1848–1926). He had wide experience of Ireland, having served Forster, Spencer, and Carnarvon as private secretary. Secretary to two missions to the Holy See in 1887.

Members and the Roman Catholic clergy to the National League. The Pope said to him in the course of this conversation, "You were Lord Carnarvon's private Secretary in Ireland?" Ross said yes. The Holy Father said, "Is he not of very high rank among the Freemasons?" Ross said yes, but he added that he had heard me say on the subject that if I thought there was anything in Freemasonry opposed to religion I should give it up immediately. Whereupon the Pope replied, "Lord Ripon was one but gave up the Society."

To which of course Ross replied that Ripon was a Roman Catholic and gave up his office "as an act of obedience."

3. Conversation with Percy Greg[1056] who came to talk to me about Irish affairs. I told him pretty much what I propose saying in public before long, only more in detail than would have been wise, and avoiding generally all criticism on the details of Gladstone's two bills. But the conversation was quite confidential.

Thursday 6 May (London)

An important conversation with Salisbury. I called on him by Sandon's advice and request and *I could see at once that he had learnt from Sandon all that had passed between us* a few days ago. I told Salisbury that I thought it right to let him know what my feelings were as to Irish matters, that he knew my original opinion, that I had not changed that opinion, but that I did not think Gladstone's proposals safe or practicable and that after his appeal to class feeling I was not disposed to strengthen the side of agitation and perhaps disorder as against the Conservative elements of Society, but that my own position was a difficult one and that it was necessary for me before long to define it, that I therefore thought it would be best that I should take some early opportunity of explaining that though I had always "hoped for a settlement of the Irish difficulties I could not accept this bill". He at once said that this would be very inconvenient before the close of the Second Reading of the Home Rule bill, that he should be obliged to reply by stating that he would never be a party to any changes and that if it came about it must be done by others, and he added that there would probably be other explanations. I replied that if this were so I would endeavour to preserve silence for the present, though of course things might be said which would compel me to speak. He

[1056]Percy Greg (1836–1889), contributor to the *Manchester Guardian*, the *Standard*, and the *Saturday Review*, author of *History of the United States from the foundation of Virginia to the Reconstruction of the Union*, 2 vols (London, 1887).

then suggested that if I made any explanations it would be best to do so by a letter to him which he could answer and that then the correspondence should go to the Papers.

So the matter ended, not perhaps very satisfactorily for me but I felt I could not refuse at his request, as the late Prime Minister, to observe silence for a time. The position however is not altogether pleasant personally, for the manner and attitude of several of my old colleagues in the House tonight was cold and rather unfriendly. This however is not the first time I have had experience of this sort of thing.

Friday 7 May (Highclere)

Herbert breakfasted with us and we had a long conversation upon what occurred yesterday with Salisbury, and as a result of it we came to the conclusion that not only should I if possible preserve silence on Irish questions till the Second Reading of the Home Rule bill is disposed of but that I should as far as possible continue this option of silence afterwards. But on the other hand we agreed that it would be well that I should let it be known in private what my position is, viz. that without going into any details it should be known that though I had always hoped to find some solution of the difficulty, some settlement, and even to agree to some extension of local self-government, I did not approve of the present separatist measure and strongly condemned Gladstone.

So it stands. I hope I may avoid all appearance of breaking with the Party. At the same time I cannot see much likelihood of being able to serve again with any safety or comfort in the same cabinet with my late colleagues. It might be possible in a mixed government, but in a reproduction of the late Government it would be very hard [. . .].

Ross of Bladensburg called on me before I left. I told him that on reflection he must *not* write the letter which he meditated to Rome.

Friday 14 May (London)

Howorth[1057] came to talk to me. He said that I had been frequently found fault with in consequence of the Maamtrasna Debate that he felt sure that it was unjust but that he had determined to ask me. I said it was unjust for it had been against my earnest protest. He asked

---

[1057] Sir Henry Hoyle Howorth (1842–1923), Con. MP for Salford South (1886–1892).

if he might tell this to Spencer *privately* as he, Spencer, was very sore.
I said yes on condition that it was private.[1058]

I called on Macmillan[1059] and opened the question of publishing my
first XII books of the *Odyssey*. We discussed and virtually settled it. He
is to send me an estimate of the expense and it is to be published by
"Commission".

Saturday 15 May (London)

The Home Rule bill seems doomed. The combination against it by
Whigs and Radicals is I think too powerful to be resisted, unless at the
last moment Gladstone should by some ingenious artifice outgeneral
his opponents. The position is a very curious one.[1060]

Sunday 16 May (London)

Lord Ashbourne called here this afternoon. He was very friendly
and cordial, said he had just returned from Ireland and that the feeling
there among all classes was one of complete gloom. He said that there
was hardly a tradesman of any importance in Dublin who was not in
dismay at the bill. He told me that Salisbury's speech yesterday, which
I have not yet seen, was "what you and I should call a very strong
one", by which I understand he means stronger than he quite agrees
with. He expressed his belief in Ulster (of which he said he knew little)
being quite in earnest in its resistance.[1061]

Monday 31 May (London)

A curious fact as to Salisbury has come to my knowledge.

[1058] See L.P. Curtis, *Coercion and Conciliation in Ireland, 1880–1892: a study in Conservative Unionism*
(Princeton, NJ, 1963), pp. 42–43.

[1059] Sir Frederick Orridge Macmillan (1851–1935), publisher and son of the founder of the
firm, Daniel Macmillan.

[1060] Gladstone had introduced the second reading of the Government of Ireland Bill on 10
May, which did little to cheer his supporters. At the beginning of May, it was calculated
that 119 Liberals would vote against the second reading (see J. Morley, *The Life of William
Ewart Gladstone*, 3 vols (London, 1903), III, p. 332). A meeting was called by Hartington at
Devonshire House on 14 May in protest against the proposed scheme for Ireland (see Cooke
and Vincent, *The Governing Passion*, p. 421).

[1061] Salisbury's speech was to the National Union of Conservative Associations at St James's
Hall (*The Times*, 17 May 1886, p. 6).

Early in the time of our government he wrote to one or two people letters in the general direction of at all events considering and entertaining some form of Home Rule. It was the time Randolph Churchill was intriguing in the same direction. It was a pity that Salisbury did not give me some better indication of what was passing in his mind.

My informant assures me he had seen the very letters.

Friday 4 June (London)

A rather interesting conversation with W.H. Smith. He is evidently not carried away by the general and popular tide of anti-Irish feeling and is aware that something better than a mere *non possumus* is necessary.[1062] A long conversation also with Greenwood on the same subject. He is I think of much the same mind though he does not see or know as much, and though he writes in his Paper in a different sense. Salisbury's speech, the "20 years' coercion" and the comparison of Irishmen with Hottentots is, as far as anything reaches me, very much disapproved.[1063]

Sunday 6 June (London)

Several long and interesting conversations today, first with Harrowby with whom I talked over the really important question whether I should speak or write anything to make my position as regards Gladstone's Irish policy clearer. At first he was strongly in favour of it and said he could not understand Salisbury binding me to silence. Afterwards when recalling my conversation last year with Parnell he said he thought it better to delay if possible any line such as I meditated till after the Elections if we are in for them.

Next a conversation with Lord Arthur Butler,[1064] mostly on Irish affairs. I explained to him a little what my position as Lord Lieutenant had been, how crippled, and tied down and a great deal of it was quite new to him [. . .].

[1062] See Douglas, *W.H. Smith*, p. 209.

[1063] A phrase used by Salisbury at the meeting on 15 May. As his daughter commented, 'For the next half-dozen years it would be safe to say that there was not one Liberal meeting in ten at which some speaker did not repeat the assertion that Lord Salisbury had declared Irishmen to be on a level with Hottentots' (Cecil, III, p. 209).

[1064] Lord James Arthur Butler (1849–1943), State Steward in Carnarvon's household in Ireland.

Next a long talk with Froude, who was very cynical as to Irish matters: but said that 60,000 copies of his *Oceana* had already been sold.[1065]

Next an important conversation with W.H. Smith, whom I much like. We spoke at length on Ireland and the present state of things and I asked his opinion as to my own position and whether I should speak or write, and his advice was not to do either unless obliged. I told him of my conversation with Parnell last year and he said that so far from blaming or thinking it unwise he would probably have done the same had he been in my place.

Wednesday 9 June (Highclere – London)

This morning at breakfast I read in the *Pall Mall* the statement that I have made overtures to Parnell and had communicated with him an offer of a statutory Parliament.[1066] After talking it all over with Elsie by her advice I came up to town, having telegraphed to Herbert, who came and met me in Portman Square and talked everything over. At first I think he was doubtful as to any explanations in the House of Lords, but as I explained to him my proposed course he gradually agreed; at last he came to the conclusion that it was the best thing I could do.

Afterwards I saw Sandon, who is so nervous about the Elections and Salisbury's position that he would have persuaded me not to speak. But I said that I really must and that I believed it was the best thing, not only for myself but for the Party and the late Government: and so the matter stands, I shall write tonight to Salisbury to say that I mean to do this tomorrow.[1067]

[1065] *Oceana, or England and her Colonies*, went through two editions on its publication in 1886. It was an account of the Australasian colonies, which Froude had visited in the winter of 1884–1885.

[1066] 'The Tory offer to the Parnellites', *Pall Mall Gazette*, 9 June 1886, p. 9. It stated, 'There is no doubt, I believe, that Lord Carnarvon did express some sort of sympathy with the Home Rule movement, but how far he was authorised to commit his colleagues is another question. There is good reason to believe that he, as well as Lord Randolph Churchill and Mr. W.H. Smith, advised the Cabinet to adopt Home Rule policy.' The paper followed Parnell's revelation on 7 June, during the twelfth day of debate on the second reading of the Government of Ireland Bill, that a senior Conservative minister had offered him home rule. Shortly after one o'clock on the morning of 8 June, the Government were defeated by 311 to 341 votes. See W.C. Lubenow, *Parliamentary Politics and the Home Rule Crisis: the British House of Commons in 1886* (Oxford, 1988), pp. 250–253.

[1067] '[Parnell's statement] reflects too much on me – and indeed on all members of the Cabinet – to allow me to remain silent' (Carnarvon to Salisbury, 9 June 1886: Hatfield House Papers, 3M/E).

Thursday 10 June (London)

My decision was taken on seeing an article in the *Daily News* which repeated the charge against me of having made this offer to Parnell and went into details.[1068] I called on W.H. Smith and told him I had made up my mind to explain in the House of Lords. He finally agreed that I was right, but telegraphed to Salisbury who came up to London and walked into my room in Portman Square at 2 p.m. He was evidently much disturbed, but I told him that my mind was clear on the subject, that I must speak but that I would take all the responsibility on myself and that he might be sure that I should not commit him or the rest of this Government. But he made various suggestions which if acceded to would have had the effect of defeating or spoiling my intentions. He tried at first to induce me to content myself with a simple contradiction, which would only have provoked Parnell to disclose the conversation with me as an unholy and secret meeting, then he proposed I could bring on my explanation on moving the adjournment of the House, when there would not be above half a dozen Peers left in it; then he said that he believed Gorst[1069] to have been the person who had made the communication and that Parnell did not mean to allude to me. However I said I must speak, and he then said, "Pray make it as dry as possible and without any sentiment," to which I replied that "I should be very short and simple but that I always eat my bread with butter": and so we parted.[1070]

I went to the House and found the best possible opportunity and made my explanation.[1071] It was listened to with the utmost attention, but with a frigidity on the part of my late colleagues that was curious. Not one of them said one word; nor when I sat down and remained sitting on the same bench for an hour and a half afterwards did any one of them say one syllable to me.

In the evening afterwards I dined with Eveline and Portsmouth,[1072] a pleasant time after all the worry and anxiety of the last two days. But

[1068]'Who Was It?', *Daily News*, 10 June 1886, p. 5.

[1069]Sir John Eldon Gorst (1835–1916), Con. MP for Chatham (1875–1892), member of the Fourth Party (1880–1884), Solicitor-General (1885). For his views on Ireland, see R. Hunter, *A Life of Sir John Eldon Gorst, 1835–1916: Disraeli's awkward disciple* (London, 2001), pp. 182–183.

[1070]Ashbourne wrote to Carnarvon the previous day also urging him not to speak 'on the eve possibly of a general election [. . .]. Statements in public from you [. . .] would to some extent involve saying what your own general views were, and would also be regarded in *some* quarters as *provocative*' (Ashbourne to Carnarvon, 9 June 1886: CP, BL 60857, fos 114–115).

[1071]The Government of Ireland Bill. The Earl of Carnarvon and Mr. Parnell. Personal Statement: *Hansard*, CCCVI, 10 June 1886, cols 1256–1260. Parliament was dissolved that day.

[1072]Isaac Newton Wallop (1825–1906), 5th Earl of Portsmouth (1854), married Carnarvon's sister, Eveline (1885).

I feel more at ease now that the statement has been made and that I have anticipated an attack that was sure to be made sooner or later.[1073]

Friday 11 June (Highclere)

The newspapers are generally friendly, the *Telegraph* particularly.[1074]

Saturday 12 June (Highclere)

In this morning's papers is Parnell's reply. I spent the morning in drawing up my answer and I have sent it off to McCraw for him to communicate to the Papers. I hope that I am right in replying but we have been obliged to act without consultation with anyone.[1075]

Sunday 20 June (Highclere)

I received today a letter from Salisbury in answer to one which I had written to him suggesting that it was desirable to make some reply to Gladstone's allegations and questions in regard to my interview with Parnell.[1076] His answer was certainly of a disagreeable and unfriendly nature and will need careful consideration. I hardly see how I can avoid replying or how I can make my reply altogether a pleasant one. "See how this man hath a quarrel against me" is the first idea that suggests itself; but it is well to take time.

[1073]Carnarvon told Harrowby, 'I never doubted the wisdom of my course. As you know, though, it was a disagreeable one to follow in the teeth of remonstrances and opposition from some of my old colleagues. But it was necessary for my own honour, and I am convinced was quite as much a gain to them as it could be to me' (Carnarvon to Harrowby, 11 June 1886: Harrowby Papers, 2nd series, lii, fos 168–169).

[1074]The leader in the paper stated, 'The clear honour, the chivalrous assumption of responsibility, the ingenuousness and fearlessness, the simplicity of purpose and policy – all in short, which we look to find in a member of our historic aristocracy – stand revealed throughout this admirable deliverance in the most brilliant and striking relief' (*Daily Telegraph*, 11 June 1886, p. 5).

[1075]Parnell repeated his claim of Carnarvon's offer of home rule at their interview (*The Times*, 12 June 1886, p. 10). Carnarvon's robust reply was printed in *The Times*, 14 June 1886, p. 10.

[1076]Salisbury's cool reply began, 'I must protest most earnestly against your making any statement of what passed between yourself and me when we were Cabinet ministers together upon official business.' It ended, 'we must leave what has been said where it is' (Salisbury to Carnarvon, 19 June 1886: CP, BL 60760, fo. 97).

Tuesday 22 June (Highclere – London)

Gladstone in this morning's papers renews his attack and we came to the conclusion that I had better go up to London and talk the whole matter over with Herbert.[1077] I telegraphed to him, went up, found him poor fellow confined to his house by gout, but talked it all over and got home in time for dinner. His opinion is that as the case now stands, silence can do me little if any harm; that it is very foolish of Salisbury when a complete answer can be given in a few words to entrench himself in silence; but that if I, contrary to Salisbury's expressed opinion, enter into fresh explanations, any difficulties or mishaps at the Elections will be laid at my door. So I am inclined to think that it may be on the whole best to write to Salisbury but to do nothing. Herbert's comment upon him was – and truly enough – that he was a selfish and ungenerous fellow to deal with, but that it was desirable to go to considerable lengths, especially now, to avoid a quarrel.

Wednesday 23 June (Highclere)

I wrote my letter to Salisbury. He will not like it much, but I do not see how I could be silent, and if I wrote anything it seemed necessary to say enough to protect myself.[1078] His object has been and doubtless is to put as much as he can upon me and his whole conduct has been very shabby. But one must make the best of the matter.

Thursday 24 June (Highclere)

My birthday – a singular mixture of angry political winds howling outside and very great domestic happiness within. But I value the latter much the most highly, and political ambition and I have so completely parted company that I have personally little care in believing as I do that I have completely ended any connection with official life. I went to Ireland sorely against my will and only because I believed it to be a matter of unquestionable duty, and though I cannot yet see that I

[1077] Gladstone had left London for Scotland on 17 June for his Midlothian campaign. He delivered speeches at Edinburgh on 18 and 21 June and at Glasgow on 22 June. Parliament was dissolved on 10 June and the general election was to begin on 11 July. For the second Edinburgh speech, see *The Times*, 22 June 1886, p. 10.

[1078] Carnarvon to Salisbury, 23 June 1886 (copy): CP, BL 60760, fos 98–100; most of the text is reproduced in Hardinge, III, pp. 227–229.

did any good by going there I suppose there was some object to be gained by it.

Monday 28 June (Highclere)

I this evening received an answer from Salisbury to my letter.[1079] It was in a very different tone, evading all the real points which I had made in my last letter and which I knew he would feel to be disagreeable and trying to seem friendly. It means, I think, that he does not, as I half thought he did, desire a break. It makes no difference of course in the actualities of the position, but it is pleasanter, as I have no wish for an open quarrel, for having gone through the vexations and troubles of a break with my Party twice in my life I do not desire it a third time. The difficulty may of course recur, but for the present at all events the sky is clearer. The bolder line is always the best.

Parnell has made another attack but I think that can be left unanswered.

Tuesday 29 June (London)

I received this morning a letter from Salisbury saying that on further consideration he thought it would be better to make some reply to Parnell's statements and Gladstone's speeches, that he was to speak tonight, and that he enclosed a memorandum of what he proposed to say.[1080] Would I telegraph or send up by messenger anything that occurred to me. I decided to go to London, telegraphed to him accordingly and came up with Elsie.

He came to me in Portman Square and I went through the memorandum with him. I suggested various alterations to which he

---

[1079] Salisbury replied on 27 June, 'I must have expressed myself very ill if I appeared to imply that you were seeking to transfer your own responsibility to me or anyone else.' See Cecil, III, pp. 161–162; Salisbury to Carnarvon, 27 June 1886: CP, BL 60760, fos 101–104.

[1080] Salisbury wrote, 'I still shrink from the statement of anything that has gone on in Cabinet. In fact I could not do so without the Queen's permission' (Salisbury to Carnarvon, 29 June 1886: CP, BL 60760, fo. 105). The letter was accompanied by a memorandum that Salisbury had drawn up the previous day, giving an account of his involvement in the Parnell–Carnarvon meeting and denying that Carnarvon had resigned over differences with the Cabinet on Irish policy. Carnarvon discussed the memorandum at the meeting and endorsed it 'Copy of Lord Salisbury's memo. Sent by him to me, with some alterations and suggestions made by me to him when we met on 29 June. He adopted them and made his speech the same evening having regard to them.' The original memorandum is at Hatfield, with a copy in CP, BL 60760, fos 108–111.

agreed, my chief points being

(1) that his words should cover the fact that I had warned him of my interview with Parnell as well before as after the event: and that I had been perfectly open with him.

(2) that whilst supporting thoroughly the Party I had my own views and must reserve them.

(3) that my resignation had been a matter decided on when we came into Office, that it was to take effect after the General Election but that at the instance of my colleagues I consented to stay on till the meeting of Parliament.

The whole tone was friendly and whether there was anything behind it I cannot tell – but certainly no wish at present to quarrel. But I could say that his look was that of a man in most questionable health. His breathing was very thick and heavy, and there seemed an increase of bulk, which cannot be satisfactory.

Wednesday 30 June (London)

Salisbury's speech appears in today's papers. All that he says of me will I think do: and I hope that things generally now stand on a fairly good footing.[1081] There appears also a letter to me from Money in the papers which I think has given satisfaction, as several people have spoken to me about it.[1082]

As far as I can learn the Party seems rather anxious and out of heart in going into the Elections. There is more *popular* support of Gladstone than was expected. It may easily happen, as I at first expected, that parties will come out much as they went in, a very unfortunate result.

A most curious circumstance has just come to my ears. Attempts have been made by *Parnell and by Gladstone* to extract from W. Forster, my lawyer, what are my views on Home Rule and Irish affairs. He replied that he did not know, and if he did should not tell. But what a commentary on Parnell's statement that I had told him, P., all these views in our conversation!

[1081] In Salisbury's speech at the annual dinner of the Constitutional Union the previous evening, defending Carnarvon's actions, he stated, 'I defy Mr. Parnell to advance the slightest proof for the slanderous assertions he has made' (*The Times*, 30 June 1886, p. 14).

[1082] An item in *The Times* the same day, headed 'The Conservative Ministry and Mr Parnell', p. 15, included mention of a letter received by Carnarvon from Walter Money, a leading member of the Conservatives in South Berkshire, supporting Carnarvon's actions in his dealings with Parnell.

Friday 2 July (Highclere)

A summer day of extraordinary beauty. The hay is so cooked by the sun that it is fit to carry almost as it is cut.

The first returns are made of the Elections. At present the general look of the case is a decided preponderance of Unionists over Home Rulers, and a fair holding of their ground by Conservatives, perhaps something more.[1083]

Monday 5 July (Highclere)

I wrote to Herbert and asked him to consider well what my position should be in the event, as seems not improbable, of a Tory majority and a Salisbury Government. In such case the alternatives were clearly two only – either an offer or not an offer of Office. In the latter case the course was simple: a frank statement of opinion and great friendliness to the incoming Government. In the former it was more difficult. Should I accept? To accept would cure the seeming differences of opinion for the time: but if a break were afterwards to come it would be impossible ever again to mend the broken china. And what are the chances of such a break? Against it my extreme wish to avoid it – but then I desired nothing more than this during the last Government. For it, the fact that I am afraid the whole Cabinet must be considered not friendly and some distinctly unfriendly. Their attitude to me personally ever since I came back from Italy has certainly been one of very great coldness. I hardly know what to wish, and I do not know what reason to assign for a refusal if Salisbury should ask me to take Office. On the other hand I dread it much, and if any very natural and quite honourable escape should present itself I should be glad.

Tuesday 6 July (Highclere)

Gladstone has written a letter to me or rather against me which I first read in the Papers – the original arrived 2 hours later.[1084] I have

---

[1083]There were thirty-three unopposed seats and one contested one declared (*The Times*, 2 July 1886, p. 5).

[1084]Gladstone complained that a letter appearing in the *Daily News* on 29 June was probably inspired by Carnarvon and that it claimed that 'I have construed your speech in the House of Lords [on 10 June] "into an acceptance of my Irish legislation." It discourteously goes on to allege that I have done this "for electioneering purposes"' (Gladstone to Carnarvon, 5 July 1886: CP, BL 60773, fos 34–35, and *The Times*, 6 July 1886, p. 5; see also Hardinge, III,

replied in as concise a manner as I can and sent it up to London.[1085] He is evidently losing temper as the Elections go against him. He is writing, telegraphing, sending messages in all directions; but the power of speech is fortunately now limited and the great organ of power is from time to time reduced to silence. It is a retribution on much mischief that he has done.

Thursday 8 July (Highclere)

My letter to Gladstone appears in the Papers. I think it is all right, though it will I believe rather irritate him.

The Elections continue to go well.

Friday 9 July (London)

I came up with Elsie for 48 hours of London. The town looks half dead, like London at the very end of the Season.

I had a long talk with Herbert as to the political situation; and after full discussion I think he agreed with me that unless in very peculiar circumstances hardly to be anticipated at present it is safer for me not to take Office if it should be offered. The real risk is the Cabinet – the many on whom no dependence can be placed and the few who for certain reasons are unfriendly.

I find that my letter to Gladstone has created a great deal of talk and is very much liked. This is the curious course of events – the best things one do pass without notice, and some little thing of this kind excites a great deal of attention. It seems somehow to have pleased a great number of people of all kinds.[1086]

Wednesday 21 July (Charlton Cottage)

Events are moving rapidly. Today's papers announce the resignation of the Government and the fact that Salisbury is on his way to England

pp. 230–231). In *The Times* of the previous day, Carnarvon had rebutted similar claims in a letter of 29 June from Gladstone to 'Mr. Tait', but it is unclear whether he was referring to the same letter: *The Times*, 5 July 1886, p. 8.

[1085] The letter was published in *The Times*, 8 July 1886, p. 12.

[1086] After receiving Gladstone's letter of 8 July, with neither man conceding ground, Carnarvon replied, 'I agree with you that there can be no advantage in prolonging this correspondence' (Carnarvon to Gladstone, 11 July 1886: Gladstone Papers, BL 44498, fo. 179).

from France to form a new one.[1087] I have been a member of 4 Governments and 3 Cabinets and my chief and most sincere wish – if it can be done honourably and conscientiously – [is] to have no part in the new administration which is forming. A short time will show.

Thursday 22 July (Highclere)

Nothing fresh politically except that Salisbury is to be in London this evening and that the town swarms with hungry place-hunters. The papers are full of articles with good advice as to how he is to construct his Government.

Sunday 25 July (Highclere)

I have had some conversation with Howorth, who is here, as to politics generally, the new Government, and Irish affairs, and incidentally as to myself, and the impression which I form is this – that Salisbury does not mean to offer me Office. Howorth is in the habit of writing to S. frequently as to the state of politics in Lancashire and is in considerable communication with him. A. Balfour is member for one of the Manchester divisions and is also in very frequent communication with Howorth, and so I feel pretty sure that he has been made aware of Salisbury's intentions and that when the conversation came round to myself he could not help letting me see it. It remains to be seen how Salisbury will intimate – or as is perhaps more likely not intimate – to me his intentions: but on the whole I am disposed to think that this solution of a possible difficulty is really the best. The risks of joining a Government in which there is perhaps more than one political gambler are too great for me; and though, old times and antecedents considered, an offer would have been graceful but I have for some time felt the extreme difficulty of formulating any satisfactory excuse for refusing Office. I think I am much safer in being outside and free.

Meanwhile I as good as settled with Howorth that I should write him a letter to be published on my general ideas upon Irish matters, etc.[1088]

[1087] At the general election, 316 Conservatives were returned, 77 Liberal Unionists, 192 Liberals, and 85 Home Rulers, an overall Unionist majority of 116.

[1088] Four days later, Carnarvon decided not to proceed with the plan, on two grounds: 'First, I doubt if people are generally ready for any considerations on Irish policy except

Tuesday 27 July (Highclere – London – Highclere)

This morning I received a letter from Salisbury written from Osborne, a very friendly and frank one, describing the differences of opinion between us on this Irish question and indicating that it would be as difficult for me as for a Cabinet formed on the basis of simple resistance and the "refusal of all national aspirations" that I should join them and adding some sort of hope that the separation was only a temporary one.[1089] Scarcely had I read this when I had a telegram from Kintore[1090] saying that he had been told to inform me of a meeting of the Party at the Carlton. After a hurried consultation with Elsie I threw myself into the train, reached London in time and went to the Carlton. It was full. Salisbury very much cheered and Northcote also when he said a few words later.

Salisbury spoke at length and gave an account of his negotiations with Hartington on two separate occasions, in which he offered to waive the Prime Ministership in his favour.[1091] He then spoke on various other more or less important points but did not go into the question of policy as he said he had formed no cabinet and "had as yet no colleagues". When he ended I got up and said I only wished to offer my best wishes to the new Government, that I made no comment on S.'s speech except to approve entirely of "his wisdom and magnanimity" in his negotiations with Hartington, that I had entertained wishes as to Ireland, but that this was not the time to explain them, that they were not such as had been represented or rather misrepresented, but that my present wishes might be summed up in one word, viz., the formation of a strong Conservative Government, that apart from the Irish question I felt this to be a paramount necessity and that I gave them my best wishes and any support that might be in my power.[1092]

those of the Government – and next I also doubt if it would be fair to the Government to anticipate their programme by any suggestion from one who had recently been their colleague' (Carnarvon to Howorth, 29 July 1886 (copy): CP, BL 60775, fo. 116).

[1089] Salisbury to Carnarvon, 25 July 1886: CP, BL 60760, fos 112–113; Cecil, III, 311–312.

[1090] Algernon Keith-Falconer (1852–1910), 9th Earl of Kintore (1880), Conservative Whip in the Lords (1885–1889).

[1091] Salisbury saw Hartington on 23 July and refused all ideas of a coalition. At a further meeting the following morning, Salisbury offered him the premiership, but this was also turned down. See B. Holland, *The Life of Spencer Compton, Eighth Duke of Devonshire*, 2 vols (London, 1911), II, pp. 169–171. In his letter of 25 July, Salisbury confided in Carnarvon, 'I have tried hard to induce Hartington to take the Prime Minister's place, but he has definitely refused and I have therefore kissed hands today. I think I ought to write to you before I write to anyone else to explain the peculiar position I am in.'

[1092] An account of the meeting was later given by a senior Conservative MP who attended: Sir J. Mowbray, *Seventy Years at Westminster* (Edinburgh and London, 1900), pp. 305–306.

I can hardly tell how this was *really* received. It lasted only a few minutes and was fairly cheered. My own impression is that my audience was not unfriendly, but not cordial. At the same time I do not think that what I said could do any harm, and I think on the whole it would probably help to put me in the position which I desire to occupy – so far as politics and I have much to do with each other at present – a certain personal independence combined with union with the Party. It is probably recognised that my views are not identical with those of the Government on Irish matters, but that in all other respects I am one of the Party. Perhaps I shall hear more of this later.

I returned here after the meeting.[1093]

Thursday 29 July (Highclere)

The Papers announce this morning the deposition of Beach from the lead of the House of Commons and the accession of Randolph Churchill.[1094] It is a curious and most rapid rise, as curious as but more rapid than that of Disraeli whom he had made his model. It is a *politique de casse-cou*, as the French say, which if Randolph can now develop higher qualities may turn out well, or in the event of a different line of conduct lead to a great smash. Anyhow I feel that there is probably a very new departure and I am sure that I am much better out of the ship. Salisbury is the only one who has ability, experience and force of character, and he sometimes seems to be only the old Robert Cecil grown older. I cannot forget my last conversation with R. Churchill, which was on his side as mad a one as I ever listened to from mortal lips and I am glad not to be tied to him as a colleague. Humanly speaking, I cannot see much probability of my being again in Office.

[1093]Carnarvon wrote to Salisbury, 'I am much obliged to you for your frank and friendly letter. I fully understand the position and appreciate all that you say. I could render you real help in the present circumstances by joining your Cabinet, but as I said today at the Carlton you have my best wishes and may count on any support that I can give' (Carnarvon to Salisbury, 27 July 1886: Hatfield House Papers, 3M/E).

[1094] *The Times*, 29 July 1886, p. 9. Hicks Beach had been leader of the Conservatives in the Commons since June 1885, in succession to Northcote. On 25 July 1886, he wrote to Salisbury stating that he wished to be relieved of the post. He was appointed Chief Secretary for Ireland. Churchill, at the age of thirty-six, became Leader of the House and Chancellor of the Exchequer.

Sunday 1 August (Highclere)

Salisbury's Cabinet is not yet formed and he must have a not very pleasant time. Randolph is already a rival that can compel or thwart, or drive or hold back. At any moment he can force Salisbury's hand in the House of Commons; and in cabinet-making he is taking a very strong part. It is thought that he opposes Cross going to the India Office, and on the ground of Cross's absolute incompetency he is quite right. Salisbury on the other hand will not give Cross up and the battle seems now to be raging. Matthews,[1095] the new Home Secretary, is probably Randolph's nominee. R. made acquaintance with him lately in his Birmingham [sic] and was much attracted by him. Matthews is said to be able as a speaker, a good lawyer, a very good linguist, French, German and Italian, an accomplished and agreeable man and a Roman Catholic. This is the pleasant side of the character, I fancy there is a less agreeable one; but I have learned all this from George Russell[1096] who is staying here with Lady R., and who is himself a very nice and pleasant companion.

Thursday 19 August (London)

In the afternoon I went down to the House of Lords, took the oath and afterwards spoke on the Address.[1097] My speech is *fairly* reported in *The Times* of today though condensed.[1098] The House listened very attentively and the general attitude on my own side was friendly. Salisbury's manner was cordial and as far as I can judge I am inclined to think that it was worthwhile speaking – that my position is somewhat more defined by what I have said than before – and that it is altogether as satisfactory as it can be.

Thursday 23 December (London)

Macdonell[1099] breakfasted with us.

[1095] Henry Matthews (1826–1913), Con. MP for Dungarvan (1868–1874) and for Birmingham East (1886–1895). He was the first Catholic cabinet minister since the Catholic Emancipation Act of 1829.

[1096] Sir George Russell (1828–1898), 4th Baronet Russell (1883), Con. MP for Wokingham (1885–1898).

[1097] The new Parliament met on 5 August. In the debate on the Queen's Speech, Carnarvon defended his Irish policy: *Hansard*, CCCVIII, 19 August 1886, cols 51–55.

[1098] For Carnarvon's full speech, see ibid., cols 55–79.

[1099] The identity of this person is not known.

He had scarcely left us when I opened *The Times* and saw the announcement of Randolph's resignation.[1100] How quiet it has been kept. Clearly the Prince of Wales knew nothing of it when he spoke to me yesterday evening, nor even Lady Randolph. It was for some time obvious that they were quarrelling; but there was nothing to indicate that the disruption was so near at hand. The Government now are quit of a dangerous colleague but it remains to be seen if outside the Cabinet he can make their position untenable. If he can he will. As for the Government themselves they have now only one really able man – all the rest are cyphers in popular estimation. The colour is taken out of the body: but I should fancy that there was no help for it and that Randolph's temper was so imperious that they had little option. But it remains to be seen whether there will be any fresh secessions and how the Cabinet will be repaired.

Tuesday 28 December (London)

An interesting conversation with Mrs Jeune who came to tea today about R. Churchill of whom she has seen much and whose cause she strongly espouses.[1101] She describes him as low, saying that he has no friend in the world, that there was an intrigue in the Cabinet against him, that Salisbury at last joined against him and that then he had no chance. He described the question at issue as only £1,300,000, that this was reduced to £1,000,000, G. Hamilton was willing to give £500,000 but that W. H. Smith stood firm to his £500,000. If so, G. H. was as I have always thought, shallow and weak.[1102]

He complained a good deal about Salisbury, said that he was always ready to conform to his judgement, that if Salisbury had only talked matters over with him it might have been adjusted but that he would

---

[1100] 'Resignation of the Chancellor of the Exchequer', *The Times*, 23 December 1886, p. 9. Churchill had delivered the notice of resignation to the offices of *The Times* in the interval of a theatre visit (see R.F. Foster, *Lord Randolph Churchill: a political life* (Oxford, 1981), p. 309).

[1101] Churchill dined with the Jeunes on 26 December. A full account of Churchill's views are described in Susan Jeune's autobiography, *Memories of Fifty Years* (London, 1909), pp. 274–275.

[1102] The immediate cause of Churchill's resignation were the estimates submitted by spending departments, which he considered to be excessive. Smith at the War Office and George Hamilton at the Admiralty were the two main culprits. For a detailed personal account of the immediate events leading to Churchill's resignation, see Lord G.F. Hamilton, *Parliamentary Reminiscences and Reflections, vol. 2: 1886–1906* (London, 1922), pp. 48–53. As Smith wrote in a letter to Cranbrook, 'The real truth is I think that it is not possible for him [Churchill] to yield his opinion or mould it so as to co-operate with his Colleagues. He must rule & my estimates have only been a pretext' (W.H. Smith to Cranbrook, 24 December 1886: Cranbrook Papers, HA3 T501/260).

not see him, or did not see him. He owned to the existence of a good deal of past friction, but seems to have laid the main stress on the financial difficulty. He said that people complained of his temper but that Lord Salisbury's was not angelic!

The conclusion I drew from it all is that Randolph was overbearing, that his head was turned by success, that he thought he could dictate his terms – that Salisbury on the other hand greatly hating him saw his opportunity, or thought he saw it, and took advantage of R.C.'s impetuosity and got rid of him.

There is a curious account of the Cabinet meeting in today's *Pall Mall*. What does it mean? How did it get there? Is it a hoax or a treachery?[1103]

[1103]'The resignation of Lord Randolph Churchill: special Cabinet meeting today at the Foreign Office', *Pall Mall Gazette*, 28 December 1886, p. 8.

1887

Friday 7 January (London)

A long conversation with Stead. He told me some curious things, amongst others that the remarkable report of the Cabinet meeting in the *Pall Mall Gazette* of ...[1104] upon R. Churchill's resignation was a transcript verbatim from an autograph letter of Salisbury's to him. S. gave him this information with his own hand, but on condition that it should not be known that it had in any way come from him. Stead did not know at first how under such conditions he would make any use of it, but at last it occurred to him that he could publish it as his own report of the Cabinet meeting leaving everyone to guess how far it was true and if so how he had got it. Randolph of course was furious at this publication as it contained Salisbury's version of the quarrel, whilst he, Randolph, was bound not to give his statement till Parliament met. At the same time he did not know how such a report had got into the paper, not knowing of this secret communication. It was a very pretty piece of jockeying.

Tuesday 11 January (London)

Holland appointed to the Colonial Office and Northcote (Lord Iddesleigh) resigned and with him his son.[1105] N. has certainly been shabbily and even cruelly treated considering his age and long service. But it is much of a piece with Salisbury's conduct to others. I cannot forget his conduct to Derby in /78 when he ousted him from the Foreign Office and then attacked him with an extraordinary bitterness. This last act as regards Iddesleigh has provoked much comment in the Press and is from all I hear a good deal resented in the Party. I hear that when Cross saw himself gazetted out of Office in the morning papers he wrote direct to the Queen to ask if it was her pleasure and hence he remains!

[1104] *Pall Mall Gazette*, 28 December 1886.
[1105] Henry Stafford Northcote (1846–1911), Baronet Northcote (1887), Baron Northcote (1900). Con. MP for Exeter (1880–1899). Financial Secretary to the War Office (1885–1886), Surveyor-General of Ordnance (1886), Governor of Bombay (1899–1903), Governor-General of Australia (1903–1908).

We have determined D.V. to start on Thursday.

Thursday 20 January (Porto Fino)

My letter on poor Northcote in yesterday's *Times*.[1106]

Thursday 14 July (London)

The Second Reading of the Coercion Bill. Ashbourne opened it –
why Cadogan did not have charge I do not know – Granville followed
in a dextrous and temperate speech, and I followed him. My speech
was listened to with very great attention and general satisfaction by
my own party, less so I think by the Unionist Liberals, but without any
signs of strong dissent from the front Opposition Bench. I am glad to
have had this opportunity of speaking on this part of the question and
on the whole I think I put my own case fairly. The Duke of Argyll's
speech was not very relevant, but was discursive and in parts good; but
very bitter. His attack on Granville for not defending Lansdowne was
as bitter as anything I have heard. The intestinal quarrels of the two
sections of the Liberal Party are growing in intensity. It is a curious
spectacle.[1107]

Friday 15 July (London)

We had a heavy thunderstorm today. How will it be for the next
forty days?

A discussion again in the House on the Coercion Bill on going into
Committee. Granville spoke again with a good deal of his usual tact
and dexterity but rather feebly. Northbrook made a violent attack on
him. At first I thought it was impromptu but it was supported by a
bundle of MSS, and it was not in very good taste though rhetorically it
was better than Northbrook's speeches generally are. He was followed
by Rosebery who made, to my mind, a very clever reply, especially if
as it seemed the greater part was made on the spur of the moment. In
it he referred at some length to my speech not only of last night but

---

[1106] *The Times*, 19 January 1887, p. 8. Northcote died suddenly on 12 January, in the ante-room
of 10 Downing Street. The event greatly shocked Salisbury (Cecil, III, pp. 343–345).
[1107] Criminal Law Amendment (Ireland) Bill: *Hansard*, CCCXVII, 14 July 1887, Ashbourne,
cols 710–724, Granville, cols 724–731, Carnarvon, cols 731–737, Argyll, cols 737–747.

of the 17 July 1885 when I assumed Office in Ireland. I was obliged
in one part to correct him. It was altogether an animated discussion,
but the spectacle of the front Opposition Bench, a very small minority
with hardly any real supporters, and having on their flanks a larger
section of their own party, bitterly enraged and ready to tear them to
pieces, is a very curious one.[1108]

[1108] Ibid., Granville, cols 899–907, Northbrook, cols 901–908, Rosebery, cols 908–918 (the
report for Northbrook's speech overlaps that for Granville because many of the speakers
interrupted one another as the debate became heated).

1888

Tuesday 1 May (London)

Dined with the Jeunes and met Buckle[1109] with whom I had a long talk as to my intended explanation in the House on Parnell's allegations and also as to my public statement in the form of a letter.[1110]

Friday 11 May (London)

My letter in *The Times* in answer to Parnell and on Home Rule and Irish affairs appeared with a fairly friendly article. It has I think made an impression and I think it will make somewhat more stir before all is over.[1111] I hardly know how far it is unacceptable to the Government and the rank and file of the Party. Salisbury said to me at the Levée that he liked it, but that does not prove much. But taking everything into account I think that the effect is on the whole good.

Attended the Levée. The Prince of Wales very civil, also the Duke of Cambridge who begged me to come and talk to him.

An extraordinary attack by Salisbury in the House of Lords on Wolseley, my impression being that he had not given Wolseley notice of it.[1112] It began by Hardinge asking a question of the Duke of Cambridge, and this, Hardinge told me, he had done at Salisbury's request.[1113]

[1109] George Earl Buckle (1854–1935), assistant editor of *The Times* (1880–1884), editor (1884–1912).

[1110] During Carnarvon's absence in Australia, the Parnellites insisted that Carnarvon had, at his interview with Parnell, offered a statutory parliament. Balfour, now Chief Secretary for Ireland, had publicly denied this. Parnell, in a recent speech at the Eighty Club, had once more repeated this statement.

[1111] 'Lord Carnarvon on Irish policy', *The Times*, 11 May 1888, p. 12. He wrote to Salisbury, 'I have been obliged to reply to Parnell's speech. You will see my letter in *The Times*, and I hope that you will like it. I have endeavoured to make it so complete that it may finally dispose of the controversy, which has lasted so long' (Carnarvon to Salisbury, 12 May 1888: Hatfield House Papers, 3M/E).

[1112] The National Defence: *Hansard*, CCCXXVI, 11 May 1888, Salisbury, cols 4–7. Wolseley had that day published an article in the *Daily Telegraph* entitled 'England in danger: our army without arms: worst guns in the world'.

[1113] Ibid., cols 1–3.

Saturday 12 May (London)

My letter in *The Times* appeared yesterday and reads satisfactorily and almost everyone whom I have seen seems pleased with it. Anyhow it puts an end, I hope, to the ambiguous and false position in which I have been through no fault of mine so long placed.

We had a breakfast party consisting among others of Lowell,[1114] Froude and Arthur Gordon. Lady D. Nevill told me that R. Churchill is spending an immense amount of money and no one knows whence it comes. He is very bitter at Goschen's success.

Friday 10 August (London)

The Parnell Commission bill read second time,[1115] a not crowded but a very attentive House. Salisbury's introductory speech was to my mind not quite up to his level. Herschell, who followed, extremely good; he handled a very difficult task with great skill. I followed him and said my say, I hope, fairly well. The Chancellor[1116] was very lawyer-like. Kimberley not very good.[1117]

Friday 12 October (Highclere)

General Hastings[1118] and Sir George Russell came.

Sir G.R. told me a curious story about Randolph Churchill. Randolph, walked with him through the Park from the Carlton and expounded to him all his wishes and aspirations, the latter being concentrated in being reinstated in the Cabinet. A few days afterwards

---

[1114]James Russell Lowell (1819–1891), American poet and diplomat, Minister to Great Britain (1880–1885).

[1115]On 18 April 1887, *The Times* had printed a letter purporting to have been written by Parnell, apologizing to a friend for denouncing the Phoenix Park murders in the Commons. Parnell demanded the paper withdrew the letter, which he claimed was a forgery. Buckle, the editor, refused to do so. Parnell's request for a Select Committee was not granted but he was offered in its place a bill appointing a Special Commission to inquire into the allegations. W.H. Smith introduced the Member of Parliament (Charges and Allegations Bill) in the Commons on 16 July 1888: *Hansard*, CCCXXX.

[1116]Hardinge Stanley Giffard (1823–1921), Baron Halsbury (1885), 1st Earl of Halsbury (1898), Lord Chancellor (1885–1886, 1886–1892, 1895–1905).

[1117]Ibid., Salisbury, cols 255–262, Herschell, cols 262–282, Carnarvon, cols 282–286, Halsbury, cols 286–291, Kimberley cols 291–296. Kimberley wrote in his journal for that day, 'A good deal of damage was done to them [Parnell and supporters] in the discussions on the bill, but on the whole, the advantage remains, I think, on their side. The further progress in the game will be interesting to watch, but in no case can any good result to the country' (Hawkins and Powell, *Journal of John Wodehouse, First Earl of Kimberley*, p. 383).

[1118]Lieut.-Gen. Francis William Hastings (1825–1914) had served in the Crimea.

he again took the opportunity to repeat all this, whereupon Sir George, understanding that this had been said for the sake of being carried on to Salisbury, told it all to Sir J. Ferguson at the Foreign Office. Sir James, being greatly excited at it, wrote it all down and sent it to Salisbury – who, however, made no reply! The fact is S. is heartily sick of Randolph and not at all disposed to take him back. Randolph on the other hand is determined if he is not readmitted to the Downing Street Olympus, according to G. Russell, to scuttle the ship from outside if he cannot do it from within!!

Sir G.R. said to me that the story that I heard the other day that Randolph when lately in Russia had told the Emperor that he could take Constantinople when he liked, provided that he left India alone, was quite correct. Randolph apparently had told him so himself.

Since writing this G. Russell has told me more of the details. Randolph hates, as he has for a long time, Edward Stanhope; and he wants the War Office. He said there were only two offices he cared to take – the War Office[1119] and Admiralty – that he could not for family reasons take the Admiralty – but that E. Stanhope was a complete failure, that he wanted the office and that Hartington desired he should have it. G. Russell was struck with this last statement and enquired from H. James[1120] whether Hartington did really wish this without giving him his reason for asking the question. H. James was much surprised but said it was perfectly true. All this was told to Salisbury who however made no reply.

It is the old case of intrigues going on right and left.

Friday 21 December (Porto Fino)

Our days slip away here peacefully and pleasantly, nothing to disturb or break the even tenour [*sic*] of the time. If it were on a river and not on the sea that my eyes so often rest with satisfaction I might write up the Prince de Ligne's[1121] pretty couplet, which he wrote on his retreat near Vienna overlooking the Danube:

Sans remords, sans regrets, sans crainte, sans envie,
Je vois couler ce fleuve, et s'écouler ma vie.

[1119] Stanhope had been appointed to the War Office in 1887.
[1120] Sir Henry James (1828–1911), Lib. MP for Taunton (1869–1885) and for Bury (1885–1895), Solicitor-General (1873), Attorney-General (1873–1874, 1880–1885), Chancellor, Duchy of Lancaster (1895–1902), created Baron James of Hereford (1895).
[1121] Field Marshal Prince Charles-Joseph de Ligne (1735–1812), soldier-poet, who settled in Vienna in 1794. See P. Mansel, *Prince of Europe: the life of Charles-Joseph de Ligne* (London, 2003), pp. 130–131.

1889

Tuesday 26 February (London)

For the last few days all London has been concentrating on the Parnell Commission where the question whether or no the famous letters were forgeries have been tried. For some days the matter has [been] very critical, and the whole affair has turned on the evidence of Pigott,[1122] a very great rascal who supplied the letters to *The Times*. Today after a vast amount of lying Pigott has absconded, having previously made and signed a confession to Labouchere[1123] that the letters were forged by him.[1124] The excitement has been great – the exultation of the Parnell party unbounded, the despondency of the Unionists great. It is anyhow a tremendous blow to *The Times*, and from the Government having tied themselves on to *The Times*, to them also. It is hardly possible to anticipate the full force of the reverse: and it remains to be seen whether the system of party which is now established in England or the democratic impulsiveness of the constituencies will prevail. A few years ago when party influences and organisation were much less it would have been easy to foretell the result. It is now more difficult. It is anyhow likely to create still more violence and bitterness on both sides.

Wednesday 27 February (London)

The break down of *The Times* case is complete and everyone is full of it and every one is very wise after the event and after lauding the action of *The Times* for the last few months they are now open mouthed upon the indiscretion which led them into such a trap. It is as strange

---

[1122]Richard Pigott (1828–1889), journalist.

[1123]Henry Du Pré Labouchere (1831–1912), Advanced Lib. MP for Windsor (1865–1866) and for Northampton (1880–1906), proprietor of *Truth*.

[1124]When Pigott failed to appear in Court on 26 February, Sir Charles Russell made the startling announcement that Pigott had, after his disastrous cross-examination, called on Labouchere on 23 February and dictated to him a full confession. See A.L. Thorold, *The Life of Henry Labouchere* (London, 1913), pp. 356–357.

and complete a break down as I can remember in the whole of my public life.[1125]

I think I have made all arrangements for the publication of the Chesterfield MSS.[1126]

I am considering rather anxiously what my next step should be as regards the Bishop of Lincoln's case.[1127]

Saturday 9 March (London)

Stead came and dined quietly with Elsie and me alone as he wished to talk to me. His first object was to talk over his own action with regard to the naval augmentations proposed by the Government. He wishes for the increase, does not much like the manner in which it is proposed, believes that he can, and he alone, stir up the country, as he did before in Northbrook's, but thinks that either this will oblige the Government to withdraw their scheme or will compel a dissolution when they will be beaten. He wished to have my advice on the subject.

He believes Randolph Churchill desires to attack the Government on their mode of proceeding, perhaps to see them turned out and then to pose as the one Tory statesman who warned them and whose advice, if they had followed it, would have saved them.

I think his view as to the Government is correct.

It is not really a large one, though in the country it will be represented as £21,000,000. It makes no provision of increasing blue jackets for the new ships, nor for guns, and is founded on a septennial principle which will be open to much objection. It is really inadequate.[1128]

[1125] On 1 March, Pigott shot himself through the head in a Madrid hotel when police entered his room (F.S.L. Lyons, *Charles Stewart Parnell* (London, 1977), p. 422).

[1126] The Memorandum of Agreement between Carnarvon, the University of Oxford, and the Clarendon Press for *Lord Chesterfield's Letters to his Godson, with Notes and an Introduction by the Author* was dated 11 August 1889 (Highclere Castle Archives, Box 1).

[1127] Edward King (1829–1910), Bishop of Lincoln, had been accused by the Church of alleged ritualist practices. Edward Benson, the Archbishop of Canterbury, had disinterred an old spiritual tribunal, the Court of Audience, to try the case. Carnarvon, together with many others, deplored this illiberal move. See Hardinge, III, p. 304; G.W.E. Russell, *Edward King, Sixtieth Bishop of Lincoln* (London, 1912), pp. 162–163.

[1128] The Naval Defence Act, introduced in March, signalled the entry of Britain into the naval armament race. The Act provided for the building of eight first-class battleships, two second-class battleships, nine large and twenty-nine smaller cruisers, four fast gunboats, and eighteen torpedo gunboats, at a cost of £21,500,000. See A.J. Marder, *The Anatomy of British Sea Power: a history of British naval policy in the pre-dreadnought era, 1880–1905* (London, 1940), p. 143; Hamilton, *Parliamentary Reminiscences and Reflections, 1886–1906*, pp. 110–114.

Alternatively, his conclusion was that he would offer Gladstone his co-operation and support if G. and the Liberal leaders would pledge themselves to such an increase as would make matters safe and would attack the form rather than the substance of the Government's proposals.

Thursday 21 March (London)

My debate in the House of Lords came off on my bill for disqualifying unworthy Peers – a full house and very attentive but evidently reluctant to adopt my proposals. A certain amount of adverse criticism was met by a good speech by Lord FitzGerald[1129] for me, and finally Salisbury made an attack on it and moved the previous question. He began quietly by saying his first disposition was in favour of it, then he proposed to postpone it: finally he assailed it. I replied by pointing this out, and said that as he had invited me to deal with the question and that as my bill was framed on the lines of his own measure of last year, his sudden face about was somewhat astounding. He did not like my remarks, I would see, and hoped that I could not divide; but I would not fall into this trap and compelled him to divide. We were 14 to 73, so the bill was lost.[1130] Another curious illustration of his falsity and untruthfulness. He is as false as he can be.

Friday 29 March (London)

I made a longish speech in the House of Lords on Army matters, praising Stanhope but arraigning the whole system of War Office organisation in almost all its branches.[1131] The Government did not much like it; but they could not complain as I worded my attack on the system rather than the individuals. Harris[1132] answered and did his

[1129] Lord John David Fitzgerald (1816–1889), Irish judge, Lib. MP for Ennis (1852), Solicitor-General for Ireland (1855–1856), Attorney-General for Ireland (1856–1858, 1859), Justice of Queens Bench, Ireland (1860–1882), Lord of Appeal and created Baron Fitzgerald (1882).

[1130] House of Lords (Discontinuance of Writs) Bill, second reading: *Hansard*, CCCXXXIV, 21 March 1889, Carnarvon, cols 333–345, Fitzgerald, cols 345–350, Salisbury, cols 353–357. Cranbrook noted the following day, 'At the House, we had Carnarvon's "black sheep" Bill, wh. was riddled with many compliments to the mover & eventually crushed by the previous question' (Johnson, p. 729).

[1131] Royal Commission on Naval and Military Depots: *Hansard*, CCCXXXIV, 29 March 1889, Carnarvon, cols 1125–1131.

[1132] George Robert Harris (1851–1932), 4th Baron Harris (1872), Under-Secretary of State for India (1885–1886) and for War (1886–1889); ibid., cols 1133–1138.

work well. But there is so poor a report even in *The Times* that the effect of what I said cannot be great in the Country.

I think that there is much discontent and some apprehension in the Government ranks. Howorth is very much out of humour and represents a certain amount of opinion, and from all I hear, R. Churchill is on the eve of a junction with Chamberlain and the Liberal Unionists in Birmingham as a first step probably to a separation from the body of the Conservatives.[1133]

Saturday 30 March (London)

We dined at the old Duchess of Marlborough,[1134] where Randolph and Lady R. were. He was extremely and unusually civil and talked a good deal to Elsie on *general* politics. He is, almost without disguise, very much out of humour with the Government and Lady Randolph does not hesitate to abuse them pretty freely. The old Duchess is not more complimentary to them, so it is not difficult to see in what direction the wind is setting.

But the Enfield Election which is rather a moral victory for the Government is disappointing to them.[1135]

Thursday 4 April (London)

Lord Justice FitzGibbon[1136] from Ireland called on me and we had an interesting conversation on Irish matters. The substance of it was briefly this:

[1133] John Bright had died on 27 March and, on the following day, Churchill told the Birmingham Conservatives that he intended to stand for selection for the constituency. Chamberlain was in fact keen for Churchill not to be invited, but the latter left the decision to Hicks Beach and Hartington. Their advice was far from encouraging and Churchill turned down the invitation. See P.T. Marsh, *Joseph Chamberlain: entrepreneur in politics* (New Haven, CT and London, 1994), p. 315.

[1134] Frances Anne Emily Churchill (1822–1899), widow of John Winston Spencer-Churchill, 7th Duke of Marlborough.

[1135] After a hard fight, the Conservative candidate, Captain H.F. Bowles, obtained 5,124 votes and his Gladstonian Liberal opponent, W.H. Fairburn, 3,612, a majority of 1,512 (*The Times*, 1 April 1889, p. 6).

[1136] Gerald Fitzgibbon (1837–1909), Solicitor-General for Ireland (1877–1878), Lord Justice of Appeal (1878). He was a friend of Churchill.

(1) It turned out that he had called, not merely *proprio motu*, but at the instance of Randolph Churchill who wished him to talk to me.[1137]

(2) He is dissatisfied with the present system of coercive or restrictive policy. He says that Balfour seems to aim only at enforcing law as a matter of Executive, and that nothing even to small improvements and necessary changes have been made. He complained a good deal of the impossibility of getting the smallest matters of improvement effected.

(3) He said that the general feeling in Ireland was in favour of some constructive measures now being taken; but he thought the opportunity had been lost and that the only measure now in prospect was a dissolution of Parliament.

(4) He said that there was a good deal of money in the country and that matters were in a fairly prosperous condition in consequence; but that one result of having given the tenants so much more interest in their holdings – and in fact of having virtually multiplied holdings – was a great increase of litigation. This however was perhaps unavoidable.

(5) He said the landowners, though much restricted in means and money, were accommodating themselves to the changed circumstances.

(6) I talked to him on self-government and he is evidently quite prepared for self-government in its subordinate features and institutions. He would not I think object to Provincial Councils provided they do not assume the character of Parliament. If only they could be bodies representing in some limited way the subordinate and more local boards of the Counties he would not, as I understand, greatly object; but on this point he was less clear than he might have been.

(7) He did not speak adversely of Ashbourne's Act[1138] but he said it was the means – and he cited a case of the Salters Company in the North where they had sold their property for £240.0.10 and taken it out of the Country – of removing from Ireland much that it was desirable to keep there.

[1137] From early 1888, Fitzgibbon urged Churchill to embark on a new initiative for Ireland. See Foster, *Lord Randolph Churchill*, pp. 351–353.

[1138] The Land Purchase Bill, introduced by Ashbourne in the House of Lords on 17 July 1885.

Sunday 7 April (London)

A curious and interesting conversation with Randolph Churchill who called on me at my invitation, that invitation being the result of the fact mentioned to me by FitzGibbon that Randolph wished to see and talk to me. I mentioned this when we met as the reason of my offer.

He was of opinion that the time had come when some constructive policy in the shape of local self-government should be given to Ireland. He said he was willing to give everything short of a Parliament. I pressed him as to Provincial Councils. He did not express the same rooted objection to them as to a General Parliament, but much preferred not to go beyond County Councils. He said he was satisfied that unless something of this kind be given the Conservative majority must go, that recent elections proved nothing on this point.

His proposals were (1) that we should make a joint move in both Houses to call attention to the state of Ireland or (2) that he should collect in the House of Commons what sympathisers he could and that I should do the same and that we should meet to confer: or (3) that he and I should draw up a memorandum and present it to Salisbury.

Of these the first seemed in both our opinions most likely, but it would need, I said, and he quite agreed, very great consideration, but in any case I said I thought the first move should be a confabulation with Hartington, and this I said I was willing to undertake if after more thought I saw no objection.

He was very friendly and anxious to please, and our conversation turned upon past as well as our present matters. He said that he much regretted in regard to my famous conversation with Parnell that the Cabinet had not been informed. I said that it was Salisbury who prevented me from communicating it, as he afterwards had induced me to remain silent, till I felt myself obliged for my own sake to explain what had passed.

He said that he believed Parnell was, for whatever reason, ready to accept very moderate terms, and he denounced Justin McCarthy as wholly untrustworthy.

He is obviously very sore with Salisbury and he said, which was quite new to me, that in /85 when forming the Government, Salisbury had sent Wynn to submit to Parnell three names for the Irish Secretaryship, Dyke, Chaplin, and he could not remember the third. I believe this must be true for Salisbury tried to persuade me to take Chaplin, which I refused and then he fell back on Dyke.

He frankly acknowledged that he had conferred with Parnell. I am not sure that he had not negotiated with him, but this was before he

was in office and he seemed quite aware that at that time Salisbury
was quite open to consider terms with the Home Ruler.[1139]

Wednesday 10 April (London)

A very long conversation with FitzGibbon who called to see me after
having evidently talked over with Randolph my late conversation with
him. The conversation came mainly to this:

(1) FitzGibbon chiefly looked at the matter in Randolph's interest
and from a personal aspect. He desires his reunion with the
Government because he thinks the Government policy will go to
pieces without Randolph and because R. alone can save them and
assume the lead on Smith's retirement.

(2) He is all against any pronouncement in the House of Commons
because R. would be beaten, alienated and thrown into the arms of
the Gladstonians.

(3) He prefers that he should state his policy at some public meeting,
hoping the Government will accept it.

(4) He evidently fears Salisbury as an enemy to R. but says Beach
and W.H. Smith are friendly.

(5) He caught at the idea of Hartington's intervention.

(6) He repeated that there is a large party in Ireland very anxious
for a settlement, that trade and industries as much as landowners fear
confiscation at the end of "the three years" lease remaining to the
Government.

(7) He is strongly opposed to Provincial Councils and would only
give County Councils – the less the better in short.

Friday 12 April (London)

Randolph Churchill came to me by appointment. I told him I
had thought over the whole question, had gleaned information and
had spoken to FitzGibbon and that if he allowed me I would speak
quite frankly to him on the personal aspect that his relations with the
Government were strained; that any action on his part either in the

---

[1139] Carnarvon considered the conversation on the state of Irish affairs so important that
he postponed a planned visit to Germany in order to meet Churchill again (Carnarvon to
Churchill, 7 April 1889: Randolph Churchill Papers, Add. MS 9248/23/3113).

H. of C. or at a public meeting would strain them more; that on the other hand by maintaining silence he would not really conciliate; but that any attack on Balfour who has at this moment a remarkable popularity would be ascribed to jealousy, that on the whole I believed it was best to profess his want in patience and wait and watch, that in so doing it might be possible to ascertain who agreed and to draw them together. Meanwhile that I will see Hartington if he liked, tell H. my own views and let him know his, Randolph's.[1140] To all this he cordially assented and said that I was free to tell H. that his opinions and mine on the situation were "identical". He was very friendly, said that he did not desire to return to office at present, but preferred his position of critic.

He then went on to speculate on future events, said that he believed Salisbury's health was very bad, that he probably had Bright's disease, that he sometimes thought that he would retire and hand over Prime Ministership to Balfour or do this and simply retain the F.O. I said that I doubted the probability of this; but that a Hartington Administration was more probable which would allow of a fresh departure in Irish policy. He agreed that this was not impossible or improbable, and that Hartington might play the role of Palmerston over again.

His feelings to Chamberlain are not very friendly. He thinks that his first object will always be his own interest.

Friday 17 May (London)

A long conversation with R. Churchill and interesting. He is as much dissatisfied with the Government as ever, but he feels that he can hardly make any move safely as regards himself. The "Tory Party" he says are just now devoted to Balfour in the H. of C. but the constituencies he believes are out of joint and growing demoralised. He believes that we should very likely lose many Landowners. He had last night a conversation with Beach, who, he said, agreed with him and with me as to the inexpediency of the present policy, and who told him that he greatly regretted that he had ever re-joined the Government. Beach and Salisbury do not hit it off. Beach very nearly resigned on the Budget, the brewing regulations and the new succession duty on real estate being very repugnant to him.

Randolph had also talked to Hartington who had listened to him very attentively. He told H. that he had talked to me and what my

---

[1140] The meeting with Hartington did not take place, owing to Hartington being out of the country and Carnarvon being laid up with an attack of gout. Carnarvon noted, 'I do not, however think that, as matters stand, there is any real loss by a short delay' (Carnarvon to Churchill, 19 April 1889: Randolph Churchill Papers, Add. MS 9248/23/3124).

general opinion was. It was finally settled that I should see and talk to Hartington. R. leaves London for the month of June to fish, but really he finds no opening for him at this moment.[141]

Friday 24 May (London)

I had this afternoon an important and interesting conversation with Hartington on Irish matters and the Government policy.

I explained to him the feeling and the capacity in which I went to Ireland as Lord Lieutenant, to fulfil a special mission, the enquiries I made as to what could and should be done, my own conviction that it was impossible to stand for much longer on the old lines and my interview with Parnell.

I explained to him my own notions, a concession of Local Government, County Councils, educational complaints considered, development of Irish industries, land settlement, though it would not be possible to do this by a mere extension of Ashbourne's Act to which he agreed.

As regards County Councils I said I should prefer to go further and accept Provincial Councils as almost the only means of protecting Ulster. He asked if I should object to two instead of four, making *Protestant* Ulster one. I said I would readily agree to this and in fact preferred it to the four. As regards land settlement I suggested that the local authorities should become landowners making some Irish tax such as Customs and Excise the first security for paying off the owners, and in fact applying it to that purpose.

He did not object, was most friendly and listened and talked with great patience and attention.

I said that for some time I had looked upon him as nearer my standpoint than everyone else and that I desired his opinion as to whether or no I should raise the question this year. He would not give an immediate answer, but desired time to consider.[142]

---

[141]After the meeting, a ten-point memorandum was drawn up by Carnarvon as a basis for future action in Ireland. It included the extension of the Local Government Act of 1888 to Ireland 'by bodies not less than County Councils', possibly to be extended to provincial councils; provisions for the purchase of freehold by the occupier; improvements in education; and the gradual relaxing of control of the police and resident magistrates by the imperial parliament and future transference to provincial councils (Carnarvon, 'Heads of changes in Irish policy drawn up in May/89 after conversation with R. Churchill': CP, BL 60828, fo. 26).

[142]Hartington was much occupied at this time as chairman of the Royal Commission on the Civil and Professional Administration of the Naval and Military Departments, to which he had been appointed in June 1888. A preliminary report, recommending important changes in the organization of the Admiralty and the War Office, and the need for greater

Monday 27 May (London)

Not feeling at all well again, but a good deal of business [. . .].

A conversation after dinner with R. Churchill, who dined here, as to my recent conference with Hartington.[1143] He said that Rothschild had told him that Hartington had informed him of my conversation with him and added that whether one agreed with me or not there was great force in my arguments.

Randolph also said that he had reason for believing that the Parnellites are meditating a parliamentary session – a contingency certainly indicated in Parnell's recent speech – but an unwise move on their part. Randolph most friendly and amiable.

Tuesday 25 June (London)

Elsie and I went up. I went almost direct to the National Society where I made a speech against the New Code.[1144] A large meeting and pretty much agreed with me on what I said. The Archbishop of Canterbury[1145] in the Chair.

Later in the House we divided against the Land Transfer Bill. The Government were all but beaten – 113 to 103 – and the 113 were almost entirely their best and most devoted supporters. Salisbury looked very much annoyed. When speaking he did not receive a single cheer from his own side.[1146]

---

co-ordination, appeared in July 1889. See P. Jackson, *The Last of the Whigs: a political biography of Lord Hartington, 8th Duke of Devonshire* (Rutherford, NJ and London, 1994), pp. 282–283.

[1143] Among the matters discussed with Hartington was whether Carnarvon should raise a debate in the House of Lords in an attempt to obtain a declaration of policy on Ireland from Salisbury (Hartington to Carnarvon, 31 May 1889: CP, BL 60828, fo. 21). Hartington advised Carnarvon 'not at this moment to stir up the question' (Carnarvon to Churchill, 5 June 1889: Randolph Churchill Papers, Add. MS 9248/24/3170).

[1144] The New Code of 1889, issued by the Committee of the Privy Council on Education, was an attempt to liberalize the system of 'payment by results' for elementary schools and allow more freedom for teachers on the subjects taught: building requirements were completely changed and class sizes were to be reduced. The voluntarists saw this as an attack on Church schools. After a bitter campaign, the Code was withdrawn. See G. Sutherland, *Policy-making in Elementary Education, 1870–1895* (London, 1973), pp. 266–277.

[1145] Edward White Benson (1829–1896), Archbishop of Canterbury (1882–1896).

[1146] Land Transfer Bill (No. 8), third reading: *Hansard*, CCCXXXVII, 25 June 1889, Salisbury, cols 687–688, Carnarvon, col. 690.

Thursday 27 June (London)

Herbert came. Murray[1147] had been with him and had told him
that there was a great desire on the part of the Cape people to have
me there, if only for a short time. Loch[1148] does not go till Christmas
and the satisfaction would be great if I could go till then, more as a
visitor than anything else. But they would not do anything without
first ascertaining my wishes in the matter. Herbert rather balanced
on the subject, on the whole more against it. After thinking it over, I
saw H. at the Colonial Office in the afternoon; he had become, on
consideration, even less in favour of my going, but agreed that if I
thought at all of it, I had best first talk it over with Loch.

Sunday 14 July (Highclere)

A great deal of conversation with Randolph on many subjects.
He has no love for Salisbury and amongst other things mentioned
that since his resignation he had been tabooed by the Queen, which he
said he probably owed to Salisbury. In foreign affairs he is convinced
that Boulanger[1149] will be at the head of things in October. He has
seen a good deal of him and next Wednesday he has Boulanger to
dinner and the Prince of Wales who desires to meet and talk to him.
In Servia [sic] he believes that the storm must soon break: there are
forces there beyond the power of Russia to control – race forces – and
he anticipates as almost certain war in the spring of 1890. One of his
anticipations is a war between France and Italy, the rest of Europe
looking on, Germany being held back by Russia. This would be a
very serious contingency, for France would certainly crush Italy.
He gave me a curious account of his interviews with the Czar, when
he was in Russia.[1150] He talked to him for nearly an hour and left the
impression on his mind of a very straightforward, simple, home loving,
peace loving, rather commonplace but resolute man.
We had a long conversation as to his own course of proceedings.
He proposes to speak at Walsall and Birmingham at the end of the
month and then to take a line as to Ireland, much in the way of our

[1147]The identity of this person is not known.
[1148]Sir Henry Brougham Loch (1827–1900), Governor of Victoria (1884–1889), Governor
of the Cape and High Commissioner in South Africa (1889–1895), Baron Loch (1895).
[1149]Georges Ernest Boulanger (1837–1891), French soldier and statesman. Served in Franco-
Prussian War (1870–1871), Minister of War (1886–1887). Committed suicide in Brussels.
[1150]For Churchill's own account of his meeting with the Czar, see W.S. Churchill, *Lord
Randolph Churchill*, 2 vols (London, 1906), II, pp. 359–366.

previous conversations in London. I advised him caution both for the sake of his object and of himself.[1151]

He said he intended to speak out, telling his audience that he could not speak freely in the House of Commons. I urged him to be very careful as to this, because he would have the House of Commons to deal with anyhow for another two years and that it was of no use to get quite angry with them. He thanked me much for all my advice, took it in excellent part and was altogether in most amiable mood. He spoke like a man who has been greatly sobered by his past reverses, with some bitterness occasionally of his old colleagues, but not very much, and he talked of his ignorance and inexperience at the time he resigned.

He is very clever – it is impossible to doubt this – and he has a very considerable attraction when he desires to put it out. He told Elsie that he had very much enjoyed his conversation with me; and I believe that it was so, for he came back half an hour before dinner to resume it, and would have talked on much longer had time allowed. I fancy that he is so cut off from his old party and friends that he is really glad of a friend, though probably he would throw the friend over without much remorse if circumstances seemed to require it.

Wednesday 24 July (London)

I lunched with the Spencers. We were alone and after lunch I had an interesting talk with Spencer for some time on Irish affairs. He seemed anxious and perplexed, not denying the improvement in affairs generally, but believing the recent disaffection to remain much the same. We touched on Ulster and Provincial Assemblies. As to Ulster he has really no expedient to suggest. He merely dwelt on the fact that Ulster is not really the Protestant Community which it is supposed to be and that an exclusion of Ulster from a general Home Rule Ireland would mean the disqualification of nearly one half the population of the province.

As to Provincial Assemblies he is not disposed to them, believing that this solution of the question would not go far enough. This I expected. The variety of opinion on this point is curious, Hartington inclining to them, Randolph thinking they go too far, Spencer not far enough.

[1151] His speech on domestic legislation at Walsall on 28 July roused the anger of publicans over the temperance issue. This overshadowed the Birmingham address on Irish policy two days later (ibid., pp. 397–398).

Monday 12 August (London)

I came up alone, and made my Egyptian speech in the House of Lords.[1152] Neither Salisbury nor the Government much liked it: at the same time it was not easy to find fault with it. Salisbury indeed misrepresented me in one part seriously by saying that I favoured repudiation, which obliged me to contradict him unequivocally,[1153] but beyond this there was nothing of consequence.

Saturday 9 November (London)

In the evening Randolph Churchill came to me and had a long talk. His notion still is that the Government is losing ground, that the bye elections show this, and that they do nothing to avert the catastrophe which is imminent. There are, as he truly says, only three men in the Cabinet who are not very inferior – Salisbury, Balfour and Goschen.

We talked much on the possibility of social reform, and I laid down in the broadest language the necessity for a policy which would at one and the same time give confidence to owners of property and would show the working classes that it was the full intention of the Government to ameliorate their lot. This I said was a difficult matter, but quite a possible one. He agreed after a good deal of conversation and said that amongst other means to such an end a Government should be formed of men, or rather containing men, who would inspire confidence to both of the two great bodies in the country.

He suggested one or two ingenious ways in which the great municipalities might be induced to undertake the sanitation of the poorer parts of large towns.

He ended by asking my advice on the following matter. When Wolff was in England he it seems spoke to Salisbury about Randolph and one day suggested that if Lytton should be obliged by health to give up Paris, whether Randolph could not go there. Salisbury said no, but added that he had thought that possibly he might go to St Petersburg, if he liked it.

[1152] Egypt. Military Operations against the Dervishes. Future Policy: *Hansard*, CCCXXXIX, 12 August 1889, Carnarvon, cols 993–1001.

[1153] Ibid., Salisbury, cols 1002–1004. Salisbury had written to Carnarvon a week earlier, at the last moment, when Carnarvon intended to introduce a debate on the Egyptian situation. 'So I sent him a few lines, good-natured but with a sting, saying I was much obliged for the letter but should have been still more grateful if he had given me an earlier intimation' (Diary, 5 August 1889; Carnarvon to Salisbury, 5 August 1889: Hatfield House Papers, 3M/E).

On this he wished for my opinion and apparently he had consulted no one else, for he said rather sadly, "I have no friend to whom I can talk." I said that I should prefer to sleep on the matter and answer him tomorrow, but *on the whole* my impression would be in favour of acceptance. He asked whether it would not cut him off from Parliamentary life, and damage him.[1154]

I said certainly not the first, and I quoted Canning accepting India and returning just as he was going; and as regards the latter I did not see that it could *really* worsen his position.

Sunday 10 November (London)

Randolph called on me this evening with regard to the question of a possible firm offer from Salisbury of the St Petersburg Embassy. I told him that I thought there were *against* acceptance:

(1) risk of political changes in the Government during his absence – undesirable.

(2) risk of his being superseded or forgotten – not very grave.

(3) risk of want of proper support at home especially if war should break out and difficulties arise. This might be avoided by great care on his part, but was a distinct risk.

On the other hand *for* accepting:

(1) it would be employment and very interesting.

(2) the difficulty of steering a safe course at home was so great that it might be well to be out of the way.

(3) it might even be easier to resume his position two or three years hence if he were now to go abroad.

But I said that taking everything into account, if the offer should be made in a fairly handsome manner I should advise acceptance. He thanked me much, said that this could determine him, and that he should accept. He said the old Duchess was averse to his going and that she was the only other person to whom he had spoken, but that what I said seemed conclusive.

[1154]Two years later, when Lytton gave up the Paris post, Balfour, after being approached by Churchill, urged Salisbury to fill the vacancy with Churchill: 'It would take him out of a sphere where, in these days of reckless electioneering promises, he is really dangerous, & put him in one where he would be relatively powerless for mischief.' Salisbury, however, would not contemplate the idea. See R.R. James, *Lord Randolph Churchill* (London, 1959), p. 356.

He talked a good deal about Salisbury, whom he neither likes nor trusts, and he reminded me in reference to Parnell of what he had once told me before – that *previous to the formation* of our Government in '85, he had talked freely to Parnell on the subject of Ireland and home rule. He said he was certain that about the time that I had my interview with Parnell, Salisbury was quite ready to go into Home Rule, but that he was deterred by the fear that he, Randolph, would turn round and trip him up.

Monday 23 December (Highclere)

We had our tenants ball, which passed off with very great success, and gave I think great satisfaction.

Froude came down from London to talk to me about Disraeli's correspondence on which he had previously written much to me. He had paid a visit to Lord Rothschild who showed him all the letters with a view to his editing them.[155]

The letters run from about 1851 to 1861 and they commence with a curious correspondence between Disraeli and old Mrs. Willyams[156] of Torquay, who at first gave him £1,000 and afterwards left him a considerable fortune. They are, Froude says, very interesting and greatly to Disraeli's credit. There is not a word of calumny or misrepresentation or malignity he says in them; they are very amusing and do justice to heart and head. Altogether it is clear that Froude is much inclined to undertake the task of editing and believes that in this particular period – from 1851 to 1861 there is nothing in Disraeli's career or this correspondence with which he would be seriously at variance.

Froude has consulted the Duke of Rutland as to Disraeli's character, but the Duke does not seem to have been able to throw much light on it, and indeed it was not likely that he should be able to do so. It is like asking a rush light to make clear an oil lamp: and from what I know of the two men I cannot conceive that Disraeli would ever feel anything but a benevolent but slightly contemptuous goodwill for John Manners. Froude is I think in want of literary work; he is

[155]In fact, the volume was published as a narrative in *The Prime Ministers of Queen Victoria* series, in octavo format, with a modest amount of quotations from Disraeli's correspondence: J.A. Froude, *The Earl of Beaconsfield* (London, 1896).

[156]Mrs Sarah Brydges Willyams (1769–1863), Sephardic Jew, wealthy widow, and owner of an estate near Torquay. She was over eighty when she first contacted Disraeli and there was a copious correspondence between them for many years. He inherited much of her estate after her death and she was buried, as she desired, at Hughenden. See Blake, *Disraeli*, pp. 414ff.

naturally taken with this correspondence and with the subject of it and I think that the end of his doubts will be to edit it. Those parts of Disraeli's career to which Froude mainly objects in 1877–8 will not come in. I thought it right to intimate, as he had virtually asked my opinion, that if he undertook to edit the correspondence he would not be at liberty to write as freely of Disraeli as he otherwise [would] be on those parts of his career outside the decade in question, and to this he quite assented.[1157]

[1157] Carnarvon commented on the project, 'I have been wary in giving advice though I have talked more or less freely of past events' (Diary, 24 December 1889).

1890

Wednesday 1 January (Highclere)

Il capo d'anno, and after a spell of unusually good health I am laid up by a sharp pain in my side, great malaise, difficulty to draw breath, altogether poorly and in pain. I was kept in bed till late and felt very miserable when up. Meanwhile nothing could exceed, for winter, the beauty of the day – a brilliant sun and blue Italian sky.

Thursday 2 January (Highclere)

Better, though not well. The morning spent in much discomfort, the afternoon in the Library, making a commencement of my Herbert Memoir, if I ever go on with it, a useful thing for the Family.[1158]

Sunday 5 January (Highclere)

There is a great deal of sickness everywhere and the accounts of the "Influenza" epidemic are bad. It is now in London. Salisbury has had it very severely, and our expedition to Greece must clearly be given up. I hope we may escape it, but it seems hardly likely.

Thursday 13 February (London)

Aubrey, Mervyn[1159] and I have had the influenza. Aubrey much the most severely, I very lightly, dear Mervyn short but sharp. All plans are disturbed. Elsie has a tiresome cough, but Dr. Granville[1160] does not think much of it and I trust it will go.

[1158] *The Herberts of Highclere*, printed for private circulation, was published by John Murray in 1908.

[1159] Mervyn Robert Howard Molyneux Herbert (1882–1929), Carnarvon's second son by his second marriage, later an attaché in the diplomatic service.

[1160] Dr Joseph Mortimer Granville of 16 Welbeck Street, Cavendish Square, London.

Saturday 8 March (Porto Fino)

We are back in our Mediterranean home,[1161] rather a cloudy day but everything looking very beautiful. We saw Dr Breiting[1162] before leaving Genoa, and the Consul paid us a little visit just to tell us that he was coming on Tuesday to welcome us.

Now for the next six weeks I hope that we shall have a time of very pleasant quiet reading and writing, and fresh air. It is a charming place, and perhaps we ought to do more with it than we do.

Saturday 15 March (Porto Fino)

Randolph Churchill has been getting into great trouble with his own Party. He is not wise about this. He gets irritated, feels the isolation of his position and possibly the slights put on him and then makes an attack on the Government as he has done in the present case on them in reference to the Special Commission.[1163] Then at once all the Party newspapers open on him and the breach becomes still wider.

If he is not careful it will end in a real quarrel and he will have to go to the Radicals.

Tuesday 25 March (Porto Fino)

Herbert writes me word that Salisbury is supposed to be unwell. I wrote a long letter to him last Thursday or Friday[1164] which I sent

[1161]The Carnarvons finally left England on 5 March, staying in Paris en route (Diary, 5 March 1890).

[1162]This person has not been identified.

[1163]The Report of the Parnell Commission was made public on 11 February; it exonerated the Irish members from some of the charges made against them in *The Times*. W.H. Smith, as Leader of the House, moved a resolution on 3 March that the Commons should adopt the Report and thank the Commissioners for their impartiality. In the subsequent debate on 10 March, Randolph Churchill bitterly attacked his former colleagues, losing the support of many of the Party. The Government had a majority of sixty-two in the division that followed. See Sir H. Maxwell, *Life and Times of the Right Honourable W.H. Smith, MP*, 2 vols (Edinburgh, 1893), II, pp. 264–272; *Hansard*, CCCXLI, 3 March 1890, Smith, cols 1656–1670; *Hansard*, CCCXLII, 10 March 1890, Churchill, cols 11–25.

[1164]Carnarvon complained of a paragraph in the *Standard* concerning a forthcoming debate in the Lords on Salisbury's motion on the Special Commission. Carnarvon wrote, 'Whenever you have spoken on the subject [of my relations in '85 with Parnell and the Irish Party] the impression has been left – very unintentionally, I doubt not – that more remained to be said, that we were not in agreement and that differences between us were extremely serious.' He also reminded Salisbury that 'it was your own opinion and wish, in to Herbert with authority to suppress or forward and this letter from Herbert today had been written before the receipt of mine.[1165]

Wednesday 2 April (Porto Fino)

I wrote my answer to Salisbury;[1166] the correspondence is now I think complete, unless he makes any reply. I do not know that it will do much good, but I do not think it can possibly do harm, and it has been a fair attempt on my part to make the personal relations, once so intimate, better. I think this was worth an effort.[1167]

It is curious that this has happened twice before to me with two Prime Ministers – Lord Derby and Disraeli. In each case I was on most friendly terms, in each case political reasons dissolved the feeling; in each case I went to see them a short time before their death and we had a *fair* reconciliation. But in these two cases I knew they had not long to live and I did not like the idea of parting ill friends.

Wednesday 9 April (Porto Fino)

I have not been feeling well, but I think I have today virtually finished my translation of *Prometheus*.[1168] What I shall now do with it is, as the Italians say *altra cosa* – not very easy for me to determine.

We are beginning to think of our homeward move.

---

which I agreed, that the affair should remain private' (Carnarvon to Salisbury, 20 March 1890: Hatfield House Papers, 3M/E).

[1165] Sir Robert Herbert to Carnarvon, 24 March 1890: CP, BL 60795, fos 188–189.

[1166] Salisbury answered Carnarvon's letter of 20 March, assuring the latter that 'I wished to dissipate from your mind the idea that I have been on any occasion backward to support your statements against the Parnellites incomparable falsehoods [. . .]. I have always deeply regretted that there should have been any divergence between us on political questions; but I should regret it much more deeply if I thought the result of it had been outside of politics, you thought more unkindly of me than you used to do' (Salisbury to Carnarvon, 27 March 1890: CP, BL 60760, fos 140–146).

[1167] Carnarvon replied, 'Your letter was very welcome to me because it expresses plainly both in tone and substance the continuation of the old feeling between us on your part, and for this reason I am glad that I wrote though under the false impression of an unfounded newspaper statement.' Nevertheless, he pointed out to Salisbury the differences that still existed between them (Carnarvon to Salisbury, 2 April 1890: Hatfield House Papers, 3M/E).

[1168] *Prometheus* was published posthumously in 1892 by John Murray.

Monday 28 April (Dover)

We left Brussels by a 10.30 train and had a prosperous journey [...].[1169]

I have a return of this detestable influenza, and what I took for rheumatism is, I do not doubt, only that. I have all the old muscular pains, and very badly. I wonder whether and when they will die out. At present I am fit for very little.[1170]

Saturday 3 May (London)

I went to the Academy dinner;[1171] the representation pictorially seemed to me very poor, the speeches except Salisbury's not very good. Salisbury's had a good deal of humour in it, and J. Morley[1172] who tried to answer it had not the lightness of touch to make the reply of the airy, easy kind that was wanted. Granville's had a ring of the *senescens equus* in it, with some of the old ease. Salisbury's faults are harshness of voice and a want of the little refinements of oratory, which link on one part of the speech to the other and with which the late Lord Derby was so endowed.

Tuesday 6 May (London)

We dined with the Jeunes, R. Churchill there, very friendly with me, and we had a good deal of general talk. He is very clever. He believes that by the end of June the Government will find themselves in a deadlock in the House of Commons, and that when the Elections take place they will be in great straits. His dislike to Salisbury is very great. He declared to Mrs. J. that there was not a Cecil who had a particle of heart or thought of anything but himself.

[1169]The Carnarvons arrived back in London on 28 April.

[1170]The following day, in conversation with his doctor, Carnarvon was told that he was still not well, 'apparently, an effect of the influenza' (Diary, 29 April 1890).

[1171]'Royal Academy Banquet', *The Times*, 5 May 1890, p. 10.

[1172]John Morley (1838–1923), Lib. MP for Newcastle upon Tyne (1883–1895) and for Montrose Burghs (1896–1908), Chief Secretary for Ireland (1886, 1892–1895), Secretary of State for India (1905–1910), created Viscount Morley of Blackburn (1908).

Wednesday 14 May (London)

I have had a really terrible time since Sunday[1173] – rheumatic gout, or rather gouty neuralgia – in one knee – pains in one side of my body everywhere – hopeless torment at night, unable to sleep – always changing position. Altogether I think the worst pain for several consecutive days that I have ever had.

Thursday 15 May (London)

Rather better but very little.

I had a visit from Gladstone[1174] who came to talk to me about Acton's Library which is to be sold.[1175] He is extremely interested in the matter and threw himself with the intense earnestness of his whole nature into it – as if he had nothing else to think of.

I also saw Verdon[1176] and said goodbye to him – probably for the last time.[1177]

[1173] On 9 May, Carnarvon was seen by Dr Granville. 'He says I shall be well again in a short time, and substantially there is really nothing the matter, but I have felt low and poorly all day' (Diary, 9 May 1890).

[1174] Gladstone called on Carnarvon at 43 Portman Square on more than one occasion during Carnarvon's last illness. His final visit was only ten days before Carnarvon's death. See Carnarvon to Gladstone, 19 June 1890: Gladstone Papers, BL 44510, fo. 106.

[1175] John Emerich Edward Dalberg Acton (1834–1902), 1st Baron Acton (1869), historian, Regius Professor of Modern History, Cambridge University (1895–1902). At the end of 1889 and the beginning of 1890, Acton was almost bankrupt. He proposed to pay off a bank loan by selling his Library at Aldenham, consisting of 70,000 volumes. To avoid this happening, Gladstone persuaded Andrew Carnegie, the philanthropist, to buy the Library for £9,000, with Acton having full use of it during his lifetime. When Acton died in 1902, Carnegie gave it to John Morley, who, in turn, presented it to Cambridge University. See R. Hill, *Lord Acton* (New Haven, CT and London, 2000), pp. 289–292; J. Morley, *Recollections*, I, pp. 231–232.

[1176] Sir George Frederic Verdon (1834–1896), politician and banker, Agent-General for Victoria (1868–1872). Verdon had had 'an important talk' with Carnarvon the week before on the latter's Sydney property (Diary, 8 May 1890).

[1177] Carnarvon died on the evening of 29 June.

INDEX

Note: all subentries appear in chronological, rather than alphabetical, order.

Abbeyleix, Thomas Veasey de Vesci, 3rd Viscount of (*see* de Vesci, Thomas Veasey)

Abdul Aziz I, Sultan of the Ottoman Empire 165, 282

Abdul Majid, Sultan of the Ottoman Empire 282

Abercorn, James Hamilton, 1st Duke of 350

Abercromby, Lady Louisa 298, 302, 311

Abercromby, Sir Robert William Duff 302

Aberdeen, George Hamilton-Gordon, 4th Earl of 2–3, 106

Abergavenny, William Nevill, 1st Marquess of 340

Aborigines Society 135

Achill, Co. Mayo 400

Acland, Sir Henry Wentworth 83

Acton, Sir John Emerich Edward Dalberg, later 1st Baron 33; proposed sale of his library 83, 471

Adderley, Charles Bowyer, 1st Baron Norton: on 1866 Reform Bill 128; receives Aborigines Society deputation 135; incompetence as Under-Secretary, Colonies 141; meeting with Canadian delegates 144; introduces Unseaworthy Shipping Bill 241, 259; possible move 266, 268; on 1884 Franchise Bill 47, 350, 362; Carnarvon visits 357–358

Adlerberg, Count Aleksandr Vladimir-ovitch 221

Adullamites 8, 127, 143, 155

Afghanistan 12, 308–309, 379, 387

Africa, South 360; Carnarvon dispatches Froude to promote federal policy 22; failure of policy 22–23, 87; Carnarvon visits 73; Confederation question 217, 249, 290

Africa, West: proposed exchange of territory with French and Dutch 136;

meeting on slave dealing 242–243; contemplated mission to Dahomey 283

Agamemnon, Carnarvon's translation of 10, 12

agricultural depression 36–38

Agricultural Distress, Royal Commission on (1879) 41–42, 314, 315

Agricultural Holdings (England) Bill (1883) 253, 258–259, 343–344

Ailesbury, Lady Maria Elizabeth 418

Akers-Douglas, Aretas, later 1st Viscount Chilston 365

Alabama, claims regarding 137–139

Albany, Prince Leopold George Duncan Albert, Duke of 217, 254, 260

Albemarle, George Thomas Keppel, 6th Earl of 349

Albert, Prince, of Saxe-Coburg-Gotha, and Prince Consort 265, 303, 327–328

Albert Edward, Prince of Wales (*see* Wales, Albert Edward, Prince of)

Alberta and *Mistletoe*, collision of 269

Alexander II, Czar of Russia 221, 249–250, 251

Alexander III, Czar of Russia 449, 461

Alington, Henry Gerard Sturt, 1st Baron (*see* Sturt, Henry Gerard)

Amherst, William Amhurst Tyssen- 164

Ampthill, Odo William Leopold Russell, 1st Baron (*see* Russell, Odo William Leopold)

Ancient Monuments Protection Act (1882) 34

Anglo-Russian Convention (1878) 303–304, 305

Annand, William 139

Anson, Augustus Henry Archibald 143

Anson, Thomas George (*see* Lichfield, Thomas George Anson, 2nd Earl of)

Anti-Slavery Society 109

Arch, Joseph 38, 316

Argyll, George Douglas Campbell, 8th Duke of: on Colonial Defence Commission 43; on Employers Liability Bill 322; and Franchise Bill (1884) 47, 351; and compromise on Franchise Bill 357, 362, 363, 367; on South African matters 360–361; speech on Coercion Bill 444

Arlington Street, London (Salisbury's London residence) 45, 51, 332, 341, 348, 352, 373, 381, 384

Armenia 313–314

Army & Navy Gazette 80, 130

Army (Purchase System) Bill (1871) 198

Arnold, Edwin 79

Arnold, Matthew 12

Arrears of Rent (Ireland) Bill (1882) 338, 339, 340; amendments to 340, 341

Ashanti War 212, 213, 215–216

Ashbourne, Edward Gibson, 1st Baron (*see* Gibson, Edward)

Astley, Maj.-Gen. Sir Jacob 419

Aston Park, Birmingham, attack on Churchill and Northcote at Conservative rally 358

Athenaeum 159, 160, 175

Aumale, Henri-Eugène-Philippe-Louis d'Orléans, Duc d' 183

Austin, Alfred 79, 80

Australia: Masonic disputes in 18, 73; Carnarvon's acquisition of property in 69–71; postal subsidy 168; Carnarvon on character of Australians 109; military assistance to 378

Aveland, Gilbert Henry Heathcote Drummond Willoughby, 2nd Baron 321

Aylesford, Heneage Finch, 7th Earl of 263

Bagehot, Walter 12, 132, 155

Baillie, Henry James 99

Baker, Richard Baker Wingfield 141

Baker, Col. Valentine 261

Balfour, Arthur James, later 1st Earl of Balfour: and Salisbury on Carnarvon's resignation 31; on 1884 Franchise Bill 48; takes hard line on Irish policy 76; relationship with Churchill 77; financial support for *National Review* 80–81, 348; his popularity 458, 463

Ball, Dr John Thomas 204

Balmoral Castle 20, 22, 51, 57, 262, 263, 264, 265, 293, 381, 403

Bank of Ireland 53, 393, 394

banking crisis, Ireland (*see* Bank of Ireland; Hibernian Bank; Munster Bank)

Barak, annexation of 24

Baring, Thomas George (*see* Northbrook, Thomas George Baring, 1st Earl)

Barkly, Sir Henry: shows poor leadership, Cape of Good Hope 22, 252, 267; as member of Colonial Defence Commission 315, 316

Barrett, Wilson 369

Barrington, George William, 7th Viscount: on Derby and Carnarvon 184; Disraeli's final illness 323, 324, 325; on Salisbury and the Arrears Bill 340

Barry, Sir Charles, and rebuilding of Highclere Castle 6

Bartley, Sir George Christopher Trout 46, 354, 358, 359, 365

Basing, George Sclater-Booth, 1st Baron (*see* Sclater-Booth, George)

Bath, John Alexander Thynne, 4th Marquess of: 27, 36, 164, 306, 330; on Carnarvon's relationship with Gladstone 40; on Disraeli and the 1866 Reform Bill 117–118; Lords' Whip on Established Church (Ireland) Bill 181; reconciliation with Carnarvon 195; at Hatfield 288; and Zulu War debate 312; tours Bulgaria 316

Bathurst, Allen Alexander, 6th Earl 330

Battenberg, Henry, Prince of 217

Baxter, Robert Dudley 130, 146, 151

Beach, Sir Michael Edward Hicks (*see* Hicks Beach, Sir Michael Edward)

Beaconsfield, Benjamin Disraeli, 1st Earl of (*see* Disraeli, Benjamin)

Beatrice, Princess 217, 254, 260, 264

Beauchamp, Frederick Lygon, 6th Earl of 93, 94, 197, 314, 350, 371

Becker, Lydia Ernestine 49, 375

Belfast 56, 412

Bell, Sir Francis Dillon 189

Benson, Edward White, Archbishop of Canterbury 460

Bermingham, Robert (*see* Leitrim, Robert Bermingham, 4th Earl of)

Bernard, Prof. Montague 136

Bernstorff, Albrecht, Count von 195

Besika Bay, Greece 26

Bethell, Richard (*see* Westbury, Richard Bethell, 1st Baron)

Billyard, W.W. 70

Bingham, Nottinghamshire 36

Bingham, George Charles (*see* Lucan, George Charles Bingham, 3rd Earl of)

Birch, Sir Arthur Nonus 262

Birch, James Wheeler Woodford 270

Birmingham 46, 78, 357, 358, 461

Bismarck, Otto Eduard Leopold, Prince von 212, 220, 247, 262, 392

Blachford, Frederic Rogers, 1st Baron (*see* Rogers, Sir Frederic, later 1st Baron Blachford)

Blackwood, Frederick Temple (*see* Dufferin and Ava, Frederick Temple Blackwood, 1st Marquess of)

Borthwick, Algernon, later 1st Baron Glenesk 300

Boulanger, Georges Ernest Jean Marie 461

Bourke, Charles Fowler 401

Bourke, Robert, later 1st Baron Connemara 288

Bouverie, Edward Pleydell- 128

Bovill, Sir William 135

Bowen, Sir George Ferguson 295

Boxall, Sir William 159

Boyle, Richard Edmund (*see* Cork and Orrery, Richard Edmund St Lawrence Boyle, 9th Earl of)

Brabourne, Edward Hugessen Knatchbull-Hugessen, 1st Baron (*see* Hugessen, Edward Hugessen Knatchbull-)

Bradford, Orlando George Charles Bridgeman, 3rd Earl of 266

Bradford, Selina Louisa Bridgeman, Countess of: letters from Disraeli: on Carnarvon's character 21, 86; on his ill-health 26; on his Cabinet triumphs 29; Disraeli attracted to 266

Brand, Henry Bouverie, later 1st Viscount Hampden 330, 332

Brand, Jan Hendrik, President of the Orange Free State 282

Brassey, Thomas, later 1st Earl 42, 315, 316

Bretby Park, Nottinghamshire 10, 35, 36, 37, 205, 206, 207, 208, 209, 216, 233, 234–235, 266, 397, 398

Bridgewater House, London 40

Bright, John 86, 173–174, 323

British Archaeological Association 33

British Columbia 102, 223, 224, 236, 240, 296, 297; need to establish civil government in 100

British North American Confederation Bill (1867) 8, 144, 145, 146, 147, 153; second reading 150

Brodrick, William St John Fremantle 355

Brown, Lancelot 'Capability' 6

Browne, Edward Harold, Bishop of Winchester 230

Browne, Lord John Thomas 400

Browning, Robert 11

Bruce, Sir Frederick William 136

Bruce, Col. Robert 384

Bryce, James, later 1st Viscount 307

Buccleuch, Walter Francis Scott, 5th Duke of 147, 164, 165, 167, 218, 321

Buckingham and Chandos, Richard Plantagenet Grenville, 3rd Duke of 154, 156, 295

Buckingham Palace 156, 165

Buckle, George Earle 447

Bulgaria, atrocities in 26–27, 285

Burgers, Thomas François 250, 252

Burghclere, Berkshire 17

Burke, Sir Bernard 52

Burma, probability of war with 12, 253

Burton Joyce, Nottinghamshire 35

Bury, William Coutts Keppel, Viscount, later 7th Earl of Albemarle 350

Butler, Lord James Arthur Wellington Foley 427

Butler, Lieut.-Gen. Sir William Francis 23

Bylandt, Charles Malcolm Ernst George 301

Cadogan, George Henry, 5th Earl 81, 301, 330, 350, 371, 444

Cadogan, Henry Charles, 4th Earl 188

Cairns, Hugh McCalmont, later 1st Earl 41, 46, 270, 324, 350; speech on Established Church (Ireland) Bill 181; wishes to relinquish Lords' leadership 15, 187–190; amendment on Irish Land Bill 194; announces compromise on Established Church (Ireland) Bill 185; on legal reform 261; on the ending of the creation of Irish Peers 271; Carnarvon's views on (1876) 85; summary of resolutions 294; Land Law (Ireland) Bill 329–330; discussion on the Arrears Bill amendments 340;

resolution on Franchise Bill 350–351; invitation to Windsor 376; death 379

Cairns, Lady Mary 376

Cairns, William Wellington 230, 243

Cambridge, Prince George William, Duke of 147, 272, 349; on vacant governorships 137; involvement in occupation of new War Office and Colonial Office buildings 223; discusses Perak with Carnarvon 273; and Salisbury's attack on Wolseley 447

Cameron of Lochiel, Donald 365

Campbell, George Douglas (see Argyll, George Douglas Campbell, 8th Duke of)

Campbell, John Douglas Sutherland (see Lorne, John Douglas Sutherland Campbell, Marquess of)

Camperdown, Robert Haldane-Duncan, 3rd Earl of 333

Canada: policy of Confederation 7–8, 87, 140, 143, 272; Carnarvon's tour of 52, 72–73; Nova Scotian and New Brunswick ministers, and schemes for federation 104; meeting of Canadian ministers at Highclere 104–105; meetings of Canadian delegates at Westminster Palace Hotel and Highclere 140, 144–146; delegates presented to Queen Victoria 153–154; Carnarvon offered Governor-Generalship 33; threatened Fenian invasion 131; possible commutation of death sentences of Fenian convicts 135, 136; Intercolonial Railway Guarantee 145, 146

Canford Manor, Dorset 49

Canning, George 464

Cape Colony 44, 227, 248, 267

Cape Town 22, 73

Cardwell, Edward 98, 140, 159

Carlingford, Chichester Samuel Fortescue, Baron (see Fortescue, Chichester Samuel)

Carlton, Nottinghamshire 35

Carlton Club 16, 48, 65, 125, 139, 185, 190, 191, 192, 194, 296, 317, 337, 363, 364, 369, 372, 374, 378, 380, 448

Carlyle, Thomas 12, 344

Carnarvon Castle 14

Carnarvon, Elisabeth Catherine Howard, Countess of (diarist's second wife) 81, 82, 83, 313, 328, 329, 331, 341, 349, 357, 364, 365, 403, 407, 409, 410, 412, 414, 415, 428, 432, 435, 437, 452, 454, 460, 467; meets and marries Carnarvon 34; invited to Windsor 375–376, 406; participates in Primrose League activities 67; and Churchill's part in removal of Northcote as Leader in Commons 59; deteriorating health in Ireland 61; commissions life of Carnarvon xv–xvi

Carnarvon, Evelyn Stanhope, Countess of (diarist's first wife) 10, 133, 154, 187, 205, 222; marries Carnarvon 5; influence on Carnarvon's political judgement 87; discussions with Lowe on Reform 134, 148; death 24

Carnarvon, George Edward Stanhope Molyneux Herbert, 5th Earl of (diarist's son) 1, 5, 219, 257

Carnarvon, Henrietta Anne Molyneux, Countess of (diarist's mother) 1

Carnarvon, Henry George Herbert, 2nd Earl of (diarist's grandfather) 11

Carnarvon, Henry Herbert, 1st Earl of (diarist's great-grandfather) 11, 35

Carnarvon, Henry Howard Molyneux Herbert, 4th Earl of: childhood, travels to the Middle East 1; lays foundation stone for Highclere Castle 6; Eton and Christ Church, Oxford 2; enters into politics, moves Address on Queen's Speech 2–3; character 3, 4; appointed Constable of Carnarvon Castle 14; Freemasonry 18–19; offered and accepts Under-Secretaryship at Colonial Office 4; on Lytton 114–115; friendship with Stanley 4; responsibilities at Colonial Office 4–5, 103–105; sends Gladstone to Ionian Islands 5, 106–108, 345–346; out of office 5–7; marries Evelyn Stanhope 5; High Steward, Oxford University 5, 13; colonial legislation 111–113; appointed as Colonial Secretary in Derby administration 7–9; views on unification of Canada 7–8; views on Richmond as Leader 118; surmises on future government 126; conferences with Disraeli 127; writes to Derby on 1866 Reform Bill 129; proposes Conservative daily paper 129–130; on Canada and the threatened Fenian invasion 131; conferences at Highclere with Disraeli on Reform 132–133; Cabinet on Reform 133, 134–135, 137; agreement with Northcote on Reform 134; attitude to *Alabama* claims 138; meets Canadian delegates on Confederation scheme 139–140, 144–146; discussions with Lowe on Reform and Confederation 140; discusses Reform Resolutions with Cranborne 143–144; joint action on the Reform Bill with Cranborne and Peel 8–9, 149–155; agrees to alliance with Cranborne 150; threatens resignation 152; sees Derby 155; resigns from government (1867) 9–10, 155–157; translates *Agamemnon* and *Odyssey* 10, 12, 71, 421; translates *Prometheus* 71, 469; writes family history 10; literary visitors to Highclere 11–12; interest in education 12–13; discusses Reform with Gladstone 158; conference with Cranborne 159; attends meetings of Peers on Reform Bill 163–164, 164–165; godfather to Cranborne's child 168; discussions with Cranborne on political prospects 169, 170; opens debate on Irish Church Bill 174–175; distrust of 14th Earl of Derby 180–181; active in leadership crisis of the House of Lords 15–16, 187–193; takes seat on front Opposition Bench 193; Greek massacre 16–17; views on Established Church (Ireland) Bill and Irish Land Bill 15, 194–195; distrusts Disraeli 197; role of secret compact with working men 197–200; illnesses 17; wishes to postpone Judicature Bill 204; speaks to Disraeli on bill 204; on conditions for taking office with Salisbury under Disraeli 208; sees Disraeli 210; Colonial Secretary in Disraeli's government 19–26, 211; conversations with Lady Derby 211, 249, 258, 272, 287, 296, 299, 302; as possible Foreign Secretary 222; on new Colonial Office building 222–223; discussions with Salisbury on future of the government 225–226, 231; conversations with Disraeli 234–235; estimate of Disraeli 235, 324, 325; effects reconciliation between Colenso and Shepstone 244; talks with Froude on confederation for South

Africa 250, 251–252; conversation with Gladstone 257; on the Chinese labour question 258; on Prince of Wales's visit to India 260, 262–263, 264; discusses government affairs with Northcote 266; South African policy 21–23; offered Viceroyalty of India 24–25, 269–271; offered Admiralty 25, 273, 274–275, 279; anti-vivisection legislation 25, 281, 314; takes on supervision of India Office in Salisbury's absence 25; on the Indian famine 283–285; discusses Eastern Question with Queen Victoria 285; meets Ignatiev 288–289; talk with Northcote on Disraeli 289; on the South African Confederation Question 290; on Russian threats 297, 298; talk with Gladstone on Eastern Question 298; important conversation with Derby 302–303; meets Froude 308; on Zulu War 311–312; attitude to the Turks 27; alliance with Derby on Eastern Question 27; growing differences with rest of Cabinet 28; on Disraeli's failing health 28; outmanoeuvred by Disraeli 29; entertains South African deputation 29; suspicious of Salisbury's changed attitude 30; resigns from office (1878) 31; personal explanation in the Lords 32; meets Gladstone 32; shunned by London society 32–33; considers joining the Liberal party 33; ambitious programme of action for British Archaeological Association 33–34; meets and marries his cousin Elisabeth 34; as landowner 35–36; effects of agricultural depression 36–38; attacks terms of Congress of Berlin 38; offered, and declines, chair of Royal Commission on Agricultural Distress 41–42, 314, 315; accepts chairmanship of Royal Commission on Colonial Defence 42, 315; proceedings and recommendations of Commission on Colonial Defence 42–45; advises Derby to remain in government 39; review of political position 317–319; friendship with Hicks Beach, Northcote, and Sandon 39; approaches from Gladstone to join Liberals 39–40; invitation to meeting of Peers under Disraeli 40, 321; Irish Land Bill 323, 325–326, 328–332; on Arrears Bill amendments 340; Agricultural Holdings Bill 343–344; leading figure in negotiations over Franchise Bill 46–50, 345–375; sees Salisbury on Churchill 352; tour of Canada 72–73; reconciliation with Queen Victoria 375–376; supports Primrose League 67–68; appointed Lord Lieutenant of Ireland 51, 383–386; health worries 52, 57; Munster Bank crisis 52–53; and Hibernian Bank 53; meets Parnell 55; tours south and west Ireland 399–400; discusses Home Rule with Churchill 59–60; outlines Home Rule plan to Cabinet 60–61, 402–403; not offered post in new administration 65, 408; sees Churchill 411; announcement of Carnarvon's retirement from Lord Lieutenancy in the *Standard* 412; discusses Queen's Speech with Ashbourne 413–414; last Cabinet 414–415; attends last Levée 416; on W.H. Smith 417; departs from Ireland 417–419; attitude to Irish Bills 423; on Home Rule Bill 424–425; possibility of publishing the *Odyssey* 426; alleged offer to Parnell 428, 429; statement in Lords on meeting with Parnell 64, 429; meets Salisbury to discuss Parnell 64–65; newspaper correspondence with Gladstone 434–435; House of Lords speech 437–438; on Churchill 441; visits South Africa and Australia 73; *The Times* letter on Parnell 447, 448; real estate and investments in Australia, New Zealand, and Canada 68–71; relationship with the press 78–81; opposes Local Government Bill (1888) 73–74; supports House of Lords reforms 75–76; publication of the Chesterfield letters 452; appointed Lord Lieutenant, Hampshire 74; co-opted as alderman, Hampshire County Council 75; meetings with Churchill on Irish self-government 76–78, 456; discussion on Ireland with Hartington 459; on Cairns, Hicks Beach, Hardy, Richmond, Gladstone, Dufferin, and Salisbury 85; on Hartington 85–86; on Bright

86; on Chamberlain 86; on his Colonial Office successors 87–88; as possible Governor of the Cape 81, 461; begins Herbert memoir 467; attempted reconciliation with Salisbury 468–469; attack of influenza 82, 470; Gladstone's last visit 471; death 83, 471

Carnarvon, Henry John George Herbert, 3rd Earl of (diarist's father) 1, 2, 6, 407

Carter, Howard 1

Cartier, Sir George-Étienne 104, 144, 153

Cartwright, Sir Richard John 272

Caulfeild, Col. John A. 387

Cave, Sir Steven 268, 275

Cavendish, Lord Frederick Charles 338

Cavendish, Spencer Compton (*see* Hartington, Spencer Compton Cavendish, Marquess of, later 8th Duke of Devonshire)

Cawdor, John Frederick Campbell, 2nd Earl 179

Cecil, Edgar Algernon Robert Gascoyne-, later 1st Viscount Cecil of Chelwood 383

Cecil, Gwendolen xv, 84

Central Board Scheme 53, 390

Chamberlain, Joseph 46, 86, 304, 323, 386, 390; Irish local government and Central Board Scheme 53, 77; on Redistribution Bill 360, 375; possible alliance with Churchill 454; Churchill's views on 458

Chaplin, Henry, later 1st Viscount: moves for Royal Commission on Agricultural Distress 314; opposes Franchise Bill 367, 372, 374; proposed as Irish Secretary 456

Charsley, Dr William Parker 260

Charteris, Lady Margaret 398

Chelmsford, Frederick Thesiger, 1st Baron 190, 191, 198, 313

Chesterfield, Anne Elizabeth Stanhope, Countess of 203, 229; death 55, 397, 398

Chesterfield, George Stanhope, 6th Earl of 10

Chesterfield, Philip Dormer Stanhope, 4th Earl of 10

Child-Villiers, Victor Albert (*see* Jersey, Victor Albert Child-Villiers, 7th Earl of)

Childers, Hugh Culling Eardley: on second
reading of 1866 Reform Bill 126;
appointed to Royal Commission on
Colonial Defence 42, 316; considers a
coalition government 309
Chinese labour question 258
Cholmondley, Hugh (*see* Delamere, Hugh
Cholmondley, 2nd Baron)
Christian, Prince of Schleswig-Holstein
262, 264
Christian, Princess Helena 262, 264
Christian Malford, Wiltshire 35, 69
Church Patronage (Scotland) Bill (1874)
218; second reading 222, 225
Churchill, Lady Jennie 264
Churchill, Lord Randolph Henry Spencer:
and Conservative Party organization
347; manoeuvring of 349, 382, 385,
397, 403, 411, 413; need for Carnarvon
and Salisbury to come to terms with
352; Aston Park meeting 358; meeting
at Northcote's 359; possible offer
of St Petersburg Embassy 78, 401,
464; conversations with Carnarvon
401, 403, 461–462, 463–465; meeting
with Salisbury 408; conditions for
joining 1885 Ministry 58; plots with
FitzGibbon 59; establishes rapport
with Parnell 59; discusses Home Rule
with Carnarvon 59–60; speech on
Carnarvon 419–420; and Parnell's
motion on Ireland 420–421, 427,
448–449; appointed Chancellor of
the Exchequer and Leader of the
Commons 66, 438; resigns 440;
ambition for War Office 449; discusses
Irish question with Carnarvon 77–
78, 456; wishes to attack the
government 452, 456–460; difficulties
with Conservative Party 468
Clarendon, George William Frederick
Villiers, 4th Earl of 169, 174, 183
Cleveland, Henry George Vane, 4th Duke
of 121, 175
Cleveland, Stephen Grover, President of
the USA 367
Clifden, Co. Galway 399
Clinton, Charles Henry Rolle, 20th Baron
330
Cochrane, Alexander Dundas Ross
Baillie-, later 1st Baron Lamington
118, 336
Coercion Bill (1881) 336

Coercion Bill (1887) 444
Colborne, Maj.-Gen. Sir Francis 271
Colchester, Charles Abbot, 2nd Baron 96
Colenso, John William, Bishop of Natal
237, 244
Collings, Jesse 63
Colonial Clergy Bill (1874) 219
Colonial Defence, Royal Commission on
42–45, 235, 315, 316, 317, 324, 326, 327,
333, 339
Colonial Office: difficulties with Treasury
20; Carnarvon's working methods at
20, 21, 86, 97; new buildings 222–
223
Colville, Charles John, 1st Baron 95, 275,
350, 371; involvement in appointment
of Leader of the Lords 189–192; on
the Irish Land Bill 194
Compulsory Church Rates Abolition Bill
(1868) 173
Connaught and Strathearn, Prince Arthur
William Patrick Albert, Duke of 403
Congress of Berlin (1878) 33, 38, 300, 305;
Disraeli's triumph 306
Congress of Brussels (1874) 224, 233, 234,
247
Conservative Party Central Organization
354, 358
Conspiracy to Murder Bill (1858) 95
Constantinople 1, 4, 25, 26, 27–28, 290, 294,
300, 305
Cooper, Anthony Ashley (*see* Shaftesbury,
Anthony Ashley Cooper, 7th Earl of)
Cooper, Col. Edward Henry 400
Copley, John Singleton (the elder) 349
Copley, John Singleton, 1st Baron Lynd-
hurst 102, 349
Cork and Orrery, Richard Edmund St
Lawrence Boyle, 9th Earl of 167
Corrupt Electoral Practices Act (1883) 66–
67
Corry, Montagu William Lowry, later 1st
Baron Rowton: writes to Carnarvon
on Fiji 232; takes over Disraeli's
correspondence 234, 235; and Dis-
raeli's illness 243; discusses Royal
Commission on Agricultural Distress
with Carnarvon 314
Courthope, William John 80
Cowley, Henry Richard Charles Wellesley,
1st Earl 169, 253
Cowper, Henry Frederick 344
Cowper, William Francis 99

Cranborne, Robert Arthur Talbot Gascoyne-Cecil, Viscount (*see* Salisbury, Robert Arthur Talbot Gascoyne-Cecil, Viscount Cranborne, later 3rd Marquess of)

Cranbrook, Gathorne Gathorne-Hardy, 1st Earl of (*see* Hardy, Gathorne Gathorne-)

Crimean War (1854–1856) 3, 4, 29

Croagh Patrick, Co. Mayo 400

Croker, John Wilson 161

Cross, Richard Assheton, later 1st Viscount 252, 271, 288, 299, 330, 335, 336, 337, 349, 381, 413, 414; first meeting with Carnarvon 84–85; on Carnarvon's resignation over Eastern Question 31; possible leadership in the Commons 202; supports Carnarvon over new Whitehall offices 223; legislative proposals 213, 234, 238, 269; on crime 241; on Irish Land Bill 261; opposed to introduction of Clôture 338; on Franchise Bill 351, 352; and Churchill's opposition to India Office proposals 439; out of office 443

Crosse, Revd John Dudley Oland 224

Cruelty to Animals Bill (1876) 25, 281

Cruelty to Animals Bill (1879) 314

Cubitt, George 130

Cunynghame, Gen. Sir Arthur Augustus Thurlow 252, 267

Cyprus, annexation of 302, 305, 307

Daily News 64, 107, 420, 429

Daily Telegraph 79, 123–124, 198, 298, 305, 430

Davitt, Michael 391

de Grey, George Frederick Samuel Robinson, Earl (*see* Ripon, George Frederick Samuel Robinson, 1st Marquess of)

de Ligne, Prince Charles-Joseph 449

de Vesci, Thomas Veasey, 3rd Viscount of Abbeyleix 164

Delagoa Bay, Mozambique 267

Delamere, Hugh Cholmondley, 2nd Baron 179

Delane, John Thadeus: invited to Highclere 79; hostility to government 117; on the state of Ireland 120–121; urges creation of new Conservative newspaper 130; on Carnarvon's resignation 160; on 1866 Reform Bill 161, 174, 177

Delaney, Revd Dr William 392

Derby, Edward George Stanley, 14th Earl of: forms new administration 4; offers Carnarvon Under-Secretaryship at Colonial Office 4, 95–96; Jewish Oaths Bill 101; fall of government 5, 110; forms another administration 7; appoints Carnarvon as Colonial Secretary 7; Carnarvon on 114, 145, 146, 167, 265–266, 469, 470; questions about Derby's leadership 117, 121; on the Oaths Bill 122; tensions between Derby and Disraeli 125–126, 150, 158; 1866 Reform Bill policy 8; Cabinet differences on Reform 134; action on Fenian convicts 135, 136; on *Alabama* claims 137; meeting of Peers in Downing Street on Reform 147, 163–164; brings forward Reform Bill in Cabinet 151; and Peel, Cranborne, and Carnarvon's joint action in the Cabinet 152–153; Carnarvon meets Derby 155; and Carnarvon's resignation 156; attacks Carnarvon 165; inflammatory speech, 'leap in the dark' 168; final illness 180; last meeting with Carnarvon 184; death 15

Derby, Edward Henry Stanley, 15th Earl of: strikes up friendship with Carnarvon 4, 93, 99; shared love of classics 10; work as Colonial Secretary 97; moves to India Office 4, 99; on Carnarvon's effectiveness 87; long discussion with Carnarvon on future leadership 125; and Reform Bills 128; discusses Reform with Carnarvon 140; as possible Leader in the Lords 187–191; as 15th Earl 201; Carnarvon's opinion that Derby would make the best Leader 202; views on taking office under Disraeli 207–208; on Langalibalele's detention 22; Queen Victoria on 265–266; his irresolute attitude to Turkey 26; and Cabinet differences over annexation of Transvaal 292; and state of Cabinet over Eastern Question 28; and Turkish atrocities 293; joins Carnarvon and Salisbury in Cabinet against war 28; reveals Cabinet secrets to

Shuvalov 30; alliance in Cabinet with Carnarvon 30; withdraws resignation 30; finally resigns 31; on Carnarvon 32; reaction to Carnarvon's proposed appointment as Governor-General of Canada 299; disapproves of Frederick Stanley's appointment to War Office 301–302, 306; discusses with Carnarvon possibilities of taking office again 302–303; joins Liberal Party 40; resigns from the Carlton 317

Derby, Frederick Arthur Stanley, 16th Earl of: Carnarvon's views on 88; attendance in the Commons 205; brother's views on 306; on Egyptian expedition 346, 348

Derby, Mary Sackville-West, Marchioness of Salisbury, Countess of 19, 24, 28, 245; on 14th Earl of Derby 201; talk with Carnarvon on future leadership of party 202; on 15th Earl of Derby 202; conversations with Carnarvon 211, 249, 258, 272, 287, 296, 299, 302; discusses break-up of the Cabinet with Carnarvon 286, 290–291; on Cabinet events 292

Denison, John Evelyn, later 1st Viscount Ossington 119

Devonshire, Spencer Compton Cavendish, 8th Duke of (see Hartington, Spencer Compton Cavendish, Marquess of, later 8th Duke of Devonshire)

Dilke, Sir Charles Wentworth, 2nd Baronet 46, 355, 360

Discontinuation of Writs Bill (1889) 75, 453

Disraeli, Benjamin, later 1st Earl of Beaconsfield: visits Highclere 6; on the 1866 Reform Bill 8, 9, 119, 120; on Party leadership 121; conversations with Carnarvon on Reform 122, 132–133, 146; and Cabinet differences on Reform 134; meets Carnarvon on Intercolonial Railway Guarantee 145; his alternative plan for franchise, 'plurality of votes' 148–149; and dissensions in Cabinet on Reform 152, 155; Derby greatly influenced by 158; political conversion to Conservatism 161; Salisbury's death and Disraeli's political isolation as Prime Minister 173; resignation 176; gives up idea of Prime Ministership 188; Salisbury's

dislike of 189, 191, 192, 193; the Judicature Bill 203; discussions with Carnarvon on Cairns 203–204; on 14th Earl of Derby and Salisbury 205; Prime Minister and Cabinet-making 210–211; supposed marriage to Lady Chesterfield 217; first meeting with Bismarck 220; the Endowed Schools Bill 228–229; apologizes to Salisbury for speech in Commons 231; attitude to Fiji question 232; allows Carnarvon free hand at Colonial Office 21, 233; sends Salisbury as plenipotentiary to Constantinople Conference 25; illness 234, 238, 243; Carnarvon's judgement of 235, 324, 325; method of working 239; complains of interference by the Queen 249; political implications of his retirement 257, 266; on Unseaworthy Ships Bill 259; relations with Lady Bradford 266; offers Board of Trade to Cave 268; offers Carnarvon Viceroyalty of India 269–271; difficulties with Ward Hunt 273; offers Carnarvon the Admiralty 273, 274–275, 279; on Carnarvon's character 86; pro-Turkish stance 26; becomes Earl of Beaconsfield 26; on naval strength in Mediterranean 281; on Salisbury 284; speculation on his retirement over Eastern Question 286; increasingly in Queen Victoria's confidence 299; attacks Carnarvon and Salisbury in Cabinet 27; absolute supremacy over Cabinet 306; triumphal return from Congress of Berlin 33, 306; Cabinet manoeuvres 28; Queen Victoria at Hughenden 28; on Carnarvon's disloyalty 29; invites Carnarvon to meeting of Peers 40; requests Carnarvon to accept chairmanship of Royal Commission on Agricultural Distress 314–315; reconciliation with Carnarvon 321; final illness 323–324; death 325; Froude on 465

Dongola, Sudan 387

Downing Street 102, 146, 147, 163

Du Cane, Sir Charles 401

Dublin 52, 57, 388, 400, 426

Dublin Castle 52, 57, 388, 391, 396, 417, 418

Duckworth, Revd Robinson 264

Dufferin and Ava, Frederick Temple Blackwood, 1st Marquess of 295; Carnarvon's admiration for 85, 225; on sentencing Lépine 239; the British Columbia difficulty 297; Dufferin's possible parentage 401

Duffy, Sir Charles Gavan: criticisms of Carnarvon on Irish policy xv; at Highclere 42; publishes article favouring Home Rule 51; meets Carnarvon on Home Rule 389; letter to Carnarvon in the *Freeman's Journal* 396

Dunraven, Edwin Richard Wyndham-Quin, 3rd Earl of 93

Dunraven, Windham Thomas Wyndham-Quin, 4th Earl of 328, 366

Earle, Ralph Anstruther 304

Edgcumbe, William Henry (*see* Mount-Edgcumbe, William Henry Edgcumbe, 4th Earl of)

Edinburgh, Prince Alfred Ernest Albert, Duke of 214, 217

Edinburgh, Princess Marie Alexandrovna, Duchess of 214

Eduard, Prince Wilhelm August 418

Edwards, Sir Henry 117

Edwards, John Passmore 130

Egerton, Wilbraham, later 2nd Baron 93

Eglinton, Archibald William Montgomerie, 13th Earl of 96

Egypt: bombardment of 339, 346, 347; proposed conference on 348; vote of censure of policy 350; Carnarvon's speech on 463

Elcho, Lord Francis Charteris Douglas, later 10th Earl of Wemyss and March 118, 124, 127, 353, 354

Elementary Education Act (1870) 13–14

Elementary Education (Compulsory Attendance) Bill (1875), defeated 248

Eliot, George (Mary Ann Evans) 12

Ellenborough, Edward Towry Hamilton Law, 1st Earl of 87, 98

Elliot, Sir George 355

Elliot, Sir Henry George 281, 289

Elliot, Sir Thomas 103

Ely, Jane, Marchioness of 24

Empire Club 374

Employers Liability Bill (1881) 41, 321–322

Endowed School Bills (1874) 14, 222, 225, 226; disagreements in Cabinet over 228, 229, 230

Enfield, George Henry Charles Byng, 2nd Viscount, and 3rd Earl of Strafford 312

Escott, Thomas Hay Sweet 304

Established Church (Ireland) Bill (1868) 15, 160, 170, 174–175, 179; Carnarvon communicates with Granville over 180; second reading 180–181; Lowe on 181–182; Kimberley on 183; committee stage 183–184; compromise solution 185

Eton College 2, 13, 253–254

Eucla, West Australia 69–70

Eyre, Edward John 240

Fawcett, Henry 257

Fayrer, Sir Joseph 260

Featherstone, Dr Isaac Earl 189, 214

Fenianism 131, 135, 136, 394, 398

Ferguson, Sir James 249, 449

Fiji, annexation of 23, 211, 216, 217, 227, 228, 229, 230, 231, 232, 236, 244, 253, 295

Finch, Heneage (*see* Aylesford, Heneage Finch, 7th Earl of)

Fisher, Charles 105

FitzGerald, Lord John David 453

FitzGibbon, Gerald, acts as intermediary between Carnarvon and Churchill on Home Rule plan 59, 76, 454–455, 456, 457

Fitzwilliam, William Wentworth, 2nd Earl 418

Forester, Revd Orlando Watkin Weld 233

Forrest, John, 1st Baron 71

Forster, William Edward 286, 299, 307

Forster, William S. 387, 419, 433

Fortescue, Chichester Samuel, later 1st Baron Carlingford 183, 300, 328

Franchise Bill (1884) 45–50, 79; conference on 346; second reading 348, 351; Conservative plans to reject 350; Carnarvon moves adjournment on 352; Gladstone's overture to Salisbury 353; Carnarvon to act as intermediary 359–360; rapidly passes through stages 367; in Lords 367; committee stage, House of Lords 375

Freeman-Mitford, John Thomas (*see* Redesdale, John Thomas Freeman-Mitford, 1st Earl)

Freeman's Journal 396

Freemasonry: Carnarvon's involvement 18–19, 283, 337, 424; Carnarvon's discussion with Prince of Wales 239

Frere, Sir Henry Bartle Edward 23, 253, 255, 312, 313

Froude, James Anthony: interviews with Carnarvon 218, 219; sent to South Africa by Carnarvon 22, 226–227; and South African matters 249, 267; dines with Tennyson and Carnarvon 286–287; character 308; on Carlyle 344; on Irish matters 428, 448; editing Disraeli's letters 465–466

Fuad Pasha 162, 165

Gallipoli 30, 294

Galt, Sir Alexander Tilloch 104, 153

Galton, Sir Douglas Strutt 261

Galway 56, 57, 399

Gambia 247, 259, 260, 267, 270, 283

Gascoyne-Cecil, James Brownlow (see Salisbury, James Brownlow Gascoyne-Cecil, 2nd Marquess of)

Gascoyne-Cecil, Robert Arthur Talbot (see Salisbury, Robert Arthur Talbot Gascoyne-Cecil, Viscount Cranborne, later 3rd Marquess of)

Gathorne-Hardy, Gathorne (see Hardy, Gathorne Gathorne-)

Gavard, Charles-René 259

Gedling, Nottinghamshire 233, 234

Gibson, Edward, later 1st Baron Ashbourne: meetings on Irish Land Bill 326, 329; appointed Lord Chancellor of Ireland 53, 384, 385, 389; views on Ireland 390; intermediary for Carnarvon–Parnell meeting 54–55; and Cabinet meetings 57, 392, 397; Carnarvon's views on 84; important conversation with Carnarvon on policy 404; supports Carnarvon in Cabinet 409; on Irish policy in Cabinet 413–414; on Home Rule Bill 426

Gibson, John George 394

Giffard, Hardinge Stanley, later 1st Earl of Halsbury 448

Gillooly, Laurence, Bishop of Elphin 400

Gladstone, Catherine 98, 131

Gladstone, William Ewart: sent by Carnarvon to Ionian Islands as High Commissioner 5, 85, 106–108, 345–346; fall of Gladstone-Russell ministry 8; involvement with Mrs Thistlethwayte 131; alarmed by 1866 Reform Bill 150, 157; sees Carnarvon on Reform 158; introduces but fails to secure Irish University Bill 15, 19; resignation 209; and collapse of opposition to Public Worship Regulation Bill 228; advocates Home Rule and disestablishment 232; pamphlet on the Bulgarian atrocities 27; Queen Victoria on 265; discusses Eastern Question with Carnarvon 32, 298; fears defection of Liberals in Commons 301; possible coalition government 309; invites Carnarvon to serve on ecclesiastical commission 324; on Irish Land Bill 335; introduces Franchise Bill 45; overtures to Salisbury on Franchise Bill 353; negotiations on Franchise Bill 356, 357, 360, 362, 366; defeat of government 50, 379; Hawarden Kite and Irish Home Rule 61; speech on the Address 415; appointed Prime Minister again 417; introduces Land Purchase and Home Rule Bills 72, 421; parliamentary opposition to Home Rule Bill 422, 423; Home Rule Bill defeated 64; resigns as Prime Minister 65, 435; newspaper correspondence with Carnarvon on Parnell interview 430, 431, 434–435; last meeting with Carnarvon 471

Glasgow 357

Globe 303

Glover, John Hawley 215, 217

Goddard, Ambrose Lethbridge 110

Gold Coast 212, 213, 216, 221, 229, 236, 295

Goodenough, James Graham 217

Gordon, Sir Arthur Charles Hamilton-, later 1st Baron Stanmore 107, 244, 295, 448

Gordon, Maj.-Gen. Charles George: discussion of estimates for Egyptian expedition 346; Conservative policy on 347; death at Khartoum 71, 377

Gordon-Lennox, Charles Henry (see Richmond, Charles Henry Gordon-Lennox, 6th Duke of)

Gorst, Sir John Eldon 58, 429

Goschen, George Joachim, later 1st Viscount Goschen 288, 313, 366, 409, 448, 463

Gower, Lord Ronald 24
Grabham, Dr Michael Comport 52, 82
Graham, Sir James 99
Granville, Granville George Leveson-Gower, 2nd Earl 42; overture to Carnarvon concerning joining Gladstone government 39–40; communications with Carnarvon on Established Church (Ireland) Bill 180; cautious approach to Bulgarian atrocities 285; on Armenian situation 314; debate on Irish Land Bill 328, 335; on French *Recidiviste* question 354; his incompetence in the Lords 356; private negotiations on Franchise Bill 357; debate on Queen's Speech 360; on second reading of Franchise Bill 367, 371; and vote of censure on Sudan expedition 378; lively speech on Coercion Bill 444; at Royal Academy dinner 470
Granville, Dr Joseph Mortimer 467, 471
Greek massacre (1870), death of Edward Herbert and companions 16–17; funeral 17
Greenwood, Frederick: weekends at Highclere 79; discusses Colonial affairs with Carnarvon 267; on Eastern Question 305; important discussion with Carnarvon on Franchise Bill 354, 369; attitude to Ireland 427
Greg, Percy 424
Gregory, Sir William Henry: interview with Carnarvon on Ceylon 222; and Prince of Wales's forthcoming visit to Ceylon 262–263, 265
Grenville, Richard Plantagenet (*see* Buckingham and Chandos, Richard Plantagenet Grenville, 3rd Duke of)
Greville, Charles Cavendish Fulke 239
Grey, Gen. Charles 133, 136
Grey, Sir Edward, 3rd Baronet, later Viscount Grey of Falloden 348
Grey, Sir George 111–112
Grey, Sir George, 2nd Baronet 126
Grey, Henry George, Viscount Howick, later 3rd Earl: memorandum on 1866 Reform Bill 134; discusses Reform Bill with Carnarvon 162; at meeting on Reform Bill 164–165; Carnarvon writes to Grey on 1867 resignation 10; depressed with politics

168; Carnarvon comments to Grey on 1878 resignation 88
Grey, Sir William 214
Grey–Seaton Constitution (1849) 105–106
Greystoke Castle, Cumberland 34, 82, 357, 409, 410
Grillion's, London 173, 203
Griqualand West, Cape Province, annexation of 22
Grosvenor, Hugh Lupus, 1st Duke of Westminster 120, 122, 126, 127
Grosvenor, Richard, 2nd Marquess of Westminster 120, 121, 122
Grosvenor, Richard de Aquila, later 1st Baron Stalbridge 362–363
Gull, Sir William Withey 178, 270, 380

Haig, Capt. Arthur Balfour 295
Halifax, Charles Wood, 1st Viscount 166
Hallett, Lilias Sophia Ashworth 49, 375
Halsbury, Hardinge Stanley Giffard, 1st Earl of (*see* Giffard, Hardinge Stanley)
Hamilton, Sir Edward Walter 40, 350
Hamilton, Lord George Francis 86, 233; reduces naval budget for Churchill 440
Hamilton, James (*see* Abercorn, James Hamilton, 1st Duke of)
Hamilton, Dr John 224
Hamilton, Sir Robert George Crookshank: member of Colonial Defence Commission 42; Permanent Under-Secretary, Ireland 389, 393, 404; possible author of Home Rule plan 421; Governor of Tasmania 73
Hamilton-Gordon, George (*see* Aberdeen, George Hamilton-Gordon, 4th Earl of)
Hampshire: Carnarvon appointed Lord Lieutenant of County and member of County Council 74–75
Hampton, Sir John Somerset Pakington, 1st Baron (*see* Pakington, Sir John Somerset)
Harcourt, George, Marquis d' 292
Harcourt, Sir William George Venables Vernon 174, 232
Hardinge, Sir Arthur xv–xvi
Hardinge, Charles Stewart, 2nd Viscount 164, 175, 447
Hardwicke, Charles Philip Yorke, 5th Earl of 295

Hardy, Gathorne Gathorne-, later 1st Earl of Cranbrook 41, 80, 81, 147, 160, 189, 208, 218, 219, 232, 258, 261, 291, 379, 403, 408, 415; attitude to 1866 Reform Bill 128; discusses Bill with Carnarvon and Cranborne 151–152; considers Carnarvon unsuitable as Leader in the Lords 16; settles with Carnarvon on workmen's compact 200; conversation with Carnarvon 201; on Public Worship Regulation Bill 214, 220, 227, 230; as possible Leader, House of Commons 225; and new Whitehall building 222–223; on Endowed Schools Bill 228, 229; appointed to India Office 301; on Indian Museum 316; on Arrears Bill 342; candidate for Chief Secretary for Ireland 62; favours proclaiming the National League 413; Carnarvon's relations with 85

Hares and Rabbits Bill (1880) 321–322
Harrel, Sir David 404
Harris, George Robert Canning Harris, 4th Baron 453
Harris, James Howard (see Malmesbury, James Howard Harris, 3rd Earl of)
Harrow School 13
Harrowby, Dudley Ryder, 2nd Earl of (see Sandon, Dudley Ryder, Viscount)
Harrowby, Dudley Francis Stuart Ryder, 3rd Earl of (see Sandon, Dudley Francis Stuart, Viscount)
Hart Dyke, Sir William, 2nd Baronet: speech on Representation of the People Bill 355; appointed Chief Secretary, Ireland 52, 456; arrives in Dublin 52, 388; complains of his subsidiary role 62; on Educational Endowments (Ireland) Bill 396; on security matters 398; hopeful on election prospects 404; discusses Irish affairs with Carnarvon 405; favours government resignation 407; meeting at Irish Office 413; resigns 414
Hartington, Spencer Compton Cavendish, Marquess of, later 8th Duke of Devonshire: attitude to Eastern Question 285; at Hatfield 288; on Russo-Turkish Treaty 300; member of Cabinet Committee on Franchise Bill 46; favours limited Redistribution Bill 363, 364; rejects Salisbury's offer

to become Prime Minister 65, 437; joins Churchill and Carnarvon in promoting Irish conciliatory policy 77, 456, 457, 458–459; supports Churchill's desire for appointment as Secretary for War 449; Carnarvon's views on 85–86; meets Carnarvon 459; favours Provincial Councils 462
Hastings, Lieut.-Gen. Francis William 448
Hatfield House, Hertfordshire 163, 169, 177, 187–188, 199, 205, 227, 242, 257, 258, 287, 288–289, 385, 397, 398, 408
Hawarden Kite 61
Hayward, Abraham 99
Head, Sir Edmund Walker 7, 104, 105, 143
Heathcote, Sir William 9, 32, 41, 50, 119, 124, 157, 158, 162; advises Carnarvon to accept office 96; possible peerage 133; urges Carnarvon to retain High Stewardship of Oxford University 168–169; on political prospects 170; told of Disraeli's high opinion of Carnarvon 19
Henley, Joseph Warner 110, 119, 124, 128
Herbert, Auberon Edward William Molyneux (diarist's brother) 3, 110, 364
Herbert, Aubrey Nigel Molyneux (diarist's son) 34, 82, 357, 467
Herbert, Edward Charles Hugh (diarist's cousin), murdered in Greece 16–17
Herbert, Lady Eveline, later Countess of Portsmouth (diarist's sister) 1, 83, 269, 305, 420, 429
Herbert, Frances G.C. (diarist's cousin) 307
Herbert, Lady Gwendoline Ondine (diarist's sister) 262, 269
Herbert, Henry Arthur 124–125
Herbert, Lady Margaret (diarist's daughter) 5, 254, 293, 412
Herbert, Mervyn Robert Howard Molyneux (diarist's son) 34, 82, 467
Herbert, Sir Robert George Wyndham (diarist's cousin) 236, 269, 276, 305, 379, 383, 397, 398, 405, 407, 412, 420, 425, 431, 435, 468, 469; on scope of Carnarvon's work at Colonial Office 20; on occupation of Cyprus 305; overseas investments 69; on Redistribution scheme 364, 365; death of Gordon 377; discusses Irish matters with Carnarvon 402; advises Carnarvon not to seek overseas post

81; on new Salisbury government 65, 434; advises Carnarvon not to return to England 72, 422; on the offer of Cape government post for Carnarvon 81, 461

Herbert, Robert Sayer 35

Herbert, Sidney, later 1st Baron 98–99

Herbert, Lady Victoria ('Vera') (diarist's daughter) 5, 409

Herbert, Lady Winifred Anne Henrietta (diarist's daughter) 5, 254, 257, 258, 313

Herberts of Highclere (1887) 10

Herschell, Sir Farrer, later 1st Baron 82, 331, 448

Herzegovina, revolt in 26

Hibernian Bank 53, 393

Hicks Beach, Sir Michael Edward, later 1st Earl St Aldwyn 176, 215, 268, 397, 458; as Chief Secretary, Ireland 270, 272, 438; appointed Colonial Secretary 32, 295, 297; friendship with Carnarvon 39; negotiates with Carnarvon on Colonial Defence Commission 315; on Franchise and Redistribution question 47, 361, 365; later parsimonious attitude to Carnarvon as Chancellor of Exchequer 56, 58, 401, 402; Cabinet dissension over the National League 419; deposed as Leader of Commons 66, 438; Carnarvon's views on 85, 87–88

Highclere Castle, Hampshire 11–12, 29, 37, 42, 67, 68, 132, 133, 168, 169, 170, 215, 216, 228, 229, 231, 236, 237, 266, 267, 270, 278, 279, 289, 290, 328, 329, 331, 332, 333, 343, 344, 345, 346, 361, 365, 375, 403, 423, 425, 428, 430, 431, 432, 434, 435, 436, 437, 438, 439, 448, 461, 465, 467; as centre for entertaining Ministers 5; rebuilding of 6; Transvaal delegates at 293

Hindlip, Henry Allsopp, 1st Baron 70

Holland, Henry Richard Vassall Fox, 3rd Baron 42

Holland, Sir Henry Thurstan, later 1st Viscount Knutsford 76, 276, 315; Carnarvon's views on 88; appointed Colonial Secretary 443

Holland House, London 162

Holmes, Sir Richard Rivington 406

Home Rule Bill (1886) 63–64, 72; introduced by Gladstone 421;

discussions over 422–423, 424–425; second reading 425; difficulties 426

Hong Kong 271

Horsford, Gen. Alfred Hastings 233

Horsman, Edward 122, 127, 157, 225

House of Lords (Discontinuance of Writs) Bill (1889) (*see* Discontinuation of Writs Bill (1889))

Howard, Sir Edward Stafford 388

Howard, Sir Esmé William, later 1st Baron Howard of Penrith 403, 409, 412

Howard, Lady Rachel 388

Howe, Joseph 139

Howorth, Sir Henry Hoyle 425, 436, 454

Hudson Bay Company 113, 143

Hugessen, Edward Hugessen Knatchbull-, later 1st Baron Brabourne 166, 167

Hughenden Manor, Buckinghamshire 28, 200

Hughes, Thomas 12

Hunt, George Ward (*see* Ward Hunt, George)

Hyde Park Riots (1866) 8

Iddesleigh, Sir Stafford Henry Northcote, 1st Earl of (*see* Northcote, Sir Stafford Henry)

Ignatiev, Nikolai Pavlovich 286, 287, 288–289

Imperial Federation League 76

Inchiquin, Edward Donough O'Brien, 14th Baron 342

India, famine in 212, 283, 284, 285, 286

India Office, Carnarvon in charge of 25, 283–286; Carnarvon chairs Indian Council 25, 284

influenza epidemic 467

Ionian Islands, British Protectorate 5; Grey–Seaton Constitution causing problems 105–106; Gladstone dispatched as High Commissioner 85, 106–108, 345–346

Irish Church Bill (1868) (*see* Established Church (Ireland) Bill (1868))

Irish Land Bill (1870) 15; committee stage 194

Irish Land Bill (1881) (*see* Land Law (Ireland) Bill (1881))

Iron Duke 269

Irving, Sir Henry 369

Ishmael Pasha, Khedive of Egypt 273, 276, 277, 278

Jamaica 109, 214
James, Henry, later 1st Baron 449
James, Sir Henry 11
Jekyll, Col. Sir Herbert: appointed Secretary, Colonial Defence Commission 42, 315, 316; work completed at the Commission 44, 333; private secretary to Carnarvon in Ireland 52, 388, 398; private secretary to W.H. Smith in Ireland 416
Jenkinson, Sir Edward George: Under-Secretary for Crime, Ireland 55–56; important conversations with Carnarvon 386, 387; on police protection for Spencer 389; discusses Fenian outrages with Carnarvon 394, 398; on his own position 405
Jenkinson, Henry T. 93
Jersey, Victor Albert Child-Villiers, 7th Earl of 81, 330, 350, 351, 354
Jervois, Sir William Francis Drummond: Governor, Straits Settlements 23–24; proclaims annexation of Perak 271, 272, 276, 277; on sending troops from India 272
Jeune, Francis Henry, later 1st Baron St Helier 83, 368, 372, 375, 409, 447, 470
Jeune, Mary Susan, later Lady St Helier 86–87, 368, 372, 375, 407, 409, 447, 470
Jewish Oaths Bill (1858) 5, 101
Jorissen, Dr Edward 293
Joyce, Myles 58
Judicature Bill (1873) 19, 203, 204, 240, 248; passed 205, 235; stormy Cabinet debate on 241–242

Kavanagh, Arthur MacMorrough 416
Keenan, Sir Patrick Joseph 412
Keith-Falconer, Algernon (see Kintore, Algernon Keith-Falconer, 9th Earl of)
Kellner, Sir George Welsh, sent to Dublin concerning collapse of Bank of Ireland 53, 394, 395, 396
Kent, John 2, 3, 102
Keppel, William Coutts (see Bury, William Coutts Keppel, Viscount)
Khartoum 347, 377
Kilkerran, Co. Cork 399
Kimberley, John Wodehouse, 1st Earl of 160, 322, 328, 448: reorganizes Colonial Office 20; on Colonial Defence Commission 43–44; con-

versation with Carnarvon 161–162; on Established Church (Ireland) Bill 183; superseded by Carnarvon at the Colonial Office 211; Zulu insurrection 223
King, Edward, Bishop of Lincoln 452
King-Harman, Col. Edward Robert 400
Kingsley, Charles 11, 344
Kintore, Algernon Keith-Falconer, 9th Earl of 437
Knebworth House, Hertfordshire 103, 104
Kneeton, Nottinghamshire 35
Knollys, Sir Francis 263, 278
Knowsley Hall, Lancashire 201, 202
Knutsford, Sir Henry Thurstan Holland, 1st Viscount (see Holland, Sir Henry Thurstan)
Kruger, Paul 293

Labouchere, Henry Du Pré 451
Lamington, Alexander Dundas Ross Baillie-Cochrane, 1st Baron (see Cochrane, Alexander Dundas Ross Baillie-)
Land Law (Ireland) Bill (1881) 50; introduced 323, 325; second and third readings 328; meetings at Northcote's 329, 330, 331, 336, 337; Gladstone's compromise 332; Committee on 335
Land League 56
Land Purchase (Ireland) Bill (1885) 54, 55, 455
Land Transfer Bill (1889) 460
Landseer, Sir Edwin Henry 173
Langalibalele 22, 237, 240
Langevin, Sir Hector-Louis 144
Lansdowne, Henry Charles Keith Petty-Fitzmaurice, 5th Marquess of 323, 331, 444; on 1866 Reform Bill 121; on Irish Land Bill 328; at meeting of Lords and Commons on Franchise Bill 354
Lathom, Edward Bootle-Wilbraham, 2nd Baron Skelmersdale, later 1st Earl of 340, 350
Law, Edward Towry Hamilton (see Ellenborough, Edward Towry Hamilton Law, 1st Earl of)
Lawley, Francis Charles 124
Lawrence, John Laird Mair, 1st Baron 112
Lees, Revd James Cameron 262
Leigh, Gilbert Henry Chandos 233
Leitrim, Robert Bermingham, 4th Earl of 340

Lempriere, C.P. 70
Lennox, Lord Henry Charles George Gordon 205, 223, 277
Leo XIII, Pope 423–424
Leopold, Prince (see Albany, Leopold George Duncan Albert, Duke of)
Lépine, Ambroise-Dydime 239, 240
Leveson-Gower, Edward Frederick 405
Leveson-Gower, Granville George (see Granville, Granville George Leveson-Gower, 2nd Earl)
Lichfield, Thomas George Anson, 2nd Earl of 122
Liddell, Henry George (see Ravensworth, Henry George Liddell, 2nd Earl of)
Liddon, Henry Parry 171
Life Peers Bill (1888) 75
Lister, Joseph, 1st Baron 254
Local Government Bill (1858) 100
Local Government Bill (1888) 5, 73–74
Loch, Sir Henry Brougham, later 1st Baron 461
Loftus, Augustus William Frederick Spencer 222
London County Council 74
Lord Chesterfield's Letters to his Godson (1889) 10–11, 452
Lorne, John Douglas Sutherland Campbell, Marquess of 47, 260
Lorne, Princess Louise, Marchioness of 260
Lothian, William Schomberg Robert Kerr, 8th Marquess of 93
Lovaine, Algernon George Percy, Lord (see Northumberland, Algernon George Percy, Lord Lovaine, later 6th Duke of)
Lowe, Robert, later 1st Viscount Sherbrooke 117, 125, 126, 127, 167, 232, 287; as leader of the Adullamites 8; views on 1866 Reform Bill 119–120, 123; at Highclere 134, 140–141; sees Lady Carnarvon on Reform 148; in despair at Reform Bill 160–161; on Established Church (Ireland) Bill 181–182, 183; on Irish Land Bill 323
Lowell, James Russell 448
Lowther, James 212
Loyd-Lindsay, Robert James (see Wantage, Robert James Loyd-Lindsay, 1st Baron)
Lubbock, Sir John, later 1st Baron Avebury 34

Lucan, George Charles Bingham, 3rd Earl of 101, 102, 160
Lumsden, Lt.-Gen. Sir Peter 387
Lygon, Frederick (see Beauchamp, Frederick Lygon, 6th Earl of)
Lyndhurst, John Singleton Copley, 1st Baron (see Copley, John Singleton, 1st Baron Lyndhurst)
Lyons, Admiral Edmund, 1st Baron 4
Lyons, Richard Bickerton Pemell, 2nd Baron: Carnarvon discusses possibility of removing Derby from Foreign Office 241–242; as possible Foreign Secretary 258; tells Carnarvon that Ignatiev is at Hatfield 287; views on Congress of Berlin 300
Lytton, Edward George Earle Lytton-Bulwer-, 1st Baron Lytton 93, 109, 112, 113; friendship with Carnarvon 4, 93; becomes Colonial Secretary 4–5; character 99–100, 114–115; illness 103, 111; Gladstone and the Ionian Islands 106, 345–346
Lytton, Edward Robert Bulwer, 1st Earl of: offered Viceroyalty of India 279; secret instructions to seize Afghanistan 309

Maamtrasna murder case (1882) 58–59, 391, 425; Parnell's motion on 393
McCarthy, Justin: meets with Vincent on Parnell 53–54; meets Carnarvon 389, 390; letter to 392; denounced by Parnell 456
McCraw, James 383, 385, 387, 430
Macdonald, Sir John Alexander: with Canadian delegates in London 139, 145–146, 153; discusses 1866 Reform Bill with Carnarvon 150; Carnarvon's visit to Canada 72; discusses Ireland with Carnarvon 370; speaks at Empire Club 374; Carnarvon writes to him on relinquishing post in Ireland 61
Mackay, Donald James (see Reay, Donald James Mackay, 11th Baron)
MacKenzie, Alexander 225
MacMillan, Sir Frederick Orridge 426
Magee, William Connor, Bishop of Peterborough, later Archbishop of York 213
Mahaffy, Sir John Pentland 418
Mahmud II, Sultan of the Ottoman Empire 282

Maine, Sir Henry James Sumner 285

Maintenance of Social Order (Ireland) Bill (1886) 421

Malcolm, William Rolle 225, 226, 282

Mallet, Sir Louis 283

Malmesbury, James Howard Harris, 3rd Earl of 106, 166, 187, 188, 191, 238

Malta 108; Indian troops sent to 325–326

Manchester, William Drogo Montagu, 7th Duke of 188, 267

Manners, Charles Cecil John, later 6th Duke of Rutland 118

Manners, Lord John James Robert, later 7th Duke of Rutland: speech in Cabinet on 1866 Reform Bill 134; offered Viceroyalty of India 24–25; attends conference on transport provision for England, Canada, and Japan 272; meetings on Irish Land bill 326, 329; active in Franchise Bill proceedings 48, 348, 368; condemns Conservative co-operation on redistribution 372; Disraeli's contempt for 465

Manning, Cardinal Henry Edward 386, 404

Mansel, Revd Henry Longueville 133

Marlborough, Frances Anne Emily, Duchess of 464

Marlborough, John Winston Spencer Churchill, 7th Duke of 211

Martin, Sir Theodore 303

Mary I, Queen of Scotland (Mary, Queen of Scots) 265

Matrimonial Causes Bill (1857) 93

Matthews, Henry, later 1st Viscount Llandaff 439

May, Sir Thomas Erskine 47, 362–363, 372

Mayhew, Henry 195

Mayne, Sir Richard 137

Mayo, Richard Southwell Bourke Naas, 6th Earl of 136, 175

Meade, Sir Robert Henry 260

Medical Practitioners Bill (1858) 5, 100

Merchant Shipping Bill (1875) (see Unseaworthy Ships Bill (1875))

Merivale, Herman 103, 111

Mill, John Stuart 170, 171

Milne, Sir Alexander 42, 43–44, 315, 316

Molloy, Father Gerard 391, 392, 396

Monck, Charles Stanley, 1st Baron: attends meeting with delegates on British North America Bill 8; and threat of

Fenian invasions in Canada 131, 135; more discussions on Confederation 144–145

Monroe, John 416

Montagu, William Drogo (see Manchester, William Drogo Montagu, 7th Duke of)

Montgomerie, Archibald William (see Eglinton, Archibald William Montgomerie, 13th Earl of)

Morley, Albert Edmund Parker, 3rd Earl of 314

Morley, John, later Viscount Morley of Blackburn 470

Morning Post 216

Morris, Michael, 1st Baron 401, 402

Mount-Edgcumbe, William Henry Edgcumbe, 4th Earl of 371

Mulhar Rao, Gaekwar of Baroda 252, 255–256

Mundella, Anthony John 63, 309

Munster Bank, financial crisis 52–53, 57, 392, 395

Murad V, Sultan of the Ottoman Empire 282

Naas, Richard Southwell Bourke (see Mayo, Richard Southwell Bourke Naas, 6th Earl of)

Napier, Field Marshal Robert Cornelis, 1st Baron Napier of Magdala 298

Natal 216, 226, 236, 240, 248, 261, 267, 273; Carnarvon's conversation with Shepstone 242; Carnarvon's conversations with Colenso 237, 244

National Association for the Promotion of Social Science 14

National Bank of Ireland (see Bank of Ireland)

National League 50, 56, 60, 63, 413, 414–415, 417, 419, 424

National Review 37, 80, 81, 348

Naval Defence Act (1889) 452

Neeld, Sir John 111

Nevill, Lady Dorothy Fanny: on Carnarvon's first wife's ambitions 87; at Highclere 141; on Churchill's extravagance 448

Nevill, William (see Abergavenny, William Nevill, 1st Marquess of)

New Brunswick 104–105

New Code (1889) 460

New Guinea 216, 267

Newcastle, Henry Pelham Fiennes Pelham-Clinton, 5th Duke of 111

Norfolk House, London 300

North American Confederation Bill (1867) (*see* British North American Confederation Bill (1867))

Northbrook, Thomas George Baring, 1st Earl: on Indian affairs 26, 255, 284, 444; possible discontinuance of Colonial Defence Commission 43; resigns as Viceroy of India 268; on Admiralty matters 374–375, 452

Northcote, Cecilia Frances, later Lady Iddesleigh 380

Northcote, Sir Henry Stafford, resigns office 443

Northcote, Sir Stafford Henry, later 1st Earl of Iddesleigh 46, 81, 212, 215, 219, 238, 239, 241, 255, 259, 272, 276, 288, 299, 330, 332, 350, 354, 403, 437; friendship with Carnarvon 39, 84, 317; on 1866 Reform Bill 119, 121; discussions with Carnarvon on party leadership 121, 122, 125; agreement with Carnarvon on Reform scheme 134; on Endowed Schools Bill 225, 228; on Public Worship Regulation Bill 227; Disraeli's state of health 253; discusses government affairs with Carnarvon 266; visits Carnarvon 267–268; Carnarvon seeks advice on Viceroy of India post 269; on Disraeli's Cabinet problems 273; gives Carnarvon advice on Admiralty post 274; talks with Carnarvon on Cabinet matters 289; on Carnarvon's objections to the size of Royal Commission on Agricultural Distress 315; appointed Leader in the Commons 41; meetings on Irish Land Bill 326, 329; ex-Cabinet meetings at Northcote's house 330, 335, 337, 338; discusses future with Carnarvon 341, 353; on Arrears Bill 342; on Franchise Bill 346, 348, 362, 364, 366, 368, 371, 372, 373–374; Aston Park meeting 358; vote of censure on the Sudan expedition 378; sounds out Carnarvon on Ireland 51; meets Carnarvon on taking office 380–381; illness 382; resigns office 443; death 444

Northumberland, Algernon George Percy, Lord Lovaine, later 6th Duke of 155, 329, 330

Northumberland House, London 155, 159

Norton, Charles Bowyer Adderley, 1st Baron (*see* Adderley, Charles Bowyer, 1st Baron Norton)

Nova Scotia 104–105, 132, 140, 272

O'Brien, R. Barry xv

O'Connell, Daniel 370

O'Donoghue, Daniel 124

Odyssey, Carnarvon's translation of 10, 71, 421, 426

O'Keefe, John 222

Osborne House, Isle of Wight 29, 65, 126, 146, 217, 248, 260, 292, 299, 437

Ossington, John Evelyn Denison, 1st Viscount (*see* Denison, John Evelyn)

Overstone, Samuel Jones Loyd, 1st Baron 337

Oxford University 2, 5, 12–13, 14, 171; Carnarvon's retention of the High Stewardship 168–169; Christ Church 2, 94, 402

Paget, Sir Richard Horner 234

Pakington, Sir John Somerset, later 1st Baron Hampton: active in 1866 Reform Bill debates 127, 134, 143; mover of secret working men's compact 197–200

Pall Mall Gazette 64, 79, 289, 300, 404, 421, 428, 441, 443

Palmer, Sir Roundell, later 1st Earl of Selborne: on the Land Bill 328; speech on Franchise Bill 352

Palmerston, Henry John Temple, 3rd Viscount 4, 110, 327, 370; becomes Prime Minister 103; method of working at Foreign Office 219

Parliamentary Oaths Amendment Bill (1866) 119, 121, 122

Parnell, Charles Stewart 50, 53, 420, 456, 465; meeting with Carnarvon 54–55; Churchill's agreement with 59; on Maamtrasna murders 393; Carnarvon on 415; Carnarvon's alleged overtures to 428, 429, 430, 432; Carnarvon's reply to Parnell in *The Times* 447

Parnell Commission (1888) 448, 451, 468

Patten, John Wilson, 1st Baron Winmarleigh 202
Pauncefote, Sir Julian, later 1st Baron 293
Peace Preservation Bill (1875) 251
Peel, Gen. Jonathan: doubts on new party leadership 121; against conference on 1866 Reform Bill 127; threatens resignation 148; compromises on plurality of votes 149; meeting with Carnarvon 152; isolated in Cabinet with Carnarvon and Cranborne 152–153; resigns from government 9, 155
Peel, Sir Robert, 2nd Baronet 161, 370
Peel, Sir Robert, 3rd Baronet 160
Peel, William Yates 210
Pembroke, George Robert Charles Herbert, 13th Earl of 257
Pender, Sir John 296
Perak, Malaysia 86, 270; rising in 271, 272, 273, 274
Percy, Algernon George (see Northumberland, Algernon George Percy, Lord Lovaine, later 6th Duke of)
Perry, Charles, Bishop of Melbourne 224
Petty-Fitzmaurice, Henry Charles Keith (see Lansdowne, Henry Charles Keith Petty-Fitzmaurice, 5th Marquess of)
Phayre, Sir Arthur Purves 295
Phillimore, Lady Charlotte 83
Phillimore, Sir Robert Joseph 173, 301, 308, 338; assists Gladstone in his appointment to Ionian Islands 106–107, 345, 346; discusses Alabama affair with Carnarvon 137; on Gladstone 158–159; meeting at his house of Carnarvon and Gladstone 32; daughter's description of Carnarvon's death 83
Phoenix Park, Dublin 391
Phoenix Park murders (1882) 338
Pigott, Richard 451
Pine, Sir Benjamin Chilley Campbell 22, 237; appointed governor of St Kitts 113; recalled as governor of Natal 240; sentences Langalibalele 22
Pitt-Rivers, Horace, 6th Baron Rivers 164
Pixton, Somerset xvi, 37, 68, 317, 378–379
Plan of Campaign 76, 357
Plevna, battle of (1877) 28, 293
Plimsoll, Samuel 241, 259, 260
Poerio, Carlo 106

Ponsonby, Sir Henry Frederick 78, 250, 264, 375, 403, 404; describes Carnarvon 3; on Carnarvon's Colonial Office working methods 20; sides with Carnarvon on Eastern Question 29; acts as intermediary in impasse over Franchise Bill 46–47, 359–360, 362, 363, 369
Pope-Hennessy, Sir John 295
Portarlington, Seymour William Dawson-Damer, 4th Earl of 329
Portofino, Italy xvii, 71–72, 75, 377, 419, 420, 421, 422–423, 444, 449, 468, 469
Portsmouth, Lady Eveline, Countess of (see Herbert, Lady Eveline)
Portsmouth, Isaac Newton Wallop, 5th Earl of 429
Powis, Edward James Herbert, 3rd Earl of 24
Primrose, Archibald Philip (see Rosebery, Archibald Philip Primrose, 5th Earl of)
Primrose League 66–68
prison reform 6–7
Prometheus, Carnarvon's translation of 71, 469
Public Worship Regulation Bill (1874) 213–214; Cabinet discussions on 218, 220, 221, 224, 226, 227, 228, 230, 231, 235
Pusey, Edward Bouverie 15, 171

Quarterly Review 80
Queen's Colleges, Dublin 391, 396

Raikes, Henry Cecil 81, 361, 362, 374
Ravensworth, Henry George Liddell, 2nd Earl of 354
Reay, Donald James Mackay, 11th Baron 364, 365, 366
Redesdale, John Thomas Freeman-Mitford, 1st Earl 102, 190, 193, 198
Redington, Christopher Talbot 418
Redistribution Bill (1884) 352, 355, 356, 357, 364, 373
Reform Bill (1832) 161
Reform Bill (1859) 109, 119
Reform Bill (1866) 117–168; committee stage, Commons 162; second reading in the Lords 165; committee stage 166–167; report stage 167; third reading 168

Register of Tithes and Judicature Bill (1874) 213

Reilly, Sir Francis Savage 144

Repton School 13, 204

Reuter, Baron Paul Julius Freiherr von 203

Richmond, Charles Henry Gordon-Lennox, 6th Duke of 9, 26, 46, 118, 223, 324, 353, 361; on joining the government 158; agrees to be Conservative Leader of the House of Lords 16, 26, 188–193; Chairman of Royal Commission on Agricultural Distress 42; disappointment in office 210–211; as possible Prime Minister 243–244, 244–245, 268; quarrel with Sandon 279; urges Carnarvon to return to Opposition Front Bench 41; on Arrears Bill amendments 342; on Agricultural Holdings Bill 343; important conversation with Carnarvon on Franchise Bill 369; Carnarvon's views on 85

Ridley, Sir Matthew White, later 1st Viscount 405

Ripon, George Frederick Samuel Robinson, 1st Marquess of 157, 160, 301, 424

Ritchie, Charles Thomson, 1st Baron Ritchie 354, 374

Ritualistic Practices in the Church of England, Royal Commission on (1868) 177, 184, 187, 192, 325

Rivers, Horace Pitt-Rivers, 6th Baron (see Pitt-Rivers, Horace, 6th Baron Rivers)

Roberts, J.D. Cramer 405, 419

Robinson, George Frederick Samuel (see Ripon, George Frederick Samuel Robinson, 1st Marquess of)

Robinson, Sir Hercules George Robert, later 1st Baron Rosmead 73, 227, 232

Robinson, Sir William Cleaver Francis 296

Roby, Henry John 225, 226

Roebuck, John Arthur 110

Rogers, Sir Frederic, later 1st Baron Blachford 144

Rolle, Charles Henry (see Clinton, Charles Henry Rolle, 20th Baron)

Rollo, John Rogerson, 10th Baron 175

Romney, Charles Marsham, 3rd Earl of 164

Rose, Sir Philip 109

Rosebery, Archibald Philip Primrose, 5th Earl of 287, 306, 444–445; and reform of House of Lords 75–76

Ross, John 104

Ross, Gen. Sir John 271, 272

Ross-of-Bladensburg, Sir John Foster George 423, 425

Rosse, William Parsons, 3rd Earl 170

Rothschild, Baron Ferdinand James de 321, 460, 465

Rowe, Sir Samuel 283

Roxburgh, Susanna Stephanie, Duchess of 254

Royal Academy 173, 219, 291, 470

Royal Commissions (see Agricultural Distress, Royal Commission on; Colonial Defence, Royal Commission on; Ritualistic Practices in the Church of England, Royal Commission on; Vivisection, Royal Commission on)

Ruskin, John 37

Russell, Sir George 439, 448–449

Russell, Lord John, 1st Earl 2; approves of Jewish Oaths Bill 101; role in debate on Reform Bill (1859) 110; on Reform Bill (1866) 129, 158; Carnarvon on his reputation 370

Russell, John Scott 197–198, 199, 200

Russell, Odo William Leopold, later 1st Baron Ampthill 249, 250

Russell, William Henry 263

Russell, William Howard 80, 130

Russo-Turkish War (1877–1878) 26–33, 88, 285, 293, 294, 300–301; secret Anglo-Russian Convention 303–304, 305

Rutland, Charles Cecil John Manners, 6th Duke of (see Manners, Charles Cecil John)

Rutland, Lord John James Robert Manners, 7th Duke of (see Manners, Lord John James Robert)

St Albans Abbey 33–34

St Helier, Francis Henry Jeune, 1st Baron (see Jeune, Francis Henry)

St Helier, Mary Susan Jeune, Lady (see Jeune, Mary Susan)

St James's Club 287

St James's Gazette 79

St James's Square (Derby's house), meetings of Conservative Peers 15, 122, 146, 178–179, 183, 184–185

St Petersburg 78, 463, 464

Salisbury, Georgina, Marchioness of 242, 302

Salisbury, James Brownlow Gascoyne-Cecil, 2nd Marquess of 96; death of 173

Salisbury, Robert Arthur Talbot Gascoyne-Cecil, Viscount Cranborne, later 3rd Marquess of: friendship with Carnarvon 93; opposes *Alabama* claims to arbitration 137; discusses Reform resolutions with Carnarvon 143–144; meets Canadian delegates on legislation 147; forms alliance with Carnarvon over 1866 Reform Bill 8, 150; on Disraeli and the Reform Bill 150; isolated with Peel and Carnarvon 152–153; resigns from government 9, 151, 155; conference with Carnarvon 159; becomes 3rd Marquess 173, 174; resumes place on Front Bench 16; refuses to stand for leadership in Lords 189, 191, 192–193, 197; discusses future position of Disraeli with Carnarvon 192; relations with Disraeli 193; views on workmen's compact 199–200; persuaded by Carnarvon to join Disraeli's government 19–20, 208; accepts India Office 210; confers with Carnarvon on future of the government 225–226, 231; rejects Foreign Office 242; on Derby 257; on Cairns 85; consulted by Carnarvon on Viceroyalty of India 269; discusses Admiralty post with Carnarvon 274; attends conference in Constantinople 25; Russo-Turkish War 26–33; with Derby and Carnarvon accused of disloyalty in Cabinet 27; favours Fleet being sent to Constantinople 27, 290; supports Disraeli 28, 30; on annexation of Transvaal 292; appointed Foreign Secretary 302; returns from Congress of Berlin 306; potential leader of Conservative party 324; meetings on Irish Land Bill 326, 329; meeting of Peers 329–330; 'riding for a fall' 366; leader of Conservative Party 41, 378; negotiations on Franchise Bill in Lords 45–50; accepts office of Prime Minister 50–51, 456; offers Carnarvon Lord Lieutenancy of Ireland 51; attitude towards Carnarvon's meeting with Parnell 54, 55, 64; interview with Carnarvon on provincial councils in Ireland 390;

sees Carnarvon's memorandum on Ireland 403; speaking on Carnarvon in Parliament 415; on Home Rule Bill 424–425, 427, 432–433; advises Carnarvon to remain abroad during Home Rule Bill debate 72; party defeated at general election 61; resigns as Prime Minister 63; preparing to form new government 435–436; reluctance in resuming office 65, 437; forms new government 439; unwell 468; Carnarvon's attempted reconciliation with 468–469

Salt, Thomas 251

Sandford, Francis Richard John, 1st Baron 296

Sandon, Dudley Francis Stuart Ryder, Viscount, later 3rd Earl of Harrowby: tours Asia Minor with Carnarvon 1; quarrel with Richmond 279; discusses Disraeli's successor with Carnarvon 26; friendship with Carnarvon 39, 84, 93; meetings on Irish Land Bill 326, 329; attitude to Franchise Bill 48, 370; on chances of a Conservative government 380; at ex-Cabinet meeting 381–382; advises on expense of Irish post 383–384; meetings with Carnarvon 385–386, 402, 419, 428; Munster Bank crisis 57; advises Carnarvon to stay in Portofino 72, 422–423; important discussion with Salisbury 423, 424

Sandon, Dudley Ryder, Viscount, later 2nd Earl of Harrowby 163, 164–165, 166, 179

Saturday Review 130

Scanderoon, Syria 302

Scarisbrick, William Benedict, Bishop of Mauritius 295

Schliemann, Heinrich 34, 292

Schwabach, Bavaria 385

Sclater-Booth, George, later 1st Baron Basing 239, 248, 268, 271, 276

Scott, Walter Francis (*see* Buccleuch, Walter Francis Scott, 5th Duke of)

Scottish Patronage Bill (1874) (*see* Church Patronage (Scotland) Bill (1874))

Seaton, John Colborne, 1st Baron 105

Selborne, Sir Roundell Palmer, 1st Earl of (*see* Palmer, Sir Roundell)

Selkirk, Dunbar James Douglas Hamilton, 6th Earl of 164

Seward, William Henry 136, 137
Shadows of the Sick Room (1873) 17
Shaftesbury, Anthony Ashley Cooper, 7th Earl of: on Reform Act 123, 164–165; speech on Archbishop's Bill 220–221; on Prince of Wales 327–328; deplores collision between the two Houses 336; death 402
Shaw, William 393
Sheffield, Henry North Holroyd, 3rd Earl of 233
Shelford, Nottinghamshire 35
Shepstone, Sir Theophilus: Carnarvon urges gradual changes in Natal 237; long conversation with Carnarvon 242; Carnarvon effects personal reconciliation between Shepstone and Colenso 244; dispatched by Carnarvon to the Transvaal 23; annexes Transvaal 23, 291
Sher Ali, Ameer of Afghanistan 308
Sherborne, James Henry Legge Dutton, 3rd Baron 167
Sherbrooke, Robert Lowe, 1st Viscount (*see* Lowe, Robert)
Shrewsbury, Henry John Chetwynd-Talbot, 18th Earl of 167
Shuvalov, Count Petr Andreievich: learns Cabinet secrets from Derby 30; dines with the Derbys 221, 240; informed of Cabinet changes 301
Sidney, Sir Henry 388
Simmons, Sir John Lintorn Arabin 42, 315, 316
Slack(e), Capt. Sir Owen Randal 411
Slave Trade Circular, proposal to withdraw 266, 268–269, 275, 276, 277
Sligo 56, 400
Smith, Sir Albert James 105
Smith, William Henry: supports founding of Conservative newspaper and journal 79, 80–81, 130; meetings on Irish Land Bill 326, 329, 335, 336–337; on purchase clauses of Land Act 337; on Arrears Bill 341; anxiety over Franchise Bill 346, 351, 356, 365, 368; member of Imperial Federation 76; on returning to office 381; troop movements in Dongola 387; Carnarvon's opinion of 402; Cabinet meeting on National League 413; appointed Chief Secretary, Ireland 62, 415; Carnarvon discloses conversation with Parnell 64;

arrives in Dublin 416; conversations with Carnarvon 427, 428; stands firm against Churchill 440; friendly towards Churchill 457
Society of Antiquaries: Carnarvon becomes member 287; Carnarvon elected president 33; Schliemann on Mycenae 34, 292
Somers, Charles Somers-Cocks, 3rd Earl 175
Somerset, Edward Adolphus Seymour, 12th Duke of 42
Sophie Friederike Mathilde, Queen of Holland 169, 255
Southampton, Charles Fitzroy, 3rd Baron 164
Spectator 80
Spencer, Lady Charlotte 415
Spencer, John Poyntz, 5th Earl: state of negotiations on Franchise Bill 47; persuaded of need for Home Rule 50; handover of Lord Lieutenancy to Carnarvon 52; contrast with security arrangements for Carnarvon 55, 389; discussions with Carnarvon on state of Ireland 386, 462; on the Maamtrasna case 391, 426; Carnarvon seeks advice on County Council work 74
Spofforth, Markham 130
Sproat, Gilbert Malcolm 224
Stalbridge, Richard de Aquila Grosvenor, 1st Baron (*see* Grosvenor, Richard de Aquila)
Standard 63, 79, 130, 412, 413, 414; publication of proposed government Distribution Bill 357, 365, 373
Stanhope, Anne Elizabeth (*see* Chesterfield, Anne Elizabeth Stanhope, Countess of)
Stanhope, Hon. Edward 256, 352–353, 449, 453
Stanhope, George (*see* Chesterfield, George Stanhope, 6th Earl of)
Stanhope, Philip Dormer (*see* Chesterfield, Philip Dormer Stanhope, 4th Earl of)
Stanhope, Philip Henry, 5th Earl Stanhope 157
Stanley, Revd Arthur Penrhyn 232
Stanley, Frederick Arthur (*see* Derby, Frederick Arthur Stanley, 16th Earl of)
Stanley, Henry Edward John, 3rd Baron Stanley of Alderley 313

Stanmore, Arthur Charles Hamilton-Gordon, 1st Baron (see Gordon, Sir Arthur Charles Hamilton-)
Stanton, Gen. Sir Edward 274, 275
Stead, William Thomas: requests report of secret Colonial Defence Committee recommendations 79; urges compromise on Franchise Bill 355; on naval expenditure 373; private letter to Carnarvon published 421; on Churchill's publication of Cabinet proceedings 443; on naval augmentations 452
Stewart, Sir Michael Robert Shaw 93
Storks, Lt.-Gen. Sir Henry Knight 108, 113
Strafford, Thomas Wentworth, 1st Earl of 370
Straits Settlements 23–24, 109, 113, 225, 296
Sturt, Henry Gerard, 1st Baron Alington 336
Sudan, debate on failure of expedition to 377, 378
Suez Canal 274, 275, 276, 277, 278

Tait, Archibald Campbell, Archbishop of Canterbury 185
Talbot, Revd Edward Stuart, later Bishop of Winchester 257
Tarleton, Admiral Sir John Walter 269
Taylor, Jeremy, Bishop of Down and Connor 380
Taylor, Thomas Edward 122
Temple, Henry John (see Palmerston, Henry John Temple, 3rd Viscount)
Ten Minute Bill (1867) 9
Tennent, Sir James Emerson 126
Tennyson, Alfred, 1st Baron Tennyson 11; Carnarvon's friendship with 12, 286–287
Teversal, Nottinghamshire 35
Thistlethwayte, Laura 131
Thorold, Anthony Wilson, Bishop of Rochester, later Bishop of Winchester 291
Thring, Edward 13
Thring, Sir Henry 261
Thynne, John Alexander (see Bath, John Alexander Thynne, 4th Marquess of)
Tilley, Sir Samuel Leonard 153
Times, The 39, 79, 84, 88, 130, 176, 209, 291, 307, 439, 440, 444, 451, 454
Townsend, Meredith White: encourages Carnarvon to take office 208–209;

believes war in Near East inevitable 301; on the Queen and Disraeli 303; important talk with Carnarvon on politics 309–310; conversation about Conservative leadership 324
Transvaal 22–23, 73, 218; annexation of 23, 250, 251–252, 291, 311, 324, 326; Frere's suggested abandonment of 312–313
Travellers' Club 397, 398, 407
Trench, H. Cooke 387
Trevelyan, Sir George Otto 422
Trinity College, Dublin 391, 392, 396
Truro, Charles Robert Claude Wilde, 2nd Baron 314
Trutch, Sir Joseph William 300
Tupper, Sir Charles 105, 153
Turner, Dr E.B. 83
Turnor, Algernon 78
Tutankhamun, Pharaoh of Egypt 1
Tyssen-Amherst, William (see Amherst, William Amhurst Tyssen-)

University College, Dublin 392
University Tests Bill (1871) 15, 19, 184
Unseaworthy Ships Bill (1875) 241, 259, 260, 261, 266, 269
Uppingham, Rutland 13

Vane, Henry George (see Cleveland, Henry George Vane, 4th Duke of)
Vanguard 268, 269, 270
Vanity Fair 87
Venables, George Stovin 276
Verdon, Sir George Frederic 471
Vernon, John Edward 392–393, 394
Vice Regal Lodge, Dublin 59, 60, 400, 401, 404, 407, 411, 415, 416, 417
Victoria, Queen of the United Kingdom of Great Britain and Ireland and Empress of India: appeals to Derby to settle Reform dispute 149–150; meets Canadian delegates 153; coldness towards Carnarvon 154; opposes Carnarvon's reasons for resignation 155; anger at resignation of Carnarvon, Cranborne, and Peel from Cabinet 9; accepts Carnarvon's resignation 156–157; Carnarvon receives seal of office as Colonial Secretary 211; on Fiji 217; godmother to Carnarvon's daughter Victoria

24; disapproves of Prince of Wales's proposed visit to India 248–249; urges letter to Czar Alexander II 251; and Carnarvon's children 254; at Balmoral 263–266; on previous Prime Ministers 265–266; discusses Eastern Question with Carnarvon 285; puts pressure on Cabinet concerning Eastern Question 27; visits Hughenden and lends support to Disraeli 28; summons Carnarvon to Osborne 29; letter to Carnarvon on Eastern Question 29–30; displeasure with Carnarvon over resignation 298–299; Disraeli's popularity with 299; on Zulu War 311; anxiety about Franchise Bill 48, 369; on Redistribution scheme 360; invites Carnarvon and Elsie to Windsor 375; reconciliation with Carnarvon 375–376; invests Carnarvon as Lord Lieutenant of Ireland 386; long audience with Carnarvon 406; sees Carnarvon on Ireland 60; assessment of Carnarvon 84

Villiers, George William Frederick (see Clarendon, George William Frederick Villiers, 4th Earl of)

Vincent, Sir Charles Edward Howard: meets McCarthy to set up Carnarvon's meeting with Parnell 53–55; arrangements for meeting with Parnell 388, 390; Carnarvon writes to 392; Carnarvon praises 397

Vivisection Bill (see Cruelty to Animals Bill (1876); Cruelty to Animals Bill (1879))

Vivisection, Royal Commission on (1875) 251, 254, 281

Vogel, Sir Julius 69

Waddington, William Henry 366

Waldegrave, Lady Frances Elizabeth Anne, Countess of 300

Wales, Albert Edward, Prince of, later Edward VII 264–265, 440, 447, 461; Masonic matters 239, 337; visit to India 248–249, 253, 255, 256–257, 263, 278; conversation with Carnarvon on Indian tour 264; returned from India 283; injudicious talk about Russia 292; displays coldness towards Carnarvon 32; criticism of his character 327–328

Wales, Alexandra of Denmark, Princess of 249, 264–265

Walewski, Count Alexandre Florian 95

Walker, Thomas 107

Walpole, Spencer Horatio: sounded out by Carnarvon on the Walewski despatch 96; on the 1866 Reform Bill 119; wishes to be Speaker 128; reaction to Reform procession 139; on London reform 144; approached by Carnarvon on chairmanship of Royal Commission on Agricultural Distress 42

Walsh, Dr William Joseph, Archbishop of Dublin 391

Walter, John 79

Wantage, Robert James Loyd-Lindsay, 1st Baron 337

Ward Hunt, George: sworn in 211; opposes revision of tax system 212; plea for more naval funds 216–217, 218, 238, 247; on Vanguard memorandum 269, 277; Carnarvon offered Ward Hunt's post 25, 273, 274–275; resignation 277

Warwick, George-Guy Greville, 4th Earl of 164

Welch, Capt. David Nairne 269

Wellesley, Henry Richard Charles (see Cowley, Henry Richard Charles Wellesley, 1st Earl)

Wellington, Arthur Wellesley, 1st Duke of 161

Wellington, Maj.-Gen. Arthur Richmond Wellesley, 2nd Duke of 147, 178

Wellow, Nottinghamshire 35

Wemyss and March, Lord Francis Charteris Douglas Elcho, 10th Earl of (see Elcho, Lord Francis Charteris Douglas)

Westbury, Richard Bethell, 1st Baron 101

Westminster, Hugh Lupus Grosvenor, 1st Duke of (see Grosvenor, Hugh Lupus)

Westminster, Richard Grosvenor, 2nd Marquess of (see Grosvenor, Richard, 2nd Marquess of Westminster)

Westport, Co. Mayo 399–400

Whitbread, Samuel 127, 336

White, Revd Henry 295

Whitworth, Sir Joseph 256

Wilberforce, Samuel, Bishop of Oxford, later Bishop of Winchester 100

Wilhelm I, King of Prussia 250

Williams, William Fenwick 295

Willoughby, Gilbert (*see* Aveland, Gilbert Henry Heathcote-Drummond Willoughby, 2nd Baron)

Willyams, Mrs Sarah Brydges 465

Winchester 171

Windsor Castle 49, 52, 211, 250, 253, 254, 285, 375, 376, 386, 405, 406

Winn, Rowland 48, 336, 346, 365, 368

Woburn Abbey, Bedfordshire 28

Wodehouse, John (*see* Kimberley, John Wodehouse, 1st Earl of)

Wolff, Sir Henry Drummond Charles 113, 463

Wolseley, Field Marshal Garnet Joseph, 1st Viscount Wolseley: victorious in Second Ashanti War 212, 215; requests more troops in Natal 261; conversation with Carnarvon on Natal and Cape 267; governor of Cyprus 305; conflict between Wolseley and Frere 313; suggested as Lord Lieutenant of Ireland 51, 62, 381; attacked by Salisbury 447

women's suffrage 49

Wood, Charles (*see* Halifax, Charles Wood, 1st Viscount)

Wright, William 35

Wyndham-Quin, Edwin Richard (*see* Dunraven, Edwin Richard Wyndham-Quin, 3rd Earl of)

Wyndham-Quin, Windham Thomas (*see* Dunraven, Windham Thomas Wyndham-Quin, 4th Earl of)

Yates, Edmund 304, 305

Yorke, Charles Philip (*see* Hardwicke, Charles Philip Yorke, 5th Earl of)

Young, Sir John 105, 107, 108

Zetland, Thomas Dundas, 3rd Earl of 164

Zulu insurrection (1874) 216, 223

Zulu War (1879) 311, 312